THE SVETLANA BOYM READER

THE SVETLANA BOYM READER

Edited by
Cristina Vatulescu,
Tamar Abramov,
Nicole G. Burgoyne,
Julia Chadaga, Jacob Emery
and Julia Vaingurt

BLOOMSBURY ACADEMIC
NEW YORK · LONDON · OXFORD · NEW DELHI · SYDNEY

BLOOMSBURY ACADEMIC
Bloomsbury Publishing Inc
1385 Broadway, New York, NY 10018, USA

BLOOMSBURY, BLOOMSBURY ACADEMIC and the Diana logo are
trademarks of Bloomsbury Publishing Plc

First published in the United States of America 2018

Cover design: Eleanor Rose
Cover image © Estate of Svetlana Boym

Library of Congress Cataloging-in-Publication Data
Names: Boym, Svetlana, 1959-2015, author. | Vatulescu, Cristina, 1976-
editor. | Abramov, Tamar, editor. | Burgoyne, Nicole G., editor. |
Chadaga, Julia Bekman, editor. | Emery, Jacob, 1977- editor. | Vaingurt, Julia, editor.
Title: The Svetlana Boym reader / edited by Cristina Vatulescu, Tamar
Abramov, Nicole G. Burgoyne, Julia Chadaga, Jacob Emery and Julia Vaingurt.
Description: New York : Bloomsbury Academic, 2018. | Includes bibliographical
references and index.
Identifiers: LCCN 2017049473 (print) | LCCN 2017054654 (ebook) | ISBN
9781501337529 (epDF) | ISBN 9781501337512 (ePub) | ISBN 9781501337505 (HB) | ISBN
9781501337499 (pbk.: alk. paper)
Classification: LCC PS3602.O974 (ebook) | LCC PS3602.O974 A6 2018 (print) |
DDC 814/.54--dc23
LC record available at https://lccn.loc.gov/2017049473

ISBN: HB: 978-1-5013-3750-5
     PB: 978-1-5013-3749-9
     ePDF: 978-1-5013-3752-9
     eBook: 978-1-5013-3751-2

Typeset by Deanta Global Publishing Services, Chennai, India
Printed and bound in the United States of America

To find out more about our authors and books visit www.bloomsbury.com and
sign up for our newsletters.

CONTENTS

PART FIVE THE OFF-MODERN (2010–17) 387

Headnote by *Tamar Abramov*

PART SIX AFTERIMAGES: SVETLANA BOYM'S IRREPRESSIBLE CO-CREATIONS 457

Headnote by *Cristina Vatulescu*

LIST OF PLATES

LIST OF ILLUSTRATIONS

ACKNOWLEDGMENTS

The editors would like to extend their heartfelt thanks to Musa and Yuri Goldberg and David Damrosch. Donald Fanger, Masha Gessen, Haaris Naqvi, William Mills Todd III, Giuliana Bruno, and Dana Villa provided greatly appreciated support along the way. This book stands as a testimony to what Svetlana Boym has taught us and been to us.

The following organizations kindly agreed to republication of Boym's work: Basic Books, Cabinet Magazine, Duke University Press, Fordham University Press, Harvard University Press, John Hopkins University Press, M. E. Sharpe Press of the Taylor & Francis Group, Princeton Architectural Press, Princeton University Press, Stanford University Press, The American Association for the Advancement of Slavic Studies, University of Chicago Press, and *Tablet* Magazine. An acknowledgment of each essay and excerpt is provided on the sources page at the end of this book.

Svetlana Boym in front of her old apartment,
St. Petersburg, Russia, 1989.

LUMINOSITIES: AN INTRODUCTION

In her 2010 essay "The Scenography of Friendship," Svetlana Boym wrote that "friendship is not about having everything illuminated or obscured, but about conspiring and playing with shadows. Its goal is not enlightenment but luminosity." Her shorthand definition of friendship, which prefers a community of "occasional lucidity and honesty" to the heroic "quest for the blinding truth," invites us to join her in a cozy conspiracy of the intellect.[1] Where many of the most influential strands of cultural studies have positioned themselves as adversaries of enlightenment, tirelessly exposing its blind spots and failures, Boym offers a homely, overlooked alternative, unfolding under the star of a playful rather than a cynical irony—the light of a kitchen lamp rather than the austere X-ray machine of the solitary philosophical mind. Her imaginary community emphasizes the peaks and troughs of an ongoing conversation rather than the implacable sequence of formal argument. Here the brilliant aperçu mixes with the obscure, half-forgotten textures of everyday life; the metaphysical insight communicates with the intimate memories of the individual and the tattered commonplaces of the decaying Soviet sphere.

Boym's implied critique of enlightenment and its intractable adversaries is embedded in a vision of creative community that is a poetics and an ethics at once, a collective participation in the making of life that looks back to the riot of historical possibilities shooting off of the main trunk of the twentieth century and looks forward to an ironic cosmopolitanism. True to form, this political and aesthetic vision of friendship—a humane and open-ended alternative to other, more totalitarian versions of utopia—is also a set of allusions to her life and work. The opposition of enlightenment, not to darkness but to the near-synonym luminosity, is typical of her attraction to phenomena that are just a little bit "off," most famously in her diagnosis of the "off-modern"—the "alternative genealogies and histories of modernity," blueprints for unconstructed buildings and ideas for unrealized polities, which seductively haunt the modernity we take for granted[2]. Luminosity suggests the warm glow that suffuses not only a cocreated community of comfort, amusement, and perception, but also the artificial lights of technological utopias and the nocturnal, Nabokovian insects that huddle round them; it suggests her efforts to liven up her own little corner in the dreary last days of the Soviet Union, but also the kitschy canopy of stars and moons that presides over the appealing, if thoroughly moth-eaten, glory of the Soviet space race. It suggests her practice as a photographer, an artist of light and shadow. It suggests Svetlana Boym herself, whose name means light, *svet*, in Russian.

The name on her birth certificate was not the name under which she entered American academia. In keeping with her critical preference for byroads and alternative visions, her account of her early life, doubtless mythologized, reads more like picaresque than autobiography. A native of Leningrad, she apparently resolved to emigrate after receiving a marriage proposal while queueing for dried fish at a kiosk on a Crimean beach, her decision catalyzed by the "perpetual identity crisis" of the enigmatic heroine in Antonioni's *Passenger*, "her hair . . . fluttering in the wind."[3] The subsequent marriage ended in divorce and in America. She had studied Spanish in Leningrad; in Boston, she adopted the fictional persona of Susana, the daughter of a Spanish Civil War refugee, in order to open doors in the Spanish department at Boston University where she eventually received an MA in Hispanic literatures.

Her biographies were not accidental inconsistencies but sustained exercises in self-fashioning, and lately, she told Cristina Vatulescu during their last conversation, self-editing. She often quoted a quip from Boris Tomashevskii, "There are writers with biographies and writers without biographies," as a prelude to her influential critique of "the death of the author."[4] She launched that critique as the polemic of her dissertation (overseen by Barbara Johnson and formalist scholar Jurij Striedter) in the 1980s, when "the death of the author" had congealed into critical dogma. The resulting book, *Death in Quotation Marks* (1991), explored the mythologies of the modern poet and critic, including her figurative and literal deaths, arguing that the "relationship between texts and life remains a vitally critical issue."[5] She pioneered then her signature critical genre, a writing that "allowed for the incorporation and superimposition of ethical, historical, biographical, and textual issues."[6] At the same time, the book already contains, smuggled inside academic prose, fragments that anticipate her later artistic practices and manifestoes:

I wish to preserve the difference between text and life and to avoid subjugating one to the other. In order to open and explore this space of difference we have to trace the ways in which the artistic constructs can, on the one hand, form and inform ordinary experiences and, on the other hand, be deformed and defied by them. This double movement invites us to see literariness or a creative aesthetic impulse in everyday life and to liberate these aesthetic experiences from the confines of "literature" and literary institutions. At the same time, it helps us to deaestheticize literature somewhat and defamiliarize again the violence, pain, and love that it contains.[7]

So it is fitting to consider Boym's writing in relation to her art and her biographies, her crafted fashioning and editing of herself. Far from any sort of *Gesamtkunstwerk*—a concept she detested—these were cocreations, whose contingent coexistence inspired thoughts on difference and a heightened sensitivity to the beauty of cracks, hinges, borderlines, and transit zones.

In her 2015 *New Yorker* profile, Masha Gessen wrote of the many self-conscious personas Boym created and cultivated—"entire new lives," in Gessen's words; "parallel lives that sometimes cross" in Boym's own.[8] She was a prolific writer, a charismatic professor, a novelist, and a public intellectual. She was a fiercely resourceful and reflective immigrant; her most resonant book, *The Future of Nostalgia*, was deeply rooted in that experience. In later years, she was an artist experimenting with point of view and media up to their sometimes literal breaking point, creating art out of nostalgic technology and human and technological errors. Even after *The Future of Nostalgia* carried her fame beyond academic circles, few readers were aware of all of the creative personas marshaled together in this book. She was simply too prolific, and her work migrated across most people's disciplinary boundaries—from literary and cultural studies through film, visual, and material culture studies, performance, intermedia, and new media.

Boym's knack for discovering aesthetic opportunities in official discourse and paradoxical third ways in the hidden junctures of cultural and political tradition was always in communication with her own self-invention, which led her to put out shoots in multifarious fields of public life. At the same time, the writings and artworks that comprise this book demonstrate not only scholarly vibrancy and versatility, but also the cohesion of Boym's intellectual pursuits. In all her endeavors, she questioned the assumptions that underlie dominant frameworks of thought. Among Boym's many theoretical contributions are: the enrichment of our understanding of the autobiographical genre via an inquiry into the alleged death of the author; the study of creative play with gender identity in the Russian context; the theoretical recuperation of the everyday, the marginal, the tacky, the mundane, and the sentimental; the investigation of the aesthetic potential of the immigrant experience; the reconceptualization of freedom as an artistic practice; and finally, the diagnosis of the off-modern. More broadly, she had a flair for making theory concrete; she excelled at coining concepts and making them an indelible part of our intellectual landscape. For all of these reasons, she is a foundational thinker. Boym's work has been a profound source of inspiration for fellow scholars, encouraging them to broaden their horizons, to rethink received wisdom, and to bring to light things previously unseen.

The aim of *The Reader* project is to make this range available to Boym's readers in one book, which spans classic essays, excerpts from Boym's monographs, and journalistic gems. Showcasing her roles as both curator and curated, *The Reader* also features interviews, excerpts from exhibition catalogs, and samples of intermedial works like *Hydrant Immigrants*, which tackles the status of the immigrant in the public sphere through diptychs of texts and photographs. Autobiographical pieces, choice documentary rarities like Boym's first graduate school essay on Russian literature (complete with marginalia by her mentor, Donald Fanger), and transcripts of her memorable last lectures and performances illuminate the genealogy of her scholarly work. Last but not least, *The Reader* includes late pieces that Boym did not live to see through publication.

Our intent throughout has been to render visible Boym's irrepressible creativity and impetus to move over boundaries—literal and figural, disciplinary and artistic—and while the bulk of the book is devoted to the cultural criticism which is likely to be Boym's most lasting legacy, her art and experimental texts help to illuminate the full context of her thought, and the many mutually tributary channels that crisscrossed her creative life. Each of *The Reader*'s six chronological sections is prefaced by a short essay that highlights, in more specific detail than this introduction can do, the period's main questions, analytical moves, and achievements;

each one coheres around a centering project while also making visible the development of key concepts, themes, and preoccupations at a given stage of Boym's career.

For example, we see the beginnings of Boym's last project, *The Off-Modern* (2017),[9] in the early drafting of her *Future of Nostalgia* (2001), which is preoccupied with ruins. Freedom as cocreation, a theme that developed into a full-blown monograph published in 2010, takes a long *via negativa* through Boym's curation of the *Territories of Terror* exhibit in 2007. An early root of that project is revealed in Boym's wry autobiographical story "My Grandmother's First Love" (2002).

Where at each stage of her writing career Boym was devoted to a penetrating exploration of a discrete theoretical concept like nostalgia, freedom, or the off-modern, her combined body of work highlights a complex genealogy of thought that questions the given, probes the absolute, seeks out the uncharted. The aesthetic fashioning of life explored in her first book, *Death in Quotation Marks*, leads her to the recuperation of the everyday; the hidden depths of everyday life's mundane, marginal, and sentimental aspects (*Common Places*, 1994) inspire her to investigate communal and personal nostalgias; the immersion in aesthetic and exilic journeys (*The Future of Nostalgia*, 2001) brings forth an attempt to define the experience of freedom (*Another Freedom*, 2012), which in turn results in an emancipatory push from the constraints of modernity, opening to us previously overlooked vistas of off-modern possibilities (*The Off-Modern*, 2017). Each text builds on her previous work, carries a trace of thoughts to come, and exhibits its author's unwavering commitment to the critique of dichotomous thinking.

A favorite passage from Viktor Shklovsky's *The Third Factory* succinctly expresses Boym's creative credo: "There is no third alternative. And that is precisely the one that must be chosen. An artist should avoid beaten paths."[10] Writing in Soviet Russia in 1926, the famous theorist of estrangement had in mind the given alternatives of retreat (writing at home for oneself, autonomy, a sacrifice of the collective for the individual) or a surrender to a "new society and correct worldview" (complacent subjection to political expediency, collaboration, the sacrifice of the individual for the collective). Both alternatives belong to the realm of necessity, which Shklovsky escapes via a creative paradox—the third alternative that does not exist, yet which an artist must imaginatively will into being.

One such alternative is a new, elective community, whether in situ or literalized as a life in emigration. Shklovsky himself, deeply committed to verbal art but fluent only in Russian, returned to the Soviet Union after a frustrating sojourn in Berlin; Boym, who forged a successful career as a comparatist in English, weaves into her work a sense of the double estrangement of theory and historical experience as a point of access onto diasporic traditions and émigré experience. A late essay[11] on Shklovsky, Hannah Arendt, and Osip Mandel'shtam reappraises the "third way" as a method of self-identification practiced by "hyphenated Jewish thinkers and writers" whose life circumstances taught them to defy binarisms, political theologies and teleologies, and look instead for lateral moves and potentialities for public "worldliness." Many of the thinkers who populate Boym's alternate history of critical and political engagement in the twentieth century are Jews whose committed non-messianism amplifies rather than restricts their engagement with the world. She reads the closing paragraphs of Mandel'shtam's *The Egyptian Stamp* as dramatizing the roots of Jewish estrangement in the moment of "great fear" in which the narrator recognizes himself as a Jew. Guided by the "Muse of Jewish Luck," the narrator embraces a personified version of terror itself, discovering that "with fear [he] has no fear." With his fear to take his hand and lead him, Mandel'shtam is able to walk Shklovsky's serpentine road of the brave, "the road of self-reflective fear which does not lead to any kind of redemption, reconciliation, feel-good palliative or a happy ending." The confrontation with fear is a part of the "honest zigzag" of his passionate thinking, which leads to an explicit rethinking of Jewish belonging in Mandel'shtam's later work, and is ultimately legible as a form of civic engagement with his "beast of a century."

This 2013 interpretation derives from a graduate school essay originally written in 1984, and Boym's reading of Mandel'shtam's confrontation with fear as the moment of self-recognition as a Jew is very much in keeping with her own long process of self-creation. Barred by Soviet policies from versing herself in Jewish traditions and texts, Boym's powerful and precise intuitions led her early on to conceive of her own intellectual resistance to that deprivation as a playful, imagined vision of what Jewishness might be. Holiday celebrations with the friends she called her "Jewish family" bore the fruit of spontaneous rituals and dietary restrictions, none of which were in the books, at least not in the precise form she practiced them, but all of which *could have been*. For Boym, Shklovsky's third way offered the freedom to resist the deprivation of a Jewish way of life by inventing it anew in the kind of imaginary community that became a central concept in her later lucid theorization of nostalgia and diaspora. The same creative courage—or "muse of luck"—guided her through her emigration and her Americanization to hold staunchly to a third intellectual way, defying trends and styles, resisting political theologies and teleologies on the one hand while debunking relativism on the other. In this she resembles her beloved forbearers, collaborators across time whose heritage she both shares and analyzes: Simmel, Arendt, Benjamin, Mandel'shtam, and of course Shklovsky—Jews who paradoxically harnessed Jewish fear. Zigzag but far from rootless, this cosmopolitanism walks an intimate, emotional path of freedom, part of a tradition to which Boym lays idiosyncratic claim, preserved from messianic teleology by its self-awareness, its ironic humor, and its embrace of paradox and oxymoron as offering escape from any given finalizing ideology.

Boym was drawn to paradox not just for an intellectual idea of freedom, but in her efforts to describe the contradictory desires at the heart of what it means to be human in human communities. In *Common Places*, a book concerned with "the utopian topography of Soviet daily existence and its secret corners . . . everyday aesthetic experiences and alternative spaces carved between the lines and on the margins of the official discourses"[12] she coins the phrase "ruins of communal utopias"— an apparent oxymoron that refers to the impeccably evoked reality of the Soviet communal apartment, as well as to artworks that reflect its indelible traces in the Soviet psyche. Thus Ilya Kabakov's installations, she writes, speak to our longings "to transcend the everyday in some kind of collective fairy tale, and to inhabit the most uninhabitable ruins, to survive and preserve memories."[13] For Boym, utopia signifies an imagined projection, a state of mind rather than a realized social order. In *Death in Quotation Marks*, her analysis of the official monument to Mayakovsky culminates in an account of "the utopian topography of Soviet daily existence" brought into being through ideologically charged buildings and monuments.

In the Soviet 1920s "art-making and life-making intersected, and the country turned into a creative laboratory of various conflicting utopian projects," Boym writes, channeling the creative energy of another time into her own, distinctly contemporary terminology of "revolutionary topography."[14] Her critical trajectory from the shining ideal to the shabby reality of the communal apartment arcs through Moisei Ginzburg's avant-garde House-Ship, "a ruin of modernist architecture, with trees growing through the half-fallen balconies."[15] Nature and culture collaborate, to cite Boym's later formulation, in an image of domestic decay that counterbalances the Petersburg myth of a battle between human works and hostile landscapes. In a close reading of the pensioner Liuba's assemblage of souvenirs—what Liuba calls her "still life"—Boym characterizes the collection as a private "monument," emblematic of Soviet people's desire for "a still life, for a sustaining everyday materiality in the face of continuing crises."[16] The Russian *natiurmort* (itself a foreign borrowing) translates into English as "still life"; Boym then estranges that translation, the second language releasing a potential for new meanings. Such wordplay was essential to Boym's translational, émigré sensibility. She showed her students that it was possible to channel one's longing for belonging into scholarship infused with creativity and play.

Private monuments such as Liuba's still life, like playful pet revisions of dictionary meanings, emerge as alternatives to the ones that watched over the utopian topography and then, as Boym documents in *The Future of Nostalgia*, became targets of popular wrath. She excavates the history of ruins and their value in different eras as material memory traces, and she shows how the monument can work to efface memory. Boym refers to the Palace of Soviets—never completed, thus indestructible—as an invisible monument to utopia "that cast a long shadow on the Moscow landscape."[17] She loved miniature monuments, like the frequently stolen one commemorating Major Kovalyov's nose in St. Petersburg, for the way they deflated the gigantomania of the official monuments implicated in what she called (after Eco) *ars obliovionalis*. On her mantelpiece at home, a tiny Palace of Soviets stood next to a photo of Boym with her parents. This assemblage conveys something essential about Boym. The Palace is finally realized, but on a charmingly small and domestic scale. The image is haunting because the Palace, which would have been built on the site of a ruin, had a memorial aura, even though it was designed as a hopeful symbol, a seed crystal around which the future utopia would grow.

Boym introduced her students to the émigré artists Komar and Melamid's project "What is to be Done with Monumental Propaganda," which proposed to creatively transform deposed Soviet monuments into history lessons. Their call for an alternative to the worship/annihilation binary resonates with Boym's fondness for the third way which the creative imagination signposts or invents. Her essay "Ruinophilia" seeks to foster an "off-modern perspective [that] allows us to frame utopian projects as dialectical ruins—not to discard or demolish them, but rather to confront and incorporate them into our own fleeting present." In *Another Freedom*, Boym continues to theorize the third way thinking that wills the impossible into being as an art of freedom, attempting to estrange and renew the perception of freedom by conceptualizing it neither as a philosophical idea nor as a political right. The idea of freedom tends to gravitate toward the absolute. And Boym's book is directed against all absolutes, all moral certainties, because they justify violence and injustice. Freedom is finite, then, but to imagine freedom as something that can be possessed is either to disengage oneself from the world in a gesture of radical individualism or to sacrifice the self by accepting the tyranny of the majority that grants political liberties. Boym opens this Shklovskian dilemma in order to seek the third way, freedom as co-creation, which sacrifices neither self nor other. Freedom, she insists, is a mode of being, an adventure, an experience, and finally, an art. The art of freedom is exercised in aesthetic acts of radical estrangement that bring forth unpredictability, not *from* but *for* the world. It is in art's ability to shock and surprise, in bursts of sudden illumination, that Boym locates the experience of freedom.

In order to perform this experience of freedom, Boym often structures her writing as a dialogue, a form that signifies openness to the unpredictable, the improbable—the "surprise of otherness," to borrow a phrase from her dissertation adviser, Barbara Johnson. Dialogue opens space for recognition of the other as well as one's own "inner plurality," bringing not conquest, but mutual liberation, or in Boym's parlance, cohabitation in the architecture of freedom. The effect is not just one of intellectual profundity that discloses portentous meaning in everyday life, but of humanizing irony that brings gentle humor to public monuments and political catastrophes. Her Harvard colleague Williams Mills Todd III describes how, in a tense historical moment, an interview broadcast on Russian television brought post-Soviet politics and American academia together in a shock of recognition that was also an exorcism of fear.

In winter 1992, just after the fall of the Soviet Union, I went to Russia to conduct archival research. Many friends advised me not to go because of the unsettled situation. Just about everything that could go wrong on my trip to Moscow did go wrong: delayed visa, delayed flight, lost luggage, confused driver, drunken porter, hotel guards wearing camouflage, accessorized with Kalashnikovs. I made my way to my room, flicked on the television, and there was our Svetlana, on Russian TV, explaining the American presidential campaign in her colorful native language. Her take on "the wimp factor"—комплекс мужской неполноценности—left me rolling on the floor in laughter. Somehow she had made the world seem smaller, less threatening, more intelligible. Her unfailing humor and courage had that effect.[18]

The luminous irreverence manifested here in a broadcast interview at a moment of geopolitical instability also appeared, in a more private sphere and on a more quotidian scale, in the verbal and written dialogue catalyzed by Boym's seminars. Boym's students are now professors themselves, and they bring into their classrooms the myriad ways—inquisitive, deeply ethical, and creative—in which she inspired them to look critically beneath the surface of the built environment, to recover the ideological longings and historical traumas concealed there and to make these objects the starting point for new conversations that bring clarity and healing.

Svetlana Boym was a professor to all of the coeditors of this book. Inside the archive behind this book is not just her first graduate school essay on Russian literature [Fig. 2, this volume], but coming full circle, her own marginalia, written in oversized, bold script, on our graduate school papers. Among our prized mementos are also her signature handouts, which she carried to class together with earmarked copies of Arendt, Brodsky, Mandel'shtam, or Tsvetaeva. We searched through graduate school folders expecting ice-breaking Nabokovian quips like her favorite, "If parallel lines do not meet it is not because they cannot but because they have other things to do"—although we knew that she did not shy away from placing Saint Teresa of Ávila next to Mallarmé at her seminar table, her kind of comparative literature. Boym left a trace of her impetuousness in her handouts' misprints. She didn't waste precious time fixing typos: instead she composed a manifesto on human error and wrote an exquisite theory of the "misprint" that addresses what she saw as a gap in our ethical reckoning with the Gulag. Her mark was also in the émigré accent that inflected all the languages on every handout and, gracing a brilliant eloquence, lured the many other accents around the table out of their respective silences. Many of us remember a class discussion that was getting progressively absurd as Svetlana probed into the creative potential of a "chaos" which her pronunciation had turned, for most of us, into "cows." The short-lived confusion was followed by illumination and general glee, without any tinge of self-consciousness or defensiveness. For some of her students, who had crossed their own borders to join her in the classroom, those chaotic cows became mascots to be remembered in moments of linguistic difficulty.

Recalling Nietzsche's warning against the danger of feeling at home in the world, she taught that being a stranger, and speaking like one, can open paths to a more creative and ethical relationship to language and reality.

The Editors

Notes

1 "Scenography of Friendship," *Cabinet Magazine*, Issue 36 Winter 2009/10, http://www.cabinetmagazine.org/issues/36/boym.php (p. 431 of *Reader* manuscript).

2 Svetlana Boym, *Another Freedom: the Alternative History of an Idea* (University of Chicago Press, 2010), p. 8.

3 From: "On Freedom: A Discussion between Svetlana Boym and Boris Groys." *Eurozine*, July 16, 2003. http://www.eurozine.com/on-freedomin-russian-there-is-no-difference-between-liberty-and-freedom-though-there-are-also-two-different-words-for-freedom-which-have-very-dif-ferent-connotations-the-authors-are-aware-of-t/

4 Svetlana Boym, *Death in Quotation Marks: Cultural Myths of the Modern Poet* (Cambridge: Harvard University Press, 1991), p. 24.

5 Svetlana Boym, *Death in Quotation Marks*, p. 243.

6 Ibid.

7 Ibid., p. 247.

8 Masha Gessen, "Postscript: Svetlana Boym, 1959-2015" in the *New Yorker Online*, August 7, 2015. http://www.newyorker.com/news/news-desk/postcript-svetlana-boym-1959-2015

9 Svetlana Boym, *The Off-Modern* (Bloomsbury Press, 2017) is, alongside this *Reader*, a posthumous publication.

10 Viktor Shklovsky, *Third Factory* (Dalkie Archive Press, 2002), p. 51

11 "Vernacular Cosmopolitanism in Shklovsky and Mandelshtam" (2013, in this book)

12 Svetlana Boym, *Common Places: Mythologies of Everyday Life in Russia* (Harvard University Press, 1994), p. 5.

13 Svetlana Boym, *The Future of Nostalgia* (Basic Books, 2001), p. 324

14 Boym, *Common Places*, p. 126

15 Ibid., p. 128

16 Ibid., p. 154

17 Boym, *The Future of Nostalgia*, p. 104

18 William Mills Todd III, Memorial Address at Harvard University, October 2015.

PART ONE

THE THEATER OF
THE SELF (1984–91)

Self-consciousness, the quintessential modernist preoccupation, is the
central concern of Boym's early works. Dissecting semi- and pseudo-
autobiographical writing of modernist poets, from Mallarmé to
Mandel'shtam, Boym revises and expands such structuralist and post-
structuralist concepts as "literary fact," "art's autonomy," and "death of
the author." Barthes's famous phrase takes on a new meaning in Boym's
first book *Death in Quotation Marks*, which analyzes literal and figurative
suicides in poets' lives and art. It is a daring enterprise to address the
author's biography amid its devaluation in literary criticism of the post-
structuralist era. Boym's aim is to map out the constellation of contradictory
impulses toward self-effacement and self-fashioning of the modern poet.
Boym argues that poets exploit and reshape numerous cultural and
literary myths and masks while creatively making and unmaking the self.
She investigates how this theater of the self affects both literature and
life, blurring the boundaries between them. Not aiming to resuscitate
the outdated notion that an artist's life can explain her writing, Boym
nevertheless puts into question the possibility of art's complete autonomy
from life, and vice versa, by demonstrating the "uncanny literariness of life
and the transgressive vitality of texts." Furthermore, Boym's case studies
of self-mythification shed light on the process of myth-making itself. In
the excerpts provided, Boym offers ingenious readings of the mutually
impactful relationships between text and tradition in Mandel'shtam,
poetry and politics in Maiakovskii, and writing and gender in Tsvetaeva.

Finally, in the last excerpt of this section, Boym turns her attention to those elements of public personas' private realm that are untheorizable, sentimental, mundane, or banal. Analyzing the diaries of Roland Barthes and Walter Benjamin, she investigates these critics' choice to write about the facets of their lives that complicate their personal myths or contradict their theories of authorship. She posits that these aspects of the everyday, when put in writing, become tools of rebellion against restrictively neat constructions of the self, a form of self-resistance.

Julia Vaingurt

1 DIALOGUE AS "LYRICAL HERMAPHRODITISM": MANDEL'SHTAM'S CHALLENGE TO BAKHTIN

Лирический поэт по природе своей,—двуполое существо, способное к бесчисленным расщеплениям во имя внутреннего диалога.

OSIP MANDEL'SHTAM, "Fransua Villon"

[*The lyrical poet is a hermaphrodite by nature, capable of limitless fissions in the name of his inner monologue.*

OSIP MANDEL'SHTAM, "François Villon"]

Развитие романа заключается в углублении диалогичности, ее расширении и утончении ... Диалог уходит в молекулярные, и наконец во внутриатомные глубины.

MIKHAIL BAKHTIN, "Slovo v romane"

[*The development of the novel is a function of the deepening of dialogic essence, its increased scope and greater precision... Dialogue moves into the deepest molecular, and ultimately, subatomic levels.*

MIKHAIL BAKHTIN, "Discourse in the Novel"]

The two epigraphs disclose a crucial "genre gap" between Osip Mandel'shtam and Mikhail Bakhtin. If for Mandel'shtam dialogue is essential to lyric, for Bakhtin the dialogical discourse identifies the novel as a genre in opposition to monologic, self-centered and self-sufficient poetic language. In his essays "Fransua Villon" ["François Villon"] and "O sobesednike" ["On the Addressee"], Mandel'shtam discusses different dimensions of dialogue—the dialogue between various historical epochs—modernity and Middle Ages, Ancient Greece and Renaissance, the dialogue between the author and the distant reader, and finally, the dialogue between the poet's diverse selves. The latter is called "lyrical hermaphroditism" and described in its multiple incarnations, including "ogorchennyi i uteshitel', mat' i ditia, sudiia i podsudimyi, sobstvennik i nishchii" ["the aggrieved and the comforter, the mother and the child, the judge and the judged, the proprietor and the beggar..."][1] Mandel'shtam's "lyrical hermaphroditism" does not signify a Platonic ideal of androgynous wholeness, a reconciliation of two polarities. On the contrary, it is viewed as a peculiar kind of poetic *dvupolost'* [hermaphroditism] that reveals multiple splittings of the poet's self and suggests an open-ended and continuous interplay of sexual and social roles, of nuances of intonation and artistic styles.

Bakhtin's early conception of dialogue is deeply rooted in the narrative structures of the nineteenth century novel. In contrast to the Russian formalists with their interest in modern experimental literature and "poetic language," Bakhtin chooses the nineteenth century novel, particularly that of Fedor Dostoevsky as a model for his theory. Yet, Bakhtin's "dialogical principle" is not a "monological" concept in itself; it acquires a different "intonation" in different contexts of discussion. In the early essay "Avtor i geroi v esteticheskoi deiatel'nosti" ["Author and Hero in Aesthetic Activity"] as well as in *Problemy poetiki Dostoevskogo* [*Problems of Dostoevsky's Poetics*], the dialogue is conceived as an interaction between "embodied consciousnesses" or "dialog cheloveka s chelovekom" ["a dialogue between human beings"] with the emphasis not so much on its psychological but on its epistemological dimension.[2] In "Slovo v romane," however, Bakhtin stresses that "dialogue" could not be reduced exclusively to the contradictions between characters; rather, it is embedded in the linguistic and social heteroglossia of narrative discourse. Furthermore, the dialogue encompasses narrativity in general, pointing beyond the novel at different contexts of literary and extraliterary communication. Such a broad understanding of the dialogical principle seems particularly applicable to modernist literature. Yet, one notices a conspicuous absence of references to twentieth century fiction and poetry and virtually no discussion of modernism in the works of Bakhtin. In his posthumously published notes, Bakhtin touches upon, in very general terms, the crisis of contemporary literature, possibly referring to the French new novel:

Поиски автором собственного слова… это сейчас самая острая проблема современной литературы, приводящая многих к отказу от романного жанра, к замене его монтажем документов, описанием вещей, к леттризму, в известной мере и к литературе абсурда. Все это в некотором смысле можно определить как разные формы молчания. Достоевского эти поиски привели к созданию полифонического романа.

[The author's quest for his own word … is the most topical problem of contemporary literature, leading many to the rejection of the novelistic genre, its substitution with the montage of documents, description of things, lettrism, and to a certain extent, the literature of the absurd. All this can be defined in a certain sense as various forms of silence. These quests led Dostoevsky to the creation of the polyphonic novel.][3]

Thus Bakhtin does not acknowledge the specificity of the twentieth century situation and the differences between nineteenth and twentieth century (modernist) conceptions of the self. Even in his later notes he does not challenge the status of Dostoevsky's text as *the* model for his theory and as *the* exemplary embodiment of the dialogical principle.

In order to bridge the gap between Mandel'shtam and Bakhtin in the context of twentieth century writing, I turn to Mandel'shtam's fictional prose, *Egipetskaia marka* (1928 [*The Egyptian Stamp*]) published in almost the same year as Bakhtin's *Problemy poetiki Dostoevskogo* (1929 [*Problems of Dostoevsky's Poetics*]). The poet's experimental narrative presents a challenge to both the lyric and the novel and blurs the established boundaries between genres. In *Egipetskaia marka* one may confront different conceptions of dialogue and genre further adulterated by cultural mythologies of gender. I will explore the practice of lyrical hermaphroditism in the novella and the ways in which it is linked to the specifically twentieth-century problems of national and sexual identity.

According to Mandel'shtam, after the revolution poetry itself demanded prose, a new kind of prose, which belongs to no one and that together with the author's personality, manages to get rid of "vse sluchainoe, lichnoe i katastroficheskoe (lirika)" ["everything incidental, personal, and catastrophic (the domain of lyric)."][4] As Bakhtin regards the novel, so Mandel'shtam regards prose as essentially multivoiced. The model for this prose is not the polyphonic novel of Dostoevsky, however; it is rather the work of Mandel'shtam's contemporaries, especially Boris Pil'niak, in whose writings the literary collage, the juxtaposition of notebooks, construction estimates, Soviet circulars, fragments, an almost completely dehumanized dialogue of things and words, substitutes for the dialogue between characters and narrators. Mandel'shtam praises this kind of prose for its radical impersonality, its attempt to efface the subjectivity of the author, and its revival of "the folkloric principle" that allows the writer to reconcile modernity and tradition. It also allows the writer to reconstruct an alternative history of Russian prose beyond and in spite of the age of great psychological novels. Moreover, in Mandel'shtam the classical image of the poet competes with the modern image of the "author as a producer," "bezymiannyi prozaik, eklektik, sobiratel'." ["the anonymous prose writer, the eclectic, the collector."] The figure of an impersonal modern author is a common modernist myth baptized by Roland Barthes as "the death of the author," which has been reenacted and described by poets from different traditions, including Stephane Mallarmé, Paul Valéry, T. S. Eliot, and, to some extent, Boris Pasternak.[5]

Mandel'shtam's own shift from poetry to prose in the late 1920s is of critical significance. Between 1926 and 1931, a period of painful cultural isolation, Mandel'shtam did not write a single poem. Yet *Egipetskaia marka,* which can be considered Mandel'shtam's exemplary prose work, does not offer us an example of an ideal prose writer, eclectic and collective. Instead, it presents a typical lyrical narrator, a would-be author, an amateur, who together with his would-be hero Parnok seeks voice and identity. The novella searches for a genre, both ironically and desperately, and reflects upon its own literary "pedigree."

Egipetskaia marka begins with an almost impersonal description of a dream in which "protivniki b'iut iz pistoletov v gorki s posudoi, v chernil'nitsy i v famil'nye kholsty." ["the opponents fired their pistols at cabinets of chinaware, at inkpots, and at family portraits."][6] The first "affair of honor" culminates in a triple destruction: of things, of writing instruments and of family memories. This beginning recurs word for word in chapter 5, this time as a literary cliché, a typical "scandalous event" of a Russian psychological novel: "skandalom nazyvaetsia bes, otkrytyi russkoi literaturoi ili samoi zhizn'iu v sorokovykh chto li godakh" (p. 27) ["Scandal is the name of the demon discovered by Russian prose or by Russian life itself sometime in the Forties" (p.150)]. In "Razgovor o Dante," Mandel'shtam associates "scandal" with the novels of Dostoevsky, with their psychological intensity and dramatic (or melodramatic) collisions. Published almost simultaneously with Bakhtin's fundamental study on Dostoevsky, *Egipetskaia marka* presents a completely different reading of the great Russian novelist. The beginning of Mandel'shtam's novella can be read as a parody of a beginning, a subtle anti-novelistic gesture. The conflict of the characters of a psychological novel becomes a conflict in the novel as a genre, a scandal not in but of literature.

In the next paragraph, the narrator appears in the first person and makes an attempt to begin again, this time in the autobiographical mode: "Sem'ia moia, is predlagaiu tebe gerb: stakan s kipiachenoi vodoi. V rezinovom privkuse peterburgskoi vody ia p'iu neudavsheesia domashnee bessmertie. Tsentrobezhnaia sila vremeni razmetala nashi venskie stul'ia i gollandskie tarelki s sinimi tsvetochkami" (p. 5).

["I propose to you, my family, a coat of arms: a glass of boiled water. In the rubbery aftertaste of Petersburg's boiled water I drink my unsuccessful domestic immortality. The centrifugal force of time has scattered our Viennese chairs and Dutch plates with little blue flowers. (p. 133)]

But here he experiences another ironic failure. In order to write an autobiography, one must have a certain noncontradictory sense of the self (*auto*), and adequate means of writing one's life (*bio-graphe*). In the novella, neither of the three is taken for granted. The self, writing, and the personal life of a Petersburg dweller in "the summer of Kerenskii" lack authenticity; his story becomes more and more fictionalized and undifferentiated from the voices of others and literary quotations. The autobiographical impulse is played out twice in the novella; first, in the narrator's desire to tell about himself and his family, and then in a curious detour of that desire, in the attempt to relate "the biography" of Parnok.[7] This biography, however, is almost completely transformed into a bibliography, a recollection of books read by any Petersburg *raznochinets*. Among the ancestors of Parnok one finds the characters of Honoré Balzac and Stendhal, and the disgraceful "little men" of Aleksandr Pushkin, Nikolai Gogol' and Dostoevsky, Petersburgian antiheroic heroes par excellence.

As has been remarked by many critics, the death sentence of the traditional hero is linked to Mandel'shtam's own novelistic theories expressed in his critical articles, especially in "Konets romana" ["The End of the Novel."] This essay proclaims with a mixture of bitterness and nostalgia that the centrifugal force of contemporary literature is no longer the individual, but time and historical necessity.[8]

The novella could hardly offer us any example of a dialogue "between human beings" in Dostoevsky's sense, because the notion of the individual and his role in literature and society has undergone important changes. The "main hero," Parnok, is merely a novelistic handicap who emerges from the doodles on the margins: "Parnok—Egipetskaia marka." Parnok is a failed Balzacian hero; he is not even lucky enough to become the "lishnii chelovek" ["superfluous man"] of a Russian novel. He is forever transferred from the rank of superfluous to the rank of marginal, both in Soviet society and in Soviet literature. The novella gradually deprives him of all literary privileges, and at the end the narrator himself switches from the third person to the first, abandoning Parnok in media res. Yet, the adventures of the failed hero Parnok exemplify the process of the literary mythification in the novella.

In fact, "Parnok" is something less than a name: Its national origins are unclear (it is definitely not Russian, but not blatantly Jewish either). It might be a first or a last name, a male or female name, a real family name or a pun, or an anagram from *parnokopytnoe* [even-toed ungulate]. Clarence Brown has suggested a reference to Viktor Parnakh, a brother of Sofiia Parnok and a man whose appearance and habits seem to have much in common with those of Mandel'shtam.[9] In my reading, the notion of a prototype for a literary hero, especially for such an unaccomplished one as Parnok, will be avoided. Instead, I will regard the extraliterary references as additional sources of allusions that contribute both richness and ambivalence to the dialogic interplays of the novella. In this case, it appears even more interesting to examine not Viktor Parnakh but his sister Sofiia, who is mentioned in the essays of Mandel'shtam, and whose names and roles present an almost ideal illustration of the multiple possibilities of dialogical splittings discussed by Mandel'shtam in "Fransua Villon."

First, Sofiia changes her name from Parnakh to Parnok, which she explains in a letter as a strange, unmotivated poetic whim: "Bukvu "kh" nenavizhu" ["I hate the letter x"].[10] Clarence Brown interprets it as a desire "to escape the disadvantages of its [letter *kh*] conspicuously Jewish sound." This points to Sofiia Parnok(kh)'s contradictory relationship with Judaism that foreshadows her future conversion to Christianity. (Ironically, the Jewish sounding letter *kh* happened to be the first letter of *Khristos* in Russian.)

Sofiia's first book of short stories was published under another pseudonym—Andrei Polianin. The choice of a male name appears to be paradoxical for a woman who confessed in a letter to Volkenstein that she never loved men,[11] and whose favorite heroine and poet was Sappho. Thus, the name Parnok itself becomes incredibly suggestive; it is a "name-transvestism" that preserves the traces of the erased letters and hints at shifting sexual identities.

Sofiia used to dislike Mandel'shtam's poetry; yet, uncannily, one of her poems of the 1930s echoes Mandel'shtam's early poem "Letaiut valkirii" ["The Flying Valkyries"] and rewrites one of his strophes in the first person.

Mandel'shtam refers to the poetry of Parnok in the essay "Literaturnaia Moskva" ["Literary Moscow"]. He sees in it the embodiment of what he described half humorously, half scornfully as "feminine poetry":

Адалис и Марина Цветаева—пророчицы, сюда же и София Парнок. Пророчество, как домашнее рукоделие. В то время как приподнятость тона мужской поэзии, нестерпимая трескучая риторика, уступила место нормальному использованию голосовых средств, женская поэзия продолжает вибрировать на самых высоких нотах, оскорбляя слух, историческое, поэтическое чутье.

Adalis and Marina Tsvetaeva are prophets, as is Sofia Parnok. Their prophesy is a kind of domestic needlework. While the elevated tone and intolerable bombastic rhetoric of men's poetry has subsided, yielding to a more normal use of the vocal apparatus, feminine poetry continues to vibrate at the highest pitch, offending the historical, poetic sense.[12]

A lyrical exaltation, falsely pathetic and exaggerated, an abusive use of metaphor and a lack of the sense of history are supposed to characterize literary femininity, from the poetry of Parnok and Marina Tsvetaeva to that of Vladimir Maiakovskii, who "is in danger of becoming a poetess." For Mandel'shtam, "feminine poetry" and "masculine poetry" are not so much references to the poet's biological sex as cultural metaphors. In fact, in this description Mandel'shtam recreates another powerful cultural myth, the myth of the "poetess," which is not uniquely limited to a Russian context.[13] The "poetess" as a cultural metaphor is usually opposed to the charismatic "poet" and romantic genius. The poetess is a "graphomaniac," who masks her lack of genius with manneristic excesses. Moreover, Mandel'shtam regards literary femininity as an unconscious parody of what, according to him, constitutes the kernel of true (virile) poetry (p. 327):

> На долю женщин в поэзии выпала огромная доля пародии в самом серьезном и формалыном смысле этого слова. Женская поэзия является бессознательной пародией, как поэтических изобретений так и воспоминаний. Большинство московских поэтесс ушиблены метафорой. Это бедные Изиды, обреченные на вечные поиски куда-то затерявшейся второй части поэтического сравнения, долженствующий вернуть поэтическому образу-Озирису свое первоначальное единство.

> [The vast realm of parody, in the most serious and formal meaning of the word, has fallen to the lot of women in poetry. Feminine poetry emerges as an unconscious parody of both poetic inventiveness and reminiscence. The majority of Moscow poetesses have been injured by metaphor. These are the poor Isises, doomed to the eternal quest after the second half of a poetic simile which was lost somewhere, and which is obliged to return its primal unity to the poetic image, to Osiris. (p.146)]

The word *bessoznatel'noi* [unconscious] here is crucial. The poetess cannot mock herself: She lacks precisely that authentic artistic subjectivity that would enable her to comment critically upon the poetic tradition. The tasteless excesses of the poetess result from her cultural uprootedness, her radical and irretrievable loss—a loss before possession—of the primordial unity of the masculine image, Osiris.

If the description of literary femininity can be seen as humorous and ironic (although this humor has important cultural implications), its opposite—the ideal of "muzhestvennost'" [manliness], "muzhskaia sila i pravda" [manly strength and truth]—is presented rather uncritically and with a suspicious seriousness (suspicious for the reader of Bakhtin):

> В отличие от старой, гражданской поэзии, новая русская поэзия должна воспитывать не только граждан, но и "мужа." Идеал совершенной мужественности подготовлен стилем и практическими требованиями нашей эпохи. Все стало тверже и громадней ... Гиератический, то есть священный характер поэзии обусловлен убежденностью что человек тверже всего в мире.

As opposed to the civic poetry of the past, modern Russian poetry must educate not merely citizens, but "Men." The ideal of perfect manliness is provided by the style and practical demands of our age. Everything has become heavier and more massive... The hieratic, that is to say, the sacred character of poetry arises out of the conviction that man is harder than everything else in the world.[14]

Masculine poetry is characterized by hieratic firmness and epic dimensions.[15] This metaphor of virility—a combination of ancient ideals and contemporary Russian prejudices—is one of the perfect Greek masks created by the poet.

In the literary works of Mandel'shtam, especially in *Egipetskaia marka*, the myths of masculinity and femininity are interwoven into the dialogical texture of the text that modifies and reshapes those myths. First of all, the very metaphor of sewing—which occurs in the above description of "feminine poetry" (the feminine poetic prophecies with their alleged mannerism and superficiality are compared to domestic needlework)—is a central metaphor for writing in *Egipetskaia marka* (although in the novella it is not explicitly linked to the feminine trade, but rather to the work of a male Jewish tailor). The metaphor of sewing is developed both in the narrator's digressions concerning the process of composing the novella and in the adventures of Parnok's coat. Another "associative chain" can be followed in the descriptions of Sofiia Parnok's "feminine poetry" and Anzhiolina Bozio's feminine death. Anzhiolina Bozio, like an exemplary poetess, seems to "vibrate at the highest pitch" and overstrain her voice. "Ona pripodnialas' i propela to chto nuzhno, no ne tem sladostnym metallicheskim gibkim golosom ... a grudnym, neobrabotannym tembrom piatnadtsatiletnei devochki-podrostka, s nepravilinoi, neekonomnoi podachei zvuka" (p. 36). ["She raised herself a bit and sang what was required, but not in that sweet voice, metallic and pliant ... but with the chesty, unpracticed timbre of a fifteen-year-old girl, with an incorrect, wasteful production of the sound."][16]

Daphne West has suggested a strong feminine presence in the images of the novella, especially those connected with death, illness and fear, and also in the figures of memory and time.[17] Even the legendary "kamennyi gost'" ["stone guest"], a guardian of the Petersburg fantastic tradition, has gone through a sex change and has turned into a terrifying "strashnaia kamennaia dama v botikakh Petra Velikogo" (p. 30) ["a terrifying stone lady 'in the high boots of Peter the Great,'" (p. 153)]. The clear opposition between feminine and masculine elements cannot be consistently preserved throughout the novella.

The images of Anzhiolina Bozio and Parnok are strikingly similar. Like her, he is completely uprooted from his country and from his time. He is an orphan of the great Russian literary tradition, unable to recover from the Petersburg influenza and prove his manliness and strength. Curiously, in the same digression in which the narrator, or rather his pen, draws the doodle of Parnok, there appears twice an androgynous image of "usataia grechanka" ["mustached Greek woman"] that remains marginal and is never completely integrated into the story. The Greek element, as well as the Egyptian, Italian, or Jewish element, represents an alien, southern intrusion in the northern capital. The Greek motif is linked to Parnok, who dreamed of becoming a dragoman in Greece with the help of Artur Iakovlevich Gofman. Also, there is an image of the Greek woman in an open grave—one of the strange memory traces shared by the narrator and Parnok. Her story, or rather fragment of a story, presents another echo, another distorted version, of the story of Parnok, the narrator, and Anzhiolina Bozio—a variation on the theme of foreignness and displacement, in which actual national and sexual identities no longer matter. They are mobile and interchangeable, or perhaps not identities at all in the conventional sense.

The narrator desperately wishes to distinguish himself from Parnok: "Gospodi! Ne delai menia pokhozhim na Parnoka! Dai mne sily otlichit' sebia ot nego" (p. 24) ["Lord! Do not make me like Parnok! Give me the strength to distinguish myself from him." (p.149)] He implores God not to make him resemble a deprived character, a poetess, a being of indeterminate sexual and national identity. The narrator tries to exorcise all Parnok-like elements from himself and to demystify his unaccomplished hero, but this demystification is never completely accomplished. The narrator partakes of the same cultural myths and practices as Parnok: He too is "guilty" of the "feminine" lyrical exaltation, and a feeling of foreignness, and a nonbelonging to the "grand cotillion" of social and political changes.

Yet the ideal of perfect virility does not triumph in *Egipetskaia marka*. The novella fails even to represent it. The extreme, almost caricatured embodiment of virility might be seen in Captain Krzhyzhanovskii. He is the only successful man in the novella and a typical novelistic villain; at the end of the novella he goes to Moscow with Parnok's coat and stops at the fashionable hotel on Malaia Lubianka (which hardly can be Mandel'shtam's ideal of virile "civic service"). Among possible Soviet literary relatives of Krzhyzhanovskii might be Babichev, from Olesha's *Zavist'* [*Envy*], another figure of inflated masculinity coupled with a profound anti-intellectualism, a figure that was soon to become the official Soviet ideal of the "real man" and citizen.

Hence, an ironic reference to Sofiia Parnok opens up other intertextual possibilities and traces new paths of reading. The analysis of Mandel'shtam's own text undermines the purity of both the myth of femininity and the myth of masculinity, and reveals how closely interwoven they are. With its ongoing painful dialogue between different contradictory voices extending to Bakhtin's "intermolecular and subatomic levels," *Egipetskaia marka* presents a striking example of the "lyrical hermaphroditism" described in "Fransua Villon."

Apart from Parnok and Anzhiolina Bozio, there are numerous other voices interwoven in the novella—the voices of the Petersburg crowd and literary voices. These voices, however, lack the proper orchestration and organizing authority of the master-director. They sound more like cacophonic chords of the "Jewish chaos" described in *Shum vremeni* [*Noise of Time*] than the elements of the harmonic Petersburg symphony or Bakhtin's utopian polyphonic novel.

Revolutionary Petersburg is seen as an embodiment of alienation. All means of urban communication are broken or disrupted. Telephones in the Petersburg pharmacies, made of "samogo luchshego skarlatinogo dereva" ["of the very finest scarlatina wood"] are disconnected, and the bridges across the Neva that are supposed to link all Petersburg's islands remain raised and inaccessible for Parnok. The search for communication reaches the extreme of dramatic intensity, but it is usually reduced to a number of urgent and desperate questions floating in the air: "Chto delat'? Komu zhalovat'sia? Kakim serafimam vruchit' robkuiu kontsertnuiu dushonku prinadlezhashchuiu malinovomu roiu kontrabasov i trutnei?" (p. 26). ["What is to be done? To whom can one complain? To which seraphim should one deliver the shy, correct-going soul belonging to the raspberry paradise of contrabasses and drones?" (p. 150)].

Thus the elements of silence, disruption, and incommunicability are present in all Mandel'shtam's dialogues, including the dialogue between the author and the reader. A mythical image of a mutilated book, the most striking in the series of book-images in the novella, that of "tortsovaia kniga s vyrvannoi seredinoi" (p. 183) ["the wooden stone-bound book, the interior of which had been ripped out" (p. 158)], appears in the last chapter. This image serves as a key figure both for *Egipetskaia marka* and for the unreadable life of revolutionary Petersburg.

This Petersburg book, however, has an international pedigree. In fact, the myth of the book—often more powerful than the myth of life—is one of the common topoi of modernist literature, linked to a peculiar version of the modernist "death of the author." Thus Mallarmé's mythical "Livre," "orphic explanation of the earth," was supposed to be the space in which the writing subject endlessly disappears and the poet becomes absolutely "pure" and "impersonal." But the Mallarméan all-encompassing Book, like Jorge Luis Borges's infinite "book of sand," could never be written and never read.[18] In fact, its very incompleteness is a source of its vitality. The impossibility of writing a perfect book or of recovering its forever missing pages, inspires many poetic narratives and guarantees the poet's survival. It prevents the ultimate modern "death of the author" from happening. Mandel'shtam's allegorical Petersburg book reveals the crucial ambiguity in the novella's relationship to modernity and tradition.

Egipetskaia marka problematizes the notions of the individual and of biography, of genre and gender and questions the validity of both biography and novel that focus on human figures and psychological conflicts. The novella, however, is not just a demonstration of "the end of the novel," nor is it an entirely avant-garde narrative. It stages the very act of collision of different values and ideas. Its sense of modernity is defined through both the reappropriation of the Russian literary tradition and a new eclecticism. In fact, *Egipetskaia marka* recreates a whole network of literary allusions, both poetic and prosaic; it participates in various genres, but does not belong to any. Mandel'shtam's prose stages a dialogue between different genres and turns it into a drama of writing in a broader sense. This drama of writing ponders the very possibility of creative expression of any kind in the specific historical moment when "temperatura epokhi vskochila na tridtsat' sem' i tri, i zhizn' proneslas' po obmannomu vyzovu, kak grokhochushchii noch'iu pozharnyi oboz" (p. 10) ["the temperature of the age shot up to 37.3 and life raced out on a false alarm like a fire brigade thundering through the night" (p. 137)]. In this respect it is of crucial importance that the action of the novella takes place in the interval between two revolutions, in the complex and pluralistic time of "two powers." The "summer of Kerensky" was a period when the Russian modernization could have taken different routes and would not necessarily have been limited to that of the Bolshevik

Revolution. The novella reflects both this plurality of modern potentials and an existential fear of the fin-de-siècle apocalyptic predicament.

Egipetskaia marka proceeds as a constant laying bare of the device of its composition. Actually, what we are reading is not a book with its definite structure and the authority of the printed word, but a work-in-progress, a draft that one day might be performed as a sonata. It is set against its own margins, in continuous interaction with accidental, nonsensical, "secondary and involuntary" creations of fantasy, comic doodles and anagrams. Probably inspired by Pushkin's manuscripts with their multiple sketches and doodles on the margins, and the critical discussion around them, Mandel'shtam intends to include the critical function in the novella, to inscribe marginality into the text, and make the text comment upon itself. Here are some of the programmatic statements that the narrator makes in one of his digressions (p. 25).

Я не боюсь бессвязности и разрывов
Стригу бумагу длинными ножницами.
Подклеиваю ленточки бахрамой.
Рукопись—всегда буря, истрепанная, исклеванная.
Она—черновик сонаты.

[I am not afraid of incoherence and gaps.
I shear the paper with long scissors.
I paste on ribbons as a fringe.
A manuscript is always a storm, worn to rags, torn by beaks.
It is a first draft of a sonata. p. 149]

Indeed, the novella makes visible and lingers upon its discontinuities—the discontinuities between the accelerated, feverish rhythm of contemporary life and the pace of traditional biographically centered fiction, between poetic subjectivity and the attempt to transmit "the noise of time." In the center of the novella is neither a hero nor a heroine, but the process of sewing and binding decentered fragments in a desire to find or create meaning. As Charles Isenberg has demonstrated, *Egipetskaia marka* operates through a series of associative chains that link it to Mandel'shtam's poetry.[19] At the same time, it lacks an overall poetic unity, and obviously enters into dialogue with novelistic conventions. The prose of Mandel'shtam can hardly be called the "novelization of poetry" or the "poeticization of the novel"—the terms frequently used by Bakhtin. Rather, it opens a "new semantic space" always before or after the distinctions between poetry and prose.[20] In "Razgovor o Dante" ["Conversation about Dante"] Mandel'shtam insists on shifting the critical focus away from the reified whole of the work to the impulses and the amplitude of fluctuation that the text reenacts, stressing "poryvoobrazovanie, a ne formoobrazovanie" ["the creation of impulses than the creation of forms"].[21] Following Mandel'shtam's advice, one should not impose a centralizing structure upon a novella about decentering. In *Egipetskaia marka* various cultural and literary myths are shaped and dissolved in the course of the narrator's self-presentation and self-effacement, opening up multiple dialogical possibilities.

Gregory Freidin, in his illuminating study of Mandel'shtam's "mythologies of self-presentation," regards *The Egyptian Stamp* as a "cruel parody of the very self that had animated some of Mandel'shtam's loftiest poetry."[22] In other words, the novella is viewed as a parody of the myth of the "charismatic author," a Joseph-Hippolytus figure, both prophet and martyr. Using Roland Barthes's notion of cultural mythologies, Freidin proposes to examine Mandel'shtam as a "complex cultural phenomenon . . . in which art extends effortlessly into biography, history and politics," stressing "the narrative continuity," or even a unity in the poet's "self-presentation" (pp. ix–x). Thus the novella can be regarded as belonging to the genre of what Freidin calls "samokritika" ["self-critique"] practiced by many intellectuals during the period of the NEP. Moreover, this samokritika "signified an attempt at reconciliation with the regime" (p. 220).

Yet, *Egipetskaia marka* presents a problem for constructing "the narrative continuity" of the poet's mythical self-presentation by acting out narrative discontinuities and pasting together different images of authorship which include a hysterical poetess, a Jewish tailor and a frustrated textual craftsman (who would hardly make company to the virile Soviet revolutionary writer). In this respect the novella goes beyond the enactment of literary envy or of self-mockery; it calls into question the very possibility of writing about the "self," as well as of the self of a modern writer and of his ability to decipher Russian or Soviet cultural myths. In fact, in Barthes's own later reconsideration of his *Mythologies* the critic warns against the easy "demystifications" that only lead to the erection of new (or temporarily forgotten) myths.[23] According to Barthes, one has to suspend demystification in order to observe the process of mythmaking itself and to capture the "hesitation" of the mythical naming. My reading foregrounds this hesitation along with various gaps in the mythical narrative of the self.

In spite of Mandel'shtam's partaking in the "classical" Russian myth of the great poet, *Egipetskaia marka* represents a genuine attempt to embrace modernity. It engages a dialogue with specifically modern mythologies that are not limited to Russian or Soviet borders. It is crucial to see both the connections and the discontinuities between various versions of modernity and modernism, particularly between that of official Soviet revolutionary literature, canonized in the late 1920s and early 1930s, and the broader project of modernity in which the acmeists actively participated in the attempt to merge "classical poetry" with "poetry of revolution." This modern project can be traced at least as far as Charles Baudelaire's and Mallarmé's attempts to abandon the traditional practice of poetry for the sake of a new kind of "poetic prose"—a response to urban experience and a reflection of the modern "crisis."[24] Mandel'shtam's autobiographical prose, together with the autobiographical prose of Pasternak and Tsvetaeva, which also problematically intertwine the issues of genre and gender (especially Pasternak's *Detstvo Luvers* [*The Childhood of Lovers*] and Tsvetaeva's *Povest' o Sonechke* [*The Tale of Sonechka*]) should not be regarded as peculiar generic miscarriages. Rather, these writings can be seen in a broader international context of modernism together with intergeneric autobiographical writings of European poets and critics, such as Walter Benjamin's *Berlin Chronicle*, Michel Leiris's *L'Age d'Homme*, Gertrude Stein's *Autobiography of Alice B. Toklas*—to name just a few examples.

On the one hand, *Egipetskaia marka* narrates the impossibility of writing a nineteenth century style polyphonic novel—the model of Bakhtin's theory of dialogue—in the feverish postrevolutionary time. The old-fashioned pistols nostalgically recreated in the first paragraphs of the novella aim at the very conception of self. Its "heteroglossia" is much more radical than the one proposed by Bakhtin, much more disjointed and dehumanized. Its disrupted dialogues re-enact the cacophonous modern rhythms and capture the destructive noise of time.

On the other hand, despite the abundance of apocalyptic imagery, *Egipetskaia marka* does not become apocalyptic. In fact, the very images of decay and disease can easily flip-flop in the text, turning into fruitful poetic metaphors. As Charles Isenberg has shown, the image of disease links the various motifs of the novella—the motifs of childhood, of the Russian literary tradition with its sickly heroes, of urban contamination, of incommunicability, as well as the motif of poetic inspiration.[25] The "Petersburg influenza" shared by Parnok and the narrator is both the sign that they do not belong to the revolutionary cotillion, and a condition of partaking in it. Ultimately, it is the fever of Petersburg influenza that also produces the creative delirium ("liubimyi prozaicheskii bred" ["dear prosaic delirium"]) and enables the narrator to experience a brief epiphany, achieving a peculiar communion with the otherwise hostile world of things: "Togda prizant'sia, is ne vyderzhivaiu karantina i smelo shagaiu, razbiv termometry, po zaraznomy labirintu, obveshannomu pridatochnymi predlozheniiami, kak veselymi sluchainymi pokupkami" (p. 40). ["Then, I confess, I am unable to endure the quarantine and, smashing, thermometers, through the contagious labyrinth I boldly stride, behung with subordinate clauses like happy bargain buys." (p. 161)].

The Petersburg disease provokes both a fear of its aggravating consequences and a desire for that liberating feverish delirium, which occurs after swallowing a spoonful of cod liver oil from beloved and hated childhood. The rhythms of the modern life are contagious like the virus of the influenza against which no vaccine has yet been invented.

Notes

1 Obviously, the idea of a poet's androgyny is not unique to Mandel'shtam; one encounters it in the writings of Samuel Taylor Coleridge, Charles Baudelaire, Stéphane Mallarmé, Marina Tsvetaeva, and other nineteenth and twentieth century poets. Osip Mandel'shtam, "Fransua Villon," in Sobranie Sochinenii, 4 vols. (New York: Inter-Language Literary Association, 1971) 2:305. All references to Mandel'shtam's essays [in Russian] follow this edition. [English translations added by the editors from Osip Mandel'shtam, Complete Critical Prose and Letters, trans. Jane Gary Harris and Constance Link (Ann Arbor, Mich.: Ardis, 1979), 56.

2 Mikhail Bakhtin, "Avtor i geroi v esteticheskoi deiatel'nosti" in Estetika slovesnogo tvorchestva (Moscow: Iskusstvo, 1979) and Problemy poetiki Dostoevskogo (Moscow: Sovetskaia Rossiia, 1979) especially, chapter 2, 54–89.

3 Mikhail Bakhtin, "Zametki," in Literaturno-kriticheskie stat'i (Moscow: Khudozhestvennaia Literatura, 1986), 526. For the discussion of Bakhtin's conception of the novel and narrativity see Michael Holquist's introduction to Mikhail Bakhtin, The Dialogic Imagination, trans. Caryl Emerson and Michael Holquist (Austin: University of Texas Press, 1982). For the most recent discussion of Bakhtin's cultural contexts and the contemporary implications of his theory see Bakhtin: Essays and Dialogues on His Work, ed. Gary Saul Morson (Chicago: University of Chicago Press, 1986). [English Translation by Julia Vaingurt]

4 Osip Mandel'shtam, "Literaturnaia Moskva: Rozhdenie fabuly" in *Sobranie Sochinenii* 2:334. Osip Mandel'shtam, *Complete Critical Prose and Letters*, 152.

5 For the theoretical discussion of the notion of the "death of the author" see Roland Barthes, "The Death of the Author," in *The Rustle of Language*, trans. Richard Howard (New York: Hill and Wang, 1986), 49–56, and Michel Foucault, "What is an Author" in *Language, Counter-Memory, Practice*, trans. Donald Bouchard (Ithaca, N.Y.: Cornell University Press, 1977), 113–139. I develop some ideas of the death of the author and the poets' mythologies in my book *Death in Quotation Marks: Cultural Myths of the Modern Poet* (Cambridge: Harvard University Press, 1991). Clare Cavanagh has elaborated the connection between Mandel'shtam and T. S. Eliot in the framework of modernism in her dissertation entitled "Mandel'shtam and the Modernist Creation of Tradition" (Ph.D. diss., Harvard University, 1988). I am grateful to Clare Cavanagh, with whom I had many stimulating and inspiring dialogues.

6 Osip Mandel'shtam, *Egipetskaia marka* in *Sobranie Sochinenii*, vol. 2. All Russian references follow this edition. [English translations added by the editors from *The Prose of Mandel'shtam*, trans. Clarence Brown (Princeton, N.J.: Princeton University Press, 1965), 150.]

7 On the problems of autobiography see Jane Gary Harris, "Autobiographical Theory and the Problems of Aesthetic Coherence in Mandel'shtam's *The Noise of Time*," *Essays in Poetics* 9, 2 (1984) and her introduction to Osip Mandel'shtam, *Complete Critical Prose and Letters*.

8 Osip Mandel'shtam, "Konets romana," in *Sobraniie Sochinenii* 2:66–70.

9 Clarence Brown, introduction, *Prose of Mandel'shtam*, 47.

10 Quoted in Sofiia Poliakova, introduction to Sofiia Parnok, *Sobranie stikhotvorenii* (Ann Arbor, Mich.: Ardis, 1979), 12. All information on Sofiia Parnok is taken from this book. Diana Burgin in her paper presented at the AATSEEL conference in San Francisco, December 1987, discussed the "triangle" Parnok-Tsvetaeva-Mandel'shtam, offering yet another interesting perspective on the relationship between Mandel'shtam and Parnok. [English translation by Julia Vaingurt].

11 Quoted in Poliakova, introduction, Parnok, *Sobranie stikhotvorenii*, 15,

12 Osip Mandel'shtam, "Literaturnaia Moskva," in *Sobranie Sochinenii* 2:328. [Osip Mandel'shtam, *Complete Critical Prose and Letters*, 146.]

13 On the poetess as a cultural construct and the ways it affects women authors, see Sandra Gilbert and Susan Gubar, *The Madwoman in the Attic* (New Haven, Conn.: Yale University Press, 1979).

14 Osip Mandel'shtam, "O prirode slova," in *Sobranie Sochinenii* 2:258. [Osip Mandel'shtam, *Complete Critical Prose and Letters*, 132.]

15 In the same essay Mandel'shtam goes further to suggest that some literary movements such as symbolism and futurism can be regarded as feminine, lacking in the historicity and cultural receptivity characteristic of a more "virile" and classic movement—acmeism.

16 Mandel'shtam, *Egipetskaia marka*, 36. [Osip Mandel'shtam, *The Prose of Mandel'shtam*, 157.]

17 Daphne West, *Mandel'shtam: The Egyptian Stamp*, Birmingham Slavonic Monographs, no. 10 (1980), 41–42.

18 For the description of mythical books see, for instance, Stéphane Mallarmé, "Autobiographie," in *Oeuvres Complètes*, 661–666, and Jorge Luis Borges, "Libro de Arena," in *Libro de Arena* (Buenos Aires: Alianza Emecé, 1984).

19 Charles Isenberg, *Substantial Proofs of Being: Osip Mandel'shtam's Literary Prose* (Columbus, Ohio: Slavica, 1987), 121–132.

20 Iurii Levin, Dmitrii Segal, et al., "Russkaia semanticheskaia poetika kak potentsial'naia kul'turnaia paradigma," *Russian Literature* 7/8 (1974).

21 Mandel'shtam, *Sobranie Sochinenii* 2:413. [Osip Mandel'shtam, *The Prose of Mandel'shtam*, 442.]

22 Gregory Freidin, *A Coat of Many Colors* (Berkeley: University of California Press, 1987), 213.

23 Roland Barthes, "Mythologies Today," in *The Rustle of Language*, trans. Richard Howard (New York: Hill and Wang, 1986), 66–67. See also Roland Barthes, "Avant-Propos," in *Mythologies* (Paris: Éditions du Seuil, 1970).

24 Charles Baudelaire, "À Arsène Houssaye," in *Petits poèmes en prose* (Paris: Flammarion, 1967), 31–32, and Stéphane Mallarmé, "Crise de vers," in *Oeuvres Complètes* (Paris: Gallimard, 1945), 360–369.

25 Charles Isenberg, *Substantial Proofs of Being*, 129–131.

Certainly, it is not just an ordinary morning coat, but a cipher of Parnok's desire for success, a desire to hide the hateful mark of alienation and become like Balzacian heroes in the good old time. The circulation of the morning coat is a circulation of that desire and of the nostalgia for the novels that made perfect sense with "physiologie" and psycology, with "real" heroes and "real" cities. It also resembles the adventures of the overcoat of poor Akakij Akakievich from Gogol's Overcoat. But unlike the ending of the Peterburg tale of Gogol where the "little man" takes a final revenge upon the "important person" (značitel'noe lico) and bring ... relief to the reader, the last scene of The Egyptian Stamp only accounts for the reader' major discomfort. Parnok's morning coat can never be retrieved, it leaves Peterburg forever together with the dream of a happy ending of the new Peterburg tale.

The lyrical narrator of the novella is not participating either in the last journey out of the city. The fear that "unharnesses horses when one has to drive" and sends the "dreams with unnecessary low ceilings" (p. 188) does not let him leave Peterburg. The fear, like the influenza, is both paralyzing and stimula- ting. It stands behind letters and lines as a constant drive and impulse for writing. Writing, however, cannot defeat fear, it can only tame it and domesti- cate a little bit playing with the ironic distancing:

> Страх берет меня за руку и ведет. Белая ни-
> тяная перчатка. Митенка. Я люблю, я уважаю
> страх. Чуть было не сказал: «с ним мне не страш-
> но!» (p. 67)

In the previous paragraph the narrator was telling us about the pleasure to switch from the third person to the first, but in the final scene we no longer hear his poetical voice. He obeys to the little words "on the beck and call" of his consciousness and seems to immerse himself completely into the rhythm of the "railroad prose:" голу бушка проза — вся пущенная в длину — обмери- вающая, бесстыдная, наматывающая на свой живоглотский аршин все шестьсот девять нико- лаевских верст, с графинчиками запотевшей водки. (p. 64)

FIGURE 2.1 An Excerpt from a Seminar Paper for Comparative Literature 206 with Prof. Donald Fanger, 1984.

2 PETERSBURG INFLUENZA: NOTES ON *THE EGYPTIAN STAMP* BY OSIP MANDEL'SHTAM: AN EXCERPT FROM A SEMINAR PAPER FOR COMPARATIVE LITERATURE 206 (Prof. Donald Fanger, 1984)

The Final Journey of *The Egyptian Stamp*

The ending of the Peterlurg novella is ironic: it is the first and the last road out of the city, a sort of illusory rupture of the city nightmare.

The dream of the voyages goes throughout the whole novella. In the first chapter Parnok is shown playing with the Il'in's map of the hemispheres and plotting "the itineraries of the grandiose voyages" to Africa, Australia and South America. In the episodes connected with Angiolina Bozio we encounter again the motive of journey–the famous transatlantic tours of the Italian singer which lead her to a tragic death in exile on the unfriendly Petersburg soil. In the last chapter there is an evocation of a childish nightmare–the journey to Malinov, an escape from the Jewish pogroms that, by a curious displacement, end in Peterburg Taurid Garden.

Thus, the voyage is both desirable and fearful. Peterburg in the novella is presented as a self-centered space, a microcosm, a no-exit labyrinth, at least for the narrator and Parnok. In the final journey they are left behind, effaced from the narrative, which follows only Captain Kržyzanwskij and the morning coat of Parnok.

Certainly, it is not just an ordinary morning coat, but a cipher of Parnok's desire for success, a desire to hide the hateful mark of alienation and become like Balzacian heroes in the good old time. The circulation of the morning coat is a circulation of that desire and of the nostalgia for the novels that made perfect sense with "physiologie" and psychology, with "real" heroes and "real" cities. It also resembles the adventures of the overcoat of poor Akakij Akakievich from Gogol's *Overcoat*. But unlike the ending of the Peterburg tale of Gogol where the "little man" takes a final revenge upon the "important person" (značitel'noe lico) and bring relief to the reader, the last scene of *The Egyptian Stamp* only accounts or the reader' major discomfort. Parnok's morning coat can never be retrieved, it leaves Peterburg forever together with the dream of a happy ending of the new Peterburg tale.

The lyrical narrator of the novella is not participating either in the last journey out of the city. The fear that "unharnesses horses when one has to drive and sends the "dreams with unnecessary low ceilings" (p. 188) does not let him leave Peterburg. The fear, like the influenza, is both paralyzing and stimulating. It stands behind letters and lines as a constant drive and impulse for writing. Writing, however, cannot defeat fear, it can only tame it and domesticate a little bit playing with the ironic distancing:

Страх берет меня за руку и ведет. Белая нитяная перчатка. Митенка. Я люблю, я уважаю страх. Чуть было не сказал: «с ним мне не страшно!» (p.67)

[Terror takes me by the hand and leads me. A white cotton glove. A woman's glove without fingers. I love terror, I respect it. I almost said, "With it, I am not terrified! p.162][1]

In the previous paragraph the narrator was telling us about the pleasure to switch from the third person to the first, but in the final scene we no longer hear his poetical voice. He obeys to the little words "on the beck and call" of his consciousness and seems to immerse himself completely into the rhythm of the "railroad prose:"

голубушка проза — вся пущенная в длину — обмеривающая, бесстыдная, наматывающая на свой живоглотский аршин все шестьсот девять николаевских верст, с графинчиками запотевшей водки. (p. 68)

[this dear little prose..., stretched out at its full length...measures, shameless thing that it is, and winds on its own fraudulent yardstick the six hundred and nine versts of the Niolaevsky road, with its sweating carafes of vodka. (p.162)]

Thus, the last journey of *The Egyptian Stamp* presents a paradox: it is an illusion of an exit out of the no-exit labyrinth of the city, a journey without the main heroes, a writing almost deprived of poetical subjectivity, an ending without resolution.

Philippe Hamon in his article on the endings has observed that "la clausule est. . .un element fondamental de la lisibilité du texte," that is supposed to satisfy the reader's desire for meaning and to open the possibility of retrospective reconstruction of the whole text.[2] In *The Egyptian Stamp* it works in an opposite way, as a frustration of the reader and a final ironic detour of the desire for meaning.

Notes

1 [English translations added by the editors from: *The Noise of Time: The Prose of Osip Mandel'shtam*, Edited and translated by Clarence Brown, New York, NY: Penguin, 1993.]

2 Philippe Hamon, "Clausules," *Poétique* 24 (1975), p. 501. Also, on the problem of ending see Peter Brooks, "Freud's Masterplot" in *Yale French Studies* 55/56 (1978).

3 THE DEATH OF THE REVOLUTIONARY POET: VLADIMIR MAYAKOVSKY AND SUICIDE AS LITERARY FACT

The Theater of the Self: Myth, Fashion, and Writing

The examination of the nuances and complexities of the modern death of the poet in writing and in life requires a construction (or a reinvention) of a dynamic critical vocabulary. We have observed that "modernism" is defined by a peculiar practice of writing which explores the boundaries of language and of the writing subject and questions linear temporality and chronology. This practice of language aims at the suspension of the cultural image repertoire, especially that of the author, who, as in the case of Mallarmé, confronts the reader with a frightening disfiguration. There develops a certain preconception of a privileged interiority of writing, which is then celebrated by the critics as the author's successful escape from the iconic profanations and popular theater of everyday life. Hence there is a need to reestablish the cultural framing of this modernist practice of writing—not to inscribe it completely within a rigid historical and ideological frame but to be able to describe it adequately from a broader cultural perspective. I would argue that the modernist resistance to framing and the privilege of the interiority of writing might be regarded as myths. The death of the author can be seen as a proclamation of his immortality, the erection of a peculiarly modernist monument.

Barthes's *cultural myth* will be a crucial concept in my discussion. Barthes did not apply his concept of cultural myth to the life of the author, or to the problem of the self in general. The Formalist notions of "literary personality" and "biographical legend" help to bridge this gap.

Cultural myth is neither an archetypal, universal, Jungian myth, nor a personal myth, a whimsical product of the individual subconscious. It is an unwritten law shared by the community, a law that is difficult to repudiate because it seems to be natural, unauthorized, given. It transforms culture into nature and aims to mask its ideological implications by erasing its historicity. According to Barthes, cultural myth constitutes a kind of anonymous depoliticized discourse which pretends to be nonideological and transparent. It masks its historicity under the disguise of universality and atemporality. As Barthes says, "Myth does not deny things, on the contrary, its function is to talk about them; it simply purifies them, it makes them innocent, it gives them a natural and eternal justification, it gives them a clarity which is not that of an explanation, but that of a statement of fact."[1]

In the first edition of his *Mythologies,* Barthes proposes a graphic model of the cultural myth whose object is the linguistic sign; accordingly it becomes a metalanguage. Later he abandoned this hierarchical model, although it survived much longer in the studies of Barthes's disciples. In my opinion, the cultural myth should not be regarded as a secondary semiotic system, that is, as a cultural sign built on the linguistic (Saussurian) sign, like a Russian doll (*matreshka*). Linguistic and cultural spheres are interdependent and culture cannot be examined as a large wooden dummy which has a smaller but identical wooden dummy (language) inside it, or even as several wooden dummies, one inside the other (subculture, sub-subculture, language, dialect, subdialect, and so on and so forth).

Cultural myth is neither a secondary linguistic system nor a metalanguage describing another language; the student of cultural myths is not a metacritic. Barthes revised his earlier conception of myth in the preface to the 1971 edition of *Mythologies.*[2] Here Barthes indicates that the problem lies not in demystifying or demythifying "bourgeois myths," which has become a convenient critical myth, but in the fissures of the representation itself, in the fluctuation of the sign. The task now consists not of *naming the myth,* but of *retracing the mythical* in phraseology, stereotypes, and references. There is a certain parallelism between the Barthesian critique of Barthes's early notion of myth and Bakhtin's critique of semiotics. The Soviet semioticians developed their own theories of the "typology of cultures." Culture is regarded as a system of information or a system of social codes that permits communication of this information by means of signs. Bakhtin criticizes the notion of code because it allows for both the development of a hierarchy of systems and the concept of metalanguage. Instead he proposes the notion of a dialogical utterance that collapses the levels of discourse and does not allow the cultural critic to establish an absolute scientific distance from the object of analysis.[3]

There is continuous dialogue, interaction, interpenetration, and superimposition of various "systems," or discourses, as well as close intertextual ties, between the linguistic and the cultural elements of myth. In fact, what are often considered to be purely linguistic conventions, such as the uses of masculine and feminine pronouns, the uses of "I," and the rhetoric of clarity, can have broad cultural implications.

[...]

What is particularly elusive about cultural myth is the fact that it does not depend entirely on written language. It is both difficult and challenging for students of literary criticism to see the limits of the verbal empire they construct around themselves. The cultural myth largely relies on unwritten but widely accepted, naturalized nonverbal discourse, on the power of the image and its semivisible, heavily codified iconography, as well as on cultural fashioning and social masks used in the "theater of everyday life."

The metaphor of the theater will be crucial in my examination of the cultural self of the poet. I assume that there is a limited cultural repertoire of roles, with their necessary visual and dramatic attributes, which are enacted and reshaped in each individual performance. There is no script for these roles, no compendium of cultural myths of the self written in the ideal metalanguage, a sort of critical Esperanto. The roles are not written anywhere in anything resembling a paradigmatic language of pure codes. Rather, they are realized in the course of individual performances, and their common attributes can be traced through their mutual superimposition. Hence, the relationship between life, art, and culture is not that of a mimesis, or a hierarchy, but rather that of a chain of rehearsals based on a certain limited repertoire (which, nevertheless, can offer a relatively unlimited number of combinations). This chain of rehearsals neither starts with the definitive original script nor ends with a final master performance. It is in a process of constant modification. Certain roles can be provisionally reified and described in order to understand the ongoing process. The death of the poet is a crucial poetic act and a crucial critical metaphor. It can be seen as an ultimate fulfillment of certain strategies and potentialities in the text, or as a provocative disruption of any unifying critical system.

To focus on the cultural myth of the poet might be particularly illuminating, because the poet is someone who is both creative and created, who is directly in touch with the language and therefore possesses maximum flexibility in role playing. At the same time, poets might stylize themselves excessively, making their attributes and theatrical makeup more visible. I wish to elaborate the notions of cultural image, cultural fashions, self-fashionings, and theatricality further, since they have been frequently excluded from the iconoclastic accounts of modernist writing.

The metaphor of the theater has emerged in various contexts in the examination of both the French and American critics, as well as the Soviet Russian Formalists and semioticians.[4] The French Structuralists and post-Structuralists focus primarily on the drama of writing, which protects its interiority and autonomy, while the Formalists begin to examine the "literary masks" of the writer and acknowledge their inescapability. The use of theatrical metaphors in everyday life and in literary criticism is tremendous. The very terms which apply both to the real-life self and to the literary self of the author (literary persona or personality) are etymologically related to the Latin word *persona,* theatrical mask. Perhaps, person, persona, personage, and personality are only different kinds of masks that suggest various degree of self-dramatization. In French *personne* also signifies "nobody," while in English "person" means precisely the opposite—"somebody." The etymological development of the two languages reflects two opposite ways of looking at the theatrical predicament of a human being, two opposites that paradoxically converge, as in the title of the Borges story about Shakespeare entitled "Somebody and Nobody."

"Mask" here does not imply a superficial disguise that hides the "real self." In fact, in traditional theatrical performances the interaction between actor and mask is very complex. The Kabuki actor, for instance, studies himself wearing the mask before a mirror for several days, for "one feels like a bamboo when one looks at a bamboo."[5] In other words, the actor identifies with his new image and becomes it (a sort of adult reenactment of the Lacanian "mirror-stage," during which a child identifies with his or her ideal flat mirror image). Greek and Roman actors undertook long silent communions with their masks before putting them on, in order to be receptive to them. Contemporary actors who work with masks note that they both hide and reveal. While they seem objects behind which one can physically hide and characterizations that "mask" one's emotions, they reveal crucial human features which go beyond individual character traits. Thus, in ancient rituals, as well as in the twentieth-century avant-garde theater of Artaud, Meyerhold, and others, the mask is often regarded as a typified image, closer to the intersubjective "self" than an actual face. In this conception the mask is no longer "outside" but rather a representation of the "inside." The paradox of the mask consists precisely in its ambivalence: in different moments in history and in different theaters it has been seen as a metaphor of exteriority, as an exterior superficial disguise, and by contrast as a metaphor of a deep, hidden, depersonalized inner self, an image of intersubjectivity.[6]

Furthermore, there are different intermediate states between being totally masked and completely unmasked. Wearing makeup, which can be subtle or ostentatious, is one example. It is no accident that one of the first major statements of modern poetics—Baudelaire's "Le Peintre de la vie moderne" ("The Painter of Modern Life")—includes a praise of makeup, in which feminine makeup is regarded as a metaphor for modern art.[7] The masks of the commedia dell'arte, for instance, are also half-masks; they reveal the mouth and chin and allow interaction between parts of the face and the mask. Thus, the metaphor of the mask, always incomplete, always in the process of transforming and being transformed by the body and face of the actor, the mask that hides and reveals all the complex interrelationships between persona, personality, and the French *personne,* serves as a useful metaphor in the discussion of literature and life. One of the central questions that will be explored in my book is precisely whether a complete "unmasking," a complete "laying bare" of cultural clothing, is possible. I will try to follow the traces of blurred makeup on the poet's defaced figure.

In fact, the Western concepts of identity and individuality are closely linked to the metaphor of the theater. Even Freud uses Sophocles' play to tell his revelatory psychoanalytical story of the self; moreover, he calls the unconscious "another theater." Elizabeth Burns writes in *Theatricality* that the actor mimes the dominant concept of "identity" in a given period, or in other words the actor's craft reflects the existential human condition.[8] The movement is from sacred to social, from the medieval notion of acting as an allegorical "personification" of moral virtues and vices that refers to human beings in relation to the unseen world of spiritual reality, to the Renaissance "impersonation" of various social types—"a portrayal of a person through imitation of behavior, derived from observation and experience of ordinary life"—from "homo sub specie aeternae" to "uomo singolare e unico."[9] It is no accident that the metaphor of *theatrum mundi* becomes a philosophical cliché precisely in the Shakespearean Renaissance world, when people become acutely aware of the theater of everyday life—not only a transcendental tragedy of the human predicament written in heaven but also a secular comedy of manners, and later even a sentimental melodrama that is acted and directed by the characters themselves. "Theatricality" here does not simply refer to the theater as one of the artistic genres or media; rather, it points to a certain ontological and social condition. In other words, it points to the "vital" element in theater, to what theater dramatizes and foregrounds in life, and to what makes us call "life" theatrical and theater "lifelike"—an interaction between playfulness and conventionality, prescriptiveness of roles and the singularity of acts.

It is curious, however, that through the centuries the obvious linguistic link between "persona" and "personality" became culturally veiled. Moreover, they were viewed in opposition to each other, the mask turning into a cover-up, a superficial disguise of the "person." On the nineteenth-century theatrical stage this opposition is reflected in the growing negative attitude toward the use of masks—they are preserved only in popular spectacles such as the commedia dell'arte. Twentieth-century theater witnesses the return of the stylized mask, as a sign of the alienated, depersonalized self and, according to Artaud, as an expression of the desire for a new, universal reintegration through the reenactment of a cruel primitive spectacle.

As Jonas Barish demonstrated in his fascinating book *The Antitheatrical Prejudice,* the "antitheatrical prejudice" runs through the whole of Western intellectual history from Plato to Artaud.[10] The argument against theatricality is at the cornerstone of Plato's *Republic.* Theatricality is a kind of human malaise, a superficial fondness of spectatordom, posing, grimacing, affection, in short, a fondness for the transient world of appearances, for the aberrant imitation of imitations. Plato builds his own utopian republic—a totalitarian philosopher-state—in opposition to what he calls "an evil sort of theatrocracy," a rein of superficially innovative poets and decadent theater people who are incapable of capturing the essential archetypes.[11] This paraphrase is an obvious vulgarization of Plato, but it helps to summarize the antitheatrical legend, a cultural prejudice that keeps reappearing throughout European intellectual history under varying disguises. My hypothesis is that the modernist practice of language—as elaborated by Flaubert, Mallarmé, and the contemporary French theorists, especially Barthes—the practice of language in which the drama of writing displaces the social theatricality of life and the "phantoms of the theater" in general, can be seen as a variation on the antitheatrical prejudice that dates back to Plato.[12]

Another term that is related to theater as well as to modernism is "fashion," both as a verb and as a noun. The attention to fashion allows us to highlight the visual attributes and characteristic attire in the cultural myth of the poet, pointing beyond the distinctions of life and art.

A problematic configuration of modernism and fashion deserves a special consideration. The word "modernism" from the Latin *modo,* "just now," which emphasizes the immanence of the present tense and capitalizes on newness, is also related to "mode" as in way of thinking, behaving, dressing, and, in Romance languages, to *mode/moda* (feminine), meaning "fashion"—an association that generates many derogative connotations, usually activated by self-righteous satirists of the "moderns." Fashion, especially in the German tradition, is seen as a "false newness," or false sublation. Even de Man insists on preserving the distinctions between "fashion" and "modernity." His description of fashion sounds rather Romantic: "Fashion (*la mode*) can sometimes be only what remains of modernity after the impulse has subsided—as soon—and it can be almost at once—as it has changed from being an incandescent point in time into a reproducible cliché . . . Fashion is like the ashes left behind by the uniquely shaped flames of the fire, the trace alone revealing that the fire has actually taken place."[13] Fashion, especially in the context of German criticism, is seen as a monstrous double of the modern quest for newness, deprived of the aura of uniqueness and converted into a "reproducible cliché."

The history of the usages of the word fashion demonstrates a spectacular cultural degradation. Stephen Greenblatt examines its cultural etymology and remarks that it gains a particular significance in the sixteenth century, concurrently with the spread of the metaphor of *theatrum mundi:* "As a term for action, or a process of making, for particular features or appearances, for a distinct style or pattern, the word has been long in use, but it is in the sixteenth century that *fashion* seems to come into wide currency as a way of *designing* and forming the self."[14]

Fashioning and self-fashioning are a kind of secular/social "self-creation," distinct from the medieval "imitation of Christ." They presuppose an increasing recognition of the theatricality of daily life and of the possibility to choose one's own repertoire, to represent oneself. Greenblatt notes that "self-fashioning derives its interest precisely from the fact that it functions without regard for sharp distinctions between literature and social life."[15] It is enacted across the border, through representations and self-representations in all the spheres of human activity. In other words, certain similar fashions traverse the culture of the period, and operate in literature and life— interlocking them and preventing the critic from compartmentalizing them. A Romantic poet, a revolutionary poet, a poetess, a martyr of writing, a poet-pariah, a poet engagé, an *enfant terrible,* a prophet, a *voyant,* a voyeur, a dandy, a bohemian, a professional writer, a poet without biography, a poet-functionary of the State, a poet-monument, an academic—these are only some of the imprecise names for cultural fashioning. Fashion designates that peculiar space of vital intertextuality, or, as Shoshana Felman puts it, "vitality of texts" and "textuality of life," that might help us reshape the figure of the poet, and give us a broader insight into the making of the self in general. The study of fashions might unveil some spectacular theatrical underwear of the self, the self that can never be "layed bare" and exempt from everyday dramas. Even the pure poet is not completely unfashionable.

In fact, "fashion" originates from the same verb as "poetry," "to make"—*facere* in Latin and *poein* in Greek. Thus in my paradigm poetry and fashion are related like person and personality, or like person and *personne.* This correspondence further complicates the distinctions between the "self" and the "mask," between the writing self and the everyday persona, between writing and acting, between the disfiguration and proliferation of images.

"Revolutionary Poet": History, Myth, and the Theater of Cruelty

Vladimir Mayakovsky is a poet with a biography par excellence, a poet who is nonexistent without it. He is one of the last in the enfilade of Soviet Russian poet-heroes whose biographical legends became well-known popular fiction. We can count among them Alexander Pushkin and Mikhail Lermontov, who depicted dramatic duel scenes in their novels as if uncannily predicting their own deaths; Sergey Esenin, the "poet-hooligan," who cut his veins in a dusty hotel room and wrote a rhymed farewell note literally in blood (not in the transemotional, metaphorical blood described by Victor Shklovsky, but in nonpoetic actual human blood); and finally Mayakovsky, who put a period at the end of his life, as in his poem, "with the bullet."

Due to peculiar cultural and political circumstances, the reaction against the Romantic myth of the poet was much less pronounced in Russia than, for instance, in France. Thus, for Russian modernism the idea of the death of the author, the disappearance of the subject in the process of writing and the "deromanticization" of the poet's life, was not at all central.[16] The persistent Russian conception of the poet's life is a curious blend of German Romantic ideas of national genius and of Russian patriotism; of the European Romantic conception of the unity of the poet's life and art and of the civic tradition of the Russian intelligentsia embodied in the writings of Vissarion Belinsky. The cult of the poet thrives on political oppression. The poet is supposed to be more than just a poet and to have a cultural mission. He can be a voice and consciousness of the nation, a martyr, dying young, a Christ-like figure, who takes upon himself the sufferings of the people. Willingly or not, every Russian writer confronts this heroic tradition that privileges dead authors and literary martyrs and often "kills" literary texts by subjugating them completely to political, biographical, social, and metaphysical concerns. The worship of the Poet with a capital P is a peculiar form of Russian religion which survives today. Perhaps the most recent manifestation of it was the cult of the contemporary Soviet bard Vladimir Vysotsky, whose untimely death in 1980 provoked the largest spontaneous demonstration in Moscow since the death of Stalin.[17]

"The revolutionary poet" can be regarded as one of the avatars of the poet-hero: it is a distinctly modern phenomenon which presents an alternative to the image of the alienated and effaced poet. The notion of revolution presupposes an acute historical conscience and points to many modern myths, such as the myth of progress—a radical rupture with tradition—the myth of action, and the myth of a man-made justice. Thus the expression revolutionary poet will activate many of the already suggested aporias of modernity that underline the relationship between literature and history, as well as between writing and life. Hegel and many others after him tried to carefully distinguish between "revolution" and "revolt," seeing in the first a collective protest against social injustice and the objective force of history, and in the second the individual reaction of an alienated intellectual.[18] For a poet, someone who constantly experiments with language, both estranging this collective tool of communication and being estranged by it, the relationship between "revolt" and "revolution" is particularly intricate and complicated.

[...]

Mayakovsky's life and death were perceived by many contemporaries as a reenactment of the Russian cultural myth of the poet's fate. Mayakovsky was one of the most theatrical, spectacular, and controversial figures on the twentieth-century Soviet Russian cultural stage and definitely the most *visible* Soviet poet in the West. It would be a cultural misrepresentation to limit oneself to a purely textual and formal analysis of Mayakovsky's verse; and it will be demonstrated later that even for one of the founders of Russian Formalism, Roman Jakobson, this task has proved impossible.

Mayakovsky is both more and less than just a poet. Everyone always describes him as a poet plus something else—a qualifying adjective or a suffix. Marina Tsvetaeva writes that even to imagine Mayakovsky simply at the writing desk is "a physical incompatibility."[19] For Tsvetaeva he is "a poet-fighter," a poet "with history." For Boris Tomashevsky, Mayakovsky is a poet "with a biographical legend"; for Yury Tynyanov, "a poet with a new will."[20] In Osip Mandel'shtam's humorous version, he acquires a feminine suffix—turning from "a poet" into "a poet-ess," an embodiment of excessive subjectivism and emotionalism.[21] Even the expression revolutionary poet, when applied to Mayakovsky by other poets and critics, is frequently qualified. Thus in André Breton's view, a revolutionary poet turns into a surrealist, revolutionary antipoet. For Louis Aragon Mayakovsky is "revolutionary" and "poetic" in accordance with the correct French Communist Party definitions of his time. The tension between the poet Mayakovsky and his multiple qualifying adjectives and spectacular attributes—the tension that might have been at the heart of the mystery of his death—will be key in this chapter.

Mayakovsky's art and life are often seen as a continuous performance on the stage of history, too large and too public for "just a poet." Mayakovsky himself in his early tragedy *Vladimir Mayakovsky* created a theatrical frame and a hyperbolic scale for all his future portraits, allowing the spectators to modify slightly the costumes and props. The only enduring requirement is to make the main hero—the Poet Vladimir Mayakovsky—monumental and immortal.

Boris Pasternak attempts to comprehend the nature of Mayakovsky's modern theatricality and its connection to the poet's suicide. He includes Mayakovsky in his own poetic autobiography, presenting him as his impossible alter ego.[22] Mayakovsky becomes an exemplary poet-phenomenon (*javlenie*) with a "spectacular Romantic biography," an "impure" poet dependent upon brilliant exterior attributes. Mayakovsky's opposite and double is Pasternak himself, an impersonal and untheatrical "pure poet."

Pasternak rebels against the cheap theatricality surrounding the figure of the poet, which he sees in opposition to truly poetic time and space that is both atemporal and atopian.[23] Pasternak shares the antitheatrical prejudice: for him, the theater is reduced to a superficial public spectacle, a variety show with lustre and heroic affectation. And yet he sees a dangerous vitality in Mayakovsky's drama: "In contrast to playing roles, Mayakovsky played with life."[24] Mayakovsky chose the most difficult pose—the pose of exterior unity, the unity of life and art joined together in a spectacular and heroic romantic legend. He selected his own life "as a plot for the lyrical drama" and intended to make it a work of art.

Although in the framework of Pasternak's poetics, the "spectacular" attributes of the poet's life are diametrically opposed to the "true poetic mystery"—understood as the poet's ability to diffuse himself spiritually in the surrounding world and remain invisibly present without putting on a heroic mask—the case of Mayakovsky goes beyond this simple opposition. Mayakovsky's mystery consists of the *transgressive nature of his theatricality,* which acquires a dangerous vitality and ubiquity, threatening to blur the differences between life and art, as well as between life and death. The doctrine of "life-creation" elaborated by the Russian Symbolists was both parodied and lived out by Mayakovsky. According to Pasternak many Symbolists and Futurists flaunted their poetic makeup, and yet their masquerade remained harmless, "soft," and undisturbing, while that of Mayakovsky "smelled of blood." We may say that Mayakovsky lived out Antonin Artaud's ideal of the Theater of Cruelty, where blood and sacrifice are real—real to the point of vertigo, hyperreal, exposing the endless chain of illusionistic effects.

My focus here will be on the connection between Mayakovsky's "spectacular biography" and his deaths—figurative and nonfigurative. The Romantic mask of a Poet-hero fighting *byt,* or a self-sacrificing revolutionary, lures the poet with a promise of immortality and future resurrection, and at the same time it threatens him with an ultimate murderous depersonalization and a loss of self.

A Portrait of the Artist in a Yellow Blouse: Metaphor and Transgression

С Маяковским произошло так ... Он раскрыл рот и сказал—Я!—
Его спросили—кто—я? Он ответил—я, Владимир Маяковский.—
А Владимир Маяковский—кто?—Я! ... Так и пошло—"Владимир
Маяковский, тот кто я." Смеялись. Но "Я" в ушах, но желтая
кофта—в глазах—оставались.

*This is what happened to Mayakovsky ... He opened his mouth
and said: I! They asked him: Who is "I"? He answered: I, Vladimir
Mayakovsky.—And who is Vladimir Mayakovsky?—I! And since then
that's how it goes—"Vladimir Mayakovsky is who is I." They laughed.
But "I" in the ears and the yellow blouse in the eyes persisted.*

MARINA TSVETAEVA, "Epics and Lyrics of Contemporary Russia"

We can represent the cultural iconography of Vladimir Mayakovsky in a series of imaginary portraits, a collage of the poet's photographs, paintings, and verbal descriptions. Here is a prerevolutionary Mayakovsky—"the handsome, twenty-two-year-old" Futurist in the yellow blouse, asking the audience "to brush his ears." He is a bit of a dandy, with a long white cigar and a cylinder hat, a passionate poseur with intense dark eyes, a stylish hooligan.

The next portrait is of a Revolutionary poet with a capital R, roaring from the tribune: "Who is there marching to the right?/Left/Left/Left!" His hair is cut short like a soldier's, without even a trace of the unyielding Romantic forelock, revealing only a majestic skull and strong virile features.

Then there is a postrevolutionary Mayakovsky who aspires to become a major Soviet poet and a messenger of Soviet Russia on all continents: we see him on a vacation boat with the secretary of the Mexican Communist Party, wearing a black bow tie and smoking a cigar, then with his former fellow Futurist, David Burlyuk, near the Brooklyn Bridge, and finally with Lily Brik's sister, Elsa, in a Parisian café.

We see the next Mayakovsky, pre- and postrevolutionary poet-lover, screaming in the streets of the city "about that" in a fit of universal jealousy "to Copernicus." He is part of Alexander Rodchenko's constructivist collage, precariously balancing on a tower of Ivan the Great raised above a modern city, Moscow or New York, with Lily Brik in the foreground and skyscrapers in the background.

Finally, there is Mayakovsky the poet-monument. He wears the official bureaucratic bronze jacket, with an officially Revolutionary Romantic forelock, and guards the streets and squares of Soviet cities.

But these images are not as consistently representational as it might seem. In fact, there is an unusual self-portrait of Mayakovsky that stands out as exceptional and does not correlate with the cultural mythology of the poet. This portrait presents a cubist disfiguration of the face; it is an exercise in representational possibilities, a game in perspectives, and a juxtaposition of different planes to the extent that the individual anthropomorphic features and idiosyncratic attributes become invisible or irrelevant. From the pictorial point of view, the portrait is quite unoriginal: Mayakovsky uses already developed cubist techniques with one important difference, the object of disfiguration is his own persona. Although this self-portrait of the artist and poet is virtually unknown, and in general is rather uncharacteristic for Mayakovsky, we will keep it in mind throughout this discussion. It will allow us to regard all the other figurative and representational images as palimpsests, which betray traces of this self-disfiguring experimentation.

Traditional visual attributes played a crucial role in Mayakovsky's myth making. They correlated with important cultural icons and served as conscious and unconscious "visual propaganda" with which the poet attempted to shock and seduce the reader. I will not trace here the development of Mayakovsky's iconographic attributes from yellow blouse to bronze jacket. Rather, I will concentrate only on the adventures of the famous yellow blouse which will function as an exemplary metaphorical texture that discloses Mayakovsky's strategies of self-creation.

Mayakovsky describes the genesis of the yellow blouse in his autobiography, *I, Myself.* The poet promises to relate only what "has a residue of words" and of course the making of the yellow blouse is one such event.

Костюмов у меня не было никогда. Были две блузы —гнуснейшего вида … Нет денег. Взял у сестры кусок желтой ленты. Обвязался. Фурор.[25]

I never had any suits. I had two blouses of a most disgusting type . . . There was no money. I took from my sister a piece of yellow ribbon. Wrapped it around. A scandal.

The tailoring of the blouse, its color and material are all the result of accident, and they reflect nothing but the poet's poverty. At first, the blouse contributed only to the shock effect of the Futurist's happenings. Subsequently, it became poeticized. In 1914 Mayakovsky dedicates to it (or to her, since the word blouse in Russian is feminine) a short poem, "Fop's Blouse" ("Kofta fata"). The poem is a typical example of Mayakovsky's early urban lyric. The poetic persona is a larger-than-life figure of the Futurist poet who goes to "rape the green springs" and converses with the Earth and the Sun on equal terms. In the first stanza, the act of sewing cloth is a significant poetic initiation.

> Я сошью себе черные штаны
> из бархата голоса моего.
> Желтую кофту из трех аршин заката.
> По Невскому мира, по лощеным полосам его,
> профланирую шагом Дон-Жуана и фата.[26]

I will make myself black pants out of the velvet of my voice. A yellow blouse out of six feet of sunset. And I'll stroll around the paved stripes of the Nevsky Avenue of the world like a Don Juan and a fop.

The yellow blouse is no longer made of the prosaic and ordinary cloth of his sister, but of "six feet of sunset." It is a sign of the poet's communion with the sun. The relationship between the poet's self and cloth grows more and more intimate. In the last stanza the yellow blouse turns into an interface between the poet and the outside world.

> Женщины, любящие мое мясо, и эта
> девушка, смотрящая на меня, как на брата,
> закидайте улыбками меня, поэта—
> Я цветами нашью их на кофту фата!

Women, who love my flesh, and this girl, looking at me as though I were her brother, throw your smiles at me, the poet. I'll embroider them like flowers on my fop's blouse!

The title, "Fop's Blouse" ("Kofta fata"), wraps around the poem, offering us an interesting interpretive thread. It presents a suggestive sound patter. The word "fat" (fop), which designates an outrageous Futurist persona of Mayakovsky's, seems to emerge from "kofta" (blouse) to strengthen the effect of the sound repetition: *kof-ta fata*. Thus it seems that even before the "I" of the poem takes control and tells us about the exciting creation of the blouse out of the sunset, the persona of the poet himself—"fat"—is already created by the suggestive and seductive sound patterns of the word "kofta." In other words, the cloth poetically motivates the figure of the poet. Moreover, if we displace the accent in the word *"fata"* and turn it into "fa*ta*" (a bridal veil)—a gesture that Mayakovsky's poetry invites us to do—we might imagine the creation of "kofta" as an important poetic ritual, a preparation for the futuristic "marriage" to the modern city.

From a seemingly insignificant article of everyday life, the yellow blouse turns into a "literary fact" and then into a cultural emblem which starts affecting the poet's daily existence. Thus, Victor Shklovsky claims that yellow, which by pure chance was the color of the poet's sister's remnant, becomes *the* color of Futurism, and Mayakovsky's yellow blouse becomes its banner. This metamorphosis of the poet's cloth, which gradually acquires a cultural significance, is a vivid example of the vital interaction between art and life.

In the long poem *The Cloud in Trousers* (*Oblako v shtanakh*) (1914–1915) Mayakovsky tries to convince us that the blouse is only a protective disguise: "Khorosho kogda v zheltuju koftu dusha ot ukusov uprjatana" ("It's good when the soul is protected from bites in a yellow blouse").[27] However, it is becoming more difficult to separate the poet's Futurist soul from his Futurist clothing; they become metaphors of each other and drift into each other's territory.

Mayakovsky creates in his various articles a parodic image of a poet in a yellow blouse that stands for Mayakovsky the Futurist. The provocative essay "O raznykh Majakovskikh" ("About the Different Mayakovskys") (1914) begins with the grotesque recreation of his Futurist persona, not only that of a fop but also of a "hooligan and cynic," in which Mayakovsky consciously rejects his Futurist attire for all sorts of bourgeois jackets.

Я-*нахал, для* которого высшее удовольствие ввалиться, напялив желтую кофту, в сборище людей благородно берегущих под чинными сюртуками, фраками и пиджаками скромность и приличие.[28]

I am a lout, for whom the highest pleasure is to put on my yellow blouse and rush into a gathering of people, who nobly guard modesty and decency under their formal suits, dress coats and jackets.

The essay is a good example of Mayakovsky's ironic criticism, a mixture of self-mockery and self-advertisement. Here the poet masterfully promotes his long poem *The Cloud in Trousers*, both flirting with and provoking the reader. Mayakovsky performs a series of *saltos mortales*, shifting back and forth between "a young man of twenty-two" and the capital *P* Poet, parodying his own image of "a publicity seeker and a scandal maker in a yellow blouse" and glorifying it in the same gesture. In the article "A Drop of Tar" ("Kaplja degtja") (1916), which playfully declares the death of Futurism, Futurism itself is personified and turned into an "eccentric pal with a red forelock" which reminds us of the young Mayakovsky.[29] But it is even more striking that the Futurist movement is personified on its death bed, about to be killed, a proof of the poet's masterful ability to personify and depersonalize, to animate and destroy cultural movements. Mayakovsky parodies and objectifies his literary personae, often to the point of vertigo.

Later, in the programmatic *LEF* article "How Are Verses to Be Made" ("Kak delat' stikhi") (1926), Mayakovsky describes his first encounter with Esenin, wearing peasant shoes and an embroidered peasant blouse like a *muzhik* from an operetta, and compares Esenin's "theatrical props" with his own yellow blouse.[30] As both the essay and the poem written on Esenin's suicide suggest, the Imaginist Esenin is a double of the Futurist Mayakovsky in life as well as death. The descriptions of Esenin's literary persona and of his actual and literary suicide help Mayakovsky to defamiliarize himself from himself and discuss, both directly and indirectly, his own tragic predicament.

In terms of rhetorical tropes, the relationship between the cloth and the skin is that of metonymy, which is a relationship by contiguity rather than by resemblance. More specifically, the yellow blouse can be seen as a synecdoche, a particular kind of metonymy that substitutes a part for the whole and the whole for a part. Paul de Man writes about the peculiar unstable status of synecdoche in the history of rhetoric.

> Classical rhetoric generally classifies synecdoche as metonymy, which leads to difficulty characteristic of all attempts at establishing taxonomy of tropes; tropes are transformational systems rather than grids . . . Synecdoche is one of the borderline figures that creates an ambivalent zone between metaphor and metonymy, and that by its special nature, creates the illusion of a synthesis by totalization.[31]

In the case of Mayakovsky we notice an obvious transformation of a synecdoche into a metaphor, into a kind of fetish-figure, which indeed promises some form of "totalization." In fact, Roman Jakobson developed his theory about metaphor and metonymy in literature using the examples of Mayakovsky and Pasternak.[32] Metaphor, according to Jakobson, emphasizes the relationships of similarity and semantic resemblance over that of syntactic contiguity. Similarity is linked with the tendency toward the symbolic (from the Greek *sum-ballein,* to throw together, to give a token for identification, to compare) which was particularly privileged by the Romantics. In Jakobson's bipolar universe, metaphor characterizes poetry as a genre and Romanticism as a movement, while metonymy distinguishes prose and Realism (although Jakobson is aware of the limitations of his model and the numerous exceptions to it). In a broad sense, the tendency toward metaphor represents the desire to make everything relevant, related, motivated, and signifying and thus to avoid the accidental, contiguous, chaotic, and uncontrollable elements that constitute the metonymic pole, or even point beyond rhetorical figuration as such.

Moreover, metaphor is at the core of what Jakobson later calls "the poetic function," based on the principle of equivalence, "promoted to the constitutive device of the system."[33] The poetic function turns language upon itself, superimposes similarity upon contiguity and forces motivation upon the unmotivated elements by including them in patterns of repetition. Jakobson notes that the poetic function is not solely confined to poetry but can also be observed in various forms of verbal communication. If we push Jakobson's notion even further, perhaps much further than Jakobson himself wished to push it, and regard the poetic function not as a unique property of the poetic text but as a peculiar way of creating meaning through patterning and repetition, then the poetic function exceeds the limits of discourse, the object of both linguistics and poetics. In the case of Mayakovsky, the poetic function, like "literariness," no longer assures the autonomy of literature, but on the contrary becomes transgressive and vital. Mayakovsky wished to motivate his life poetically, presenting it as a series of metaphorical knots in a single design, creating a biography in which each everyday occurrence is written as something significant and signifying. The orientation toward the poetic function, toward the patterning and metaphorization in life and art, promises the poet some form of control over his immortality. It serves as an antidote to the contingency and entropy that he would have to face were his life only metonymically related to his art.[34] The poetic yellow blouse offers some existential protection, and yet with time it also becomes worn out, full of unpatchable holes.

The figure of metaphor is ambiguous. On the one hand, it seems to assure the transfer of signification and to inscribe the elements of resistance into a pattern, making gaps a part of the ornament. On the other hand, to quote Jakobson, it "deepens the fundamental dichotomy of sign and object."[35] The poet driven by what I will call *"metaphor compulsion"* (analogous with "the repetition compulsion") sooner or later confronts an abyss of displacements and discontinuities and a perpetual noncoincidence of words and things, which for him is tragic. The *metaphor compulsion* does not allow him to account for the heterogeneity and multiplicity of elements in everyday life (the *byt*, the daily grind which the poet saw as his worst enemy), the elements that do not yield to even the most unconventional poetic meters, and to accept with an appropriate balance of humor and wisdom the limitations of human control and the limits of intelligibility. When the lights in the theater go off, the poet is alone in the darkness and there is no space for chiaroscuro.

In the case of Mayakovsky, the metaphor compulsion functions like the Derridean *pharmakon* discovered in Plato's pharmacy: it is both a cure and a poison, it provides some temporary relief from the destructive effects of the untamable and nonsignifying chaos and, at the same time, further aggravates the disease, feeding its very roots.[36] Excessive personification and depersonalization become closely interwoven, and the poet's self-metaphorizing "I" turns into a discontinuous series of personae, in which it is impossible to distinguish between mask and face, cloth and skin.

Hence certain devices in Mayakovsky's poetry—"direct speech with a living target," the intrusive use of his proper name, self-parodying, and an overwhelming use of metaphors, particularly metaphors of the self—contribute to his peculiar understanding of the poet's life and to the genesis of a spectacular "biographical legend." The yellow blouse is only one example of Mayakovsky's transgressive metaphors, the tenor of which is located on the fragile border between literature and life.

Mayakovsky's chef d'oeuvre—the yellow blouse—originally an ordinary item in the poet's life, has become a literary fact and then a critical metaphor. Mayakovsky's contemporaries, his fellow poets and writers, appropriated and altered it in different ways. They, together with the yellow blouse, inherited that contagious *metaphor compulsion* which it provokes. The blouse appears in almost all the articles on Mayakovsky's suicide and serves as a metaphor in various paradigms. Kornely Zelinsky, one of the Constructivist theorists, remarks that Mayakovsky's yellow blouse is better known than his poetry.[37] The Constructivists see the yellow blouse as a Futuristic atavism that does not allow Mayakovsky to embrace fully Soviet revolutionary art, an anonymous process of production and not an individual subversive act of "épater les bourgeois." Similarly, André Breton, the poet and theoretician of the Surrealist revolution, argues with Lev Trotsky, the practitioner of political revolution and later theoretician of revolutionary art, over the significance of the yellow blouse. Breton tries to convince Trotsky that even if the blouse can be regarded as "bohemian" it is not necessarily "counterrevolutionary."[38] The implied opposition is between the individualistic yellow blouse and the proletarian uniform of the author-producer.

Pasternak places the yellow blouse in yet another series of binary oppositions. Superficially, he contrasts it with the "philistine's jacket," while on a deeper level with the "black velvet of the poet's talent contained within himself."[39] The use of cloth as a metaphor for poetic talent is a curious case of the "textualization" of the poet's "inner self." In the clothing of the inner self we find a parallel with Mallarmé's "Igitur" and the same allusion to Hamlet. It seems that Pasternak himself is affected by the rhetorical powers of the yellow blouse so that, instead of laying bare any poetic talent, he clothes it again in a new metaphoric disguise.

That a blouse is at the center of a serious poetic debate is not as strange as it might appear at first glance. The obsession of male poets with clothes, both literary and actual, has a long tradition. It is enough to remember *le gilet rouge* of the poetic circle *La Jeune France,* the black attire of dandies and *poètes maudits,* Baudelaire's famous praise of makeup, which laid the foundation of modern poetics, and Mallarmé's fashion magazine.

Mayakovsky, in both his poetry and life, was extremely preoccupied with clothing. Perhaps that is one of the reasons why Osip Mandel'shtam and later Yevgeny Zamyatin derogatively call him a "poetess." In the essay "Literary Moscow" ("Literaturnaja Moskva") Mandel'shtam writes that "Mayakovsky . . . is in danger of becoming a poetess, which is already half-done."[40] (In the same essay he calls the Formalist School— in Russian it is the feminine "formal'naja shkola"—a woman critic, but grants it a privileged position among the not so flatteringly described poetesses: "It is the only woman who entered the circle of poetry as a new muse.") It is interesting to note that "poetess" is not defined entirely by biology. Rather it is a cultural metaphor of femininity, a metaphor for poetic inferiority, for lyrical indecency and emotional excess, jarring like an excess of tawdry makeup. The lyrical poet with a spectacular biography is in danger of becoming a poetess, in danger of imitating the female figure of Vanity trying on beautiful, richly embroidered attire before a mirror.

In the essay "Moscow-Petersburg" Zamyatin classifies Futurism, a movement "based on the image," specifically the emotional image, as "feminine." This classification applies primarily to Mayakovsky, who according to Zamyatin could have claimed that "Futurism—is I."[41] According to Zamyatin, the postrevolutionary Mayakovsky never quite overcame Futurist image making; he merely dyed his yellow blouse red: "The inventors of the yellow blouse were the first to win the red mandate— the right *to represent* the Revolution in literature."[42] Here Zamyatin addresses a crucial problem of revolutionary and postrevolutionary representation, whether the Soviet modification of the yellow blouse should be a symbolically red attire, a kind of new "gilet rouge" of the French Romantics, or a colorless and unspectacular worker's uniform. The yellow blouse circulates, therefore, between many paradigms of class, gender, poetics, and politics, intricately tying them together: bohemian blouse vs. bourgeois jacket, feminine blouse vs. masculine shirt, Futurist yellow vs. Revolutionary red, the exteriority of cloth vs. the interiority of the poetic self, the rich black velvet of talent vs. the cheap yellow satin of the poseur, and—most dangerous of all—the remarkable, lively singularity of the yellow blouse vs. anonymity, the absence of mark, the erasure of the image, the death of the poet.

The image of the modern author as producer, a functionary of the state, appears to be absent from Mayakovsky's cultural iconography in spite of his efforts.[43] Only a few weeks before his suicide Mayakovsky organized a photograph exhibition, "Twenty Years of Work," in an attempt to present his new and distinctly Soviet iconography. But again he wished to author his own antiauthorial image, to impersonate the new myth and even document it photographically, in the best of modern traditions. The exhibit offered a carefully documented reflection of his artistic persona as defined by the author himself at the end of his creative period. This persona of the literary "latrine cleaner and water carrier" or "Soviet factory producing happiness" was largely derived from Mayakovsky's association with the organization LEF, which saw itself both as a child of

Futurism and its killer. An excerpt from the LEF program, written in the euphoric collective "we" of an avant-garde manifesto, is illustrative.

Раньше мы боролись с быками буржуазии. Мы эпатирова-ли желтыми кофтами и размалеванными лицами. Теперь мы боремся с жертвами этих быков в нашем советском строе. Наше оружие—пример, агитация, пропаганда.[44]

Before we were fighting against the bulls of the bourgeoisie, jarring [épater] it with the yellow blouses and made-up faces. Now we are fighting against the victims of these bulls in our Soviet regime. Our arms are: setting an example, agitation, and propaganda.

Sergey Tretyakov, one of the ideologues of LEF, suggests the necessity of "rational costume" for "workers of art" (*rabotniki iskusstva*) who should be seen as "psycho-engineers" and "psycho-designers." He argues for what he calls *"the americanization of the writer's personality* [the development of a businesslike, efficient matter-of-factness], which runs parallel to the electrification of the industry."[45] In accordance with Tredyakov's description, Mayakovsky tries to present himself in his last exhibition as a writer as deprived of any Futuristic exhibitionism, a fully integrated functionary of the state working in the artistic industry and cultivating the modern consciousness. And yet there is something threatening about this technocratic model. The anonymity associated with the process of production does not simply jeopardize the possibility of representing the figure of the poet by depriving him of any spectacular attributes; it actually questions the poet's right to exist.

Walter Benjamin, in his famous article "The Author as a Producer," in which he sympathetically describes Sergey Tretyakov as an exemplary "operating writer," draws a parallel between Plato's *Republic,* a perfect community in which the poet is considered to be harmful and superfluous, and the Soviet state: "The Soviet state, it is true, will not banish the poet like Plato, but it will . . . assign him tasks that do not permit him to display in new masterpieces the long-since counterfeit wealth of creative personality."[46] (Benjamin's attitude toward this creative personality is ambiguous. On the one hand, Benjamin is aware that its extreme embodiment is the fascist "superman" mentality. On the other, in its more moderate "liberal" and somewhat anti-Romantic expression, the creative personality can also refer to a figure dear to the critic's heart—a free-floating flâneur, a collector of poetic fragments and urban illuminations, who as Benjamin nostalgically remarks in the essay "Moscow" has turned into an almost extinct species in the revolutionary state.) Thus the murder of the poet-Futurist dressed in spectacular attire is a necessary death, a necessary sacrifice in service of the state for the birth of the new rational "worker of art."

The making of a new Soviet author is linked to the final purge and death of the poet. If the LEF's radical ideas were to be followed consistently, the poet both as inspired Romantic prophet and as subversive avant-garde explorer of language would be replaced by the journalist, the reporter, the propagandist *au service* not of the Revolution but of the postrevolutionary state. Or maybe the poet's replacement would be an "americanized" poet who saves his neologisms and puns for political advertisement. There is a tragic irony in the fact that Tretyakov himself fell victim to one of the first Stalinist purges and died in a camp. Perhaps he, like Mayakovsky, was too much of a poet in his radical rhetoric and vision of the technocratic utopia. The official Soviet death of the poet was more grim and literal than the LEF's and the Constructivists' joyful collective depersonalization through the process of production. Its style was party academism (that is, Socialist Realism), which turned the poet not simply into a reporter but into an informer—in the Soviet sense of the word—and threatened him with both figurative death and actual physical destruction.

The image of the author as a producer, the poet as a Soviet factory producing happiness, was something Mayakovsky both desired and feared. He felt that he was "the last poet," flattering himself with this peculiar singularity. His contemporaries had rightly distinguished the worn-out yellow blouse behind all Mayakovsky's "rational costumes." In Soviet Russian cultural history Mayakovsky's avant-garde and revolutionary repertoire was reduced to traditional literary masks. Tynyanov compared him to Gavril Derzhavin, Jakobson to Pushkin; Pasternak, Lidiya Ginsburg, and others saw him as the new embodiment of the old Romantic spectacular biography. Mayakovsky's obsession with "life-creation" ("zhiznetvorchestvo") links him also to his immediate predecessors—the Symbolist poets Andrey Bely and Alexander Blok. Yet, the historical specificity of Mayakovsky's fate, his confrontation with modern conditions in their peculiar Soviet variation, has to be taken into consideration. His repertoire of cultural masks is much wider than that of the Romantic poet, and much more contradictory and pluralistic. It includes among others the masks of a Futurist-urbanist, of a technology lover (as opposed to the Romantic nature lover), and of an author-producer, a functionary of the technocratic postrevolutionary state.

In his description of the poet on his death bed, Victor Shklovsky returns to Mayakovsky, as a last gift, his bright spectacular attributes and a new blue blouse. In Shklovsky's presentation the dead Mayakovsky is surrounded by an atmosphere of heightened theatricality, heightened to the point of uncanniness: "There lay Mayakovsky, in a light blue blouse, on a colorful sofa, near the Mexican shawl."[47]

Suicide as a Literary Fact: "Vladimir Mayakovsky" by Roman Jakobson

In 1926 Mayakovsky wrote about the suicide of Sergey Esenin, whose farewell verses were signed in blood: "Esenin's death has become a literary fact."[48] Thus Mayakovsky suggests that the poet's death can be easily fictionalized and mythified. It can be considered a part of literature, a final mysterious dénouement of the poet's work.

[…]

In 1930 Roman Jakobson, confronted with the tragedy of Mayakovsky's death, uncannily echoes the poet's own words. He writes that the motif of suicide in Mayakovsky's work has become "literature of fact."[49] It contains a curious inversion, an interesting shift in syntax from the suicide in life viewed as "literary fact" to the suicide in poetry considered "literature of fact"—which in the formulation of the LEF theorists meant a document, a vital and timely element that goes beyond the traditional boundaries of the "literary." In the case of the poet's suicide the literary fact and the literature of fact mirror each other, creating an enigmatic chiasmus.

[…]

Mayakovsky's final message, "To All of You," together with Esenin's poem in blood, forms a peculiar genre of *auto-moribundia*—to borrow an expression of the Spanish avant-garde writer Ramón Gómez de la Serna. Here is the text of Mayakovsky's suicide note:

To All of You:
     Don't blame anyone for my death, and please, don't gossip about it. The deceased hated gossip.

Mama, sisters, comrades, forgive me. This is not a good method (I don't recommend it to the others), but for me there is no other way out. Lily, love me.

Comrade Government, my family consists of Lily Brik, mama, sisters and Veronica Vitoldovna Polonskaya.

If you can, provide a decent life for them. Thank you.

The verses which I have begun, give to the Briks. They'll figure them out. As they say, the incident is closed.

Love boat
has crashed against the daily grind
I don't owe life a thing
and there is no point
in counting over
mutual hurts,
harms
and slights.

Best luck to all of you!

Vladimir Mayakovsky
4/12/30

Comrades from the Proletarian Literary Organization, don't think me a coward. Really, it couldn't be helped.

Greetings!

Tell Yermilov it's too bad he removed the slogan: we should have fought over it.

V.M.

In the desk drawer I have 2,000 roubles. Use them to pay my taxes. The rest can be obtained from the State Publishing House.[50]

In an almost schizoid fashion Mayakovsky displays in a short message to his contemporaries the entire repertoire of his cultural personae. This suicide note is a strange document that consists of verses, solicitations of love, jokes, and promises to pay taxes. It addresses both the poet's lovers and his comrade government with the same intimate and informal *you*, second person singular. What strikes us at first glance is the note's heterogeneity, a clash of different discourses. It contains high poetic diction, contemporary Soviet speech, colloquialisms, and some expressions which seem to come from popular urban romances and sentimental melodramas, linking death with kitsch. Such is for instance the much quoted sentence "Ljubovnaja lodka razbilas' o byt" ("Love boat has crashed against the daily grind"), which does not allow us to distinguish between pathos and irony. (It seems that the English expression "the love boat" with all its television connotations is an adequate cultural translation of this expression in Russian.) Political and poetic effects of Mayakovsky's love boat are discussed with much seriousness by André Breton, while Marina Tsvetaeva describes it rather ironically as an alien vessel on the poet's carefully styled Soviet "ship of modernity." In her poetic epitaph to Mayakovsky she writes: "Lodka-to tvoja, tovarishch, iz kakogo slovarja?" ("That love boat, comrade, what language does it come from?")[51]

Perhaps it is precisely this nontotalizable heterogeneity of Mayakovsky's note, its combination of poetic and antipoetic elements, a very modern, transient matter-of-factness of its discourse—which explains nothing but rather covers up the enigma—that tantalized his contemporaries. The note has many intertextual allusions, mostly to the poetic work of Mayakovsky himself. In this way Mayakovsky the author of poems and Mayakovsky the author of the suicide note become inseparable. The note reveals the poet's desire to estrange himself from his own death, to fictionalize it. At the same time, it proves the impossibility of that ultimate literary distance in the haunting proximity of the revolver.[52]

[…]

Modern suicide exceeds any precise classification: it is at once a reenactment of certain cultural myths, especially in the case of a poet's suicide, and a result of alienation not only from society, from "others"—*altrui*—but also from oneself, within one's own ego, from one's rapidly proliferating masks. Thus, in the case of Mayakovsky, we wonder who was killing whom: the Futurist in the yellow blouse killing the postrevolutionary poet-functionary, the poet-lover killing the poet-bureaucrat, the poet killing the conformist, the man killing the poet, or the reverse of any of these possibilities. Was it an act of a monomaniac, a "Mayakomorphist" as Trotsky once put it, a schizoid lost in his multiple incompatible masks, or else of an artist-aesthete finding the perfect ending to his own eclectic drama? One wonders if the poet's suicide signifies a desire for self-effacement, more radical than "the elocutionary disappearance of the poet," or on the contrary whether it reveals the astute gesture of a myth maker wishing to reenact culturally glorified poetic martyrdom in hopes of resurrection.

[…]

The official Soviet version of Mayakovsky's suicide conveys ideological clarity. The death is seen as a "strictly personal matter," something that has nothing to do with the Soviet Poet of the Masses, Poet-Revolutionary. The journalist Koltsov expresses "public opinion" on the poet's death: "Someone else was shooting; someone who temporarily and by mistake took over the weakening psyche of the poet, the public figure and the revolutionary."[53] The Soviet revolutionary poet has become immortal; he is community property, property of the socialist state. He cannot be accidentally murdered by the weak and impressionable individual Vladimir Mayakovsky. In the duel between the official Vladimir Mayakovsky and his flickering double, the first always wins. The poet is no longer in control of the dynamic and playful process of self-creation; some of his masks are already "patented" by the literary establishment with all rights reserved.

It is against this cultural background that Roman Jakobson launches a morbid attack on his generation in "On a Generation That Squandered Its Poets." Jakobson's article is not written from the omniscient point of view of the literary scientist. It uses the first person plural *we* and presents a kind of cultural autobiography of the generation that "squandered its poets." In this article the complexities of Jakobson's own perspective become visible: He is both a scholar and a personal friend of the poet, a defender of the Russian revolutionary avant-garde and an émigré from postrevolutionary Russia. The pathos of the essay comes from the clash of those perspectives, from the inability to allegorize the poet's death completely, comfortably enclosing it within the necrological or critical frame; and from the impossibility of defamiliarizing oneself entirely from the subject of analysis, protecting the autonomy of literature and of the literary scientist. The blood of the poet—Shklovsky's favorite Formalist metaphor and a powerful Surrealist image—becomes all too real, tinging the poet's lines with red.

Jakobson's article opens with a set of important dilemmas:

О стихе Маяковского. О его образах. О его лирической композиции. Когда-то я писал об этом. Печатал наброски ... Но как писать о поэзии Маяковского сейчас, когда доминантой не ритм, а смерть поэта, когда (прибегаю к поэтической терминологии Маяковско-го) "резкая тоска" не хочет сменится "ясною осознанною болью"?[54]

Mayakovsky's poetry—his imagery—his lyrical composition—I have written about these things and published some of my remarks . . . But how is it possible to write about Mayakovsky's poetry now, when the *dominanta* is not the rhythm, but the death of the poet, when (if I may resort to Mayakovsky's poetic terminology) "sudden grief" is not yet superseded by "a clearly realized pain"?

Curiously, even in talking about the poet's death Jakobson uses the literary term "dominanta" and in describing his own very personal grief he resorts to the poetic terminology of Mayakovsky. The essay demonstrates that in Mayakovsky's case it is impossible to separate the strictly personal and the social, the collective, the public, as well as the personal and the poetic. "Personal motives about the common *byt*" ("Po lichnym motivam ob obshchem byte") was Mayakovsky's poetic motto. The very notion of the strictly personal, of bourgeois individual privacy, is alien to Mayakovsky. (It is interesting to note that the word "privacy" cannot be directly translated into Russian, nor can the word "identity." The Russian culture has never absorbed this "individualistic" jargon.) Mayakovsky vacillates between two extremes, both equally removed from the nineteenth-century bourgeois individual privacy: between the hyperreal, hyperbolic, but always ironic exhibitionism and the constructivist self-effacing uniformity of the process of production—two extremes that intricately converge in the moment of death.

Jakobson describes how Mayakovsky acts out the suicide under different disguises, parodying and glorifying it at the same time. Yet as a critic he disbelieves the superficial histrionics. Revealing his own peculiar antitheatrical prejudice, Jakobson argues against all those who lost "the real Mayakovsky" behind the "masquerade" and remain blind to the only true mask, hardly visible behind the temporal disguises, the tragic death mask. Jakobson attempts to devise an almost archetypal design of the poet's fate, which manifests itself through Mayakovsky's seemingly eclectic repertoire. He describes it in the avant-garde genre of a literary montage:

В душе поэта взрощена небывалая боль нынешнего племени. Не потому ли стих его начинен ненавистью к крепостям быта, и в словах таятся "буквы грядущих веков"? ... С каждым шагом все острее сознание безысходности единоборства с бытом. Клеймо мучений выжжено.[55]

The poet nurtured in his heart the unparalleled anguish of the present generation. Is that why his verse is charged with hatred for the strongholds of *byt*, and in his words "the alphabet of coming ages" languishes? . . . The hopelessness of his lonely struggle with the strongholds of *byt* becomes clearer and sharper with every step. The brand of martyrdom is burned into him.

The poet reenacts the cosmic drama, a heroically uneven struggle between the future sun's reflections and the earthly strongholds of *byt*. His death is seen as a ritual sacrifice in the ceremony of radical historical change. It seems that behind Jakobson's literary montage of the poet's biography lurks the ghost of Romantic genius, the belief in the ahistorical, archetypal fate of the poet-prophet, poet-messiah, who takes upon himself the brand of martyrdom to redeem the generation that would otherwise be doomed to remain songless, locked forever in the slimy fortresses of *byt*.

The Death of the Poet—the title of the book in which the essay first appeared—echoes the title of Mikhail Lermontov's famous poem on the tragic death of Pushkin, Russian poetry's "slave of honor" who was "slandered by the mob," an exemplary Russian genius. Jakobson's Mayakovsky reenacts the eternal return of the Russian genius, the poet-savior. The critic styles his own, the only "true" and "real," Mayakovsky according to the archetypal tragic mask designed by the Romantics. This heroic rendering covers up many unromantic contemporary details, allowing Jakobson to ignore the concrete circumstances of Soviet history in the late 1920's and early 1930's—the beginning of the ideological persecutions of intellectuals, constant attacks on LEF and the other avantgarde groups, and the malicious critique of fellow Formalists and friends from the OPOJaZ. On the one hand, Jakobson seems to have had very little regard for the historical specificity and the peculiar modernity of the poet's suicide. On the other, this in itself can be seen as a reaction against the official politicization of all the discourses in the Soviet context, be they on literature, life, or an author's death.

In Jakobson's version of the story, Mayakovsky's suicide is something predetermined by the poetic autobiography as a system. Suicide is one of the elements of its grammar—to use Jakobson's later terminology—that is destined to be realized with a greater degree of vitality and less and less literariness. Jakobson writes that "Mayakovsky's poetry from his first verses to the last lines is one and indivisible."[56] Although he sees certain dialectical oppositions behind the motifs of Mayakovsky's poetry—such as between rational and irrational, present and future, "I" and "not I"—the structure of the system and the interrelationship between "the grammar of life" and "the grammar of poetry" seem to remain continuous.

Yet even within Jakobson's argument, the continuity between systems is challenged. His article both perpetuates and blurs the opposition between poetry and personal life, between literary science and biographism. Jakobson demonstrates that the motif of suicide pervades Mayakovsky's corpus and actually transgresses it, losing its literariness.

> Этот мотив теряет литературность. Сперва из стиха он уходит в прозу. "Деваться некуда"—ремарка на полях "Про это." Из прозы в жизнь—"мама, сестры простите—это не способ, но у меня выходов нет."[57]

This motif [of suicide] loses its literariness. First, from the poetic passage it found its way into prose—"there is no way out" turns up as the author's remark on the margins of the long poem *About That*. And from prose it moves to the poet's life—"Mama, sisters, forgive me—this is not a good method, but for me there is no other way out."

The motif of suicide, according to Jakobson, is the most "unpoetic," that is, the least formal and most personal, element in Mayakovsky's work, which makes the literary scientist reconsider the strict boundaries between the disciplines. These statements of Jakobson's comment upon and paradoxically complement his 1919 radical Formalist proclamation that "to incriminate the poet with ideas and emotions is as absurd as the behavior of the medieval audience that beat the actor who played Judas."[58]

The loss of literariness prevents us from drawing a line between the literary mask of the poet and his nonliterary self. Suicide, a voluntary loss of life, is a particularly striking example of the loss of literariness because it entangles art with death and makes the limits of identity less and less tangible. It is no longer clear, therefore, whether the motif of suicide in Mayakovsky's poetry anticipates and predetermines his death or whether the poet's actual suicide allows the critic to reorganize the elements of his poetry and in retrospect see it as dominant and prophetic.

For Jakobson the moment of extreme uncanniness comes when the boundaries of systems are blurred, making it impossible to protect the autonomy of art proclaimed by the Formalists.

> Формализм брал в кавычки лирический монолог, гримировал по-этическое "я" под псевдоним. Непомерна жуть, когда внезапно

вскрывается призрачность псевдонима, и смазывая грани, эмигрируют в жизнь призраки искусства, словно в давнишнем сценарии Маяковского—девушка похищенная из фильма безумцем художником.[59]

Formalism placed the lyrical monologue in quotation marks and masked the poet's "I" under a pseudonym. What an unbound horror and uncanniness result when suddenly the elusiveness of the pseudonym is disclosed, and the phantoms of art emigrate into life, blurring all the boundaries—just as in Mayakovsky's scenario *Bound in Film* a girl is captured from a film by a mad artist.

The most dangerous effect of this emigration is that the elusiveness of the pseudonym and the phantoms of art reveal neither the true self nor the real life of the poet, but a chain of simulacra. Perhaps the source of Jakobson's uncanniness resides not only in the loss of literariness but also in the loss of reality. Or, rather, it suggests a broader notion of literariness that goes beyond Jakobson's early definition, hinting at the complex intertextuality among life, art, and politics. There is a danger that the face of the real or archetypal Mayakovsky clings too intimately to literary and cultural masks—almost to the point of inseparability.

One of the untrue and pseudo-Mayakovskys, a Mayakovsky impostor, that Jakobson tries to exorcise is "the drummer of the October Revolution" glorified in the West. According to Jakobson "the West"—this peculiar Russian generalization is a mixture of provincialism and self-centered patriotism, a unique definition of all the countries lying to the west of the Russian border—knew only Mayakovsky's mask that was created by propagandistic oversimplification, that of a drummer of the October Revolution.

Jakobson satirizes the Western view of Russian culture and presents Mayakovsky as the last tragic genius of Russian and of Western literature, the last inspirer of the generation, the prophet of modernity. Jakobson sees that the division between Russia and the West is not purely geographical; it passes through the same frontier as the division between the literal and figurative meanings of words. In delineating these borders Jakobson juxtaposes by analogy male courtship, the practice of Marxist Leninism, and the poet's Golgotha.

Есть страны, где женщине целуют руку, и страны где только говорят "целую руку." Есть страны, где на теорию марксизма отвечают практикой ленинизма, страны где "безумство храбрых," костер веры и Голгофа поэта не только фигуральные выражения … И в конечном счете, особенность России не только в том, что сегодня магически перевелись ее великие поэты, как и в том, что они еще были. У великих народов Запада после зачинателей символизма, думается не было большой поэзии.[60]

There are some countries where men kiss women's hands, and others where they only say "I kiss your hand." There are countries where Marxist theory is answered by Leninist practice, and where "the madness of the brave," the martyr's stake, and the poet's Golgotha are not just figurative expressions . . . In the last analysis what distinguishes Russia is not so much the fact that her great poets have ceased to be, but rather that not long ago she had so many of them. Since the time of the first Symbolists, the West seems not to have had great poetry.

And now we will cross the Russian border and turn to the Western Mayakovskys, who according to Jakobson are much more figurative and unauthentic. We will examine the mask of the revolutionary poet made in France—an inspiring Surrealist *cadavre exquis* who is elaborately made-up and animated.

Poetics of Mistranslation: "Vladimir Mayakovksy" by André Breton

[…]

The Surrealists' response to Mayakovsky's death is particularly interesting because it addresses different aspects of Mayakovsky's myth. André Breton adds some surrevolutionary layers to the old yellow blouse, trying to defend the poet, to save him at least from a figurative death, giving him back his privileged position in society.

[…]

In the year of Mayakovsky's death the Surrealists voted unanimously to change their journal's name from *La Révolution surréaliste* to *Le Surréalisme au service de la Révolution,* stressing the new understanding of the word revolution and its relationship to Surrealism. The central article of the first issue is dedicated to Mayakovsky. Breton gives it a title in Russian—a language he did not know: "Ljubovnaja lodka razbilas' o byt" ("Love boat has crashed into *byt*").[61] (The French title, translation by the sister of Lily Brik, Elsa Triolet, is "La Barque de l'amour s'est brisée contre la vie courante.") It is a quote from Mayakovsky's poem *About That*, which reappears in his final message, "To All of You." The essay is both *article de circonstance* and a programmatic Surrealist document which raises major philosophical and political issues. Like Jakobson's "On a Generation That Squandered Its Poets," it attempts to transgress the necrological frame and place Mayakovsky among "the living intellectuals." It is also written in the first person plural—Breton's privileged *we*, the glorious *we* of "the Surrealist voice" that disguises its single-voicedness behind the collective mask.

The essay is quite eclectic: it juxtaposes almost Shakespearean questions, "to love or not love," with responses to slanderous articles in the Parisian newspapers. It was printed with large margins filled with all sorts of material about and by Mayakovsky. These included the poet's suicide note; the articles of his fellow LEF members, proclaiming Mayakovsky a true "revolutionary proletarian poet" and reenforcing his image as a poet-producer working for the Revolution; fragments from *About That*, a poem about love, suicidal despair, and murderous everyday *byt*; "Notre Dame," a poem which envisions a Russian-style proletarian revolution in Paris; and finally the Surrealists' responses (both in words and fists) to the ignominious articles against Mayakovsky. Breton's essay suggests a parallel, but sometimes conflicting, reading with its marginalia. It proceeds as a polemical dialogue with several interlocutors, including the anonymous *monsieur*, a kind of generalized image of the petit bourgeois liberal; Trotsky; the editor of the Communist newspaper *Humanité*; and fellow Surrealists.

The framework of the article is very peculiar: on the one hand, Breton presents Mayakovsky from the poetic "inside," that is, from the point of view of an avant-garde poet; on the other hand, it regards the Soviet Russian poet "outside" his immediate historical and cultural context. Breton defines his own fragile ground by fluctuating between different poles. In the realm of politics, he defends Mayakovsky from the bourgeois press, which regarded his suicide as a failure of the revolutionary ideal, and from the Communist *Humanité*, which converged with the former in deploring the voluntary death of the poet. For *Humanité* the suicide was an ultimately counterrevolutionary manifestation, an act that unmasks Mayakovsky as a "bourgeois, who never accepted the ideas of proletarian emancipation." In the realm of poetics, as in the realm of politics, Breton defends the Russian poet on both fronts. Paradoxically, in the polemical discussions of the time Mayakovsky was accused of being at once "too lyrical for a revolutionary poet" and "too engagé" for a lyrical poet. Breton argues against the logic that separates politics and poetry, personal and public personae, revolutionary activities and love—the logic that produces both the bourgeois image of the poet-lover, creator of beautiful lyrical verses, and the ascetic ideal of the Communist revolutionaries. The power of the revolutionary avant-garde poet, according to Breton, resides precisely in his ability to poeticize politics and politicize poetry, thus subverting the fundamental structures of the dominant ideology. Breton argues, both in this essay and in *Misère de la poésie,* that the "poetic drama" and the "social drama" can and must coexist. He desires to create a new Surrealist revolutionary ideal, one that would grant a poet a privileged, active social status.[62]

[…]

If in Jakobson's understanding Mayakovsky's suicide is seen as something predetermined by the poetic autobiography and by Russian fate, in Breton's view it becomes the act of a free will, perhaps its ultimate expression: "Sommes-nous au monde, oui ou non, c'est-à-dire y nous avons-nous été mis par des personnes qui s'entendaient plus ou moins à nous-y mettre et . . . ne pouvons-nous par nous même juger d'opportunité d'y rester ou d'en sortir?" ("Are we in the world, yes or no, that is to say were we put here by those who more or less agreed to put us here and . . . can't we judge for ourselves whether to stay here or to get out?").[63] Suicide clearly plays a very important role in Surrealist discussions. In the second issue of *La Révolution surréaliste* the Surrealists were invited to answer a questionnaire on suicide. Although there is no glorification of suicide, it is viewed as a peculiar liminal experience, a transgression of all boundaries.[64]

[…]

If Jakobson's version of Mayakovsky's suicide is a literary montage Russian style, then Breton's is a Surrealist melodrama. Already in the first paragraph Breton develops a contradiction between revolutionary devotion and love and, in the case of Mayakovsky, love for a counterrevolutionary woman. Breton presents his reader (a male reader, an anonymous *monsieur* with whom the author pretends to have a coffee-table chat) with a drama of love, a drama that somewhat resembles a soap opera. The heroine is, as usual, an ideally beautiful woman with ideally beautiful breasts ("des seins trop jolis"). She is one of those unknown beautiful women whose names often appear in Surrealist manifestos at the end of a long list of male poets and artists.

Love, according to Breton, offers an instant resolution of all contradictions, unachievable in a social struggle oriented toward a future utopian society. Love is something that is equally repressed by bourgeois hypocrisy and revolutionary asceticism. Ultimately, what matters for the poet is to be a Surrealist revolutionary, to be in love with love rather than with a specific woman. In Mayakovsky's case the woman happened to be a sort of *femme fatale* who "dans l'incompréhension toute féminine" created obstacles in the revolutionary activities of the man.

> Il va sans dire que la situation faite aux femmes dans la société contemporaine expose les plus favorisées physiquement d'entre elles à souséstimer l'action révolutionnaire . . . je répète qu'en outre le socialisme pourrait-il changer cela?—elles ont l'horreur congenitale de tout ce qui ne s'entreprend pas pour leur beaux yeux.[65]

> It goes without saying that the situation made for women in contemporary society leads the physically most favored among them to underestimate the revolutionary action . . . I repeat, can socialism, moreover, change this?—they have a congenital horror of all that is not undertaken for their beautiful eyes.

The woman is seen as apolitical if not antipolitical by definition. She and indirectly the society that formed her are found guilty in the poet's tragedy. Breton's popular story of Mayakovsky's suicide hints at the poet's love affair with a Russian émigré, Tatyana Yakovleva, whom Mayakovsky met in Paris. According to Elsa Triolet, Aragon's future wife, Yakovleva appeared "rather anti-Soviet." The relationship between her and Mayakovsky ended half a year before his suicide when the Soviet government denied Mayakovsky an exit visa; two months later Yakovleva married a French diplomat.

In Breton's account, the story of Mayakovsky's death becomes symbolic. If in Jakobson's version it was the archetypal Russian fate of the poet-prophet, here it is the universal drama of a revolutionary poet in love with a counterrevolutionary woman (of course, this "universal" is based on the French Surrealist model). Mayakovsky is compared with Rimbaud, and his death is inscribed in the French context and examined in the Surrealist discussions of the 1930's on the relationship between love and revolution, poetry, and politics.

The only trace of Russian present is in the title of Breton's essay, which is printed in the Cyrillic alphabet. It is the only foreign sentence in the whole article and Breton curiously mistranslates it. There appears to be a certain tension between the title and the rest of his essay. In the Mayakovsky quote the revolution is not even mentioned; rather it is "la vie courante," the daily grind, that engulfs and destroys the "love boat." The Russian original for "la vie courante" is *byt*—a very common word that according to Jakobson is all too Russian, hence untranslatable, not linguistically but culturally. Jakobson explains:

Творческому порыву в преображенное будущее противопоставлена тенденция к стабилизации неизменного настоящего, его обрастание косным хламом, замирание жизни в тесные окостенелые шаблоны. Имя этой стихии—быт. Любопытно что в русском языке и литературе это слово и производные его играют значительную роль ... а в европейских языках нет соответствующего названия—должно быть потому что в европейском массовом сознании устойчивым формам и нормам жизни не противопоставлено ничего такого, чем бы эти стабильные формы исключались.[66]

Opposed to this creative urge toward the transformed future is a tendency toward stabilization of an immutable present, covered over by a stagnating slime, which stifles life in its tight hard mold. The name of this element is *byt*. It is curious that this word and its derivatives should have such a prominent place in the Russian language, while Western European languages have no word that corresponds to it. Perhaps, in the Western European collective consciousness there is no concept of such a force as might oppose and break down the established norms of life.

Byt is everyday routine, the things surrounding us which are deprived of any aura, of any latent capacity for the illumination of the marvelous. It is a tantalizing presence of omnipotent ordinariness in its most static and conservative forms, pettiness, philistinism, and slime, that are all too real to inspire any nostalgia. At the same time, there is another, non-Romantic conception of *byt: byt* relates to "byt'" (to be), and in nonpoetic speech it often signifies simply everyday existence. Perhaps, it is this everyday existence that resists the metaphor compulsion and the heroic designs of life-creation.

In many of Mayakovsky's poems about love, death, and revolution, it is *byt* that is the main hero, as Jakobson remarks, a primordial enemy of the poet. *Byt* for Mayakovsky is the most petrifying and deadening force of "la vie courante." *Byt* as his primary "other" appears in both his prerevolutionary and postrevolutionary poems. In the famous poem "On Trash," Mayakovsky writes: "The revolution is by philistine meshes entangled, the philistine meshes are more dangerous than Vrangler" ("Oputali revoluciju obyvatel'shchiny niti /strashnee Vranglera obyvatel'skij byt").[67] (The Russian for "philistine" is "obyvatel'skij," which shares the same root as *byt*.)

In Mayakovsky's works *byt* appears to be immune to the most radical social revolutions. This uncontrollable sphere of everyday practices and ordinary routines resists both political change and poetic metaphorization. *Byt* creates a gray area between the two poles— revolutionary and counterrevolutionary—complicating the relationship between them. Is the everyday counterrevolutionary and antipoetic by definition? Or does it challenge the utopian political constructs of revolutionary theories and revolutionary poetics? What does it mean to be a *revolutionary* ten years after the revolution? How can one survive the everyday bureaucracy in the country where the Bolshevik revolution was already won and where "revolutionary" discourse has become a discourse of power? Is there any difference between being at the service of the revolution in the country where revolution is still an ideal and serving in the country where revolutionary ideals are merging with philistine *byt* and certain dreams about the future are becoming politically dangerous?

In his book *Theory of the Avant-Garde* Peter Bürger questions whether the revolutionary avant-garde can exist in a socialist society and whether art can be totally integrated into the "praxis of life."[68] He raises this issue, however, only in a footnote, thereby acknowledging it and at the same time placing it outside the main body of his text, in which he elaborates the theory of the avant-garde exclusively on the Western European, particularly Surrealist model. It seems that the "practice of poetry"—to use Breton's term—in the Soviet Russia of the 1930's demonstrates the impossibility of the utopian ideal of a complete integration of revolutionary art into revolutionary, or rather postrevolutionary, society. The Soviet literary establishment turned to the most conservative "bourgeois" art forms, and the exciting and euphonic word "revolutionary" became part of the official bureaucratic "speak." The gap between being revolutionary "in line" and being revolutionary "beyond the line" became unbridgeable. During Stalin's purges of the mid and late 1930's this seemingly metaphorical delineation of frontiers led to a life-and-death dilemma for many poets and writers.

By staging the drama *Vladimir Mayakovsky* in the Surrealist context, Breton does poetic justice to the Soviet Russian poet, giving him a chance of surrevolutionary resurrection. At the same time, while defending Mayakovsky from both the bourgeois press and *Humanité*, he immerses him completely in the French context; he dresses him as a Soviet Rimbaud, overlooking the cultural and historical specificities of Mayakovsky's suicide. If, as Walter Benjamin says, "the translation is a somewhat provisional way of coming to terms with the foreignness of languages," it is precisely this foreignness that Breton fails to take into account.

Notes

1 Barthes, *Mythologies* (Paris: Editions du Seuil, 1957). The quoted essay is reprinted as "Myth Today," in *A Barthes Reader*, ed. Susan Sontag (New York: Hill and Wang, 1982).

2 See Roland Barthes, "Change the Object Itself," in *Image, Music, Text*, New York: Hill and Wang, 1978, pp. 165-170.

3 Mikhail Bakhtin, "Iz zapisej, 1970-1971" and "Problema teksta v Iingvistike, filologii i drugikh gumanitarnykh naukakh," in his *Estetika slovesnogo tvorchestva* (Moscow: Khudozhestvennaja literatura, 1979).

4 The notion of "theatricality" underlines Lotman's concept of culture as a system of codes, which determines the "script" of individual performance. If in Saussure's linguistics the central metaphor is the game of chess, in Lotman's semiotics it is the theatrical stage. One wonders if in the discussions of postmodern self-fashioning a cinematic or video metaphor would be more appropriate.

5 Bari Rolfe, *Behind the Mask* (Oakland: Personabooks, 1977), p. 10.

6 Actors have reported that wearing a mask in a theater performance makes one aware of the theatricality of everyday life and teaches one to regard one's face as one disguise among others. In this respect, the advice that the director Mikhail Chekhov gave his actors is particularly relevant: he recommended that they "wear the face as if it were make-up" (ibid., p. 6).

7 Charles Baudelaire, "Le Peintre de la vie moderne," in *L'Art Romantique, Oeuvres completes*, IV (Paris: Gauthier, 1923).

8 Elizabeth Burns, *Theatricality* (New York: Harper and Row, 1972). For the uses of the theatrical metaphor in psychology see Erwing Coffman, *The Presentation of Self in Everyday Life* (New York: Donbleday, 1959).

9 Burns, *Theatricality*, p. 63.

10 Jonas Barish, *The Antitheatrical Prejudice* (Berkeley: University of California Press, 1981). This prejudice is reflected in ordinary language in the peculiar use of many theatrical metaphors, which, unlike metaphors borrowed from the other arts, tend to be "hostile and belittling." Here are a few examples: "to be theatrical," "to put on an act," "to make a scene," "to play to the gallery," or in French simply that an action is "du theatre." These and many other expressions in European languages reveal vestiges of a prejudice against the theater that is as old in European history as the theater itself. See also David Marshall, *The Figure of Theater* (New York: Columbia University Press, 1986) in which he discusses the theatricality involved in publishing a book and in the relationships between authors and readers in eighteenth- and nineteenth-century examples.

11 For the reading of Plato's and Mallarme's theater see Jacques Derrida, *Dissemination,* trans. Barbara Johnson (Chicago: University of Chicago Press, 1971). See Chapter 1 for a fuller discussion.

12 Interestingly in Barthes's discussion of the traditional Japanese theater, which he constructs as an imaginary other, a space for staging cultural difference, he describes the Japanese mask as a kind of writing on the face and celebrates this ultimate escape from Western naturalist theatricality. (Roland Barthes, *Empire of Signs,* trans. Richard Howard, New York: Noonday Press, 1982.)

13 Paul De Man, "Literary History and Literary Modernity," *Blindness and Insight,* Minneapolis: University of Minnesota Press, 1983, p. 147.

14 Steven Greenblatt, *Renaissance Self-Fashioning* (Chicago: University of Chicago Press, 1980), p. 2.

15 Ibid. Rather than appear in the traditional biography, this life in quotation marks surfaces in biographical fictions such as Vladimir Nabokov's *The Real Life of Sebastian Knight,* Jorge Luis Borges's "Borges and Myself," Milan Kundera's *Life Is Elsewhere,* and Christa Wolf's *The Quest for Christa T.*

16 As late as the first third of the twentieth century the consistent critique of Romantic biographical myths is still offered in the writings of Mandel'shtam and Pasternak, which however did not significantly affect the Russian cultural consciousness. Moreover, Mandel'shtam and Pasternak themselves, in spite of their desire to be "poets without a biography," as expressed in their theoretical writings, were transformed into "poets with a biography."

17 In Europe and in the United States the Romantic cult of the poet disappeared with the heroic deaths of Byron, Hugo, Leopardi, Rimbaud, and Whitman, yet on a smaller scale it persists in Spanish-speaking countries with Federico Garcia Lorca and Pablo Neruda as its main twentieth-century representatives. Every Russian poet, willingly or not, has to respond to this unwritten but widely shared Russian-Soviet cultural myth, to this heroic tradition that privileges dead poets and deemphasizes the literariness of literature.

18 Friedrich Hegel, *Phenomenology of Spirit*, trans. A. V. Miller (Oxford: Oxford University Press, 1977), pp. 111-118. See also Pierre Miquel, *La Révolte* (Paris: Bordas, 1971), p. 17.

19 Marina Tsvetaeva, "Epos i lirika sovremennoj Rosii," in *Nesobrannye Proizvedenija*, ed. Gunter Wytrzens (Munich: Wilhelm Fink, 1971), p. 661.

20 Boris Tomashevsky, "Literature and Biography," in *Readings in Russian Poet. ics*, ed. Ledislav Matejka and Krystyna Pomorska (Ann Arbor: Michigan Slavic Publications, 1973), pp. 47-56; Yury Tynyanov, "O Majakovskom. Pamjati Poeta," in *Poetika, Istorija literatury, Kino*, ed. V. A. Kaverin and A. S. Myasnikov (Moscow: Nauka, 1977), pp. 196-197.

21 Osip Mandel'shtam, "Literaturnaja Moskva," in *Sobranie sochinenij*, 11 (New York: Inter-Language Literary Associates, 1971), p. 329.

22 Boris Pasternak, "Okhrannaja gramota," in his *Vozdushnye puti* (Moscow: Sovetskij Pisatel', 1983). Pasternak's paradoxical love-hate relationship with Mayakovsky's literary persona allowed him to define his own literary identity, find his own romantically anti-Romantic "originality." On the comparison between Pasternak and Mayakovsky see Tsvetaeva, "Epos i lirika sovremennoj Rossii," and Roman Jakobson, "Randbemerkungen zur Proza des Dichters Parsternak," *Slavische Rundschau* 7 (1935), 357-374.

23 Pasternak, "Okhrannaja gramota," p. 273.

24 Ibid. On "life-creation" among the Symbolists see Vladislav Khodasevich, *Nekropol'* (Paris: YMCA Press, 1976).

25 Vladimir Mayakovsky, *Ja sam*, in his *Sobranie sochinenij*, I (Moscow: Pravda, 1978), p. 54. All further references to Mayakovsky are from this edition.

26 Vladimir Mayakovsky, "Kofta fata," I, p. 89.

27 Mayakovsky, "Oblako v shtanakh," p. 242.

28 Vladimir Mayakovsky, "O raznykh Majakovskikh," II, p. 70.

29 Vladimir Mayakovsky, "Kaplja degtja," II, p. 74.

30 Vladimir Mayakovsky, "Kak delat' stikhi," XI, p. 248.

31 Paul de Man, *Allegories of Reading* (New Haven: Yale University Press, 1979), p.63n.

32 Jakobson, "Randbemerkungen zur Proza des Dichters Parsternak" and Roman Jakobson, "Two Aspects of Language and Two Types of Aphasia," in his *Fundamentals of Language* (The Hague: Mouton, 1956).

33 The Soviet semioticians Pyatigorsky and Uspensky would call this phenomenon "a semiotic type of behavior," which is characteristic of a type of personality that tends to transform "nonsign elements into signs." See A. M. Pyatigorsky and B. A. Uspensky, "The Classification of Personality as a Semiotic Problem," in *Soviet Semiotics*, ed. David Lucid (Baltimore: Johns Hopkins University Press, 1988), p. 140.

34 For more on metaphor and metonymy see de Man, *Allegories of Reading.*

35 Roman Jakobson, "Poetics and Linguistics," in *Fundamentals of Language,* p356. In "White Mythology" Jacques Derrida writes that metaphors "exist only in plural": "If there were only one possible metaphor, the dream at the heart of philosophy, if one could reduce their play to the circle of family or group of metaphor, that is to one 'central,' 'principal' metaphor, there would be no more true metaphor, but only through the one true metaphor the assured legibility of the proper" (in his *Margins of Philosophy,* trans. Alan Bass, Chicago: University of Chicago Press, 1971, p. 268). But since there can be no "assured legibility" in the process of designing artistic patterns, the poet, while yielding to repetition compulsion, or metaphor compulsion, is inevitably faced with the impossibility of fulfilling his poetic desire.

36 Jacques Derrida, "Plato's Pharmacy," in his *Dissemination,* trans. Barbara Johnson (Chicago: University of Chicago Press, 1981).

37 Komely Zelinsky, "O konstruktivizme," in *Literaturnye manifesty,* I, ed. Karl Eimennacher (Munich: Wilhelm Fink Verlag, 1969).

38 See Andre Breton, "Ljubovnaja lodka razbilas' o byt," *Le Surréalisme au service de la révolution* 1 (1930). Also reprinted in his *Point du Jour* (Paris: Gallimard, 1934).

39 Pasternak, "Okhrannaja gramota," p. 262.

40 Mandel'shtam, "Literaturnaja Moskva," p. 327.

41 Yevgeny Zamyatin, "Moskva-Pererburg," *Novyj Zhurnal* 72 (June 1 96-). In English it appeared in Mirra Ginsburg, ed. and trans., *A Soviet Heretic* (Chicago: Chicago University Press, 1970). Obviously, one should take into account that both Mandel'shtam's essay of 1922 and Zamyatin's essay of 1933, written in exile in Paris, reflect the attitudes of writers who were culturally marginalized from a much more officially accepted "revolutionary poet." In their way, they attempt to subvert Mayakovsky's own argument— his flaunting Futurist virility as opposed to the Symbolist "effeminization"— and turn it upside down.

42 Ibid., p. 147. Italics mine.

43 On Mayakovsky's image making see Halina Stephen, "The Myth of the Revolutionary Poet: Mayakovsky in Three Modem Plays," *SEEJ* 30 (Summer 1986).

44 Sergey Tretyakov, "Lef," in Eimermacher, *Literaturnye manifesty,* I, p. 235.

45 Ibid., p, 242.

46 Walter Benjamin, "The Author as a Producer," in *Reflections,* trans. Edmund Jephcott, ed. Peter Demetz (New York: Harcourt Brace Jovanovich, 1979).

47 Victor Shklovsky, *O Majakovskom* (Moscow, 1940), p. 220.

48 Roman Jakobson, "O pokolenii rastrativshem svoikh poetov," in his *Smert' Vladimira Majakovskogo* (Berlin: Petropolis, 1931), p. 2.

49 Jakobson, "O pokolenii rastrativshem svoikh poetov," p. 25.

50 Vladimir Mayakovsky, "To All of You," trans. Edward Brown, in Brown, *Mayakovsky: A Poet in the Revolution* (Princeton: Princeton University Press, 1973) p. 352. The tone of the note is somewhat similar to the tone of Mayakovsky's letters, which reflect a peculiarly modem telegraphic way of letter writing. Mayakovsky's letters, particularly those addressed to Lily Brik, are not letter-essays with a declaration of major poetic principles. They are not written for posterity, but rather for the pleasure of the moment. However, in these letters Mayakovsky invents many neologisms-mostly derivations of Lily's name, Lilenok, Lisenok, and so on–which are terms of endearment. Moreover, Mayakovsky hardly ever signs them with his full name, which has become a worn-out literary pseudonym, but rather with little nicknames, such as "Shchen" ("Doggy").

51 Marina Tsvetaeva, "Majakovskomy," in *Nesobrannye proizvedenija*, p. 56.

52 Edward Brown writes that "the note is a kind of re-capitulation of his life and work, composed during the period of deep peace ... The poet is calm and self-possessed; and though almost all of his other poems express a towering and intransigent egotism, in this one he attends entirely to the 'others': Lily Brik, mama, sisters, Polonskaya, his new 'comrades from RAPP' and even 'Comrade Government'" (Brown, *Mayakovsky*, p. 352).

53 Quoted in Jakobson, "O pokolenii rastrativshem svoikh poetov," p. 29.

54 Ibid., p. 8.

55 Ibid., p. 25.

56 Ibid., p. 10.

57 Ibid., p. 25.

58 Roman Jakobson, *Novejshaja russkaja poezija* (Prague, 1921). In English it appeared as "The Newest Russian Poetry," in Brown, *Major Soviet Writers*, p. 66.

59 Jakobson, "O pokolenii rastrativshem svoikh poetov," p. 28.

60 Ibid., pp. 32-33.

61 Breton, "Ljubovnaja lodka razbilas' o byt."

62 Andre Breton, *Misère de la poésie: L'Affaire Aragon devant l'opinion publique* (Paris: Editions Surrealistes, 1932).

63 Breton, "Ljubovnaja lodka razbilas' o byt," p. 18.

64 See *La Révolution surréaliste* 2 (1925).

65 Breton, "Ljubovnaja lodka razbilas' o byt," p. 17. On the myth of femininity in Surrealism, see Xaviere Gauthier, *Surréalisme et sexualité* (Paris: Gallimard, 1971); Ferdinand Alquie, *Philosophie du surréalisme* (Paris: Flammarion, 1977). On the representation of women, particularly in

Surrealist photography and painting, see Mary Ann Caws, "Ladies Shot and Painted: Female Embodiment in Surrealist Art," in *Female Body in Western Culture,* ed. Susan Rubin Suleiman (Cambridge, Mass.: Harvard University Press, 1986).

66 Jakobson, "O pokolenii rastrativshem svoikh poetov," p. 12.

67 Vladimir Mayakovsky, "O drjani," I, p. 212.

68 Peter Bürger, *Theory of the Avant-Garde,* trans. Michael Shaw (Minneapolis: University of Minnesota Press, 1984), p. 114n.

4 MARINA TSVETAEVA AND THE CULTURAL MASK OF THE POETESS

Marina Tsvetaeva's *The Tale of Sonechka* (*Povest' o Sonechke*, 1937), an unconventional love story written in Russian and in French, invites us to rediscover a few pages in the forgotten history of female literary eroticism with all its digressions, silences, fragmentations, paradoxes, double entendres, and poetic excesses. The novella is also a story of exile that crosses the borders of Russia and France through desperate lover's discourse. *The Tale of Sonechka* describes multiple relationships between women: between a woman writer and her stereotypical cultural other, the poetess; a woman poet and her female beloved; a woman playwright and her actress-heroine. It is an attempt to reinvent love and "women in love" from a feminine perspective. Yet it remains to be seen whether any form of love or passion can exceed its cultural inscriptions and whether self-conscious texts of the woman poet can completely estrange the ghostwriting of the grotesque "poetess."

The word "poetess," like the word "sexuality," will be used here in quotation marks. It does not refer to women's nature or to the nature of feminine writing. Rather "poetess" designates a specific cultural mask, or, to use Tynianov's term, a specific "literary personality" whose caricaturesque portrait can be found in many Russian, European, and American texts of the nineteenth and twentieth centuries. The "poetess" is an impure poet; a poet plus an excess; a poet plus a feminine suffix, a mark of cultural inferiority and artistic nonbelonging. She is only an impostor in the world of letters. Obviously, the notion of the "poet" is not at all monolithic, shared as it is by everyone. It is rewritten differently by each major poet of the time and in each artistic manifesto. However, in terms of gender, there seems to be a good deal of agreement: the poet is either virile or asexual (the latter acquired the poetic name of "spiritual androgyny"). We read the texts written by a "poet" differently from those composed by a "poetess." In the mind of the reader, the word "poet"— grammatically masculine in all European languages that preserve grammatical gender—is often perceived as culturally neutral and unmarked, that is, as above and beyond sexual difference. Masculinity, in this case, simply signifies normality, universality, and linguistic convention. On the other hand, the "poetess" is seen as a deviation from the norm, clearly marked and excessive. As we shall see, the root and the suffix of the word "poetess" are perpetually at war.

[...]

The "poetess" is not a uniquely Russian cultural myth but a commonly shared European and American phenomenon with diverse culturally specific manifestations. The "poetess" is not a genius by definition; rather she is seen as a sort of literary *nouveau riche* who lacks the genetic blue blood of the artistic aristocracy. ("Genetic" has the same root as "genre," "gender," "genius," and "genitalia.") If we are to trace the genealogy of the twentieth-century myth of the "poetess" and her inevitable "lack of taste" we will have to reconsider the conception of "good taste" as developed in seventeenth-century France and reexamine Kantian foundations of the aesthetic based on the judgment of taste. In seventeenth- and eighteenth-century Europe the so-called "skepticism of tastes"—best expressed in the famous Roman proverb translated into English as "There's no accounting for tastes"—is gradually superseded by a more defined conception of a "good taste." The imposition of the ideals of good and bad on the plurality of sensual pleasures has connections to moral philosophy. According to Hans Georg Gadamer, there is a classical and classicizing element in the conception of taste that dates back to Greek notions of ethics of measure from Pythagoras to Plato, the ethics of proportion, restraint, balance, which is clearly reflected in the Kantian description of the beautiful.[1] As Mandel'shtam's poetic rewriting of this paradigm demonstrates, the Greek notion of measure and beauty, which has directly and indirectly shaped Kantian views, is linked to the conception of ideal virility. The Kantian "beautiful" is not to be confused with the agreeable, with its lack of "vigor," its languid appeal to the senses, and its propensity for decoration.[2] Moreover, genius was also conceived as "a virile spirit"; hence the gendered metaphor is at the very core of aesthetics.

Perhaps it is not by chance that the Russian word *poshlost'*, which signifies simultaneously artistic triviality, bad taste, sexual indecency, and lack of spirituality, is feminine in gender. In Sasha Cherny's 1910 poem entitled "Poshlost," *poshlost'* becomes personified as a tacky salon goddess.[3] She is presented as a middle-aged, sexually loose woman, a pretentious amateur painter of watercolor roses and a *nouveau riche* who is enamored of tacky bric-a-brac and foreign fashions. Sexual indecency, excessive "feminine" propensity for decorativism, "cosmopolitanism," and pretentious artistic practices in bad taste are joined together in this grotesque figure of Madame Poshlost'. Any woman poet, and especially a woman poet in love, both in life and in the text is perpetually haunted by the caricaturesque figure of Madame Poshlost'.

Once we begin to disentangle the cultural preconceptions behind the exotic configuration of "women, love, and passion," we see why the story of feminine love told in the first person the way the story is culturally engendered is doomed to a peculiar "stylistic miscarriage" that is at the same time irreducible to matters of style. "For a woman to be a poet is an absurdity" ("Byt' poetom zhenshchine—nelepost'"), Alexander Blok supposedly said to one of the most distinguished women poets of the time, Anna Akhmatova; and she ironically, yet reverentially, rewrites his lines in one of her famous poems dedicated to Blok.[4]

Tsvetaeva's prose writings arouse much criticism, even from the otherwise favorable Tsvetaeva scholars, like D. S. Mirsky and Simon Karlinsky. Mirsky, for instance, calls her prose "the most pretentious, unkempt, hysterical and altogether the worst prose ever written in Russian."[5] Thus, there is something in the very structure of Tsvetaeva's prose works, especially the *Tale of Sonechka,* that insults the notion of "good taste" and appears shocking to many literary critics. It reveals itself in its excessive "hysteric" lyricism, "the excess in the world of measures," overflowing subjectivism, and the impossibility of distinguishing between writing about the self and writing about others. Tsvetaeva's prose goes beyond many acceptable boundaries of genre and does not allow us to draw comfortable distinctions between criticism and autobiography, prose and poetry, fact and fiction. In these eclectic, intergeneric writings Tsvetaeva does not simply describe but also acts out the roles of lover and analyst, critic and poet, poet and "poetess." First we will observe Tsvetaeva's ambivalent attitude toward the cultural myth of femininity as manifested in her essays: on the one hand, her attempt to distance herself from the traditional feminine heroines—be it a "beautiful woman or a poetess"—and on the other hand, her infatuation with aesthetically obscene "oversweetening," an overly romantic "feminine" discourse in which she partakes and which she tries to reinvent against all critical taboos. Finally, the *Tale of Sonechka* will enable us to explore the links between literary femininity and aesthetic conventions, as well as the relationship between feminine love story and feminine sexuality in the Russian context.

In her essay "The Hero of Labor," Tsvetaeva mocks the very idea of the "evening of poetesses." She claims she has always been appalled by anything that bears a mark of "female separatism . . . and the so-called women's question," except for (she continues unpredictably) "its military resolution" in the legendary kingdom of the Amazons and the no less legendary Petrograd Women's Battalion. As Karlinsky remarks, "Tsvetaeva might have wanted to dissociate herself from any kind of feminism in response to the trend in the Soviet Union towards segregating women poets into a somewhat inferior critical category."[6]

What is particularly interesting in the essay is Tsvetaeva's ambiguous perspective. On the one hand, she sees herself as a member of the universal fraternity of poets, and on the other hand she also belongs to the sorority of tragic female heroines. Her description of the "poetesses" presents a kaleidoscope of visual impressions with occasional brief comment on their poetry. For instance, she says about a "poetess" named Susana that she was such a beauty that she did not seem to write poetry at all. This is an interesting twist: from a subject of discourse, the "poetess" is turned into an object for sight. This objectified feminine beauty is a reduction to absurdity of the poetess's mask. Tsvetaeva's description alternates between ridicule and sympathy. Her gaze shifts constantly between distance and involvement, between her estrangement from "poetesses" and her identification with them. Contemporary film critic Laura Mulvey calls the ambiguous viewpoint of a female author that includes the perspectives of a woman director and a woman spectator "a bisexuality of the gaze."[7] Tsvetaeva's prose stages the drama of female authorship and female spectatorship.

In the essay "Natalia Goncharova" (1932), Tsvetaeva addresses again the question of the relationship between art and gender. The focus of the essay is the contrasting juxtaposition of the two Goncharovas.[8] On the one hand, Natalia Goncharova the wife—first of Pushkin and then of Lanskoi—is an exemplary feminine beauty (*krasavitsa*), empty and wordless (*besslovesnaia*), "without a soul, intelligence, or a heart." Her biography is "the everyday [*zhiteiskaia*] biography," that is, a biography consisting entirely in the events of everyday life. On the other hand, Natalia Goncharova the artist does not condescend to beauty, just as

Natasha Rostova in *War and Peace* "does not condescend to intelligence." Her biography is "purely masculine," "a biography of the creator through the creation." Tsvetaeva writes that the other side of the beauty is not the beast, the monster, but "the essence, the personality, the mark" ("sushchnost', lichnost', pechat'"). This quote curiously paraphrases some of Flaubert's pronouncements in which he opposes the artist to the woman. Unlike "a woman," who is intuitive, natural, voiceless, and entirely absorbed in everyday life, the artist has to be a monster in everyday life, a sort of "homme-plume" (man-pen), a martyr of writing. Thus, it appears at first glance that Tsvetaeva shares the common cultural metaphors of femininity and masculinity. Yet it is crucial to note that Tsvetaeva's "pure masculinity" is exemplified by female artists and writers (Goncharova, George Sand, and others). Hence, what interests her is not "pure masculinity" per se but rather a "purely masculine side" of the split *female* personality.

In Tsvetaeva's imagination, the image that links her and Goncharova is that of Goncharova's grandmother swinging in Tsvetaeva's yard (they happened to be neighbors in Moscow) because she did not wish to meet her potential fiancés: "The grandmother is swinging on the swing in the garden because she does not want any fiancés! The grandmother who does not want fiancés because she is swinging on the swing in the garden! The grandmother escaping from a wedding into the air. Tossing not the bonnet [*chepets*] but her own self into the air! . . . My verses written at age fifteen, aren't they the swing of Goncharova's grandmother?" (p. 117).

Here of course we recognize the famous literary bonnets of Griboedov's women from *Woe from Wit* (*Gore ot uma,* 1823–27), the pathetic feminine pieces of clothing used to express women's patriotic cheer for heroic men: "The women shouted 'hurrah' and tossed their little bonnets [*chepchiki*] into the air."[9] This can be characterized as a revisionary intertextuality, a polemical rewriting of the images of femininity, which is practiced by many women poets. The flying bonnet turns into a flying feminine self, a feminine self flying away from traditional feminine roles and prescriptive family romances and marriages, or not even necessarily flying *away* from something but simply enjoying flight for its own sake. Tsvetaeva wishes to adopt Goncharova's grandmother and become her granddaughter-in-art (not in-law) and the blood sister of Natalia Goncharova. The Natalia Goncharova of the essay incarnates Tsvetaeva's exemplary artist. The peculiar kind of artistic "bisexuality" Tsvetaeva advocates here is female virility, a flight away from the fragile and beautiful heroine-poetess with her seductive disguises designed by sympathetic male artists.

In the *Tale of Sonechka*, a tale about love, theater, and revolution, Tsvetaeva stages a large repertoire of gender roles, and plays many of them herself.[10] To quote Sonechka's nanny: "It's a revolution now, a great cataclysm [*velikoe sotriasenie*]. . . . One does not distinguish men from women, especially among the deceased" (p. 265). In fact, most of the characters of the novella have ambiguous sexual identities. All the relationships among the characters, who are professional actors, poets, and playwrights, are at least triangularized. Hence, it is possible to talk not only about bisexuality but about a general fluidity of sexual identities.

In the center, however, is Tsvetaeva's ideal tragic couple: a poet and an actress ("a woman, an actress, a flower, a heroine"). (To avoid lengthy discussion of the author and narrator and their conflation and differentiation in the autobiographical fiction, I will call the self-styled autobiographical narrator of the *Tale of Sonechka* Marina, while referring to the author as Tsvetaeva). For Marina, Sonechka exemplifies unliterary femininity: the unidealized, the unstructured, and the excessive.

In Tsvetaeva's novella, Sonechka appears in two feminine roles: she speaks like a "poetess" and functions like a traditional female addressee of the poet. But both of those roles are rewritten by the playwright Marina. Sonechka is unashamed of being aesthetically obscene, and of transgressing the norms of established "good taste." One day she confesses to Marina her love for "bad poetry": melodramatic gypsy romances and popular urban songs, what we might now call "kitsch"—something like "And I sharpened my knife in the dark, for the count was devilishly handsome" ("A ia v pot'makh tochila nozh, a graf byl demonski khorosh"). According to Marina, this is the reason why Sonechka is "unloved by men" and intellectuals: her peculiar, deeply feminine intelligence goes beyond "pseudo-feminine pseudo-Beatrice and pseudo-Carmen." Even her name "Sonechka," a diminutive from Sophia, appears significant, almost symbolic. It is one of those unpremeditated, uncanny coincidences that easily yield to allegorization. According to the philosopher of the Russian Eros, Vladimir Solovyov, Sophia is the name of the Eternal Feminine, Feminine Wisdom, the symbolist muse, which then metamorphosed into Blok's famous Beautiful Lady (*Prekrasnaia Dama*). The name "Sonechka," flaunting its endearing diminutive suffix, belongs to a different discourse. It is a feminine term of endearment, an element of feminine "speak" inappropriate for an incorporeal, ideal Beautiful Lady.

It is a part of Sonechka's own discourse, which, as Tsvetaeva writes, was full of diminutive suffixes, imploring and endearing.

Marina recreates by memory the long monologues of her beloved, which form almost one third of the tale. For instance:

> And Marina, while loving your poems so much, I madly, hopelessly, disgustingly, shamefully love bad verses—those verses, Marina, which nobody wrote but everyone knows, . . . like "The blue balloon is turning and spinning / blue balloon, stay with me / it is turning and spinning and wishing to fall / a young man wishes to kidnap a girl." No, no, Marina, I can't, I'll sing it to you! (She jumps, tosses her head and sings the same.) . . . And now, tell me, Marina, do you understand it? Can you love me the way I am? Because it's just bliss (she recites as if asleep)—a balloon—in the blue of the sky—is spinning, a fire balloon, in the net of blue silk, and it itself is blue, and the sky is blue, and he looks at it and is scared to death that it might fly away forever! And from his glance the balloon is beginning to spin more and more, and it is about to fall down and all the fire balloons will die. (pp. 305–8)

Sonechka's speech reveals all the mannerisms of the actress and "poetess": extremely passionate diction, immoderation, excessive use of exclamations, repetitiveness, flights of fancy. It curiously intertwines various clichés from literary and popular culture, even paraphrasing Pushkin's poem "I Loved You" ("Ia vas liubil," 1829) and popular "cruel romances" in one line. Sonechka is a professional actress, and potentially an exemplary "poetess," since the "poetess" is primarily seen as an actress, a heroine of her own masquerade. Sonechka's monologues display genuine poetic insights, emotional generosity, and a passion for cheap melodrama that comes from Dostoevsky's hysterical and sentimental heroines whom she impersonated on stage. As Karlinsky remarks, it is possible that Tsvetaeva never read *Netochka Nezvanova* since she was generally not interested in Dostoevsky, yet the discourse of Dostoevsky's exalted girls in love with each other—one of the first such instances in Russian literature—enters the novella through Sonechka's speeches. For Marina the poet (and not the "poetess," as Sonechka argues), Sonechka becomes a living embodiment of what used to be the empty and idealized female addressee of male lyric, the muses, and the beloved. However, the relationship between Marina and Sonechka goes beyond the traditionally unbalanced relationship between the eloquent poet and his ideally silenced beloved, the female beauty as embodied in Tsvetaeva's mythology in Pushkin's wife, Natalia Goncharova the first. Unlike her brother poets, Tsvetaeva lowers her voice and allows us to hear Sonechka's speech with all its childish cuteness, diminutive suffixes, sighs, and exclamations. Marina starts as a playwright writing parts for Sonechka and ends up speaking in Sonechka's voice. Sonechka often exposes Marina's aesthetic credo rather as Alice B. Toklas exposes Gertrude Stein in Stein's *Autobiography of Alice B. Toklas* (1932). Among other things, Sonechka comments on the impossibility of calling Marina "poetess" or a member of the intelligentsia because her life and writing exceed those notions: "How can one call Marina a member of the intelligentsia? [*intelligentnyi chelovek*] This is almost as stupid as to call her a poetess. What a disgusting thing to say!" (p. 293).

This radically modified relationship between the poet and *her* addressee, and the continual transvestism of all the characters, influences the very structure of the novella. In fact, Tsvetaeva writes: "In my tale there were no characters. There was love. It (she) characterized the action" ("Deistvuiushchikh lits v moei povesti ne bylo. Byla lyubov'. Ona i deistvovala—litsami," p. 354). Thus the novella is not structured like any literary genre; it is structured, or rather obsessively unstructured and destructive, like love itself. Tsvetaeva's prose is full of contradictions: it is both excessively lyrical and novelistically polyphonic, written in Russian and French; it consists of seemingly disjointed fragments from diaries, letters, and postcards, multiple parentheses, and discontinuous recollections; it participates in many genres, such as the epistolary novel, the memoir, the essay, the novella, but does not belong to any of them. In this respect it can be compared to another generic monster—Mandel'shtam's autobiographical prose, particularly *The Noise of Time* (*Shum vremeni,* 1925), *The Egyptian Stamp* (*Egipetskaia marka,* 1928), and *The Fourth Prose* (*Chetvertaia proza,* 1930–31?).

Tsvetaeva herself is aware that the structure of love goes against the grain of the conventions of literariness: "I know, I know, that with my love I 'diminish' the 'effect' . . .," she writes in one of the parentheses, using estranging quotation marks around the word "effect" (p. 227). Her writing with the urgency of love seems more like an emotional exorcism, a lament, than a composition of a "work of art." It seems that in our culture the lover's discourse is always aesthetically compromised: it is situated in the rift between the abstractions and poetic generalizations of "high culture" and the sentimental kitsch of "lowbrow culture." It is possible to claim that Tsvetaeva structurally reinvents feminine love in her obsessive intergeneric narrative. The logic of the novella is what in Russian is scornfully called *zhenskaia logika* ("feminine logic"), an expression that is commonly used to characterize something irrational, illogical, anarchic, capricious, inconsistent, paradoxical, and excessively emotional. But in Tsvetaeva's writings this cultural stigma of "female logic" is reevaluated. It does not simply exceed but transgresses gentlemanly literary taste.

However, in terms of Tynianov's concept of literary evolution, defined as a continuous shifting of the boundaries between literature and *byt*, Tsvetaeva's prose appears to be very innovative. It questions the established notion of literariness and mixes high and low genres, including examples of "bad verse," lowbrow urban folklore, and the excessively emotional "feminine" speeches of Sonechka. In this way, she self-consciously (unlike the Mandel'shtamian "poetess") parodies the traditional literary relationship of genders, which usually consists of a male poet addressing a silent or silenced female love object. As if haunted by a ghost of the beloved, the novella becomes aesthetically obscene, or as Tsvetaeva self-consciously remarks, "oversweetened." Sonechka is not only Marina's muse, but also an author and an exemplary "poetess," one of those female literati who are so often ridiculed and insulted by male poets, but one whom Marina nonetheless cherishes in herself and refuses to exorcise. The playwright Marina no longer censors the voice of the "poetess"; instead, she falls in love with it.

But what kind of love relationship is described in this text? Is it a love affair with love, a romance with feminine lover's discourse, or a love affair with Sonechka as a person? Can we really distinguish between them in any of Tsvetaeva's relationships with women or men? Is the relationship between Marina and Sonechka "sexual" or Platonic? How does it participate in Russian cultural myths of love and sexuality?

The novella has inspired a lot of criticism for both aesthetic and ideological reasons—it was aesthetically obscene for some critics and not radical enough sexually for others. On the one hand, it is saturated with feminine eroticism and excessive sentimentality, characteristics that seem to repulse some readers, and on the other hand, its depiction of sexual relationships between women has enraged others. The novella does not present a fully sexual relationship between two women. Furthermore, it declares the impossibility of a happy ending in the relationship between women, claiming that Sonechka was doomed to fulfill her "women's fate . . . to love a man, whoever he may be and him alone" (p. 347). Sophia Poliakova has read the novella as "Tsvetaeva's theater of oneself" and as revenge on Sophia Parnok.[11] In a similar vein, Karlinsky infers from the novella that Tsvetaeva's relationship with Sonechka Holliday took the form of a passionate schoolgirl crush and did not have the "dimension of unbridled sensuality" that characterized her affair with Parnok. Indeed, there is a muted intertext in *Tale of Sonechka*—the poetic cycle "Girlfriend" ("Podruga," 1914–15), dedicated to Sophia Parnok, which Tsvetaeva, as Diana Burgin suggests, never published, as if attempting to erase Sophia Parnok from her artistic corpus and from her personal memory. In my opinion however, the novella, with its complex intergeneric status both invites and challenges a biographical reading, never allowing clear distinctions between biography and what Boris Tomashevsky calls "biographical legend."[12] The interpretation of the novella as an act of personal revenge does not take into account Tsvetaeva's erotic textuality, the painful pleasure of writing and loving. It is a "theater of oneself" in the sense that it is an act of self-dramatization, one could almost say of self-melodramatization, in which Tsvetaeva's life as a person and her life as a poet are closely intertwined. At the same time, Tsvetaeva's theater is not monologic: it is permeated by the discourse of the other and by the other's erotic presence. Perhaps, rather than focusing on Tsvetaeva's potential homophobia, or what constituted her cultural prejudices, especially concerning the relationships between women, it would be more challenging to discuss what can be called "gynophobia," or aesthetic misogyny, a prejudice against writing in the feminine that structures our whole aesthetic value system and therefore perpetuates a certain understanding of gender and sexuality.

The novella continues to be a perfect site for the contemporary critical debate that reveals the historicity of the conceptions of sexuality and gender as well as the politics of sexual orientation and conventions of literariness. Tsvetaeva's self-mythification, as well as her mythification of feminine sexuality, both gives us some insight into the very process of mythmaking and shows how difficult it is even for the most unconventional woman poet to escape pervasive Russian cultural myths.

From the outset, Marina confesses that describing Sonechka and their relationship presents a linguistic problem. She has to use the vocabulary of three languages because Russian lacks the words to relate her love story. Among other things this suggests the lack of female discourse of love written by women, and not simply translated from French and from the feminine, as is Tatiana Larina's letter in Alexander Pushkin's *Eugene Onegin*. Tsvetaeva frequently uses the French word *amant* ("lover"), which is linked to *amour* ("love") and to *âme* ("soul"). Of course, the "soul" (*dusha*) in Tsvetaeva is never incorporeal but, as she puts it in the *Tale of Sonechka*, "soul with flesh" (*dusha s miasom*). The French vocabulary does not prevent Tsvetaeva from partaking in Russian cultural paradigms and transforming them through her own, Tsvetaeva's, syntax.

From the first pages of the book Marina both defers and anticipates the description of Sonechka. Characteristically, in their first encounter the two women blush. This hot blush is a blush of passion, of mutual recognition and embarrassment. This embarrassment is a combination of self-consciousness and loss of control, a recognition of one's own physicality and the physical bond with the other. The uncontrollable fire is Marina's key metaphor for Sonechka—from the fire of embarrassment to the fire that burned her to ashes. The other central image is its opposite—the ocean, which has literal and poetic meaning, referring on the one hand to a specific place on the ocean where Marina is writing her memoirs and on the other hand to a poetic image of Sonechka's tears and laughs, which generate the overflow of narrative. The description of Sonechka in itself is a perpetual aesthetic embarrassment; it is at once fragmentary and overflowing, incomplete and excessive. It is not by chance that Tsvetaeva was regarded by Hélène Cixous as a predecessor of what 50 years later was to be called *l'écriture feminine,* not to be confused with the discourse of the "poetess."

The novella constantly circulates around the possibility of the physical relationship between Marina and Sonechka, obsessively trying to justify the lack of it in two languages—Russian and French. In the following passage I translate only the Russian and leave the French:

We never kissed, only when saying hello and goodbye. But I often embraced her with a gesture of protection, seniority . . . in a fraternal embrace. . . . No, this was a dry fire, pure inspiration, without an attempt to discharge, spend, realize. A sorrow with no remedy. . . . Je ne me souviens pas de l'avoir embrassée hors de le baiser usuel, presque machinal du bonjour et de l'adieu. Ce n'était pas de la mauvaise—ou bonne—honte, c'était—mais la même chose que avec le tu: je l'aimait trop, tout était moins. . . . Commençant par baiser une âme, on continue par baiser une bouche et on finit par baiser—

le baiser. Anéantissement. Mais je l'embrassais souvent de mes bras, fraternellement, protectionnellement, pour la cacher un peu à la vie, au froid, à la nuit. C'était la Revolution, donc pour la femme: vie, froid, nuit. (pp. 230–31)

The paragraph reiterates and paraphrases a number of poetic paradoxes—including François Villon's "dying of thirst near the stream"—and the Romantic notion of love as insatiable. Here we observe a familiar constellation of the metaphors of fire and water, a peculiar coupling of two languages, and a curious, untranslatable ambiguity of the French *baiser/embrasser*, where *baiser* means both a kiss and sexual intercourse. Interestingly, the feminine fraternal embrace is a woman's protection of another woman from the Revolution, from that kind of revolutionary brotherhood that for a woman signifies "life, cold, night."

Within the novella the kiss is associated with casual unloving relationships with men, in which an overabundance of kisses covers up a lack of words and a lack of love. Sonechka tells Marina the story of one of her failed theatrical love affairs, this one with her young student admirer, whom she kissed in excess to compensate for the lack of words: "Everything lasted for a very short time. We had nothing to talk about. At first I was talking, talking, and talking, and then I fell silent. Because one can't, I can't stand it when in response to my words there are only eyes, only kisses" (p. 243).

Hence in the novella the substitution of kisses for words and words for kisses is thematized; the first kind of relationship—a casual affair between a man and a woman—is called *poshlost'*, and is opposed to the second kind of relationship, that exemplified by the true love between Marina and Sonechka, with its continuous flow of verbal caresses. The novella itself can be read as an excess of lover's discourse that substitutes for the loss of the heroine and addressee, Sonechka, who first leaves Marina and then dies prematurely. But the overwhelmingly "oversweetened" dialogues between Marina and Sonechka do not simply compensate for their lack of physical contact. Neither do they merely present an ideological statement on the (asexual) nature of relationships between women—this would be a trivialization of the poetic and emotional force of the work. These dialogues recapture and redeem that culturally ostracized feminine erotic discourse that tends to exceed narrative and sexual conventions. To regard that discursive excess as a "sublimation" of a failed sexual relationship would be an oversimplification; indeed the relationship between Marina and Sonechka is not conventionally sexual, it is both more and less than that.

The paradox of possession (*obladanie*) and nonpossession is also exemplified in the numerous acts of gift giving and theft in the novella. Marina and Sonechka give each other material and immaterial things, things to wear and thing to write. Thus Marina mentions several times that she "plagiarizes" Sonechka, steals lines from her, while Sonechka promises to give Marina as a gift her favorite book, *Netochka Nezvanova*, which, symptomatically, someone later steals from her. Marina offers Sonechka a number of symbolic gifts: the dress that supposedly was given to her by Sophia Parnok, and the coral necklace. One of the most erotic moments of the novella occurs when Marina offers Sonechka a dress that belonged to her grandmother. Marina's description of Sonechka's undressing, however, focuses not on the romantic beauty of feminine forms but on the poverty of Sonechka's underwear, which is treated here with almost maternal endearment.

The farewell present that Marina gives Sonechka, a token of their mutual possession and foreboding of their mutual loss, is the coral necklace. The corals turn into a love fetish—both Marina and Sonechka cover it with kisses and tears; it is a kind of materialization of that hot blush with which they greeted each other during their first encounter. Furthermore, the necklace is linked to the story of a mythical Undine, a story of two women—not in love with each other, but in love with the same man—which ends tragically. Apart from the presents, Marina often perceives Sonechka herself as a gift. Thus physical nonpossession is redeemed by Marina's possession of Sonechka through language, and the novella demonstrates that this fragile possession can turn out to be more durable than the physical one.

Hence the relationship between Marina and Sonechka can be read in light of *Lettres à l'Amazone* (1932), where Tsvetaeva argues that after the relationship of maternity, love between women is the "truest" kind of love. The relationship between Marina and Sonechka follows many conventions of a Romantic love affair, and in this respect it shares some features with Tsvetaeva's other romances with men and women. Moreover, Tsvetaeva is quite conscious of this *erotic intertextuality* in the novella, and she reveals her Romantic references as well as her stylization of Sonechka as a heroine of her eighteenth-century plays. In fact, the novella vacillates between stylization of the characters of what she calls "Jacobean Moscow" and quite precise description of post-revolutionary poverty and *byt*. The element of being in love with love, and in love with the words of love, characteristic of all Tsvetaeva's infatuations, is definitely present here. Yet what distinguishes the *Tale of Sonechka* is the fact that Marina's relationship with her female addressee is based on dialogue with the beloved and not on the traditional lyrical appropriation of the beloved by the poet. This dialogue is realized here to a much larger degree than in any other of Tsvetaeva's love stories. Marina allows her lover to speak in her own voice, and she lets that feminine discourse dominate the novella. In the *Tale of Sonechka*, "unbridled sensuality" is displaced into discourse.

Tsvetaeva's narrative is indeed very telling: it both reinforces some cultural stereotypes of women's Romantic love and exceeds them, by attempting to speak feminine eroticism in the feminine, by problematizing the "lover's discourse" in the Russian tradition, and by challenging self-consciously aesthetic and social preconceptions. Ultimately, Tsvetaeva's *Tale of Sonechka* is not a story of "sexuality" in the Foucauldian sense of the word. One wonders in general whether this kind of "sexuality" and literariness are inevitably in conflict. Yet Tsvetaeva's novella remains one of the most unconventional love stories ever written in Russian, the one that combines modern eroticism and "outmoded" Romantic pathos and challenges the aesthetic conventionality of a "poet" with no "ess," a poet lacking the suffix.

Maximilian Voloshin once suggested to Tsvetaeva that she should adopt a male pseudonym, like Petukhov, who would be author of the poems about Russia, or even several pseudonyms: genius twins, brother and sister Kryukovs, the creators of Romantic verses.[13] Unlike many famous women poets of the time, including Gippius and Parnok, who started writing under male pseudonyms, Tsvetaeva refused. She wished to keep her female identity, but to stretch it, to push it to the limit, deviating from the established conventions of literary femininity and literary maleness.[14] Hers was an uncommon one-woman show, a polysexual masquerade that staged a continuous passionate dialogue between poet and poetess.

Notes

1 Hans Georg Gadamer, *Truth and Method*, trans. Garret Barden and John Cummings (New York, 1975), pp. 33–39.

2   Immanuel Kant, *Critique of Judgement,* trans. Werner Pluhar (Indianapolis, 1987), pp. 68–73, 79–85, 126–41. In *Death in Quotation Marks* and in "Obscenity of Theory: Roland Barthes's 'Soirées de Paris' and Walter Benjamin's Moscow Diary" (*Yale Journal of Criticism* [Spring 1991]), I elaborate a concept of aesthetic obscenity that is applicable to Tsvetaeva's prose. The etymology of the word "obscene" is obscure: it can relate both to *obcaenum* (Latin *ob* [on account of] + *caenum* [pollution, dirt, filth, vulgarity]) and to *obscenum* (*ob* [in a relation of tension] + *scena* [scene, space of communal and ritual enactment, sacred space]). "Ob-scene" is defined as something "in a relation of tension" to the (aesthetic) scene. In the context of my work it points to something that has been perceived as culturally marginal and marginalized, as something played offstage with respect to the performance of a male genius. The *American Heritage Dictionary* defines "obscene" first as "offensive to accepted standards of decency or modesty" and second as "inciting lustful feelings, lewd." Perhaps it is the exposed genderedness of the "poetess's" writing, the laying bare of sexual difference, that offends the accepted universal standards of literary decency. Obscenity here is not a pornographic exposure but a manneristic sentimentality that disguises the fundamental lack. Barthes suggests in *A Lover's Discourse* that contemporary obscenity is not pornography or shocking transgression, but sentimentality, sentimentality that is less strange and therefore even more "abject" than Sade's classic example of transgression, the story of the pope's sodomizing of a turkey (*A Lover's Discourse,* trans. Richard Howard [New York, 1987], p. 175). It is this sentimental "lover's discourse," this excess of affect and lack of structure, that disrupts the aesthetic dignity of literary discourse and shapes the modern cultural myth of writing in the feminine.

3   Sasha Chernyi, "Poshlost," in Sasha Chernyi, *Stikhotvoreniia* (Moscow, 1977), p. 6.

4   Anna Akhmatova, "We met the last time . . ." ("V poslednii raz my vstretilis' togda . . ."), in Anna Akhmatova, *Stikhi i proza* (Leningrad, 1976), p. 63.

5   Quoted in Simon Karlinsky, *Marina Cvetaeva, Her Life and Art* (Berkeley, 1966), p. 272. The American Association for the Advancement of Slavic Studies conference, the American Association of Teachers of Slavic and Eastern European Languages conference, and other Slavic conferences in the past few years have demonstrated an increasing interest in Tsvetaeva's poetry and prose in the work of many American Slavists: Olga Peters Hasty, Katherine O'Connor, Catherine Ciepiela, Greta Slobin, Stephanie Sandler, Michael Naydan, Jane Taubman, Laura Weeks, Pamela Chester, and others have greatly contributed to the recent reappraisal of Tsvetaeva's work.

6   Simon Karlinsky, *Marina Tsvetaeva: The Woman, Her World, and Her Poetry* (Cambridge, Eng., 1985), p. 97.

7   Laura Mulvey, "Visual Pleasures and Narrative Cinema," in Philip Rosen, ed., *Narrative, Apparatus, Ideology: A Film Theory Reader* (New York, 1986), pp. 198–210.

8   Marina Tsvetaeva, "Natal'ia Goncharova," in Marina Tsvetaeva, *Moi Pushkin* (Moscow, 1974), pp. 143–87.

9   Aleksander Griboedov, *Gore ot Uma*, in A. S. Griboedov, *Sochineniia* (Moscow, 1988), p. 66.

10 Marina Tsvetaeva, *Povest' o Sonechke*, in Marina Tsvetaeva, *Neizdannoe* (Paris, 1974). All references follow this edition.

11 Sofiia V. Poliakova, *Nezakatnye ony dni: Tsvetaeva i Parnok* (Ann Arbor, Mich., 1983). Diana Burgin's forthcoming book will give us a more in-depth view of Parnok's life and work.

12 Boris Tomashevsky, "Literature and Biography," in Ladislav Matejka and Krystyna Pomorska, eds., *Readings in Russian Poetics* (Ann Arbor, 1973), pp. 255–70.

13 Marina Tsvetaeva, "Zhivoe o zhivom. (Voloshin)," in Tsvetaeva, *Sochineniia*, vol. 2, pp. 166–224.

14 As the two Tsvetaeva scholars Kroth and Gove have observed, Tsvetaeva seeks to go beyond gender roles and gender limitations. See Antonina Filonov Gove, "The Feminine Stereotypes and Beyond: Role Conflict and Resolution in the Poetics of Marina Tsvetaeva," *Slavic Review*, 36 (June 1977), pp. 231–55, and Anya Kroth, "Dichotomy and *Razminovenie* in the Work of Marina Tsvetaeva" (Ph.D. diss., University of Michigan, 1977). Also see Kroth's article "Androgyny as an Exemplary Feature in Marina Tsvetaeva's "Dichotomous Poetic vision," *Slavic Review*, 38, no. 4 (1979), pp. 563–82. Kroth suggests that at the center of Tsvetaeva's "dichotomous vision" is the notion of androgyny, a desire for a "sexlessness of the soul," for ultimate reconciliation of the terrestrial sexes in one transcendental being. As Hélène Cixous pointed out in her essay "Laugh of the Medusa," the concept of androgyny, dating back to Plato's *Symposium* and Ovid's *Metamorphosis*, is a very controversial one: in spite of its implied sexlessness and reconciliation, the root of the first syllable in the words "androgyne" and "hermaphrodite" always remains male. Moreover, "androgyny" suggests a final reconciliation of the sexes, the absence of conflict, of dialogue, an ultimate self-sufficiency. Tsvetaeva's theoretical pronouncements, tinged with Romantic Platonism, might suggest the figure of the androgyne as an embodiment of the desire to transcend sexual stereotypes existing in culture. However, true to her defiant spirit, Tsvetaeva often deviated from her own critical pronouncements, and her writings remain controversially and unconventionally gendered. Tsvetaeva's gender theater is not necessarily "dichotomous" or "dualistic," but rather, truly dramatic, characterized by—to use Bakhtin's term—"heteroglossia," what we might call sexual multi-voicedness or polysexuality. This polysexuality, like Dostoevsky's "heteroglossia" celebrated by Bakhtin, is not devoid of cultural prejudices and myths; in Tsvetaeva's case, it reveals many conflicting attitudes, especially with regard to relationships between women.

5 PUBLIC PERSONAS AND PRIVATE SELVES OF CULTURAL CRITICS

The Obscenity of Theory: Roland Barthes' "Soirées de Paris" and Walter Benjamin's Moscow Diary

Subtracted from the book, his life was continuously that of an unfashionable subject; when he was in love (by the manner and the fact) he was unfashionable; when he loved his mother . . . he was unfashionable; when he felt himself to be a democrat, he was unfashionable, etc. . . .

"THE UNFASHIONABLE," IN *ROLAND BARTHES*[1]

This essay is about the "unfashionable" in life, love, and politics. It attempts to recover the unfashionable subjects of such fashionable critics as Roland Barthes and Walter Benjamin by reading their diaries: accounts of sentimental attachments and everyday politics. My focus will be on the relationship between the writers' theoretical and everyday discourses and on the ways in which a certain inscription of the critic's "banal" body goes against the grain of the accepted body of his criticism and exceeds the conventions of theoretical "good taste." Turning away from what can be called "theoretical necrophilia"—that literary and critical discourse which performs the modern ritual of the "death of the author," while preserving a certain kind of modernist autonomy of art and theory—I will explore the minor arts of living and writing and everyday "techniques of the self" that compose an "ethnography" of the private writer and intellectual. I will move not only towards a rethinking of the critic's subjectivity but even further, towards such embarrassing subjects as the inscription of the critic's body and everyday trivia in his personal texts. Thus the ordinary, the incidental, the awkward, the private, the sentimental, as well as their place in the cultural fashioning of the theorist, will be central to my discussion.

Obviously, the "unfashionable" is not a stable category: the ordinary can become extraordinary when expropriated for a critical discussion, the private can be viewed as a public ill, and the outmoded can turn stylishly postmodern. The reading of the critics' diaries reveals an elusive dance of resistance and desire: a resistance to being fashionably central and then to being fashionably marginal, a desire to suspend theorizing and then to theorize this resistance to theory.

In Barthes, the "unfashionable" is curiously linked to the "obscene" through his own redefinition of the latter term. In A Lover's Discourse, Barthes writes: "Whatever is anachronic is obscene. As a (modern) divinity, History is repressive. History forbids us to be out of time. . . . The lover's sentiment is old-fashioned, but this antiquation cannot even be recuperated as spectacle. It is in this that it is obscene."[2] Barthes' discussion of "obscene" polemically couples together "sentimental" and "ideological" discourses, the discourses of the lover and the theorist. The etymology of the word "obscene" is obscure: it can be related both to the Latin ob (an account of) + caenum (pollution, dirt, filth, vulgarity) = obcaenum. But it may also be related to ob (in a relation of tension) + scena (scene, space of communal ritual enactment, sacred space) = obscenum.[3] Barthes' own enjoyment of etymologies, not as a search for the truth and origin of words but as a revelation of the palimpsest present in the linguistic conscience of the speaker, inspires my speculation on obscenity. In Barthes and Benjamin's diaries, the "obscenity" is not simply thematic but also aesthetic: it resides in the sentimental triviality of their notes and their inscription of an everyday, unglamorous body—a "private" body— that resists the canons of literariness and turns out to be too "vulgar" and "in a relation of tension" to the "fashionable" theoretical scene. ("Fashionable" here might stand for the modern version of "communal," "ritualistic," "sacred.") The everyday errands, detours, and dead ends of Barthes' and Benjamin's diaries will lead us to eavesdrop on different theoretical scenes of obscenity.

The juxtaposition of the names of Benjamin and Barthes, critics of two different generations, is not completely accidental. In spite of the fact that Barthes—somewhat surprisingly—never directly refers to Benjamin, both writers were controversial exponents of literary modernity who elaborated theories of the author's sacrifice, either in his textual death (Barthes) or in the process of production (Benjamin). Moreover, the two critics themselves had a similar "borderline" status as authors and scholars: they were both more and less than scholars (neither Benjamin nor Barthes ever received a doctorate). Both partook of various systems of belief (Marxism and Jewish mysticism in the case of Benjamin, and Marxism and structuralism in the case of Barthes) but never entirely belonged to a single theoretical school. Barthes and Benjamin can be called "post-systematic" thinkers who enjoyed the rigors of modern systems of thought and explored their limits in the peculiar hybrid genre of the essay. The critical personae of Benjamin and Barthes are also similar: Benjamin's flâneur, the collector of fragmentary urban illuminations who moves inside and outside the city crowd, vacillating between engagement and estrangement; and Barthes' cultural mythologist, especially in its later version, no longer an iconoclastic and demystifying theorist-outsider but a rigorous amateur, an anti-authoritarian observer who lingers on the nuances of mythification.[4]

The recent publication of the critics' personal diaries—Roland Barthes' "Soirées de Paris" in the collection *Incidents* and Walter Benjamin's *Moscow Diary* (neither one intended for print)—is of particular critical interest.[5] Walter Benjamin's diary was composed during his two-month stay in Moscow in the winter of 1926 and Barthes' during two weeks in August and September 1979, not long before his death. The two texts have an eccentric place in the corpora of the two critics.[6] The diaries' very existence is somewhat paradoxical, since their authors in theory do not believe in any kind of confessional, sincere, and unmediated self-expression; they theoretically question the whole genre of diary writing, its illusory calendar coherence, its lack of literariness. At first glance their own two texts appear surprisingly un-literary and lacking in insight. In their mapping of Moscow and Paris, urban illuminations, suggestive allegorical exhibits, and mythological artifacts are quite rare. Barthes' and Benjamin's diaries are not shaped by aesthetic principles but rather by personal frustrations and the descriptions of the body's minor needs. But though they appear completely untheoretical, both diaries articulate their discontent with certain kinds of modern theoretical practices and search for a redefinition of the "factual," the "real," and the "private."[7] Hence *Moscow Diary* and "Soirées de Paris" will be treated here as symptomatic "paroxysms of criticism" (to use Barthes' expression) and read in the light of the notion of the "everyday" and its ability to subvert gently powerful metanarratives of criticism.

[. . .]

Barthes' diary does not offer any sexual "shock encounters" but only minor sentimental incidents: missed rendezvous, awkward embraces in the elevator, the "imperfect response" of the other, nuances of misunderstanding, small insensitivities, holding hands in the taxi ("till Clichy") the recording of amorous details, frustrated voyeuristic scenarios in the cafés, and forever interrupted romantic readings. Reported to us are the details of gastronomic seduction: "un rôti (trop cuit), des avocats, avec une sauce vinaigrette très noire, des melons français et espagnols"— all those minor sensual ciphers that do not even amount to a love story.

In *A Lover's Discourse*, Barthes states that contemporary obscenity is neither pornography nor erotic transgression. Rather, it is pathos and sentimentality that have become more "abject" than Sade's famous story of the pope sodomizing a turkey.[8] Barthes writes, "The sentimental obscenity is less strange, and that is what makes it more abject: nothing can exceed the unseemliness of a subject who collapses in tears because his other behaves distantly, 'when there are still so many men in the world who are dying of hunger, when so many nations are struggling for their freedom,' etc. . . ." (179). Barthes' sentimental obscenity is forever "ideologically incorrect": sentimentality is a transgression of transgression, a transgression of the modernist, avant-garde sexual politics and philosophies of sexuality, elaborated by Bataille and the surrealists. This kind of postmodern obscenity is characterized by an excess of affect and by the lack of the modernist literary decorum; it disrupts what can be called the aesthetic dignity of the discourse of the author.

In *A Lover's Discourse*, the lover's speaking in the first degree produces a "dutiful, discreet, conformist delirium tamed and banalized by literature" (177). Thus literary decorum tames and banalizes individual excess, turning a private discourse into a public language. Barthes is searching for something that he calls "individual," something indivisibly singular—not to be confused with the American cultural myth of individualism. Barthes' notion of the "individual" resists the paradigm of "personal vs. collective," and it invites us to question and suspend the Western understanding of personhood and subjectivity. In a way, what Barthes is proposing in his late works and interviews is a kind of new individualism (neither a humanism with its universalizing concept of the "human" nor the modern "de-humanization"). Moreover, this individual and his body are not self-assertive; instead they rather gently jam the social codes. However, Barthes resists his own tendency to gently idealize the "private." Barthes himself ironically remarks that his private migraines and mild obsessions remind him of a jeune fille bourgeoise. The figure—not only of femininity, already culturally devalued, but of effeminacy as well—haunts anyone plunging into the private sphere, the sphere of everyday insignificances, domestic chores, and affections, that are neither central nor eccentric enough for theoretical discourse.[9]

Is this figure of the *jeune fille bourgeoise* an inescapable, uncanny double of any "private self"? Are there any ways of describing the private trivial sensations, amorous frustrations, ennui, loneliness, and awkwardness that are not always already clichés? Why is it that these instances of human affectation, empathy, and discomfort are relegated to the backyard of theory? Can the "private" be constituted as a resistance to theory?

[. . .]

Let us turn to Barthes' other seemingly antimodernist statements in Roland Barthes. (Writing on Barthes, one always runs a risk of adopting Walter Benjamin's utopian strategy of quotation: one hopes that a sheer collection of Barthes' quotes will be self-explanatory.)

His "ideas" have some relationship to modernity, i.e., with what is called the avant-garde, (the subject, history, sex, language) but he resists his ideas; his "self" his ego a rational concretion ceaselessly resists them. Though consisting apparently of a series of "ideas," this book (RB) is not the book of his ideas but the book of the Self, the book of my resistance to my own ideas, it is a recessive book (which falls back, which also may gain perspective thereby). (119)

The sheer separation of "self" and "ideas" and the absence of the notion of the "text," in which the two are indivisible, might seem rather unlike Barthes, but we can interpret this separation as provisional and somewhat exaggerated. This paragraph is indeed about Barthes' resistance to Barthes. In fact, the whole book *Barthes by Barthes* could have been entitled, in Borges' paradoxical fashion, Barthes and Myself. The name "Barthes" here stands for many contradictory and often almost mutually exclusive discursive practices.

The notion of "modernity" in this paragraph is linked to the discourse of theory in a broad sense and, more specifically, to the doctrine of the death of the author (which has to be resisted in order to write the book of self). "Theory," as Heidegger pointed out, shares one of its Greek roots with the word "theater"—the theater which both fascinates and frustrates Barthes.[10] In this case it is the theater that stages the violent death of the author, precluding his "vulgar" private inscriptions and everyday affections.

Death plays an important part in the diary. The text is preceded by a suggestive epigraph, the words written by Schopenhauer right before his death: "Eh bien, nous nous en sommes bien tiré" (*Incidents*, 72). It might be possible to see the figure of death behind the everyday metonymic and insignificant observations of the diary and the ordinary ripplings of desire. This figure manifests itself in an occasional "lapsus" (to use Barthes' own word), often linked to involuntary memories of Barthes' deceased mother:

> J'ai eu le coeur gonflé de tristesse, presque de désespoir; je pensais à mam, au cimitière où elle était, non loin, à la "Vie." Je sentais ce gonflement romantique comme une valeur et j'étais triste de ne pouvoir jamais le dire, "valant toujours plus que ce que j'écris" (thème du cours); désespéré aussi de ne me sentir bien ni à Paris, ni ici, ni en voyage: sans abri véritable. (90)

Here death is linked to the impossibility of writing "life" without quotation marks. The romantic *gonflement*, which is unspeakable or aesthetically obscene, is undercut by irony. And yet the notion of homelessness that is suggested at the end, homelessness in the face of death, might be seen as a powerful force that brings all the author's voyages through Paris to a frustrating anticlimax. This figure of death that dominates some of the entries in "Soirées," reminding us that this diary is one of the last texts written by Barthes before his own tragic, accidental death, is the single element that is most capable of transforming Barthes' insignificant memoirs into what Blanchot calls *le récit*.[11]

But there is a crucial structural difference between "Soirées" and Barthes' other late texts dominated by the figure of death, such as *Camera Lucida*. The diary form seems to propose the most prosaic antidote for the death drive: the simple continuity of the calendar; it alleviates the anxiety of closures. The daily practice of filling the page with insignificant, unnecessary, inessential, and "infinitely supressable" details—to paraphrase Barthes' own description of a diary in "Deliberation"—preserves the "effects of the real." The kind of real that Barthes strives to capture is a real that goes beyond conventions of realisms and verisimilitude. That evasive real relates to the "true to life" and the "lifelike" as well as to all sorts of affects and effects of the body—

which are in opposition to "intelligibility," "meaning," and "signification" ("as if," Barthes writes, "by some statutory exclusion, what is alive cannot signify").[12] And yet, it is possible to suggest that the "lifelike" practice of recording "lifelike" events," exemplified in the personal writing, embarrasses that currently dominant aesthetic which privileges non-presence (re-presentation) and the metaphorical death of the subject in the elegant ruins of the text.

Finally, Barthes' "obscenity" in the diary upsets many contemporary theoretical paradigms of the obscene. The most currently fashionable one is that of Baudrillard who regards obscenity as "omnipresent visibility," which is opposed to playful seduction and its dialectic of revelation and concealment.[13] Although Baudrillard's universe is technologically postmodern, it is quite old-fashioned in its moral paradigm, a Manichean paradigm of good and evil. Obscenity is morally valorized in a traditional manner; together with banality it is placed on the side of evil, and it is regarded as a fatal outcome of the hyper-real powers of simulacra and the "evil demons of images." The obscene displaces the scene of seduction, the domestic scene with its mirrors and secrets, as well as the scene of critical alienation and social conflict: the "hot" seduction of the public by the alienated, socially-minded critic. Baudrillard's texts betray a nostalgia for the theater of theoretical violence performed by a "drunken demiurge of power," alias the intellectual.[14] Baudrillard's own insistence on the "omnipresent visibility" and the fatal banality of the postmodern world often does not allow him to see beyond his own metaphors and "panic" prophesies of doom into the particularity and complexity of the everyday. In Barthes, the obscene is not morally valorized; it functions more as a concept of nonviolent resistance to the very (modernist) scene that Baudrillard celebrates. Throughout Barthes' writings we find a consistent suspicion of the "scene" or what, after Bacon, he would call "the phantoms of the theater."[15] The "scene" is "a confrontation of codes," which in Barthes' writings, like in those of Baudrillard, is associated with violence, with the entrance into the public sphere. According to Barthes, however, the only interaction with the other that occurs on the scene is an interaction on the level of the image-repertoire. Moreover, in the scene the self turns into a character in a tableau vivant; "I" becomes an actor—even if his theater is the most self-consciously estranged Brechtian drama. For Barthes, the scene is not a site of communication. Here we can see Barthes' difference not only from Baudrillard, but also from Bakhtin, a celebrated metaphysician of dialogue and an apologist for Dostoevsky's "scandal scenes." In Bakhtin's book on Dostoevsky, the dialogue is structured as a scene and defined as an exchange between "two human beings" and two "embodied consciences," as exemplified in Dostoevsky's "scenes of scandal," often punctuated by violence and hysteria. (Even in Bakhtin's later work we can observe the traces of his earlier conception of the dialogue based primarily on the nineteenth-century novel. Bakhtin never confronts the problems of twentieth-century subjectivity.)[16]

Unlike Bakhtin, Barthes is very cautious about the scandal scene as a site of dialogue or polyphony. The relationship between "scene" and "obscene" is not simply one of difference but one of hierarchy, inequality, the privilege of one over the other. Thus the obscene is not in a dialogical relationship to the scene. The obscene "pollutes" the very structure of the scene; it disfigures the *p. 97* actors, resists the representation of the body as a public image-repertoire, as *Caenum* a product of the codes of beauty and unity. Barthes' personal journal lacks scenic roads, sexual transgressions, and explicit metaphysical scandals. For Barthes, the communication occurs in private, in a desire to reconquer and reinhabit common places, in a loving exchange between the reader and the author, and in the fragmented remembrances of a lover.

[. . .]

Like Barthes', Benjamin's diary (in spite of its occasional descriptions of prominent Soviet writers and theater-directors and literary debates) is mostly structured as a series of frustrated travelogues, about museums that happen to be closed, theater shows in an incomprehensible foreign language, and his woman friend, Asja Lacis, who is usually absent, sick, or in a bad mood.

[. . .]

As a way of conceptualizing his own silence and lack of definitive statements on Moscow, Benjamin states, in a letter to Buber:

> I want to write a description of Moscow at the present moment in which "all factuality is already theory" and which will thereby refrain from any deductive abstraction, from any prognostication, and even within certain limits from any judgement. . . . Moscow as it appears at the present reveals a full range of possibilities in schematic form: above all, the possibility that the Revolution might fail or succeed."
> (*Moscow Diary*, 132)

Benjamin's "factuality" reflects his interest in the Soviet Russian "literature of fact"—a type of documentary writing advocated by Tretiakov, Pil'njak, and the editors of Left Front—and the German movement in photography called "the new matter-of-factness." In the description of Moscow, Benjamin's "antitheoretical" stance is pregnant with controversial ideological significance. On the one hand, as the critic states in the opening paragraphs of the essay "Moscow," one has to come to Moscow with a self-conscious ideological position. Benjamin calls himself "a left-wing intellectual," and he makes his own position—that of a highly sympathetic fellow-traveler who considers the possibility of entering the German Communist Party—clear. On the other hand, Benjamin becomes aware of the necessity to suspend ideologization for the sake of a radical materialism (more radical than Marx's), and he focuses on the very materiality of Soviet daily existence. His point of view differs from that of a distanced scholar or a "bourgeois" objectivist observer. But neither is it that of a blind ideologue who does not see beyond the official slogans. (To become the latter, unfortunately, was the fate of many well-meaning communist intellectuals, such as Rolland and Aragon, who visited Russia in the 1930s and silently consented to many Stalinist purges of the intellectuals, including those mentioned in Benjamin's diary—Tretiakov, Meyerhold, and others.) As a result, in spite of Benjamin's unilluminating love relationship, his myopia, his lack of knowledge of the language, and the "rigors of Moscow daily life," Benjamin's account of the situation in Moscow in 1926, both in the diary and in the essay "Moscow," has proven to be more insightful, prophetic, and courageous—courageous for its resistance to easy ideologizing on the right and on the left—than any other foreign account of Soviet life written at that time.

Like Barthes' diary, Benjamin's is marked by embarrassing awkwardness. The feeling of unprotectedness on Moscow streets, the lack of balance, of orientation, of privacy, and a longing for intimacy and personal contact permeate the text. These desires and occasional "bundled actions"—to paraphrase Freud—are not merely eccentric elements in the diary; rather, they are part of that intimate "factuality" that Benjamin is faithfully reporting.[17] We remember some glimpses from the diary: Benjamin's stolen pleasures of reading Proust and eating marzipan, of discovering naive Russian folk toys (which present such a striking contrast to the Constructivist hymns to technology and the official post-Revolution industrialization), of kissing Asja on the threshold of his Moscow apartment. These incidents constitute minimal proofs of the materiality of existence, that dense materiality of personal and collective experiences in the present that seem to counteract Benjamin's fascination with allegorical ruins, monuments to the things of the past, and emblems of death.

[. . .]

The most recent interdisciplinary work on the everyday is Michel de Certeau's *L'Invention du quotidien / arts de faire*, which combines references to Wittgenstein, Bourdieu, and Foucault with discussions of walking, reading, cooking, and other daily activities that fall into the category of what Certeau calls "ruse" and "braconnage."[18] Certeau attempts to displace the dichotomy of theory and practice; he regards theory in terms of the paradigm of daily activities and their historical transformation. While examining the Western cultural practice of theory from the sixteenth century on, he demonstrates how *savoir* (knowledge) gradually dissociates itself from *savoir-faire* (knowledge of skills); in a similar fashion "art" becomes divorced from the "art of" (saying, doing, inhabiting space, walking, cooking—all the practices of the body and the techniques of the self). These developments lead to the cultural oppositions between theory and practice and between art and everyday life, which are often attacked in theory and yet followed in practice by many contemporary literary critics and readers. (Curiously, both Lefebvre and Certeau use literature extensively, discussing mostly modernist masterpieces—Joyce in the case of Lefebvre and Mallarmé in the case of Certeau—and never refer to diaries or other writing. So, while upsetting many social hierarchies, these critics of the everyday continue to preserve the aesthetic ones.) Certeau focuses on the rhetoric of the everyday practice, on daily usages of discourse (and not only of discourse) that account for the heterogeneity of modern culture, which is always "culture in plural." These daily tactics and strategies of the participants in culture undermine purist theoretical concepts and allow for a multifaceted understanding of the contemporary cultural processes. Certeau's subject is "a very ordinary person," neither a great self-effaced artist, nor a nineteenth-century unified human being, but a modern subject traversed by multiple cultural voices and perpetually engaged by the ethics of intersubjective interaction. The study of the modern everyday converges with the new ethnography where "ethnikos" no longer refers to the exotic other ("ethnikos" in Greek means heathen) and where the other is conceptualized neither as a marginalized outsider nor as a mysterious "unconscious self." The "heathen," the "ethnic," in ourselves can be that frustrated petit(e) bourgeois(e) with his or her minor sentimental failures, the clumsy loner who excels in the arts of writing but not always in the arts of survival.

In this light, reading diaries as examples of ordinary writing, juxtaposing them with critics' other texts, reveals an interesting paradox: the everyday practices of discourse both carry out and embarrass the critic's theoretical projects. Instead of acting out the death of the author, the diaries stage authors' desperate lives and expose various unglamorous spheres of human experience. The corpus of a critic's work, which includes his personal writings, demonstrates the ultimate fragmentation of authorship and opens up the whole laboratory of "usages" of literary and non-literary discourses. This extensive corpus affects the image of the author: the modern ideal, Flaubertian *homme-plume* and martyr of scriptures, glorified by early Barthes and Foucault, is on the verge of turning into a feminine or effeminate figure—the figure that has been culturally associated not only with *une fille bourgeoise* but also with a woman writer, with her "anxiety of authorship," madness, eclecticism, and sentimental kitsch.

Ultimately, the expression "obscenity of theory" can be read in two ways: The everyday "non-literary" writing can be regarded as obscene in relation to a certain kind of modernist and postmodernist literary theory that uncritically depends on the death of the author. The diaries "vulgarize" the central scandal of modernism: the noble and heroic sacrifice of the author's affects and everyday chores. On the other hand, cultural theory itself should aim at obscenity; in other words, it should off-stage itself, constantly exploring its limits of intelligibility—not only in the vertical axes of the ineffable but also in the horizontal dimensions of the everyday. The critics' diaries teach us to unlearn many of our critical myths and, perhaps, to reconsider the relationship between critical thinking and "theory," between aesthetic experiences and "art," and between our intimate individual trivia and public clichés of the private. The mapping of Barthes' incidents and inscriptions of the atopical body, together with Benjamin's slippery routes and awkward insights, opens up an alternative space at the crossroads of aesthetics, theory, and the everyday and helps us to design a new, more inclusive, critical geography with obscene sites, unfashionable exhibits, and trivial illuminations.

Notes

1 Roland Barthes, "The Unfashionable," in *Roland Barthes*, trans. Richard Howard (NY: Hill and Wang, 1977), 125. Quotations throughout this essay appear in English if translations exist; otherwise, they appear in the original.

2 Roland Barthes, *A Lover's Discourse*, trans. Richard Howard (New York: Hill and Wang, 1987), 177–78.

3 I am grateful to Leslie Dunton-Downer for helping me with the etymologies of the word "obscene." See her forthcoming doctoral dissertation, *"Scripting Vulgarities: The Obscenic in Medieval Fabliaux"* (Harvard University).

4 Benjamin and Barthes share a single literary love that colors their writing in the first person: Proust, whom they both are re-reading at the time of writing their diaries. Also both writers stage a continuous, agonistic dialogue with Brecht. The other (this time, non-literary) object for the love-hate relationship that Barthes and Benjamin share is the photographic image. For the two "men of letters" who never used any expressive medium other than writing, photography exerts a peculiar fascination. For Barthes, the photographic surface reflects the "myth of life" as well as the apparition of death, the illusion of documentarity and of singularity, the affirmation of being there, as well as the recognition of loss. For Benjamin, the photograph is an exemplary modern document that records the destruction of aesthetic aura. Both critics' reflections on photography are highly relevant to the writing of their own personal documentaries—the diaries—singular recordings of everyday occurrences.

5 Roland Barthes, *Incidents* (Paris: Éditions du Seuil, 1987). Walter Benjamin, *Moscow Diary*, trans. Richard Sieburth (Cambridge: Harvard University Press, 1987). All the references in the text refer to these editions.

6 The ambivalence about the diary as a way of writing and living is reflected in the texts themselves. Numerous entries of both diaries start with a statement about the insignificance of a diary and about the lack of events or insights worthy of being put on paper. Compare Barthes' "soirée pas grand chose à dire" or "vaine soirée" (*Incidents*, 111) and Benjamin's nearly identical sentences: "There is almost nothing to report about this day" or "futile trip to the toy museum" (*Moscow Diary*, 95, 85).

7 The diary as a genre of writing particularly flourished in the romantic period, with its stress on individual introspection and self-expression. The diary form has never been an exclusively everyday genre; rather it travels in and out of "literature," creating many hybrid forms like the stylized fictional diary, such as Dostoevsky's "Notes from Underground," or Gogol's "Diary of a Madman," or the personal but highly literary diary. According to Maurice Blanchot, in modern times, the diary is a "livre sans avenir," "an *anti-récit*. (By "récit" Blanchot means a peculiar, transgeneric, but essentially literary kind of writing generated by the desire to retell the experience of the ineffable.) Blanchot regards the diary as a "piège" for the writer, "garde feu d'écriture" (trap of writing), as something in-between literature and life, which in fact is an inauthentic surrogate for both. (Maurice Blanchot "Le journal intime et le recit," in *Livre à venir* (Paris: Gallimard, 1959), 274–75). Also see Béatrice Didier, *Le journal intime* (Paris: Presses universitaires de France, 1977) and Stephen Rendall, "On Diaries," *Diacritics* (Fall 1986).

8 Barthes, *A Lover's Discourse*, 178.

9 The question of the gender and sexuality of Barthes' "body" is quite problematic. Is this body, as Barthes ultimately desires it to be, "neuter" and beyond the binary opposition of masculine and feminine? Is it radically heterogeneous? In the light of Eve Sedgwick's discussion "Across Gender, Across Sexuality: Willa Cather and Others" (*SAQ* 88 [Winter 1989]) that urges us not to subsume all examination of sexuality under the category of gender, this issue becomes further complicated. In fact, in *Roland Barthes*, Barthes mentions in passing some of his future projects, which include, together with the collection of "incidents" (which the editors of "Soirées de Paris" used to justify their publication), the project of writing discourses of homosexuality or rather, always in plural—homosexualities. Had Barthes written it, we would have had a more subtle insight into this issue.

Barthes' very interest in writing the body—an anti-phallic and non-unifiable one—and his insistence upon an unforceful seduction and profoundly anti-authoritarian discourse brings his theoretical enterprise close to that of the French feminists. However, as Naomi Shorr observes, Barthes' discourse of radical heterogeneity and pure difference borders on indifference, appropriation of the feminine for the subject that remains—symbolically—masculine ("Dreaming Dissymmetry: Barthes, Foucault, and Sexual Difference," in *Men in Feminism*, ed. Alice Jardine and Paul Smith [New York: Methuen, 1987]). Furthermore, Barthes' discourse re-essentializes the feminine without reconsideration of what constitutes feminine specificity and feminine difference. Without disagreeing with this argument, I would like to slightly shift the focus. What interests me here is not so much the issue of how Barthes' writings—especially *S/Z*—re-essentialize the feminine but rather how they help us to re-think cultural myths of the feminine and its links to domesticity, privacy, and everydayness. Often unconsciously, or uncritically, one internalizes a cultural value-system that marks everything "feminine" or "effeminate" as inferior and excludes it from "high theory." "Private," domestic," "sentimental," "affectionate" seem to fall into the category of the culturally inferior, which explains why they become relegated to the sphere of "aesthetic obscenity." I am grateful to Andrew Parker for drawing my attention to the relationship between gender and sexuality.

10 Martin Heidegger, "Science and Reflection," in *The Question Concerning Technology*, trans. William Lovitt (New York: Harper and Row, 1977).

11 Despite the general lack of what one conventionally calls "artistic quality" in the diary, there are several explicit gestures towards literariness and attempts to give the everyday a certain literary framing. Thus, in one of the few footnotes to the text, Barthes wrote "mettre au passé composé" (*Incidents*, 85), suggesting a possibility not only of re-reading the diary but of revising and unifying it by deferring the immediacy of the events.

12 Roland Barthes, "The Reality Effect," in *The Rustle of Language*, trans. Richard Howard (NY: Hill and Wang, 1986) 146. See also Roland Barthes, "The Rhetoric of the Image" and "The Third Meaning" in *Image, Music, Text*, trans. Stephen Heath (New York: Hill and Wang, 1977).

13 The "obscene" is discussed throughout Baudrillard's work. See especially, Jean Baudrillard. *De la séduction* (Paris: Edition Galilée, 1979); *Stratégies fatales*, (Paris: Bernard Grasset, 1983); and "Ecstasy of Communication," in *The Anti-Aesthetic: Essays in Postmodern Culture*, ed. Hal Foster (Port Townsend: Bay Press, 1983).

14 Baudrillard, "Ecstasy of Communication," in *The Anti-Aesthetic*, ed. Foster, 127.

15 On the "scene" see Roland Barthes, "Diderot, Eisenstein, Brecht," in *Image, Music, Text; Roland Barthes*; and *S/Z*, trans. Richard Howard (New York: Hill and Wang, 1974).

16 Mikhail Bakhtin, *Problems of Dostoevsky's Poetics*, trans. Caryl Emerson (Minneapolis: University of Minnesota Press, 1984). Later Bakhtin sees the dialogue as a linguistic heteroglossia, but the phenomenon of heteroglossia is still often made anthropomorphic. Moreover, Bakhtin's notion of the human subject differs from the modernist decentered self. In fact, Bakhtin carefully avoids references to twentieth-century writings. I have developed these issues in my article "Dialogue as Lyrical Hermaphroditism: Mandel'shtam's Challenge to Bakhtin," *Slavic Review* (Spring 1991).

17 This can be compared with the description of Benjamin's childhood awkwardness and "impotence in front of the city" (4) in "Berlin Chronicle," which later translates into an illuminative urban re-mapping.

18 Michel de Certeau, *L'invention du quottdien/arts de faire* (Paris: Union Générale d'Éditions, 1980). Surprisingly, perhaps, the work of Certeau is not discussed in the special issue of *Yale French Studies*. On the further elaboration on the relationship between "art" and "arts" and on the critical reevaluation of the concept of culture, see James Clifford, *Predicament of Culture* (Cambridge: Harvard University Press, 1988).

PART TWO

LIVING IN COMMON PLACES AND RETHINKING WHAT MATTERS (1992–95)

Boym's book, *Common Places: Mythologies of Everyday Life in Russia*, as well as her other writings at this time, liberated scholars of culture to range more broadly than ever before, emboldening them to challenge critical assumptions, and inspiring them to shed light on the heretofore invisible. Boym uncovers a treasure trove of cultural artifacts rescued from neglect and shown to be well worth our attention, from a 1952 painting titled *The New Apartment* (whose analysis reveals not only the workings of official ideology but also an "iconographic blemish on the image of Socialist Realist domestic bliss [that] can function as a trigger of cultural memory and a key to the archeology of Soviet private and communal life") and the bric-a-brac of average Soviet citizens to the collapsing monuments and ascendant matryoshki of the post-Soviet cityscape. The works in this section were written during a major historical transition; as Boym documents "the end of the Soviet world," she seeks to preserve monuments (broadly defined) from destruction, presenting them in new, defamiliarizing contexts so that they may serve as history lessons, akin to the émigré artists Komar and Melamid's *Monumental Propaganda* project. At the same time, by focusing on the spaces that people inhabit and the built environment that both reflects and shapes our world, Boym shows the ways in which the Soviet legacy is more tenacious than we might think, defying the triumphalist declarations of Cold War victory that resounded in the early 1990s, and that strike one today as perhaps premature.

A major keyword in Boym's writing at this time is "utopia," a story about a place that is both perfect and nonexistent. For Boym, utopia signifies an imagined projection rather than a realized social order. Boym contrasts the utopian sphere of visual propaganda with private spaces in which individuals can carve out alternative forms of freedom; "utopia" thus comes to signify not just top-down social engineering but also private worlds into which ordinary individuals can escape from the violence of those inhuman designs. Boym's attention to words, their historical trajectories, and their (un)translatability is part of her long-term project of tracing the links between word and worldview. She highlights a particular set of terms pertaining to "bad taste" as a category that blends ethics and aesthetics: kitsch, cliché, and the uniquely Russian *poshlost'* as well as the opposition between *byt* (the daily grind, grounded in the fallen/feminized material world) and *bytie* (spiritual being that is situated on a higher plane). Writing in a voice that ranges from intimate to magisterial—and wielding the first-person singular without apology—Boym challenges binaries and other received wisdom, and in the (carnivalesque) spirit of inverting hierarchies, she brings readers face to face with the marginal, the tacky, and the everyday, while showing that the stakes are deeply ethical throughout. Boym's gift for visceral description allows her to capture the texture of lived experience, which in its own way helps her to oppose the *ars obliovionalis* that she would address head on in *The Future of Nostalgia*; her deep empathy for her interlocutors depicts them in all their human complexity.

In an essay we have included here, Boym delineates the peculiar "Russian conception of national culture" whose heroic self-definition excluded "the sphere of the everyday" to which women were habitually consigned. Boym juxtaposes the works of a writer, a filmmaker, and a visual artist to consider how women artists grapple with the association between femininity and bad taste that they have inherited. Visual culture, iconography, materiality, and play serve as key critical concepts in Boym's approach to these diverse artists. Challenging the commonplaces of gender ideology, she depicts women working in a post-Soviet context who offer "alternative framings of poshlost', kitsch, and everyday culture," each creatively rehabilitating the objects of customary scorn, as Boym herself does in her scholarly practice. Sometimes wordplay drives the point home, as in the description of the woman writer traditionally relegated to the (debased) material realm who is viewed as "someone who can excel only in textiles, not in texts." Via history and theory, Boym demonstrates the urgent need to question the assumptions that underlie the dominant frameworks within which we define what—and who—is valuable, worthy of attention and respect.

Another essay included here recounts how in Stalin's time, "the advocacy of *kulturnost'* (culturalization)" was embodied in cultural artifacts that served to translate ideology into the everyday. In examining the workings of culturalization, Boym focuses on a popular song and a lacquer box; she excavates their origins and takes account of their intended meaning as well as alternative readings that neither the objects' creators nor their doctrinaire Soviet commentators could fully control. Boym's analysis of the fairy-tale associations of both song and box is part of her larger project of unpacking cultural mythologies; and she anticipates affect theory in her critical concern for the emotional and sensory appeal of these artifacts. We see, too, how the song and the box endure into the present, taking on new meanings in a post-Soviet context, as in the memorable image of Boym's father, whose mother spent five years at hard labor, humming his own version of the song while washing dishes in his American kitchen. The scene's musical tribute to an oppressive regime captures the irony that is crucial to Boym's historical consciousness; this keen attentiveness to the paradoxical essence of being human informs *Common Places*' approach to the power of collectively imagined common ground, and the irony that such imaginings can generate: "The common place is a mythical site from which intellectuals perpetually displace themselves, only to write elegies to the lost communality."

Julia Chadaga

6 THE POETICS OF BANALITY: TAT'IANA TOLSTAIA, LANA GOGOBERIDZE, AND LARISA ZVEZDOCHETOVA

In response to a questionnaire on mass culture distributed among prominent Soviet writers, artists, and intellectuals, Tat'iana Tolstaia wrote that mass culture is "by definition not culture." "Mass culture," in other words, is a contradiction in terms, and Tolstaia dismisses its Soviet variant as "kitsch" (*Iskusstvo kino* 6 [1990]: 69–70). Yet elements of "mass culture" and of what at various moments in history has been considered kitsch, banality, bad taste, and petit-bourgeois *poshlost'* are woven into the artistic texture of many works and creatively reinterpreted in Tolstaia's own artistic works as well as in the works of many other contemporary women artists, filmmakers, and writers.

Vladimir Nabokov considered the Russian conception of banality (*poshlost'*) culturally untranslatable into other languages: it combines artistic triviality and spiritual deficiency, an attitude toward love as well as toward mass culture ("Philistines and Philistinism," 309–14). The untranslatable aspect of *poshlost'* has to do with the Russian conception of national culture echoed in Tat'iana Tolstaia's response, which is always culture in the singular, Culture with a capital C. The sphere of the everyday is not part of Russian culture in its heroic self-definition. *Poshlost'* has been frequently represented as a woman, an impertinent goddess of bad taste. Nabokov writes that the *o* of *poshlost'* is "as round as the bosom of a bathing beauty on a German picture postcard" (*Nikolai Gogol*, 70). The history of *poshlost'*, which reveals many connections with the cultural myth of femininity and feminine writing, illuminates the relationship between aesthetics, politics, and everyday culture. The poetics of *poshlost'* is conceived here as a double movement between the historical metamorphosis of the concept and its transformation within a single contemporary work of art. Works by the writer Tat'iana Tolstaia, the film director Lana Gogoberidze, and the painter Larisa Zvezdochetova offer alternative framings of *poshlost'*, kitsch, and everyday culture. Rethinking kitsch and *poshlost'* and revisiting some theoretical commonplaces will give us new insight into shifting cultural hierarchies and conceptions of taste in contemporary Russian art.

Poshlost' comes from *poshlo*—something that has happened. In Vladimir Dal''s dictionary, the obsolete meaning of *poshlyi* is, in fact, "old, traditional, common, ancient, ancestral" (374). Initially *poshlyi* had no moral or aesthetic connotation. The history of the use of the words *poshlyi* and "banal" demonstrates how a descriptive term can turn into a term of discrimination; it reflects a changing conception of communality and of artistic convention, a transformation of a "common good" into a commonplace. This transformation occurs with the advent of Romanticism and its aesthetics of originality, authenticity, and individual genius. At the core of the problem of *poshlost'* is the paradox of repetition, of communality, and of tradition. *Poshlost'* is repetition gone sour, a convention turned into a cliché, into an infinitely exploitable set of devices that preclude the critical aesthetic process. It closes off experimentation and experience. It is often difficult, however, to distinguish between "good" and "bad" repetition and to draw a line between a convention that is needed to reflect our cultural predicament and the triteness and trivialization that create culture's malign doubles.

The struggle against *poshlost'* plays a crucial role in Russian cultural history; it is linked to mythologies of social class (a perpetual war between the intelligentsia and the *meshchanstvo*, or bourgeoisie), attitudes toward material culture and the everyday, and conceptions of national identity and sexuality. The evolution of the concept of *poshlost'* reveals a remarkable metamorphosis. The Soviet Academy Dictionary lists the following meanings for *poshlost'*: "1. Lacking in spiritual qualities, ordinary, insignificant, worthless, paltry. 2. Not original, worn-out, banal. 3. Indecent, obscene, tasteless, vulgar" (*Akademicheskii*, 476). It is amazing that a single concept can embrace sexual indecency, artistic triviality, and lack of spirituality. In Russian culture the separation of the sexual, spiritual, and artistic spheres, or the split between the ethics of behavior, metaphysics, religion, and aesthetics, did not occur in the same way as it did in the West. Art never became completely autonomous; rather, the nineteenth-century Russian intelligentsia regarded Russian literature as always more or less than literature—a voice of national consciousness, the foundation of Russian identity.

In the Russian tradition *poshlost'* is also linked to the discourse of love, as we see in Anton Chekhov's short story "A Lady with a Dog." Here Chekhov turns a Western-style affair into a typical Russian love story complete with tears, gray dresses, autumnal landscapes, and yearning for a happy ending.[2] *Poshlost'* might refer both to sentimentality construed as tastelessness and to obscenity, often construed as any explicit expression of sexuality. The discourse on banality in the Russian context reveals a quasi-religious discourse on good and evil superimposed on the Romantic discourse on what is original or common, so that *poshlost'* becomes a peculiarly syncretic concept. It also has to do with the perpetual cultural opposition of *byt* (daily grind) and *bytie* (spiritual being)—the Russian symbolist version of the Orthodox Christian paradigm. The everyday is a modern secular concept. The opposition between *byt* and *bytie* fosters a peculiar cultural ostracism of diverse experiences associated with everyday culture, from "private life" to attitudes toward material objects.

While the Russian intelligentsia launched a war on *poshlost'*, Russian writers from Pushkin to Chekhov derived a great deal of pleasure from describing and savoring it.[3] In this respect they are not unique. Baudelaire wished to "create a cliché," and Flaubert from his very first letter at the age of ten claimed that his artistic impulse was to record banalities (Baudelaire 23). *Poshlost'* in Russia, like banality in France, has been conceived as opposed to the creative force of art, but in fact the relationship between the two is symbiotic and paradoxical. I am interested less in defining "banal" than in tracing its adventures through history and examining how an element of the habitual becomes defamiliarized and reclaimed by art, and then turns into an artistic cliché that in turn has to be reinvented. What is the relationship between banality and irony, banality both with and without quotation marks? How do we distinguish between artistic and self-conscious references to *poshlost'* and its involuntary uses? Where is the line between *poshlost'* with an aura and *poshlost'* without an aura, good "bad taste" and simply bad taste?

Poshlost', according to Nabokov, is "an unobvious sham"; it is "not only the obviously trashy but also the falsely important, the falsely beautiful, the falsely clever, the falsely attractive" (*Nikolai Gogol*, 70). In other words, *poshlost'* is false not only artistically but also morally; yet it is also very seductive. *Poshlost'* is an older sister of German kitsch. In Western Europe and the United States, the critique of kitsch reached its peak in the 1920s and 1930s in reaction to the commercialization of art and later to totalitarian fascist art.[4] What is fascinating and disturbing about kitsch is that it blurs the boundaries between art and life, denying autonomy to art. Kitsch is not merely bad art but also an unethical act, an act of mass manipulation. Kitsch is presented as "the debased and academic simulacra of genuine culture" (Greenberg 10), as "a parody on catharsis" (Adorno 340), and as a "sentimentalization of the finite ad infinitum" (Broch 75). Certain stylistic elements characterize kitsch—a propensity for ornamentation, eclecticism, and sentimentality. But, as Clement Greenberg points out, more important are the mechanisms by which kitsch imitates art's effects and not its inner processes (15). Yet the examples that critics cite betray their own cultural tastes and the climate of the time, and warn us against an uncritical reification of a single conception of kitsch. Milan Kundera, one of the great critics of totalitarian kitsch, has written that "none of us is superman enough to escape kitsch completely. No matter how we scorn it, kitsch is an integral part of the human condition" (256). So instead of trying to be supermen or rather superwomen fighting the empire of kitsch, we will examine kitsch and *poshlost'* as syntactic phenomena that depend on context and angle of vision. At the center of our attention will be neither the universal "structure of bad taste" that Umberto Eco began to discern (180–216) nor the "timeless beauty of *poshlost'*" that Nabokov ironically sought, but its historical and fictional transformations by three women—a writer, a filmmaker, and a painter—in works that reveal instances of cultural intolerance as well as of poetic generosity.

From the eighteenth century on (in Russia from the nineteenth), "bad taste" became increasingly feminized. In Sasha Chernyi's poem "Poshlost'" (1910), *poshlost'* is personified as a tacky salon goddess. She is presented as a middle-aged sexually loose woman, a nouveau riche who probably bought herself a title of nobility. Madame Poshlost' dresses in lilac and yellow, paints watercolors of roses, and sleeps with her cabby:

Lilac corset and yellow bow on her bosom;
Eyes like navels—eyeless eyes.
Someone else's curls cling thick to her temples
And greasily hang down her sides.

... In her salons *everyone,* the audacious crowd,
Having torn the skin off virginal ideas,
Clutch in their paws the unfeeling body
And zealously neigh like a herd of horses.

There they say eggs went up in price
And over the Neva a comet fell,—
Self-admiring, like mantelpiece Chinamen,
They nod to the beat of the gramophone's wail. . . .

She sings, and paints a watercolor rose.
She follows fashions of all sorts,
Saving up jokes and rumors, phrases, poses,
Corrupting the muse, corrupting love.

She's in kinship and in constant friendship
With effrontery, nonsense, talentlessness.
She's familiar with flattery, pathos, betrayal,
And, it seems, love affairs with dunces. . . .

The only ones not to know her are . . . who?
Of course: children, beasts, and common people.
The first when they don't look like grownups,
The last when away from their masters.

The portrait is ready. As I throw down my pens,
Please don't make a scene about my crassness:
When you paint a pig beside its shed—
No belle Hélène can appear on the canvas.

(Chernyi 27–29)

Cheap eroticism, infatuation with foreignness, and the vanity of a nouveau riche in art and life happily merge in this grotesque female figure who embodies all aspects of *poshlost'*—its relation to sexuality, Western influences, and the mythology of social class. She is a guardian of a pseudo-artistic salon and of a hearth of hypocritical bourgeois domesticity, with its tacky attributes: fashionable porcelain "Chinamen" on the fireplace, elaborate satin comforters on the queen-size bed, the "howling" of gramophone records in the background. The proliferation of material objects from the eclectic urban domestic culture at the turn of the century goes hand in hand with the profanation of "ideals." The major sin of Madame Poshlost' is her eclecticism; she mixes lilac and yellow, the works

Possibly speaks to "the intolerable" (?) that Deleuze speaks of in cinema

of the erotic writer Ivan Barkov and gramophone romances, watercolor roses and clichés about political "crises." But a close reading of the poem demonstrates the ambiguous position of the poet himself and unintentional ironies in the war against banality. In fact, the new Pygmalion of Madame Poshlost' is implicated in her bestial salon scene, and does not completely escape the dated charms of the goddess of bad taste.

In the Russian tradition the figure of Madame Poshlost' threatens any woman writer of prose or poetry.[5] What is important here is less the writer's gender than the use of gendered metaphors in aesthetics, and the ways in which femininity, effeminacy, decadence, excessive ornamentation, and cosmopolitanism become entangled with the idea of bad taste. "Feminine" writing has been described as excessive lyrical exaltation, perpetual lovesickness, an abusive use of metaphor, and a lack of a sense of history or historical responsibility. The woman writer has been conceived as a kind of nouveau riche who lacks the blue blood of literary aristocracy. She is an exalted weaver who by mistake picked up the wrong materials for her knitting, someone who can excel only in textiles, not in texts. All women writers and poets, including Tsvetaeva and Akhmatova, were accused of displaying various kinds of "feminine genetic deficiency," and each responded to the threats of Madame Poshlost' in her own way.

In Russia in the 1920s a campaign was launched against "petit-bourgeois *poshlost'*," which encompassed everything associated with private life, love, and domesticity—everything that went against the virile ascetic spirit of the revolution. The poet Vladimir Maiakovskii decried the effeminate interiors of the new Soviet middle class, with their porcelain elephants on the mantelpiece, phonographic love songs (*romansy*), lace curtains, yellow canaries, and Marx in a crimson frame. By the late 1920s any art not sponsored by the state was prohibited and the heterogeneous culture of the early 1920s was displaced by the doctrine of socialist realism, coupled with a sanitized version of nineteenth-century Russian high culture, which in a cruel and paradoxical manner realized the old dream of the Russian intelligentsia, the dream of creating a unified "people's culture." Jeffrey Brooks has convincingly analyzed particularly hostile attitudes toward "popular literature" on the part of the state, the church, and the intelligentsia in the nineteenth century—attitudes that were perpetuated by the new Soviet state (295–99).

This process culminated in a peculiar pact between the Stalinist state and the new Soviet middle class and two decades of middlebrow art, which Milan Kundera defined as "totalitarian kitsch." The postwar Stalinist culture of the 1950s was marked by a return of the repressed: the despised coziness of the "bourgeois interior." The fashionable color of the Soviet 1950s was no longer red but pink: pink lampshades and postcards with exotic views substituted for Marx in a crimson frame (Dunham 41–48). The semiotics of color, and especially shades of red (from pink to crimson), played a crucial part in the construction of "good revolutionary taste" or "petit-bourgeois" effeminate taste. In the 1960s the intelligentsia of the thaw generation rebelled against the "bad taste" of the 1950s, which smacked of Stalinism and philistinism, and rediscovered in a somewhat distorted form the heritage of revolutionary modernism. In the eclectic age of Mikhail Gorbachev, "totalitarian kitsch" or the "high Stalinism" of the 1930s, old *poshlost'* from the time of NEP, 1950s middlebrow art, and the neomodernist euphoria of the 1960s all reappeared as aesthetic and political styles, occasions for nostalgia and laughter.

Contemporary Soviet women artists—both of the thaw generation and of the 1980s—have inherited and often internalized the conceptions of effeminate "bad taste" and are still haunted by the grotesque female figure of Madame Poshlost'. For Tat'iana Tolstaia "women's prose" is synonymous with superficiality, philistinism, commercial psychology, and excessive sentimentality—a "saccharine air" (McLaughlin 77–80). At the same time, in Tolstaia's short stories we easily find elements of what she describes as "women's prose"—a term that has to be reevaluated and considered without its deprecating quotation marks; here *poshlost'* mingles with poetry, and the boundaries between irony and banality are often blurred.

Everyday trivia, minor rituals, and tacky domestic objects with an aura of time past occupy a central place in Tolstaia's stories and provide a major writerly "pleasure of the text." As Helena Goscilo remarks, "the most striking effects of her prose issue precisely from the dramatic contrast between the seemingly lackluster characters and events of her stories, on the one hand, and, on the other, the lush, colorful prism of multiple perspectives through which they are glimpsed and conveyed" (283). In this respect Tolstaia follows the tradition of Gogol', Flaubert, and Nabokov: she both decries *poshlost'* and takes a special writerly delight in describing it. Yet the flashes of "high culture" do not fully illuminate Tolstaia's fictional world; her central subtext is Soviet urban folklore, especially slightly outmoded urban romances and sentimental songs.

The word *poshlyi* actually occurs in Tolstaia's "Okkervil River," one of her most poetic stories, about a man's dream romance with a recorded singer in an imaginary land on the banks of the Okkervil River. The area bordering the Okkervil River is a peculiar margin, the folkloric "end of the world" and the limit of Simeonov's everyday existence, with its bachelor's feasts of pasteurized cheeses and bits of bacon served on yesterday's newspaper. But how does one imagine the limit of one's world, the marginal? The story offers us two equally hypothetical pictures—the ideal Okkervil valley as a land of "blue mists" and an imaginary Petrine landscape of clear waters, nasturtiums on the windowsills, little bridges with towers and chains, on the one hand; and on the other the Okkervil as the edge of the city, a land of urban trash, pollution, excrement, and residue, "something else hopeless, provincial, and trite" (*chtonibud' eshche beznadezhnoe, okrainnoe, poshloe* [Tolstaya 21]). Thus the limit of the world poetically embodied in the "Okkervil River" (which actually exists in Leningrad/St. Petersburg) can be seen as an ideal escape or as something inescapably banal and paltry, something inescapably of *this* world—its residue, its poisonous triviality. In other words, the euphonious Okkervil River has two banks—the bank of the blue misty ideal and the bank of *poshlost'*.

At first glance a similar duality is to be found in the images of two women: Vera Vasilievna, the heroine of Simeonov's heroic solitude, of sentimental songs about withering chrysanthemums, the ephemerality of being, and unrequited love; and Tamara, an ordinary woman, with domestic flowery curtains and home cooking. (Both women have their flowery attributes, but the flowers are of distinctly different styles: Vera Vasilievna's are pseudo-aristocratic chrysanthemums and nasturtiums, while Tamara's are standard Soviet flowers on homey curtains.) This opposition of ideal beauty and *poshlost'*, however, does not hold throughout the story. In fact, even the ideal Vera Vasilievna is depicted at the beginning as a queen of turn-of-the-century *poshlost'* (not a nouveau riche like Sasha Chernyi's Madame Poshlost' but a true queen of démodé). She is described as a "languorous naiad," which reminds us of turn-of-the-century soft-porn postcards and the German bathing beauty, the bosom of Nabokov's *poshlost'*. At the end of the story Vera Vasilievna is not even a queen of old-fashioned *poshlost'* bathing in the aura of past ideals, only the tacky and vulgar Soviet prima donna Verunchik, who ends up taking a bath in Simeonov's house—bathing, but not a beauty. (But then, the distinction between *poshlost'* with an aura and *poshlost'* without an aura is tenuous at best.)

The narrative both distances itself from and engages with the sentimental discourse of "romances"—those popular songs that Maiakovskii and the writers of the Left Front considered the embodiment of bad taste. Two that play a prominent part in the text are "The Chrysanthemums" and "No, It's Not You I Love So Passionately."[6] Here is the refrain from "The Chrysanthemums," which resounds throughout Tolstaia's story: "The chrysanthemums have withered in the garden long ago, / but love is still alive in my ailing heart." (Otsveli uzh davno, chrizantemy v sadu, / no liubov' vse zhivet v moem serdtse bol'nom). The other romance begins like this: "No, it's not you I love so passionately, / it's not for me the shining of your beauty, / I love in you my past suffering / and my perished youth." (Net, ne tebia tak pylko ia liubliu / ne dlia menia krasy tvoei blistan'e / liubliu v tebe ia proshloe stradan'e / i molodost' pogibshuiu moiu). The second song is in fact based on a Lermontov poem. The romance as a genre moved down from high culture to become a part of people's oral culture, an urban and middle-class folklore, and then turned into a *meshchanskii,* a petit-bourgeois artifact that the new high culture wished to suppress. At last it is recovered, now that it is completely outmoded, within the eclectic texture of a self-conscious artistic text.

The distinction between Tolstaia's defamiliarizing ironic narrative and the free indirect discourse that incorporates the perspective of Simeonov, the romance lover, is often difficult to trace. The story is a wistful meditation on the "hopelessness, the *poshlost'*" of existence, to the accompaniment of the powerful, larger-than-life voice of Vera Vasilievna on the phonograph. The last paragraph of "Okkervil River" incorporates some lines from old romance songs, and recycles and poetically rewrites clichés about rivers, lives, loves, and beautiful stories that can wither like chrysanthemums in autumn.

Tolstaia's "Sonia" is yet another meditation on romance and bad taste. Let us examine the first paragraph of the story:

A person lived—a person died. Only the name remains—Sonya. "Remember, Sonya used to say . . . " "A dress like Sonya's . . ." "You keep blowing your nose all the time like Sonya. . . ." Then even the people who used to say that died, and there was only a trace of her voice in my head, incorporeal, seeming to come from the black jaws of the telephone receiver. Or all of a sudden there is a view of a sunny room, like a bright photograph come to life—laughter around a set table, like those hyacinths in a glass vase on the tablecloth, wreathed too with curly pink smiles. Look quickly before it goes out. Who is that? Is the one you need among them? But the bright room trembles and fades and now the backs of the seated people are translucent like gauze, and with frightening speed, their laughter falls to pieces, recedes in the distance—catch it if you can. (Tolstaya 144–45)

The first sentence of the story is a cliché, a trivial statement about life and death: "A person lived—a person died." It could be uttered by a *skaz*-narrator, a wisewoman storyteller in a communal apartment. In the first paragraph the narrator does not merely describe but acts out the difficulty of recovering the story and the characters from oblivion. The first cliché actually reveals to us what the story is about: about death and revival by fiction—what is poetically called "festively dressed-up immortality" (*nariadnoe bessmertie*). The disembodied voices, traces of overheard conversations, conjure up some visual memory: "All of a sudden there is a view of a sunny room, like a bright photograph come to life." The room emerges like a scene from an amateur home movie, and the characters appear as projections of light, fragile and semitransparent, "like gauze." The space of the story is presented to us not according to realist conventions as a three-dimensional space in perspective but rather as a space of memory that is fragile and on the verge of vanishing. But what this fragile representation brings us is a picture of an old-fashioned *meshchanskii byt,* a private banal scene with tacky objects. The little glass vase and the hyacinths with their curly pink smiles remind us of some evil flowers of *poshlost'*. It is difficult to say whether this *poshlost'* is with or without quotation marks. (The color pink figures prominently in Tolstaia's fiction. We find it, for instance, in the first paragraph of another story in the collection—"Sweet Shura.") The smiling curly hyacinths in a little vase function as the main triggers of memory. It is a memorable tacky object and some everyday clichés in overheard conversations that make the story possible.

Sonia, whom the female narrator of this story wishes to recover from the blurred background of an old photograph, is radically unphotogenic, like her fictional sisters in the world of Tolstaia stories—Shura, Zhenia, and others, all those old women from a different era who inhabit tiny rooms in godforsaken communal apartments in Leningrad. Sonia is a kind of blessed fool whom everyone considers unattractive, stupid, and always guilty of bad taste. The two main female characters are described in terms of their taste: Ada Adolfovna (the alliteration is hellish: *ad* means "hell" in Russian) is said to possess "a serpentine elegance," whereas Sonia is dressed very "unbecomingly" (*bezobrazno*).

One detail of Sonia's clothing becomes particularly important in the story—the little enamel brooch in the form of a dove, which she never takes off. In the context of the history of Soviet taste this little enamel dove is an emblem of bad taste and *poshlost'*. In the story it is ridiculed as an ultimate embodiment of Sonia's lack of style. Sonia falls victim to a party joke orchestrated by the powerful Ada Adolfovna, who invents a passionate epistolary lover for Sonia named Nikolai. The clichés of a tacky romance work for poor Sonia, who falls in love with Nikolai, a product of Ada Adolfovna's powerful "feminine prose." At the moment Ada is ready to "kill" Sonia's imaginary romantic lover, Sonia encloses her enamel dove, her most intimate and sacred object, in one of her letters. This gesture allows the epistolary romance to continue just a bit longer. At the end, the narrator, wishing to reconstruct Sonia's story from fragmentary tales and old blurred photographs, asks Ada for Sonia's letters. Considerable time has passed. There has been a war, a siege; Sonia and her mythical love have died their natural or unnatural deaths; and Sonia's letters may have been burned along with the books to heat the house during that impossible first winter of the siege of Leningrad. In the end the only thing that has survived, or at least is believed to have survived, is the enamel dove. The last line of the story—"After all, doves don't burn" (Ved', golubkov ogon' ne beret)—is introduced by the colloquial and affective Russian *ved* (after all, just, you know). The line also paraphrases the proverbial phrase in Bulgakov's *Master and Margarita*, "manuscripts don't burn" (rukopisi ne goriat), which perpetuates the myth that art survives all purges and repression. In Tolstaia's story, however, it is not a work of art that does not burn but a tacky enamel dove.

The adventures of the enamel dove parallel the adventures of *poshlost'* and the complex shifts in the narrative perspective on it. Not only does the dove make the epistolary romance more "physical," saving the lover from premature death; it also triggers both the romance and the narration of the story itself. From an emblem of ridiculed old-fashioned tackiness it turns into a sympathetic sentimental object, a souvenir, imbued by personal warmth. At the end it is reframed as a poetic thing par excellence, the last eccentric romantic survivor of the world of daily *poshlost'*. Sonia's little brooch suggests the infinite powers of poetic metamorphosis, of the metamorphosis of *poshlost'* into poetry and back. The dove can be regarded as a symbol of spirituality, but it is a mass-reproduced one and a clichéd element of decoration that has frequently been used in book illustrations, architectural bas-reliefs, and cheap women's jewelry since the late nineteenth century. It is associated with popular versions of the eclectic and art nouveau style in the applied arts and in crafts. Strongly disliked by the intellectual arbiters of taste, it is beloved by many people who are deprecated as having the tastes of the *meshchanstvo*.

That kind of trashy jewelry is not valuable, but it is priceless. Tolstaia has admitted to a particular affection for trash; she said that she found the inspiration for her story "Sweet Shura" in the discards thrown from a communal apartment into the trash in one of Leningrad's asphalt yards. Sonia's dove can be seen as this kind of trashy found object, with a special fictional charisma. The dove becomes a metaphor for the protean powers of fiction. From a spiritual symbol the dove is transformed into a romantic cliché, embodied in a tacky artifact that suddenly reveals itself as pregnant poetic metaphor. The narrative adornment and the meaning the enamel dove acquires depend on the context; it defies a clear-cut opposition between *byt* and *bytie* (everyday existence and spiritual being, the opposition particularly promoted by the Russian symbolists in their reinterpretation of traditional Russian spirituality). The dove appears as an ideal narrative gift that ensures the imaginary exchange between the fictional lovers of the story and between the writer and her readers. But gifts should not be overinterpreted. The enamel dove will "burn" and disappear the moment we attempt to reduce its poetic suggestiveness and rich textuality to any kind of universal symbolism.

Through its narrative perspectives the story invites us to rethink any one-sided mockery of sentimental kitsch. Tolstaia's own writing, full of ornamental excesses and artistic density, vacillates between poetic clichés and poetic discoveries, and the clear distinction between the two tends to evaporate in the "blue mist" of the narrative streams.

We observe that most of the kitschy items in Tolstaia's stories are not contemporary; they belong to another time and are colored by the aura of memory. In Walter Benjamin's conception, the experience of an aura is the experience of distance, of involuntary memory and historical temporality. It is that element of uniqueness which art objects preserve.[7] Yet in Benjamin's own thought, an aura escapes a single critical framework. Photography, which is an example of art in the age of mechanical reproduction, may seem to be antithetical to traditional oil painting, which possesses an artistic aura. But the photographs of Atget, a professional photographer and a poet of emptied domestic interiors, a pioneer of modern nostalgia, are, in Benjamin's view, suffused with an aura, and so are the tacky objects of the old communal apartments that Tolstaia describes. Susan Sontag characterizes this particular attitude of eroticization, or in Tolstaia's case poeticization, of daily life and tacky trivia as a "campy sensibility." Camp is described as anything outrageously inappropriate, old-fashioned, out of date, *démodé*, all those things that, "from a 'serious' point of view, are either bad art or kitsch." Camp sensibility is based on the conception of "Being-as-Playing-a-Role," of the metaphor of life as theater. It is also "a triumph of the epicene style," of playful reversals of gender and sexual impersonations, often associated with gay sensibility (Sontag 280–81). Sontag remarks that "camp taste is by nature possible only in affluent societies, in societies or circles capable of experiencing the psychopathology of affluence" (291). Affluence is hardly a feature of Soviet life even among the privileged circles of the intellectual elite. Although Tolstaia's framing of trivial objects and her affection for artifice may coincide with Sontag's description, *theatrum mundi* is hardly her metaphor. Sexual playfulness is not her forte either. In Tolstaia's fictional world sympathy and morality are as important as literary artifice (Goscilo 281). Perhaps one should not simply ally Tolstaia with camp, since she has expressed her strong dislike for any kind of "group activities," however theatrical they may be. Rather, we can reread her stories and examine her particular way of poeticizing the everyday, her playful transformation of some stereotypes and unplayful preservation of others.[8]

Lana Gogoberidze's film *Turnover* (1987) also pays tribute to the ordinary marvelous; it shifts the relationship between cultural categories, between public and private spheres, between history and the everyday. The title of Gogoberidze's film may be seen as a rewriting of the *perestroika* metaphor; rather than a directed linear movement—from destruction to reconstruction or vice versa—"turnover" suggests an unpredictable dynamic force in human life that is played out in a series of fragmented narratives, intertwined and entangled like lines of fate. At the center of the film are a pair of "unphotogenic women," the aging actress Manana and the spinster and would-be playwright Rusudan. Although Gogoberidze confessed that she never saw *Sunset Boulevard,* her *Turnover* can be viewed as a peculiar remake of that famous film presented from a woman's perspective.

At the beginning Manana, with all her tacky clothes—fake furs, black lace, scarves—seems to be a parody of idealized femininity. She is perpetually "too much"—overdressed, over-made-up, and hysterical. In another film these two women might have been caricatures, parodies, and embarrassments. Yet in Gogoberidze's film they emerge as sympathetic and problematic characters who can laugh at themselves and at their absurd, unfortunate turns of fate. In this respect the two explosive scenes of women's laughter are of great importance. After one of them, Manana and Rusudan turn into would-be authors and write a play about "two mature women." Hence "feminine excess" is played out with humor throughout the film and turned into potential creativity.

Turnover was released at a time when films denouncing Stalin and Stalinism were flooding the Soviet screen after the unshelving of *Repentance*. In a scene in which Manana, after an unsuccessful audition for a film, stops in at a shoemaker's shop, a photograph of Stalin appears—briefly, in the background. Here we see a new, interesting way of using cinematic depth of field for a peculiar subversion of high political discourse. A tacky collage in the shoeshine booth, made up of a jumble of found objects and outmoded images, includes a picture of the young Manana—the superstar of the 1950s—and the portrait of Stalin, perpetually young and smiling through his handsome mustaches.

After a showing of the film at Boston University, when Gogoberidze was asked about the political meaning of her use of Stalin's picture, she replied that it is simply a "documentary element" of the film, something one sees in Tbilisi in most shoe-shine booths, and as a decoration in trucks and cars. Gogoberidze pointed out that she did not intend to make a straightforward political statement. The picture of Stalin hanging in the background in the mid-1980s reveals the persuasiveness of the Stalin myth (and of the cult of personality in general) and shows how "unreconstructed" Soviet daily experiences really were. Gogoberidze commented that for her "cultural liberation" does not consist exclusively of the opportunity to make more openly political films; it also represents a chance to make films that resist the overpoliticization of culture. In many ways the film is about women's invention of the everyday, the famous prosaic *byt*, the site of *poshlost'* par excellence. Whereas the film's male characters escape to search for truth away from home (the cliché of the male quest for abstract truth), women learn ironically and sympathetically to reestablish the everyday. Ultimately the film is not simply about the turnover of a series of fragmentary narratives, which has become a mark of the new Georgian school of cinema, but also about the possibility of recovering alternative forms of communication and sympathy that badly need recovery.

Larisa Zvezdochetova also takes part in a magic turnover of everyday kitsch objects, childhood memories, and high art clichés. She has said that she wants to recover in her work everything that art history has ignored: amateur embroidery by provincial women on collective farms, 1950s postcards, "deer" carpets from communal apartments, matchbox labels showing the battleship Aurora, chocolate foil wrappers (*fantiki*) bearing Ivan Shishkin's classic painting *Three Bears,* badges with the logo "Be Ready for Labor and Defense" and a gilded athlete covered with rust, black-and-white reproductions of Nefertiti, the beauty queen of ancient Egypt, who became the most popular Soviet pinup after Ernest Hemingway. All of these found objects disclose the minor aesthetic delights of bleak Soviet everyday culture and were doubly censored, by high art and high politics.[9] Just as Tolstaia found inspiration for "Sweet Shura" in Leningrad trash, Zvezdochetova affectionately excavates Soviet dumps—and finds there not only all those *poshlye* objects, the petit-bourgeois "domestic trash" scorned from the 1920s to the 1960s, but also reproductions of high art torn out of popular magazines. In her works "the feminine" and "bad taste" are placed within quotation marks and creatively reinterpreted.

A dialogue with the avant-garde—and, between the lines, with some Soviet conceptualists of the older generation—is played out in some of her key works. Her installation with fragile paper angels hanging from trees, programmatically titled *The End of the Avant-Garde,* was presented at the exhibition "Aptart—Beyond the Fence" in 1983. The angels, cut out of white paper like the ready-made snowflakes familiar to all Russian schoolchildren, evoke both children's art and turn-of-the-century mass culture, which was populated by angels, "fat flirtatious cupids," and the other whimsical winged creatures against which the avant-gardists fought so ferociously (Malevich 123). The flimsy angels in the natural setting signal the end of the seriousness and stylistic purity of the newly fetishized historical avant-garde. In her work Zvezdochetova wants to confront high avant-garde culture, predicated on originality, with everyday culture—the mass-reproduced and repetitive female arts and crafts, the communal apartment decorations, the Soviet wallpaper designs that frame one's memories of childhood.

Zvezdochetova's artistic work can be placed in the context of the younger generation of conceptual artists that includes Konstantin

Zvezdochetov and Mariia Serebriakova, but she also has cross-cultural references of other kinds. Zvezdochetova remembers an amateur "aesthetic therapist," a woman she got to know during her work with craftsmen in the small towns near Odessa. With her followers the woman made large embroideries patterned on reproductions of paintings that had become Russian and Soviet classics—from the nineteenth-century *End of Pompeii* by Aleksandr Briullov to the portrait of Lenin in his study. When Zvezdochetova asked why she embroidered portraits of Lenin rather than her own designs, the woman explained that this was the true way to bring art to the masses: when the embroiderers followed the lines and brush strokes of the great artists, they were both propagating art and raising the prestige of the embroidery. Zvezdochetova wants to do exactly the opposite—to copy embroidery into art and challenge cultural hierarchies. Moreover, unlike constructivists of the 1920s such as Varvara Stepanova, she is trying not to impose her pure, nonobjective patterns upon mass design but rather to learn from women's unofficial mass culture itself.

In a recent work Zvezdochetova touches—and invites us to touch, literally sense—one of Russia's main avant-garde icons, Kazimir Malevich's *Black Square.* Imagine the *Black Square,* which was supposed to be an ultimate pure nonobjective painting, "zero degree of form," as an attractive object of soft velour in a gilded frame—an avant-garde antique. Zvezdochetova goes further, however—what she offers us is zero degree of painting; the Suprematist surface is nothing but a folding velour curtain that invites us not to search for avant-garde absolutes but to look right behind the cover—only to find an enlarged reproduction of a common embroidery. Moreover, the black squares themselves are reproduced and repeated three times. The work, called *Classical Genres of Art: Portrait, Landscape, Still Life,* is a kind of trompe-l'oeuil or trompe genre. It appears at first as a perfect classical ensemble: a gray monumental pedestal in the center and three black squares. On three sides of the pedestal are three little embroideries—a portrait of a girl, a landscape, and a still life. The embroideries are actual found objects: one was found on an old pillowcase; the others were rescued from the trash or bought at a cheap store. They are the products of craftswomen, collective and anonymous. Moreover, they are incomplete, nothing but fragments, unfinished because of lack of time and the burden of domestic chores or simply badly preserved, ruined, unvalued. The three black-square velour curtains cover up, like the most precious museum artifacts, the enlarged photographic projections of the embroideries, merely mechanical reproductions, even less original than their anonymous originals.

The work has many tricks, devices and levels of irony. It plays with and humorously and creatively borrows not only from Malevich, the suprematist master, but also from the master of embroidery, the amateur "aesthetic therapist" from a small town near Odessa. Moreover, it is the embroidery that is given the most prestigious place and cherished as a found masterpiece, while the black square, the icon of high avant-garde art, serves only as the frame and cover. The most unoriginal collective craft is positioned as unique, while the avant-garde art is reproduced. The space also creates a trompe l'oeil museum space, because what is covered by the rich velour is in fact reproductions or projections of the originals. And the frame, which appears to be of sumptuous gold, is actually made of a gold tablecloth that Zvezdochetova found at a Turkish flea market in Germany. In a museum, a painting is untouchable; its aesthetic distance is carefully patrolled and protected by watchful guards. Zvezdochetova's installation is supposed to be touched. But many viewers have internalized the conventions of museum behavior and are too embarrassed to play erotic games with a work of art—the status that Zvezdochetova's installation, composed of many found objects, has certainly acquired. The work is a clash of tactile experiences—the embroidery, a very tactile art, is turned into a flat photograph that is covered by the luxurious velour. So one is invited to touch the curtain, while the photograph itself is immaterial.

According to Zvezdochetova, she was attempting to make what she calls "erotic art," but art with a particular kind of tactile female eroticism. It is not sexually explicit at the level of visual representation—the obligatory nude scene of any recent Soviet or post-Soviet film. Nor is it eroticism in quotation marks, a kind of intertextual eroticism. Her erotic art is not violent but playful; it consists of a variety of tactile experiences, including tactile trompe l'oeil, the games of revealing and concealing the "body of work." The installation plays not only with arts and crafts, high and low styles, but with aesthetic distance itself. Zvezdochetova's is the art of tactile conceptualism. Of course, it is up to the viewer to decide whether to touch or not.

Classical Genres of Art is one of Zvezdochetova's more explicitly conceptual works. It is also more of an ensemble than a fragmented souvenir, the lost memory that some of her other works resemble. The silhouettes, cut out of paper covered by a lace curtain, offer us again a clash between the immateriality of the silhouette and the ostensibly tactile quality of the lace. The work reminds us of a child walking through the streets of her native city, peeking through the brightly lit windows and eavesdropping on the lives of strangers, and never resolving the plots of their dramas. Not kitsch but something prior to it—a childhood surprise, a gust of curiosity, naive admiration, wonder and bewilderment, before the categories and hierarchies of art and culture, the distinctions between high and low, original and common, are irrevocably ingrained in the mind.

One of Zvezdochetova's mottos is a proverb that may have come from prison jargon: "candy out of shit" *(iz govna konfetku)*, which means to make something out of nothing. While reading *The Encyclopedia of Bad Taste*, which is based exclusively on American mass culture, I discovered that making "treasures from trash" is a common occupation of lower-class suburban American housewives, an activity that has moved from hippy art and the counterculture into suburban mass culture (Stem and Stem 293–94). In the United States this is a kind of popular recycling program, a reaction against a culture of wasteful overabundance of commercial goods. In Russia, by contrast, the idea of making something out of nothing is a result of material scarcity, not a countercultural gesture but an expression of a need—and not simply a material need, but also an assertion of minimal aesthetic necessity and self-affirmation. Zvezdochetova associates it not with housewives' culture but with "prison art and the prison mentality——[. . .] a kind of all-Soviet aesthetic therapy—making something out of nothing, 'candy out of shit.'"

In Zvezdochetova's artistic quilt two cultural levels are absent—the official socialist realism of high Soviet political icons and the media culture and Western mass culture with which Zvezdochetova has become increasingly familiar. "Mickey Mouse is uninteresting," she said in an interview. "He's just too cold." Instead of working with major political events or major historical figures in the manner of the artists of the *sots art* movement, who play ironically with socialist realist icons, she recovers another level of culture—the everyday, forgotten and yet familiar. At this level of culture there are no heroes or antiheroes, only endless tacky ornaments of communal apartments, standardized Soviet children's books, women's needlework, icons of official commemoration (Tupitsyn 35–53). The everyday represents resistance to artistic defamiliarization; it is both too familiar and too uncanny. Yet, unlike Il'ia Kabakov, a founding father of Soviet conceptual art and producer of stark works,

Zvezdochetova enjoys the banal ornaments of the old-fashioned Soviet communal carpet and the material details of standard Soviet furniture and mass-produced objects. It is not Kabakov's metaphysical "emptiness" but the material particularity of detail, with its aura of outmoded ordinariness from the totalitarian past, that motivates her work. Her creative recuperation of the everyday is not totalizing but an invitation to a forgotten children's game, a childhood secret framed by the artificially aged golden foil.

Zvezdochetova's art, as well as that of the other conceptual artists, reminds one of American art of the 1960s and 1980s that incorporates and reinterprets many elements of American mass culture. The cross-cultural artistic comparison, however, makes clear the striking difference between the two mass cultures. Whereas the American cultural text is heavily televisual, full of references to commercial and consumer culture, Soviet mass culture has plenty of high art and high politics; it includes Pushkin and Stalin, political slogans, school manuals, and bureaucratic clichés. The commonplace of Soviet mass culture is not the shopping mall but the communal apartment.

The works of women artists of the former Soviet Union demonstrate that the relationship between irony and sympathy, distancing and engagement, material and conceptual, is far from simple. *Poshlost'*, like beauty, is in the eye of the beholder. Beauty is often embodied in the female figure, and so is *poshlost'*. In the women's artistic works that we have examined *poshlost'* no longer appears as a reified goddess of bad taste. Rather, its effects and affects are paradoxically interwoven in the artistic texture. If, as Clement Greenberg claims, kitsch can be defined as a mere mechanical reproduction of the effects of art, here we observe how women's artistic works meditate upon the effects of kitsch and *poshlost'*, challenge cultural hierarchies, and creatively reinvent that illegitimate and untranslatable Russian and Soviet everyday which is so often a blurred background to a larger historical tableau.

Notes

1 The French and then English word "banal" underwent a similar shift in meaning. In medieval French *banal* referred to something shared and common in the feudal jurisdiction; thus one spoke of banal fields, mills, and ovens.

2 After the mid-nineteenth century the word *poshlyi* developed many derivatives—*poshliak, poshliatina,* etc.—all linked to sexual indecency and obscenity. *Poshlost'* determines attitudes toward sexuality and femininity. The fear of *poshlost'* reflects less a fear of sex per se than fear of sexuality as an autonomous sphere of existence, independent of love and social concerns—in other words, fear of sexuality as a Western cultural construct. For more on this topic, see "Loving in Bad Taste: Eroticism and Literary Excess in Marina Tsvetaeva's 'The Tale of Sonechka,'" in Costlow et al.

3 Pushkin was one of the first to use *poshlyi* to refer to conventional poems of high society and to epigones of the Romantics who fancied themselves as Russian Mephistopheleses or Russian Napoleons of German descent, such as Herman in *The Queen of Spades* (Pushkin, ch. 5, XLIV, 99). To Gogol', *poshlost'* and banality are connected to the idea of realism, and Belinskii, in his discussion of *Dead Souls,* rewrote Gogol''s *poshlyi* as "realistic" (293). So Russian realism could have been called *poshlizm.* Chekhov is also a powerful explorer of *poshlost'* and banality in love, art, and boredom. Late in the nineteenth century, with the emergence of commercial culture, *poshlost'* was used in reference to popular artistic genres—sentimental romances, books by women, English drawing room stories.

4 In contemporary Russian, *poshlost'* and "kitsch" are occasionally used as synonyms, although kitsch can be seen as only one instance of *poshlost',* referring to pseudo-artistic phenomena as well as to the elements of Western popular culture that have begun to make their way into Russia. "Kitsch" comes from the jargon of Munich art dealers of the 1870s, to whom it signified cheap artistic stuff.

5 In the essay "Literary Moscow," Mandel'shtam poetically synthesizes the attributes of the cultural mask of the "poetess." She is described as a parody of the poet, a conglomeration of lack and excess—lack of true genius, hence suffering from a perpetual "genetic deficiency," and an emotional and sentimental excess. This notion actually goes back to the Romantic concept of genius as a virile spirit, and the Kantian description of the beautiful (not to be confused with the agreeable, with its languid appeal to the senses and its propensity for decoration). See Svetlana Boym, "Loving in Bad Taste," in Costlow et al.

6 Several versions of these romances are still known by heart and sung in Russia. I quote the texts from the 1989 edition of *Russkie pesni i romansy,* 200, 390.

7 For Benjamin's shifting concept of aura, compare "Some Motifs in Baudelaire" (188–89) and "The Work of Art in the Age of Mechanical Reproduction" (222–23).

8 Occasionally Tolstaia's journalism, once she abandons narrative and other subtleties, appears as a reiteration of clichés about "Russia and the West," the intelligentsia, and the *meshchanstvo.* One would like to think that perhaps Tolstaia the journalist is only one of the writer's stylized personae, whose straightforwardness counteracts the ambiguities of her fictional narrators.

9 Interest in everyday culture is not exclusive to women artists. In fact, this
movement in Soviet conceptualism was pioneered by Il'ia Kabakov. In *The
Communal Apartment* Kabakov uses a female character—his mother, a longtime victim of the housing shortage—as his invisible guide to the communal
labyrinths. The walls of the corridors in Kabakov's communal apartment
are covered by his mother's autobiography, awkwardly typed on an old
manual typewriter. Yet Kabakov's communal apartment is a realm of Soviet
uniformity and of badly executed socialist realist paintings produced by an
"untalented artist." It is an overcrowded place from which the artist escapes
into the white emptiness of the canvas, and there is no place in it for the
decorative tacky and old-fashioned objects that come from the "feminine"
culture of the communal apartment.

References

Adorno, Teodor. *Aesthetic Theory.* Trans. C. Lenhardt. London and New York:
Routledge & Kegan Paul, 1984.
Akademicheskii slovar' russkogo iazyka. Moscow, 1957.
Baudelaire, Charles. "Fusées." In *Oeuvres complètes.* Paris, 1965.
Belinskii, Vissarion. *Polnoe sobranie sochinenii.* Moscow, 1953.
Benjamin, Walter. *Illuminations.* New York: Schocken, 1985.
Boym, Svetlana. *Death in Quotation Marks: Cultural Myths of the Modern Poet.*
Cambridge, MA: Harvard University Press, 1991.
Broch, Hermann. *Kitsch: The Anthology of Bad Taste.* Ed. Gillo Dorfles. London:
Studio Vista, 1969.
Brooks, Jeffrey. *When Russians Learned to Read.* Princeton, NJ: Princeton
University Press, 1985.
Chernyi, Sasha. *Stikhotvoreniia.* Moscow, 1991.
Costlow, Jane, Stephanie Sandler, and Judith Vowles, eds. *Sexuality and the Body
in Russian Culture.* Stanford, CA: Stanford University Press, 1993.
Dal', Vladimir. *Tolkovyi slovar' zhivago velikorusskogo iazyka.* St. Petersburg:
Volf, 1882.
Dunham, Vera. *In Stalin's Time.* Cambridge: Cambridge University Press, 1976.
Eco, Umberto. *The Open Work.* Trans. Anna Cancogni. Cambridge, MA:
Harvard University Press, 1989.
Flaubert, Gustave. *Correspondances.* Paris, 1942.
Goscilo, Helena. "Tat'iana Tolstaia's 'Dome of Many-Coloured Glass': The World
Refracted through Multiple Perspectives." *Slavic Review* 47, no. 2 (Winter
1988): 280–90.
Greenberg, Clement. *On Art and Culture.* Boston, MA: Beacon, 1965.
Kundera, Milan. *The Unbearable Lightness of Being.* Trans. Michael Heim. New
York: Harper & Row, 1984.
McLaughlin, Sigrid. "Contemporary Soviet Women Writers." *Canadian Woman
Studies* 10, no. 4 (Winter 1989): 77–80.

Malevich, Kazimir. "From Cubism and Futurism to Suprematism." In *Russian Art of the Avant-Garde*, ed. John Bowlt. New York: Thames & Hudson, 1991.

Mandel'shtam, Osip. *Sobranie sochinenii*, vol. 2. New York: Inter-Language Literary Associates, 1971.

Nabokov, Vladimir. "Philistines and Philistinism." In *Lectures on Russian Literature*. New York: Harcourt Brace Jovanovich, 1981.

Nabokov, Vladimir. *Nikolai Gogol*. Norfolk: New Directions, 1944.

Pushkin, Aleksandr. *Sochineniia*, vol. 3. Moscow, 1955.

Russkie pesni i romansy. Moscow, 1989.

Sontag, Susan. *Against Interpretation*. (1961.) New York: Dell, 1969.

Stern, Jane, and Michael Stern. *The Encyclopedia of Bad Taste*. New York: Harper Perennial, 1991.

Tolstaya, Tatyana. *On the Golden Porch*. Trans. Antonina W. Bouis. New York: Knopf, 1989.

Tupitsyn, Margarita. *Between Spring and Summer: Soviet Conceptual Art in the Era of Late Communism*. Ed. David Ross. Cambridge, MA: MIT Press, 1991

7 COMMON PLACES

Theoretical Common Places

There used to be a saying among Soviet intelligentsia—"to understand each other with half-words." What is shared is silence, tone of voice, nuance of intonation. To say a full word is to say too much; communication on the level of words is already excessive, banal, almost kitschy. This peculiar form of communication "with half-words" is a mark of belonging to an imagined community that exists on the margin of the official public sphere. Hence the American metaphors for being sincere and authentic—"saying what you mean," "going public," and "being straightforward"—do not translate properly into the Soviet and Russian contexts. "Saying what you mean" could be interpreted as being stupid, naive, or not streetwise. Such a profession of sincerity could be seen, at best, as a sign of foreign theatrical behavior; at worst, as a cunning provocation. There is no word for authenticity in Russian, but there are two words for truth: *pravda* and *istina*. It is possible to tell the truth (*pravda*), but *istina*—the word that, according to Vladimir Nabokov, does not rhyme with anything—must remain unarticulated. In this form of indirect communication, quasi-religious attitudes toward language, devices of romantic poetry, revolutionary underground conspiracies, and tactics of dissident intelligentsia strangely converge.

Communication with half-words secures the unspoken realm of cultural myths and protects the imagined community from outsiders and, in a way, from its own members. Among the dissidents of half words very little dissent is permitted. If all at once those other halves of words were to be spoken intimate gatherings of friends might end—in fistfights.

At the risk of disturbing some of the imagined communes that I myself once cherished, I will try to describe them in a language foreign to them, in more than half-words. I write from the double perspective of a cultural critic and a former Leningrader, a resident of a communal apartment who often forgot to turn off the lights in the communal closet, earning severe scoldings from the watchful neighbors. This is a poignant historical moment, when all the imagined communities of Soviet culture are in a twilight phase. Some members of the post-Soviet intelligentsia perceive it as the end of a millennium of Russian culture, not merely of the Soviet Union but of the whole Russian literature-centered empire, with its centralized cultural text and shared double-speak.

In all the voluminous discussion one subject is generally left out: the everyday mythologies and rituals of ordinary life. They are hidden behind political, ideological, or artistic screens, deemed irrelevant for the heroic conception of the national identity in Russia or for Soviet ideology, inscrutable to many Western political scientists and journalists. The inner workings of the culture thus remain a mystery. In Russia, a country which during the past two centuries went through extreme calamities, wars, revolutions, and epochs of terror, everyday existence has often been precarious for the majority of the population. At the same time, in Russian intellectual tradition as well as in Soviet official ideology, a preoccupation with everyday life for its own sake was considered unpatriotic, subversive, un-Russian, or even anti-Soviet. Conversely, a central thread is an unusually strong, almost Romantic, fear of banality and "lack of culture," of anything that smacks of middlebrow or middle-class values. In this respect, both the Russian dream described by many Russian philosophers and writers, as well as the Soviet vision of the future, were radically different from the mythical American dream which was based on the American lifestyle rather than on education, spiritual or ideological commonality, or the cultural canon.

I intend to put at the center what is marginal to certain heroic or apocalyptic self-definitions of Russian culture: the attitudes toward ordinary life home, material objects and art, as well as expressions of emotion and ways of communication. In Russia the history of relations between culture and nation, art and life, society and individual, public and private, commodity and trash, often diverges from familiar Western European or American versions of modernity. To examine these differences is one subject of this book.

We might think, for instance, that banality is a global phenomenon and the banal is the banal is the banal. Vladimir Nabokov insists, however, on the originality of Russian banality and on its untranslatability. In his view, only Russians were able neatly to devise the concept of *poshlost'*-a word that encompasses banality, lack of spirituality and sexual obscenity.[1] In a similarly patriotic manner the distinguished linguist Roman Jakobson claims that the Russian word for the everyday—byt—is culturally untranslatable into Western languages; according to Jakobson, only Russians among the European nations are capable of fighting "the fortresses of *byt*" and of conceptualizing a radical alterity to the everyday (*byt*).[2] Russian, and later Soviet, cultural identity depended on heroic opposition to everyday life.

One could compile a Dictionary of Untranslatables that would include all the words that are (or were proudly claimed to be) culturally untranslatable into another language.[3] Perhaps every cross-cultural study should begin with a glossary of untranslatables and cultural differences, to prevent the transformation of a culture into a mere exotic movie backdrop or kitsch object. Until recently, many words used in Western public and private spheres lacked Russian equivalents: among them are the words for "privacy," "self," "mentality," and "identity."[4] The distinction between "policy" and "politics" is also incomprehensible in Russian, since they both translate as *politika*.

Conversely, various Russian thinkers from the nineteenth to the twentieth century insisted with a great zeal on the untranslatability of certain Russian words into Western languages. Among such specifically Russian words are *sobornost'* (a spiritual community, from *sobor*, which refers both to cathedral and to a gathering)—the Russian mythical alternative to private life, advocated by nineteenth-century Slavophile philosophers and contemporary nationalists-and the Russian form of compassion, sostradanie, literally co-suffering. And, of course, one could never forget Russian *toska*—a form of acute homesickness and yearning, celebrated in poems and heartbreaking gypsy romances. On a more heroic note, the Russian word for a feat, *podvig*, was also thought to be unique: it emphasizes dynamic heroic impulse, courage and self-sacrifice, not merely a specific accomplishment suggested in the English word "feat." Perhaps the untranslatable Russian everyday depended too much on this Russian *podvig* and its near-inability to acknowledge the ordinary.

My book is organized around several Russian cultural "untranslatables" that reflect common places of everyday life. I write "common place" as two words when I wish to preserve all the multiple historical significations and poetic allusion of the word, from public architecture to topography of memory. I write it as one word ("commonplace") when I have in mind the modern derogative use of the term in reference to a worn-out banality, or cliché. (The distinction between "common place" and "commonplace" is not wholly translatable into French, Spanish, or

Russian, whereas in English the derogatory use of the term prevails, and the historical memory of different "common places" is forgotten.)

Mythologies are cultural common places, recurrent narratives that are perceived as natural in a given culture but in fact were naturalized and their historical, political, or literary origins forgotten or disguised.[5] In Russia and the Soviet Union, where there is a long tradition of extreme political, administrative, and cultural centralization, those mythologies played a particularly important role. Myths are discernible in a variety of literary and historical texts as well as in everyday practices. A myth fragment could slip into a love letter in verse memorized in a Soviet high school, or into a reference to a slogan that used to hang in front of the entrance, or a mildly political joke told by a friend in the break between a lecture on "scientific atheism" and a seminar on "the history of the Communist Party." To understand Russian mythologies it is not enough to trace their origins in intellectual history, state policy, or actual practice. It is necessary to remember that they function in the culture as magical incantations, memorized or paraphrased but rarely interpreted critically. Cultural myths could also be defined as cultural obsessions. Looking for everyday mythologies one is tempted to see certain continuities in the history of concepts between Russian and Soviet intellectual traditions-- continuities which, however, reveal themselves to be paradoxical. My aim is neither to perpetuate cultural myths nor merely to demystify them, but to identify them, to show how they were appropriated by various ideologies, both Communist and nationalist and how they seduced native and foreign scholars and might have obscured a cultural tradition that is in truth diverse and hybrid. Myths are sites of a shared cultural memory, of communal identification and affection; and while they shaped the national imagination, they did not always correspond to actual everyday practices and people's preoccupations.

One of the prominent Russian myths of the past two centuries is the myth of the national unity of Russian culture based exclusively on the heritage of the great literary classics of nineteenth and twentieth centuries. (The actual list of national literary geniuses has been altered several times throughout the twentieth century, but the myth of a unified canon survived.) "Culture" will be used both in its traditional sense as literature and the arts (which could be linked to the imagined community of a nation) and in a broader anthropological sense, as a way of making sense of the world and a system of patterns of behavior and signs. We will examine together the philosophical and literary texts, mass entertainments, and popular artifacts. We will walk down the streets of Moscow and Leningrad, eavesdrop on domestic life, and examine jokes, films, TV programs, popular songs, and even the realm of post-Soviet advertising—new Russia's Wild West. At the center of our concern is the utopian topography of Soviet daily existence and its secret corners, from the Palaces of Culture to communal apartments, from public subways in the magnificent Stalinist style to not-so-private closets. These are spaces of illegitimate privacy, of forbidden kitschy souvenirs, of practiced indirection. The study of the Russian everyday reveals some centuries-old mechanisms of cultural survival, arts of minor compromise and resistance. This book is not about Soviet politics or Russian art but about the unwritten laws of everyday existence, about everyday aesthetic experiences and alternative spaces carved between the lines and on the margins of the official discourses.

Archaeology of the Common Place: From Topos to Kitsch

Common place refers to both the organization of space and the organization of speech. This trope has degraded through history: from the noble Greek *topos*, a site of classical argument, it has turned into the modern commonplace, the synonym for a cliché. Common places (*koinos topos*) date back to the ancient art of memory; they were familiar sites in a building or on a habitual walk through the city, to which one attached memory images. They also preserved the traces of occult topography of the ancient Theater of Memory and provided a common spatial arrangement for the architecture of the world, the interior designs of memory, and, occasionally, of the cosmological theater of the universe. The art of memory was invented–or remembered–by Simonides of Ceos, the first professional poet in ancient Greece, the first one to take money for his poetry.[6] In Aristotle's writings common places (topics) are seen exclusively as devices of rhetoric and refer to arguments used by a skillful orator or politician.[7] In Renaissance rhetorical treatises classical common places are rediscovered as the memory of antiquity, their rhetorical role is reestablished, and they are regarded as necessary elements of a learned and elevated style. "Common place" could refer to a quotation of ancient wisdom; the quotation marks—two severed heads—were not always marks of originality and individual authorship, rather, they "decapitated" an individual author or, from another point of view, they authenticated his participation in the cultural commonality. In the sixteenth century studious young men were supposed to collect quotations of ancient wisdom in books; in the eighteenth century sensible young ladies cherished their "books of commonplaces" with dried flowers and perfumed letters from "dear friends." But in the nineteenth century the attitude toward the common place changed drastically: from something to be collected, it turned into something to be avoided. People still collected aphorisms-literally "off boundaries" (*apo-horos*)-and maxims, but not for long.

A certain anxiety surrounds the definition of common place in the eighteenth and nineteenth centuries. As the derogatory connotation of the word "common" gained ground, so did a philosophical nostalgia for a more idealized, purified, and euphorically positive redefinition of commonality-from the Kantian *sensus communis*, which fostered the judgment of the beautiful, to the early American conception of commonwealth, to the Saint-Simonian (and later Marxist) political ideal of a new world order founded on the communes and culminating with communism. Communality usually becomes precious at the moment it is perceived to be in crisis. (But we need not fall into an elegiac mode and lament the Golden Age of the Common Place, conceived as some kind of pastoral Arcadia. Under close historical scrutiny, neither the collectivity of primitive societies, called by Marx "primitive communism," nor the Greek polity, idealized by many twentieth-century philosophers as a pretechnocratic paradise of democracy, nor the peasant communes in Russia would qualify as this kind of ideal community.) The crisis of the common place is accompanied by a resurgence of utopian thought. "Utopia" is full of linguistic ambiguity; it can refer to "no place" or to a "good place"; the "u" can be a Latin negation (u) or a Greek euphoric affirmation of goodness (eu).[8] Utopia is the ultimate insular conception of the ideal Common Place.

Kant attempts to draw a clear distinction between the usual formulation of common sense, which borders on vulgarity, and a philosopher's conception of a "common human understanding." *Sensus communis*—often used in Latin to distinguish it from its slippery colloquial counterparts in modern European languages—is what allows a human being to perceive, through reflexive aesthetic judgment, the universal purposefulness of nature. *Sensus communis* emerges through the blurred images of intuition, which are not private but shared:

"Humanity means both universal feeling of sympathy and the ability to engage universally in very intimate communication."[9] At times it seems that Kant's concept of *sensus communis* in itself is not a concept but a sense, a poetic metaphor for the problematic hide-and-seek of human commonality. What is "common" to all humanity is not the primary sensory reflexes, "languid affects," but precisely the ability to detach oneself from the senses in order to apprehend the beautiful. Sympathy is a step toward the perception of the beautiful. Yet this perception, and the experience of human commonality, become more and more indistinct, and the shapes of the beautiful more blurred. The last paragraphs of *The Critique of Aesthetic Judgment* declare that in future centuries it will be ever more difficult to form a concept of the beautiful and of the common.

In earlier eighteenth-century discussions *sensus communis* is connected to Roman understanding of common morality and civic duty.[10] In Kant it is linked to the judgment of taste—specifically to aesthetic taste. "Taste" itself, used primarily as a metaphor, is taken directly from the numerous culinary treatises of the seventeenth century, suggesting an important connection between the arts of cooking and the arts of thinking. From the so-called skepticism of tastes, best expressed in the universally famous Roman proverb, "there is no arguing about tastes," we move toward a more refined concept of "good taste." The imposition of the ideals of good and bad on the range of sensual pleasures has connections to moral philosophy.[11] There is a classical and classicizing element in the notion of taste, one which dates back to the Greek conception of "ethics of measure," from Pythagoras to Plato: the ethics of proportion, restraint, and balance. "Common places," thus, are the sites of ancient good taste. The cultivation of good taste and the increasing emphasis on cultural distinction, rather than a distinction of birth, grew more important in the seventeenth and eighteenth centuries. The history of the idea of taste parallels the history of absolutism in Spain, France, and England, and it is closely bound up with the development of the third estate.

With the Romantics, the idea of good taste is superseded by the idea of genius, which drastically affects the conception of the common place. At the turn of the eighteenth century a virtual "revolution in the common place" took place. One result of this change has been the modern crisis of cultural consensus, a crisis in the very understanding of the human community and commonality. Romantic aesthetics for the first time drew a sharp opposition between commonality and originality, triviality and authenticity. The common place, once merely a trope of normative classical rhetoric, a mark of learned elevated style shared by the privileged aristocrats of taste, took on a literal meaning associated with a public place, which in turn became a vulgar site. Formerly an aristocratic privilege, common place turned into "commonplace"; it became devalued and associated with unoriginality and ordinariness. Romantic originality was an enterprise dedicated to forgetting the complex rhetorical structure of the common place.

Romanticism thus brought about a degradation of the common place, which became synonymous with cliché, the word that embodies the devaluing effects of modern technology and mechanical reproduction. The French *cliché* referred originally to the typographic plate that allows multiple printings of pages, and also to the photographic negative. It is a modern word par excellence, which moves from technology to aesthetics. The reproducibility of the cliché and the availability of mass reproduction form a necessary background for the Romantic search for newness and for the cult of individual self-expression. Cliché ensures the proliferation of a work, but deprives it of an aura surrounding the uniqueness of the masterpiece. Cliché both perpetuates and prostitutes, both provides a grid for originality and devalues it.

We live nowadays in a "clichégenic society"; it is our inescapable cultural predicament. "One of the main reasons that clichés manage to evade reflection and its potential relativization, lies in the fact that they're as catching as laughter, or if you want, as stuttering."[12] Clichés preserve traces of cultural institutions, one of which is the very institution of the common sense that is a foundation of capitalist society. Moreover, in modern society clichés constitute the necessary incantatory noise of the everyday. They provide a guarantee of everyday survival that would not otherwise be possible in our age of oversaturation of information and stimuli. Clichés protect us from facing the catastrophe, the unbearable, the ineffable; thus for the major inexplicable areas of human existence— birth, death, and love—we have the maximum number of clichés. Responses to death and declarations of love are the most clichéd and ritualistic in every culture. Clichés often save us from despair and embarrassment by protecting the vulnerability and fragility of our way of life and social communication. In social situations we often blush and recite cliché excuses, cliché formalities, or no less cliché informalities, in order to cover up a frightening realization of the limits of language. One can estrange the common place, but then one has to estrange one's own estrangement.

Throughout European history the many levels of the "common place" were gradually forgotten, together with the art of memory itself. No longer a part of ancient art or of the rhetorical organization of the world, the common place was devalued and literalized. But on the ruins of the classical common place, the dreams of ideal communality—in art, politics, and society—emerged with a new force, taking their various shapes from the aesthetic *sensus communis,* whether communist utopia or democratic commonwealth. The new topographies of an ideal communality also produced its converse, the "bad communality": Palaces of Culture versus the Shopping Malls of Kitsch, architectural utopia versus communal apartments and housing projects, the sublime versus the banal. According to American modernist critic Clement Greenberg, not the "beautiful" of aesthetic judgment but the "agreeable" of kitsch has produced the "universal culture" of the twentieth century.[13]

"Kitsch," the Bavarian slang word that possibly translates as "sketch" or "cheap stuff," has received its share of cultural critique.[14] It was described as "the debased and academic simulacra of the genuine culture" (Greenberg), "a parody on catharsis" (Theodor Adorno), and a "sentimentalization of the finite ad infinitum" (Hermann Broch).[15] In this view kitsch is not merely bad art but also an unethical act, an act of mass manipulation. It blurs the boundaries between art and life and stands in the way of artistic autonomy. Kitsch appears as a sort of modern parasite, a virus of art and modernization to which there is no single antidote or counterconcept. Many critics attempted to discern the stylistic elements that characterize kitsch and shape the structure of bad taste—the propensity toward ornamentation, eclecticism, and sentimentality. But kitsch is not merely a sum of stylistic features; in fact, the specific examples of kitsch given in critical studies are often problematic. Through them the critics betray their own cultural tastes and times. Greenberg's example of kitsch is Ilia Repin's battle scenes, which, he claims, merely imitate the effects of artistic battles and battles of consciousness and turn into didactic objects of official Stalinist art. Much as one might agree with his assessment of Soviet reframing of Repin's art, however, the fact is that Repin never painted any battle scenes. Possibly Greenberg is confusing Repin with another painter or rehearsing someone else's clichés and effects of criticism. Clearly, particular examples of kitsch change from country to country, from one historical context to another, and an uncritical choice of kitsch artifacts can turn the critique itself into kitsch.[16]

Much more important than specific stylistic devices are the mechanisms of kitschification. Greenberg writes: "If avant-garde imitates the processes of art, kitsch ... imitates its effect..."[17] Kitsch manipulates through objectification of the effects of art, and through ready-made formulas that function like premodern magical incantations known to trigger specific emotional responses. Such responses often have the effect of mass hypnosis, even if a particular consumerist kitsch item advertises individual improvement. This sort of individualism is mass-produced and ready-made, available to the many at a discount price. The mechanisms of kitsch are directed toward pacifying and sweetening the contradictions of human existence. Kitsch neither resolves nor critically exposes the conflicts; instead, it offers fragile bridges of commonplaces over the unbridgeable abyss. "Kitsch expresses the sensibility of a public that no longer believes in hell, but still worships paradise," writes Yaron Ezrahi.[18]

What is at stake in the modernist Western critiques of kitsch of the 1930s-1950s is, first of all, the responsibility of the intellectual, the intellectual's response to the uses of kitsch by the culture industry and by the totalitarian state, in both its fascist and Stalinist models. Hannah Arendt, in her report on the Eichmann trial, presents Adolf Eichmann as a kind of fascist kitschman who speaks exclusively in officialese, "because he was genuinely incapable of uttering a single sentence that was not a cliché."[19] Even at his execution Eichmann came up with cliché phrases from funeral oratory—he surrounded himself with clichés to protect him against the words and worlds of others, against life and death. In Arendt's view, Eichmann's story, "the lesson of this long course in human wickedness," is the "lesson of the fearsome, word-and-thought-defying banality of evil." The psychological "normality" of Eichmann, diagnosed by Israeli psychiatrists, and even his conventional morality are particularly frightening: from the "banality of evil" to the "normality of evil" is only one step. (In prison Eichmann refused to read Nabokov's *Lolita*, considering it an "immoral book," a judgment which Nabokov would probably have taken as an ironic compliment.) In Arendt's discussion ethical and aesthetic judgments converge; Eichmann's inability to use words in an imaginative and individual manner reflects on his inability to think critically. The modernist critique of the banality of evil offers a powerful, if controversial, defense of the ethical foundation of aesthetics, as well as of the aesthetic judgment of morality.[20]

At the same time that intellectuals launched their critique of kitsch, artists and poets began to search for another sort of banality, which does not necessarily qualify as "evil." In the mid-nineteenth century artists developed a fascination for bad taste and the démodé.[21] Baudelaire declared his desire to "invent a cliché," thus offering us a paradox of the Romantic ideal of poetic invention that both defies and responds to the modern challenge of technological anonymity.[22] Baudelaire's fascination with bad taste is a reaction against bourgeois propriety and good taste that has less to do with aesthetic judgment than with moralistic common sense. The bourgeois good taste that Baudelaire attacked was a kind of "kitsch in good taste" to which he opposed the vulgarity of the grotesque and of low-class entertainment. For post-Romantic French poets and writers banality offered the infinite pleasures of writing, as well as an exploration of the limits of culture and the exotic journey from "high" to "low."[23] The English aesthetes, led by Oscar Wilde, cultivated artifice and artificiality, challenging Victorian good taste in art and life. They also claimed to be superior aristocrats of taste, going beyond the dull bourgeois norms of "good," "bad," and "evil." In the twentieth century the Surrealists cherished the ordinary marvelous, old-fashioned and useless "found objects" that prompted "profane illuminations." Surrealist art is excluded from Greenberg's definition of the "good avant-garde." Surrealists were the "bad boys" of the avant-garde because they were excessively seduced by bad taste.

Finally, in the 1960s, art criticism began to catch up with art and belatedly paid homage to "camp sensibility," which could be defined as kitsch in quotation marks, or aestheticized bad taste. Susan Sontag describes camp as a taste for everything "off," old-fashioned, out-of-date, démodé, all those things which, "from a 'serious' point of view, are either bad art or kitsch."[24] Camp sensibility is based on the eroticization of daily life; its key metaphor is that of life as theater, of "being-as-Playing-a-Role." Camp celebrates "a triumph of the epicene style" and playful reversals of gender and sexual impersonations, often associated with gay sensibility. Sontag remarks that "camp taste is by nature possible only in affluent societies, in societies or circles capable of experiencing the psychopathology of affluence. "[25] "Camp sensibility" coincides with Pop art, which plays with the signs of commercial culture and with modernist theoretical clichés about the autonomy of art. Flirting with kitsch is a way of exploring the boundaries of art and of institutionalized good taste, which itself can turn into a cliché.

"None of us is superman enough to escape kitsch completely. No matter how we scorn it, kitsch is an integral part of the human condition," writes Milan Kundera, author of one of the most powerful invectives against both totalitarian and democratic kitsch.[26] The "we" of this sentence is seductively inclusive—it is at once the "we" of the universal brotherhood of kitsch-people and the "we" of the ironic critics of kitsch; it includes those who live it and those who scorn it. In Kundera's description of kitsch sentimental and political images blur, and so do the ironies and nostalgias of critics. Kitsch is defined by Kundera as a "dictatorship of the heart," as the "universal brotherhood of men" who celebrate a life in which the existence of shit is denied. The writer's own generalization suggests that not even he is "superman enough" to claim a space outside kitsch. Kundera's prophetic verdict on the human condition enacts the paradox of kitsch, is simultaneous repulsion and seduction, power and weakness, its ability to universalize and to discriminate.

I will not attempt to get to the very heart of kitsch—a cheap holiday balloon heart made of red foil paper—and pierce it with a sharp critical arrow. Such heart-breaking criticism is both too violent and too sentimental. To confront the phenomenon of kitsch does not necessarily mean to discern its essence and to universalize the structure of bad taste. On the contrary, I seek to understand kitsch as an experience and to recover precisely what kitsch tries to cover up: its history, its cultural mythology, and its contexts.

The history of kitsch is as different in Eastern and Western Europe as is the history of modern art. What is countercultural discourse in one part of the world can turn into officialese in the other. In our cross-cultural exploration of banality and kitsch we will find some untranslatable cultural aspects of the commonplace and of bad art, as well as of their critique. In Russia the word "kitsch" was adopted in the 1970s in a special sub-genre of books on Western mass culture. It is characteristic of various foreign words in Russian that the word in translation is less insulting than the native equivalent. This is true of "banality" (*banal'nost'*) as well as of "kitsch." Furthermore, kitsch is mistranslated in Russian, and its critical history is virtually unknown. Whereas many modernist critics emphasized that kitsch is not merely bad art but an unethical act, in the Russian usage kitsch has no moral connotations. The Russian word *poshlost'* partly overlaps both banality and kitsch, but it has its own dramatic cultural history connected to the Russian encounter with Western "progress," the pace of change and modernization.

Sontag's "camp," in contrast, would not include Russian artists until the late 1980s. In Russia the metaphor of camp would be definitely unpopular; nobody would like to be in any sort of camp voluntarily. The mark of self-imposed aesthetic exclusionism turns into its opposite—an image of enforced political isolation—when it crosses the American-Russian border. Sontag's examples of supposedly shared and recognizable "camp sensibility" now appear dated; one of the few that I was able to recognize, *Swan Lake*, I would hardly call playful: for me it is associated with official Soviet culture. The postmodern elements in late Soviet and post-Soviet art, which will be explored in the last chapter, have little to do with the "psychopathology of affluence" and consumerism; they relate instead to the psychopathology of totalitarian daily life. Hence the communality of camp is culturally exclusive; not everyone can share the same quotation marks.

The common place is not as transparent as it might seem; it is a barricade, a battleground of warring definitions and disparate discourses-philosophical, political, aesthetic, and religious. By the twentieth century the common place has turned into a complex palimpsest, a museum of the Romantic ruins of authenticity and of modern homesickness. The common place is where the Romantic poet stages his rebellion and where the modernist searches for anonymity; in the twentieth century it has sharply contrasted political meanings, from the communist paradise of the common citizen to the commercial bliss of the common consumer. The common place is a mythical site from which intellectuals perpetually displace themselves, only to write elegies to the lost communality.

Living in Common Places

Family Romance and Communal Utopia

This is another version of the Soviet family romance; it could be entitled "In the Old Apartment." Instead of a portrait of Stalin there is a televisual image of Brezhnev, but no one listens. My parents are having foreign guests for the first time in their life in our room in the communal apartment. Our neighbors, Aunt Vera and Uncle Fedia, are home. (Russian children call their neighbors "aunt" and "uncle," as if they were members of one very extended family.) Uncle Fedia usually came home drunk, and if Aunt Vera refused to let him in, he would crash right in the middle of the long corridor—the central "thoroughfare" of the communal apartment-obstructing the entrance to our room. As a child, I would often play with peacefully reclining and heavily intoxicated Uncle Fedia, with his fingers and buttons, or tell him a story to which he probably did not have much to add. This time we were all in the room, listening to music to tone down the communal noises, and my mother was telling our foreign guests about the beauties of Leningrad: "you absolutely must go to the Hermitage, and then to Pushkin's apartment-museum, and of course to the Russian Museum." In the middle of the conversation, as the foreign guest was commenting on the riches of the Russian Museum, a little yellow stream slowly made its way through the door of the room. Smelly, embarrassing, intrusive, it formed a little puddle right in front of the dinner table.

No one seems to remember what happened afterwards. In the apartment Uncle Fedia and Aunt Vera were displaced by lonely Aunt Valia, who worked in a bread factory, and her mentally ill son Yura, and then by a couple of homonymic drunkards—Aunt Shura and Uncle Shura, who endearingly called themselves "Shurenkis." And if it were not for the benevolent foreign guest enjoying the beauties of the Soviet public places, and for my mother's deeply personal embarrassment, the story would not have been particularly exceptional. After all, as one of my Soviet friends remarked, some neighbors peed into each other's teapots. Yet this scene, with its precarious coziness of a family gathering, both intimate and public, with a mixture of ease and fear in the presence of foreigners and neighbors, remained in my mind as a memory of home. The family picture is thus framed by the inescapable stream of Uncle Fedia's urine, which so easily crossed the minimal boundaries of our communal privacy, embarrassing the fragile etiquette of communal propriety. (And it smells too much to turn it into a mere metaphor. This is something that is hard to domesticate.)

If there had been such a thing as a Soviet cultural unconscious, it would have been structured like a communal apartment—with flimsy partitions between public and private, between control and intoxication. The Soviet "family romance," now in melancholy twilight, was adulterated by the fluttering sound of a curious neighbor's slippers in the communal apartment, or by an inquisitive representative of the local Housing Committee. It was a romance with the collective, unfaithful to both communitarian mythologies and traditional family values.

The communal apartment was the cornerstone of the now disappearing Soviet civilization. It was a specifically Soviet form of urban living, a memory of a never implemented utopian communist design, an institution of social control, and the breeding ground of police informants between the 1920s and the 1980s. This is a place where many battles for reconstruction at daily life were launched and most of them were lost. Here the neighbors engaged in quite un-Marxist class struggles; "domestic trash" triumphed; and privacy was prohibited only to be reinvented again against all odds. *Kommunalka*—a term of endearment and deprecation—came into existence after postrevolutionary expropriation and resettlement of the private apartments in the urban centers. It consisted of all-purpose rooms (living rooms, bedrooms, and studies became a "decadent luxury") integrated with "places of communal use," a euphemistic expression for shared bathroom, corridor, and kitchen, spaces where hung schedules of communal duties and where endless complaints were exchanged among the fellow neighbors. The communal neighbors, most often complete strangers from different classes and social backgrounds thrown together by the local Housing Committee, were joined in a premodern practice of "mutual responsibility." (Every communal apartment dweller is probably scarred for life by that symbolic "mutual responsibility"—a double bind of love and hatred, of envy and attachment, of secrecy and exhibitionism, of embarrassment and compromise.)

The communal apartment was not merely an outcome of the postrevolutionary housing crisis but also of a revolutionary experiment in living, an attempt to practice utopian ideologies and to destroy bourgeois banality. Hence this is a Soviet common place par excellence, which reveals all the paradoxes of the common place and of Soviet communality. The archeology of the communal apartment reveals what happens when utopian designs are put into practice, inhabited, and placed into history—individual and collective.

The communal apartment stands as a metaphor of the distinctive Soviet mentality. It was a favorite tragicomic setting for many Soviet jokes. Thus when Stalin was taken out of the mausoleum, people joked that Khrushchev had "resettled Lenin's communal apartment" (which in the post-Soviet time might be further "privatized").[27] More recently, the behavior of Russian national-patriots and members of the Russian Parliament was compared in the press to "communal apartment tactics" of boorish intimidation, conformism, and collective guilt.[28]

Actually, the communal apartment was conceived in Lenin's head. Only a few weeks after the October Revolution of 1917 Lenin drafted a plan to expropriate and resettle private apartments. This plan inspired many architectural projects of communal housing and new revolutionary topography. The "rich apartment" is defined by Lenin as "the apartment where the number of rooms equals or surpasses the number of residents who permanently inhabit this apartment."[29] A minimum living space of about 10 square meters per person and 13 square meters per family was established. In his memoirs Joseph Brodsky calls his family's living quarters, poetically and quite literally, "a room and a half."[30] What appears striking in Lenin's decree is that it suggests a different understanding of home and space than one is used to in Western Europe or in the United States. A person, or rather a statistical unit (in Lenin's expression, "the soul of the population"), was not entitled to a room or to a private space but only to a number of square meters. The space is divided mathematically or bureaucratically as if it were an abstract problem in geometry, not the real space of existing apartments. As a result, most of the apartments in the major cities were partitioned in an incredible and often unfunctional manner, creating strange spaces, long corridors, and so-called black entrances through labyrinthine inner courtyards.

The communal apartment is not to be confused with a kibbutz or merely an apartment with roommates. Since the late 1920s and especially during the Stalin years the communal apartment had become a major Soviet institution of social control and a form of constant surveillance. At that time the "separate apartment" became a sign of special privilege, or occasionally, of special luck. Only in the late 1950s was there a new revolution in Soviet daily life, consisting of resettlement out of communal apartments to outlying "micro-districts," where people were able to live in separate, albeit state-owned, apartments—many for the first time in their lives. The building blocks received the unflattering name of *Khrushchoby* (a combination of Khrushchev and slums. Ironically, in Brezhnev's time the older construction became an example of high quality). These bleak versions of "garden cities" still did not end the housing shortage. In the 1970s some people were allowed to purchase cooperative apartments in the outskirts; in some cases it took decades of waiting. But it took forty more years and the end of the Soviet Union to put an end to the communal apartment as a social institution.

My "thick description" of the communal apartment will include projects for collective living and utopian architectural house-communes, literary anti-utopias and tragicomedies of actual communal living, and personal observations of present-day communal apartments and the daily practices of their residents. An archeology of the communal apartment helps to uncover the ruins of Russian and Soviet communality and the once illegitimate private life. We will eavesdrop on the elusive private behavior of Soviet citizens behind the communal partitions and visit exhibits of ideologically incorrect domestic trash, precarious possessions that challenge many theoretical "systems of objects." The observation of the cultural ethnographer will be occasionally disrupted by memories of the communal apartment survivor, frequently scolded by the neighbors for all her unfulfilled communal duties.

From the House-Commune to the Communal Apartment

The 1920s in Soviet Russia was a unique moment in history when art-making and life-making intersected, and the country turned into a creative laboratory of various conflicting utopian projects. "Utopia" in Russia was never perceived merely as a work of art; fictional utopias were guides to life and blueprints for social change. Revolutionary architects dreamed of turning architecture into an arch-art and more: into a material embodiment of the revolutionary superstructure, which would impose order on a chaotic world.[31] Since Marx and Engels did not develop a specific blueprint of communist life, it was necessary to go back to the utopians-More and Campanella, Owen and Fourier-and to their various Cities of Sun and Ikarias. They inspired a variety of projects for socialist cities that would bring about the "socialist resettlement of mankind." A new revolutionary [u]topography was going to alter radically the commonplaces of culture and public and private spaces; in the avantgarde designs not only the places themselves but the very way of creating the space was to be revolutionized. Masters of photomontage, experimental film makers, and Formalist theorists dreamed of a space created by a montage of perspectives, a truly revolutionary prospect that would open new dimensions of living free from the bourgeois realist illusion of three-dimensionality.[32]

In the utopian map of the "land of the Soviets" House-Communes, Palaces and Parks of Culture, Workers' Clubs and Artists' Labor Collectives, and later also collective farms supplant old forms of sociability in apartments and barracks, cafes and pubs. Walter Benjamin commented that together with "private life" and "petit-bourgeois homeliness" what disappeared in Russia were the cafes: "Free trade, like the free intellect, was abolished."[33] The worker should prefer the swimming pool. In fact a few postrevolutionary avant-garde groups announced a war on cafes, salons, and cabarets where "the public demands frivolity and poshlost."[34] The café relationships are too intimate and too accidental, collective in an ideologically incorrect manner, eccentric but in a wrong style, not classless but déclassé (if not bourgeois). The cafe is a place for conversation, not for conversion, a place for minor theatrical revolts, not for revolutions. Instead of the cafe the revolutionary artists wished to go out to the streets. The slogan of their day was: "Revolution carries the art of good taste from the palaces to the boulevards."[35] By the late 1920s the emphasis shifts from the unruly streets to the "organized outdoors" in the Parks of Culture and Rest and in sports stadiums. The "boulevard" that evokes the dynamism of the early avant-garde and its foreign accent gives way to the square, the place for parades and collective festivities. The Soviet park and the subway station compose the Soviet urban iconography. The Moscow Metro of the 1930s becomes a material embodiment of a new utopia— this one located not on the island of utopia but under the ground.

The house-commune was a kind of microcosm of the socialist city, and the city a microcosm of the "land of the Soviets" as a whole.[36] They were avant-garde matreshka-dolls, one inside the other, repeating the same utopian designs. One of the first projects proposed in 1918 borrowed its name directly from Fourier's Phalanstery.[37] Interestingly, some seventy-five years earlier Fourier's design inspired the Parisian Arcades—a site of mythical modernity par excellence, serving the passage of commerce and providing a display of commodities; a place where the modern urban flaneur catches his fragmentary illuminations during his leisurely walks.[38] The French utopian's idea proved adaptable enough to inspire the Soviet house-communes, which were meant to eradicate the commodity culture along with the leisurely strolls of the intellectual fellow-travelers. In this way the same utopian element characterizes both early capitalism and early socialism.[39]

The designs for new collectivity and new ways of living demanded a new language. The architectural writings of the time contain a whole series of neologisms: "block-commune," "dwelling space," "socialist settling," and so on. (Unfortunately, some of them later became part of Soviet bureaucratic jargon.) The word apartment, in fact, is rarely used. The central nucleus was the house-commune, a model of "socialism in one building" to use Richard Stites's expression. The house-commune would radically reconstruct the individualist bourgeois quarters, "defamiliarize" them in a literal sense of the word by subverting the structure of the bourgeois family and instituting the relationships of proletarian comradeship. In the house-commune kitchens and children were to be shared, to avoid the burdens of the bourgeois family. One of the slogans of the time was "Down with the dictatorship of the kitchen!" The individual kitchen was the symbolic space of the nuclear family and the cause of women's enslavement by the daily grind. (Although the "woman question" was widely debated in the first years after the Revolution, in practice the division of labor within the family in the communal as in the individual kitchen remained very traditional.)[40]

Although many house-communes were established in the countryside and in the cities during the 1920s, they did not become widespread and by the 1930s were abolished, together with other leftist excesses. Paradoxically, the few house-communes that were built in Moscow and Petrograd were never turned into communal apartments but became privileged housing for members of the intellectual elite. They offered more spacious and luxurious family housing than the partitioned communal rooms, and were inhabited by the architects and writers who later became part of Stalin's establishment. A few of those house-communes, like the famous House-Ship, an exemplary avant-garde project by Ginzburg, turned into a ruin of modernist architecture, with trees growing through the half-fallen balconies, revealing the poor quality of the Constructivist building materials.

Instead of building new "dwelling massifs" and "garden cities," in the late 1920s the government gave orders to reconstruct and partition already existing bourgeois quarters, renaming them with important designations like "dwelling comradeships" and "workers' communes." These were transitional communal arrangements later institutionalized as the communal apartments. The Soviet kommunalka shares more than a linguistic resemblance to the house-commune; it includes elements of revolutionary topography such as the communal kitchen and other places of communal use. Yet the topography of the communal apartment often also presented a peculiar superimposition of old and new hierarchies. In many cases, when the owner of the apartment did not leave the country, he or she and the family took the former master bedroom while the new neighbors took the dining room, study, guest rooms, and maids' rooms. Occasionally the former servants of the apartment owner continued living in the same apartment, hence the old structure of the bourgeois household appeared transplanted into the communal apartment. (The survival of the domestic servants and nannies until the 1950s is a peculiar feature of Soviet everyday life that does not fit the ideological self-image of the socialist system.[41]) In due course some Party enthusiast might inform on the "bourgeois class origins" of the former owner of the apartment; he might be sent to a camp and his room might be appropriated by ideologically correct neighbors, who would continue employing the same servants and acquire new prestige in the communal hierarchy.

While housing shortages, urban poverty, and various forms of collective living were a part of Russian life before and after the Revolution (recall Dostoevsky's heroes Makar Devushkin and Raskolnikov and their squalid St. Petersburgian quarters), collective living was never a specific ideological institution. In the Soviet Union it did become codified, and by the mid-1930s the communal apartment had turned into a prominent Stalinist institution of social control. The new laws enforced the passport system and *propiska*—resident permits that tied the individual to a specific place–and established new privileges that allowed certain groups—Party apparatchiks or members of the intellectual elite that collaborated with the regime (and were not arrested)—to have additional "living space." Under these conditions the local bureaucrats of the Housing Committee (ZhEK) acquired the power to "educate" Soviet men and women and became an important local institution of Sovietization. Lidiia Ginzburg describes the Housing Committee as an "institution of denial of human rights-rights to air, to toilet, to space."[42] The other important figure in a Soviet communal apartment house was the janitor (dvornik); this official was also connected to the Housing Committee and to local authorities. Janitors had usually moved to the city recently and were given resident permits in exchange for performing a number of services-least of which was any actual yard cleaning. They informed, supervised, drank with the members of the Housing Committees, and occasionally swept the staircases.

During the Stalin years the communal apartment was both omnipresent and invisible. It was everywhere in daily life and nowhere in its official representation. Only the idealized *New Apartment*, albeit spoiled by the bourgeois rubber plant, appears in the painting of 1952. *Kommunalka* was a kind of mockery of ideal Soviet communality, but an ideal place to look for actual everyday ways of Soviet communal living. It inspired writers and artists in the 1920s and later in the 1980s but did not attract the imagination of the historians, neither in Russia nor abroad.

Whereas the house-commune had been a microcosm of the ideal revolutionary universe, the communal apartment was an actual Soviet microcosm, a non-idealized image of Soviet society in miniature. The economic circumstances are not alone responsible for the transformation of a socialist idyll into a social farce. A more fundamental problem is that any utopia is a u-chronia; in other words, it assumes a certain atemporality, a cessation of the time-flow and an immutability of life.[43] What an architectural utopia does not take into account is history and narratives about inhabiting places. Thus the utopian Common Places run into "places of communal use" in the apartment, a shabby stage for many scandals between the neighbors and a ruin of utopian communality.

Welcome to the Communal Apartment

"Black Entrance"

A few years before returning to Russia, I had my first dream of homecoming. In the dream I stand in front of my house and I try to enter it but I can't. I don't remember what the doorknob looked like.

Then somehow I manage to enter and quickly rush through the dark corridor fearing there is someone hiding behind the elevator right near the door of the mysterious office named "Little Red Corner," the office of the Housing Committee, which seems to be forever locked or forever in the middle of a meeting. I am scared of a familiar ghost, a wicked stranger, a drunk man in the dark. I hear his resounding laughter followed by his stinking, spitting threats: "Fuck your mother in the mouth, you little bitch ... Stinking ass." If I could only twist my tongue to repeat the curses with pleasure and self-confidence, if I could only forgo my shamefully proper intelligentsia habits and linger on every guttural sound "kh," the drunkard would stop laughing at me. I could enter my house fearlessly and give the hallway stranger a wink of complicity. I could have been home by now. My compressed lips are ready for the forceful "u" sound, my throat is about to utter the guttural sound. But somehow, the air is blocked, the sound freezes on my lips, and my obscenities remain mute, harmless, unheard and unheard-of—defenseless.

The entrance that I have just failed to take used to be the main entrance to the house. To enter the communal apartment requires a long "rite of passage": in and out through a dark hallway with ruined mosaics and pieces of beer bottles and across the interior yards full of communal trash, with occasional graffiti and half-erased hop-scotch on the asphalt.

Visiting a Soviet home one is struck not only by a deep contrast between the public and private spheres, between official communality and the community of one's own inner circle, but also by that strange no-man's-land, the space that belongs to everybody and to nobody but that creates discomfort in both public and private existence. Since the communal restructuring of the building one rarely enters the old house from the front door; the front hallway is merely a space to cross.

The hallway occupies a special place in the Soviet mythical topography; it is a space of transition, a space of fear, the dark limit of the house. It could preserve traces of a building's former elegance: fragments of mosaics and ruined, not-so-classical pilasters with obscene graffiti scribbled all over. The hallways are usually inhabited by old drunks, local fools, youth gangs, and teenagers in love. Here all sorts of unofficial initiations take place. (In the romantic version we would imagine the last farewell kiss in the hallway, a little poem by Sergei Esenin, perhaps "Life's a lie, but with a charming sorrow" recited by one teenager to another, with the sound of benevolent laughter in the background, of a couple of slightly tipsy comrades, old war veterans with a bottle of Stolichnaya ... For the darker side, we would have to picture all sorts of unreported crimes happening in the hallways–from rape to murder, committed in a state of total intoxication.)

The Soviet bard Bulat Okudzhava dedicated a song to communal "black staircases" inhabited by black cats and ghosts of fear. The black entrance to the communal apartments leads to a dark corner of the Soviet unconscious. In the song the black cat that "never cries nor sings" embodies the suspicions of Stalin's times, the mutual fears and occasional tragic complicity of informants and victims who often inhabited the same communal apartment. The end of the song is a poetic reflection on the Soviet collective mentality. All it will take is "to put a new light bulb on the black staircase" —one collective illumination, metaphorically speaking, and then some of the dark fears can be eliminated. But somehow collective inaction conspires to keep the public spaces dark. The black staircase is a Soviet public site par excellence, a space that is everybody's and therefore nobody's responsibility; it is where the ghosts of a collective fear are kept alive much longer than they needed to be. In Soviet Russia there was no interface between public and private, no space of conventional socialization, the space that is governed neither by the official decorum, like the Soviet subway, nor by the unwritten rules of intimacy that reign in the overcrowded domestic nooks. The space between is the space of alienation-the Soviet zone—the space on the outskirts of the Soviet topography.

My house, a typical old St. Petersburgian building partitioned into many communal apartments, was located on Bolshoi Avenue near the Karpovka River, which in the nineteenth century constituted the urban frontier. The building was rumored to have belonged to a wealthy St. Petersburg engineer, a nouveau riche with a non-Russian name and cosmopolitan, eclectic tastes. After the Revolution all the apartments— now communal property—were partitioned; only the ornamental front hallway reminds us of the past. As for the engineer, he was forever erased from history and from the well-kept list of house residents in the Building Committee Office. (It was rumored that he was a liberal. He even collaborated with the revolutionary government. But around 1926 he obtained a foreign passport and "went traveling." He may have died of consumption on the French Riviera with a little volume of Pushkin's poems in his hands. Perhaps he suffered a heart attack in a small Mexican village while making love to a beautiful member of the local Trotskyist group ... I am glad he did not turn into an anonymous neighbor in the partitioned and subdivided apartment on the third floor, vanishing in the purges of 1937 or 1942.)

With the engineer's disappearance, the single narrative of the house becomes infinitely subdivided like the space inside; it bifurcates into the interrupted, aborted narratives of the countless neighbors in the communal apartments. The shabby facade of the house with its whimsical and eclectic bas reliefs of the turn of the century was an embarrassing reminder of the engineer's cosmopolitan tastes incompatible with the new Soviet style.

When I worked as a Leningrad tour guide, mostly for the Young Pioneers from provincial towns, I was supposed to take my tourists away from the Petersburg eclecticism to the harmonious classical ensembles on the squares around Neva, the monuments to Lenin with his hand outstretched and the revolutionary cruiser Aurora. (Leningrad in the Brezhnev era had a precise iconography immortalized on a series of official postcards, where even the clouds had Soviet classical shapes— not too fluffy and not too thin—and the sky had the proper blue of East German color film.) When the bus passed by my house, I would inevitably recite the memorized lines from the "Guide's Instruction Manual": "This building on the right with strange beasts on the facade derives from foreign models, lacks classical proportions, and does not present any real architectural value." Hence the obscenity of the entrance, the curses of the drunks, and the "bad taste" of the facade marked the road to the communal apartment.

Communal Neighbors: Oral History and Class Struggles

Imagine entering one of the communal apartments in Leningrad/St. Petersburg, not mine but the one across the street. We pass by the back staircase and stop in front of the massive door with several separate bells: "three rings for Petrov, two for Khaimovich, one for Skripkina, four for Genalidze." This is the first affirmation of separateness—if we don't have a separate door, at least we've got a separate doorbell—if we don't have a separate kitchen, at least a separate gas burner. If we share the same electric light, then each of us should have a switch; even if it is completely irrational and inconvenient, we will go all the way along the long corridor to our room in order to turn on the lights in the toilet. In circumstances of extreme overcrowdedness and imposed collectivity there is an extreme—almost obsessive—protection of minimal individual property. Just be sure to remember how many times you have to ring the bell, and God forbid you ring the wrong one! As you enter the communal corridor you hear the flutter of slippers and the squeaking of the floors and you notice many pairs of eyes scrutinizing you through half-opened doors. Some look at you indifferently, others with suspicion or with basic self-defensive hostility, just in case. When a guest comes to the apartment it is everyone's business, a mini-event, a source of gossip and argument. Please don't forget to clean your feet, right on the threshold of the communal apartment—do it thoroughly and just a bit longer than needed, otherwise you will violate the schedule of communal duties, especially the time-table of corridor-cleaning, and bring a lot of communal misfortune to your host.

Meet the neighbors of this exemplary composite communal apartment: most of them come from my grandmother's large communal flat, others come from shared Soviet folklore, perhaps not exactly the way they really were, but the way they could have been. The collective of the communal apartment included an old woman named Glebovna, who claimed to have swept the floors of the Winter Palace, and had been a maid of the first owner of the apartment; she hid a little photograph of Tsar Nikolai II in the back of a drawer. There was Gertruda Genrikovna, a piano teacher of German descent, who was exiled during the war to a special camp for russified Germans in Kazakhstan and had nineteenth-century porcelain figurines representing all the nations of Great Russia; there was the former Stakhanovite and now drunkard Uncle Kolia, who occasionally watched TV with Gertruda Genrikovna; the old maid Aleksandra Ivanovna, a member of the intelligentsia with the manners of a governess and the complete works of Russian and French classics, and her retarded aunt, Raisa; there was Uncle Vasia, who walked down the hall half-naked, exuding the cheap eau-de-cologne "Red Moscow"; and finally, the sailor Nikita, who sailed abroad, brought Peruvian panties to his longtime fiancée Galia, and was promised a new cooperative apartment in the new year. Galia is the daughter of one of the first neighbors of my grandmother's, Aunt Klava, who left the village and went to Petrograd after the Revolution together with her friend Aleftina. Both became devoted Bolsheviks; Aleftina worked as an accountant in Smolny—briefly after the Revolution the headquarters of the Soviet government and later of the Leningrad Party Committee—and she used to enjoy special vacations in the Party sanatorium; Klava became a secretary of the local district Party organization, and was the communal apartment's authority on "ideological correctness." In the 1950s, during the purges of Jewish doctors, Aleftina stopped talking with my grandmother in the communal kitchen, while Klava publicly announced in the communal corridor in the presence of Aleftina and my grandmother that she never believed that all Jews were guilty "of using the blood of Christian children." After this authorial statement Aleftina got scared and just in case started to chat with my grandmother again, at least when Aunt Klava was there.

But this was more than thirty years ago, and now Klava's daughter Galia hangs her foreign underwear on Aleksandra Ivanovna's personal laundry line in the communal bathroom because she objects to Aleksandra's "imperialist attitude towards communal property." Nikita periodically screams at Gertruda Genrikovna calling her "German swine" or a "kike" (she was not Jewish, but she said it just in case, since she had a non-Russian last name), and asks her what she was doing in 1941. Retarded Aunt Raisa spits at Uncle Kolia because she does not like the smell of alcohol.

One amazing version of Russia's oral history would show the whole country as a gigantic communal apartment with many mysteries and secrets. Old Glebovna tells stories of everyday life in the Russian Imperial court from the perspective of someone who swept the floors and the staircases—a cinematic perspective worthy of Eisenstein. But another story is that of the neighbor who informed on old Glebovna and her monarchist affections at the local Housing Committee meeting in 1937 and temporarily took over her shabby little room while she was taken away for investigation. Another neighbor, Elena, who moved away and gave her room to Galia, used to tell and retell this obsessive story: in 1938 she saw Fanny Kaplan, the woman who shot at Lenin, twenty years after her execution for her failed attempt to kill the great leader. The woman our neighbor saw wore a little jacket, the color of young grass ... "no, it was more like the color of sea wave, and she was brutally treated by the guards on the ship but she behaved herself with the dignity of a true revolutionary ... and there was blood on her aqua jacket."

Stories were told about war defectors and about Stalinist informers—in the 1950s and 1960s the former victims began to inform on the informers—and then in the 1970s a story circulated about Galia, and her illegitimate children fathered by a leader of a "developing country" studying in Russia. Then there were stories of the "new traitors," the victims of Zionist propaganda who tried to emigrate to Israel or to America. And now there are stories of the communal survivors and the limitchik—the new marginals of post-Soviet society who arrived in the city from the country for temporary jobs and live on limited permits and on the margins of urban communality. Thus in addition to being the site of class conflicts and kitchen wars, the communal apartment was a place of old-fashioned story-telling and myth-making, where the now-vanishing Soviet folklore was preserved and cherished.

Psychopathology of Soviet Everyday Life

Once I was asked what were my earliest memories of growing up in the same room with my parents. The first thing I remembered was the texture of the curtain (*port'era*) that partitioned our shared room. The *port'era* of my childhood was heavy and dark yellow, with an ornamental applique. I remember overhearing the voices of my parents and their friends and the songs of Okudzhava and Vysotsky, but most of all I remember the *port'era* itself. So much for the primal scenes.

The partition is the central architectural feature of the communal apartment. Most of them are made of plywood and they mark the intersection of public and private spheres within the apartment. After the expropriation of property, the old rooms and hallways were partitioned and subdivided, creating weird angular spaces, with a window opening into a sunless back yard or without any windows. Every tenant exercised her imagination in inventing curtains and screens to delineate their minimum privacy. A plywood partition was so much flimsier than a wall, more a sign of division than a division itself. It let through all the noises, the snoring, the fragments of conversations, the footsteps of the neighbor, and everything else you can think of. The partition served not so much to preserve intimacy as to create an illusion that some intimacy was possible.

Secrecy is one of the most important ways of keeping the illusion of privacy. But secrecy in the communal apartment was a game of searching for alternative communalities. There used to be an unofficial children's game we played in the kindergarten, called "the game of burying secrets" which had nothing to do with the official collective "hide-and-seek" orchestrated by the teacher, a game in which there were no secrets and nothing particular to seek or to find:

Our unofficial game consisted in a ritual burial of our little fetishes; the ceremony was performed by a group of close friends and hidden from the kindergarten authorities. The buried "secret" might be a piece of colored glass found in the trash, an old stamp, a piece of the glittering foil wrapping of chocolates, an old badge. The point is that something had to be hidden in order to be shared to be a bond between friends, a perfect something to be exposed as a seal of another, unofficial, communality. This secrecy is not solitary; it has to be dramatized in public. As for the secret itself, the fetishized useless souvenir preserved only for the sake of the game, it parallels some styles of personal collecting in the communal apartments.

Games of secrets were played by adults in their attempts to establish an alternative community and communality, but not necessarily individual privacy. The places of communal use—kitchen, corridor, bathroom—were both the battlegrounds and the playgrounds for the communal neighbors. The use of the toilet, as the fictional and nonfictional accounts of communal life attest, was the most frequent ground for communal disagreement. Toilet paper, a rare commodity in the Soviet Union, was kept in the room and carried inconspicuously to the toilet. Next to the toilet were neatly cut up sheets of *Pravda*, to be read or put to another functional use. The figure of the intellectual in the closet—in the literal rather than literary sense— is prominently featured in many communal apartments. (The toilet was often occupied by some avid reader. The neighbors tried to be discreet, not lining up for the toilet but watching and eavesdropping through the half-opened doors of their rooms, planning when to make their strategic move. Sometimes, though, the wait went beyond the limits of their patience and they would bang ferociously on the door. And, of course, the neighbor who did not turn off the lights in the toilet was considered "an enemy of the people.") Until the 1970s very few apartments had bathrooms (usually separate from the toilet). And where there were bathtubs, they were used for much more important occupations than mere self-indulgent washing. When my mother was a secondary school student, she and the neighbor's daughter used to do their homework on a shelf put across the never-functioning bathtub. The bathtub became my mother's study, her only private space in the crowded apartment.

The communal kitchen hardly resembles the dream of the utopian architects: to be a place of women's liberation from the daily chores. The kitchen is not a communal meeting place, rather it is a place that exemplifies the kind of communality to be avoided. One of the recently interviewed communal apartment residents called it a "domestic Nagorno-Karabakh." Because communal life was endlessly bureaucratized according to schedules dictating in detail the use of each oven and sink, the potential for friction was unending. The burden of the communal interactions and negotiations rested entirely on women: the world of the communal kitchen has often been called matriarchal but I would add that it has been matriarchal by necessity and not by choice.

In the 1960s an alternative "kitchen culture" emerged. The members of Moscow intelligentsia who happened to live in their own separate flats (in Leningrad this was more rare) started to have unofficial kitchen gatherings at their homes. The kitchen became a kind of an informal salon for the culture of the 1960s, of the thaw generation. The most important issues were discussed in the overcrowded kitchen, where people "really talked," flirted, and occasionally ate.[44] The kitchen provided a perfect informal setting for the subtle, casual but friendly intimacy that became a signature of that generation. The kitchen gathering of the 1960s represents a different form of collectivity—it is neither utopian nor forced, like that of the communal apartment. It was a company of friends, unofficial though not antiofficial; in this collective the bonds of affection and friendship constituted its ideology. (But these friendships too were affected by the cultural myths of the time.) The kitchen salon of the 1960s was where grown-up children continued to bury their secrets and to celebrate their shared escapes from the predictability of Soviet life.

The communal apartment is a perfect stage for displaying various forms of theatricality of daily behavior. The main feature of communal interaction can be called "performance disruption." The communal intrusion into the intimate life of a couple is comically featured in many Soviet literary works and films. Soviet sexologists consider the lack of privacy and an internalized fear of interruption as one of the major sources of sexual dissatisfaction and neurosis. Embarrassment is the most characteristic feature of communal life: it does not happen in solitude. Embarrassment is the painful awareness of one's loss of control in the presence of the others, the self-consciousness of loss of confidence, and an exemplary trope of social theatricality.[45] The word "embarrassment" initially referred to a physical obstruction of passage, and only since the eighteenth century has it been applied in reference to people. In this respect the incident with Uncle Fedia urinating in the communal corridor and violating the codes of propriety and social etiquette in front of foreign guests is a typical case of embarrassment, which my mother internalized as a kind of personal shame. Embarrassment was so frequent it almost turned into a ritual in itself. The consequences of ritual embarrassment varied: It could lead to establishing communal tolerance, to making a compromise of minimal plausible conviviality in the impossible circumstances, or to continued intolerance and repressed anger.

[…]

Interior Decoration

The campaign against "domestic trash" did not triumph in the majority of the communal apartments. Instead, as in Mayakovsky's play entitled *The Rebellion of Things*, the so-called domestic trash rebelled against the ideological purges and remained as the secret residue of privacy that shielded people from imposed and internalized communality.

Ode to the Commode

Walter Benjamin wrote that "to live means to leave traces."[46] Perhaps this is the best definition of the private—to leave traces for oneself and for others, memory traces of which one cannot be deprived. A Soviet room in the communal apartment reveals an obsession with commemoration and preservation in the most ostensible fashion. The minimum of privacy is not even a room but a corner in a room, a hidden space behind the partition. The cherished object might be something almost immaterial: a pen, a writing table, a letter in the drawer, a sea shell, little fetishistic objects, embodiments of human desires and aesthetic and ideological imperfections.

Let us enter the room of an aging widow, Liuba, who lives in a communal apartment next door to my old house in Leningrad. Although she has lived here for almost thirty years, her room was not "reconstructed" in the sixties. It appears untouched by the recent changes in taste and in ideology; instead, Aunt Liuba's room preserves a sense of a long duration of time of a certain domestic mentality that survives historical upheavals. It also illustrates almost literally everything that was considered to be in bad taste from the 1920s to the 1970s, including the rubber plant.

Aunt Liuba's room (approximately 13 square meters) contains a sideboard, a version of a commode made in the early 1960s, a bed, a table, and an old-fashioned TV set. The television stands in the center of the table on a Russian shawl like an altar of modern conveniences. The console is covered with a special golden velvety cloth that used to cover icons and later gramophones, all of which were treated with a special reverence. Aunt Liuba's room reminds us of traditional homes of peasants and *meshchanstvo*. In the central space of a Russian village home, which has been framed and idealized by the ethnographers so many times that it has become hard to imagine what it was really like, there was a stove, the symbol of an old Russian hearth, used for cooking and for sleeping during the cold nights. Right across from the stove there was another source of light and warmth, this one spiritual. It was the so-called red corner, where the icons were kept and the candles for the icons were lit. In the Soviet public spaces the "red corner" was turned into "Lenin's corner," still with a lot of red—the color of blood, the color of the Russian icons, the color of the Revolution. In the rooms of the communal apartment the functions of the stove and the red corner were taken up by the TV and the display shelf of the commode, where the most precious items were kept. The artificial light of the TV is reflected in the glass doors of the sideboard, casting bluish shadows upon the personal possessions.

The commode (called also servant or bufet) is the most important piece of furniture in the old-fashioned communal apartment room. It survived all the ideological purges—the campaign against domestic trash, the civil war on *meshchanstvo*, and literary irony. Perhaps a nostalgic poet from the former Soviet Union should write an elegy or even an "Ode to the Commode."

The genesis of the item is of great historical importance. It symbolizes bourgeois commodity and the conceptions of comfort, home, and interiority.[47] According to Mario Praz the commode was invented in the early eighteenth century, out of the "confluence of bourgeois and patrician tastes," and it contributed greatly to giving rooms "a more intimate character."[48] In mid-nineteenth century, as Walter Benjamin put it, "the private individual enters the stage of history."[49] In contrast, in the mid-1920s in Russia the private individual goes backstage. Yet the old and not so luxurious commode in the room of the communal apartment remains the site of personal pride, a display of one's externalized interior and of the desire for individuation.

Aunt Liuba has carefully arranged the objects on her sideboard. There is a big plastic apple brought from her native Belorussian village, a Chinese thermos with bright floral ornaments, a naturalistic porcelain dog, three bottles containing different glass flowers—daisies and some exotic red flowers not without a touch of elegance—a samovar, a set of folk-style Soviet-made porcelain cups. "You see, I have it all here—it's my still life," she said proudly when I photographed her room. It is curious that she would use the artistic term "still life" to describe it. (She called it *nature morte*, a term familiar from the obligatory high-school excursions to the museum.) To her, the display is obviously imbued with an aesthetic quality as much as with personal memories. She almost never drinks from her beautiful porcelain cups. They are precious objects of decoration, not for everyday use. Indeed there is something pleasing and cheerful in the brightness and unabashed eclecticism of the objects, in contrast to the bleak uniformity of the communal corridors.

The still life appears to be removed from historical narrative and from narrative as such; it reflects a conception of time as habit, repetition, and long-duration; it is, to use Norman Bryson's expression, "the sleep of culture."[50] But it is hard to imagine a still life in a culture where one major devastation follows the other—revolutions, wars, housing crises, famine, Stalin's purges—where habit, repetition, and everyday stability are so difficult to sustain. In Russia one can only speak about nostalgia for a still life, for a sustaining everyday materiality in the face of continuing crises. Liuba's collection of Soviet ready-mades, objects of trivial private utopias and of mass aesthetics, framed by the glass of the commode as if it were a museum exhibit, is a kind of monument to that desire for a still life, for a life that does not rush anywhere in a whirlpool of uncontrollable change.

In Aunt Liuba's room ornaments clash: the carpet with its oriental motifs, the standard roses on the wallpaper, the bright country flowers on the tablecloth, the big polka dots on the pillow covers, and the geometrical

FIGURE 7.1 Aunt Liuba's "still life" (photo by Svetlana Boym).

FIGURE 7.2 Aunt Liuba's "still life": detail (photo by Svetlana Boym).

decoration of the modern blanket on the bed. Obviously she did not choose them to match; she simply collected what she could get and tried to imbue it all with warmth and vitality, recreating distant images of the village home and prerevolutionary images of cozy merchants' dwellings whose covers, napkins, and laces gave the feeling of "completeness and personal touch" that Benjamin decries in bourgeois interiors.

Liuba's room is full of flowers: Soviet roses on the wall; exotic red glass flowers and simple plastic daisies on the shelf, and stylized golden and yellow daisies painted on the porcelain objects, and even red floral patterns on the wooden *khokhloma* spoon. Obviously, many of the objects themselves are ideological artifacts and products of cultural myths. For instance, the little busts of Pushkin, Tchaikovsky, and other great Russian geniuses that have persistently decorated apartments from the late nineteenth century to now represent the popular prestige of high culture. The glass flowers are cultural hybrids, impure flowers of degraded art nouveau and low-brow urban culture, artifacts that annoy intellectual ethnographers in search of authentic popular culture. The porcelain cups and plates come from the Leningrad porcelain factory, a former imperial factory. Its designers changed the tsarist insignia, Victorian roses, and floral chinoiseries for more democratic and folkloristic national motifs. And what could be more national and expressive of "simple folk taste" than daisies, the flowers of the field! The daisies on Aunt Liuba's porcelain, however, are stylized, abstract 1960s daisies.

Next door to Aunt Liuba lives a documentary filmmaker Olia with her twelve-year-old daughter. Her room too is overcrowded with personal memorabilia: portraits of Pushkin in the bookcase, reproductions of Hindu goddesses, sea corals, calendars with Soviet actresses in foreign black lingerie, images of prerevolutionary St. Petersburg. There is the usual clash of ornaments and conflicting styles. Olia is not happy with my taking pictures in her room: "Do you think I like all these pictures torn out of old journals and calendars? I have to cover the holes in the wall. Do you think I like this wallpaper? But how can I change it?" Indeed, who can afford here to have "good taste"?

In the rooms of the intelligentsia one finds similar "still lives" of personal memorabilia. Instead of cupboards and chests of drawers, there are bookcases built to occupy the whole wall, designed in a modern and functional fashion and made in the so-called developed Socialist countries like Hungary or Yugoslavia. These shelves seem to lack the fetishistic quality of the other pieces of furniture, having none of the ornamental details of the commodes. However, the bookcases themselves became fetishes of the intelligentsia and items of social status. The bookshelves display many hard-to-get hardcovers and collected works of foreign authors that are the mark of belonging to the intelligentsia. Yet the most important space here is the space between the folding glass doors on the bookshelf for the display of one's most personal objects—postcards, baby pictures, portraits of a bearded Hemingway or Vysorsky with or without a cigar, snapshots of faraway friends, toys or souvenirs from Crimea or Susdal, envelopes with foreign stamps, loose pages from old books, dated newspaper clippings. This narrow, nearly one-dimensional space behind the glass of the bookcase reflects the image of the resident; it is his or her carefully arranged interface with the world. The narrative of treasured objects cannot be easily reconstructed by the outsider: it is nonlinear, full of blank spots, oddly meaningful banalities, and minor obsessions. This life history is not a biography but rather a biographical legend, a story of inner life externally fashioned, a story of what really matters, what leaves traces and survives the drudgery of dailiness. Often it is also a story of travels, real or imaginary—of journeys to exotic places, of escapes into wishful thinking. In the 1960s and early 1970s, when traveling abroad was nearly impossible, Soviet citizens engaged in "virtual travels" through the popular television program "The Club of Cine-Travelers" (a Soviet version of "National Geographic"), or through collecting foreign stamps and pictures of Western writers, artists, and intellectuals.

The objects on personal display on the bookshelves are not completely individual: some unwritten law tells everyone when Hemingway is out and Vysotsky is in, when Pasternak is out and Solzhenitsyn is in. Then Solzhenitsyn himself is out and in his place reigns exotic and apolitical Nefertiti, the beautiful queen of ancient Egypt. The reproduction is from the traveling exhibit "The Treasures of Tutankhamen," to which hardly anyone could purchase tickets. Now side by side with Nefertiti there is a picture of a half-dressed foreign pin-up girl with a non-Russian smile, which seems to supplant the political and poetic heroes of the past and present.

The private memorabilia are steeped in cultural myths; they are separated from the dominant discourses by a mere plywood partition. But in that space the elements of those myths can be reconstructed in a creative personal collage; it doesn't matter that it lacks aesthetic unity. The objects/souvenirs are the minimal repositories of personal memory.

Both priceless and cheap, conspicuous and private, they make us question certain commonplaces of the commodity theory.

Poverty of Sociology and the Aesthetics of Survival

Pierre Bourdieu begins his chapter "Social Critique of the Judgment of Taste" with an epigraph from Alain Besançon's *The Russian in the Nineteenth Century*: "And we do not know whether cultural life can survive the disappearance of domestic servants."[51] The sociologist goes on to analyze the French "aristocracy of culture," subordinating the delights of art to a class-based construction of taste. Yet the seamless passage from the epigraph to the main body of the text glosses over the fact that Russian cultural life survived not only the disappearance of the servants but even the rise and disappearance of a variety of sociological approaches to art and to everyday living. Bourdieu contrasts the "popular" movement to translate art into daily life with the "aristocratic" movement to "confer aesthetic status on objects that are banal or even common." In his view, "Popular taste applies the scheme of ethos which pertains in the ordinary circumstances of life to legitimate the works of art, and so performs a systematic reduction of the things of art to the things of life."[52]

Yet as some of the Russian examples demonstrate, the opposition between aesthetics and ethics, disinterestedness and empathy, elite and popular, does not function so neatly. In fact, popular aesthetic is often escapist and fantastic rather than entirely realistic; or rather, the elements of fantasy and verisimilitude in it tend to interact in a complex and ambiguous manner, as they do in the folk tales or science-fiction movies. Moreover, popular tastes are eclectic– together with urban middlebrow culture they often preserve a trace of peasant pre-realist or slightly primitive sensibility (which should not be exaggerated, to avoid falling into the trap of folk exoticism). Popular tastes frequently incline to bright colors and fantastic ornaments. In Russia the culture of icons–their spiritual and also their pictorial and ornamental qualities–influenced both popular tastes and the taste of the avantgarde elite. Bourdieu takes two reductive steps: reducing popular culture to ethical projection and equating ethical projection with realistic representation.

In the everyday, especially in the highly politicized and semioticized Soviet everyday, the aesthetic and the ethical are indistinguishable in the ordinary micropractices. Moreover, it can become unethical to deny the aesthetic experience of the impoverished residents of the communal apartment.

The personal domestic objects of Aunt Liuba are difficult to categorize: they are too useless for both use-value and exchange-value theories, not authentically primitive or exotic enough for transgressive modern theories, too trivial and banal—in a nonfatal manner—to be turned into a simulacrum à la Baudrillard. The fetishistic aspect of these objects is not sufficiently perverse to make interesting psychoanalytical reading.[53] In other words, these objects are impure and outmoded on all grounds.

In Soviet Russia, the experience of material scarcity for the majority of the population and the official critique of bourgeois commodities (combined with thinly disguised social inequalities) endows private objects with a different cultural significance. While in Western Europe the critique of commodity is a marginal oppositional discourse, in Soviet Russia it is the mainstream. At the time of the campaign against domestic trash, Osip Mandelshtam made the cultivation of "domestic object" the cornerstone of his poetics of remembrance and his "nostalgia for world culture." Mandelshtam's autobiographical novella, *The Egyptian Stamp* (1928), opens with a toast to lost domesticity: "I propose to you, my family, a coat of arms; a glass of boiled water. In Petersburg's boiled water, with its rubbery aftertaste, I drink to my unsuccessful domestic immortality. The centrifugal force of time has scattered our Viennese chairs and the Dutch plates with little blue flowers."[54]

The same centrifugal force disperses the domestic objects and shatters the "I" of the hero. The fate of the things is parallel to the fate of persons. Those Viennese chairs and Dutch plates with little blue flowers exist in the past perfect or future indefinite of literature; lost domestic objects that can only be recovered through art. The poet has to be "a good housesitter."[55]

Of course, the artifact on display in the communal apartment is less the trace of world culture than a mass-reproduced object. Yet it is aesthetically commemorated. Aunt Liuba's perfectly functional porcelain cups are made useless, and therefore beautiful. These cups and glass flowers have something in common with Mandelshtam's Viennese chairs and Dutch plates; they partake of the same aesthetics of survival.[56]

In her book *The Body in Pain* Elaine Scarry talks about the object in a world that is always in danger of being "unmade," where materiality is fragile and not to be taken for granted.[57] The object is treated not as a commodity or fetish but as an artifact, a product of human creativity that helps to make the world and undo the suffering. It is this conception of the object that is particularly suited for Soviet circumstances. There, the artifact is a personal souvenir and a souvenir of privacy itself; it is an object displaced from a common into an individual history. The owner of the souvenir becomes the author, who reinvents the use of the object and makes it memorable. As Susan Stewart points out, the tragedy of the souvenir is the death of memory, the nightmare of the "unmarked grave."[58] It is another way of describing the impossibility of "leaving traces."

The objects in the personal display cases of the communal apartments are neither bare essentials nor merely objects of status and conspicuous consumption. If they do represent a need, it is first and foremost an aesthetic need, a desire for beauty met with minimal available means, or the aesthetic "domestication" of the hostile outside world. They are not about defamiliarization, but rather about inhabiting estranged ideological designs.

[...]

The End of the Communal Apartment

By the late 1980s a few completely dilapidated communal apartments had been taken over by artists. But suddenly almost like in downtown Manhattan they began to be reconquered by newly emerging shady cooperatives and businesses, branches of heretical Buddhist sects prospering in Russia, or some mysterious astrologists anonymous. After the adoption of the 1991 law allowing for privatization of domestic property, a new wave of "gentrification" of the communal apartments began; it turned out to be one of the most intricate exercises for the emerging post-Soviet legal culture. The law inevitably got tangled in the unpredictable (or rather very predictable but never legally accountable) webs of Soviet everyday practices.[59] The privatization policy met with a lot of popular criticism, however, some of it the result of seventy years of building communism, and some the continuation of old Russian folkways and particular attitudes toward property and privacy. A friend reports a conversation on the trolley in 1991: "They are going to give out vouchers; we are going to privatize!"–To which his comrade replies, "Don't use such words in the presence of women." An aging schoolteacher wrote a letter of complaint to the journal *Ogonek*, describing how she was ostracized by the other dwellers of her apartment block when she decided to privatize her one-room standard apartment. She was called "NEP woman, capitalist, and private property owner"–insults that, in Stalin's time, could have deprived people of the rights of citizenship. In popular slang privatization is ironically called prikhvatization (grab-what-you-can, from *prikhvatit*, to grab).

Here is a story about privatization. Our heroine is newly rich: a young woman who works as a financial director for an international "joint venture." She falls in love with an old and fairly dilapidated Moscow communal apartment with bay windows and a neoclassical façade. She would need to pay each communal apartment neighbor a significant fee and also to offer each one a satisfactory place in another apartment. Moreover, she would have to deal with the surviving Soviet bureaucrats of the Housing Committee, an old institution of control that is now becoming obsolete. There are still many Soviet atavisms in law, especially in bureaucratic practice. One of them is the requirement of the resident permit, which now functions as a kind of permit for bribery, or what can be described as the unwritten sanctioning of state bureaucracy racketeering. In this privatization story of one of the communal apartments on Arbat Street, the apparatchik from the Housing Committee demanded a bribe of no less than $20,000 (more, probably, than a year's income for all the residents of the building put together). When the bribe was declined, threatening phone calls and other practices of harassment began. The harassment ceased only when the aspiring owner of the building came back accompanied by the prime minister's wife.[60] The Housing Committee members still understand best the language of the old system of power, protection, and favoritism.

The would-be buyer said that in the eyes of many communal apartment members she took on the role of the former government and offered them what the government always promised but never delivered—apartments of their own. She had to follow all the old rules, overcome attitudes of dependency and entitlement, and fight against the new structures of the shadow economy. Furthermore, the work of resettling a communal collective turned out be more personal than professional; she had to provide psychological as well as financial assistance. The new owner of the apartment had to become a part of that collective, entering the old communal structures of mutual responsibility and becoming responsible for the future of former neighbors. These were the first experiences of the post-Soviet "lawful practices" of domestic privatization. On the one hand, a few brave members of the post-Soviet elite mobilized superhuman efforts to overcome the old Soviet bureaucracy and achieve their dream of a Western-style private dwelling; on the other hand, though, the great number of former communal apartment dwellers, taught by both the long tradition of subsistence economy and the recent experience of unstable political power, learned that they might survive capitalism but not necessarily inhabit it or make it work for them. Russian privatization follows a crooked path between new and untested democratic laws and old practices of bureaucracy and bribery (which had many precedents and unwritten rules). According to the official statistics of 1993, on the Russian territory 30 million people continued to live in the communal apartment.[61] So the communal apartment ceased to be a primary institution of social control, but it still remains a necessity of life in post-Soviet Russia.

A Homecoming, 1991

Ten years after I left the USSR, I went to visit the house where I had lived in Leningrad. The main entrance was blocked, and on the broken glass door an outdated poster advertised a videosalon featuring *Rambo II, Emmanuelle*, and a Brazilian soap opera, *The Slave Isaura Part IV*. The house at 79 Bolshoi Avenue looked the same, but that first impression was disappointing and unevocative. This house was not my home but an impostor, a look-alike, which imitated the "original" so literally as to be uninteresting. "What is happening here" I asked an elderly woman standing on the street where there used to be a bus stop. "Repairs," she answered. (*Remont* was the first word Walter Benjamin learned on his travels in Russia, when everything seemed to be in the process of being repaired.) "When did it start?" "About ten years ago, or earlier."

So I failed to enter my house through the front door and had to sneak in through the broken wooden fence on the other side of the yard. This altered my narrative of entrance and made the yard look different. I was surrounded by heaps of trash, telephone wires, pieces of old furniture, worn-out slippers (that might have belonged to Uncle Fedia), the pages of a 1979 calendar, mysterious schedules and graphics–all fragments of perfect organization whose purpose was now entirely lost, along with pieces of a broken record by a once-popular French singer of the 1960s. Oh, I think I know the song: "Tombait la neige / Tu ne viendrais pas ce soir / Tombait la neige / Tout est blanc de désespoir."

Climbing through the trash, I made my way upstairs. The apartment looked uncanny. Some of the partitions had been taken off, and the whole framework of our interpersonal and communal interactions was broken. All the wrong doors, which once were locked and hidden behind the wallpaper to keep separate entrances for the neighbors, were open. The communal kitchen, our apartment forum, seemed to have shrunk in size, and so had our interminable corridor, where the communal telephone was located. As a teenager I used to conduct my personal conversations here using elaborate codes and suggestive hints to irritate curious Aunt Shura, who was eavesdropping tactfully behind a half-opened door. The apartment looked like a stage set, and my whole trip seemed predictable and obvious. It was not the space itself, not the house, but the way of inhabiting it that had made it home, and that was forever lost. But a few insignificant things remained: silly white squares on our yellow wallpaper and the floral bas relief on the ceiling, the last remainder of the decadent tastes of the first owner of the house. Suddenly I noticed something painted on the wall paper—a window frame, with a vase of flowers and an open book on the sill, and an empty center. It had been painted by my friend some twelve years ago around a glossy poster of a faraway Mediterranean country; something that I would now consider to be tourist kitsch. The dark room did not have a window and we used to joke that this was our "window to Europe." It was at a difficult time when we were trying to emigrate to what then appeared as a mythical West, but often thought that the escape from the communal apartment would be virtually impossible. Now the poster was gone, a foreign or pseudo-foreign commodity, probably stolen by a local drunkard, only the dream-frame had somehow remained to evoke us and our communal neighbors.

I looked through a cracked kitchen window into the yard: black balconies with holes were still precariously attached to the building and a few uprooted plants continued to inhabit them. An old lonely drunk wandered into the gaping hole of the back entrance, which used to be an unofficial gathering place of the local youth. He stopped to urinate near the skeleton of the old staircase. I took just a few snapshots of the apartment and the yard: the balconies, the trash, the floral bas reliefs. In the center of the yard there was an old truck, looking like it could be from the 1940s, inscribed with the single word DEATH. I thought it would make a good picture, but I decided never to show it to my parents. They had spent most of their adult life in this apartment. However, when I came back and told them that our old house on Petrogradskaia is in repairs, they seemed remarkably indifferent, as if far removed from my somewhat artificial search for memories.

"We heard they were making a movie in the yard. Lenfilm, I think. And they brought an old and rusty truck in. It must have been something about the war and the Leningrad blockade."

"No, no, it was a film about a poet Daniil Kharms who wrote about a man who went to the forest one day and never came back. And then Daniil Kharms left his house one day in 1937 to buy a pack of cigarettes and never came back…"

Notes

1   Vladimir Nabokov, "Philistines and Philistinism," in *Lectures on Russian Literature* (New York: Harcourt, Brace, Jovanovich, 1981), p. 313.

2   Roman Jakobson, "On the Generation That Squandered Its Poets," in *The Language in Literature,* ed. Krystyna Pomorska and Stephen Rudy (Cambridge, Mass.: Harvard University Press, 1987).

3   Even the word "neighborhood" does not have a comfortable Russian translation (the word *sosed* is now too compromised by communal apartment life, where a good neighbor is defined, in Soviet folklore, as someone who pees in the communal neighbor's teapot only occasionally). After glasnost', however, americanisms and gallicisms have begun to enter the language.

4   Dmitrii Likhachev quotes Nikolai Rerikh's complaint that the *Oxford English Dictionary* includes only two Russian words, *ukaz* and *sovet,* both connected to Russian and Soviet systems of power and bureaucracy. Likhachev, *Zametki o russkom* (Moscow: Soviet Russia, 1984), p. 11; conversely, *volia,* "freedom," and *udal,* "courage," are connected to the Russian landscape, and particularly to the great central Russian plain.

5   My conception of "cultural myth" derives from Lévi-Strauss and Roland Barthes, particularly the latter's *Mythologies* (Paris: Seuil, 1957). See also the revised preface to the 1970 edition, translated into English as "Change the Object Itself" in Barthes, *Image, Music, Text,* trans. Stephen Heath (New York: Hill and Wang, 1978). In a later revision of "cultural myth" Barthes writes that the task of the cultural mythologist is not to "demystify" but rather to reveal the process of myth-making.

6   See Frances Yates, *The Art of Memory* (Chicago: University of Chicago Press, 1966).

7   Aristotle, *Topica* and *Rhetorica* in *Basic Works,* ed. Richard McKeon (New York: Random House, 1941).

8   More, *Utopia.* For the explanation of the linguistic neologism see Frank E. Manuel and Fritzie P. Manuel, *Utopian Thought in the Western World* (Cambridge, Mass.: Harvard University Press, 1979), p. 1.

9   Immanuel Kant, *Critique of Judgment,* trans. Werner Pluhar (Indianapolis: Hackett, 1987), p. 231.

10 Hans-Georg Gadamer, *Truth and Method* (New York: Continuum, 1975), pp. 19–29.

11 Ibid., p. 38.

12 Anton Zijderveld, *On Clichés: The Supersedure of Meaning by Function in Modernity* (London: Routledge and Kegan Paul, 1979), p. 66. See also Ruth Amossy and Elisheva Rosen, *Discours du cliché* (Paris: CDU SEDES, 1982) and Ruth Amossy, *Les Idées réçues: Sémiologie du stereotype* (Paris: Editions Nathan, 1991); see Umberto Eco, "The Structure of Bad Taste," in *The Open Work,* trans. by Anna Cancogni (Cambridge, Mass.: Harvard University Press, 1989), pp. 180–217.

13 Clement Greenberg, "Avant-Garde and Kitsch" in *On Art and Culture* (Boston: Beacon Press, 1965). Theodor Adorno, *Aesthetic Theory,* trans. C. Lenharardt (London: Routledge and Kegan Paul, 1984).

14 For a survey of the possible etymologies of kitsch and a bibliography, see Matei Calinescu, *Five Faces of Modernity* (Durham: Duke University Press, 1987), pp. 225–265.

15 Hermann Broch, "Notes on the Problem of Kitsch" in *Kitsch: The Anthology of Bad Taste,* ed. Gillo Dorfles (London: Studio Vista, 1969), pp. 69–70.

16 Clement Greenberg himself acknowledges his mistake in the 1970 edition of his essays and attributes it to intellectual ignorance of Russian art and its contexts. In a discussion of modern aesthetics Theodor Adorno made an infamous attack on American jazz, which he evaluated with comparable acumen.

17 Greenberg, "Avant-Garde and Kitsch," p. 15.

18 Yaron Ezrahi, in *Salmagundi,* 85–86 (Winter-Spring 1990), p. 309. This is a special issue dedicated to kitsch. For the distinction between democratic and fascist kitsch see Saul Friedlander's preface to this issue. See also Abraham A. Moles, *Le Kitsch: l'art du bonheur* (Paris: Mame, 1971).

19 Hannah Arendt, *Eichmann in Jerusalem: Report on the Banality of Evil* (New York: Viking, 1963), p. 48.

20 For the contemporary discussion see Saul Friedlander, *Reflections of Nazism: An Essay on Kitsch and Death* (New York: Harper and Row, 1984).

21 If kitsch comes from the Bavarian slang word for "sketch," it illustrates Baudelaire's point that modern beauty can be captured only in the dynamic, unfinished sketches that embody transience itself. Kitsch-sketch is a kind of reification of that unrevelatory but gratifying transience that both mimics and mocks universal beauty.

22 Charles Baudelaire, "Fusées," in *Oeuvres complètes* (Paris: 1965), p. 23.

23 Rimbaud cultivates the aesthetics of bad taste, which is not at all satanic but the soft, sentimental seduction of provincial art, of the old-fashioned decorations of village churches, popular calendars, and postcards of the opera. Flaubert morally decries the banality of bourgeois life and at the same time perpetuates it within his perfectly crafted, beautiful sentences.

24 Susan Sontag, "Notes on Camp," in her *Against Interpretation* (New York: Pantheon Books, 1989), p. 117.

25 Ibid., p. 118.

26 Milan Kundera, *The Unbearable Lightness of Being,* trans. Michael Heim (New York: Harper and Row, 1989), p. 256.

27 The anecdote is from *Istoriia SSSR v anekdotakh* (Smolensk: 1991), p. 77.

28 Alexander Kabakov, "Na chuzhom pole," in *Moskovskie novosti, 49,* December 6, 1992, p. 5.

29 Quoted in Vladimir Paperny, *Kul'tura Dva* (Ann Arbor: Ardis, 1984), p. 83.

30 Joseph Brodsky, "Room and a Half" in *Less Than One: Selected Essays* (New York: Farrar, Straus & Giroux, 1986).

31 El Lissitsky, "Basic Premises, Interrelationships between Arts, the New City and Ideological Superstructure" in *Bolshevik Visions,* ed. William Rosenberg (Ann Arbor: The University of Michigan Press, 1990), vol. 2, pp. 194–195.

32 The evolution of the concept of place was similar to that of photomontage itself, which recreates the revolutionary topos with its deliberate cuts and seams. At first, as in the early photographic experiments of Klutsis, Lissitsky, and Rodchenko, the construction of space calls for a radical reversibility of perspectives and multiplicity of viewpoints: "to be looked at from all sides," reads the caption on Gustav Klutsis's first revolutionary photomontage, "Dynamic City." Later, the play of perspective becomes more fixed, the montage more explicitly ideological, and the organization of space more hierarchical. By the 1930s the photomontages are dominated by the figures of the party leaders, Lenin and Stalin, who indicate one route through the space, the route of "communist victory." See Margarita Typitsyn, "From the Politics of Montage to the Montage of Politics," in *Montage and Modern Life,* ed. Matthew Teitelbaum (Cambridge, Mass.: MIT Press, 1992), pp. 82–128.

33 Walter Benjamin, "Moscow," in *Reflections,* p. 109.

34 Grigorii Kozintsev, Leonid Trauberg, Georgii Kryzhitsky, Sergei Iutkevich, *Ekstcentrism 1922* (Ekscentropolis (formerly Petrograd): 1922), p. 10. Cafés,

like salons, could be seen as institutions of artistic communication, and revolutionary artists wished to avoid this mode of artistic self-reference.

35 The "boulevard," like the "street" is often personified; it appears as a metonymic substitution for the "crowd." The emphasis on the crowd as the main actor of modernity brings us back to Baudelaire's "The Painter of the Modern Life," Apollinaire's Parisian "Calligrams," and Mayakovsky's early poems "Street," "Street Signs," and others. In other words, boulevard brings us back to the prerevolutionary international avant-garde, while the crowd is too anarchistic a concept to serve the new order. A short time later, however, the ideas of the eccentric manifesto become marginal in Soviet culture, and the foreign word "boulevard" ceases to be relevant to the Soviet public place. For an inspiring article on Surrealist topography and the movement from the street to the salon, see Susan Suleiman, "Between the Street and the Salon: The Dilemma of Surrealist Politics in the 1930s" in *Visual Anthropology Review*, 7, 1 (Spring, 1991).

36 For a historical description of revolutionary utopias, see Richard Stites, *Revolutionary Dreams: Utopian Vision and Experimental Life in the Russian Revolution;* V. E. Khazanova, *Iz istorrii sovetskoi arkhitektury, 1917–1925* (Moscow: A.N.S.S.S.R., 1963); *Sovetskaiia arkhitektura pervykh let oktiabria* (Moscow: Nauka, 1970); *Sovetskaiia arkhitektura pervoi piatiletki* (Moscow: Nauka, 1980); Christina Lodder, *Russian Constructivism* (New Haven: Yale University Press, 1983); Moisei Ginzburg, *Style and Epoch* (Cambridge: MIT Press, 1982). For theory and comparative views on utopia see Frank and Fritzie Manuel, *Utopian Thought in the Western World* (Cambridge, Mass.: Harvard University Press, 1979) and Lars Kleberg and Richard Stites, eds., *Utopia in Russian History, Culture and Thought* (Special issue of *Russian History*, 11/2–3, Summer–Fall 1984).

37 The authors of the project were the architects Vengerov, Tverskoi, and Buryshkin. See Richard Stites, *Revolutionary Dreams*, pp. 200–204.

38 See Walter Benjamin, "Paris, the Capital of the Nineteenth Century," in *Charles Baudelaire: A Lyric Poet in the Era of High Capitalism* (London: Verso, 1983), pp. 155–177.

39 Many revolutionary architects who called themselves "dis-urbanists" planned socialist suburbs. Among the most interesting projects are Leonid Vesnin's garden court apartment complex, and Konstantin Melnikov's Green City (1929)—a peculiar suburban Arcadia in which people lived in private rooms in hotels, and communal interaction took place in the huge railroad station. Melnikov, who comes from a peasant background, was one of the more "individualist" among the designers of the house communes: he paid special attention to the areas of transition between public and private and created long corridors that connected small private sleeping rooms with the communal spaces. One of the most imaginative of Melnikov's spaces were aroma-therapeutic sleeping chambers called euphonically "sonnaia sonata" (sleep sonata) where the air would be crystal clean and the poets and musicians would sing ideologically correct lullabies to the fatigued laborers. The idea was partially plagiarized by the American architect Wallace Harrison and his benefactor and New York showman "Roxy" Roth. It led them to create a special atmosphere of ozoned, ultra-solarized air in Radio City Music Hall—another kind of workers' paradise. Melnikov's sleeping chambers were both poetic and imaginative yet imbued with revolutionary teleology: in the very center of Green City there was an Institute for Changing the Form of Man, a behaviorist laboratory that was supposed to model an ideal socialist laborer of the future. Russian utopias in general tend to be less pleasure- and leisure-oriented than their Western counterparts. (Nobody could compete with the grand gourmet Fourier's imagined pleasures of eating and of leisure.) And in contrast to the French Surrealists' program, especially the first manifesto published four years before Melnikov's project for the Green City, which centers on the unconscious, Russian utopian dreams were both more outlandish and more controlled, subservient to the overruling teleology of the revolution. See S. Frederick Starr, *Melnikov: Solo Architect in the Mass Society* (Princeton: Princeton University Press, 1978), pp. 49–50.

40 Alexandra Kollontai in her novellas presents working women caught between their intimate and their public life, matters of the heart and matters of duty. Vasilisa Malygina, the heroine of one of Kollontai's stories, leaves her unfaithful husband, a new Soviet apparatchik who has a petit-bourgeois mistress, and finds her self-realization in the building of collectives for women and men. The story ends at the start of the construction of a housecommune; we learn about the difficulties of dreaming but not about the consequences of those dreams. The novella is also a didactic lesson, a moral tale in the Tolstoyian tradition of fairy tales for the common people. Yet it reveals some of the crucial ambiguities in the foundations of the new byt.

Housing dreams were not limited to writers or avant-garde architects. The newspapers of the 1920s were full of the amateurish utopian projects suggested by the readers. One of the articles, "Give Us the House-Commune," quotes the workers from the "Red Chemist" factory: "We don't need little English houses, we don't need private apartments, give us a whole house where a worker's family could be in touch with the other workers' families, where they could meet in one common room." See *Komsomolskaia Pravda*, Oct. 13, 1928. The writer stresses that this is "not a matter of utopia" but a project for the future. Many authors of utopian projects preferred to emphasize collective authorship and the rational and practical base of their ideas.

41 I am grateful to Maya Turovskaya, a specialist on everyday life of Stalin's times, for bringing this to my attention.

42 Lidiia Ginzburg, *Chelovek za pis'mennym stolom* (Leningrad: Sovetskii pisatel', 1989), pp. 492–493.

43 There is a game theory of utopia: it is presented as a playground for the escapist ideas of a specific historical period and an enactment of political programs. But utopian thinking has to pass through a non-playful leap of faith that cuts the connection between everyday life and imaginary existence. Utopias often present a "paradise on earth" in a corrupt land, which might help to redeem it. Hence utopias tend to be didactic rather than playful. See James Michael Holquist, "How to Play Utopia: Some Brief Notes on the Distinctiveness of the Utopian System" in *Science Fiction*, ed. Mark Rose (Englewood Cliffs: Prentice Hall, 1976).

44 I am indebted to Moscow writer and journalist Alla Gerber, who told me about kitchen culture.

45 See Erving Goffman, *The Presentation of Self in Everyday Life* (New York: Doubleday, 1959).

46 Walter Benjamin, "Paris, the Capital of the Nineteenth Century," in *Reflections*, p. 155.

47 The Russian word for furniture, *mebel'*, comes from the French *meuble* meaning movable property, in contrast to land or buildings. Gradually a mere storage chest turned into an object of craft and art, a prototype of the modern chest of drawers and glass cabinets.

48 Mario Praz, *An Illustrated History of Interior Decoration*, p. 56. The glassed cabinet, a stronghold of bourgeois coziness, was locked with a key to protect the private treasures and opened only to the private delights of the family and of selected guests. By the end of the century, the glass cabinets turned into a home *kunstcamera*, a private collections of curios and bric-à-brac, a privileged site of bibliomania and occasionally of rarefied and morbid fin-de-siècle erotomania. The private collection was the primary display of bourgeois self-fashioning. See Emily Apter, "Cabinet Secrets: Peep Shows, Prostitution and Bric-a-Bracomania," in *Feminizing the Fetish: Psychoanalysis and Narrative Obsession in Turn-of-the-Century France* (Ithaca: Cornell University Press, 1991), pp. 15–39.

49 Walter Benjamin, "Paris, the Capital of the Nineteenth Century," p. 154.

50 Norman Bryson, *Looking on the Overlooked: Four Essays on Still Life Painting* (Cambridge, Mass.: Harvard University Press, 1990), p. 8.

51 Pierre Bourdieu, *Distinction: A Social Critique of the Judgement of Taste*, trans. Richard Nice (Cambridge, Mass.: Harvard University Press, 1984), p. 9.

52 Ibid., p. 5.

53 For an extensive theoretical discussion of fetishism see William Pietz, "The Problem of Fetish I," *Res* 9 (Spring 1985); "The Problem of Fetish II," *Res* 13 (Spring 1987), pp. 23–45; and "The Problem of Fetish IIIa," *Res* 16 (Autumn, 1988), pp. 105–123. Emily Apter, *Feminizing the Fetish*, p. 5. Sigmund Freud, "On Fetishism," in *The Standard Edition of Complete Psychological Works and Letters*, 24 vols., trans. James Strachey (London: Hogarth Press, 1953–

1974), vol. 21, pp. 152–157. Karl Marx, *Capital,* trans. Samuel Moore and Edward Aveling, ed. Frederick Engels (New York: Modern Library, 1906). For a discussion of the fetishization of the concept of fetish, see W. J. T. Mitchell, "The Rhetoric of Iconoclasm: Marxism, Ideology and Fetishism," in *Iconology: Image, Text, Ideology* (Chicago: University of Chicago Press, 1986), pp. 160–208. See also Naomi Shor, "Female Fetishism: The Case of George Sand" in *The Female Body in Western Culture,* ed. Susan Suleiman (Cambridge, Mass.: Harvard University Press, 1986). British psychoanalyst D. W. Winnicot has a useful and complex theory of the "transitional object." See also Jean Baudrillard, *For a Critique of the Political Economy of the Sign,* trans. Charles Lewin (St. Louis, Mo.: Telos Press, 1981), and *De la séduction* (Paris: Galilée-Denoel, 1979). For the discussion of culture collecting see James Clifford, *The Predicament of Culture* (Cambridge, Mass.: Harvard University Press, 1988).

54 Osip Mandelshtam, "Egipteskaia marka," in *Sobranie sochinenii v trekh tomakh,* vol. 2, p. 5.

55 Mandelshtam reacts against both Futurist utopianism and Symbolist metaphysics, commenting that the latter were "the bad house sitters" of language, who wished to transcend the materiality of language and of the world too quickly.

56 A kind of empathetic everyday aesthetics is needed to account for the cultural significance of ordinary precarious possessions. This aesthetics is not ahistorical and universally human: the appeal to the precariousness and preciousness of the objects can in itself be rhetorically abused. Yet this aesthetics ought to be developed alongside theories of commodity fetishism.

57 Elaine Scarry, "The Interior Structure of the Artifact," in *The Body in Pain: The Making and Unmaking of the World* (Oxford: Oxford University Press, 1985), pp. 278–326. Following from the context of alienated labor and economic production, thinking about things is displaced into the context of reception, projection of reciprocity, responsibility, and responsiveness. The object is seen as a projection of human sentience, as a projection of the awareness of aliveness. The denial of the object is not only a social deprivation but also a sensory deprivation, a thwarting of sentience, human contact, powers of projection, and reciprocity. Although Scarry does not wish to draw a clear distinction between art objects and artifacts, it seems that a creative impulse is crucial for her reading, and this creative impulse and affirmation of aliveness constitute the aesthetics of daily existence.

58 Susan Stewart, *On Longing: Narratives of the Miniature, the Gigantic, the Souvenir, the Collection* (Baltimore: Johns Hopkins University Press, 1984).

59 In 1988 Soviet ministers approved an amendment allowing citizens to buy their apartments, but the process went exceptionally slowly: only 0.03 percent in 1989, and 0.07 percent of apartment residents, turned their apartments into their "private property." Only in July of 1991 did the Supreme Soviet adopt the law allowing for full privatization of apartments. *Ogonek,* 38 (September 1991), p. 18.

60 See Celestine Bohlen, "Moscow Privatization Yields Privacy and Problems," *Sunday New York Times,* Feb. 28, 1993.

61 This statistic was given in a Russian news program (*Novosti,* August 10, 1993).

8 PARADOXES OF UNIFIED CULTURE: FROM STALIN'S FAIRY-TALE TO MOLOTOV'S LACQUER-BOX

In the last years of the Soviet Union a Moscow journalist observed: "The unique Russian character is shaped by Russian bread lines, Russian inefficiency, as well as Russian culture... a powerful word, which has replaced everything—democracy, law, education, food."[1] In Russia, "Culture"—defined in the singular and with a capital "C"—has survived as an emblem of national identity for nearly 150 years. It has become a kind of civic religion that has led to many contradictory phenomena, to the flourishing of both literature and censorship, to the cult of the poet as a national hero and to poets' physical extermination. In the nineteenth century, "culture" was often synonymous with literature, and Russians were defined less by blood or class than by being a unique community of readers of Russian literature.[2] According to Vissarion Belinsky, who masterminded the cult of literature in Russian society, "Our literature has created the morals of our society, has already educated several generations . . . has produced a sort of special class in society that differs from the 'middle estate' in that it consists not of the merchantry and commoners [*meshchanstvo*] alone but of people of all estates who have been drawn together through education, which, with us, centered exclusively in a love of literature."[3] These words and those of the perestroika journalist encompass the birth and twilight of the literature-centric and culture-centric Russian universe, from the intelligentsia's quasi-religious cult of culture to the avant-garde dreams of an aesthetic transformation of the world, from the Soviet policy of mass culturization to the dissent of underground art. The Russian intelligentsia creatively reinterpreted the German Romantic idea of "culture," defined in opposition to the French and English Enlightenment idea of "civilization." This unique spiritual culture, the foundation of Russian national identity, was opposed to transnational "Western" individualism and its "civilizing process," often perceived as "artificial," false and inauthentic.[4] Socialist realism represents the last organized attempt at creating an "all-people's culture," translating into life the old dream of the Russian intelligentsia, with an ironic or tragic twist.

In Stalin's time the word "culture" acquired an important suffix, and the slogan of the 1920s, "cultural revolution," turned into an advocacy of *kulturnost* (culturalization). This term included not only the new Soviet artistic canon, but also manners, ways of behavior, and discerning taste in food and consumer goods. Culturalization was one way of translating ideology into the everyday; it was a kind of Stalinist "civilizing process" that taught Marxist-Leninist ideology together with table manners, mixing Stalin with Pushkin. Material possessions, crêpe-de-chine dresses, old-fashioned dinnerware, and household decorations were no longer regarded as petit bourgeois; rather, they were presented as legitimate awards for the heroes and heroines of labor, for the marching enthusiasts of the new Stalinist order. Moscow was proclaimed the premier communist city of the future, the most "cultured city in the world." Moscow citizens were encouraged to discover new pleasures in Metro rides or walks in the Parks of Culture and Leisure, where they could taste delicious, newly imported ice cream. Culturalization offered a way of legitimating the formerly despised bourgeois concerns about status and possession; it both justified and disguised the new social hierarchies and privileges of the Stalinist elite.[5]

The aim of socialist realist mass culturalization was to synthesize—in a peculiar Hegelian-Marxist-Stalinist manner—the old opposition between culture and civilization, high and low art, public and private genres. Yet unified socialist realist culture hardly presented a unity of grand style. It was rather a kind of monstrous hybrid of various inconsistent elements from right and left: aristocratic and proletarian culture; radical avant-garde rhetoric and the chaste Victorian morals of nineteenth-century realism; happy endings and nature descriptions from popular fiction of the turn of the century; and "positive heroes" from the Russian classics and Slavic hagiographies.[6] The only thing that was consistent and unified about it was its dependence on Soviet power.

To understand the paradoxes of unified culture we might look at two newly revived genres of Stalinist art that could be easily incorporated into everyday life: the "mass song" (*massovaya pesnya*) and the lacquer box. The song reflected the futuristic aspirations and technological dreams of the recently defeated avant-garde, while the box embodied the desire to preserve and rewrite Russian national traditions and the "peasant art" that avant-gardists opposed. The song flirted with the future, while the box recreated the allure of the past; the song affirmed that "fairy tales would come true," while the box made fairy tales look realistic. Furthermore, in the last years of Stalin's power, the lacquer box became a kind of Pandora's box for Stalinist criticism, reflecting the debates over mimesis in socialist realism and the "lacquering (or "varnishing") of reality" (*lakirovka deistvitelnosti*), and testing the limits of socialist realist doctrine.

"March of the Aviators": Singing the Unreadable

The song helps us build and live,
It is like a friend who leads us ahead.
The one who marches through life with a song
Will never be stranded again!

This popular song from one of the most celebrated musicals of the 1930s celebrates itself: it is self-referential, a "mass song" about the importance of mass singing. Indeed, singing was an important part of the Stalinist *Bildung*. Stalinism was not merely a political system, but also a mentality, a way of life and a grand totalitarian spectacle that needed to be continually reenacted. The favored genres were no longer poetry or even the novel, but rather the arts of mass spectacle—film, ballet, and organized popular festivities. The move was toward a collectivization of the utopian vision, as in the words of the popular song entitled "The March of the Aviators":

We were born to make fairy tales come true
To conquer distances and space
Reason gave us steel wings for arms
And a flaming motor for a heart.
And higher, and higher, and higher
We aim the flight of our wings,
And the hum of our propellers
Spreads peace across our borders.

Our sharp gaze pierces every atom
Our every nerve is bold and resolute
And trust us: to any ultimatum
An answer will give our Air Fleet!

Here the romantic metaphor of the flaming heart is wedded to love for the machine; these cheerful humanoids with wings and motors in their chests are the product of Futurist and Constructivist imaginations. One is reminded of avant-garde ballets in which the dancers impersonated machine parts and made mechanical gestures instead of the undulating, organic movements of classical dance. The protagonist of the song is not a Whitmanesque poet or a modern Icarus. It is rather a collective, patriotic "we," projected onto the millions of people who were supposed to fall in love with the song—and they did. The song has an amazing history that reveals a continuity between the art of the 1920s and the 1930s and kinship with other totalitarian cultures.[7] Written in 1920 by the little-known team of poet B. German and composer D. Hait, the song became popular in the 1930s and in 1933 was adopted as the official march of aviators. It was translated into German and sung by the German communists; later, its catchy melody captured the imagination of the Nazis, who took the song for their own. After the words "and higher and higher and higher," they sang "Heil Hitler and dethrone the Jews," which was particularly ironic since the song's composers were Jewish. What it shows is how easily the words of a catchy patriotic tune can circulate from one totalitarian culture to another. The phrase "we were born to make fairy tales come true" became one of the central slogans of the time; it functioned like an advertising logo and was frequently recycled as a caption for paintings and for newspaper articles. These words were sung during the years of collectivization and hunger, of purges and war. The march was frequently played on the radio to cheer up the Soviet youth as they performed heroic feats of labor. (My father, a Soviet émigré whose mother spent five years in a Stalinist labor camp, still occasionally hums his own version of the "March of the Aviators" as he washes dishes in his well-equipped American kitchen, with the TV on.)

According to the most popular songwriter of the 1930s, Lebedev Kumach, what people needed during those years was a song "with distinct patriotic character," a song-slogan, a "song-poster" (*pesnyaplakat, pesnya-lozung*). The march, like the songs he composed for the "Stalinist musicals" of the 1930s, was "from the musical point of view, . . . a cheerful [*bodryi*] march with robust rhythm; from the verbal point of view, . . .

lines not connected by inner plot, lines patriotic in content . . . with lyrical tonality."[8] The new Soviet song was not supposed to present a coherent narrative but to offer a series of life-affirming punch lines and slogans. A close reading of the song points out its elements of absurdity and incongruity. Among other things, the "flaming motor for a heart" makes us apprehensive about the general success of this flight. But a mass song was not created to be read closely. The art of mass spectacle was not made for interpretation; indeed, it was extremely suspicious of interpretation and of any attempt at individual comprehension instead of shared experience. And one of those shared experiences was fear. The incantatory power of the song could only be enhanced by the fear of interpretation internalized by the participants in the optimistic march. The song was made not to be read, but only to be memorized and repeated as an incantation of fairytale magic. The commonplaces of socialist realist art, the slogans and punch lines, functioned collectively as a magic force that programmatically aroused a certain predictable emotional, even behavioral, quasi-Pavlovian response. To understand the "March of the Aviators" it is necessary, first of all, to sing it in a crowd.

Boris Groys claims that Stalinist art is not merely a return to academism and conservatism, but an even more radical continuation of the avant-garde project.[9] Avant-garde theorists and Russian Formalists regarded every new period in art in terms of how it managed to lay bare its modes of operation and devices, seeing art in terms of undoing, defamiliarizing, and critical negativity. Socialist realist art did not simply, unselfconsciously, believe in the transparency of language, as did some of the realists of the nineteenth century. Rather, it self-consciously promoted the manipulation of consciousness, using the techniques that automatically secure specific emotional responses. Moreover, there was an ideological and theoretical justification for that radical self-conscious "automatization of consciousness," turning it into a collective unconscious not in a Freudian or Jungian sense, but in a Pavlovian sense. According to Groys, "Stalinist culture [was] very interested in different models of the formation of the unconscious, without exposing its mechanisms, as in the theories of Pavlov, or in Stanislavsky's method, which required the actor to enter the role so completely as to forget his identity."[10]

To read socialist realist texts as texts, revealing their strategies of manipulation, can yield important insights into the Stalinist coverup. But this approach, in turn, covers up the central blindness of such analysis—its failure to theorize or to incorporate into the framework of critical inquiry *emotion,* that "demon" of Russian literature and culture. In fact, Vladimir Propp, in his pioneering study of fairy tales, analyzed them merely as *tales,* as narratives, failing to confront the element of the marvelous which explains how they could have operated in society. The Stalinist fairy tale cannot be read merely on a textual level. Otherwise, one would be confronted with its sheer absurdity and fail to comprehend how it could have come true, even if only in the imagination. Stalinist magical commonplaces only became commonplaces when they were enacted in popular spectacular rituals; they were hypothetical commonplaces that existed nowhere; they were omnipotent because circumscribed and guarded by fear. And there was no child who would have innocently disclosed them as the emperor's new clothes. This happy dénouement belongs in a foreign fairy tale.

Saul Friedländer has proposed a distinction between the kitsch of death characteristic of Nazi Germany and the more innocuous and "life-affirming" kitsch of Stalinist Russia.[11] Indeed, in the socialist realist universe of the 1930s the emphasis on death was not crucial. Early socialist realist novels written before World War II were motivated neither by love nor by death—*pace* Freud—but rather by the drama of labor, of overcoming the petit-bourgeois self and partaking of the heroic collective spirit.[12] After the war, however, many war heroes entered the Soviet pantheon, and the scene of the death of a hero became crucial for postwar iconography—be it Alexander Matrosov, the pilot Gastello, or the partisan Zoya Kosmedemyanskaya. Not death as such, but a heroic feat, an ultimate victory, and the official resurrection of the tortured hero were brought to the fore. In spite of this difference in emphasis, victory over death in the communist socialist realist universe and the glorification of death in Nazi art manipulated the same emotional and behavioral structures. Milan Kundera has described a socialist realist revolutionary festivity in which the French communist and surrealist poet Paul Eluard joins the Czech people in a dance around the scene of a public execution of another poet, the Czech surrealist Zavis Kalandra.[13] So the dancing ring of a new generation of youthful enthusiasts hid the scene of execution from view. After all, it is hard to say whether there was much difference between being killed with Wagner's "Death of Isolde" blaring in the background or with the sounds of a life-affirming collective march. (This is metaphorically speaking, of course, because most of the victims of Hitler and Stalin were killed in much less theatrical settings.)

It was not by chance that so many songs celebrated the utopian, life-affirming spaces of the new Stalinist culture—as did, for example, a well-known song from another Alexandrov musical, *The Circus*:

Our country is the land of beauty,
Our country is the land of glee,
I don't know any other country
Where a man is so gloriously free.[14]

In Stalin's time, geography was perhaps the most political of all sciences: in the song, the multinational Soviet Union is completely remapped and deterritorialized; the spaces of terror, the camps, are hidden from view and absent from the maps. Instead, another utopian ideological map of the motherland is created, that of a "land of beauty and a land of glee." The utopian iconography of the "greatest country in the world" was reflected on both micro and macro levels—in the monumental mosaic *panneaux* of the Stalinist subway and on the black lacquer miniatures that Maxim Gorky called "the little miracles of the Revolution."

"Lacquering Reality": Molotov's Lacquer Box

At a Moscow flea market I recently came across a unique gadget, a perfect fetish of Stalinist culturalization, which illustrates many paradoxes of the idea of unified culture. It is a traditional *Palekh* box representing Molotov and Stalin as folk-heroes (*bogatyrs*) on a black lacquered background. The Palekh box is an example of the official reinvention of Russian national culture that began in the 1930s, as well as a sample of the everyday rituals of the Stalin era. Inside the box is a little visiting card that reads: "Mrs. Molotov has the honor of inviting you for an afternoon tea on September 13 at 5 o'clock."[15] The writing is in the old-fashioned script—elegant, ceremonious, and refined. Afternoon tea chez Madame Molotov, wife of the general and hero of the Civil War and the "Great Patriotic War" (World War II) perfectly exemplifies the rituals of the Stalinist haut monde, the last aristocratic revival by the grand-style Soviet nouveaux riches. The box provides a rich insight into the everyday life of the Stalinist elite and embodies some quite old-fashioned ideals of "culture" and "culturalization."

It might come as a surprise that the "traditional Russian lacquer box" was in fact a very recent invention. After the Revolution the craftsmen and icon painters organized themselves into the *Artel* (Workshop) of Proletarian Art and began to use Russian icon-painting techniques to depict revolutionary fairy tales on traditional Japanese lacquer boxes. Gorky called it "a little miracle of the Revolution" and praised the transformation of the "craft into true artistic mastery."[16] Palekh box makers, in turn, followed the example of nineteenth-century *kustars,* who had organized an industrialized production of Russian crafts primarily for the new middle class, nostalgic for premodern Russian ways and eager to consume them in prefabricated (modern) packaging. This contributed to the creation of pseudo-Russian style and to a national revival. Much of the "folk art" was intended for international exhibitions abroad and was consumed by foreigners as Russian premodern picturesque objects. Hence there was a continuity between the consumer culture at the turn of the nineteenth century and that of the Stalin era.

When Walter Benjamin visited Moscow in 1926, he was fascinated not by the future-oriented technology and pace of progress, but by the old-fashioned Russian toys and the black lacquer boxes from the Museum of Popular Crafts. Here is how Benjamin described it:

There are the heavy little boxes with scarlet interiors; on the outside on a gleaming-black background, a picture. . . . A *troika* with its three horses races through the night, or a girl in a seablue dress stands at night beside green flaring bushes, waiting for her lover. No night of terror is as dark as this durable lacquer myth in whose womb all that appears in it is enfolded. I saw a box with a picture of a seated woman selling cigarettes. Beside her stands a child who wants to take one. Pitch-black night here too. . . . On the woman's apron is the word "Mosselprom." She is the Soviet Madonna with cigarettes.[17]

This exemplary Soviet allegorical artifact, with its dark background and red interior, had a contemporary surface: the Mosselprom Madonna with cigarettes was the perfect salesgirl for Soviet ideology.

For socialist realist critics, blind to the black terror of the night, these were examples of life-affirming, colorful popular art, at once useful and decorative. Yet in the last years of Stalinism the lacquer box turned into a controversial object of ideology that represented the terror of Stalinist criticism. One of the key terms in socialist realist criticism, "the varnishing of reality," came from the critical discussion of ideologically incorrect lacquer boxes, which we can dub "the critique of the pure lacquer box." The lacquer box was a unique product of Stalinist arts and crafts, exactly the kind of object that was burned during avant-garde "campaigns against domestic trash" in the 1920s and 1960s, yet one that would become a decorative objet d'art in the 1970s—the ideal gift for foreign guests, a beautiful, well-packaged box of Russian exotica.

In the early 1950s the boxes became a focus of the discussion of "people's culture," as well as of the critique of "conflictlessness" (*bezkonfliktnost*). Ideological correctness was at that time a complex balancing act. The boxes were supposed to reflect the Soviet "people's spirit" (*narodnost*) but not the "common people's spirit" (*prostonarodnost*); to give examples of "refined artistic quality" (*tonkii artistizm*) but not of mannerism (*mannerizm*); to reflect taste (*vkus*) but not "pseudo-tastefulness" (*vkusovshchina*). All the ambiguities of Stalinist mimesis found their reflection on these lacquered surfaces:

> The overcoming of some mistakes by certain Palekh painters consists not in the escape into naturalism, into mere copying [*kopirovka*] into a "light" stylization "à la Palekh." What is required is further study of reality, a development of the progressive tradition of Palekh arts, which consists of ideological wholeness [*ideinaya nasyshchennost*] of the works, their life-affirming spirit, festive brightness of coloring, and subtle artistry, along with great artistic taste, wise mastery of composition, expressive laconic drawing, and finally, attention to different kinds of decorative art.[18]

Everything that appeared in quotation marks in the criticism of the Stalin era was meant to be an insult; it parodied the words of the invisible enemy that was everywhere. In this case, the enemies were "naturalism," on the one hand, and "stylization," on the other. The words "craft," "artifact," and "copy" tended to be negatively valorized in Stalinist criticism. While copying and reproduction were central to socialist realist practice (as to most artistic practices in general), they were vehemently criticized in theory. "Stylization" posed a great threat to socialist realist aesthetics by explicitly deploying the evil scare quotes of irony and aesthetic distance and thus putting "ideological wholeness" in doubt. The ritual nature of the work, its reenactment of ideological and aesthetic formulas, was carefully "varnished" by the critics. Hence the explicitly stated intentionality of the miniature painter, his or her creative revolutionary impetus, was of central ideological importance. While in the capitalist world craftsmen were "poor beggars deprived of rights," in Soviet Russia the "people's painters [affirmed] their creative personality."[19] The artist was a "genius of the people," and despite the traditional nature of the work, artists were called "original treasures" (*samorodki*). They received praise for being both decorative and useful, but their utility was defined quite vaguely as "certain everyday meaning" (*nekii bytovoi smysl*). For instance, one of the lacquer boxes representing the traditional troika was described as "a useful traveler's item" (*dorozhnyi predmet*). Yet it is somehow difficult to imagine that a cultured Soviet citizen would have used the lacquer box painted with a troika for travel on the crowded Soviet train (unless, of course, he or she never had to take the crowded train and instead traveled in a black car with the black lacquer box).

The Palekh craftsmen were frequently criticized for trying to embody a "new revolutionary content in the old form." The conflict of form and content haunted the miniature-painters for thirty years. The debates around lacquer boxes reveal certain important hierarchies among artistic genres of Stalinist culture. Since literature was the arche-art, the model for both the nineteenth-century idea of an "all-people's culture" and the socialist realist culture, the Palekh painters worked on many illustrations of Russian and Soviet classics. Pushkin was a common favorite; the hundredth anniversary of his death was celebrated in 1937 by the production of hundreds of lacquer boxes depicting scenes from his fairy tales. Other Soviet classics that were illustrated were Blok's long poem *Twelve* and Gorky's romantic tales. The lacquer boxes, miniatures, and small objects in general presented a great problem for the unified epic style of socialist realism. Its creative geniuses were urged to tackle new, ambitious subjects such as "The Battle of Stalingrad" or "Comrade Stalin giving a speech on the meeting of Batumi workers in 1902," all in the space of a small lacquer box. Critics instructed the miniature-painters to learn from the epic styles of urban sculpture (*uchitsia u Vucheticha*) and to think further about the boxes' "architechtonics." (The boxes' "plumpness" was criticized, perhaps for being incompatible with the modern age of physical culture.) However, some modern genres like photography were rejected. One critic denounced the use of photographs for portraiture on the lacquer boxes and appealed to the Palekh artists to make their lacquer miniature "in *plein air* and from the original [*pisat s natury!*]"[20] Here we encounter one reductio ad absurdum of Stalinist criticism: to paint lacquer boxes in "plein air" is equivalent to flying with a "flaming motor." The key here is that Stalinist criticism functioned quite similarly to the "March of the Aviators": not to be read for meaning, but rather reenacted, an obligatory ritual of invoking familiar formulas with mild variations that are understandable to the initiated few and feared by the uninitiated many. Even the clichés themselves were borrowed from different discourses and layers of culture—from right and left, radical and conservative idioms—including the writings of the nineteenth-century intelligentsia, the conventions of academia, Bolshevik slogans, and, occasionally, the campaign slogans of the avant-garde. Behind the eclecticism of Stalinist culture, one can see similar rules of the game and mechanisms of collective performance.

Socialist realist critics insisted on their crucial educational role in the life of the artists; they presented themselves as responsible for the artists' ideological Bildung:

> One should not think that the Palekh artists arrived at their perfect mastery, their great life-affirming art, without individual creative failures, without a struggle of opinions around their wonderful work. In those periods Palekh artists experienced doubts over whether their chosen route was the right one; they experienced bitterness at the just charges of mannerism, of narrowness (at first) in their themes, in their unjustified attempts to reveal new content in the old canonical form (also, only at first). With the help of well-wishing critics [*dobrozhelatelnye kritiki*], the Palekh artists successfully overcame their mistakes and grew to be excellent masters in their field.[21]

The cautious tendentiousness of this critical self-praise requires no comment. The adjective "well-wishing" was frequently used as a euphemism for informers, whom the KGB referred to as "well-wishers." Yet in this case, "well-wishing" criticism might also appear to be a kind of self-defense and self-justification. "Art criticism" in Stalin's time was a peculiar balancing act, more about the art of survival than about art; criticism could cost the artist his life, and a lack of criticism could cost the critic his job. Thus he usually had more training in ideology and the propaganda of culturalization than in art history. The high seriousness of socialist realist criticism bordered on absurdity because it did not acknowledge the distinction between literal and metaphorical levels; art could become life, and vice versa; metaphors had to be practiced—often in the most "naturalistic" fashion. While some painters of the lacquer miniature might have been forced to work in plein air, it was not the consistency of vision that mattered, but the gusts of power and its whims. At the end, the "varnishing of reality" was not a critique of representation, but rather a polishing up of that critique; it was an internal critique within the system. Evgeny Dobrenko sees "lacquered reality" as "a mechanism of literary politics": "Everything that was later called 'the theory of conflictlessness' [bezkonfliktnost] was a part of an apology for the system, characteristic of totalitarian culture. On the other hand, the system itself was based on the mentality of conflict and confrontation, the cult of struggle and the search for the enemy."[22] In the 1960s, when totalitarian culture began to lose its magic spell and its clearly delineated boundaries of power, the slogan "varnishing of reality" was used again, but with a different signification. In the era of Khruschev's thaw, the slogan was still taken literally and its reflective aesthetic surface was not questioned. The intelligentsia of the 1960s proposed to substitute one kind of "impossible aesthetic" of life for another, which would be more "sincere." In 1980s art, the critique of varnished reality went through a more radical perestroika, and the songs, boxes, and metaphors of socialist criticism seemed to acquire the necessary estranging quotation marks.[23]

Having survived all the balancing acts of moribund Stalinist criticism, the Molotov Palekh box has now become a perfect totalitarian antique, a Stalinist objet de *folk* art, sold at the flea market together with the more expensive czarist eggs. The addressee of this refined invitation for tea and the history of this Stalinist family souvenir remain unknown. Yet one doesn't have to throw out the idea of culture with the Molotov lacquer box. The end of the culture-centric epoch does not have to lead to the decline of the arts at the turn of the next century, but only to the decline of their central educational and ideological role in society. In a sense, there are more ways now of dreaming "world culture"—or, to paraphrase Osip Mandelshtam, of "longing for the world culture"—than there ever were before, although this longing itself is becoming outmoded. It remains to be seen whether it will be possible to reinvent a Russian identity that will not depend on a unified Russian culture: an identity that would acknowledge differences and paradoxes beyond polished-up picturesque reflections in pseudo-Russian style.

Notes

1   A. Bossart, "A ia ostaiusia s toboiu," *Ogonek,* No. 44 (1989): 31; quoted in Irina Corten, *Vocabulary of Soviet Society and Culture* (Durham, 1992), 73. Corten offers many wonderful examples of the Soviet usage of the word "culture." Apparently the word entered post-perestroika slang, and "cul'turno" is now synonymous with "cool."

2   This explains why the word "culture" does not get much attention in Dal's *Dictionary,* where the first meaning given is "cultivation" (*obrabotka i ukhod, vozdelyvanie, vozdelka*), and the second is moral and intellectual "education" (*obrazovanie umstvennoe i nravstvennoe*); see Vol. 2, p. 217.

3   Vissarion Belinsky, "Thoughts and Notes on Russian Literature" (1846).

4   Here is how Norbert Elias described this opposition, in *The History of Manners,* trans. Edmund Jephcott (New York, 1982), 5: The French and English concept of civilization can refer to political or economic, religious or technical, moral or social facts. The German concept of *Kultur* refers essentially to intellectual, artistic and religious facts. . . . "Civilization" describes a process or at least the result of the process. . . . The German concept of *Kultur* has a different relation to motion. The concept of *Kultur* delimits. To a certain extent, the concept of civilization plays down the national differences between peoples; it emphasizes what is common to all human beings or—in the view of its bearers—should be. In contrast, the German concept of *Kultur* places special stress on national differences and particular identity of the group. See also Jean Starobinski, "The Word Civilization," in *Blessings in Disguise; or The Morality of Evil,* trans. Arthur Goldhammer (Cambridge, MA, 1993), 1–36. From Ivan Kireevsky to Nikolai Berdiaev, Russian culture was viewed in opposition to "civilization," which was described as "mercantile" and individualistic. This polarization is problematic, however, in that the history of both words themselves internalize this opposition. In other words, the history of "civilization" in French exposes the battle between true and false civilization, and the same applies to the idea of culture. Thus no good or evil attaches to either "culture" or "civilization" as such; it depends entirely on the context. Starobinski writes that in mapping civilizations and cultures, "what matters is the shifting patterns of boundaries and distinctive systems of value, not the qualitative judgement we might make." In his view, "civilization"— and I will add "culture" as well—has to be seen both as "threatening and threatened, persecutor and persecuted. It is no longer a safe haven for those who shelter beneath its roof." Culture in the Russian context is this kind of a double-edged sword; it can be seen as a way of survival and of domination, of creating a community and of delimiting it, a way of dreaming of aesthetic emancipation and of taming those dreams. For more detailed discussion, see Svetlana Boym, *Common Places: Mythologies of Everyday Life in Russia* (Cambridge, MA, 1994).

5 On the concept of *kul'turnost'*, see Vera Dunham, *In Stalin's Time* (Cambridge, 1976); and Sheila Fitzpatrick, "Becoming Cultured: Socialist Realism and the Representation of Privilege and Taste," in *The Cultural Front: Power and Culture in Revolutionary Russia* (Ithaca, 1992), 216–17. I am grateful to Golfo Alexopoulos for bringing Sheila Fitzpatrick's new project to my attention.

6 Evgeny Dobrenko offers an insightful history of the "sources of Socialist Realism," which he finds not only in classical Russian literature or in high avant-garde art, but also in less canonical cultural stratas and subcultures, especially in the works of poet-proletarians and peasants of the early twentieth century; see "Levoi, levoi, levoi! Metamorfozy revoliutsionnoj kul'tury," *Novyi mir*, No. 3 (March 1992).

7 I am grateful to Felix Rosiner for sharing with me the information about this song. See Vladimir Frumkin, "Ran'she my byli marksisty: Pesennye sviazi dvukh sotsializmov," in *Obozrenie*, No. 17, to *Russkaia Mysl'* (Paris), November 1985.

8 Grigory Alexandrov, *Epokha i Kino* (Moscow, 1976), 286.

9 Boris Groys, *The Total Art of Stalinism*, trans. Charles Rougle (Princeton, 1992). The relationship between the avant-garde and socialist realism is one of the central issues in the contemporary debate about Soviet postmodernism. Indeed, what did occupy the space between the prefix "post" and the root of the word "modernism"? What is the place of socialist realism, which comes directly after modernism in Soviet culture? In the 1960s and 1970s many writers and critics emphasized the break between the two, the war of languages and tastes between the avant-garde's nomadism and the socialist realist establishment. In the 1980s it was more fashionable to emphasize the continuity between the two, while insisting on the radical discontinuity between "Russian" and "Soviet." This led some Russian postmodern theorists to claim that Russians invented postmodernism and the practice of simulation, as described by Jean Baudrillard. Socialist realism is postmodern in one sense only: historically, it comes after modernism; ideologically, it discards its heritage.At first glance, avant-garde art seems to be about reflection on language and defamiliarization, while socialist realism seems to be about precisely the opposite: a cover-up of rhetoric and an attempt at a new familiarization. This familiarization is even more uncanny than the avant-garde's defamiliarization because it seeks to make the most impossible and the fantastic into the familiar. The "realism" part of socialist realism has virtually nothing to do with the everyday existence of Soviet citizens; it does not even attempt to mimic or imitate it. The point is to enact the mythical and utopian world and thus bring it into existence. On the other hand, what socialist realism shares with the avant-garde is its total—and potentially totalizing—vision and the rejection of art as an autonomous domain of the beautiful in favor of the idea of art as a "road to life," to use the title of a popular film of the 1930s. Of course, the avant-garde has never achieved, and perhaps never could have achieved, its project of bringing art into the praxis of life; it is too caught up in the creative search for a new language and a new, antisubjective subjectivity. See Peter Burger, *The Theory of the Avant-Garde* (Minneapolis, 1984).

10 Groys, *Total Art of Stalinism*, 67.

11 Saul Friedländer, "Kitsch and Apocalyptic Imagination," *Salmagundi* 85/86 (1990): 201–6.

12 This is discussed in Katerina Clark, *The Soviet Novel: History as Ritual* (Chicago, 1981).

13 Milan Kundera, *The Book of Laughter and Forgetting* (London, 1983).

14 I am using a Soviet translation of the song from the time of stagnation, which was learned by heart in Soviet English schools of the 1970s to be performed for foreign visitors. The English translation is somewhat unfaithful to the Russian original, but it rhymes!

15 I do not exclude the possibility that the box was an artful fake made for the foreign market. Yet many similar boxes were produced in Stalin's time and many old-fashioned parties were held in the Kremlin for Party members.

16 Quoted in G. Zhidkov, "Laki," *Iskusstvo*, No. 2 (1947):33.

17 Walter Benjamin, "Moscow," in *Reflections*, ed. Peter Demetz, trans. Edmund Jephcott (New York, 1978), 114.

18 N. Sobolevskii, "Iskusstvo Palekha," *Iskusstvo*, No. 6 (1955): 28.

19 Ibid., 26.

20 Ibid., 30.

21 Ibid., 28.

22 Evgenii Dobrenko, "Pravda zhizni" kak formula real'nosti," *Voprosy literatury*. No. 1 (1992):23.

23 In the 1990s, the new, self-proclaimed "elite" of the Russian cinema has created nostalgic visions of the festive and macabre life of Stalinist elites. This retro art reflects a peculiar kind of nostalgia—not for Stalinism, but for the last grand style of Russian culture. Once it became stylized—an operation that Stalinist critics decried—the socialist realist world looked much more aesthetically unified in those films than it actually was. For further discussion, see my "Stalin's Cinematic Charisma: Between History and Nostalgia," *Slavic Review* 51 (1992): 536–43.

PART THREE

THAT HISTORICAL EMOTION (1996–2001)

Boym's work on the "historical emotions" which charge everyday experience with political and aesthetic potential culminated in *The Future of Nostalgia*, a 2001 book that reached far beyond academic circles. More than a cultural archaeology, the book is a paean to "a freedom to remember." For Boym, this entails not just the recreation of a monolithic and idealized past but also the liberty to "choose the narratives of the past and remake them." The analysis of everyday life carried out in *Common Places*, which revealed the aesthetic dimension to such homely installations as a mantelpiece display in a Soviet collective apartment, now extends to the larger project of modernity, whose breaks and discontinuities are perpetually, though never permanently, healed by invented traditions and personal investments of creative feeling into the humdrum panorama of passing years. Looming especially large is the collapse of the Communist world, whose painful history becomes, with its passage, retrievable as kitsch, commercialization, playfulness, and pastiche—disturbingly or gloriously inauthentic reformulations of the life that millions of people lived. In Boym's nuanced readings of public monuments and private memorials to the end of this era, the nostalgic afterlife of Soviet power becomes paradigmatic of a distinctly modern condition that has come to undergird political paranoia and resurgent nationalism, the enlightenment project of accumulated knowledge, and the simultaneous restoration and falsification of everything from mineral water to the Sistine Chapel.

Key to the discussion is the distinction between two modes of looking back, "restorative" and "reflective" nostalgia. Boym takes clear sides. Restorative nostalgia is paranoid; it reacts to the forces of degradation that conspire to erode what it imagines as essential character and purity of tradition; in pining for the good old days, it creates a political community that is united by fear of loss and a hope that the past can be restored by brute force. Where restorative nostalgia is self-serious, imitative, and dogmatic, reflective nostalgia is—like its author—ironic, creative, and cosmopolitan. An expansive and ultimately insatiable longing, it takes pleasure in its own failure to be entirely constrained by a single image of authenticity. Reflective nostalgia is not nationalist but global and, in Boym's reading, essentially urban; the megalopolis becomes a site of contested remembrance, the screen on which natives and newcomers alike project kaleidoscopic illusions of authenticity, narratives of decay, and spontaneous recreations of the public sphere within a phantasmal geography of commercial capital and political conspiracy.

Boym is especially drawn to a canon of figures who, like her, intellectually engaged their own condition of displacement in order to create imaginary homelands out of the double consciousness or "double exposure" of exile, which superimposes the specters of another land, life, and language onto material surroundings that become in the same stroke unreal. In one essay, Boym shows how the Serbian author—and Parisian exile—Danilo Kiš reframes the nationalist, conspiratorial confabulation that is the *Protocols of the Elders of Zion* within a rootless and cosmopolitan ethics of estrangement. In our selection from *The Future of Nostalgia*, she turns to Vladimir Nabokov's "syncopal kick" of exile: a missed heartbeat and a heartsick missing, which puts the time out of joint by vanishing into an imagined time and place. This impossible time and space of the aesthetic is the heart of that perfectly intimate "textual labyrinth" of longing into which we too are drawn, a dreamy home in which the author casts himself at once as a monstrous minotaur, victorious hero, and abandoned lover.

In the conclusion of her book, Boym projects nostalgia forward, noting that "cyberspace" is already a dated term for the technological shifts that have exacerbated the modern condition of virtuality and displacement, to the point of upending time and space. Kant wrote that "space is public and time is private," but the contemporary global elite inhabits spacious dwellings rather than communal apartments; at the same time, even our moments alone are colonized by multitasking, virtual friendships, one-click shopping, and working from home. Her meditations on cyberspace are echoed in a more personal essay on Russian myths of space exploration; originally written to accompany a photographic exhibit, "Kosmos" shows how the glorious extraplanetary future of cosmonautics makes outer space into a memory of Earth, and makes the progress of technology into a sentimental myth of heroism. We are already nostalgic, Boym notes, for a present that is palpably dissolving into a virtual or inaccessible future. In the blur of that same border between lost and looming time, however, we still find the "creative emotion of nostalgia" and the cherished if always ironized ideals it furnishes us: the delights of art and an ethics of freedom.

Jacob Emery

9 ON DIASPORIC INTIMACY: ILYA KABAKOV'S INSTALLATIONS AND IMMIGRANT HOMES

Russian émigré writer Nina Berberova tells a story of domestic embarrassment. Some time in the early 1930s the writer Ivan Bunin paid a visit to Berberova and poet Vladislav Khodasevich in their little flat in the working-class outskirts of Paris that were populated by immigrants. The apartment hardly had any furniture and no particular dinner was served that night. Yet Bunin was irritated by Berberova's precarious domesticity: "'How do you like that! They have an embroidered cock on the teapot!' exclaimed Bunin once as he entered our dining room. 'Who could have imagined it! Poets, as we all know, live in a ditch, and now it turns out they have a cock on the teapot!'"[1] The embroidered cock symbolized a certain intimacy with everyday objects that appeared to be in profoundly bad taste for Russian intellectuals in exile. For Bunin, it was an example of domestic kitsch that compromised the purity of Russian nostalgia. The embroidered cock seemed like a cover-up of exilic pain; it betrayed a desire to inhabit exile, to build a home away from home. Berberova confesses to love that other deliberately chosen and freely inhabited domesticity that "is neither a 'nest' nor biological obligation" but something "warm, pleasant, and becoming to men."[2] She did not give up her embroidered teapot, whose decorative cock turned out to be a dangerous exilic bird. This embroidery was a handmade gift sent to Berberova from the Soviet Union by a woman friend who ended up in Siberian exile for having contacts abroad. Hardly an item of domestic kitsch, it was a souvenir of transient, exilic intimacy.

The notion of intimacy is connected to home; *intimate* means "innermost," "pertaining to . . . one's deepest nature," "very personal," "sexual."[3] I will speak about something that might seem paradoxical—a diasporic intimacy that is not opposed to uprootedness and defamiliarization but constituted by it. In the late twentieth century millions of people find themselves displaced from their places of birth, living in voluntary or involuntary exile. Their intimate experiences occur against a foreign background, where they are aware of the unfamiliar stage set whether they like it or not. Immigrants to the United States, moreover, often bring with them different traditions of social interaction, often less individualistic than those they encounter in their new surroundings. In contemporary American pop psychology one is encouraged "not to be afraid of intimacy," with a presumption that intimate communication can and should be made in plain language. You'd have to feel at home to be intimate, "to say what you mean." Immigrants—and many alienated natives as well—can't help but dread this kind of plain language. To intimate also means "to communicate with a hint or other indirect sign; [to] imply subtly."[4] Diasporic intimacy can be approached only through indirection and intimation, through stories and secrets. It is spoken in a foreign language that reveals the inadequacies of translation. Diasporic intimacy does not promise an unmediated emotional fusion but only a precarious affection—no less deep, while aware of its transience. In contrast to the utopian images of intimacy as transparency, authenticity, and ultimate belonging, diasporic intimacy is dystopian by definition; it is rooted in the suspicion of a single home. It thrives on unpredictable chance encounters, on hope for human understanding. Yet this hope is not utopian. Diasporic intimacy is not limited to the private sphere but reflects collective frameworks of memory that encapsulate even the most personal of dreams. It is haunted by images of home and homeland, yet it also discloses some of the furtive pleasures of exile.

Intimacy has its own historical topography. In the Western tradition it reflects the colonization of the world by a private individual. The maps of intimacy expand through the centuries: from precarious medieval retreats—a corner by the window or in the hallway, a secluded spot behind the orchard, a forest clearing—to the ostentatious bourgeois interiors of the nineteenth century, with their innumerable curio cabinets and chests of drawers, to the end of the twentieth century's transitory locations—the back seat of a car, a train compartment, an airport bar, a home page on the web. It might appear that intimacy is on the outskirts of the social;

it is local and particular, socially superfluous and noninstrumental. Yet, for better or for worse, each romance with intimacy is adulterated by a specific culture and society. The revulsion against the embroidered cock on the teapot might surprise an American reader for whom the pursuit of domestic happiness goes together with spiritual fulfillment, not in opposition to it. While intimate experiences are personal and singular, the maps of intimate sites are socially recognizable; they are encoded as refuges of the individual.[5] Intimacy is not solely a private matter; it may be protected, manipulated, or besieged by the state, framed by art, embellished by memory, or estranged by critique.

The twentieth century embraced intimacy as an ideal and also rendered it deeply suspicious. Hannah Arendt, for instance, criticizes intimacy as a retreat from worldliness. Whether the middle-class cult of intimacy or a special relationship cherished by a pariah group, a form of brotherhood that allows one to survive in a hostile world, intimacy, as Arendt sees it, is the shrinking of experience, something that binds us to a community (even if it is a pariah community), to home and homeland, rather than to the world.[6] Similarly, Richard Sennett argues that in contemporary American society the cult of intimacy has turned into a form of seductive tyranny that promised warmth, authentic disclosure, and boundless closeness and effectively led to the detriment of the public sphere and sociability.[7] Sennett's critique is directed against the late twentieth-century commercialized version of the Protestant cult of authenticity that could make everyday life inartistic, humorless, divested of worldliness and public significance. In this case intimacy is no longer a retreat from but a fulfillment of the dominant cultural ideology. This ideology of intimacy—not so much as actual experience but as promise, even as an entitlement—pervades all spheres of American life, from slick fresh breath advertisements of family values to informal support groups and minority communities.

The diasporic intimacy that interests me is neither the touchy-feely imperative of the fresh breath commercial nor the fraternal/sororial warmth of a minority group. Diasporic intimacy does not promise a comforting recovery of identity through shared nostalgia for the lost home and homeland. In fact, it's the opposite. It might be seen as the mutual enchantment of two immigrants from different parts of the world or as the sense of the fragile coziness of a foreign home. Just as one learns to live with alienation and reconciles oneself to the uncanniness of the world around and to the strangeness of the human touch, there comes a surprise, a pang of intimate recognition, a hope that sneaks in through the back door, punctuating the habitual estrangement of everyday life abroad.

A cultural genealogy of diasporic intimacy leads us away from the history of private life. We have to look for its modern beginnings in the alienating and illuminating experiences of the metropolis, in the double consciousness of the urban wanderers at once estranged from and engaged with the life around them. In his well-known essay on Baudelaire, Walter Benjamin speaks of a love at last sight in which a wanderer encounters an unknown woman in an urban crowd and experiences a shock of recognition and a sexual shudder.[8] The passerby disappears into urban anonymity, leaving behind a few declarations of love in the future perfect. This intimate shock occurs in the impersonal city crowd, not in the designated private refuge. Yet this extravagant love at last sight could be quite gratifying. Rather than seeming a melancholic sorrow, it reveals itself as a miracle of possibilities. Love at last sight strikes urban strangers when they realize they are on stage, at once actors and spectators. Georg Simmel, too, describes modern sociability as a playful and artistic form of association, "related to the content-determined concreteness of association as art is to reality."[9]

What might appear as an aestheticization of social existence to the "native," strikes the immigrant as an accurate depiction of the condition of exile. That is, of course, when the first hardships are over and the immigrant can afford the luxury of leisurely reflection. Immigrants always perceive themselves onstage, their lives resembling a mediocre fiction with occasional romantic outbursts and gray dailiness. Sometimes they see themselves as heroes of a novel, but such ironic realizations do not stop them from suffering through each and every novelistic collision of their own lives. As for the sexual shock, it becomes a commonplace. What is much more uncommon is a recognition of a certain kind of tenderness that could be more shuddering and surprising than a sexual fantasy. Benjamin's love at last sight is the spasm of loss after the revelation; the tenderness of the exiles is about a revelation of possibility after the loss. It is when the loss has been taken for granted that one can be surprised that not everything has been lost. Tenderness is not about complete disclosure, saying what one really means, getting closer and closer. It excludes absolute possession and fusion. It defies symbols of fulfillment and is not very goal oriented. In the words of Roland Barthes, "Tenderness . . . is nothing but an infinite, insatiable metonymy" and a "miraculous crystallization of presence."[10] In tenderness, need and desire are joined. Tenderness is always polygamous, nonexclusive. "Where you are tender you speak your plural."[11] The reciprocal enchantment of exiles has a touch of lightness about it. And, as Italo Calvino points out, lightness does not mean being detached from reality but cleansing it from its gravity, looking at it obliquely but not necessarily less profoundly.[12]

Diasporic intimacy is belated and never final; objects and places were lost in the past, and one knows that they can be lost again. The illusion of complete belonging has been shattered. Yet, one discovers that there is still a lot to share. The foreign backdrop, the memory of past losses, and the recognition of transience do not obscure the shock of intimacy but rather heighten the pleasure and intensity of surprise.

I would leave the reciprocal enchantment of exiles for future scholarly elaboration and focus, instead, on the imagination of home and on deliberate domesticity in exile. My site of diasporic intimacy is the "second home," which preserves many archeological layers of underground homemaking, fantasmic habitats, clandestine spaces of escape and intimacy. Here aesthetic and everyday practices become closely intertwined. One cannot theorize intimacy without exploring a few particular instances that have to be culture specific. My examples should not be seen as exemplary but rather as contradictory and somewhat contingent on my own background and research. However, I hope that, while particular, they will not be seen as local and exceptional. After all, it is precisely the common experience of dislocation that makes intimacy possible. We will start with home as art and then visit the homes of exile and their displays of diasporic souvenirs.

Intimate Art: Ilya Kabakov's Toilets and the Palace of the Future

The Russian word for intimacy—*intimnost'*—is of foreign origins and is registered only in twentieth-century dictionaries. Intimacy was decried as a dangerous bourgeois remainder in the 1920s during the campaigns against "domestic trash" and the aftereffects of the New Economic Policy. *Intimnost'* came to be fashionable in the 1960s when private life became a kind of escape from the official public life. Intimate spaces were created with the help of those much coveted Yugoslav standing lamps with bright lampshades, which provided a focalized lighting, illuminating the secret spaces of unofficial interaction. Yet, *intimnost'* was neither a family value nor even the experience of a couple, but was staged against some sort of collective background. This background might have been the official collective or a communal apartment, where most urban dwellers resided and from which they dreamed of escaping, or it might have been an intimate circle of friends that carved out their own alternative communality within the official edifice.[13] In the early 1960s, at the time of Khrushchev's thaw, such gatherings were humorously called "kitchen salons" and could be seen as the nucleus of civil society under the Soviet regime. In Brezhnev's time the kitchen salons gave way to the apartment exhibits of unofficial or antiofficial art.

Artist Ilya Kabakov pays tribute to those shared experiences of paradoxical Soviet intimacy. In the 1990s he created a series of labyrinthine "total installations" that represented the Soviet home in exile. Defamiliarizing home and inhabiting the uninhabitable are the two main obsessions that drive his work. Each installation stages an intimate encounter of the artist with his past and invites the viewers to do the same. Yet, this kind of intimate encounter with the past is never strictly personal; rather, it unfolds against the background of Soviet ruins, the ruins of the last modern utopia. One of his most "intimate" projects, *The Toilets*, provoked a national scandal after which he never returned to Russia.

In the 1970s Kabakov was close to the Moscow conceptualist movement, the last unofficial and occasionally underground art group, which became known in that decade through a series of apartment art exhibits (called aptart), samizdat editions, and events, some of which resulted in direct confrontations with the Soviet police and arrests. These artists created a rebuslike language of Soviet memory in which the official ideological symbols coexisted with trivial *objets trouvés*, unoriginal quotes, slogans, and domestic trash. The works of the conceptualists were often regarded as a Soviet parallel to pop art, but there was one significant difference: instead of advertisement culture they used the trivial and drab rituals of Soviet everyday life, too banal and insignificant to be recorded anywhere else, made taboo not because of their potential political explosiveness but because of their sheer ordinariness, their "all-too-human" scale. The conceptualists "quote" both the Russian avant-garde and socialist realism, as well as amateur crafts, kitsch, and collections of useless objects by ordinary people.

Kabakov's work always contains a dialogue between the ordinary and the utopian. If in the Soviet Union his work took the form of albums and fragmentary collections of Soviet *objets trouvés*, in exile Kabakov embraced the genre of total installation. Yet this totality is always precarious, and there is always something incomplete in his works, something about to break or to leak.[14] The artist's fate embodies many of the paradoxes of post-Soviet memory—from his own personal identification to the public reception of his work. Kabakov, according to the fifth line ("Nationality") in the Soviet passport, is Jewish; he was born in Dnepropetrovsk, the area in the Ukraine most heavily populated by Russians, and spent most of his life in Moscow. Even after the breakup of the Soviet Union and his departure from Russia, he called himself neither a Russian nor a Ukrainian artist, but a Soviet artist. That, of course, is an ironic self-definition. The end of the Soviet Union has put an end to the myth of the Soviet dissident artist. Sovietness, in this case, does not refer to politics but to a common culture. In what way is Kabakov a nostalgic Soviet artist? He embraces the idea of collective art; his installations offer an interactive narrative that could not exist without the viewer. Moreover, he turns himself into a kind of ideal communist collective made up of his own embarrassed alter egos, which include untalented artists, amateur collectors, and the "little men" of nineteenth-century Russian literature—Gogolian characters with Kafkaesque shadows—as well as the Soviet "little men," the anonymous communal apartment dwellers. Kabakov's installations evoke collective memories of intimate experiences of the Soviet era.

We will begin our tour of the Kabakovian home with its most private part—the toilet. Kabakov's installation *The Toilets* was presented at the 1992 Kassel *Documenta* show. An exact replica of provincial Soviet toilets, the kind that one encounters in bus and train stations, was brought to Kassel (fig. 1).[15] Kabakov describes them as "sad structures with walls of white lime turned dirty and shabby, covered by obscene graffiti that one cannot look at without being overcome with nausea and despair."[16] The original toilets didn't have any stall doors: everyone could see each other answering the call of nature in what in Russian was called "the eagle position," to be assumed while perched over the black hole. Like ordinary people's residences, toilets were communal. Voyeurism became nearly obsolete; rather, one developed the opposite tendency, less tempted to eavesdrop than to close one's eyes. Everyone who used the toilet had to accept the conditions of total visibility. Women's and men's toilets looked alike.

The toilets were placed behind the main building of *Documenta*, just where the outside toilets would normally be. Viewers had to stand in line to enter. Once inside, they find themselves in an ordinary Soviet two-room apartment, one that might be inhabited by "some respectable and quiet people" (*I*, p. 162) (figs. 2 and 3). Here, side by side with the black hole, everyday life continues uninterrupted. There is a table with a tablecloth, a glass cabinet, bookshelves, a sofa with a pillow, a reproduction of an anonymous Dutch painting, and children's toys, creating the sense of a captured presence: the dishes have not yet been cleared; a jacket has been dropped on a chair. Where are the apartment residents? They might have just stepped out for a moment to visit the *Documenta* exhibit.

Kabakov's exhibits are never entirely site-specific; rather, they are about displaced homes. They never include the human figure: it is the visitor to the exhibit who becomes a protagonist in Kabakov's narrative by inhabiting his empty interiors. In an interview, Kabakov declares that the project had two points of origin: his childhood memories and the circumstances that brought the installation to life. The artist tells the following story: After he was accepted as a child to a boarding school for art in Moscow, his mother decided to quit her job and move from Dnepropetrovsk to be with him. But she could not rent anything in the city, not even a corner, without a residence permit. So she became a laundry woman in the boarding school and slept in the laundry room, actually an old bathroom in which the toilets still remained. She arranged her folding bed there and kept the room meticulously tidy. Then the cleaning lady informed on her to the director and she was chased out. In Kabakov's own words, his mother felt "homeless and defenseless vis-à-vis the authorities, while, on the other hand, she was so tidy and meticulous that her honesty and persistence allowed her to survive in the most improbable place. My child psyche was traumatized by the fact that my mother and I never had a corner to ourselves" (*I*, p. 163).

Yet, Kabakov does not dwell for too long on his childhood sorrows but displaces the story onto another level. His tale of the project's conception is a tongue-in-cheek story of a poor Russian artist summoned to the sanctuary of the Western artistic establishment, the *Documenta* show, much to his embarrassment and humiliation:

With my usual nervousness I had the impression that I had been invited to see the Queen or to the palace where the fate of the arts is decided. For the artist this is a kind of Olympic Games. . . . The poor soul of a Russian impostor was in agony in front of these legitimate representatives of great contemporary art. Finding myself in this terrifying state, on the verge of suicide, I distanced myself from those great men, approached the window and looked out. . . . "Mama, help"—I begged in silence. . . . At last, my mother spoke to me from the other world and made me look through the window into the yard—and there I saw the toilets. Immediately the whole conception of the project was in front of my eyes to a minute detail. I was saved. [*I*, pp. 163–64][17]

This is a Cinderella tale of a post-Soviet artist who, with the help of his mom—at once a fairy and a muse—discovers his miracle toilets. The two origins of the toilet project are linked—the mother's embarrassment is reenacted by her artist son, who feels like an impostor, an illegal alien in the home of the Western contemporary art establishment. The toilet becomes the artist's diasporic home, an island of Sovietness with an insuppressible nostalgic smell that persists even in the most sanitized Western museum. Yet, for Kabakov, the museum is not simply a space of institutional alienation; quite the contrary, the museum can be intimately inhabited, turned into a perfect stage for diasporic intimacy. In his museum installation of Soviet toilets, Kabakov redeems the panic and embarrassment of his childhood through humor and aesthetic play. This redemption, of course, remains tantalizingly incomplete.

Another point of origin for Kabakov's toilets is to be found in the Western avant-garde tradition. There is a clear toiletic intertextuality between this project and Marcel Duchamp's *Fountain,* the mass-produced porcelain pissoir that Duchamp placed on a pedestal, signed with a pseudonym (R. Mutt), and proposed to exhibit at the American Society for Independent Artists (fig. 4). The exhibition's jury rejected the project, saying that while the urinal was a useful object, it was "by no definition, a work of art." In twentieth-century art history, this rejection has been seen as the birth of conceptual art and as an artistic revolution—one that happened to take place in 1917, a few months before the Russian Revolution. Subsequently, the original "intimate" pissoir splashed by the artist's signature vanished under mysterious circumstances, and the artistic photograph by Alfred Stieglitz made from the "lost original" added the aura of uniqueness to radical avant-garde gesture, making the pissoir look "like anything from a Madonna to a Buddha."[18] In 1964, Duchamp himself made an etching from Stieglitz's photograph and signed it with his own name. The permutations of the best-known toilet in art history perform a series of defamiliarizations, both of the mass-produced everyday object and the concept of art itself, ending with a paradox: by the end of the century, Duchamp's artistic cult imbued everything he touched—if only by a signature—with an artistic aura, securing him a unique place in the modern museum.

In comparison with Kabakov's toilet, Duchamp's pissoir really does look like a fountain—clean, Western, and individualistic. Besides, scatological profanity itself became a kind of avant-garde convention—part of early twentieth-century culture as represented by Bataille, Leiris, and so forth. Kabakov's installation is not merely about radical defamiliarization and recontextualization but also, more strikingly, about inhabiting the most uninhabitable space, in this case the toilet. Instead of Duchamp's sculpturelike ready-made, we have here an intimate environment that invites walking through, storytelling, and touching. The artist's own artistic touch is visible throughout. Kabakov took great care in arranging the objects and things in the inhabited rooms side by side with the toilet, those metonymical memory-triggers of Soviet everyday life.

It is revealing, though, that there is no representation of a human figure in Kabakov's work. One is reminded of Benjamin's description of his memory work in *Berlin Chronicle,* where the writer speaks about remembering places of his childhood but not the faces of people. The place appeared emptied, estranged, devoid of its inhabitants, but it preserved the aura of their glances, traces of encounters, many archeological levels of recollections. Kabakov offers a similar kind of topography of memory with his domestic interiors, inhabited oases next to the toilet.

Kabakov tried to resist the interpretation of the project as a single symbol or metaphor. This, however, was beyond his control. In the Russian press he was reviewed very negatively: in spite of the political differences among his reviewers, they all seemed to agree that the toilets were an insult to the Russian people and to Russian national pride. Many reviewers invoked a curious Russian proverb, "Do not take your trash out of your hut" ("ne vynosi sor iz izby"), which counsels not to criticize one's own people in front of strangers and foreigners. The proverb dates back to an ancient peasant custom of sweeping trash into a corner of the dwelling and burying it inside rather than outside, since it was feared that evil people might use the trash to cast spells on the occupants.[19] In recalling this superstition, the reviewers called for intimate memories— in Kabakov's case, shared intimate memories with clear collective Soviet frameworks—to be hidden, especially from the international community or from one's own estranging gaze. Kabakov's domestic trash from the Soviet era was regarded as a profanation of Russia.

Kabakov shunned this negative symbolic interpretation of his project. It is hard to imagine Duchamp's pissoir being interpreted as an insult to French culture. It was seen as a slap in the face of art in general, beyond national boundaries. Kabakov re-created his toilets with such meticulousness—working personally on every crack on the window, every splash of paint, every stain—that the inhabited toilet turned into an evocative memory theater, irreducible to univocal symbolism. Yet, the insults that Kabakov received are part of being a "Soviet artist"—a role that he chose for himself not without inner irony and nostalgic sadomasochism. Russian critics expropriated the artist's toilets and reconstructed them as symbols of national shame. Russian national mythology had no place for ironic nostalgia.

The largest of Kabakov's total installations, shown at the Centre Pompidou in Paris in the summer of 1996, was, in a way, his ironic homage to the never realized Palace of the Soviets, the most grandiose of Stalin's projects, imagined on the site of the destroyed Cathedral of Christ the Savior. The installation, entitled *This Is How We Live,* represents a major construction site of the Palace of the Future, with a grand panel representing the city of the future in the center and workers' barracks around it (figs. 5 and 6).[20] As one walks through the exhibit one begins to realize that the construction of the Palace of the Future has long been abandoned and that the scaffoldings are nothing but ruins and debris. The temporary workers' houses became permanent; everyday life took root on the site of an unfinished utopia. When Benjamin visited Moscow in 1927 one of the few Russian words he learned was *remont* (repairs) from the signs that were everywhere. In Kabakov's exhibit repair becomes a key metaphor—the exhibit is a utopia under repair. A utopia tends to be sanitized and antiseptic. Its ruins, on the other hand, are intimate and domesticated.

The exhibit uses the actual basement of the Centre Pompidou, and the imported trash of the Palace of the Future peacefully coexists with the garbage of the palace of modern art. The museum, for Kabakov, is at once a sanctuary and a dump for cultural trash. A visit to the exhibit is all about trespassing the boundaries between the aesthetic and everyday life. One is never sure where the total installation begins and ends. Visitors begin by not being able to find the exhibit: instead of feeling they have come across workers' barracks, they might think they have mistakenly wandered into the Pompidou's storage area, where someone has collected funky furniture from the 1950s (figs. 7, 8, and 9). Paradoxically, these nostalgic oases of interrupted Soviet life are the only seemingly unguarded spaces in the museum. Here the museum officials actively encourage you to touch everything you wish. Visitors to the exhibit are invited to inhabit the workers' barracks, to relax on the plush sofas, to touch the personal souvenirs.[21] Indeed, wandering through the exhibit one might always find a couple of exhausted tourists or immigrants reclining here and there. After all, the museum is still a relatively inexpensive urban refuge; it is cheaper than going to a cafe, and sometimes even free. Kabakov promotes tactile conceptualism; he plays hide-and-seek with aesthetic distance itself.

Kabakov remarks that of all utopian palaces under repair, the Centre Pompidou will probably survive the longest. His total installations reveal a nostalgia for utopia, but they return utopia back to its origins—not in life but in art. While dwelling on his own diasporic souvenirs from his Soviet childhood, Kabakov goes to the origins of modern utopia and reveals two contradictory human impulses: one to transcend the everyday in some kind of collective fairy tale, and the other to inhabit the most uninhabitable ruins, to survive and preserve fairy tale, and the other to inhabit the most uninhabitable ruins, to survive and preserve memories. Post-Soviet nostalgia is not the same as nostalgia for the Soviet Union. "Sovietness" in this case is not merely a political reference but rather a reference to the common culture of childhood and adolescence, to the shared cultural text that is quickly forgotten in the current rewritings of Russian history.

Total installations are Kabakov's homes away from home; they help him dislocate and estrange the topography of his childhood fears and domesticate it again abroad. Jean-Francois Lyotard suggests an interesting category, "domestication . . . with no *domus*," which I understand as a way of inhabiting one's displaced habitats and avoiding the extremes of both the domus of traditional family values and the megalopolis of cyberspace.[22] While some of the works of post-Soviet artists reveal the postmodern strategies of multiple narrative, hybridization, and pastiche, they do not engage in euphoric celebrations of nomadism and perpetual identity play. Kabakov's commemorations speak of the pain of estrangement, the embarrassment of memory, and the panic of oblivion; they reveal the precariousness of the human habitat and the fragility of intimacy. In his essay "On Emptiness," written after his first departure from Russia, Kabakov remarks in the Russian prophetic mode that at the end of the twentieth century we all seem to live on tiny islands in the midst of the oceans of emptiness, like scholars in "tents in the uninhabited and icy Antarctic": "Of course, one can go visiting, drink tea or dancing, moving from one tent to another, from the Soviet to the American and vice versa," but we must never forget the emptiness that surrounds us."[23]

Notes

1   Unless otherwise indicated, all translations are my own. Nina Berberova, *The Italics Are Mine*, trans. Philippe Radley (New York, 1991), p. 338. Historically, the term *émigré* has referred to political exiles. Hence, it would apply to Berberova and the Soviet exiles who came to the United States as refugees and until glasnost could never go back. However, my discussion of diasporic intimacy has broader implications and in this context I use the terms *immigrants, exiles,* and *émigrés* interchangeably. It is not within the scope of my paper to discuss the social, political, and economic differences among them (which are often far from obvious: not all émigrés belonged to the upper or middle class, and not all immigrants are poor). It should be noted however that exiles and emigres usually cannot go back "home." Diasporic intimacy is an inclusive rather than an exclusive category. For further inspiring discussion of diaspora, cosmopolitanism, homeland, and immigrant poetics, see the journal *Diaspora,* and *Nation and Narration,* ed. Homi Bhabha (New York, 1990).

2   Berberova, *The Italics Are Mine*, p. 338.

3   *American Heritage Dictionary,* s. v. "intimate."

4   Ibid.

5   See Philippe Ariès, introduction to *Passions of the Renaissance,* trans. Arthur Goldhammer, ed. Roger Chartier, vol. 3 of *A History of Private Life* (Cambridge, Mass., 1989), 3:1–7, and Orest Ranum, "The Refuges of Intimacy," in *A History of Private Life,* 3:207–63.

6   See Hannah Arendt, "On Humanity in Dark Times: Thoughts about Lessing," trans. Clara and Richard Winston, *Men in Dark Times* (New York, 1968), pp. 15–16.

7   See Richard Sennett, *The Fall of Public Man* (New York, 1977), pp. 337–40.

8   Walter Benjamin, "On Some Motifs in Baudelaire," *Illuminations,* trans. Harry Zohn, ed. Arendt (New York, 1968), p. 169.

9   Georg Simmel, "Sociability," *On Individuality and Social Forms: Selected Writings,* ed. Donald N. Levine (Chicago, 1971), p. 130. I am grateful to Gabriella Turnaturi for bringing it to my attention. See Gabriella Turnaturi, *Flirt, seduzione, amore: Simmel e le emozioni* (1994).

10 Roland Barthes, *A Lover's Discourse: Fragments,* trans. Richard Howard (New York, 1978), pp. 224, 225.

11 Ibid., p. 225.

12 See Italo Calvino, "Lightness," *Six Memos for the Next Millennium* (Cambridge, Mass., 1988), pp. 3–31.

13 For a further discussion of the campaign against domestic trash, the communal apartment as a cultural site, and the conception of public and private, the aesthetic and the everyday in Russian and Soviet contexts, see my "The Archeology of Banality: The Soviet Home," *Public Culture* 6 (Winter 1994): 263–92 and my *Common Places: Mythologies of Everyday Life in Russia* (Cambridge, Mass., 1994).

14 This progression from fragment to totality is not a one-way street. Moreover, each total installation in itself embodies the Kabakovian work of memory, creating a complete environment which includes Kabakov's earlier works, fragments from his albums, paintings, everyday objects, the collectibles of obsessive communal apartment neighbors, sketches by untalented artists, and communal trash. Each installation becomes a kind of museum for Kabokov's earlier work, something like *matreshka* dolls, with many layers of memory.

15 [Unfortunately the figures from this article could not be reproduced for *The Svetlana Boym Reader.* The original article with illustrations is available at http://www.jstor.org/stable/1344176. -JE]

16 Ilya Kabakov, *Installations 1983–1995* (Paris, 1995), p. 162; hereafter abbreviated *I.*

17 Then Kabakov proceeds to argue with Dante that it is not love that inspires art but fear and panic.

18 Quoted in Dalia Judovitz, *Unpacking Duchamp: Art in Transit* (Berkeley, 1996), pp. 124, 125; see also pp. 124–35.

19 See Vladimir Dal', *Tolkovyi slovar' zhivago velikorusskogo iazyka,* 4 vols. (St. Petersburg, 1882), 4:275.

20 The construction site is surrounded by barracks of different shapes and forms where workers and their families lived. In the basement where the foundations of the unfinished Palace of the Future have been laid are several "public rooms" in which cheerful Soviet songs are playing, each room decorated by a single socialist-realist painting representing labor, leisure, and the bright communist future.

21 These souvenirs are not exclusively Soviet; Kabakov has internationalized his nostalgia. One may find Soviet journals from the 1970s, a Russian translation of a Hungarian novel, or a post-Soviet business quarterly. One may touch the shaded glass of the cabinet and the French family photo that stands side by side with a Disney souvenir. The visitors to the exhibit seem to have accepted Kabakov's invitation to touch and to inhabit.

22 Jean-Francois Lyotard, *"Domus* and the Megalopolis," *The Inhuman: Reflections on Time,* trans. Geoffrey Bennington and Rachel Bowlby (Stanford, Calif., 1991), p. 199. Andreas Huyssen in his new book *Twilight Memories* claims that the current memory boom is not a result of further kitschification of the past, but "a potentially healthy sign of contestation; a contestation of the informational hyperspace and an expression of the basic human need to live in extended structures of temporality, however they may be organized. . . . In that dystopian vision of a high-tech future, amnesia would no longer be part of the dialectic of memory and forgetting. It will be its radical other. It will have sealed the very forgetting of memory itself: nothing to remember, nothing to forget" (Andreas Huyssen, *Twilight Memories: Marking Time in a Culture of Amnesia* [New York, 1995], p. 35).

23 Kabakov, "On Emptiness," trans. Clark Troy, in *Between Spring and Summer: Soviet Conceptual Art in the Era of Late Communism* (exhibition catalog, Tacoma Art Museum, 15 June–9 Sept. 1990; Institute of Contemporary Art, Boston, 1 Nov. 1990–6 Jan. 1991), p. 59.

10 THE FUTURE OF NOSTALGIA

From Cured Soldiers to Incurable Romantics

The word nostalgia comes from two Greek roots, yet it did not originate in ancient Greece. Nostalgia is only pseudo-Greek, or nostalgically Greek. The word was coined by the ambitious Swiss doctor Johannes Hofer in his medical dissertation in 1688. He believed that it was possible "from the force of the sound Nostalgia to define the sad mood originating from the desire for return to one's native land."[1] (Hofer also suggested nosomania and philopatridomania to describe the same symptoms; luckily, the latter failed to enter common parlance.) Contrary to our intuition, nostalgia came from medicine, not from poetry or politics. Among the first victims of the newly diagnosed disease were various displaced people of the seventeenth century, freedom-loving students from the Republic of Berne studying in Basel, domestic help and servants working in France and Germany and Swiss soldiers fighting abroad.

Nostalgia was said to produce "erroneous representations" that caused the afflicted to lose touch with the present. Longing for their native land became their single-minded obsession. The patients acquired "a lifeless and haggard countenance," and "indifference towards everything," confusing past and present, real and imaginary events. One of the early symptoms of nostalgia was an ability to hear voices or see ghosts. Dr. Albert von Haller wrote: "One of the earliest symptoms is the sensation of hearing the voice of a person that one loves in the voice of another with whom one is conversing, or to see one's family again in dreams."[2] It comes as no surprise that Hofer's felicitous baptism of the new disease both helped to identify the existing condition and enhanced the epidemic, making it a widespread European phenomenon. The epidemic of nostalgia was accompanied by an even more dangerous epidemic of "feigned nostalgia," particularly among soldiers tired of serving abroad, revealing the contagious nature of the erroneous representations.

Nostalgia, the disease of an afflicted imagination, incapacitated the body. Hofer thought that the course of the disease was mysterious: the ailment spread "along uncommon routes through the untouched course of the channels of the brain to the body," arousing "an uncommon and everpresent idea of the recalled native land in the mind."[3] Longing for home exhausted the "vital spirits," causing nausea, loss of appetite, pathological changes in the lungs, brain inflammation, cardiac arrests, high fever, as well as marasmus and a propensity for suicide.[4]

Nostalgia operated by an "associationist magic," by means of which all aspects of everyday life related to one single obsession. In this respect nostalgia was akin to paranoia, only instead of a persecution mania, the nostalgic was possessed by a mania of longing. On the other hand, the nostalgic had an amazing capacity for remembering sensations, tastes, sounds, smells, the minutiae and trivia of the lost paradise that those who remained home never noticed. Gastronomic and auditory nostalgia were of particular importance. Swiss scientists found that rustic mothers' soups, thick village milk and the folk melodies of Alpine valleys were particularly conducive to triggering a nostalgic reaction in Swiss soldiers. Supposedly the sounds of "a certain rustic cantilena" that accompanied shepherds in their driving of the herds to pasture immediately provoked an epidemic of nostalgia among Swiss soldiers serving in France. Similarly, Scots, particularly Highlanders, were known to succumb to incapacitating nostalgia when hearing the sound of the bagpipes—so much so, in fact, that their military superiors had to prohibit them from playing, singing or even whistling native tunes in a suggestive manner. Jean-Jacques Rousseau talks about the effects of cowbells, the rustic sounds that excite in the Swiss the joys of life and youth and a bitter sorrow for having lost them. The music in this case "does not act precisely as music, but as a memorative sign."[5] The music of home, whether a rustic cantilena or a pop song, is the permanent accompaniment of nostalgia— its ineffable charm that makes the nostalgic teary-eyed and tongue-tied and often clouds critical reflection on the subject.

In the good old days nostalgia was a curable disease, dangerous but not always lethal. Leeches, warm hypnotic emulsions, opium and a return to the Alps usually soothed the symptoms. Purging of the stomach was also recommended but nothing compared to the return to the motherland believed to be the best remedy for nostalgia. While proposing the treatment for the disease, Hofer seemed proud of some of his patients; for him nostalgia was a demonstration of the patriotism of his compatriots who loved the charm of their native land to the point of sickness.

Nostalgia shared some symptoms with melancholia and hypochondria. Melancholia, according to the Galenic conception, was a disease of the black bile that affected the blood and produced such physical and emotional symptoms as "vertigo, much wit, headache, . . . much waking, rumbling in the guts . . . troublesome dreams, heaviness of the heart . . . continuous fear, sorrow, discontent, superfluous cares and anxiety." For Robert Burton, melancholia, far from being a mere physical or psychological condition, had a philosophical dimension. The melancholic saw the world as a theater ruled by capricious fate and demonic play.[6] Often mistaken for a mere misanthrope, the melancholic was in fact a utopian dreamer who had higher hopes for humanity. In this respect, melancholia was an affect and an ailment of intellectuals, a Hamletian doubt, a side effect of critical reason; in melancholia, thinking and feeling, spirit and matter, soul and body were perpetually in conflict. Unlike melancholia, which was regarded as an ailment of monks and philosophers, nostalgia was a more "democratic" disease that threatened to affect soldiers and sailors displaced far from home as well as many country people who began to move to the cities. Nostalgia was not merely an individual anxiety but a public threat that revealed the contradictions of modernity and acquired a greater political importance.

The outburst of nostalgia both enforced and challenged the emerging conception of patriotism and national spirit. It was unclear at first what was to be done with the afflicted soldiers who loved their motherland so much that they never wanted to leave it, or for that matter to die for it. When the epidemic of nostalgia spread beyond the Swiss garrison, a more radical treatment was undertaken. The French doctor Jourdan Le Cointe suggested in his book written during the French Revolution of 1789 that nostalgia had to be cured by inciting pain and terror. As scientific evidence he offered an account of drastic treatment of nostalgia successfully undertaken by the Russians. In 1733 the Russian army was stricken by nostalgia just as it ventured into Germany, the situation becoming dire enough that the general was compelled to come up with a radical treatment of the nostalgic virus. He threatened that "the first to fall sick will be buried alive." This was a kind of literalization of a metaphor, as life in a foreign country seemed like death. This punishment was reported to be carried out on two or three occasions, which happily cured the Russian army of complaints of nostalgia.[7] (No wonder longing became such an important part of the Russian national identity.) Russian soil proved to be a fertile ground for both native and foreign nostalgia. The autopsies performed on the French soldiers who perished in the proverbial Russian snow during the miserable retreat of the Napoleonic Army from Moscow revealed that many of them had brain inflammation characteristic of nostalgia.

While Europeans (with the exception of the British) reported frequent epidemics of nostalgia starting from the seventeenth century, American doctors proudly declared that the young nation remained healthy and didn't succumb to the nostalgic vice until the American Civil War.[8] If the Swiss doctor Hofer believed that homesickness expressed love for freedom and one's native land, two centuries later the American military doctor Theodore Calhoun conceived of nostalgia as a shameful disease that revealed a lack of manliness and unprogressive attitudes. He suggested that this was a disease of the mind and of a weak will (the concept of an "afflicted imagination" would be profoundly alien to him). In nineteenth-century America it was believed that the main reasons for homesickness were idleness and a slow and inefficient use of time conducive to daydreaming, erotomania and onanism. "Any influence that will tend to render the patient more manly will exercise a curative power. In boarding schools, as perhaps many of us remember, ridicule is wholly relied upon. . . . [The nostalgic] patient can often be laughed out of it by his comrades, or reasoned out of it by appeals to his manhood; but of all potent agents, an active campaign, with attendant marches and more particularly its battles is the best curative."[9] Dr. Calhoun proposed as treatment public ridicule and bullying by fellow soldiers, an increased number of manly marches and battles and improvement in personal hygiene that would make soldiers' living conditions more modern. (He also was in favor of an occasional furlough that would allow soldiers to go home for a brief period of time.)

For Calhoun, nostalgia was not conditioned entirely by individuals' health, but also by their strength of character and social background. Among the Americans the most susceptible to nostalgia were soldiers from the rural districts, particularly farmers, while merchants, mechanics, boatmen and train conductors from the same area or from the city were more likely to resist the sickness. "The soldier from the city cares not where he is or where he eats, while his country cousin pines for the old homestead and his father's groaning board," wrote Calhoun.[10] In such cases, the only hope was that the advent of progress would somehow alleviate nostalgia and the efficient use of time would eliminate idleness, melancholy, procrastination and lovesickness.

As a public epidemic, nostalgia was based on a sense of loss not limited to personal history. Such a sense of loss does not necessarily suggest that what is lost is properly remembered and that one still knows where to look for it. Nostalgia became less and less curable. By the end of the eighteenth century, doctors discovered that a return home did not always treat the symptoms. The object of longing occasionally migrated to faraway lands beyond the confines of the motherland. Just as genetic researchers today hope to identify a gene not only for medical conditions but social behavior and even sexual orientation, so the doctors in the eighteenth and nineteenth centuries looked for a single cause of the erroneous representations, one so-called pathological bone. Yet the physicians failed to find the locus of nostalgia in their patient's mind or body. One doctor claimed that nostalgia was a "hypochondria of the heart" that thrives on its symptoms. To my knowledge, the medical diagnosis of nostalgia survived in the twentieth century in one country only—Israel. (It is unclear whether this reflects a persistent yearning for the promised land or for the diasporic homelands left behind.) Everywhere else in the world nostalgia turned from a treatable sickness into an incurable disease. How did it happen that a provincial ailment, maladie du pays, became a disease of the modern age, mal du siècle?

In my view, the spread of nostalgia had to do not only with dislocation in space but also with the changing conception of time. Nostalgia was a historical emotion, and we would do well to pursue its historical rather than psychological genesis. There had been plenty of longing before the seventeenth century, not only in the European tradition but also in Chinese and Arabic poetry, where longing is a poetic commonplace. Yet the early modern conception embodied in the specific word came to the fore at a particular historical moment. "Emotion is not a word, but it can only be spread abroad through words," writes Jean Starobinski, using the metaphor of border crossing and immigration to describe the discourse on nostalgia.[11] Nostalgia was diagnosed at a time when art and science had not yet entirely severed their umbilical ties and when the mind and body—internal and external well-being—were treated together. This was a diagnosis of a poetic science—and we should not smile condescendingly on the diligent Swiss doctors. Our progeny well might poeticize depression and see it as a metaphor for a global atmospheric condition, immune to treatment with Prozac.

What distinguishes modern nostalgia from the ancient myth of the return home is not merely its peculiar medicalization. The Greek nostos, the return home and the song of the return home, was part of a mythical ritual. As Gregory Nagy has demonstrated, Greek nostos is connected to the Indo-European root nes, meaning return to light and life.

There are in fact two aspects of nostos in The Odyssey; one is of course, the hero's return from Troy, and the other, just as important, is his return from Hades. Moreover, the theme of Odysseus's descent and subsequent nostos (return) from Hades converges with the solar dynamics of sunset and sunrise. The movement is from dark to light, from unconsciousness to consciousness. In fact the hero is asleep as he floats in darkness to his homeland and sunrise comes precisely when his boat reaches the shores of Ithaca.[12]

Penelope's labor of love and endurance—the cloth that she weaves by day and unravels by night—represents a mythical time of everyday loss and renewal. Odysseus's is not a story of individual sentimental longing and subsequent return home to family values; rather, this is a fable about human fate.

After all, Odysseus's homecoming is about nonrecognition. Ithaca is plunged into mist and the royal wanderer arrives in disguise. The hero recognizes neither his homeland nor his divine protectress. Even his faithful and long-suffering wife does not see him for who he is. Only his childhood nurse notices the scar on the hero's foot—the tentative marker of physical identity. Odysseus has to prove his identity in action. He shoots the bow that belongs to him, at that moment triggering recollections and gaining recognition. Such ritual actions help to erase the wrinkles on the faces and the imprints of age. Odysseus's is a representative homecoming, a ritual event that neither begins nor ends with him.

The seduction of non–return home—the allure of Circe and the sirens—plays a more important role in some ancient versions of Odysseus's cycle, where the story of homecoming is not at all clearly crystallized. The archaic tales around the myth, not recorded in the Homeric rendering of the story, suggest that the prophecy will come true and Odysseus will be killed by his son—not Telemachus, but by the son he bore with Circe— who would later end up marrying Odysseus's wife, Penelope. Thus in the potential world of mythical storytelling there might be an incestuous connection between the faithful wife and the enchantress that delays the hero's homecoming. After all, Circe's island is an ultimate utopia of regressive pleasure and divine bestiality. One has to leave it to become human again. Circe's treacherous lullabies are echoed in the melodies of home. So if we explore the potential tales of Odysseus's homecoming, we risk turning an adventure story with a happy ending into a Greek tragedy. Hence even the most classical Western tale of homecoming is far from circular; it is riddled with contradictions and zigzags, false homecomings, misrecognitions.

Modern nostalgia is a mourning for the impossibility of mythical return, for the loss of an enchanted world with clear borders and values; it could be a secular expression of a spiritual longing, a nostalgia for an absolute, a home that is both physical and spiritual, the edenic unity of time and space before entry into history. The nostalgic is looking for a spiritual addressee. Encountering silence, he looks for memorable signs, desperately misreading them.

The diagnosis of the disease of nostalgia in the late seventeenth century took place roughly at the historical moment when the conception of time and history were undergoing radical change. The religious wars in Europe came to an end but the much prophesied end of the world and doomsday did not occur. "It was only when Christian eschatology shed its constant expectations of the imminent arrival of doomsday that a temporality could have been revealed that would be open to the new and without limit."[13] It is customary to perceive "linear" Judeo-Christian time in opposition to the "cyclical" pagan time of eternal return and discuss both with the help of spatial metaphors.[14] What this opposition obscures is the temporal and historical development of the perception of time that since Renaissance on has become more and more secularized, severed from cosmological vision.

Before the invention of mechanical clocks in the thirteenth century the question, What time is it? was not very urgent. Certainly there were plenty of calamities, but the shortage of time wasn't one of them; therefore people could exist "in an attitude of temporal ease. Neither time nor change appeared to be critical and hence there was no great worry about controlling the future."[15] In late Renaissance culture, Time was embodied in the images of Divine Providence and capricious Fate, independent of human insight or blindness. The division of time into Past, Present and Future was not so relevant. History was perceived as a "teacher of life" (as in Cicero's famous dictum, historia magistra vitae) and the repertoire of examples and role models for the future. Alternatively, in Leibniz's formulation, "The whole of the coming world is present and prefigured in that of the present."[16]

The French Revolution marked another major shift in European mentality. Regicide had happened before, but not the transformation of the entire social order. The biography of Napoleon became exemplary for an entire generation of new individualists, little Napoleons who dreamed of reinventing and revolutionizing their own lives. The "Revolution," at first derived from natural movement of the stars and thus introduced into the natural rhythm of history as a cyclical metaphor, henceforth attained an irreversible direction: it appeared to unchain a yearned-for future.[17] The idea of progress through revolution or industrial development became central to the nineteenth-century culture. From the seventeenth to the nineteenth century, the representation of time itself changed; it moved away from allegorical human figures—an old man, a blind youth holding an hourglass, a woman with bared breasts representing Fate—to the impersonal language of numbers: railroad schedules, the bottom line of industrial progress. Time was no longer shifting sand; time was money. Yet the modern era also allowed for multiple conceptions of time and made the experience of time more individual and creative.

Kant thought that space was the form of our outer experience, and time the form of inner experience. To understand the human anthropological dimension of the new temporality and the ways of internalizing past and future, Reinhart Koselleck suggested two categories: space of experience and horizon of expectation; both are personal and interpersonal. The space of experience allows one to account for the assimilation of the past into the present. "Experience is present past, whose events have been incorporated and could be remembered." Horizon of expectation reveals the way of thinking about the future. Expectation "is the future made present; it directs itself to the not-yet to the non-experienced, to that which is to be revealed."[18] In the early modern era new possibilities of individual self-fashioning and the quest for personal freedom opened a space for creative experimentation with time that was not always linear and one-directional. The idea of progress, once it moved from the realm of arts and sciences to the ideology of industrial capitalism, became a new theology of "objective" time. Progress "is the first genuinely historical concept which reduced the temporal difference between experience and expectation to a single concept."[19] What mattered in the idea of progress was improvement in the future, not reflection on the past. Immediately, many writers and thinkers at the time raised the question of whether progress can ever be simultaneous in all spheres of human experience. Friedrich Schlegel wrote: "The real problem of history is the inequality of progress in the various elements of human development, in particular the great divergence in the degree of intellectual and ethical development."[20] Whether there was indeed an improvement in the humanities and arts, and in the human condition in general, remained an open question. Yet progress became a new global narrative as a secular counterpart to the universal aspirations of the Christian eschatology. In the past two centuries the idea of Progress applied to everything—from time to space, from the nation to the individual.

Thus nostalgia, as a historical emotion, is a longing for that shrinking "space of experience" that no longer fits the new horizon of expectations. Nostalgic manifestations are side effects of the teleology of progress. Progress was not only a narrative of temporal progression but also of spatial expansion. Travelers since the late eighteenth century wrote about other places, first to the south and then to the east of Western Europe as "semi-civilized" or outright "barbarous." Instead of coevalness of different conceptions of time, each local culture therefore was evaluated with regard to the central narrative of progress. Progress was a marker of global time; any alternative to this idea was perceived as a local eccentricity.

Premodern space used to be measured by parts of the human body: we could keep things "at arm's length," apply the "rule of thumb," count the number of "feet." Understanding nearness and distance had a lot to do with kinship structures in a given society and treatment of domestic and wild animals.[21] Zygmunt Bauman writes, somewhat nostalgically,

That distance which we are now inclined to call "objective" and to measure by comparing it with the length of the equator, rather than with the size of human bodily parts, corporal dexterity or sympathies/antipathies of its inhabitants, used to be measured by human bodies and human relationships long before the metal rod called the meter, that impersonality and disembodiment incarnate, was deposited at Sevres for everyone to respect and obey.[22]

Modern objectivity is conceived with the development of Renaissance perspective and the need for mapping the newly discovered worlds. The early modern state relied on a certain "legibility" of space and its transparency in order to collect taxes, recruit soldiers, and colonize new territories. Therefore the thicket of incomprehensible local customs, impenetrable and misleading to outsiders, were brought to a common denominator, a common map. Thus modernization meant making the populated world hospitable to supracommunal, state-ruled administration bureaucracy and moving from a bewildering diversity of maps to a universally shared world. With the development of late capitalism and digital technology, the universal civilization becomes "global culture" and the local space is not merely transcended but made virtual. It would be dangerous, however, to fall into nostalgic idealization of premodern conceptions of space with a variety of local customs; after all, they had their own local tradition of cruelty; the "supracommunal language" was not only that of bureaucracy but also of human rights, of democracy and liberation. What is crucial is that nostalgia was not merely an expression of local longing, but a result of a new understanding of time and space that made the division into "local" and "universal" possible. The nostalgic creature has internalized this division, but instead of aspiring for the universal and the progressive he looks backward and yearns for the particular.

In the nineteenth century, optimistic doctors believed that nostalgia would be cured with universal progress and the improvement of medicine. Indeed, in some cases it did happen, since some symptoms of nostalgia were confused with tuberculosis. While tuberculosis eventually became treatable, nostalgia did not; since the eighteenth century, the impossible task of exploring nostalgia passed from doctors to poets and philosophers. The symptom of sickness came to be regarded as a sign of sensibility or an expression of new patriotic feeling. The epidemic of nostalgia was no longer to be cured but to be spread as widely as possible. Nostalgia is treated in a new genre, not as a tale of putative convalescence but as a romance with the past. The new scenario of nostalgia was neither battlefield nor hospital ward but misty vistas with reflective ponds, passing clouds and ruins of the Middle Ages or antiquity. Where native ruins were not available artificial ruins were built, already half-destroyed with utmost precision, commemorating the real and imaginary past of the new European nations.

In response to the Enlightenment, with its emphasis on the universality of reason, romantics began to celebrate the particularism of the sentiment. Longing for home became a central trope of romantic nationalism. The romantics looked for "memorative signs" and correspondences between their inner landscape and the shape of the world. They charted an affective geography of the native land that often mirrored the melancholic landscape of their own psyches. The primitive song turned into a lesson in philosophy. Johann Gottfried von Herder wrote in 1773 that the songs of Latvian peasants possessed a "living presence that nothing written on paper can ever have." It is this living presence, outside the vagaries of modern history, that becomes the object of nostalgic longing. "All unpolished people sing and act; they sing about what they do and thus sing histories. Their songs are archives of their people, the treasury of their science and religion. . . . Here everyone portrays himself and appears as he is."[23]

It is not surprising that national awareness comes from outside the community rather than from within. It is the romantic traveler who sees from a distance the wholeness of the vanishing world. The journey gives him perspective. The vantage point of a stranger informs the native idyll.[24] The nostalgic is never a native but a displaced person who mediates between the local and the universal. Many national languages, thanks to Herder's passionate rehabilitation, discovered their own particular expression for patriotic longing. Curiously, intellectuals and poets from different national traditions began to claim that they had a special word for homesickness that was radically untranslatable. While German heimweh, French maladie du pays, Spanish mal de corazon have become a part of nostalgic esperanto, the emerging nations began to insist on their cultural uniqueness. Czechs had the word litost, which meant at once sympathy, grief, remorse and undefinable longing. According to Milan Kundera, litost suggested a "feeling as infinite as an open accordion where the "first syllable when long and stressed sounds like the wail of an abandoned dog."[25] The whispering sibilants of the Russian *toska*, made famous in the literature of exiles, evoke a claustrophobic intimacy of the crammed space from where one pines for the infinite. Toska suggests, literally, a stifling, almost asthmatic sensation of incredible deprivation that is found also in the shimmering sounds of the Polish tesknota. Usually opposed to the Russian *toska* (even though they came from the same root), tesknota gives a similar sense of confining and overwhelming yearning with a touch of moody artistry unknown to the Russians, enamored by the gigantic and the absolute. Eva Hoffman describes tesknota as a phantom pregnancy, a "welling up of absence," of all that had been lost.[26] The Portuguese and Brazilians have their saudade, a tender sorrow, breezy and erotic, not as melodramatic as its Slavic counterpart, yet no less profound and haunting. Romanians claim that the word dor, sonorous and sharp like a dagger, is unknown to the other nations and speaks of a specifically Romanian dolorous ache.[27] While each term preserves the specific rhythms of the language, one is struck by the fact that all these untranslatable words are in fact synonyms; and all share the desire for untranslatability, the longing for uniqueness. While the details and flavors differ, the grammar of romantic nostalgias all over the world is quite similar.[28] "I long therefore I am" became the romantic motto.

Nostalgia, like progress, is dependent on the modern conception of unrepeatable and irreversible time. The romantic nostalgic insisted on the otherness of his object of nostalgia from his present life and kept it at a safe distance. The object of romantic nostalgia must be beyond the present space of experience, somewhere in the twilight of the past or on the island of utopia where time has happily stopped, as on an antique clock. At the same time, romantic nostalgia is not a mere antithesis to progress; it undermines both a linear conception of progress and a Hegelian dialectical teleology. The nostalgic directs his gaze not only backward but sideways, and expresses himself in elegiac poems and ironic fragments, not in philosophical or scientific treatises. Nostalgia remains unsystematic and unsynthesizable; it seduces rather than convinces.

In romantic texts nostalgia became erotic. Particularism in language and nature was akin to the individual love. A young and beautiful girl was buried somewhere in the native soil; blond and meek or dark and wild, she was the personification of nature: Sylvie for the sylvan imagination, Undine for the maritime one, Lucy for the lake region and a poor Liza for the Russian countryside. (Male heroes tended more toward bestial representations than pastoral, ranging from Lithuanian bearcounts in Prosper Mérimée's novellas to Ukrainian and Transylvanian vampires.) The romance became a foundational fiction for new national revivals in Latin America, where countless novels bear women's names.

Yet the song of national liberation was not the only melody chosen in the nineteenth century. Many poets and philosophers explored nostalgic longing for its own sake rather than using it as a vehicle to a promised land or a nation-state. Kant saw in the combination of melancholy, nostalgia and self-awareness a unique aesthetic sense that did not objectify the past but rather heightened one's sensitivity to the dilemmas of life and moral freedom.[29] For Kant, philosophy was seen as a nostalgia for a better world. Nostalgia is what humans share, not what should divide them. Like Eros in the Platonic conception, longing for the romantic philosophers and poets became a driving force of the human condition. For Novalis, "Philosophy is really a homesickness; it is an urge to be at home everywhere."[30]

Like the doctors before them, poets and philosophers failed to find a precise location for nostalgia. They focused on the quest itself. A poetic language and a metaphorical journey seemed like a homeopathic treatment for human longing, acting through sympathy and similarity, together with the aching body, yet not promising a hallucinatory total recall. Heinrich Heine's poem of prototypical longing is about sympathetic mirroring of nostalgia.

A spruce is standing lonely
in the North on a barren height.
He drowses; ice and snowflakes
wrap him in a blanket of white.

He dreams about a palm tree
in a distant, eastern land,
that languishes lonely and silent
upon the scorching sand.[31]

The solitary northern spruce dreams about his nostalgic soulmate and antipode—the southern palm. This is not a comforting national love affair. The two rather anthropomorphic trees share solitude and dreams, not roots. Longing for a fellow nostalgic, rather than for the landscape of the homeland, this poem is a long-distance romance between two "internal immigrants," displaced in their own native soil.

The first generation of romantics were not politicians; their nostalgic world view was weltanschauung, not real politik. When nostalgia turns political, romance is connected to nation building and native songs are purified. The official memory of the nation-state does not tolerate useless nostalgia, nostalgia for its own sake. Some Alpine melodies appeared too frivolous and ideologically incorrect.

Whose nostalgia was it? What used to be an individual emotion expressed by sick soldiers and later romantic poets and philosophers turned into an institutional or state policy. With the development of Swiss nationalism (that coincided with the creation of a federal state in the nineteenth century), native songs were rewritten by schoolteachers who found peasant melodies vulgar and not sufficiently patriotic. They wrote for the choral repertoire and tried to embrace patriotism and progress. The word nation was one of the new words introduced into the native songs.

"To forget—and I would venture say—to get one's history wrong, are essential factors in the making of a nation; and thus the advance of historical study is a danger to nationality," wrote Ernest Renan.[32] The French had to forget the massacres of St. Bartholomew's night and massacres of the Cathars in the south in the thirteenth century. The nostos of a nation is not merely a lost Eden but a place of sacrifice and glory, of past suffering. This is a kind of inversion of the initial "Swiss disease": in the national ideology, individual longing is transformed into a collective belonging that relies on past sufferings that transcend individual memories. Defeats in the past figure as prominently as victories in uniting the nation. The nation-state at best is based on the social contract that is also an emotional contract, stamped by the charisma of the past.

In the mid-nineteenth century, nostalgia became institutionalized in national and provincial museums and urban memorials. The past was no longer unknown or unknowable. The past became "heritage." In the nineteenth century, for the first time in history, old monuments were restored in their original image.[33] Throughout Italy churches were stripped of their baroque layers and eclectic additions and recreated in the Renaissance image, something that no Renaissance architect would ever imagine doing to a work of antiquity. The sense of historicity and discreteness of the past is a new nineteenth-century sensibility. By the end of the nineteenth century there is a debate between the defenders of complete restoration that proposes to remake historical and artistic monuments of the past in their unity and wholeness, and the lovers of unintentional memorials of the past: ruins, eclectic constructions, fragments that carry "age value." Unlike total reconstructions, they allowed one to experience historicity affectively, as an atmosphere, a space for reflection on the passage of time.

By the late nineteenth century nostalgia acquired public style and space. The "archive" of traditions that Herder found in folk songs was no longer to be left to chance. The evasive locus of nostalgia, the nomadic hearth of the imagination, was to be fixed for the sake of preservation. Memorative signs of the nation were to be found in card catalogues. The elusive temporality of longing was encased and classified in a multitude of archival drawers, display cases and curio cabinets. Private collections allow one to imagine other times and places and plunge into domestic daydreaming and armchair nostalgia. The bourgeois home in nineteenth-century Paris is described by Walter Benjamin as a miniature theater and museum that privatizes nostalgia while at the same time replicating its public structure, the national and private homes thus becoming intertwined. Public nostalgia acquires distinct styles, from the empire style favored by Napoleon to the new historical styles—neo-Gothic, neo-Byzantine, and so on—as the cycles of revolutionary change are accompanied by restorations that end up with a recovery of a grand style.

Nostalgia as a historical emotion came of age at the time of Romanticism and is coeval with the birth of mass culture. It began with the early-nineteenth-century memory boom that turned the salon culture of educated urban dwellers and landowners into a ritual commemoration of lost youth, lost springs, lost dances, lost chances. With the perfection of album art, the practice of writing poems, drawing pictures and leaving dried flowers and plants in a lady's album, every flirtation was on the verge of becoming a memento mori. Yet this souvenirization of the salon culture was playful, dynamic and interactive; it was part of a social theatricality that turned everyday life into art, even if it wasn't a masterpiece. Artificial nature begins to play an important part in the European imagination since the epoch of baroque—the word itself signifies a rare shell. In the middle of the nineteenth century a fondness for herbariums, greenhouses and aquariums became a distinctive feature of the bourgeois home; it was a piece of nature transplanted into the urban home, framed and domesticated.[34] What was cherished was the incompleteness, the fossil, the ruin, the miniature, the souvenir, not the total recreation of a past paradise or hell. As Celeste Olalquiaga observed for the nineteenth-century imagination, Atlantis was not a "golden age" to be reconstructed but a "lost civilization" to engage with through ruins, traces and fragments. The melancholic sense of loss turned into a style, a late nineteenth-century fashion.

Despite the fact that by the end of the nineteenth century nostalgia was pervading both the public and private spheres, the word itself was acquiring negative connotations. Apparently there was little space for a syncretic concept of nostalgia during a time in which spheres of existence and division of labor were undergoing further compartmentalization. The word appeared outmoded and unscientific. Public discourse was about progress, community and heritage, but configured differently than it had been earlier. Private discourse was about psychology, where doctors focus on hysteria, neurosis and paranoia.

The rapid pace of industrialization and modernization increased the intensity of people's longing for the slower rhythms of the past, for continuity, social cohesion and tradition. Yet this new obsession with the past reveals an abyss of forgetting and takes place in inverse proportion to its actual preservation. As Pierre Nora has suggested, memorial sites, or "lieux de memoire," are established institutionally at the time when the environments of memory, the milieux de memoire, fade.[35] It is as if the ritual of commemoration could help to patch up the irreversibility of time. One could argue that Nora's own view is fundamentally nostalgic for the time when environments of memory were a part of life and no official national traditions were necessary. Yet this points to a paradox of institutionalized nostalgia: the stronger the loss, the more it is overcompensated with commemorations, the starker the distance from the past, and the more it is prone to idealizations.

Nostalgia was perceived as a European disease. Hence nations that came of age late and wished to distinguish themselves from aging Europe developed their identity on an antinostalgic premise; for better or worse they claimed to have managed to escape the burden of historical time. "We, Russians, like illegitimate children, come to this world without patrimony, without any links with people who lived on the earth before us. Our memories go no further back than yesterday; we are as it were strangers to ourselves," wrote Petr Chaadaev in the first half of the nineteenth century.[36] Not accidentally, this self-critical statement could well apply to the young American nation too, only with a change in tone that would supplant Russian eternal fatalism with American eternal optimism. Ignoring for a moment the massive political differences between an absolute monarchy and a new democracy, we can observe a similar resistance to historical memory (albeit with a different accent). Early-nineteenth-century Americans perceived themselves as "Nature's Nation," something that lives in the present and has no need for the past—what Jefferson called the "blind veneration of antiquity, for customs and names to overrule the suggestions of our own good sense."[37] The lack of patrimony, legitimacy and memory that Chaadaev laments in the state of the Russian consciousness is celebrated in the American case as the spirit of the new, at once natural and progressive. Intellectuals of both new nations share an inferiority-superiority complex vis-à-vis old Europe and its cultural heritage. Both are antihistorical in their self-definition, only Russians lag behind and Americans run ahead of it. Chaadaev, discoverer of the nomadic Russian spirit, was declared a madman upon his return from abroad and became an internal immigrant in his motherland. Slavophiles appropriated Chaadaev's critique of the Russian mentality and turned spiritual longing (*toska*) and the lack of historical consciousness into features of the Russian soul and a birthmark of the chosen nation. In the American case this youthful forgetfulness allowed for the nationalization of progress and the creation of another quasi-metaphysical entity called the American way of life. On the surface, little could be more different than the celebration of Russian spiritual longing and the American dream. What they share, however, is the dream of transcending history and memory. In the Russian nineteenth-century tradition it is the writer and peasant who become carriers of the national dream, while in the American case the entrepreneur and cowboy are the ultimate artists in life. Unlike their Russian counterparts, they are strong and silent types, not too good with words. Wherein in Russia classical literature of the nineteenth century viewed through the prism of centralized school programs became a foundation of the nation's canon and repository of nostalgic myths, in the United States it is popular culture that helped to spread the American way of life. Somewhere on the frontier, the ghost of Dostoevsky meets the ghost of Mickey Mouse. Like the characters from The Possessed, they exchange wry smiles.

Restorative Nostalgia: Conspiracies and Return to Origins

I will not propose a wonder drug for nostalgia, although a trip to the Alps, opium and leeches might alleviate the symptoms. Longing might be what we share as human beings, but that doesn't prevent us from telling very different stories of belonging and nonbelonging. In my view, two kinds of nostalgia characterize one's relationship to the past, to the imagined community, to home, to one's own self-perception: restorative and reflective. They do not explain the nature of longing nor its psychological makeup and unconscious undercurrents; rather, they are about the ways in which we make sense of our seemingly ineffable homesickness and how we view our relationship to a collective home. In other words, what concerns me is not solely the inner space of an individual psyche but the interrelationship between individual and collective remembrance. A psychiatrist won't quite know what to do with nostalgia; an experimental art therapist might be of more help.

Two kinds of nostalgia are not absolute types, but rather tendencies, ways of giving shape and meaning to longing. Restorative nostalgia puts emphasis on *nostos* and proposes to rebuild the lost home and patch up the memory gaps. Reflective nostalgia dwells in *algia*, in longing and loss, the imperfect process of remembrance. The first category of nostalgics do not think of themselves as nostalgic; they believe that their project is about truth. This kind of nostalgia characterizes national and nationalist revivals all over the world, which engage in the antimodern myth-making of history by means of a return to national symbols and myths and, occasionally, through swapping conspiracy theories. Restorative nostalgia manifests itself in total reconstructions of monuments of the past, while reflective nostalgia lingers on ruins, the patina of time and history, in the dreams of another place and another time.

To understand restorative nostalgia it is important to distinguish between the habits of the past and the habits of the restoration of the past. Eric Hobsbawn differentiates between age-old "customs" and nineteenth-century "invented traditions." Customs by which so-called traditional societies operated were not invariable or inherently conservative: "Custom in traditional societies has a double function of motor and fly wheel. . . . Custom cannot afford to be invariant because even in the traditional societies life is not so."[38]

On the other hand, restored or invented tradition refers to a "set of practices, normally governed by overtly or tacitly accepted rules and of a ritual of symbolic nature which seeks to inculcate certain values and norms of behavior by repetition which automatically implies continuity with the past." The new traditions are characterized by a higher degree of symbolic formalization and ritualization than the actual peasant customs and conventions after which they were patterned. Here are two paradoxes. First, the more rapid and sweeping the pace and scale of modernization, the more conservative and unchangeable the new traditions tend to be. Second, the stronger the rhetoric of continuity with the historical past and emphasis on traditional values, the more selectively the past is presented. The novelty of invented tradition is "no less novel for being able to dress up easily as antiquity."[39]

Invented tradition does not mean a creation ex nihilo or a pure act of social constructivism; rather, it builds on the sense of loss of community and cohesion and offers a comforting collective script for individual longing. There is a perception that as a result of society's industrialization and secularization in the nineteenth century, a certain void of social and spiritual meaning had opened up. What was needed was a secular transformation of fatality into continuity, contingency into meaning.[40] Yet this transformation can take different turns. It may increase the emancipatory possibilities and individual choices, offering multiple imagined communities and ways of belonging that are not exclusively based on ethnic or national principles. It can also be politically manipulated through newly recreated practices of national commemoration with the aim of reestablishing social cohesion, a sense of security and an obedient relationship to authority.

Cultural identity is based on a certain social poetics or "cultural intimacy" that provides a glue in everyday life. This was described by anthropologist Michael Herzfeld as "embarrassment and rueful self recognition" through various common frameworks of memory and even what might appear as stereotypes. Such identity involves everyday games of hide-and-seek that only "natives" play, unwritten rules of behavior, jokes understood from half a word, a sense of complicity. State propaganda and official national memory build on this cultural intimacy, but there is also a discrepancy and tension between the two.[41] It is very important to distinguish between political nationalism and cultural intimacy, which, after all, is based on common social context, not on national or ethnic homogeneity.

National memory reduces this space of play with memorial signs to a single plot. Restorative nostalgia knows two main narrative plots— the restoration of origins and the conspiracy theory, characteristic of the most extreme cases of contemporary nationalism fed on right-wing popular culture. The conspiratorial worldview reflects a nostalgia for a transcendental cosmology and a simple premodern conception of good and evil. The conspiratorial worldview is based on a single transhistorical plot, a Manichaean battle of good and evil and the inevitable scapegoating of the mythical enemy. Ambivalence, the complexity of history and the specificity of modern circumstances is thus erased, and modern history is seen as a fulfillment of ancient prophecy. "Home," imagine extremist conspiracy theory adherents, is forever under siege, requiring defense against the plotting enemy.

To conspire means literally to breathe together—but usually this collective breath doesn't smell very good. Conspiracy is used pejoratively, to designate a subversive kinship of others, an imagined community based on exclusion more than affection, a union of those who are not with us, but against us. Home is not made of individual memories but of collective projections and "rational delusions."[42] Paranoiac reconstruction of home is predicated on the fantasy of persecution. This is not simply "forgetting of reality" but a psychotic substitution of actual experiences with a dark conspiratorial vision: the creation of a delusionary homeland. Tradition in this way is to be restored with a nearly apocalyptic vengeance. The mechanism of this kind of conspiracy theory is based on the inversion of cause and effect and personal pronouns. "We" (the conspiracy theorists) for whatever reason feel insecure in the modern world and find a scapegoat for our misfortunes, somebody different from us whom we don't like. We project our dislike on them and begin to believe that they dislike us and wish to persecute us. "They" conspire against "our" homecoming, hence "we" have to conspire against "them" in order to restore "our" imagined community. This way, conspiracy theory can come to substitute for the conspiracy itself. Indeed, much of twentieth-century violence, from pogroms to Nazi and Stalinist terror to McCarthy's Red scare, operated in response to conspiracy theories in the name of a restored homeland.

Conspiracy theories, like nostalgic explosions in general, flourish after revolutions. The French Revolution gave birth to the Masonic conspiracy, and the first Russian revolution of 1905 was followed by mass pogroms inspired by the spread of the theories of Judeo-Masonic conspiracies exacerbated after the October revolution and recovered during perestroika. *The Protocols of the Elders of Zion*, which supposedly relate the Jewish plot against the world, is one of the best-documented fakes in world history. The original text, entitled Dialogues Between Montesquieu and Machiavelli, was written by a liberal French journalist, Maurice Joly, as a political invective against the policies of Napoleon III (the Elders of Zion were nowhere present). The pamphlet was prohibited and taken out of print, with one copy only remaining in the British Museum—that will later prove the fictional origins of the *Protocols*. The pamphlet was appropriated by an agent of the Tsarist secret police, transported to Russia, and rewritten by a devoted Russian monk, Nilus Sergius (a pro-Western libertine in his youth turned extreme nationalist), who transformed a political text into a quasi-religious invective of the Antichrist by attributing the words of Machiavelli to the Jewish conspiracists. This presumed Jewish conspiracy was used to instigate and legitimize mass pogroms that were supposed to restore purity to the corrupt modern world. In this extreme case, conspiracy theory produced more violence than conspiracy itself, and a premodern restorative nostalgia turned out to be bloody.

The end of the second millennium has witnessed a rebirth of conspiracy theories.[43] Conspiracy theories are as international as the supposed conspiracies they are fighting against: they spread from post-Communist Russia to the United States, from Japan to Argentina and all around the globe. Usually there is a secret, sacred or conspiratorial text—*The Book* of *Illuminati*, *The Protocols of the Elders of Zion* or, for that matter, the Turner Diaries, which functions like a Bible among the American militia movement.[44] Russian ultranationalists used to claim, for instance, that a truly sacred book, not the Bible but *The Book of Vlas*, had been long concealed from the Russian people. This book supposedly dates back to about 1000 B.C. and contains the true gospel and protocols of pre-Christian pagan Slavic priests. Were the book to be recovered, the primordial Slavic homeland could be recovered as well, were it not for the evil "Jewish Masons" intent on distorting Russian history.[45] It is not surprising that many former Soviet Communist ideologues have embraced a nationalist worldview, becoming "red-and-browns," or Communist-nationalists. Their version of Marxism-Leninism-Stalinism was revealed to have the same totalizing authoritarian structure as the new nationalism.

Nostalgia is an ache of temporal distance and displacement. Restorative nostalgia takes care of both of these symptoms. Distance is compensated by intimate experience and the availability of a desired object. Displacement is cured by a return home, preferably a collective one. Never mind if it's not your home; by the time you reach it, you will have already forgotten the difference. What drives restorative nostalgia is not the sentiment of distance and longing but rather the anxiety about those who draw attention to historical incongruities between past and present and thus question the wholeness and continuity of the restored tradition.

Even in its less extreme form, restorative nostalgia has no use for the signs of historical time—patina, ruins, cracks, imperfections. The 1980s and 1990s was a time of great revival of the past in several projects of total restoration—from the Sistine Chapel to the Cathedral of Christ the Savior in Moscow—that attempted to restore a sense of the sacred believed to be missing from the modern world.

The Sistine Chapel: Restoration of the Sacred

That intimate and forever suspended touch between God and Adam on Michelangelo's frescoes of the Sistine Chapel is perhaps the best known artistic image of all time. There is a crack in the fresco, right above Adam's fingers, like the thunderbolt of history that underscores that familiar gesture of longing and separation. The artist strove to paint the act of divine creation itself and to play God for his artistic masterpiece. Michelangelo's image of spiritual longing turned into the ultimate site of the European sacred, both the religious sacred and the sacred of art, guarded in the world-famous chapel-museum. Later it became a tourist sacred, expensive but not priceless. The crack right above the two longing figures of God and man is now reproduced on innumerable T-shirts, plastic bags and postcards.

That scar on the fresco that threatened to rip apart God and the first man highlights the mysterious aura of the painting, the patina of historical time. Aura, from the Hebrew word for light, was defined by Benjamin as an experience of distance, a mist of nostalgia that does not allow for possession of the object of desire. If aura is intangible, patina is visible: it is that layer of time upon the painting, the mixture of glue, soot, dust and incense from the candles. When it became clear that the Sistine Chapel was in need of restoration, the Vatican's museum authority made a radical decision: to return "back to Michelangelo," to the original brightness of the frescoes. The restoration of the Sistine Chapel became one of the remarkable superprojects of the 1980s that made sure that historical time would no longer threaten the image of sacred creation. The Museums of the Vatican made the deal of the century with Nippon TV Networks of Japan, known primarily for its quiz shows. In return for the millions needed for the restoration, Nippon Networks acquired exclusive rights to televise the restoration all over the world. It seemed to be a mutually beneficial transaction: the treasure of the Vatican was restored in the sacred museum space and at the same time democratized through mass reproduction and televisual projection.

With the help of advanced computer technology, most of the cracks in the background and even the loincloths on the male figures in the foreground were removed to get back to the original "nakedness" and freshness of color. The restorers left no seams, no signs of the process of restoration that is so common for restoration work in the other Italian museums. They had no patience for the patina of time made of candle smoke, soot, cheap Greek wine and bread used by ingenious seventeenth-century restorers and a few hairs from the artist's brush that were stuck in the painting. Actual material traces of the past might disturb the total recreation of the original, which was to look old and brand-new at the same time. The total restoration and the return "to the original Michelangelo" attempted to extinguish the myth of dark romantic genius in agony and ecstasy, forever haunted by Charlton Heston. The new, improved Michelangelo was presented as a rational man, a modern craftsman who did not merely display the miracle of genius, but performed a feat of exceptional labor that was reenacted by twentieth-century scientists. The bright, almost cartoonish colors of the restored fresco bestowed upon Michelangelo the gift of eternal youth.

The work of restoration was not a self-conscious act of interpretation, but rather a transhistoric return to origins with the help of computer technology–a Jurassic Park syndrome all over again. Only this time contemporary scientists did not reconstruct a primordial natural habitat but the vanishing Garden of Eden of European art itself. [46]

The restoration provoked controversy, in which all sides accused the other of distorting Michelangelo and engaging either in nostalgia or in commercialism. In One argument by a group of American art historians brought forth the issue of remaking the past and returning to origins. They claimed that the contemporary restorers in their search for total visibility had removed Michelangelo's "final touch," "l'uluma mano" creating a Bennetton Michelangelo." Through that "final touch" Michelangelo might have projected the historical life of the painting, as if partaking in the aging process. While the accuracy of this accusation is open to discussion, it raises the question of the artist's testimony. If indeed the original painting projected its own historical life, how can one remove the last wish of the artist who left his masterpiece open to the accidents of time? What is more authentic: original image of Michelangelo not preserved through time, or a historical image that aged through centuries? What if Michelangelo rejected the temptation of eternal youth and instead reveled in the wrinkles of time, the future cracks of the fresco?

In fact, Michelangelo himself and his contemporaries loved to restore and recreate the masterpieces of antiquity that survived in fragments and ruins. Their method of work was the opposite of the total restoration of the 1980s. The artists of the sixteenth and early seventeenth century viewed their contribution as a creative collaboration with the masters of the past. They attached their sculptural limbs right to the body of the ancient statues. adding a missing nose or an angel's wing, or even a contemporary mattress, as did Bernini in his sculpture of reclining Hermaphrodite. Renaissance and early Baroque artists never disguised their work as the past. They left the scars of history and reveled in the tactile intimacy of marble and the mystery of distance at the same time. They conscientiously preserved different shades of marble to mark a clear boundary between their creative additions and the fragments of the ancient statues. Moreover, unlike the computer craftsmen of the twentieth century, Michelangelo's contemporaries did not shy away from the individual touch of artistic whim, imperfections and play. While adhering to the time-tested technique, they never strove for blandness and homogeneity that plagued the new restoration of the "original."

When I visited the Sistine Chapel after the restoration. I was struck by a strange and moving spectacle. In spite of the vivid corporeality of the fresco, it revealed a mysterious cosmological vision, an allegory that escapes modern interpreters. Inside the Chapel hundreds of people were staring up at the blindingly bright artwork equipped with all kinds of binoculars and tape recorders, trying to make sense of what they could and could not see. Semi-dark, the space was drowned in multilingual whispers, transforming the Sistine Chapel into a Tower of Babel. The moment the whispers mounted to a crescendo, armed guards loudly admonished the tourists, requesting silence. The tourists here felt like disobedient high school children in front of an incredible miracle. They were in awe and never sure in awe of what Michelangelo's oeuvre or the tour de force of the modern restorers.

Why was the Chapel so poorly lit? After all, so much money and effort went into brightening up the masterpiece. A guide explained to me that the museum had to save on the electricity after such an expensive restoration. The mystique had its price tag. Keeping the Chapel semi-dark was the most economic way of recreating the aura, of having it both ways, bright in the exclusive light of the TV camera and mysterious in the heavily guarded museum space. The total restoration of the Sistine Chapel found a permanent cure for romantic nostalgia and accomplished the definitive repackaging of the past for the future. After this scientific restoration, the original work has been laid bare to the extreme. the protective coating that had shrouded it in mystery having been permanently removed. There is nothing more to discover in the past. The restorers, however, might not have reached their desired end. Believing that their own final touch is invisible, the scientists didn't take into account that modern airborne toxins might begin to corrode the perfect work of restoration in ways that Michelangelo could never have predicted.

My journey to the restored sacred culminated with an embarrassment, if not a sacrilege. On my way to St. Peter's Cathedral, I was stopped by the Vatican fashion police. A young guard indicated to me very politely that my bare shoulders would be completely inappropriate for the visit to the cathedral. I joined a group of other miserable rejects, mostly American tourists in shorts or in sleeveless tops, hiding in the shade on that exhaustingly hot day. Unwilling to take no for an answer, I remembered the old Soviet strategy of camouflage and found a hiding place where I fashioned for myself short sleeves out of a plastic bag adorned with a reproduction of Michelangelo's frescoes (with the crack) and the elegant inscription musei di Vaticano. I then passed nonchalantly by the group of other rejected tourists, paying no attention to their comments about my fashion statement. Mounting the majestic staircase I again came face to face with the vigilant young policeman. My far-from-seamless outfit would have fallen apart with a single touch. But my shoulders were covered and the dress code was restored. Besides, I was wearing the name of the Vatican on my sleeve. The guard let me pass in a ceremonial fashion, maintaining the dignity of the ritual and not condescending to a wink of complicity.

Reflective Nostalgia: Virtual Reality and Collective Memory

Restoration (from re-stoure–re-establishment) signifies a return to the original stasis, to the prelapsarian moment. The past for the restorative nostalgic is a value for the present; the past is not a duration but a perfect snapshot. Moreover, the past is not supposed to reveal any signs of decay; it has to be freshly painted in its "original image" and remain eternally young. Reflective nostalgia is more concerned with historical and individual time, with the irrevocability of the past and human finitude. Re-flection suggests new flexibility, not the reestablishment of stasis. The focus here is not on recovery of what is perceived to be an absolute truth but on the meditation on history and passage of time. To paraphrase Nabokov, these kind of nostalgics are often "amateurs of Time, epicures of duration," who resist the pressure of external efficiency and take sensual delight in the texture of time not measurable by clocks and calendars.[47]

Restorative nostalgia evokes national past and future; reflective nostalgia is more about individual and cultural memory. The two might overlap in their frames of reference, but they do not coincide in their narratives and plots of identity. In other words, they can use the same triggers of memory and symbols, the same Proustian madelaine pastry, but tell different stories about it.

Nostalgia of the first type gravitates toward collective pictorial symbols and oral culture. Nostalgia of the second type is more oriented toward an individual narrative that savors details and memorial signs, perpetually deferring homecoming itself.[48] If restorative nostalgia ends up reconstructing emblems and rituals of home and homeland in an attempt to conquer and spatialize time, reflective nostalgia cherishes shattered fragments of memory and temporalizes space. Restorative nostalgia takes itself dead seriously. Reflective nostalgia, on the other hand, can be ironic and humorous. It reveals that longing and critical thinking are not opposed to one another, as affective memories do not absolve one from compassion, judgment or critical reflection.

Reflective nostalgia does not pretend to rebuild the mythical place called home; it is "enamored of distance, not of the referent itself."[49] This type of nostalgic narrative is ironic, inconclusive and fragmentary. Nostalgics of the second type are aware of the gap between identity and resemblance; the home is in ruins or, on the contrary, has been just renovated and gentrified beyond recognition. This defamiliarization and sense of distance drives them to tell their story, to narrate the relationship between past, present and future. Through such longing these nostalgics discover that the past is not merely that which doesn't exist anymore, but, to quote Henri Bergson, the past "might act and will act by inserting itself into a present sensation from which it borrows the vitality."[50] The past is not made in the image of the present or seen as foreboding of some present disaster; rather, the past opens up a multitude of potentialities, nonteleological possibilities of historic development. We don't need a computer to get access to the virtualities of our imagination: reflective nostalgia has a capacity to awaken multiple planes of consciousness.[51]

The virtual reality of consciousness, as defined by Henri Bergson, is a modern concept, yet it does not rely on technology; on the contrary, it is about human freedom and creativity. According to Bergson, the human creativity, élan vital, that resists mechanical repetition and predictability, allows us to explore the virtual realities of consciousness. For Marcel Proust, remembrance is an unpredictable adventure in syncretic perception where words and tactile sensations overlap. Place names open up mental maps and space folds into time. "The memory of a particular image is but regret for a particular moment; and houses, roads, avenues are as fugitive, alas, as the years," writes Proust at the end of Swann's Way.[52] What matters, then, is this memorable literary fugue, not the actual return home.

The modern nostalgic realizes that "the goal of the odyssey is a rendez-vouz with oneself."[53] For Jorge Luis Borges, for instance, Ulysses returns home only to look back at his journey. In the alcove of his fair queen he becomes nostalgic for his nomadic self: "Where is that man who in the days and nights of exile erred around the world like a dog and said that Nobody was his name?"[54] Homecoming does not signify a recovery of identity; it does not end the journey in the virtual space of imagination. A modern nostalgic can be homesick and sick of home, at once.

As most of the stories in this book suggest, the nostalgic rendezvous with oneself is not always a private affair. Voluntary and involuntary recollections of an individual intertwine with collective memories. In many cases the mirror of reflective nostalgia is shattered by experiences of collective devastation and resembles-involuntarily-a modern work of art. Bosnian poet Semezdin Mehmedinovic offers one of such shattered mirrors from his native Sarajevo:

> Standing by the window, I see the shattered glass of Yugobank. I could stand like this for hours. A blue, glassed-in facade. One floor above the window I am looking from, a professor of aesthetics comes out onto his balcony; running his fingers through his beard, he adjusts his glasses. I see his reflection in the blue facade of Yugobank, in the shattered glass that turns the scene into a live cubist painting on a sunny day.[55]

Bar Nostalgija: Reflections on Everyday Memories

In 1997 I visited a cafe in the center of Ljubljana, located not far from the famous Cobbler's Bridge decorated by stylized freestanding columns that supported nothing. The ambiance was vaguely familiar and comforting, decorated in the style of the 1960s. The music was Beatles and Radmila Karaklaic. The walls were decorated with Chinese alarm clocks, boxes of Vegeta seasoning (which was considered a delicacy in the Soviet Union) and posters of Sputnik carrying the unfortunate dogs Belka and Strelka, who never came home to earth. There was also an enlarged newspaper clipping announcing Tito's death. When I got my bill, I didn't believe my eyes. The name of the place was Nostalgija Snack Bar.

"There would never be a bar like that in Zagreb or Belgrade," a friend from Zagreb told me. "'Nostalgia' is a forbidden word."

"Why?" I asked. "Isn't the government in Zagreb and Belgrade engaging precisely in nostalgia?"

"'Nostalgia' is a bad word. It is associated with the former Yugoslavia. Nostalgia is 'Yugo-nostalgia.'"

The Nostalgija Snack Bar was a friendly place. Its very definition was international—"snack bar"—something that the current owners might have dreamed about in their youth while watching old American movies on Yugoslav TV. The American version of the Nostalgija Snack Bar would not arouse much scandal. One could imagine a cozy place decorated with 1950, lamps, jukeboxes and pictures of James Dean. This is an American way of dealing with the past-to turn history into a bunch of amusing and readily available souvenirs, devoid of politics. More provocative would be to refer to the emblems of the divided past, especially the imagery of segregation. The Nostalgija Snack Bar plays with the shared Yugoslav past that still presents a cultural taboo in many parts of the former Yugoslavia. Nationalist restorers of tradition find unbearable precisely this casualness in dealing with symbolic politics, in mixing the political with the ordinary.

Dubravka Ugresic, a native of Zagreb who declared herself "anational," wrote that the people of the former Yugoslavia, especially those who now live in Croatia and Serbia, suffer from the "confiscation of memory." By that she means a kind of everyday memory, common corpus of emotional landmarks that escapes a dear chart. It is composed of both official symbols and multiple fragments and splinters of the past, "a line of verse, an image, a scene, a scent, a tune, a tone, a word." These memorial landmarks cannot be completely mapped; such memory is composed of shattered fragments, ellipses and scenes of the horrors of war. The word nosta181ja, the pseudo-Greek term common to all the new languages of the country–Croatian, Serbian, Bosnian, Slovene–is linked together with the word Yugoslavia that Milosevic had confiscated from the common memory.

The ordinary fearful citizen of former Yugoslavia, when trying to explain the simplest things, gets entangled in a net of humiliating footnotes. "Yes, Yugoslavia, but the former Yugoslavia, not this Yugoslavia of Milosevic's ..." "Yes, nostalgia, perhaps you could call it that, but you see not for Milosevic, but for that former Yugoslavia ..." "For the former communist Yugoslavia?!" "No, not for the state, not for communism ..." "For what then?" "It's hard to explain, you see..." "Do you mean nostalgia for that singer, Djordje Balasevtc, then?" "Yes, for the singer. ." "But that Balasevic of yours is a Serb, isn't he!?"[56]

One remembers best what is colored by emotion. Moreover, in the emotional topography of memory, personal and historical events tend to be conflated. It seems that the only way to discuss collective memory is through imaginary dialogues with dispersed fellow citizens, expatriates and exiles. One inevitably gets tongue-tied trying to articulate an emotional topography of memory that is made up of such "humiliating footnotes" and cultural untranslatables. The convoluted syntax is part of the elusive collective memory.

The notion of shared social frameworks of memory is rooted in an understanding of human consciousness, which is dialogical with other human beings and with cultural discourses. This idea was developed by Lev Vygotsky and Mikhail Bakhtin, who criticized Freud's solipsistic view of the human psyche.[57] Vygotsky suggested that what makes us human is not a "natural memory" close to perception, but a memory of cultural signs that allows meaning to be generated without external stimulation. Remembering doesn't have to be disconnected from thinking. I remember therefore I am, or I think: I remember and therefore I think.

Psychic space should not be imagined as solitary confinement. British psychologist D. W. Winnicott suggested the concept of a "potential space" between individual and environment that is formed in early childhood. Initially this is the space of the play between the child and the mother. Cultural experience is to be located there, and it begins with creative living first manifested in play.[58] Culture has the potential of becoming a space for individual play and creativity, and not merely an oppressive homogenizing force; far from limiting individual play, it guarantees it space. Culture is not foreign to human nature but integral to it; after all, culture provides a context where relationships do not always develop by continuity but by contiguity. Perhaps what is most missed during historical cataclysms and exile is not the past and the homeland exactly, but rather this potential space of cultural experience that one has shared with one's friends and compatriots that is based neither on nation nor religion but on elective affinities.

Collective memory will be understood here as the common landmarks of everyday life. They constitute shared social frameworks of individual recollections. They are folds in the fan of memory, not prescriptions for a model tale. Collective memory, however, is not the same as national memory, even when they share images and quotations. National memory tends to make a single teleological plot out of shared everyday recollections. The gaps and discontinuities are mended through a coherent and inspiring tale of recovered identity. Instead, shared everyday frameworks of collective or cultural memory offer us mere signposts for individual reminiscences that could suggest multiple narratives. These narratives have a certain syntax (as well as a common intonation), but no single plot. Thus the newspaper clipping with Tito's portrait in the Nostalgija Snack Bar might evoke the end of postwar Yugoslavia, or merely a childhood prank of a former Yugoslav, nothing more. According to Maurice Halbwachs, collective memory offers a zone of stability and normativity in the current of change that characterizes modern life. [59] The collective frameworks of memory appear as safeguards in the stream of modernity and mediate between the present and the past, between self and other.

The historians of nostalgia Jean Starobinski and Michael Roth conclude that in the twentieth century nostalgia was privatized and internalized.[60] The longing for home shrunk to the longing for one's own childhood. It was not so much a maladjustment to progress as a "maladjustment to the adult life." In the case of Freud, nostalgia was not a specific disease but a fundamental structure of human desire linked to the death drive: "The finding of an object is always a refinding of it."[61] Freud appropriates the vocabulary of nostalgia; for him, the only way of "returning home" is through analysis and recognition of early traumas.

In my view, nostalgia remains an intermediary between collective and individual memory. Collective memory can be seen as a playground, not a graveyard of multiple individual recollections. The turn, or rather return, to the study of collective memory in contemporary critical thought, both in the social sciences and the humanities, is in itself a recovery of a certain framework of scholarly references that has been debated for two decades and now appears to have been virtually forgotten. Collective memory is a messy, unsystematic concept that nevertheless allows one to describe the phenomenology of human experience. The study of collective memory defies disciplinary boundaries and invites us to look at artistic as well as scholarly works. It brings us back to the reflections on "mental habitus" (Panofsky and Lefèvre) and "mentality" defined as "what is conceived and felt, the field of intelligence and of emotion," and on "cultural myth, understood as a recurrent narrative, perceived as natural and commonsensical in a given culture, seemingly independent from historical and political context."[62] Cultural myths, then, are not lies but rather shared assumptions that help to naturalize history and makes it livable, providing the daily glue of common intelligibility.

Yet no system of thought or branch of science provides us a full picture of human memory. The interpretation of memory might well be a "conjectural science," to use Carlo Ginzburg's term.[63] Only false memories can be totally recalled. From Greek mnemonic art to Proust, memory has always been encoded through a trace, a detail, a suggestive synecdoche. Freud developed a poetic concept of a "screen memory," a contextual contiguous detail that "shades the forgotten scene of private trauma or revelation." Like a screen of a Viennese writing pad, it keeps traces, doodles, conjectures, distracting attention from the central plot imposed by an analyst or interpreter of memory. Often collective frameworks function as those screen memories that determine the contexts of an individual's affective recollections. In exile or in historic transition, the signposts from the former homeland themselves acquire emotional significance. For instance, former East Germans launched a campaign to save their old traffic signs representing a funny man in a cute hat, Ampelmann, which was supplanted by a more pragmatic West German image. Nobody paid much attention to Ampelmann before, but once he vanished from the street signs, he suddenly became a beloved of the whole nation.

One becomes aware of the collective frameworks of memories when one distances oneself from one's community or when that community itself enters the moment of twilight. Collective frameworks of memory are rediscovered in mourning. Freud made a distinction between mourning and melancholia. Mourning is connected to the loss of a loved one or the loss of some abstraction, such as a homeland, liberty or an ideal. Mourning passes with the elapsing of time needed for the "work of grief." In mourning "deference to reality gains the day," even if its "behest cannot be at once obeyed." In melancholia the loss is not clearly defined and is more unconscious. Melancholia doesn't pass with the labor of grief and has less connection to the outside world. It can lead to self-knowledge or to continuous narcissistic self-flagellation. "The complex of melancholia behaves like an open wound, draining the ego until it is utterly depleted."[64] Reflective nostalgia has elements of both mourning and melancholia. While its loss is never completely recalled, it has some connection to the loss of collective frameworks of memory. Reflective nostalgia is a form of deep mourning that performs a labor of grief both through pondering pain and through play that points to the future.

The Nostalgija Snack Bar restores nothing. There was never such a cafe in the former Yugoslavia. There is no longer such a country, so Yugoslav popular culture can turn into self-conscious style and a memory field trip. The place exudes the air of Central European cafe culture and the new dandyism of the younger generation that enjoys Tito-style gadgets and Wired magazine. This is a new kind of space that plays with the past and the present. The bar gently mocks the dream of greater patria while appealing to shared frameworks of memory of the last Yugoslav generation. It makes no pretense of depth of commemoration and offers only a transient urban adventure with excellent pastries and other screen memories. As for the labor of grief, it could take a lifetime to complete.

Vladimir Nabokov's False Passport

Nabokov goes to the origins of early modern nostalgia—both as a physical ache and as a metaphysical longing for the lost cosmology of the world. Not surprisingly, the journey home in Nabokov's poetics is linked to many mythical journeys—to the underworld or to the "other shore," to another life or to death. Yet this is never a one-way trip. The writer never becomes a newborn patriot or a convert to a single religious or metaphysical system, thereby tremendously irritating some of his critics, who would be glad to pin him down like a butterfly. "My" Nabokov is not a dual citizen of this world and another world, but a passportless wanderer in time as well as in space, who knows all too well that the object in the mirror is closer than it appears—and if you come too close you will merge with your reflection. He is closer to a poetic mystic who believes in patterns and the gaps between them, in ellipses that should never be spelled out. "It's a mystery—ta-ta-ry-ry / and I can't be more explicit."[65] Nabokov transforms the irreparable loss of exile into his life work. This is not merely aesthetic or metaliterary play, but an artful mechanism for survival. The writer had many second homes, not only "comfortable hotels" and the inexpensive sabbatical houses that he rented, but homes in his art that uncannily evoke the architecture of this Italianate mansion, badly in need of repair. The homes and museums in his texts inevitably open into another dimension and into a time warp of sorts.

Back home in the United States, I pulled out the English and Russian editions of Nabokov's autobiography to verify the quote about the passportless spy. I did not believe my eyes. In the Russian version, the passportless spy did not appear in the "stereoscopic dreamland" that transports the writer from the United States to Russia. The Russian text spoke only of doubles, not of spies—leaving in the fantastic element, but not the political.[66] Intrigued by this divergence, I decided to follow the trail of the passportless spy in Nabokov's works—which bifurcates, leading us to the writer's recreated homeland and through the labyrinths of exile. The false passport becomes a password for the writer's reflective nostalgia.

Speak Memory opens with two visual representations of home—a diagram of the Nabokovs' country estates in Vyra and Batovo that the writer drew from memory, and a photograph of the house in St. Petersburg-Leningrad, accompanied by an explanatory caption that reads like an invitation to a detective story:

> This photograph, taken in 1955 by an obliging American tourist, shows the Nabokov house, of pink granite with frescoes and other Italianate ornaments, in St. Petersburg, now Leningrad, 47 Morskaya, now Hertzen Street. My room was on the third floor, above the oriel. The lindens lining the street did not exist. Those green upstarts now hide the second-floor east-corner window of the room where I was born. After nationalization the house accommodated the Danish mission, and later, a school of architecture. The little sedan at the curb belongs presumably to the photographer.[67]

The caption refuses to accept the literal truth of the photograph. Instead, Nabokov questions documentary evidence, dwelling on renaming and imprecision. The writer becomes a detective who explores the hidden territories behind the "green upstarts." He takes humorous delight in photographic opacity, for which no revelatory blow-up is possible. The writer focuses our attention on a foreign sedan at the curb, which helps locate a point of view in the image—namely, that of a well-wishing tourist photographer, who took risks in taking the picture. The existence of the photograph itself is precarious and cannot be taken for granted. Roland Barthes wrote that the photographs he loved most possessed, besides social meaning and a sense of "being there," a certain capacity to prick one's emotions a punctum (a wound or a mark made by a pointed instrument).[68] A punctum "is this element which rises from the scene, shoots out of it like an arrow and pierces me. "A punctum is a singular accident that joins the viewer and the image and reveals something about both; it points at the scars in the viewer's psyche and imagination. For Nabokov, this punctum is not in what is represented, but in what remains invisible. In other words, what makes these images so poignant is not a pang of recognition, but a realization of difference.

The story of the snapshot is itself remarkable. It was given to Nabokov's sister, Elena Sikorsky, not by a passportless spy but by a friend. Nabokov writes her back with gratitude and sadness: "Thank you very much for the heartwrenching pictures. The lindens, of course, were not there, and everything is greyer than the painting of memory, but still very detailed and recognizable."[69]

In the face of these heartwrenching images, the writer clings desperately to his written word. He refuses to accept this ready-made image of home. The photograph pales in comparison with memory and imagination. The literal is less truthful than the literary. A return home does not involve only a journey in space, but also an adventure in time. And no snapshot can capture that. Susan Sontag wrote that photography is an "elegiac art, a twilight art."[70] It is a memento mori, an inventory of mortality that inevitably sentimentalizes the past and the present. "The knowledge gained through still photography will always be some kind of sentimentalism, whether cynical or humanist. It will be a knowledge at bargain prices."[71] Nabokov is suspicious of elegiac art. The snapshot of his Petersburg home becomes an uncanny image of nostos without algia. The photograph is black and white and cannot capture that nebulous "pink granite" of the building and its patina of time past, lost and regained. Nabokov's texts, however, are permeated with the "mauve remoteness"— the twilight aura of the abandoned house in the Baltic "pink granite." In his memoirs Nabokov takes over the photographic medium and turns it into his metaphor, he puts technology to his own use, multiplying "virtual planes" of imagination. If the photograph is an example of a restorative nostalgia that offers an illusion of completeness, the writer's text presents a drama of nonrecognition and reflective longing.[72]

The temporary homes of émigrés are described with equal uncanniness in another caption:

A snapshot taken by my wife of our three-year-old son Dmitri (born May 10, 1934) standing with me in front of our boardinghouse, Les Hesperides, in Mentone, at the beginning of December 1937. We looked it up twenty-two years later. Nothing had changed, except the management and the porch furniture. There is always, of course, the natural thrill of retrieved time; beyond that, however, I get no special kick out of revisiting old émigré haunts in those incidental countries.

The winter mosquitoes, I remember, were terrible. Hardly had I extinguished the light in my room than it would come, that ominous whine whose unhurried, doleful, and wary rhythm contrasted so oddly with the actual mad speed of the satanic insect's gyrations. One waited for the touch in the dark, one freed a cautious arm from under the bedclothes—and mightily slapped one's own ear, whose sudden hum mingled with that of the receding mosquito. But then, next morning, how eagerly one reached for a butterfly net upon locating one's replete tormentor—a thick dark little bar on the white of the ceiling![73]

Nabokov gets a kick out of remembering, not revisiting. This is a lyrical photograph, with the dark shadows of the dandy émigré hat upon the writer's eyes, and the piercing eyes of his little son shying away from the camera. Nabokov humorously deflects attention from the elegiac pleasure of nostalgia to the art of memory. The caption guides us beyond the closed door, where the buzz of the invisible mosquito orchestrates the scene of memory. Nabokov's mosquitoes are often intertextual. Flies and moths, it turns out, are both poetic and antipoetic things par excellence that inspire both literature and philosophy.[74] In Nabokov flies, moths and especially butterflies are, first and foremost, messengers of memory. They are not symbolic but singular. This particularly jarring winter mosquito, whose rhythmic whining conceals its "satanic gyrations" and timing of attacks, is a creature that inhabits "old émigré haunts." This winter mosquito is an antidote to nostalgia, disrupting any elegiac recollection of the past.

Yet the mosquito is more than an accidental annoyance; it represents a strategy of "cryptic disguise" or mimicry that defines Nabokov's narratives of homecoming. The mosquito is killed with a butterfly net in the morning when it loses its powers of mimicry and reveals itself as a black cipher on the white ceiling. In the end, Nabokov defies photographic objectivity by creating his own black-and-white contrast in the recollection of the irritating mosquito, thereby turning photographic mimesis into a kind of poetic mimicry performed by the writer himself. In a perpetual quixotic battle with deterministic modern ideologies, from Darwin's theory of evolution to Freudian psychoanalysis, Nabokov develops his own conception of mimicry—as an aesthetic rather than natural survival. Mimicry is based on repetition, but an uncanny repetition that entails difference and the unpredictability of imagination. It is opposed to the struggle for survival and class struggle, as the principal drives of human existence. Mimicry does not simply represent, but also disguises and conceals nature. Homo poeticus is most important for Nabokov; without him, homo sapiens would not have been possible. "A colored spiral in a small ball of glass, this is how I see my own life. . . . In the spiral form, the circle, uncoiled, unwound, has ceased to be vicious; it has been set free."[75] Mimicry corresponds to Nabokov's idea of the "spiritualized circle." Mimicry, then, revisits without a return, marking the singularity of cryptic disguise.

While cryptic disguise is a foundation of Nabokov's exilic art, it is also a version of the immigrant art of survival and adaptation. The immigrant mimics the natives, sometimes excessively, becoming more European than Europeans or more American than Americans, more desperate in his eagerness to please. Only in the writer's case, the pain of "passing" is transformed into an imaginative play that allows him to criss-cross the borders between his former homeland and the adopted land.

Nostalgia, Kitsch and Death

Why is it that for Nabokov certain cures for nostalgia are more dangerous than the disease itself? Prefabricated images of home offer an escape from anxiety of loss. "Kitsch is an antidote to death," claimed Milan Kundera, noting that "none of us is a superman enough" to escape kitsch entirely, since it is part of the human condition. Nabokov's stories and novels are filled with nostalgic heroes and heroines that walk a fragile line between banality and survival, allowing the writer to dramatize his longing. One of the most striking nostalgic characters in Nabokov's memoirs is his Swiss governess, Mademoiselle O., whose story is intimately connected to his own.

A poor, stout Swiss governess arrives in the "hyperborean gloom of remote Muscovy" in the early twentieth century, mumbling one of the few Russian words that she knows—the word for "where," gde, pronounced by her as "giddy-eh." In parallel, Nabokov recalls his own return to Russia at the age of five on board the Nord Express: "An exciting sense of rodina, 'motherland,' was for the first time organically mingled with the comfortably creaking snow."[76] Apart from the explicit message, we notice here a presence of Russian words that compose a cryptic message "spoken" by both narrator and Mademoiselle: gde rodina—where is the homeland?

While in Russia Mademoiselle sighs about the silence of her native Alps and recreated a little Swiss home in her Russian dwelling, complete with postcard images of the castle, a lake and a swan, and pictures of herself as a young woman with thick braids. After the revolution, as the Nabokovs fled Russia, Mademoiselle returns "home" to Switzerland, where she recreated a dreamlike version of her Russian dwellings. Following the exemplary nostalgic route, Mademoiselle went back to the Alps, but the homecoming didn't cure her at all; it rather aggravated the longing.

Visiting his aging governess in Switzerland, the young Nabokov finds Mademoiselle nostalgic for Russia. Instead of the Château de Chillon, her room is decorated with a picture of a garish troika. The only place Mademoiselle could call home is the past—mainly, the past that she framed for herself, or for which she found a convincing ready-made image. Mademoiselle changed the souvenirs, but not the overall design of her self-pitying nostalgia: "What bothers me, is that a sense of misery, and nothing else, is not enough to make a permanent soul," confesses the young writer. At first glance it might seem that Mademoiselle's nostalgia is restorative while the narrator's is ironic, and yet he cannot survive without her. Nabokov's own nostalgic and antinostalgic revelations— from the nightmare of passportless spy to the memory of his father's death—run in parallel montage to the story of Mademoiselle, often with unpredictable turns.

As a young writer leaves his Swiss governess, disappointed by her inability to listen to him and confront his and her own past, he unexpectedly finds himself an uncanny heir to Mademoiselle's language and imagery. It is not by chance that the story was first written in French, the language that Mademoiselle taught him. Moreover, the Swiss nature itself seems to imitate Mademoiselle's nostalgia. The rain falls over the mountain lake with a castle in the background, just like in Mademoiselle's French lessons—Il pleut toujours en Suisse. What's most alarming is that in the middle of the mountain lake the writer sees a solitary swan flapping its wings, sending ripples through the water, defying its own reflection.

Why should one be afraid of swans and swan lakes? For Nabokov the swan is a dangerous bird of kitsch. In his essay on Gogol, the swans exemplify ready-made melancholia and poshlost—the Russian word for obscenity and bad taste. Poshlost is described as one of those untranslatable Russian words meaning "cheap, sham, common, smutty, pink-and-blue." Poshlost is an unobvious sham that deceives not only aesthetically but also morally. Nabokov retells Gogol's story of a German gallant who devised a special way to impress his maiden, whom he has been courting to no avail. This is how he decided to "conquer the heart of his cruel Gretchen":

> Every evening he would take off his clothes, plunge into the lake and, as he swam there, right under the eyes of his beloved, he would keep embracing a couple of swans which had been specially prepared for that purpose. I do not quite know what those swans were supposed to symbolize, but I do know that for several evenings on end he did nothing but float about and assume pretty postures with his birds.[77]

What is kitschy is not the swan itself but the predictability of this dance of seduction, which relies on ready-made emotional and aesthetic effects. Nabokov calls it by the Russian word poshlost and insists patriotically on its Russian originality. Russian poshlost in fact is a twin sister of the German word kitsch, as described by Clement Greenberg and Hermann Broch. Kitsch imitates the effects of art, not the mechanisms of conscience. In the words of Theodor Adorno, it is a "parody of catharsis," a secondhand epiphany. Kitsch is often associated with a nostalgic vision of the middle-class home; it domesticates every possible alienation, satiates the insatiable thirst with artificially sweetened drinks that quench the very need for longing. For Nabokov, sentimentality of this kind is not merely a matter of taste, but an atrophy of reflective thinking; and thus an ethical as well as an aesthetic failure.

Yet the swan near Mademoiselle's Swiss home haunts the writer. It was "an aged swan, a large, uncouth, dodo-like creature, making ridiculous efforts to hoist himself into a moored boat." It is as if the swan were looking for home, maybe his last one. The aging swan, caught in an act of transient futility, evokes many allegories of beauty and melancholy. The swan lake is at once Swiss and Russian. The swan is a bird of kitsch and high culture, an allegorical being and a living creature, ridiculous yet touching. Nabokov triangulates his and Mademoiselle's memories by literature, evoking all the melancholic birds of French poetry that Mademoiselle might have read to him.[78] By describing his bird as "dodo-like" Nabokov interrupts all the clichés and poetic references to the swans of other times. The detail turns the predictable swan into a creature of individual memory and anticipatory nostalgia. He evokes something that hasn't happened yet, at least not at the time of his strange apparition. The "impotent flapping of his wings" was "laden with that strange significance which sometimes in dreams is attached to a finger pressed to mute lips."[79] Years later, the image of this aging swan is what the writer remembers when he learns of Mademoiselle's death.

The encounter with the uncouth swan brings the ironist a moment of self-doubt. In trying to distinguish desperately between his own reflective memory and Mademoiselle's sentimental nostalgia, the writer wonders if he himself had committed the sin of poshlost by making Mademoiselle's story into a predictable nostalgic cliché and thereby missing some of her deeper sensitivities and intuitions. Was his inability to hear her a response to her failure to listen to him? Were both of them equally inattentive and not curious about the other?

The apparition of the homeless swan is the moment of an ironic epiphany in the story in more ways than one. An ironic epiphany is a kind of imperfect moment, a fateful coincidence and a misrecognition. Ironic epiphanies reveal the patterns of memory and fate but don't allow the author to master them by creating a redemptive unified vision. What's ironic about them is that the master ironist himself cannot control the vertigo of fate.

Only after having told the story of Mademoiselle's misery does Nabokov allow himself to drop hints about his own tragic loss that he would have liked to share with his old governess. It concerned the tragic death of his father, the event that haunts the autobiography: "[T]he things and beings that I had most loved in the security of my childhood had been turned to ashes or shot through the heart."[80] The cryptic or explicit references to the death of the writer's father occur at the end of almost every chapter.[81] The murder of his father does not allow the writer to go back and beautify the past. The ashes are reminders of the impossibility of homecoming.

The ironic epiphany had even more unforeseen echoes. At the time of the story's writing, Nabokov could not have imagined foreseeing that almost half a century later, he, like Mademoiselle, would make his home by a Swiss lake. Nor did he know that he had already dreamed up the landscape of his own death. Vladimir Nabokov died, not far from his former governess, in the grand hotel Montreux Palace, decorated with swans.

Exile by Choice

"The break in my own destiny affords me in retrospect a syncopal kick that I would not have missed for worlds," writes Nabokov in his autobiography. Syncope has a linguistic, musical and medical meaning. Linguistically, it refers to "a shortening of the word by the omission of a sound, letter, or syllable from the middle of the word." Musically, it indicates a change of rhythm and a displacement of accent, "a shift of accent in a passage or composition that occurs when a normally weak beat is stressed." Medically, it refers to "a brief loss of consciousness caused by transient anemia, a swoon."[82] Syncope is the opposite of symbol and synthesis. Symbol, from the Greek syn-ballein, means to throw together, to represent one thing through another, to transcend the difference between the material and immaterial worlds. The syncopal tale of exile is based on sensuous details, not symbols. Nabokov was notoriously suspicious of symbols, believing that they "bleach the soul," numb "all capacity to enjoy the fun and enchantment of art."[83] Details, however, are "asides of the spirit" that animate curiosity, making life and art unpredictable and unrepeatable. Syncopation does not help to restore the lost home. What it accomplishes is a transformation of the loss into a musical composition, a ciphering of pain into art.

Nabokov was very worried that his nostalgia would be misinterpreted as the eternal Russian *toska*, or even worse, as the whining of a Russian landowner who lost his estate and fortune in the revolution.[84] "The nostalgia I have been cherishing all these years is a hypertrophied sense of lost childhood, not sorrow for lost banknotes. And finally: I reserve for myself the right to yearn after an ecological niche:

. . . Beneath the sky
Of my America to sigh
For one locality in Russia.[85]

The object of Nabokov's nostalgia, then, is not "Russia," but one locality in Russia, an ecological niche. He claims to have discovered the "delights of nostalgia long before the Revolution had removed the scenery of his young years."[86] In the end, Nabokov made his nostalgia personal and artistic, independent of external circumstances. Imposed exile becomes voluntary. To the question of an intrusive interviewer about whether he believed in God, Nabokov answered: "I know more than I can express in words, and the little I can express I would not have expressed had I not known more." Nabokov, till his death, did not belong to an organized church and never wrote anything resembling a metaphysical treatise or a total system of thought. Literary writing was his worldview and his philosophy. Expressing everything would be tantamount to destroying the writer's precocious design of immortality; it is like a forced return to a reconstructed home. The writer chose exile.

When it came to chance, Nabokov was unusually optimistic, believing that lines of fate, like waves, offer the attentive wanderer more than one opportunity for a fortuitous encounter. Suspicious of any teleology, Nabokov nevertheless trusted that memory had its own watermarks and designs. The double exposure of exilic consciousness became such a watermark. Initially a political catastrophe and a personal misfortune, exile became the writer's destiny, which he discerned and realized. In interviews Nabokov stressed that he was not miserable in exile, adding on one occasion that his own life has been "incomparably happier and healthier than that of Genghis Khan who fathered the first Nabok, a petty Tatar Prince."[87] Nabokov retrospectively rewrote his own biography as a tale of a "happy expatriation" that began at his birth.[88] Algia, longing, helped the writer to inhabit virtual planes of existence. Nostos was what he carried with him, light as ashes and dreams.

Nostalgia and Global Culture

When I returned to Leningrad-St. Petersburg, I found myself wandering around the miniature rockets rusting in the children's playgrounds.

FIGURE 10.1 The Last Sputnik, 1999. Photo by Svetlana Boym.

Crash-landed here three decades ago, they reminded me of the dreams of my early childhood. I remembered that the first thing we learned to draw in kindergarten in the 1960s were rockets. We always drew them in mid-launch, in a glorious upward movement with a bright flame shooting from the tail. The playground rockets resembled those old drawings, only they didn't fly very far. If you wanted to play the game, you had to be prepared to glide down, to fall, not to fly. The playground rockets were made in the euphoric era of Soviet space exploration, when the future seemed unusually bright and the march of progress triumphant. Soon after the first man flew into space, Nikita Khrushchev promised that the children of my generation would live in the era of communism and travel to the moon. We dreamed of going into space before going abroad, of traveling upward, not westward. Somehow we failed in our mission. The dream of cosmic communism did not survive, but the miniature rockets did. For some reason, most likely for lack of an alternative, neighborhood kids still played on these futuristic ruins from another era that seemed remarkably old-fashioned. On the playgrounds of the nouveau riche, the attractions have been updated in the spirit of the time. Brand-new wooden huts with handsome towers in a Russian folkloric style have supplanted the futuristic rockets of the past.

Before cyberspace, outer space was the ultimate frontier. More than merely a displaced battlefield of the cold war, the exploration of the cosmos promised a future victory over the temporal and spatial limitations of human existence, putting an end to longing. Now that the cosmic dream has become ancient history, new utopias are neither political nor artistic, but rather technological and economic. As for politics and philosophy, they play a minor role in the imagination of the future. Once opium, leeches and a return home was a panacea for nostalgia. Now it is technology that has become the opiate of the people, that promises speed, ease and oblivion of everything except the technological products themselves. In its original meaning, the word technology, from the Greek techne, shares the same root with the word art. Technology is not a goal in itself but an enabling medium. While nostalgia mourns distances and disjunctures between times and spaces, never bridging them, technology offers solutions and builds bridges, saving the time that the nostalgic loves to waste.

Yet fundamentally, both technology and nostalgia are about mediation. As a disease of displacement, nostalgia was connected to passages, transits and means of communication. Nostalgia—like memory—depends on mnemonic devices. Since the invention of writing in ancient Egypt, these memory aids have been viewed with ambivalence as tools of forgetting as well as remembering. In the nineteenth century, many believed that railroads would take care of displacement and that the speed of transportation would accommodate trips to and from home. Some thought that the modern metropolis would provide enough excitement and stimuli to quell people's longings for the rustic life. Yet this did not come to pass. Instead, nostalgia accompanied each new stage of modernization, taking on different genres and forms, playing tricks with the timetables.

Each new medium affects the relationship between distance and intimacy that is at the core of nostalgic sentiment. In the early twentieth century, Russian avant-garde poets hailed the radio as a revolutionary medium that would provide a universal understanding and bring the world into everyone's home. It turned out that the radio was used by democratic politicians and dictators alike, who loved to promote their own messages of "progress," the bright future, as well as of community and traditional charisma. Radio technology brought back oral culture, yet the community of radio storytellers and listeners was decentered, transitory and not at all traditional. When the first films made by the brothers Lumière were shown some hundred years ago, awestricken viewers screamed while watching a train approaching head on. The cinema too was hailed as a universal language, but its uncanniness wasn't lost on the first reviewers, who saw film as both amazingly lifelike and terrifyingly ghostly. Film marked a return to the visual culture that had dominated Europe before the advent of print media.

Cyberspace now appears to be the newest frontier. The Internet is organized in a radically spatial manner; it is datacentric and hypertextual, based on simultaneity, not on continuity. Issues of time, narrative and making meaning are much less relevant in the Internet model. Computer memory is independent of affect and the vicissitudes of time, politics and history; it has no patina of history, and everything has the same digital texture. On the blue screen two scenarios of memory are possible: a total recall of undigested information bytes or an equally total amnesia that could occur in a heartbeat with a sudden technical failure.

At first glance, hypertextual organization eliminates the very premise of nostalgia—that of the irreversibility of time and of the inability to revisit other times and places. Here it is merely a matter of access. Time in cyberspace is conceived in terms of speed: speed of access and speed of technological innovation. There is simply no time for temporal experiments of remembering loss and reflecting on memory.

It is now up to eccentric East Europeans to lament the loss of slowness: "In existential mathematics . . . the degree of slowness is directly proportional to the intensity of memory; the degree of speed is directly proportional to the intensity of forgetting."[89] Internet patriots would claim that cyberspace unfolds in another dimension, beyond the rules of existential mathematics and the dialectic of memory and forgetting. Cyberspace makes the bric-a-brac of nostalgia available in digital form, appearing more desirable than the real artifacts. Jorge Luis Borges wrote a story about a map of an empire that is made the size of the empire; at the end the storyteller dreams of walking on the ruins of the map. One day one might be able to walk around the ruins of a webpage surrounded by new colonial houses.

There is a hidden paradox in the Internet philosophy of time: while internally the system relies on hypertext and interaction, externally many info-enthusiasts rely on the nineteenth-century narrative of progress with occasional eliminational pathos. The extreme version of the eliminational model of progress (which believes, for example, that e-book will supplant the book altogether rather than that the two can happily cohabit in the same household) presents a kind of tunnel vision of the road toward the future. It presumes that there is no environment around that tunnel, no context, no other streets and avenues that take a detour from the underground speed lanes and traffic jams. Reflective nostalgia challenges this tunnel vision, backtracking, slowing down, looking sideways, meditating on the journey itself.

Moreover, the cultural archeology of the cyber world reveals that it too had its own nostalgic genesis. The discoverers of cyberspace inherited some of the ideas of the 1960s of "real space" experience and experimentation in love and politics, coupled with a critique of technology. Now these ideas of "free communication" and grassroots political protests have immigrated and taken root in virtual space. No wonder there is such a phenomenon as dot.communism on the web, a suspicion of the "bourgeois institutions" of private property and copyright.[90] The very creation of the new media was a curious collaboration of the cold war military-industrial complex and the aging hippies who turned into computer scientists. In the 1980s, cyber travel empowered people who had ceased to seek empowerment in other spaces. This peculiar chicken-and-egg logic produced some of the paradoxes of cyberspace. It is not by chance that the hero of 2000 is a digitized Marshall McLuhan, giving a new twist on the old saying, "(digital) medium is the message."

The discoverers of the Internet borrowed key metaphors of philosophical and literary discourse—virtual reality comes from Bergson's theory of consciousness, hypertext, from narrative theories of intertextuality— which were then regarded as the exclusive property of the new media. The Internet also took over elements of pastoral imagery and "Western" genres (e.g., the global village, homepages and the frontier mentality). The new media redefined the architecture of space with a "superhighway," villages and chatrooms—all evidence that the Internet foregrounds pastoral suburbia and the romance of the highway and domestic morality tales over the ruins of the metropolis. E-mail, however, offered the possibility of instant intimacy; the more distant the correspondents, the more intensely they shared their innermost secrets in all late-night languages. I don't think I would have been able to write this book without the virtual support of my friends, nostalgics and antinostalgics from all over the world. Romances of the 1990s also took place online and often resulted in disappointment, embarrassment at best, violence at worst, the moment the computer interface was substituted by face-to-face encounter. The computer medium is largely tactile, not merely visual; and when two strangers meet on the web, their fingers unwittingly search for that erotic keyboard of their own beloved computer, not for the other person's hand. Somehow the e-lovers discovered that when the distance of cyberspace was gone, so too was the intimacy.

The recent phenomenon of video recording someone's home life on a homepage gives a whole new meaning to the expression "being at home." Being at home in this self-imposed panopticon scenario means being watched or being a voyeur, for no particular political reasons. For all participants in this interaction, privacy becomes vicarious and virtual; no longer the property of a single individual, it turns into a space of projection and interaction. No wonder an Internet artist recently named her daughter E (reminding me of the Russian dystopian novel We written eighty years ago, where the citizens of the Single State were called by a single letter). The mother did not wish to oppress her daughter with her choice of a name and left it as interactive as possible, remarking only that for her, E stands for "entropy."[91]

Recently the prefix cyber has itself become nostalgic, as Jeffery Nunberg observes; the new prefix is e, as in e-world.[92] Cyberspace had a sense of open spaces and conquering frontiers; e- is more about marking territories, and is particularly beloved by corporations that try to fix you to their site and limit your cyber wanderings. Airport and suburbia terminology (with new words such as e-hub) supplanted the romantic vocabulary of space exploration and the dream of uncorrupted communication.

Electronic mediation traverses national borders, creating different kinds of virtual immigrations. If the nation-state has begun to yield to the forces of globalization, the debate about regulating the Internet between Europe and the United States echoes the debates about their real-life systems of government and attitudes toward violence, hate speech and the public-private distinction. Similarly, recent discussions in the United States about public Internet and Internet constitution that would establish etiquette and rules of conduct in the cyber world reveal a preoccupation with the disappearing public sphere that occurs in real as well as virtual spaces. Since the late 1980s, there has been a widespread belief among promoters of globalization that the economy and technology determine politics, and culture is nothing more than a consumer item and the icing on the cake. The economic and political developments in post-Communist countries as well as in Asia and Latin America in the 1990s revealed that the opposite might be true: cultural mentality and political institutions could affect the economy both locally and globally.

It is not surprising, then, that the dream of the nation-state is alive and well among the virtual citizens of cyberspace—not all of whom have chosen to become citizens of the world. Many sites representing minority communities perpetuate ethnic and racial animosities, cyber hype notwithstanding. The Balkan war of the early 1990s was replayed in cyberspace when in November 1998 Serbian hackers destroyed the web site of a Croatian magazine, and Croat hackers immediately retaliated. Around the same time, an Albanian site was "desecrated" by cyber graffiti alleging "ethnic Albanian lies." Ethnic attachments and stereotypes did not turn out to be virtual even in virtual space.

The "millennial" piece of Russian cyber postmodernism was the revisionist cartoon representing Beavis and Butthead. During NATO's intervention in Yugoslavia, Russian hackers destroyed the NATO site. The image they sent showed Beavis and Butthead with captions such as "From Russia with Love," "Down with NATO," and "KPZ" (the abbreviation of kamera predvaritel'nogo zakliucheniia—the pretrial holding cell of the Russian-Soviet police and KGB). The cartoon was quite witty. It projected an anti-Western message in the global language of Western popular culture that struck back at the West like a boomerang. The ability to speak the global language and use the web is no guarantee of shared culture, democratization or mutual understanding. The message from the Russian hackers taken in the Russian context of that moment was neither controversial nor countercultural—in fact it represented the view of the Russian government, a national knee-jerk reaction. The cartoon was subversive vis-à-vis the assumed global patriarch, NATO, but it also nostalgically and unselfconsciously affirmed the imperial aspirations of the local big brother, Russia.

In Europe those who resist globalization American-style often appeal to the traditional European social structures of welfare, a balance of work and leisure, market values and cultural values. The most recent movements that have emerged in 2000 often have the word slow in their names, such as the movement for Slow Eating, which is a part of the Gastronomic Left, who try to influence the future through gastronomic nostalgia. Having begun, predictably, in Italy and France, the movement focuses on the politics of food, and protests what they call "franken food" (referring to GM products) made with utmost efficiency for fast consumption. Yet even the movement against globalization that culminated with protests in Seattle and Washington was organized globally and widely used the World Wide Web for the dissemination of information. Some activists tried to argue that they were not against globalization altogether; rather, they were against technological and economic globalization and for globalization with a human face (and the freedom to eat slowly). Nostalgia in fact has always spoken a global language, from the nineteenth-century romantic poem to the late- twentieth-century e-mail.

The excitement of cyber exploration notwithstanding, when it comes to nostalgia, the medium is never the message. At least not the whole message. To examine the uses and abuses of nostalgic longing one has to look for mechanisms of a different kind—mechanisms of consciousness. Reflection on nostalgia allows us to reexamine mediation and the medium itself, including technology.

Nostalgia is about the virtual reality of human consciousness that cannot be captured even by the most advanced technological gadgets. Longing is connected to the human predicament in the modern world, yet there seems to be little progress in the ways of understanding it. Indeed, there is a progressive devaluation of all forms of comprehensive, noncompartmentalized forms of knowledge. Culture is increasingly squeezed between the entertainment industry and religion, while education is understood more and more as management and therapy, rather than the process of learning to think critically. With the waning of the role of the art and humanities, there are fewer and fewer venues for exploring nostalgia, which is compensated for with an overabundance of nostalgic readymades. The problem with prefabricated nostalgia is that it does not help us to deal with the future. Creative nostalgia reveals the fantasies of the age, and it is in those fantasies and potentialities that the future is born. One is nostalgic not for the past the way it was, but for the past the way it could have been. It is this past perfect that one strives to realize in the future.

No political scientist or Kremlinologist could have predicted the events of 1989, even though many of them were dreamed in the 1970s and 1980s and were prefigured in popular nostalgias, aspirations and nightmares, from the visions of democracy to national community. The study of nostalgia might be useful for an alternative, nonteleological history that includes conjectures and contrafactual possibilities.

Kant once wrote that space is public and time is private. Now it seems that the opposite is true; we might have more private space (if we are lucky) but less and less time, and with it less patience for cultural differences in understanding time. Space is expandable into many dimensions; one has more and more homes in the span of one's life, real and virtual; one criss-crosses more borders. As for time, it is forever shrinking. Oppressed by multitasking and managerial efficiency, we live under a perpetual time pressure. The disease of this millennium will be called chronophobia or speedomania, and its treatment will be embarrassingly old-fashioned. Contemporary nostalgia is not so much about the past as about the vanishing present.

While finishing this book, on May 1, 2000, I received an e-mail from the International Decadent Action Group urging me to live slowly but boldly, to reclaim my right to idleness, to protest the "dwindling quality of life" and the "erosion of leisure" by the exploitative work ethic of the international corporations. "Phone a sick day today!" insisted the decadent activists, "make it a holiday." I wasn't sufficiently radical but, moved by global solidarity, I turned off my computer and took a long walk.

The Last Homecoming

I have returned there
where I had never been.
Nothing has changed from how it was not.
On the table (on the checkered

tablecloth) half-full
I found again the glass
never filled. All
has remained just as
I had never left it[93]

This poem by Giorgio Caproni is about a classical homecoming: "I have returned there . . . nothing has changed . . . on the table (on the checkered tablecloth) half-full I found again the glass . . . All has remained." Only in this case it is a return to a negative space (where I have never been, where the glass was never filled and which I never left). John Ashbery wrote about a return to a point of no return. Caproni speaks of a return without a departure. The lost home and the found home have no relationship to one another.

The only specific detail in the poem capable of evoking Proustian involuntary memories appears in parentheses. It is the checkered tablecloth, an embodiment of domesticity, evoking an Italian countryside trattoria or its fast-food version in Moscow or Brooklyn. If you daydream for a moment you can see the fresh tomato stains and smell the aroma of basil and smoke—but then you are not sure whether you are remembering your last vacation to Italy or a TV commercial for tricolor fettucini. The checkered tablecloth is generic: it is a one-size-fits-all approach to home; it is like a chessboard where you can move your own pawn and knights according to the rules of the game. The homecoming too turns into a generic dream, like that checkered tablecloth, that exists independently from any particular home. I have never owned a checkered tablecloth, yet it makes me vicariously nostalgic. Maybe it is not a tablecloth at all but the rhythms of Italian verse that don't translate well into English or Russian; they convince me that the longing is real, even if there is no there there.

Indeed, every return to our actual birthplace or ancestral land gives us the same sensation of returning to where we have never been. We have simply forgotten the fear of the initial border crossing and the dreams of departure. I too experienced something similar to that German couple who came "home" to Kaliningrad, and smelled the toxic waste together with the dandelions, although mine was altogether less dramatic.

I came back to Leningrad for the first time during the exceptionally hot summer of 1989. I used to spend summers in the country, so such urban heat was new to me. My friend recommended that I not drink any water: "The more you drink in the heat, the more you want to drink," she said philosophically.

The first thing I did when I escaped my friend's stiflingly cozy apartment was to wander into a half-empty grocery store. There were a few Turkish juices and the greenish bottles of local mineral water standing on the shelf in the "canned foods" section. "Poliustrovo"—I read the label on the bottle and a wave of memories overcame me: smells of Leningrad yards, the salty taste of a bread crust, the lukewarm sweetness of the tea of yesterday. I rushed to buy several bottles of Poliustrovo in spite of the surprised expression of the saleswoman who tried to dissuade me, pointing at the expensive foreign fruit juices. I opened it like an experienced drunk, knocking off the nontwist cap against the granite steps on the Neva embankment, and drank it straight from the bottle, wondering about the wisdom of the common sense that varies so much from culture to culture. The Poliustrovo was warm and green, or maybe it was just the color of the bottle. When I arrived back at the apartment smiling triumphantly, my friend burst out laughing.

"What happened to your teeth?" she asked. "Did you kiss the stones or something?"

Looking into the mirror, I realized that my teeth had acquired a dark grayish stain, the color of the Neva embankment.

"Don't you remember? We never liked Poliustrovo," my friend said. "We always tried to buy Borjomi, the one made in the Caucasus, or the drink Baikal, a version of Pepsi. And now you come all the way here for the Poliustrovo. You've become so Americanized."

The only thing I forgot about Poliustrovo was that I had never liked it. In a similar way, people remember their high school friends, hometown, or party leaders of their childhood, Stalinist musicals, handsome soldiers on the streets in fitted uniforms—all tinged with the same affection and colored in soft sepia hues of the past. There should be a special warning on the sideview mirror: The object of nostalgia is further away than it appears. Nostalgia is never literal, but lateral. It looks sideways. It is dangerous to take it at face value. Nostalgic reconstructions are based on mimicry; the past is remade in the image of the present or a desired future, collective designs are made to resemble personal aspirations and vice versa. Linda Hutcheon has suggested that nostalgia bears a "secret hermeneutic affinity" to irony; both share a double structure, an "unexpected twin evocation of both affect and agency—or emotion and politics."[94] Nostalgia, like irony, is not a property of the object itself but a result of an interaction between subjects and objects, between actual landscapes and the landscapes of the mind. Both are forms of virtuality that only human consciousness can recognize. Computers, even the most sophisticated ones, are notoriously lacking in affect and sense of humor.[95] Contrary to common sense, irony is not opposed to nostalgia. For many underprivileged people all over the world, humor and irony were forms of passive resistance and survival that allowed affection and reflection to be combined. This kind of irony was never cool or lukewarm. For many former Soviets and Eastern Europeans irony has persisted as a kind of identity politics that they employ to create a cross-cultural intimacy among the survivors of doublespeak in a world where everything has to be translatable into media-friendly sound bites. Now they are nostalgic for the critical political edge of their own ironic stance.

Etymologically, irony means "feigned ignorance." Only a true ironist knows that her ignorance is not feigned but understated. To confront the unknown, particular and unpredictable, one has to risk embarrassment, the loss of mastery and composure. On the other side of ironic estrangement might be emotion and longing; they are yoked as two sides of a coin. In this moment of nostalgic embarrassment one can begin to recognize the nostalgic fantasies of the other and learn not to trample on them. The border zone between longing and reflection, between native land and exile, explored by the Nabokovian passportless spy, opens up spaces of freedom. Freedom in this case is not a freedom from memory but a freedom to remember, to choose the narratives of the past and remake them.

In the end, the only antidote for the dictatorship of nostalgia might be nostalgic dissidence. While restorative nostalgia returns and rebuilds one homeland with paranoic determination, reflective nostalgia fears returning with the same passion. Instead of recreation of the lost home, reflective nostalgia can foster a creative self. Home, after all, is not a gated community. Paradise on earth might turn out to be another Potemkin village with no exit.

Nostalgia can be both a social disease and a creative emotion, a poison and a cure. The dreams of imagined homelands cannot and should not come to life. They can have a more important impact on improving social and political conditions in the present as ideals, not as fairy tales come true. Sometimes it's preferable (at least in the view of this nostalgic) to leave dreams alone, let them be no more and no less than dreams, not guidelines for the future. Acknowledging our collective and individual nostalgias, we can smile at them, revealing a line of imperfect teeth stained by the ecologically impure water of our native cities.

"I write of melancholy by being busy to avoid melancholy," claimed Robert Burton in his Anatomy of Melancholy.[96] I have tried to do the same with nostalgia. Survivors of the twentieth century, we are all nostalgic for a time when we were not nostalgic. But there seems to be no way back.

Notes

1 Johannes Hofer, *Dissertatio Medica de nostalgia* (Basel, 1688). An English translation by Carolyn Kiser Anspach is given in the *Bulletin of the History of Medicine*, 2 (1934). Hofer concedes that "gifted Helvetians" had a vernacular term for "the grief for the lost charms of the Native Land"—*heimweh*, and the "afflicted Gauls" (the French) used the expression *maladie du pays*. Yet Hofer was the first to give a detailed scientific discussion of the ailment. For the history of nostalgia see Jean Starobinski, "The Idea of Nostalgia," *Diogenes*, 54 (1966): 81–103; Fritz Ernst, *Vom Heimweh* (Zurich: Fretz & Wasmuth, 1949); and George Rosen, "Nostalgia: A Forgotten Psychological Disorder," *Clio Medica*, 10, 1 (1975): 28–51. For psychological and psychoanalytic approaches to nostalgia see James Phillips, "Distance, Absence and Nostalgia," in D. Ihde and H. J. Silverman, eds., Descriptions (Albany: SUNY Press, 1985); "Nostalgia: A Descriptive and Comparative Study," *Journal of Genetic Psychology*, 62 (1943): 97–104; Roderick Peters, "Reflections on the Origin and Aim of Nostalgia," *Journal of Analytic Psychology*, 30 (1985): 135–48. When the book was finished I came across a very interesting study of the sociology of nostalgia that examines nostalgia as a "social emotion" and suggests the examination of three ascending orders of nostalgia. See Fred Davis, *Yearning for Yesterday: A Sociology of Nostalgia* (New York: The Free Press, 1979).

2 Dr. Albert von Haller, "Nostalgia," in Supplément to the Encyclopédie. Quoted in Starobinski, "The Idea of Nostalgia," 93.

3 Hofer, *Dissertatio Medica,* 381. Translation is slightly modified.

4 Curiously, in many cases throughout the eighteenth and even early nineteenth century during the major epidemics of cholera as well as what we now know as tuberculosis, the patients were first described as having "symptoms of nostalgia" before succumbing to the other sicknesses.

5 Jean-Jacques Rousseau, *Dictionary of Music*, W. Waring and J. French, trans. (London, 1779), 267.

6 Robert Burton, *The Anatomy of Melancholy: What it is, with all the kinds, causes, symptomes, prognostickes & severall cures of it,* Lawrence Babb, ed. (1651; reprint, East Lansing: Michigan State University Press, 1965).

Melancholy was also a popular allegorical figure of the Baroque age, best represented by Dürer's engraving. Writing under the pseudonym Democritus Junior, Robert Burton proposes a fictional utopia as a potential cure for melancholia, but he admits that the best cure could be writing itself. The author confesses himself to be a melancholic. At the end, Burton extends a less flattering and less philosophical melancholia to those whom he describes as religious fanatics (as well as people of a religious faith different from his, from "Mahometans" to Catholics). While melancholia often overlaps with nostalgia, particulary with what I have called reflective nostalgia, the study of nostalgia allows us to focus on the issues of modernity, progress and conceptions of the collective and individual home.

7   Starobinski, "The Idea of Nostalgia," 96. The reference comes from Dr. Jourdan Le Cointe (1790).

8   Theodore Calhoun, "Nostalgia as a Disease of Field Service," paper read before the Medical Society, 10 February 1864, *Medical and Surgical Reporter* (1864), 130.

9   Ibid., 132.

10 Ibid., 131.

11 Starobinski, "The Idea of Nostalgia," 81. Starobinski insists on the historic dimension of some psychological, medical and philosophical terms because it "is capable of dislocating us somewhat, it compels us to observe the distance which we have poorly apprehended up to now." The historian of nostalgia thus embraces the main rhetoric of nostalgic discourse itself for critical purposes.

12 Gregory Nagy, *Greek Mythology and Poetics* (Ithaca: Cornell University Press, 1990), 219.

13 Reinhart Koselleck, *Futures Past,* Keith Tribe, trans. (Cambridge, MA: MIT Press, 1985), 241.

14 Johannes Fabian, *Time and Other* (New York: Columbia University Press, 1983), 2.

15 Matei Calinescu, *Five Faces of Modernity* (Durham, NC: Duke University Press, 1987), 19.

16 Quoted in Koselleck, *Futures Past, 15.*

17 Ibid., 18.

18 Ibid., 272.

19 Ibid., 279. On the idea of progress see most recently *Progress: Fact or Illusion?* Leo Marx and Bruce Mazlich, eds. (Ann Arbor: University of Michigan Press, 1998).

20 Ibid., 279.

21 Edmund Leach, "Anthropological Aspects of Language," in Eric Lenenberg, ed., *New Directions in the Study of Language* (Chicago: University of

Chicago Press, 1964). See also Zygmunt Bauman, *Globalization: The Human Consequences* (New York: Columbia University Press, 1998), 27–29.

22 Ibid., 27.

23 Johann Gottfried von Herder, "Correspondence on Ossian," in Burton Feldman and Robert D. Richardson, comps., *The Rise of Modern Mythology* (Bloomington: Indiana University Press, 1975), 229–30.

24 "Heart! Warmth! Humanity! Blood! Life! I feel! I am!"—such are Herder's mottoes. Yet the expressivity of multiple exclamation marks cannot obscure from us the profoundly nostalgic vision. Romantic nationalism places philology above philosophy, linguistic particularism over classical logic, metaphor over argument.

25 Milan Kundera, *The Book of Laughter and Forgetting* (New York: King Penguin, 1980), 121.

26 Eva Hoffman, *Lost in Translation: A Life in a New Language* (New York and London: Penguin, 1989), 115.

27 I am grateful to Cristina Vatulescu for sharing with me her knowledge of the Romanian *dor.*

28 It is unfortunate that this shared desire for uniqueness, the longing for particularism that does not recognize the same longing in the neighbor, sometimes prevents an open dialogue between nations.

29 The melancholic, according to Kant, "suffers no depraved submissiveness and breathes freedom in a noble breast." For a discussion of Immanuel Kant's "Observations on the Sense of the Beautiful and Sublime" and *Anthropology* see Susan Meld Shell, *The Embodiment of Reason* (Chicago: University of Chicago Press, 1996), 264–305. See also E. Cassirer, *Kant's Life and Thought* (New Haven: Yale University Press, 1981); and Georg Stauth and Bryan Sturner, "Moral Sociology of Nostalgia," in Georg Stauth and Bryan S. Turner, eds., *Nietzsche's Dance* (Oxford and New York: Basil Blackwell, 1988).

30 Quoted in George Lukacs, *The Theory of the Novel,* Anna Bostock, trans. (1916; reprint, Cambridge, MA: MIT Press, 1968), 29.

31 Heinrich Heine, *Selected Works.* Helen Mustard, trans. and ed. Poetry translated by Max Knight (New York: Vintage, 1973), 423. The original is in Heine's *Lyrisches Intermezzo* (1822–23).

32 Ernest Renan, "What Is a Nation?" in Omar Dahboure and Micheline R. Ishay, eds., *The Nationalism Reader* (Atlantic Highlands, NJ: Humanities Press, 1995), 145.

33 Alois Riegl, "The Modern Cult of Monuments: Its Character and Its Origins," K. Forster and D. Ghirardo, trans., *Oppositions,* 25 (Fall 1982): 21–50.

34 For more on romantic kitsch see Celeste Olalquiaga, *The Artificial Kingdom: A Treasury of the Kitsch Experience* (New York: Pantheon Books, 1998). Olalquiaga's distinction between melancholic and nostalgic kitsch is akin to my distinction between reflective and restorative nostalgia.

35 Pierre Nora, "Between Memory and History: Les Lieux de Memoire," *Representations*, 26 (1989).

36 Petr Chaadaev, *Philosophical Letters and Apology of a Madman*, Mary Barbara Zeldin, trans. (Knoxville: University of Tennessee Press, 1969), 37; in Russian, *Stati i pisma* (Moscow: Sovremennik, 1989).

37 Quoted in Michael Kammen, *Mystic Chords of Memory* (New York: Vintage, 1991), 42.

38 Eric Hobsbawm, "Inventing Traditions," in E. Hobsbawm and T. Ranger, eds., *The Invention of Tradition* (Cambridge: Cambridge University Press, 1983), 2. See also *Commemorations: Politics of National Identity*, John R. Gillis, ed. (New Jersey: Princeton University Press, 1994).

39 Ibid., 5.

40 Benedict Anderson, *Imagined Communities* (New York: Verso, 1992), 11.

41 Michael Herzfeld, *Cultural Intimacy: Social Poetics* in *the Nation-State* (New York: Routledge, 1997), 13–14.

42 Paranoia has been described as a "rational delusion." The rational quality of delusion is very important; every element and detail makes sense within a closed system that is based on a delusionary premise. In Freud's description, paranoia is a fixation on oneself and a progressive exclusion of the external world through the mechanism of projection.

43 See Svetlana Boym, "Conspiracy Theory and Literary Ethics," *Comparative Literature* (vol. 51, no. 2 Spring 1999).

44 The history of the making of one of the most popular secret books translated into fifty languages—*The Protocols of the Elders of Zion*—demonstrates how a certain blueprint plot travels from medieval demonology to gothic fictions, then to the classical nineteenth-century novel, and finally to right-wing popular culture.

45 This is discussed in my article "Russian Soul and Post-Communist Nostalgia," *Representations*, no. 49 (Winter 1995): 133–66. See also Walter Laqueur, *Black Hundred: The Rise of the Extreme Right in Russia* (NewYork: Harper Perennial, 1993).

46 Contrary to Michelangelo's belief in individual creativity, the restorers were not allowed to leave any personal or human touch. Every color shade was computer controlled. The fresco, it was claimed, is not an oil painting, it requires an accelerated speed of brush strokes.

47 Vladimir Nabokov, "On Time and Its Texture," in Strong Opinions (New York: Vintage International 1990), 185–86.

48 Roman Jakobson proposed a distinction between two types of aphasia, the linguistic disorder of "forgetting" the structure of language. The first pole was metaphorical–a transposition through displacement and substitution. For instance, if a patient is asked to make an association with a red flag, he might say "the Soviet Union." The patient remembers emblems, not contexts. The second pole was metonymical–a memory of contextual, contiguous details that didn't amount to symbolic substitution. The patient might remember that the red flag was made of velvet with golden embroidery that he used to carry to those demonstrations and then got a day off and went to the countryside to gather mushrooms. The two types of nostalgia presented herein echo Jakobson's aphasia: both, after all, are side effects of catastrophic forgetting and a desperate attempt at remaking the narrative out of losses. See Roman Jakobson, "Two Types of Apbassa," in *Language in Literature*, (Cambridge, MA, Harvard University Press), 1987.

49 Susan Stewart, *On Longing* (Baltimore: Johns Hopkins University Press, 1985), 145.

50 Bergson suggested the metaphor of a cone that represents the totality of virtual pasts that spring from a moment in the present. Bergsonian duration is "defined less by succession than by coexistence." Henri Bergson, *Matter and Memory*, N. M. Paul and W S. Palmer, trans. (New York; Zone Books, 1996); Gilles Deleuze, Bergsonism (New York: Zone Books, 1991), 59–60.

51 "Between the plane of action and-the plane in which our body condenses its past into motor habits-and the plane of pure memory-we believe that we can discover thousands of different planes of consciousness, a thousand of integral yet diverse repetitions of the whole of the experience through which we lived." Bergson, Matter and Memory, 241.

52 Marcel Proust, *Swann's Way*, C. K. Scott Moncrieff and Terence Ktlmatrinm, trans. (New York: Vintage International, 1989), 462.

53 Vladimir Yankelevitch, *L'Irrevérsible et la nostalgie* (Paris: Flammarion, 1974), 302.

54 "Ya en el amor del compartido lecho duerme la clara reina sobre el pecho de su rey, pero dóndeesta aquel hombre que en los dias y noches des detierro erraba por el mundo como un perro y decía que nadie era su nombre." Jorge Luis Borges, *Obras poéticas completas* (Buenos Aires: Emece, 1964).

55 Semezdin Mehmedinovie, *Sarajevo Blues*, Ammiel Alcalay, trans. (San Francisco: Cit) Lights Books, 1998), 49.

56 Dubravka Ugresic, "Confiscation of Memory," in *The Culture of Lies* (University Park: Pennsylvania State University Press, 1998).

57 Lev Vygotsky, *Mind in Society* (Cambridge, MA: Harvard University Press, 1978). Psychologists of individual memory following Vygotsky distinguish between *episodic memory*, defined as "conscious recollection of personally experienced events," and *semantic memory*, knowledge of facts and names, "knowledge of the world." The distinction roughly corresponds to Jakobson's distinction between "metonymic" and "metaphoric" poles. See E. Tulving, "Episodic and Semantic Memory," in E. Tulvig and W. Donaldson, eds., *Organization of Memory*, (New York: Academic

Press, 1972), 381-403. For psychological and psychoanalytic approaches to nostalgia see James Phillips, "Distance, Absense and Nostalgia," in Don Ihde and Hugh J. Silverman, eds., *Descriptions* (Albany: SUNY Press, 1985).

58 D. W. Winnicott, *Playing and Reality* (London: Routledge, 1971), 100.

59 Unlike the "common places" of classical memory, the modern topoi are themselves constantly in flux: "The social frameworks of memory (les cadres sociaux de memoire) . . . are like those woodfloats that descend along a waterway so slowly that one can easily move from one to the other, but which nevertheless are not immobile and go forward. . The frameworks of memory... exist both within the passage of time and outside it. External to the passage of time, they communicate to the images and concrete recollections... a bit of their stability and generality. But these frameworks are in part captivated by the course of time." Maurice Halbwachs, *On Collective Memory*, Lewis Coser, trans. and ed. (Chicago: University of Chicago Press, 1992), 182. For the most recent work see Simon Schema, *Landscape and Memory* (New York: Knopf, 1995); and Peter Burke, "History as Social Memory," in Thomas Butler, ed., *Memory: History, Culture and the Mind* (Oxford and New York: Basil Blackwell, 1989), 97-115.

60 Michael Roth, "Returning to Nostalgia," in Suzanne Nash, ed , *Home and Its Dislocation in Nineteenth-Century France*, (Albany: SUNY Press, 1993), 25-45.

61 Roth, "Returning to Nostalgia," 40.

62 Collective memory also informs Roland Barthes' cultural myth-in its later redefinition-where Barthes no longer tries to "demystify" but rather reflects on the processes of signification and the inescapability of mythical common places, in which the mythologist himself is endlessly implicated.

63 Carlo Ginzburg, *Clues, Myths and the Historical Method*, John Tedeschi and Anne Tedeschi, trans. (Baltimore: Johns Hopkins University Press, 1986).

64 Sigmund Freud, "Morning and Melancholia," in General Psychological Theory (New York: Macmillan, 1963), 164-80.

65 Vladimir Nabokov, *Poems and Problems* (New York: McGraw Hill, 1970), 110-11. *Eto taina, ta-ta, tata-ta-ta- a tochnee skazat' ia ne v prove.* The translation from Russian is mine. For a different interpretation see Vladimir Alexandrov, *Nabokov's Otherworld* (Princeton, NJ: Princeton University Press, 1991). This interpretation elaborates on Vera Nabokov's remark about the role of *potustornonnost* in Nabokov's art and life. In my view, *potustornonnost* is more accurately translated as "otherworldliness," as a quality, state, aura or condition, but never as the "other world" as such. In fact, the other world in Russian is *inoi mir* or *drugoi mir*. For Nabokov, who believed in the precision of language and translation, the difference is crucial. (Professor Alexandrov himself acknowledges difficulties in translation.) Nabokov insisted on leaving things unsaid; this was his main "metaphysics."

66 Vladimir Nabokov, *Speak, Memory: An Autobiography Revisited* (New York: Vintage International, 1989) 99. The expression *podlozhnyj pasport* (fake passport) does appear in the Russian text, but in a different place, at the end of chapter 11. "Passportless spy" is added to chapter 5 in the 1966 version of the English autobiography, but it is not added to the Russian version of *Drugie Berega*—a curious gesture of caution on the writer's part. The only way of traveling to Soviet Russia in the late 1920s and 1930s was by means of illicit border crossings. In the 1930s, a return to Soviet Russia most often signified some form of collaboration with the KGB, which engaged many Eurasians and nostalgic patriots (like Tsvetaeva's husband, Sergei Efron); in the postwar period of late 1940s and 1950s, many émigrés inspired by the Soviet victory in the war were lured back and promised safety and employment. Many were arrested at their arrival or lived for years in fear of arrest. In the 1960s and early 1970s, however, the threat to personal safety had diminished and many émigrés ventured to the Soviet Union as members of foreign tour groups.

67 Nabokov, *Speak, Memory*, 18.

68 Roland Barthes, *Camera Lucida* (London: Flamingo Press, 1984), 26–27.

69 Vladimir Nabokov, *Perepiska s sestroi* (Ann Arbor, MI: Ardis, 1985), 93.

70 Susan Sontag, On *Photography* (New York: Penguin, 1977), 15.

71 Ibid., 24.

72 At a time when actual photographs of home were not yet available, Nabokov created imaginary photographs of his abandoned house: "[I]n the gathering dusk the place acted upon my young senses in a curiously teleological way, as if this accumulation of familiar things in the dark were doing its utmost to form the definite and permanent image that repeated exposure did finally leave in my mind. The sepia gloom of an arctic afternoon in mid winter invaded the rooms and was deepening to an oppressive black. A bronze angle, a surface of glass or polished mahogany here and there in the darkness, reflected the odds and ends of light from the street, where the globes of tall street lamps along its middle line were already diffusing their lunar glow. Gauzy shadows moved on the ceiling. In the stillness, the dry sound of a chrysanthemum petal falling upon the marble of a table made one's nerves twang." Nabokov, *Speak, Memory*, 89. This description resembles a film Tarkovsky could have made, of sculpting in time with many reflective surfaces for the fleeing shadows. These "odds and ends of light," this diffused lunar glow, illuminates the elusive scene of memory. The dry sound of the chrysanthemum petal falling on the marble table is a synesthetic image of sound, taste and smell, defying the two-dimensional stillness of a photograph. The description seems to transcend both the verbal and the visual. This is a singular sensuous image of the lost home of one's childhood and can never become a symbol of a lost homeland.

73 Ibid., 256.

74 This is a comic reference to Pushkin's remarks about nature and pastoral imagination: "Oh, lovely summer, how I would have loved you, were it not for the mosquitoes, flies, and moths..." In the philosophical tradition flies are messengers of daily banality. Nietzsche's Zarathustra despises the "flies of the market-place": "Flee, my friend, to your solitude, I see you stung by the poisonous flies. Flee to where the raw, rough breeze blows." Quote from Friedrich Nietzsche, *Thus Spoke Zarathustra*, R. J. Hollingdale, trans. (NewYork: Penguin, 1962), 79.

75 Nabokov, *Speak, Memory*, 275.

76 Ibid., 96.

77 Idem, *Nikolai Gogol* (New York: New Directions), 66.

78 Rhetorically, this is close to *tmesis* (from the Greek "to cut"), which refers to the separation of a compound word or a cliché as a means of defamiliarizing it and drawing attention to its parts. For a discussion of *tmesis* see Peter Lubin, "Kickshaws and Motley," *Triquarterly*, 17 (1970): 187–208.

79 Ibid., 116. His narrative of nostalgia is both personal and intertextual. The swan is a favorite allegorical bird in turn-of-the-century French poetry. In Baudelaire's "Le cygne," the swan becomes a mournful figure of modernity, the displaced messenger of *vieu Paris*. In Mallarmé's sonnet "Le vierge, le vivace et le bel aujourd'hui," the swan, haunting a forgotten and frozen lake, is a sign of exile itself (*Exil inutil du cygnet*–futile exile of the swan– are the last lines of the sonnet). Swan (*le cygne*) and sign (*le signe*) are pronounced the same in French. Mallarmé suggests the exile of both, an alienation of meaning itself. Stéphane Mallarmé, *Oeuvres complètes* (Paris: Gallimard, Pléiade, 1945), 67–68; John Burt Foster, Jr., *Nabokov's Art of Memory and European Modernism* (Princeton, NJ: Princeton University Press, 1993), 39–40. Foster discusses in detail the intertextual dialogue between Nabokov, Baudelaire and Nietzsche.

80 Nabokov, *Speak, Memory*, 117.

81 Perhaps Nabokov's violent opposition to Freud's theory of the Oedipus complex is due to the fact that the writer's father was murdered for political, not symbolic, reasons. (Nabokov frequently ridiculed the vulgar Freudians.)

82 *American Heritage Dictionary* (Boston: Houghton Mifflin, 1985), 1232-33.

83 *The NewYork Review of Books*, 7 October 1971; Nabokov, *Strong Opinions*, 304–7.

84 In a little chapter included not for the general reader but for an "idiot," he stresses: "My old (since 1917) quarrel with the Soviet dictatorship is wholly unrelated to any question of property. My contempt for the émigré who 'hates the Reds' because they 'stole' his money and land is complete." Nabokov, *Speak, Memory*, 73.

85 Ibid.

86 The New Yorker, 28 December 1998 and 4 January 1999, 126.

87 Nabokov, Strong Opinions, 119.

88 Ibid., 218.

89 Milan Kundera, *Slowness,* Linda Asher, trans. (NewYork: HarperCollins, 1995), 39.

90 After writing this section I came across Andrew Sullivan's essay on dot. communism in the *New York Times Magazine,* 11 June 2000, 30–36.

91 The name of the artist is Natalie Jeremijenko, *New York Times Magazine,* 11 June 2000, 25.

92 Interview with Jeoffrey Nunberg on National Public Radio, "All Things Considered," 13 November 1998.

93 Giorgio Caproni, *Poesie* 1932–1986 (Milano, 1989), 392. Translated by Toma Tasovac and Svetlana Boym.

94 Linda Hutcheon, "Irony, Nostalgia and the Post-modern," paper presented at the Modern Language Association conference, San Francisco, December 1997.

95 Ibid., 9.

96 Robert Burton, The Anatomy of Melancholy: What it is, with all the kinds, causes, symptoms, prognostickes & severall cures of it, Lawrence Babb, ed. (1651; reprint, East Lansing: Michigan State University Press, 1965), 9.

11 CONSPIRACY THEORIES AND LITERARY ETHICS: UMBERTO ECO, DANILO KIS AND *THE PROTOCOLS OF ZION*

Danilo Kiš and the Ethics of Estrangement

"My intention was to summarize the true and fantastic—'unbelievably fantastic'—story of how *The Protocols of the Elders of Zion* came into existence and to chronicle the work's insane impact on generations of readers and its tragic consequences," wrote Danilo Kiš ("Postscript" 196-97). He began by composing a documentary essay but then realized that knowledge of the facts of the story was not likely to stop its influence. He thus decided to resort to fiction in order to dramatize the absurdity and danger of the Plot, imagining "the events as they might have happened" and changing the title of his text from *Protocols* to *Conspiracy*.[1] If for Eco conspiracy theory is interesting as a problem of interpretation, for Kiš it is an actual historical threat. Kiš's characters cannot afford the playful and ambiguous repertoire of Eco's computer games. Eco's novel is about the desire for a plot. In contrast, "The Book of Kings and Fools," Kiš's fictional history of the *Book of Zion,* is about the urge to interrupt conspiratorial logic. His heroes are the anonymous Mr. X and the no less anonymous victims of conspiracy theories. Instead of looking for analogies and connections, Kiš's narrator looks for the breaks in the transmission of the conspiracy theories from text into life. "A Book is interrupted discourse catching up with its own breaks. But the books have their fate; they belong to the world they do not include, but recognize by being printed . . . They are interrupted and call for other books and at the end are interpreted in a saying distinct from the said"—these words of Emmanuel Levinas could serve as an epigraph to the story. Kiš's aesthetic-ethical project is deeply concerned with the interruptions and breaks that inform the fate of the "sacred" book and with the violence that could result from prophetic rather than ethical reading.[2]

"The Book of Kings and Fools" is narrated by an anonymous essayist who only at the very end tells us "that conspiracy loosely affects him as well," and that after the new Hungarian edition of the book in 1944 someone shot at the window of his house. This is a very different positioning from that of Eco's characters. The story itself appears to have a circular structure, as it is framed by two scenes of violence and destruction. From the very beginning we enter Kiš's dense fictional woods:

the crime, not to be perpetuated until some forty years later, was prefigured in a Petersburg newspaper in August 1906. The articles appeared serially and were signed by the paper's editor-in-chief, a certain Khrushevan, A.P. Kruscheva, who, as the instigator of the Kishinev pogroms, had a good fifty murders on his conscience. (Throughout the darkened rooms, mutilated bodies lie in pools of blood and raped girls stare wild-eyed into the void from behind heavy, rent curtains. The scene is real enough, as real as the corpses; the only artificial element in the night-marish setting is the snow.) *"Pieces of furniture, broken mirrors and lamps, linen, clothing, mattresses and slashed quilts are strewn about the streets. The roads are deep in snow: eiderdown feathers everywhere; even the trees are covered with them."* ("The Book of Kings and Fools," 135; italics are Kiš's)

The first long paragraph is a tortured narrative montage of various scenes, voices, and quotes. The documentary style of the description is immediately interrupted by the parenthesis, a sudden traumatic memory of mutilated bodies and the wide-eyed stare of an anonymous girl. Then there is a quote, without a source, of an anonymous witness who describes the destruction of objects and the depopulated scene of a pogrom. Although the scene might remind us of Eco's laundry list of furniture to be repaired, this is not a conspiratorial message but the description of the consequences of a conspiracy theory. In place of Sergius Nilus's museum of the Anti-Christ, Kiš shocks us with a display of violence. "The scene is real enough, as real as the corpses"; violence is the only measure of reality, and the broken mirrors bear witness to the event. One is reminded of Borges' story "Tlon Uqbar and Orbis Tertius," explicitly alluded to by Kiš, which opens with the "conjunction of mirror and encyclopedia." But in Borges the mirror haunts and distorts; in Kiš the broken mirror actually bears witness. It does not let us escape into a hypothetical world, but rather forces us to remember the unimaginable but actual world of twentieth-century violence. The Borgesian "fallacious and plagiarized Anglo-American encyclopedia" is replaced by a similarly plagiarized and fallacious—but much more dangerous—guide to life, a "new Bible" called "Conspiracy."

In Kiš's work the word "real" is juxtaposed to theatrical metaphors, the last of which appears at the end of the story in another eye-witness account of senseless murders perpetrated by the Nazis: "In 1942, thirty six years after Krushevan's articles first appeared in his Petersburg newspaper, a witness to the crime noted in his journal: I cannot comprehend the judicial bias for these murders—men killing one another in the open, as if on stage. But the stage is real, as real as the corpses" (174). The stage is real, "as real as the corpses." The phrase turns into an obsessive refrain. The unimaginable can be real, and the only way to make sense of its senselessness is to compare it to fiction.

"The only artificial element in this nightmarish setting is the snow"—the kind of decorative white snow that is indispensable for any picturesque Russian setting, a touch of Russian exotica such as is found in *Doctor Zhivago* with its teary-eyed Omar Sharif. It is a kitschy theatrical snow, mixed with the feathers from sliced-open pillows. But this artificial snow triggers Mr. X's memory throughout the story and so helps him to reconstruct the scene of violence. In particular, it helps him remember the soldiers gathered around the fire listening to an officer reading from Nilus's prophesies and *The Conspiracy* before the pogrom, the silence between words interrupted only by the whisper of large snowflakes: "The officer lowers the book to his side for a moment, marking the place with his index finger. 'That, gentlemen, is the kind of morals they preach.' (The officer's orderly takes advantage of this break to brush the newly accumulated snow off the tent flap over his head.)" (145).

Mr. X recalls this scene while reading Joly's "Dialogues in Hell" and discovering its similarities to *The Conspiracy.* At this moment, as on that wintry night, he feels "the snow slide into the sleeve of his greatcoat" (p. 154). The snow brings back those moments of interruption in the reading of the Book of Revelation, when the authorial reader made his fingernail marks on the margin. Although those breaks in inspirational communal reading were intended to recharge the energy of hate, in the case of this witness, they permitted moments of reflection and doubt that disrupted the incantatory self-justification of violence. It is neither political ideology nor abstract morality that drives Mr. X, a white Russian officer, constitutional monarchist, and Orthodox Christian to act against the conspiracy theory of his fellow officers, but rather basic honesty and elementary humane responsiveness, something akin to what Levinas calls "anarchic responsibility," that is, responsibility for the other individual in the present moment and "justified by no prior commitment."[3]

Kiš's story dramatizes those interruptions in reading that preclude the transference of text into life and estrange its incantatory spell. The book is described as a material object with fingernail markings, reader's notes—including the swastika signs that the Empress of Russia drew in her three favorite books: the Russian Bible, *War and Peace,* and *The Conspiracy.* At the end of the story an ordinary German, the Nazi officer Captain Wirth, places *The Conspiracy* next to his heart in the hope that the book will protect him from enemy bullets. The book is for him a magic talisman and a protective shield; its message goes straight to the heart. This is not a case of a victim identifying with his victimizer, but a dangerous and often ignored reversal—the victimizer thinking himself a victim. The perpetrator of violence employs the logic of paranoiac projection where "we are killing them" and "they wish to kill us" is interchangeable. In this way Kiš's story helps us understand the vicious circles of conspiratorial projection. Moreover, if a given conspiracy theory seems short of proof, the dedicated theorist tries hard to provide it. To give a contemporary example: after Ashahara, the leader of the Japanese sect Aum, told his followers to wear gas masks in their compound and prepare to defend themselves against a poisonous gas attack, he went on to prepare just such an attack. Conspiracy theories predicting the end of the world thus inevitably lead to attempts to conjure up and ensure that such a catastrophe will indeed occur.

For the narrator-witness in Kiš's story it is important not to succumb to the other's paranoiac fantasy, not to look for a paranoiac within oneself, but to affirm one's separateness from the paranoiac other. Any East European writer has a well-nourished paranoiac within—that's no revelation. It's the resistance to communal paranoia that has to be nourished. Levinas writes that one has to recognize the humanism of the other man; in Kiš's story one also has to recognize his paranoia.

Kiš's story unfolds as a series of face-to-face encounters between men and books, and as a clash of various quotations.[4] The witnesses help to interrupt the conspiratorial chain, even if this interruption is only temporary. An ironic magician, Kiš reveals to us the obsessive refrains and patterns in his story as well as incidents, chance encounters, accidents, and individual singularities. In fact, there are two mythical books in Kiš's collection—both intertextually linked to Borges—*The Conspiracy* and *The Encyclopedia of the Dead*. The first one describes the hypothetical new world order, while the second one records all the minor particular details and incidents of human lives, omitting only the famous names that might have appeared in other books. Unlike the encyclopedia of Tlon, which records impossible but not improbable idealist theories of immaterial objects and anonymous subjects, *The Encyclopedia of the Dead* is, in fact, an encyclopedia of unrecorded lives, a collective Proustian *oevre*, the redemption of the lost time of ordinary people who never became famous and never wrote. It salvages individual ir-replaceability—to borrow Michael Holquist's term. Kiš formulates his own ethically maximalist vision of human history, in which "each individual is a star unto himself, everything happens always and never, all things repeat themselves ad infinitum yet are unique" (Baranczak 42). His stories are always poised on the brink between allegory and a chance encounter.

"The Book of Kings and Fools" is at once tragic, violent, and playful. Kiš gives wonderful evocations of émigré nostalgia, with cockroaches in a third-class hotel under an embalming Mediterranean sky, and excels in Dostoevskian descriptions of double agents and anti-Semites like Rachkovsky. Almost every West-European and American critical discussion of ethics and narrative opens with Dostoevsky's moral pronouncements. In contrast, for many East-European modernist writers Dostoevsky is not a model of ethics; he is held responsible for conflating ethics with melodrama in a way that became so ubiquitous in a Russian and East-European context, where sentimentality and cruelty, preaching and prejudice went hand in hand.

In fact, the ethical dimension of Kiš's story resides in the way it undercuts both tragedy and melodrama. The ethical in Kiš is connected with the aesthetic; Kiš's stories present a peculiar dialectical, or rather ethical, montage of multilayered literary allusions and aesthetic palimpsests disrupted by violence. Realist or pragmatic ethics are unavailable to him, as are rational, positivist solutions. After all, the facts have been revealed but the violence persists. Hence, the reader is left to confront the absurdity of evil and experience devastating powerlessness, what Hannah Arendt describes as an experience of "radical evil": "When the impossible was made possible it became the unpunishable, unforgivable absolute evil which could no longer be understood and explained by evil motives of self-interest, greed, covetousness, resentment, lust for power and cowardice; and which therefore anger could not revenge, love could not endure, friendship could not forgive. Just as the victims in the death factories or the holes of oblivion are no longer 'human' in the eyes of their executioners, so this newest species of criminals is beyond the pale even of solidarity in human sinfulness" (Arendt 459).

Kiš's Russian contemporary, Joseph Brodsky, notes in his memoir the untranslatability of that Russian and East-European sense of the absurdity of evil. He observes that "such advanced notion of Evil as happens to be in possession of Russians has been denied entry into [Anglo-American] consciousness on the grounds of having a convoluted syntax. One wonders how many of us can recall a plain-speaking Evil that crosses the threshold saying "Hi, I'm Evil. How are you?" (Brodsky 31). Perhaps Kiš's convoluted syntax owes something to his no less convoluted encounter with Evil. One of Kiš's favorite Russian critical tropes is an old-fashioned and, in the Western context, mostly forgotten term: Shklovskian defamiliarization. Kiš uses defamiliarization both as an artistic device and as a strategy for survival. His poetics are, he states, based on the "defamiliarizing effect of history on the destiny of the Jews." For him, among other things, "Judaism is an 'effect of defamiliarization.'"[5] (Kiš goes on to say that Judaism in his case "is a persistent sentiment that Heine called Familienungluck, the family misfortune.")

The poethics of East-European art is informed by defamiliarization as a device central to both art and life. Victor Shklovsky's o-stranenie (estrangement or defamiliarization) both *defines* and *defies* the autonomy of art.[6] In the Russian and East-European context, the call for defamiliarization and the "autonomy of art" was not depoliticized but rather a political issue. It was an attempt to sever the connection between art and despotic power, and to prevent a quasi-religious reading of literary texts as revelations and grids for life. Defamiliarization is an ethical stance for Kiš; he both acknowledges the primary role of art in the discussion of ethics and affirms the separateness of text and life, the intransitivity of fiction or at least the chance to interrupt its transmission which, in the extreme case of the *Protocols,* is a matter of life and death.

At the same time, for a writer-survivor there is no question that literature has to exist after the Holocaust. For better or for worse, literature remains an ideal space for the ethical encounter.

In recent newspaper reviews in the West of East-European fiction, reviewers frequently complain about the frequent literary references, intertextual play, disconnectedness, and convoluted syntax characteristic of these works. What the reviewers fail to understand is that this seemingly excessive literariness is not so much about literature as it is about an autonomous sphere of cultivated bourgeois entertainment. Dense literary intertextuality in recent East-European texts signals membership in an alternative imagined community of East-European cosmopolitans, who share, in Mandel'shtam's words, "nostalgia for world culture" and nomadically inhabit that alternative universe that goes beyond national borders. The alleged "plagiarism" and cosmopolitanism for which the Belgrade literary establishment attacked Kiš was his way of belonging to that highly individualized literary cult. In this respect, he follows the tradition of early twentieth-century modernists such as Witold Gombrowicz and Osip Mandel'shtam, not the avant-garde.[7]

Kiš begins his postscript to *The Encyclopedia of the Dead* by saying that he first wished to call his collection of stories "The East-Westerly Divan" "for its obvious ironic and parodic undercurrent" (p. 191). Indeed, all of the stories present interesting East-West encounters. Moreover, the word "divan" is a curious Eastern import into Western languages. Both Persian and Turkish in its origins, "Divan" at first referred to the privy council of the Ottoman Empire and then came to signify a sofa or a couch as well as, in Persian and Arabic, a collection of poems (*Webster's New College Dictionary* 333). The history of the word reveals, through a series of metonymic substitutions, the shrinking influence of an imperial power. From a secret council of the powerful, "divan" came to mean a hedonistic piece of furniture, and also a collection of tales one could read or write while lounging upon it. The early title also alludes to Goethe's poem cycle *Der Westostliche Divan,* suggesting that Goethe's dreams of world literature and aesthetic cosmopolitanism has been reappropriated by Kis over a century later.

As we leave Kiš's ethics on the divan—his version of philosophy in the boudoir—one is tempted to suggest a certain didactic conclusion. While paranoia might be critical, the critical enterprise should not be reduced to a singular paranoia. Because for a conspirator the other remains only another conspirator, an encounter between individuals is impossible or else results in the violence of broken mirrors. As far as books are concerned, Kiš remarked: "Books in quantity are not dangerous; a single book is" (p. 197). And if by a rare chance one becomes a possessor of a book that aspires to supersede all others and give a total explanation of the world, one should find courage to return it to the library, where it can be lost among other books with and without secret fingernail messages in their margins.

Notes

1 Kiš claims to work "on the fringe of facts" and never betrays them entirely. The story takes its own direction "where data [is] insufficient and facts unknown, in the penumbra where objects acquire shadows and outlines" (197). Kiš quotes Borges, Cortazar, and Hawthorne to justify his desire "to give the story a bit of drama."

2 Although in "The Book of Kings and Fools" Kiš restrains himself from writing a confessional autobiographical narrative, even ironically, the way Eco does, his own biography is rather novelesque. The son of a Jewish father and Montenegrin mother, he was born in Hungary in 1936. While Kiš was still a young boy, his family moved from Hungary to Serbia where, for the sake of survival, he was baptized as an Orthodox Catholic. Later, the family returned to Hungary where he attended a Catholic school. After the Second World War they once again returned to Yugoslavia. When Kiš's novel *The Tomb of Boris Davidovich* first appeared in 1976, the Yugoslavian literary establishment accused him of plagiarizing Borges, Solzhenytsyn, Nadezhda Mandel'shtam, Joyce, and Koestler. The collected title of the essays criticizing Kiš—"Should we burn Kiš?" ("Treba li spaliti Kisa?")—should remind us of many previous book burning campaigns on the right and left. Obviously someone who could plagiarize Borges, Solzhenytsyn and Joyce must already be a genius.

   In the case of Kiš we are dealing with a peculiar genre that he himself called "faction"—a hybrid of fact and fiction. Similarly, one could speak about Kiš's "poethics"—the poetics and ethics of using facts and fictions together, questioning and reasserting their boundaries depending on context. Kiš thus combines the Russian post-revolutionary avant-garde idea of the "literature of facts" used by, among others, Isaak Babel in *Red Cavalry* with the fantastic metahistoriography characteristic of Borges.

3 This responsibility "that summons me from nowhere into the present time, is perhaps a measure or the manner or the system of immemorial freedom that is even older than being, or decisions, or deeds" ("Ethics as First Philosophy," p. 84). Anarchic responsibility is "justified by no prior commitment, in the responsibility for another" (92).

4 Moreover, the circularity of the story should not be taken as Borgesian repetition. While employing refrains and repetitions, Kiš's story defies any

neatly constructed form. The narrator makes an observation that two books, that of Joly and that of Nilus, are separated by "the cabalistic distance (and I tremble as I write the word 'cabalistic') of four letters of the alphabet" (p. 157). Cautious of analogies, the narrator refrains from making more "cabalistic connections." This hesitancy contrasts the rather superficial cabalistic arrangement of chapters in Eco's novel.

5   "Judaism in *The Tomb to Boris Davidovich* has a twofold [literary] meaning; on the one hand . . . it creates a necessary connection and expands the mythologeme I am involved with, and on the other hand . . . Judaism is simply an 'effect of defamiliarization'" (quoted in Longinovic 140).

6   It also acknowledges the unique role of art and literature in the national conscience. Estrangement is what makes art artistic, but by the same token it makes everyday life lively, or worth living. By making things strange the artist does not simply displace them from an everyday context into an artistic framework; he also helps to "return sensation" to life itself, to reinvent the world, experience it anew. Estrangement in this sense mediates between art and life. See Striedter, Erlich, and Steiner. On the connection between the theory of estrangement and romantic aesthetics, see Todorov. See also Boym, "Estrangement."

7   These writers could be also compared with Latin American authors of the Boom generation, authors whose literary games were also perceived as controversial within their highly politicized contexts.

Works Cited

Arendt, Hannah. *Origins of Totalitarianism*. New York: Harcourt Brace Jovanovich, 1966.

Bakhtin, Mikhail. *Estetika slovesnogo tvorchestva*. Moscow: Iskusstvo, 1979.

—. *Art and Answerability: Early Philosophical Essays*. Ed. Michael Holquist and Vladimir Liapunov. Austin: University of Texas Press, 1990.

Baranczak, Stanislaw. "Fearful Symmetry." *New Republic*. 22 Oct. 1990: 42.

Bernstein, Herman. *The Truth about "The Protocols of Zion."* New York: Covici Firede Publishers, 1935.

Booth, Wayne. *The Company We Keep: An Ethics of Fiction*. Berkeley: University of California Press, 1988.

Boym, Svetlana. "Russian Soul and Post-Communist Nostalgia." *Representations* 49 (1995): 133-66.

—. "Estrangement as Lifestyle: Shklovsky and Brodsky." *Poetics Today* 17.4 (1996): 511-30.

Brodsky, Joseph. *Less Than One*. New York: Farrar, Strauss and Giroud, 1984.

Céline, Louis-Ferdinand. *Bagatelles pour un massacre*. Paris: Denoel, 1937.

Cohn, Norman. *Warrant to Genocide: The Myth of the Jewish World Conspiracy and* The Protocols of the Elders of Zion. Providence, RI: Brown Judaica Studies 23, 1981.

Culler, Jonathan. "In Defense of Overinterpretation." *Umberto Eco, Interpretation and Overinterpretation.* Ed. Stefan Collini. Cambridge: Cambridge University Press, 1992. 109-25.

Eco, Umberto. "Ars Oblivionalis." *PMLA* 103.3 (1988): 254-61.

—. "Master of Semiotic Thrillers." (interview) *U.S News and World Report* 20 Nov. 1989: 78-79.

—. *Foucault's Pendulum.* New York: Ballantine Books, 1990.

—. "Fictional Protocols." *Six Walks in the Fictional Woods.* Cambridge and London: Harvard University Press, 1994.

Erlich, Victor. *Russian Formalism: History-Doctrine.* 3rd ed. New Haven: Yale University Press, 1981.

Freud, Sigmund. "On the Mechanism of Paranoia." *General Psychological Theory.* New York: Macmillan, 1963. 29-49.

Kiš, Danilo. "The Book of Kings and Fools." *The Encyclopedia of the Dead.* Trans. Michael Henry Heim. New York: Penguin, 1991. 133-75.

—. "Postscript." *The Encyclopedia of the Dead.* 191-99.

—. "On Nationalism." *Why Bosnia?* Ed. Rabia Ali and Lawrence Lifschultz. Stony Creek: The Pamphleteer's Press, Inc., 1993.

Kristeva, Julia. "Ethics of Linguistics." *Desire in Language: A Semiotic Approach to Literature and Art.* New York: Columbia University Press, 1980. 23-26.

Laplanche, Jean and J.B. Pontalis. *The Language of Psychoanalysis.* Trans. Jeffrey Mehlman. London: Hogarth Press, 1973.

Laqueur, Walter. *Black Hundred: The Rise of the Extreme Right in Russia.* New York: Harper Perennial, 1993.

Levinas, Emmanuel. *Justifications de l'étique.* Bruxelles: Éditions de Université de Bruxelles, 1984.

—. "Ethics as the First Philosophy." *The Levinas Reader.* Ed. Seán Hand. Oxford and Cambridge: Blackwell, 1989. 75-88.

Longinovic, Tomislav. *Borderline Culture: The Politics of Identity in Four Twentieth-Century Slavic Novels.* Fayetteville: University of Arkansas Press, 1993.

Miller, J. Hillis. *The Ethics of Reading.* New York: Columbia University Press, 1987.

Morson, Gary Saul and Caryl Emerson, eds. *Rethinking Bakhtin: Extensions and Challenges.* Evanston: Northwestern University Press, 1989.

Newton, Adam Zachary. *Narrative Ethics.* Cambridge and London: Harvard University Press, 1995.

Rorty, Richard. "Pragmatist's Progress." *Umberto Eco, Interpretation and Overinterpretation.* Ed. Stefan Collini. Cambridge: Cambridge University Press, 1992. 89-109.

Steiner, Peter. *Russian Formalism: A Metapoetics.* Ithaca: Cornell University Press, 1984.

Striedter, Jurij. *Literary Structure, Evolution and Value: Russian Formalism and Czech Structuralism Reconsidered.* Cambridge: Harvard University Press, 1989.

Todorov, Tzvetan. "Three Conceptions of Poetic Language." *Russian Formalism: A Retrospective Glance: a Festschrift in Honor of Viktor Erlich.* Ed. Robert Louis Jackson and Stephen Rudy. New Haven: Yale University Press, 1985. 130-48.

12 KOSMOS

When I returned to Leningrad (now St. Petersburg) in the early 1990s, I was struck by the presence of small rockets, strewn across the urban playgrounds. Miniature models of the Soviet universe, these playgrounds were created in the 1960s, during the euphoric era of space exploration. The rockets placed there resembled our kindergarten pictures of rockets, one of the first things we learned how to draw. Using all of the available colored pencils, from red to gold, we depicted these fairytale vehicles with bright flames shooting from their tails and the proud "USSR" written on their bodies. Poised between heaven and Earth, our colorful rockets ecstatically defied the force of gravity. Today the children of St. Petersburg play on the same playgrounds, amidst the futuristic ruins shipwrecked here three decades ago. Sliding down the rusting shafts, they confirm, rather than defy, earthly gravitation, receiving a few black and blue marks on their backsides in the process,

Born at the time of the Soviet cosmic triumph in space, my generation learned to look at the world as if from outer space. The word *sputnik*, Russian for "satellite," is not a technical term. It means a "companion," or even, a "significant other." Indeed, Sputnik, first launched in 1957, was one of our first companions and favorite toys. Soviet children of the 1960s did not dream of becoming doctors and lawyers, but cosmonauts (or, if worse came to worst, geologists). We were encouraged to aim upward and not westward. Indeed, a trip to the Moon seemed more likely than a journey to America, "Would you like to have a million? No" sang a chorus of Soviet children. "Would you like to go to the Moon?–Yes!"

In retrospect, I recognize striking differences between the Soviet and the American concepts of space exploration. The American term "outer space" is descriptive, referring to something contiguous to Earth, a new frontier–not so much the wild West, but the wild sky. The Soviet notion of cosmos, on the other hand, comes from the Greek, meaning "order, ornament, harmony," and suggests a harmonized chaos, where human or divine presence is made manifest. The word "cosmos" links Soviet space technology with the mystic theories of Russian cosmism from the late-nineteenth century. Soviet "cosmonautics" developed not merely out of the Cold War arms race; it was part of a history of technology, an *enchanted technology*, founded on charisma as much as calculus, on premodern myth as well as modern science, In the exploration of the cosmos, science merged with science fiction, and ideology sounded like poetry.

In the twentieth century, Soviet advances in space exploration were directly linked to the advent of Communism. "This generation of Soviet citizens will live in the era of Communism," proclaimed the New Program of the Communist Party on July 30, 1961. Only three months earlier, on April 12, 1961, the first man flew into space. Yuri Gagarin (1934-1968), the exemplary Soviet citizen of the future, became known all over the world for his larger-than-life smile, framed in the halo of a space helmet. When Gagarin made his flight, the Soviet Union was about to proclaim itself the winner of the Cold War. His triumph in the cosmos promised a victory over time and space, ensuring a radiant future and the transcendence of all earthly hardships.

One of the veterans of the Soviet space program remembers the excitement of the day Sputnik was launched into space:

> The words "beginning of the Space Age" were not spoken by any of us. They were the contribution of journalists. In the evenings, all of us poured out onto the street, away from the light sources, and awaited the appearance of the quickly moving, pale asterisk that we had thrown into the sky. By some deep intuition we understood that this asterisk marked a star moment in each of our individual lives.[1]

Sputnik appeared to mark a victory over nature itself. In this recollection, the word "asterisk" is striking; it refers both to the little satellite in the sky and to the reference mark used in printing. Sputniks engineers had a feeling they were able to write in the sky. They were not merely observing the remote stars but creating new ones, and they were in awe of their own creation.

Every fairy tale we read in our early childhood spoke to us about a space journey. Whenever the Russian hero Ivan the Fool found himself on the crossroads, ordered to go "there nobody knows where" to find "that nobody knows what," we suspected that he had traveled into space, just like Gagarin. In high school, our cosmic fascination turned into a romance. The first Soviet cosmonaut became the object of popular adoration. When he died a tragic, early death in 1968, a song addressing him with the intimate "you" was sung nationwide:

The earth is empty without you.
How can I survive these lonely hours?
Only the stars share with you their ten-der-ness.

This cosmic romance, however, did not survive our teenage years. The seeds of its demise date back to the early 1960s, when we started to prefer the yellow submarine of a smuggled Beatles album to yet another rocket, which seemed to fly only on the front page of the newspaper *Pravda*.[2] Like the cosmonaut himself, the dream of cosmos proved mortal.

By the time we became teenagers, many rumors about the Soviet space program always shrouded—in—secrecy abounded. The history of space exploration read like a detective novel, filled with daring discoveries, chance encounters, and untold victims. It was as if the exploration of black holes within the universe aimed to cover up the black spots of Soviet history. In the late 1980s, at the time of perestroika, Russians had enormous difficulty sustaining their commitment to space travel, not only because they lacked the necessary resources but because the intimate connection between technological development, state ideology, and utopian myth had been broken.

With some trepidation I realize that we were the generation that was supposed to live in the era of Communism and travel to the moon. We did not fulfill our mission. Instead we were forced to confront the ruins of utopia; Soviet icons, recycled into souvenirs and totalitarian antics. The fairy tale of our childhood was deprived of a happy ending, as if Ivan the Fool, ordered to go "there nobody knows where," remained stranded at the crossroads. Cosmic paraphernalia now appears like memorabilia from another civilization, like those rusting rockets on the urban playgrounds.

The metamorphosis of the cosmic myth, which in the Russian and Soviet context was closely linked to the actual history of space exploration, is the topic of this essay. The story reveals a paradoxical relationship between individual imagination and collective aspiration, between poetry and technology. Cosmic exploration began as a philosophical, scientific, and artistic quest for free space and the defiance of earthly gravitation; it culminated in a Soviet megaindustry that made dreams come true and, inadvertently, put an end to all collective dreaming.

[...]

COSMOS CONQUERED

The 1968 "moon walk" of the American astronauts was etched into the American consciousness through the vehicle of television. Russians my generation and older remember a different walk, captured on film, which took place seven years earlier; Yuri Gagarin moved slowly, as if unsure of the Earths gravitation, along the red carpet–that unmistakable Soviet status symbol–after his 108 minutes in space. In the next shot he appears on the tribune in Red Square next to Comrade Khrushchev, who makes a memorable speech about the Soviet citizens "born to make the dreams come true." I was too young to remember the original walk, so my memory of these events has been formed through TV reruns. By the time I studied the history of the Soviet "break into space" in school, both Gagarin and Khrushchev were dead, and so was the myth. Dying a political death before the actual one, Khrushchev was removed from the historic footage; Gagarin now walks alone down the carpeted path and into the living rooms of the whole world.

The "Space Age" began not with Gagarin's flight but with the moment the flight was reported. From then on, the age was associated with the triumph of communism on Earth. On April 12, 1961, *Pravda* proclaimed, "Gagarin flies on the wings of the Great October," asserting a direct continuity between the triumph of the Great October Revolution on Earth and the triumph of the Soviet Union in space. Like the space flight itself, the great revolution of 1917 remained largely undocumented at the time it occurred. The "ten days that shook the world," in the words of the American journalist John Reed, went practically unnoticed. Judging from his diary, Reed himself overslept on the morning of October 26 and missed the storming of the Winter Palace. Indeed, the unobserved assault on the palace that initiated "the Age of the Great October" was restaged for the masses in October of 1919 as a grandiose spectacle. Choreographed by the theater director Nikolai Evreinov, the event incorporated ten thousand extras who stormed the Winter Palace while Wagnerian themes played in the background. Something similar happened with the "Space Age", only the medium was different. When the first Sputnik was launched into space, Khrushchev had little confidence in its potential for media success. Once the leader began to comprehend the ideological leverage of the man-made asterisk, however, he ordered his chief designer, Sergei Korolev (1906-1966), to send another into space to coincide with the anniversary of the October Revolution. Similarly, after the successful launch of Gagarin into space, Khrushchev summoned Korolev to his dacha by the Black Sea and advised him to send another man into space by August of 1961, to distract world attention from the erection of the Berlin Wall. Just as the achievements of Soviet aviation were Stalin's personal trophy, space exploration was Khrushchev's.

The "Peaceful Kosmos" program developed by Khrushchev during the 1950s and 1960s was, in fact, a continuation of Stalin's military initiative of an earlier era. That initiative had translated the early Bolshevik vision of utopia into the practical goals of the Stalinist state. Inspired, and indeed enraged, by Charles Lindbergh's flight, Stalin had focused national efforts on the training of pilots and on the engineering of rockets and missiles. After unsuccessful offensives in the Spanish Civil War and Finnish War, however, Stalin's wrath fell upon his falcons. The hero pilots, as well as top military generals such as Marshall Tukhachevsky, chief defender of space technology, and A. N. Tupolev, chief designer of the aerospace industry, were arrested during the purges of 1934 and 1937. In 1938 Korolev, then a young engineer, was placed along with many other prominent space scientists in the special labor camp known as "Tupolev's *sharaga*."

Korolev was one of the last cosmic visionaries. Like Tsiolkovsky, whom he met with in the 1930s, the engineer was in many respects a dreamer who combined eccentric beliefs, romantic faith, and scientific devotion with cosmic exploration. He held fast to his dream of space flight throughout his many years in the camps. Years later, Korolev revealed the story of his survival to the young cosmonauts Gagarin and Titov. He told them about how he contracted scurvy while working near Magadan and was sent to Khabarovsk, on the northern Chinese border. During the journey he was taken off the train and abandoned to die in the snow. He would have frozen to death had it not been for a random act of kindness; an elderly man found Korolev and nursed him back to health using traditional Siberian herbs and medicines, which the exemplary Soviet engineer should have scorned as the unscientific product of superstition. Korolev's near-death experience strengthened his will to conquer space and his hope to achieve immortality in the process.

In the early 1940s, Stalin summoned Korolev to the Kremlin to ask him what he thought about UFOs, which were becoming a popular topic of interest in the West. Suspecting that UFOs were part of a plot to develop the American military industry, Stalin asked the scientist to review several new books on the subject. Korolev, by his own account, proceeded to give the books away as gifts to the pretty young women who worked in his office as translators. He told Stalin that he did not believe in UFOs but that he did have faith in the development of rocket science. As a result, Stalin sent Korolev to Germany to explore rocket technology at the end of World War II and to develop rockets for the Soviet Union that would be capable of carrying missiles and other weapons of mass destruction.[3] Paradoxically, the vision of immortality motivating early Russian space exploration gave way in Soviet times to an initiative to develop deadly weapons. Individual escapes into free space were transformed into collective self-sacrifice for the motherland. Once the ultimate space of dreams, cosmos became an ideological battlefield.

While Sputnik, triumphantly orbiting the Earth, was visible with the naked eye, the earthly circumstances of its production were shrouded in mystery. The Soviet space center, the cosmodrome Baikonur, was a secret space, off limits to foreigners and to most Russians as well. Even the immediate families of Baikonur employees often had little perception of what kind of work was being done there. Baikonur veterans tell a story about the relative of a space engineer who lived in Moscow. He sent a letter to the engineer at the cosmodrome right after Gagarin's flight saying, You live out there in the wilderness. The news might not have reached you that we have sent a man into space.[4] Gagarin himself kept his flight a secret from his own family. His mother learned about his space odyssey by listening to the radio. Reportedly, she nearly fainted when the familiar voice of the wartime announcer Yuri Levitan revealed the frightening truth that her own son had been launched into space. She cried for him, repeating over and over again, "What's he gone and done, my Yura," as if she were talking about a naughty boy.[5]

Baikonur was part of the secret geography of the Soviet Union, the invisible heart of the Soviet motherland. The cosmodrome was founded on the eve of the twentieth Party Congress in 1955. At that congress the "excesses of the Stalin era" were denounced, and information about the Gulag, reluctantly released. Ironically, the complex lay in the area of "internal exile," in the Kazakh desert of Tyuratam, close to the Aral Sea, where many enemies of the state were sent during the epoch of the Terror. Like the Gulag, Baikonur constituted a state within a state. The largest cosmodrome in the world, its population reached about 150,000 by 1985. The complex included fifty-two launching plazas, thirty-four scientific laboratories, ten factories, and a school for cosmonauts, as well as three Palaces of Culture, a Palace of Young Pioneers, a lycée, fifteen schools (two specializing in music, an agricultural system, some of the best-equipped hospitals in the country, three movie theaters, a stadium, a luxury swimming pool, resorts, and beaches built on artificial lakes. In the golden age of Baikomur in the early 1960s, the secret complex appeared for the first time on the world map. While its geographic location was left imprecise, its mythical magnitude was by then immense. The cosmodrome had come to embody the Soviet fairy tale come true. A garden city in the midst of an arid desert, Baikonur itself appeared to be a victory over nature; a triumph of Soviet technology, ideology, and human labor made all the more mythic by its subsequent success launching men and satellites into space.

The dialectic of invisibility and conquest was characteristic of the whole Soviet space program, and the symbolic use of space exploration, almost as powerful as the scientific one. The dream had to be thoroughly choreographed and the making of the dream, kept mysterious. Secrecy did not merely surround scientific discoveries or processes of production related to the space industry but most of its daily practices as well. The work of thousands of people who made the space program possible–from the chief designer to the cleaning women who made up Gagarin's bed–remained outside official representation. The memoirs of Baikonur veterans reveal how conscious many of them were of their invisibility and how painful it was for them to be excluded from the picture of national triumph, which created the illusion that cosmonauts just flew by themselves.

The cosmonaut became the central hero, not an American-style star but a representative of the Soviet people and a mythical being. Gagarin, the most important Soviet icon and the human face of Socialism, was worshipped all over the nation. The real-life story of Gagarin–that of a self-made man from a peasant background who, like many other Soviet children of his generation, lived through the hardships of war in territory occupied by the Nazis and who developed admiration for partisans and war pilots–turned from a biography into a hagiography. His premature death during a training flight became a kind of martyrdom,

As a child, Gagarin worshipped Alexei Meresiev, the wartime pilot who crawled through the woods without his legs to become a Soviet hero and protagonist of a Socialist Realist novel. Soviet space exploration inherited the rhetoric of war; it was about "the storming of space," and the cosmonaut was the peacetime hero who was ready to dedicate himself to the motherland and, if necessary, sacrifice his life for her sake.

Gagarin's brother remembers Yuri's legendary return to his native village. A delegation of elderly women came to see the first cosmonaut. Only for them, he was not a hero but a heretic.

'Tell us, Yura, did you see Him?'
'Whom?' asked Gagarin.
'Him. The Lord. And how did He ever let you get so close to him?'[6]

Another woman proceeded to pull his hair and check if he had burns on his face.

'Excuse me, Yura, but there's been so much talk, you know. They said that the Lord punished you and took off all your hair, and that you had to wear a wig made of dog's hair.'[7]

Gagarin laughed heartily. He persuaded his compatriots that he had not seen anybody there and that the Earth was blue and beautiful. The official image of Gagarin remained that of an exemplary Soviet man, not of a fallen angel.

The cosmonaut's triumph was portrayed as a victory for the Soviet state. Before flying into space, cosmonauts had to become members of the Communist Party, just in case they met some Trotskyites on the other red planet. They also had to go through a terrestrial rite of passage and visit the Soviet "underworld" – Lenin's mausoleum in Red Square. In the case of Gagarin, his earthly pilgrimages before his "break into space" were revealed only after his flights and would have remained secret had he not come back. Those rituals became a blueprint for the trips of future cosmonauts. Titov, the second cosmonaut to be launched into space, went to the Kremlin Wall, to Lenin's tomb, and then placed flowers at the pedestal of Pushkin's monument, thus paying tribute to Russia's cultural heroes—the leader and the poet.

While the solitude of the cosmonaut during the flight must have been of the most intense kind, cosmonauts had little privacy on Earth. Gagarin's journey into space became a major publicity event, not only for the Soviet Union but for Communists everywhere. The cosmonaut was represented as the "dove of peace" for the Cold War world. "Brothers from Warsaw Pact countries" cheered his accomplishment, and "friends from the developing countries" applauded the Soviets' success, while journalists in capitalist countries like the United States only begrudgingly acknowledged Gagarin's feat.

Both Soviets and Americans praised the victory of peace and science, while continuing to prepare for the battles of the Cold War. One of the first letters published in *Pravda* came from Paul Robeson, the famous African-American actor, singer, and athlete and a laureate of Stalin's Peace Prize. On behalf of "progressive humanity," Robeson glorified the name of the Soviet space shuttle "Vostok," meaning "East," writing, "The space shuttle of Soviet progress is called 'Vostok!' How symbolic! It points to the colossal achievements of that part of the world that is called 'the East' and especially to the heart of the East, the Soviet Union."[8] The fact that Gagarin flew into space on the Day of the Freedom of Africa was also regarded as symbolic. "The East is the Sun and light," Robeson pronounced. "The space shuttle 'East' flying over Africa is the light of the future freedom of the African continent, the source of faith and strength of the millions of Africans fighting for their independence."[9] The space trip was equated with political liberation itself.

Soviet cosmonauts became national diplomats and missionaries. Gagarin's flight coincided with the early days of the Cuban Revolution, and the cosmonaut became a friend both of Fidel Castro and of the revolutionary cause. The flight also coincided with the building of the Berlin Wall, which the West–intimidated by Soviet might–did not oppose. Gagarin made friends with Walter Ulbricht of the German Democratic Republic. Titov traveled to the United States after his flight, where he met with students protesting the Vietnam War. He remained unimpressed by New York, the legendary city of the future. He disliked its skyscrapers, which "[hid] the sun from the people" and its neon signs, which he said do not "attract the viewer but rather repulse and exhaust him."[10] Titov also disliked the "absurd" landscapes in the Museum of Modern Art; like Khrushchev, who once contended that a donkey paints better with its tail than does an abstract artist, Titov was not a fan of modern art. He did not recognize the dream of cosmos in the adventures of its modern form.

Soviet cosmonauts were, however, poets at heart. As conceived by Korolev and by Tsiolkovsky before him, a cosmonaut had to be able to make sense of the never-before seen beauty and deep solitude of space. Gagarin's favorite poet was Sergei Yesenin, the "peasant poet" famous for his lyrical and melancholic images of Russian nature. Yesenin made himself immortal by writing his last poem in blood, after cutting open his veins. Gagarin's brother remembers the cosmonaut's favorite lines from Yesenin's poem "Anna Snegina":

Past me there sweep in hectic flight
Grey clouds, a dark day's tousled tresses.
The sadness of approaching night
Upon my heart, resistless, presses.
Down to the very church domes drops
The hazy veil of dusk and twilight.[11]

Yesenin's lines are written from the viewpoint of a poet looking upward from the Earth into the moody sky, not that of a modern aviator gazing down at earth. The poem has no avant-garde imagery; its tone is nostagic, rather than futuristic. The hazy veil of dusk is but a projection of the poet's own internal melancholia.

Titov's favorite poets were Lermontov and Mayakovsky. He particularly liked Lermontov's line, "I walk to the solitary road where the Milky Way glistens and the star speaks to another star."[12] If, before the development of the space program, most of the imaginary cosmic journeys described by artists, writers, and scientists were futuristic adventures in outer space, at the time that space exploration actually took place the destination of the cosmonaut's poetic dreams seems to have reversed. Amateur poets from Baikonur, as well as the cosmonauts themselves, still wrote about the beauty of the world as seen from outer space, but more often they appeared nostalgic for the earthly landscape of Russian birch trees, forest paths, melting snowflakes on a child's palm.

The cosmonauts would eventually bring a piece of Earth with them into space. During a flight in the 1980s, they cultivated a small garden in a pot filled with native soil. Earlier, in the nineteenth century, the fashion for greenhouses and house plants among middle-class apartment-dwellers represented a domestication of nature, the displacement of the external landscape onto interior space, the introduction of a miniature paradise into the domestic realm. At the end of the twentieth century, this miniature paradise was further deterritorialized, yet it served a similar purpose; to domesticate space. The small garden—like the tape recording of Russian birds played by the cosmonauts while tending it—humanized the cosmos, It made technology, and the ideology that drove its development, appear cozy. The birdsong, once compared to the heavenly melody of sirens luring travelers away from home, now served as a memory of Earth.

Notes

1   Adam Bartos' interview with Svyatoslav Sergeevich Lavrov. For the best overview of the Soviet space program in English, see Walter A. McDougall, *The Heavens and the Earth: A Political History of the Space Age* (New York: Basic Books, 1985). See also James Harford, *Korolev: How One Man Masterminded the Soviet Drive to Beat America to the Moon* (New York: John Wiley and Sons, 1997), *Nikolai Rynin, Russkii izobretatel' i uchenyi Konstantin Tsiolkovsky* (Leningrad: Profintern, 1931), and Ivan Slukhai, *Russian Rocketry*, trans. E. Vilim (Jerusalem: Israel Program for Scientific Translation, 1968).

2   The carnal humor of popular songs, or *chastushki*, poked fun at the tragic romanticism of official culture: "I was born on a collective farm. I slept with a cosmos man. O-ooh ... A-aaah ... Aren't we all cosmonauts!"

3   Harford, *Korolev*, 234.

4   M. N. Mal'kov, N. S. Narovliansky, A. P. Zavalishin, and B. B. Vymekaev, *Baikonur prodolzhaetsia* (Moscow: ADB, 1997); K. B. Gerchik, ed., *Kosmodrom Baikonur: nachalo kosmicheskoi e.ry. Proryv v kosmos* (Moscow: ADB, 1994), 28. From more on the history of Baikonur, see K. B. Gerchik, ed., *Legandarnyj Baikonur* (Moscow: Veles, 1995).

5   Recounted in Valentin Gagarin, *My Brother Yuri: Pages from the Life of the First Cosmonaut*, trans. Fainna Glagoleva (Moscow: Progress Publishers, 1973), 40.

6   Gagarin, *My Brother Yuri*, 212.

7   Gagarin, *My Brother Yuri*, 212.

8   Paul Robeson, "Vostok-eto gluboko simvolichno," *Pravda* (13 April 1961). See also, V. Mayevsky, "Den' svobody Afriki," in *Pravda* (15 April 1961).

9   Robeson, "Vostok-eto gluboko simvolichno."

10   German Stepanovich Titov, *Golubaio moia planeto* (Moscow: Voenizdat, 1977), 202-03.

11   Sergei Yesenin, "Anna Snegina," cited in Gagarin, *My Brother Yuti, 218.*

12   Cited in Titov, *Goluhaia moio planeta.*

PART FOUR

FREEDOM, SUBJECTIVITY, AND THE GULAG (2002–10)

After *Nostalgia*'s success, Boym moved on to the weighty topic of the Gulag. Her engagement with the Gulag had an autobiographical root, which she self-reflexively explored in "My grandmother's First Love," (2002), as well as in the introduction to "Art of the Gulag" (2007), an essay for an exhibit that she curated at the Boston University Art Gallery. In the "'Banality of Evil,' Mimicry, and the Soviet Subject" (2008), Boym started by identifying the intellectual departure point of her engagement with the topic in the "persistent difficulty in coming to terms with the gulag:" "The experience of Auschwitz profoundly influenced western political philosophy of the twentieth century, but the experience of the Soviet gulag did not." (343) In that essay, she turned to Hannah Arendt, her long-term philosophical inspiration, and Varlaam Shalamov, a new figure in her pantheon, to provide signposts for a "mutually illuminating relationship between art and politics." (344) For while Boym started with Adorno's dictum about poetry being "barbaric" after the Holocaust, she chose to emphasize Adorno's paradoxical adage: "Literature, he insists, 'must resist this verdict. For it is now virtually in art alone that suffering can still find its own voice without immediately being betrayed by it'" (342). Closely reading Shalomov's tactics of "deaestheticizing evil," in a literature that he presents to us not as "understanding of life" but as "document," Boym argues for the necessity of preserving art in the context of the Gulag not in its traditional role in Russian culture, "as the unofficial cultural legislator (342). Rather, literature is "the space where the practice of imagination becomes a 'weapon of the weak,' that teaches lesson in non-collaboration and tactics of survival" (342). From Arendt's last book, *The Life of the Mind*, Boym chooses to emulate the practice of passionate thinking, which, as opposed to "professional thinking," explores "the limits of knowledge and engages in a double movement between different modes of knowledge and between theory and experience" (345). Boym's lifelong preoccupation with methodology is here revealed to be not just a professional but primarily an ethical preoccupation: "understanding the camp experience requires this kind of thinking that is at once interdisciplinary and passionate" (345).

This interest in the conjunction of methodology, ethics, and contemporary politics also drew her in the most polemic of her positions at this time: her criticism of "the important trend in studies of Soviet subjectivity associated with the work of Igal Halfin and Jochen Hellbeck." In an *Ab Imperio* article titled "How is Soviet Subjectivity Made?" (2002) Boym argued that the new approach to Soviet subjectivity conflates the Kantian notion of the subject with its post-structuralist critique. Foucauldian analysis suggests that the formulaic language cited in Soviet diaries is a result of propaganda rather than the conscious sharing of a narrative with the regime. She charged that proponents of the new approach miss an opportunity to truly engage in post-structuralist analysis in order to explore the heteroglossia that is evident in the texts. Furthermore, she identified an Orientalist dimension to the new approach, arguing that hardly imagine a similar study of, for example, American subjectivity based on FBI employees' diaries during the J. Edgar Hoover era. Revisiting and upholding her position in the polemic in her 2008 "Banality of Evil," Boym once more directly linked it to political commitment: "In the contemporary Russian situation, the excess of liberal subjectivity is hardly a threat, nor does it determine current historical paradigms. Rather the situation is determined by the closing of archives and the rewriting of history books, by the censorship and self-censorship that is imposed on most political debate" (344).

Significant parts of Boym's work on the Gulag were incorporated in her major achievement of the last decade: *Another Freedom* (2010). Reached through *the via negativa of* Boym's deep engagement with the Gulag, this book blossomed into a richly researched and creatively conceived cross-cultural history of freedom. To the brilliance, gusto, and irony that had become part of her signature in her previous books, *Another Freedom* adds a wisdom and humaneness that makes the reading experience a bracing intellectual journey. Boym explored the cultural myths of Russian and Soviet freedom from Pushkin's "other better freedom" that doesn't depend on political rights, to Dostoevsky's "freer freedom" in prison to the Soviet idea of freedom as "well-recognized necessity," to artistic and dissident freedom based on the "art of estrangement." She returned with an expert archaeology of everyday practices of politics and aesthetics in Russia, tracking how they conformed or deviated from its myths and how they surprise us. *Another Freedom* is also the worldliest of Boym's books, wandering far from Russia to the United States and deep in time to ancient Greece. Its brilliant, subtle, and ultimately exhilarating history of freedom from a cross-cultural viewpoint focuses on the relationship between public and private freedom as well as on Boym's lifelong fascination with the relationship between aesthetics and politics, artistic estrangement and political dissent.

Cristina Vatulescu

13 MY GRANDMOTHER'S FIRST LOVE

In 1995, shortly before my grandmother's death, I recorded our conversations,

"You know, my first love was shot by the Bolsheviks," says my grandmother.

"Really? What for?" I ask. "What for? Nothing. What was I in the camps for? For my good luck..." Was he handsome?" "Yes, he was very handsome and a trumpet player, too. All the girls in the Gymnasium were enamored of him. They used to tease me, because everyone was in love with him and I wasn't. He took us to the matinee shows at the Bolshoi Drama Theater to see Catherine's fairy tales."

"Catherine who?" "Catherine the Great. You probably don't know that she wrote fairy tales in her free time."

"And what happened afterwards?" "Afterwards? The trumpet player went away. The World War had just started, you know. I remember all my friends were crying and bidding him farewell. Even our French schoolmistress in the Gymnasium cried. What a charming woman she was. I was her favorite: a good figure skater with my golden hair coming down to here, right below my waist. She used to call me Baroness Sophie Feigelson. So everyone was crying at the farewell party, except me. You've got no heart, my girlfriend Anya scolded me. You know what I did? I ran away and splashed some water on my eyes, and it looked like I was crying. With tears in my eyes, I waved the trumpet player a long goodbye."

I don't listen to the end, I know it by heart. The story of my grandmother's first love has very little to do with the rest of her life. The trumpet player never came back, the French schoolmistress died of the Espagnole virus while escaping to the Whites, and my grandmother lived to the age of ninety-five, surviving two wars, two revolutions, six years in the camps, forty years in communal apartments, and ten years in America. She was no baroness.

"Mama liked to make things up," my father said. "Especially after she came back from the camps. You see, here in America, it's fashionable to remember the past, but it was very different in Russia. We didn't know and didn't want to know who our grandparents were, out of fear. What if they turned out to be enemies of the people: merchants, kulaks, petty traders, or even worse, rootless cosmopolitans or foreigners–Our family surely had a few of them."

"You don't even know that in Stalin's time it was a crime to keep newspapers that were more than five years old," my mother adds. I remember already in the 1960s we discovered a Pravda from 1938 under the old wallpaper. It talked about the great friend of the Soviet Union, Adolf Hitler–We couldn't believe our eyes. We hadn't known anything about the Molotov-Ribbentrop Pact and the Soviet-Nazi friendship."

"Did you keep it" "No, we read it and then covered it up again with the new wallpaper, just in case. It was a communal apartment, after all. So, if your grandma lived in a parallel world, it might have been better for her that way."

I remember how during my childhood my grandmother would stand by the kitchen window right next to the stove in the steam of the boiling chicken soup, looking like a diminutive forgotten actress from a silent melodrama. She would stretch out her hands and whisper to herself or to an imagined sympathetic listener in the grey clouds. As a little girl watching my grandmother, I became obsessed with the steam, which I tried to shape with my hands. She talked to the clouds and I talked to the steam. I believed that the steam was a magic material, parovoe polotno, that could take any shape, and steal you away like a flying carpet in a fairy tale. My grandmother didn't pay attention to my games. One overcast day in Brighton, Massachusetts, I caught her again whispering to herself in front of a window. It was in her room in the Jewish elderly housing center. The room was much more comfortable than where she'd lived before, but there was no gas stove there. Gas stoves were considered a health hazard.

I am not sure my grandmother was aware that she was actually in America. She followed my parents to a strange world, preoccupied mostly with her daughter, whom she was leaving behind. As for her, she knew how to travel light. She moved from one tiny room in a communal apartment in Leningrad to Boston via Vienna and Rome with the same portable altar of old photographs on a French bureau cabinet, the last surviving piece of a set from her departed brother. This was the world of her dreams, a world with no farewells, where all the loved ones crowded together happily in one narrow space. There was a picture of her younger self, a tiny woman in a dark lilac suit and her favorite high-collar blouse. With her large gray-green eyes, Louise Brooks haircut, and what was called in Russia jokingly a "Roman nose," she looked like an aged college student the many hurts that shed endured and inflicted over the years were nowhere in sight.

Besides photographs, the altar contained my grandma's notebooks with quotes from great men and women, seven tiny ivory elephants–carriers of happiness–miniature portraits of Chaliapin and Schubert, a postcard of Leningrad with a view of the frozen Neva River and the wrought-iron fence of the Summer Garden, a gilded pendant of the Eiffel Tower, which my grandmother never visited, and busts of her best friends–Tchaikovsky and Beethoven. Unlike many Jews of her generation, my grandma had sympathies neither with the communists nor with the Zionists. If anything, she was a Beethovenist. In a way she had exactly the same taste as Lenin, who once complained to Dzerzhinsky, the future head of the Secret Police, that he loved Beethoven's Fifth so much that it made him want to pat everyone on the head. But we, the revolutionaries, he must have added, cannot afford that. My grandmother could. At first she listened to Beethoven; then, when she began to go a little deaf, she would talk to his little bust. It turned out that he was not only a great composer but also a patient listener. And my grandmother was much more frank with strangers than with relatives because it was easier to charm them recounting the same stories over and over again.

She became a virtual orphan at an early age, cared for by her elder brother who married and escaped to Paris in the late 1920s, leaving my grandmother behind. The exact time and place of her birth remain uncertain. According to her Soviet passport, she was born in 1902, but she always claimed to be three years younger. She also claimed that her family lived somewhere near Novaya Ladoga, even though it was not in the Pale of Settlement. The story of her parents, reiterated through the years, was always the same: My poor mother worked all day long in a shop and one day was run over by a tram in St. Petersburg, My father never finished his studies to become a rabbi. All he did was slaughter chickens for Passover, thats all he was good for. If only my poor mother had lived longer," she would sigh. If only my brother didn't marry that woman..."

The story of her marriage to my grandfather was equally filled with lost possibilities, You know, I really wasn't in love with Isaiah, your grandfather. Another very interesting man was courting me at that time. His name was Boris Iosifovich. He kept bringing me flowers, but never proposed, I was a proud girl, so when your grandpa proposed I said yes. I didn't keep in touch with Boris Iosifovich, but he died relatively young. From cancer, which ran in his family. It might be good, after all, that he never proposed to me. Neither you nor your father would have existed. But I brought flowers to his grave many years after his death, just like he used to bring flowers to me, and I cried by his grave all by myself."

My grandmother confided in me when I was little and her fears became mine. Sshhhh... don't tell anyone... Its our secret, she would say, Now did you check under the bed? Did you hear the strange footsteps below? Always check what's under your bed. That's a good place to hide. Use a wet mop. And put some chlorine on it, don't mind the smell. You just don't but the less I knew, the more I was afraid. Wherever I have lived since then, I have looked for a secret place to hide. From time to time, I still hear the susurration of "their" slippers. They are coming to get someone, and one day it might be me.

They came for my grandmother several times. First in the 1930s to interrogate her about her brother, and then in 1948 to arrest her. If it wasn't for her brother in France, would she have been arrested? Who knows? It was in the midst of an anti-cosmopolitan campaign, and my grandmother was a schoolteacher with a sharp tongue. "And her daughter Inna, my fathers sister, was dating a Yugoslav unaware of Titos treacherous revisionism." And then there was a mysterious story that my father remembers hearing: in the corridors of the KGB my grandmother ran into her neighbor who had been arrested half a year earlier. He ran to embrace her and profusely apologized. "He might have pronounced her name among other cosmopolitans" during the interrogations, possibly under torture. But my grandma didn't hold a grudge against him. While she blamed many relatives and friends for things they had and hadn't done, she suppressed her good neighbors story from her later accounts of her arrest and imprisonment.

"I was lucky, they put me with the thieves," my grandmother used to say. "Much better than murderers." As a relief from hard labor on the construction site, she was temporarily sent to work in the thieves colony as an assistant librarian. This seemed like a great vacation. "The thieves were avid readers. Sometimes they even returned the books." My grandma was very fond of her camp mates. She told a story about sharing a prison cell with Tatiana, a relative of the famous TV anchor. She was arrested because Stalins daughter was enamored of her father. The third woman in the cell was an informer who was supposed to build a case against Tatiana. She would talk about how the Jews used the blood of Christian children during Passover. Poor Tatiana grew outraged, while my grandmother staged scenes to distract the informer and prevent Tatiana from compromising herself and ending up with a longer prison sentence.

"I met very cultured people there," my grandmother liked to say, with a sense of pride. "Do you know the famous actress Okunevskaya, a great beauty, adored even by Marshall Tito? We were in the same barracks. We used to recite *Uncle Vanya* together. 'One day we, too, will see diamonds in to the sky, my dear.'" My grandmother would pause here, according the Stanislavsky method. "'One day we will see diamonds in the sky.'"

It happened that Stalin died soon after their camp performance of Uncle Vanya. My grandma loved to tell the story of the letter she got from my father about Stalin's death: "Dear Mamochka," he wrote, "What a tragedy! What a great man we've lost. What a great loss for our country." I was reading it not knowing whether to laugh or cry," she would add, sighing. My father wasn't a fervent Stalinist, just a normal Soviet war child who grew up on Cold War movies about good guys and bad guys, brave Soviet soldiers and evil spies. As a young teenager he was cared for by frightened relatives who were embarrassed that his mother had been arrested as an enemy of the people, regardless of whether she was guilty or not. After Khrushchev's secret speech, my father embraced the Thaw and destalinization in all its manifestations, organizing numerous clubs and voluntary associations, from the (a fan club for the forever-losing Leningrad football team, Zenith) to a film lovers' club, Film and You, which invited great Polish film divas and New Wave Czech directors to visit. Mostly, my parents wanted to live in a club of their own, a grey zone of non-lying, not haunted by the ghosts of the past. My father said that he went through a crisis, not during destalinization, but a decade later in 1968, when Soviet tanks entered his favorite city of Prague, the capital of film-lovers.

I remember spending August 1968 at a seaside resort with my parents, listening to the Voice of America speaking about somebody named Dubcek and some sort of tanks. Their unusual anxiety, their secret whispers on a windy beach, and the background noise of the jammed radio signaled to me a radical change in climate and mood. My parents did not talk politics at home, trying not to burden me at a young age with a double conscience. As a result, I inherited their sense of secrecy, and in the sixth and seventh grade I began to organize secret societies of my own. The Black Mimosa club was followed by the Club of Great Intriguers and the Society of Subjective Idealists, which never boasted more than five members. The intimate scale never bothered me, though, for we learned in the seventh grade that the first Congress of Russian Social Democratic Workers' Party, which took place in 1898, twenty years before the victorious revolution, had only nine participants. The most dedicated member of all my secret societies was my best friend Natasha, whose grandfather had also spent a long time in the camps. In the 1920s he was a proletarian poet, a friend of Yesenin and Mayakovsky, but in 1918 he voted for Trotsky, a fact that somebody remembered in 1938. I knew Natasha's grandfather; he recited to us forbidden decadent poems about "pineapples in champagne." Like my grandmother's, he too lived in a parallel world.

Whether accurate or not, my grandmother's stories produced the first crack in my picture of the world. Yet nobody in my family, myself included, ever managed to find out exactly what had happened to her. After my grandmother's death, I tried to get my father to probe into uncomfortable regions of our family memory.

"It was like in the movies," my father says. Two men in gray suits came at night for my mother. They began with a house search, throwing everything on the floor, turning every paper and book upside down. They were happy when they found a French book. That was evidence against her.

"Mama went out of the room, and suddenly we heard a scream. A man in a grey suit dragged her down the corridor, bandages on her wrists. She had tried to cut her veins. After that I didn't see her for six years."

"And what happened when she returned?" "I don't remember," he said. "Your mother and I, we were dating already, I guess we were happy she was alive. She didn't want to talk to us about her experience. It was a different era. You know, she came back, but she didn't go out into the streets for half a year," he adds suddenly. "For half a year?" "Yes, she just couldn't. And then somehow things went back to normal. She started her job again as a schoolteacher and the first stories started to come out. They were cheerful, upbeat stories. Mostly about the great actress Okunevskaya and the other cultural figures. We never pushed her. We didn't know how to ask questions about the past. Maybe we were afraid that it would upset her too much, or that she would make a scene."

My grandmother spent the next two decades teaching her secondary school pupils the fundamentals of math, Russian grammar, and self-mastery. Developing will power must have been a fashionable pedagogical slogan of my grandmothers time. I only remember that you were supposed to take cold showers, eat Antonovka apples, and count to ten if you were about to lose your patience or your mind. She always had her favorite pupils, liubimchiki, whose thank you cards and pictures in cute figure skating outfits she preserved on her bureau. They were the only ones who appreciated her and loved her, she used to say.

But side by side with this life of an exemplary Soviet schoolteacher, my grandma had a secret nocturnal life. When she moved to our communal apartment, I would often see her alone in our kitchen at night trying to catch the "enemy voices" of the BBC and the Voice of America, fighting with the antennas of the old radio transmitter like Don Quixote with his windmills. I don't think she ever succeeded. But she enjoyed the fight. It gave her an an opportunity to bash and curse "our idiots." Sometimes she would doze right there next to the noisy radio, filling the kitchen with the staticky sounds of foreign voices. My grandma, the dissident. She was sad about my emigration in 1981. She sold her French bureau to help pay for my ticket, and told me that she hoped I would become what I wanted to become and travel the world, because she had never been able to. Of my whole family I was the one she felt closest to, yet I was never sure if she was really talking to me and not at me, seeing in me her own imaginary stranger.

When I went back to Russia after ten years, I found myself retracing more and more my grandmas elusive steps. It happened almost unwittingly at first. By chance I met an archeologist of the Baltic region who did excavations in the town of Novaya Ladoga, uncovering a Jewish cemetery. Those buried there were mostly of German and Baltic ancestry, and many were descendants of Jewish military recruits. "We were surprised," he said. This wasn't the Pale of Settlement. We didn't know that Jews had ever lived there." My archeologist friend had never met a single Jew born in Novaya Ladoga and wanted to record my grandmother's story. She will someday appear on display in an ethnographic museum in the town of her youth, becoming the honorary Jew of Novaya Ladoga. It occurred to me that while whispering at the grey clouds in our communal kitchen she, in fact, might have been praying, in her own unconventional way.

Traditional Jewish life, idyllically imagined by some American Jews, was something she escaped from, hoping to study, live in a big city, and travel the world. Later that life was made impossible by the state. It survived as a childhood memory and a series of strange, clandestine practices that my grandmother reinvented throughout her life. During the war, when she was evacuated to Siberia, she made hamantaschen cookies for Purim, went to synagogue for matzos, and fasted very quietly once a year. At the same time, my grandma spoke perfect schoolteacher's Russian and claimed to have studied French and German, but not "the dialect," which was her way of referring to Yiddish.

As for her arrest, I haven't yet been able to find my way through the vagaries of the post-Soviet archival access laws to obtain her KGB file. The only document I have is her release form, which says that she was rehabilitated and released from the camps for "lack of incriminating evidence." On my last trip to Moscow, I was surprised to see the famous actress Okunevskaya on television, very much alive, an avid yoga practitioner and the author of bestselling memoirs. When I tuned in, she was speaking eloquently about the disappearance of beauty in the contemporary world. At the end of her own life, my grandmother's dream to see the world came true. Only I am not sure whether she was fully aware of it. She was more preoccupied with settling scores with "our idiots." On the day of emigration she took a crazy risk, nearly endangering everybody's safe journey. Protesting the Soviet customs regulations that allowed her to carry abroad only two blouses, she took the matter into her own hands and put on three of them, one on top of the other. "Like a cabbage" she said proudly. Our idiots noticed nothing. Thus my grandma arrived in the West dressed in three smuggled off-white blouses, grayed by time and tough Soviet detergent. That did not embarrass her in the least. A few days later, she was wandering the streets of Vienna practicing the long-forgotten German that she had learned in school. A polite Viennese gentleman who escorted her home one night informed my parents that she spoke Yiddish, not German. Of course she got lost, but this didn't prevent her from finding the free concert she was looking for.

Once in Boston, my grandmother lived with me in my student apartment for a brief time. From a schoolteacher she turned into a giggling girlfriend, sharing with me some slightly off-color gossip. But like a partisan she revealed no new information about the dark parts of her life, instead telling me the same stories about her beloved French schoolmistress and the lilac silk dresses that her dear brother had bought for her, about Beethoven and Tchaikovsky, Boris Iosifovich and the actress Okunevskaya who seemed to be perpetually performing the monologue about diamonds in the sky. The handsome trumpet player, the darling of all the schoolgirls of Novaya Ladoga, fell silent over and over again in the midst of tears and farewells.

Her memory loss happened very quickly. Once we came to visit her in the Jewish Rehabilitation Center with my father, but she barely recognized us. Moreover, she no longer spoke Russian, but Yiddish, the dialect that she supposedly didn't know. It must have been, after all, the language of her youth. This is where she returned to at the end. To the happy Sophie who didn't know how to cry and hadn't cut her golden hair. To that slender little girl who was yet to experience her first love.

My grandmother died on the tenth anniversary of her arrival in America. On her deathbed she appeared uncannily young. She was lying in her favorite blouse with rouge on her cheeks and a little color on her lips. The rabbi who kindly agreed to say the final vows tried to find out something about her from us. We felt dumbfounded and awkward and couldn't say much. So the rabbi tried to humor us with a joke about the strange fate that makes people go places.

"You know how I came to America? My father and mother had no luck with children. So their rabbi recommended that they either divorce or change places in order to change their luck. That is why they left Russia for America, and a few years later I was born. Your grandma, too, had some good luck dying surrounded by her children at the age of ninety-two" At the funeral the rabbi said a few simple, general things: that my grandma loved her family, that she was a good storyteller and a great teacher, and that this was already a lot. Strange as it might seem, he got it almost right. It is not by chance that my grandmother was always kinder to strangers than to members of her own family. The strangers understood her better. I inherited her portable archive, which I set aside for a few years. I knew that she had several notebooks, filled with her tortured scribbles and punctuated with multiple exclamation marks breaking the lines, demanding attention. Sometimes she would put as many as eighteen at the end of one line, usually when she wished us all the best: Be happy and healthy!!!!!!!!!!!!!!!!!!!" I guess I was afraid that there might be something in her scribbled pages that would compromise my father, embarrass or terrify us all, revealing some dark family secret that we had all helped to cover up.

Nothing could have been further from the truth. It turned out that she was endlessly writing letters to her daughter Polina and her great-granddaughter Anechka, letters that for the most part she never mailed, telling them how much she missed them. My pictures and postcards sent from different parts of the world were there too. The only revelation was a small photo of my father as a teenager dating from 1950. He must have sent it to her in the camps. I was prepared to read some official lines on the back, knowing that all camp mail had to go through the censor. Instead there was only one sentence written in pencil on the back of the picture: "Dear Mamochka: I am always with you everywhere, wherever you are." Strange, people usually embellish their pasts. In my fathers case, he presented himself as more of a conformist than he really was, as if assuming some collective guilt. "I am with you always and everywhere, wherever you are," seemed an uncanny line, since neither then nor now does anyone know where she has been.

For better or worse, the whole family lived out my grandmother's fears and ambitions, following her roads not taken. Her stories protected her and us from her past, and we ended up inheriting that past without confronting it. My father and mother experienced their own share of fear during frequent interrogations by the KGB when they were refuseniks in the 1980s. My mother tells her own stories of this now-historic past, only instead of a monologue by actress Okunevskaya about diamonds in the sky they feature a dialogue with a young Vladimir Putin, then employed by the Leningrad KGB.

"You know, the moment I saw Putin on TV here in Boston I immediately recognized him."

"How so?"

"He came to ask us a few questions in our apartment in Leningrad in the early 1980s."

"What makes you think it was Putin?"

"Well, the man was rather short, without distinct qualities, but very polite. I am sure it was him!"

"Really?" (My mother thinks that I am doubtful about her story.)

You don't believe me, why? I'm not your grandma Sonia . . ."

"Messengers from the old world," we all become storytellers. Only our audience is shrinking. The new world is already oversaturated with the dreams and fears of other people and their endless chatter about themselves. Tales of strangers' first loves are consumed and forgotten in an expedient manner with the dying sounds of a remote trumpet in the thin background. I tried to pierce through my grandma's tales to see what was behind them, but I found no smoking gun there, only the ebb and flow of daily survival, a few crossroads that defy lifes staunch inevitability, and one or two happy moments that punctuate time like those pauses that my grandma staged so well. One day we will see diamonds in the sky..."

My grandmother's past continues to play tricks on us, influencing our future. I owe to her my decision to emigrate, not only into texts but also into another country. I became a teacher, just like her, although I am not sure I succeed in the exercise of self-mastery. I remain obsessed by infinite potentialities, the "what-ifs" of life. I love dark lilac, while my fathers favorite color remains red. No one in our family is fond of Beethoven.

As I listen to the end of my grandmothers recording, I realize that I got it all wrong.

"Babushka, was the trumpet player in love with you" "I don't know," "What do you mean? What happened between you and him" "I told you, he took us to see a matinee performance of Catherine's fairy tales."

"And then?"

"Nothing. Then he brought us all home and said good-bye. We were just girls, what do you want? I never saw him again."

"And then he was shot by the Bolsheviks?"

"Why are you confusing me? The trumpet player just went away . . . with a circus or something. It is my first love who was shot by the Bolsheviks. Venia, a young cadet. If only he had survived… (sigh, pause). Who knows what would have happened with my life . . .

14 HOW SOVIET SUBJECTIVITY IS MADE (KAK SDELANA "SOVETSKAIA SUB'EKTIVNOST")

"There were many victories and defeats. The class enemy, the kulak, did not sleep, organizing the backward mass of the bedniaki and seredniaki against the kolhozes. Thus in a bitter skirmish with the obsolete and dying capitalist elements, our kolhozes have been born, reared, strengthened. A lot of struggle still lies ahead..."
FROM THE DIARY OF A.I ZHELEZNIAKOV

Even the Gulag camps, staffed with large libraries and other educational facilities were conceived of as construction sites of the New Man.
FROM JOCHEN HELLBECK,
"WORKING, STRUGGLING, BECOMING"

In the Beatles' song "Back in the USSR" Soviet girls have long "caught up and outpaced" the Western ones. The singer is dreaming how one of these beautiful Soviets will "bring [him] to [her] daddy's farm" where they will spend a beautiful weekend listening to the sounds of balalaika. We forgive John Lennon his political incorrectness, lack of knowledge about collectivization and interest in "class-alien elements". His USSR is as real as America in the song "Goodbye, America" where the balalaika is replaced with the banjo. These are imaginary countries, the looking glass of the Cold War. However, starting from 1920s "Back in the USSR" became a certain topos of Western imagination, and every Western historian knows that when he writes about the USSR, whether he wants it or not, he must conceptualize his historiographical context and his attitude towards the mythical country of the USSR. Especially, if such a historian deals with the problem of cognition and subjectivity in the Stalinist period – the problem that is the stumbling block of the leftist intellectual thought. Thus, the study of Soviet subjectivity, as through the looking glass, reflects Western intellectual-professionals' subjectivity of the beginning of the twenty first century. Every study of this kind should be considered in two contexts: the Soviet context of the 1930s, and the Western and post-Soviet scholarly context of the 1990s-2000s.

One of the central problems of modern history is the relationship between history and theory. On the one hand, innovative theoretical and philosophical approaches open new vistas, lead to fundamental historiographical reflection, and help remove clichés and taboos on certain types of research. This is especially the case when it comes to difficult historical periods such as the Soviet 1930s. On the other hand, in the context of Western academic market there is a wolfish law "publish or perish" which stimulates the industry of "new approaches" to history. The definition of "professional thinking" given by Hannah Arendt helps understand this phenomenon. Professional thinking seeks inner consistency within its own narrowly delimited parameters but at times has very little relationship to personal or historical experience. "Professional thinking" uses theory not for expanding the borders of cognition, but rather in purely utilitarian purposes: theory becomes so to speak the "surplus value" of an academic product making it more attractive (speaking in Marxist terms, in the spirit of Hellbeck's and Halfin's works). Hannah Arendt contrasts such absolutely logical pseudo-professionalism to professionalism of a different kind, the one that is creative and reflexive and which can be characterized by responsibility for the research material and at the same time engagement with the world beyond the limits of disciplinary frames. So, theory and history should not be perceived as "class enemies" or "two incompatibles" (this time I'll paraphrase Pushkin, not Marx). It is not so important whether historians read Foucault, what is important is how they read him. "Professional thinking" can be distinguished from reflective thinking, which operates through the estrangement of disciplinary clichés, intellectual passion and engagement with the world. The current academic climate in the West with its slogans "publish or perish" and the industry of "new approaches" contributes to the development of "professional thinking" which arms itself with technical proficiency and the appropriate style of academic humorlessness. Yet, not all new trends can be dismissed in such a fashion since they open new vistas in the human understanding. I propose to examine the movement of "Soviet subjectivity" using its own theoretical vocabulary taking as an example one of Jochen Hellbeck's articles. In my brief close-reading I will employ some of the structuralist and post-structuralist techniques and will refer to Mr. Hellbeck as 'the author" in the Foucauldian sense, a producer of the discourse, not a specific biographical subject. In the spirit of the Russian Formalists, I ask the question "how is the Soviet subjectivity" made?

1. *Conceptual apparatus.* The author claims to redress the imbalance in scholarship on the Stalinist period and argues that "the primary effect on individuals' sense of self of the revolution of 1917 and of the Soviet revolutionary practices was not repressive but productive." In the center of attention are diaries of communists, active participants of collectivization, and soviet functionaries. The author argues against the "assumptions deeply ingrained in the Western imagination," based on a commitment to the type of "the tenacious liberal subject," as well as against the conclusions of Russian and Western scholars who believe that "the Soviet regime sought to subjugate individual's sense of selfhood." Indeed, a large number of Soviet citizens benefited from the regime and were its supporters, so the analysis of their private writing is an important historical endeavor that contributes to the understanding of the re-forging of the Soviet self. Such an approach does not seek sincerity and authenticity and does not ask the insoluble question of what the Soviet citizens actually thought and felt. Instead, the author directs our attention to the statements of the Soviet citizens about themselves and views them as a form of self-expression, not repression. As a methodology, Hellbeck proposes some of the postulates of Michel Foucault and, above all, his notion of "technology of the self" and technology of powers. Since my doctoral dissertation at Harvard University focused on issues of subjectivity and authorship and partially on the work of Michel Foucault, I was pleased to find some familiar references in the work of a historian.

To my surprise, on page 1 the author defines subjectivity as "a capacity for thought and action derived from a coherent sense of self." Where does this definition of subjectivity come from? Anyone even vaguely familiar with the work of Michel Foucault realizes that this stands in complete contradiction to the Foucauldian concept of the subject, which is anything but "coherent". The author proceeds throughout the article to conflate the Cartesian and Kantian concept of subject with its post-structuralist critique.

Similarly, there is complete conceptual confusion around the concept of "private self." The author rightly remarks that the concept of privacy presents a major problem in both Russian and Soviet context, yet in making his argument he cannot decide between valorizing private self expression and conflating it with the Bolshevik conception of "free subjectivity" where freedom is "a well-recognized necessity." As a result, Soviet communists, the authors of the diaries, are endowed with Kantian creative subjectivity and "private self" which somehow embrace "the modern agenda of subjectivization. " This "tenacious liberal subject," however, is reserved only for those who were not "class aliens" and persons of "impure Soviet origin." (I quote the expressions used in the article.) The study of other categories of the Soviet citizens remains entirely outside the scope of this investigation. They are denied any type of "subjectivity".

The author might be reminded of an interesting comment made in the diary of the German critic on the left, Walter Benjamin who travelled to Moscow in the winter of 1926-1927: "The Bolsheviks have abolished private life." Fortunately, Walter Benjamin exaggerated, defining the tendency, not the outcome, yet most of his observations and his own tenacious attempts to preserve a modicum of privacy and reflective thinking in Moscow deserve some attention. After his trip, Benjamin made a decision not to join the Communist Party, and his beloved communist theater director and actress Asia Lacis and her German comrade Reich stayed in Moscow and ended up in the Gulag).

The result of Hellbeck's persistent conceptual confusion is anything but coherent, but this in itself might not have been a problem. A thoughtful student of Foucault would focus on such discursive discontinuities, as well as gaps and inconsistences in the diaries, which are most revealing in any study of subjectivity. In fact, Foucault spoke about powers in plural and never presented an argument which would show a continuity between the subject's techniques of the self and the dominant state ideology (in the Soviet case, Bolshevik, then Stalinist state) But incoherence is always a challenge to a professional thinking, it requires a reflection on one's own methodology that is absent from the article.

I have observed a series of paradoxes in the recent appropriation of Foucault for Russian and Soviet studies. They tend to ignore the progression of Foucault's own work and twenty years of internal critique of his work in the French context. They sort of freeze the theory in the early 1980s and present this stale frozen product as the last word in science. Literary critics of the post-structuralist theory (I identify myself as one of them to a certain extent, as my doctoral dissertation in Harvard was dedicated to the theory of subjectivity in literature, the problem of an author's death, and among others, works of Foucault) have long abandoned such narrow discursive understating of the subject. A "friendly" critique of Foucault in works of Michel de Certeau, late Barthes, Derrida, Nancy and Lyotard returns exactly to the question of resistance to the practices of power (Certeau), of humanism/individualism (Barthes and Nancy) which cannot be reduced or collectivized, of the new ethics and responsibility (Derrida, Lyotard and Levinas), which is not reduced to a hateful caricature of the liberal of the nineteenth century. Although, Foucault himself turned out to be quite a caricature in their interpretations. Instead of the discussion of methodology there was a scene of a social realistic nature or a preachy American comedy with good guys and bad guys. It is known that Foucault didn't have much use for the distinction between authoritarian regime and Western style democracy, yet in his time, he presented a creative and provocative critique of the Western subjectivity in the Western context. The scholars of Russia and the Soviet Union do not follow Foucault's method (that would require the critique of Russian subjectivity from within the Russian and the Western context). Instead they merely mimic the effects of Foucault's work and apply his critique of the Western subjectivity to justify its Soviet or Russian counterpart. (This reminds me of an old Soviet joke which dates back to the time of the thaw. "An American and a Russian meet and discuss who has more freedom of expression. The American says: "I can go to the White House and criticize the American president any time." "Big deal," says the Soviet citizen. I too, can go to the Red Square and criticize the American president any time.")[1]

2. Analysis of the Historical Documents. Let us examine one of the author's examples that comes from the 1930s diary of A/I Zhelezniakov:

> "There were many victories and defeats. The class enemy, the kulak, did not sleep, organizing the backward mass of the bedniaki and seredniaki against the kolhozes. Thus in a bitter skirmish with the obsolete and dying capitalist elements, our kolhozes have been born, reared, strengthened (no Russian original is provided)."

The author's comment on the passage is that the diary writer begins with a macro frame in which he then places events from his personal life. This is an example of "autobiographical record" as a chronicle of class struggle which "bespeak an extraordinary involvement of their authors in the development of the Soviet system." No discursive analysis of the text was called for by the critics of the Soviet subjectivity. A closer look at the passage reveals that virtually every element of the sentence, from the use of the adjectives ("backward mass of bedniaki, "bitter skirmish, dying capitalist elements) to the syntax is 100% formulaic. The author is not quoting the original Russian, which would reveal this more clearly. Not a single grammatical or stylistic feature in these sentences (as far as I could judge from the English) presents even a minor variation on the official iconography. The degree of the formulaic quality is truly amazing and cannot be compared even with the premodern folkloric literature or icon painting that has a higher degree of variation. This robotic reproduction of the official ready-mades of the political language by somebody who was a direct witness to the events is a frightening and reveals psychological phenomenon. The diary writer seems to know instinctively that a minor deviation from official iconography might cost him dearly. This is not even repetition but a form of incantation [the order of the sentences is switched in the Russian version].

I note one incongruity here (not noted by the author): the capitalist elements are described as "obsolete and dying." The common sense logic would suggest that something is dying first and only then becomes obsolete. However, here works a different logic. The Marxist-Leninist-Stalinist telos of history already made them "obsolete" but there is still a gap between revolutionary theory and the revolutionary practice, hence these bad elements keep "dying" a long and painful death, but cannot become obsolete, as it was demanded by Marx, Engels, Lenin, and Stalin. Indeed, as the author remarks some of the diary writing didn't merely describe but reshaped the reality. But how? How exactly were those "capitalist elements" consisting of "backward bedniaks," seredniaks, and kulaks made to conform to the new state telos and move from 'dying to obsolete?' Why did Western historians-Foucauldians suddenly forget Foucault's main idea of powers in plural and turn the discourse of powers into a form of self-expression?

I cannot even begin to speak about what's at stake here. Those of us with some knowledge of the Soviet history of collectivization (as it was said in the Soviet poems: not everyone "learned history by Hegel") and elementary human compassion can imagine what happened to all those 'seredniaks" and kulaks silenced forever by this description. Indeed, the literary became literal. The "dying capitalist elements" to whom the formulaic passage refers, most likely died unnatural deaths. Some didn't even get a chance to check out those excellent library facilities in the Gulag camps referred to in the article. We don't have their diaries to quote them here as historical documents. This kind of study of the Soviet subjectivity that excludes them from the sphere of inquiry kills them all over again. A historian should not forget "the price of the metaphor" in the Soviet context.

Had the author been the student of structuralist and poststructuralist analysis that he claims to be, he would have paid more attention to the close reading of the documents (which is really the only original part of his work). He might have looked at the "heteroglossia" in the diarists' texts (speaking Bakhtin's language), many voices present there from ideological cliches of the Bolshevik propaganda to the melodramatic locutions of the prerevolutionary popular culture. There in those discontinuities, he might have found the features of "private self expression" which should have concerned him. The analysis of the Soviet subjectivity (and not a superficial and didactic reading of a few highly selective texts that speak about the making of the Soviet self) would juxtapose and oppose one type of text to another and place together the diaries, secret NKVD accounts (the study of which the author ridicules and makes a caricature of), the words of the interrogators and interrogators. One could have found, for example, a "macro context" and looked at how the same event is reflected differently in different diaries. But such an approach would require an open mind, responsibility, above all, for the historical material, certain professional fearlessness, willingness to sacrifice wholeness and coherence. The task of the historian is not to operate on an agonistic academic principle "whoever is not with us is against us," which is the mode of this article, forgetting the broader historical contexts. Otherwise, it turns out just like in the old Russian saying: "all for the sake of a witty remark".

Had the author placed different kinds of texts side by side, his current argument might have fallen apart like the house of cards, but the honest discussion of the Soviet subjectivity would have been born out of this provisional failure.

3. *Professional Methodology/Analysis of the article as a text/ Contexts of history.* Since the author doesn't reflect on the nature of Stalinist discourse, he seems unaware of the fact that it begins to penetrate his own vocabulary without quotation marks. In the brief historical descriptions he makes use of the same terminology. (Thus poor Marieta Shaginian and Vera Inber are presented in the text as "writers of impure, non-Soviet origins," this definition is not used in quotation marks as somebody else's description, but as the author's own characterization.)

The author doesn't know the meaning of quotation marks, which have an interesting history: originally they represented two severed heads. The device of blurring the distinction between the voice of the narrator/author and that of his characters/subject was pioneered by Flaubert and has a particular name in literary studies: "free indirect discourse." The author uses it unselfconsciously, thus rhetorically embracing the vision of the 1930s that he finds in the diaries. If we were Martians or for that matter American first year students of Russian history, we would come out from reading this article with a peculiar vision of the 1930s where collectivization was triumphant, hunger minor, seredniaki were class enemies, the Gulag had very good libraries, and capitalism was becoming progressively obsolete. Interestingly, the article ends with a quote "I categorically reject the slanderous claims." While a normal practice in many essays, in this rhetorical environment, it seems to stand for the author's emphatic position. When the author uses quotation marks around the words it is usually to define class enemies. This incidentally is a rhetorical practice of the Socialist realist criticism from 1930s throught 1950. Or rather, as they used to say in Soviet times, this is "not by chance." Eto nesluchajno. Official socialist realist criticism in the Soviet Union was preoccupied with a very similar Soviet subjectivity, without a footnote to Foucault. (As the joke of Stalin's time goes, With Soviet critics it's difficult to fight—you fight them with quotes, they fight you with exile. S sovetskimi kritikami trudno sporit'. Ty im –tsitatu, oni tebe ssylku...)

The author calls his method "historicist" yet I was not sure what was the referent to the word "history" here. He uses interchangeably and ahistorically such terms "Bolshevik," Revolutionary," Stalinist." For instance in the sentence like "Soviet revolutionaries also promoted diary as a subjectivizing technique" it is unclear who are the "Soviet revolutionaries." (In Russian an expression "sovetskie revoliutsionery" sounds ridiculous. " The other term "class aliens" (no Russian equivalent provided) is equally amusing. To my knowledge, there were "class enemies" (klassovye vragi), but nobody was outside the class system. The expression 'class alien" suggests to my American ear either an infatuation with Hollywood horror movies (Aliens Aliens II or Aliens III, etc) or a reference to the immigrant status and visa problems.

The author has published a number of articles that use exactly the same primary materials and are based on just a few diaries from which he extrapolates and makes broad generalizations. The author creates strawmen out of his adversaries through vague generalization ("in the Western imagination," some literary specialists, etc.) about them or through caricature. Moreover, the author often falls into exactly the same pitfalls that he criticizes. Thus, he remarks that most studies focused on the concealed or repressed selves" of the Soviet citizens were based on limited sources (i.e. secret NKVD reports and interrogations) but then makes an even vaster generalization based on a couple of diaries.

This brings me to question one of the article's claim of originality. Supposedly it is redressing the balance in the studies of the Soviet Union. This seems to ignore all of the Soviet historical writing done in the Soviet Union for at least fifty years and in Eastern Europe that did a very similar analysis of the Soviet experience without unnecessarily implicating Michel Foucault into it. As a methodology this can be described as cliches dressed into a new terminology masquerading as innovation.

As for the use of clichés in that type of text and their broader implications, I recommend rereading *Eichmann in Jerusalem* by Hannah Arendt (of course, this is not meant to suggest any similarities between Eichmann and the diary writers.) We remember that Eichmann, the architect of the final solution in Nazi Germany was not a monster. He was considered normal by the trial psychiatrists and even rejected Vladimir Nabokov's novel "Lolita" offered to him by the Israeli librarian as an "immoral book." (great compliment to Vladimir Nabokov). Arendt' analysis reveals the crucial feature in the excessive reliance on the clicheistic discourse in the formation of subjectivity; it helps to domesticate political evil. Alas, the Gulag camps did not exist merely in the Western imagination.[2]

If a similar study was conducted based on the German material, say, on diaries of the fascist functionaries, it is highly unlikely that a Western historian would fall into a trap of a rhetorical blur of the vocabulary of his diary writers and his own? I do not think that the author of this hypothetical study would begin to identify German critics and writers, say, Adorno or Brecht, as "impure German subjects" (without quotation marks), even if he found this definition in some diary or a Nazi document. One should think about these double standards. Aren't they a form of *orientalism* of a kind? What will be called political coercion in Western context, in Russian context is perceived as "a required sacrifice" (I do not accuse the author of orientalism, but only of the absence of reflection on his own rhetoric and methodology). I hope young Russian scholars who are now writing interesting papers using new documents and theoretical approaches, will not follow the way of the new orientalism and won't "domesticize" without reflection western prepacks of the Soviet subjectivity.

Jochen Hellbeck claims originality and stands for the restoration of balance in the study of the Soviet Union. At the same time, polemicizing with the new Western (and partly – post-Soviet) historiography, it seems that he is ignoring all the historical literature published in the Soviet Union in the last 50 years as well as works of the Eastern European historians who did a similar analysis of the Soviet experience without drawing on Foucault.

Of course, one can ask the question: in what context are professional historical texts being written and read? Maybe scholarly texts should be accompanied by the tag "the author is not responsible for the contexts"? A description of the Soviet subjectivity based on the limited sources in the narrowly professional Western context appears to be quite congenital to the current climate in Russia where a larger attempt is being made to rewrite the Soviet history (I do not attempt to judge whether it is accidental or not). Putin's Russia is experiencing massive rewriting of Soviet and Russian pre-evolutional history. Today references to Gulag are treated with the greatest suspicion by the new state functionaries. The recent discovery by Memorial of major mass graves near St. Petersburg was met with hostility and indifference. The new Russian anthem and an attempt to restore Felix Dzerzhinksy's monument in front of the KGB building on Lubjanka serve as examples of nostalgia for the Russian-Soviet great power and attempts to forget the events of 1991. Liberalization of the market became an official discourse while liberal values are now almost swearwords, reminding of the caricatured usage of liberal categories by the latest Western scholars of Soviet subjectivity. The balanced history of the 1930s is still not written, neither in Russia, nor in the West.

Any scholar of subjectivity' should be aware of the slippery nature of his subject, it reveals more than the author bargained for. The contradictions and incoherencies of the author's method, discourse and analysis are very telling. They reveal an unreflective nostalgia for the Soviet Union that never existed but could have if there was no such gap between revolutionary theory and revolutionary practice. Now the only drug for this unreflective nostalgia is to write professional texts that might conjure this phantom back to life.

I write this in the name of all those impure Soviet subjects who remained marginalized in the article and for those exemplary Soviet subjects whose recorded lives remain unfortunately misread. As the Russian predecessor of poststructuralism Victor Shklovsky said in 1926: "Existence defines consciousness, but conscience remains unsettled."

4. Contemporary Context of the debate in Russia and in the West. I hope my analysis won't discourage young scholars in Russia and abroad from engaging with contemporary theory and with the important legacy of the Soviet diaries, both of those who embraced the Soviet way of life and those who didn't. In fact, my recent participation in the workshop of young scholars from Russia and Eastern Europe revealed to me that some excellent work is being done using contemporary methods in the European University of St. Petersburg, as well as in Tallinn and in Ekaterinburg. The study of the Soviet subjectivity is an important topic, but these articles are merely tangential to this enterprise. I don't wish to imagine how Prof. Hellbeck teaches the history of the 1930s in the Soviet Union.

What worries me is that this type of analysis is quite congenital to the current climate in Russia where a larger attempt is made in the rewriting of the Soviet history. The president of Russia remarked in his well-publicised 1999 interview that he was not aware of the purges when he decided to join the KGB. Today references to Gulag are treated with the greatest suspicion by the new state functionaries. Recent discovery by Memorial of major mass graves near St. Petersburg was encountered with hostility and indifference. The debate around the return of Felix Dzerzhinksy to his home in Lubjanka reflects another epoque in rewriting of the most recent history, specifically the events of 1991. In fact, the balanced history of the 1930s still does not exist in the Russian context. This type of the limited study of the forging of the Soviet self (spiced with a few Foucauldian-sounding terms) advances one's professional career in the West and might sell in Putin's Russia. In my (old-fashioned) view, the responsibility of a historian is not to be caught in the minor academic controversies and to be able to have a broad balanced analytical perspective on Soviet history.

This, however, is not the goal of the scholars of Soviet subjectivity. Something else is going on here. Most of the diaries quoted in the text come from Communist and Comsomol functionaries yet the extrapolations are made for all of the "Soviet subjectivity." Can one imagine a discussion of American subjectivity based on the diaries of, say, J. Edgar Hoover's FBI employees or a discussion of the German subjectivity based on the diaries of fascist functionaries done with the same methodology and rhetoric? If so, would a Western historian fall into the same rhetorical blur of the vocabulary of his diary writers and his own? Can one imagine a similar discussion of "impure subjects" in the German context? I don't think so.

Soviet Russia functioned in the Western imagination as the place of the privileged projection, a utopia and hell, a laboratory of communism or a space for the future dreams. Occasionally this more or less cheerful orientalizing vision was projected back onto Russians themselves, some of whom accepted it as theirs. In this vision, that is partially embraced by Hellbeck's article, Russians were supposed to be "self sacrificial" and treat political injustices and horrors that they survived in the twentieth century as mere "obstacles" and occasions for sacrifice en route to self-transformation.

Any scholar of subjectivity should be aware of the slippery nature of his subject, it reveals more than the author bargained for. The contradictions and incoherencies of the author's method, discourse and analysis are very telling. They reveal an unreflected nostalgia of those pining for the Soviet Union that could have been if only those ready-mades of the "Soviet revolutionaries" had more relation to the actual historical practices. Now the only drug for this unreflective nostalgia is to write professional texts that might conjure this phantom back to life. I write this in the name of all those impure Soviet subjects who remained marginalized in the article and for those exemplary Soviet subjects whose recorded lives remain unfortunately misread.

Notes

1 I note that the author's only references to Foucault offered in his footnotes are to introductions to Foucault's major works. Perhaps this explains what I tried to demonstrate above.

2 I note that Igal Halfin refers to the work of Hannah Arendt but does her a complete injustice. He presents a highly selective extraction of a few notions, just the way Hellbeck reads Foucault, ignoring larger questions of the nature of the political as well as intellectual's responsibility that are so crucial to Arendt's work and goes way beyond her earlier reflection on totalitarianism.

15 "BANALITY OF EVIL," MIMICRY, AND THE SOVIET SUBJECT: VARLAM SHALAMOV AND HANNAH ARENDT

One of the most frequently quoted statements about art after the Holocaust is Theodor Adorno's comment, "I have no wish to soften the saying that to write lyric poetry after Auschwitz is barbaric."[1] What is less commonly known is that Adorno continues his reflection in a paradoxical manner. Literature, he insists, "must resist this verdict. For it is now virtually in art alone that suffering can still find its own voice without immediately being betrayed by it." Varlam Shalamov, a survivor and a brilliant and unflinching storyteller of the Kolyma camps, claims a similar paradoxical imperative for art after the gulag: "In the new prose—after Hiroshima, after Auschwitz and Kolyma, after wars and revolutions—everything didactic should be rejected. Art does not have a right to preach. Art neither ennobles nor improves people. Art is a way of life, not a way of understanding life [*poznaniia zhizni*]. In other words, it is a document . . . a prose lived through like a document."[2]

But what kind of literature can be "lived through like a document"? Does this emphasis on art have something to do with the grand role of literature in Russian culture, the role of the unofficial cultural legislator, or does the practice of imagination become a "weapon of the weak" that teaches lessons in noncollaboration and tactics of survival?

There is something radically inassimilable in Shalamov's prose: it confronts the experience of extremity but does not offer redemption through labor, suffering, religion, or national belonging. It proceeds through precise descriptions of life in the gulag, paying close attention to the historical facts, yet presents no history of the camps. The narrators of the *Kolymskie razzkazy* (Kolyma tales) often resort to apparent mimicry of Soviet discourse and the technologies of the gulag, but only to challenge any coherent conception of "Soviet subjectivity," whether enthusiastic or defiant. Instead of performing ideology, Shalamov's documentary prose exposes the breaking points of cultural myths that reveal possibilities for paradigm shifts.[3]

The experience of Auschwitz profoundly influenced western political philosophy of the twentieth century, but the experience of the Soviet gulag did not. The persistent difficulty in coming to terms with the gulag, besides complex historical and political circumstances, lies in large part in its dual image: it was represented as both paradise and hell, an ideal socialist construction site and a slave labor camp.[4] During the gulag's thirty-year existence, artists, writers, and filmmakers from the Soviet Union and abroad were recruited by Stalin's state to celebrate the utopian land "where men breathe most freely."[5] All the gates and watchtowers of the gulag zone, where an unknown number of millions of prisoners perished, were decorated with the refrain from a popular song: "Labor is a matter of honor, glory, courage, and heroism." Socialist realist art mass-reproduced a hypnotic simulacrum of the ideal Soviet territory through Soviet musicals, the twins of Broadway and Hollywood, which still enjoy frequent reruns on state television in contemporary Russia. This seductive, euphoric, and entertaining art helped to distract from and domesticate the powerful teleology of revolutionary violence that justified sacrifice for the sake of paradise on earth. Thus not only does the history of the gulag conjure up memories of terror, it also tampers with one of the most powerful utopian dreams of the twentieth century that extended far beyond the Soviet border. Legitimation of the gulag in Soviet life proved to be stranger than fiction; it estranged the commonsense perceptions and everyday experiences of ordinary citizens. They could only be "rehabilitated" through a double estrangement—from actual Soviet everyday life and from the official state fiction that supplanted it. Shalamov, like Primo Levi and Hannah Arendt, speaks repeatedly about "changed scales" for understanding the camp experience that apply to all human emotions and relationships—friendship, love, decency, freedom—and require new modes of understanding.

Shalamov's gulag stories confront the reader with their "inhumanity," and yet the author himself claimed that "there is nothing in *Kolyma Tales* that does not involve the overcoming of evil and the triumph of good—if we understand it in the plane of art."[6] To understand this paradoxical affirmation of humanism *via negativa,* one has to remember that Shalamov's subject matter is not universal human nature but "the relationship between the individual and the state."[7] I propose to read the Shalamov stories not only in the Soviet context but also as a broader twentieth-century philosophical and literary reflection on totalitarianism and the confrontation with terror. Of particular interest is the work of Hannah Arendt (not only *The Origins of Totalitarianism,* 1951, but also *The Life of the Mind,* 1978; *Lectures on Kant's Political Philosophy,* 1982; and *Essays in Understanding, 1930–1954,* 2005). Such a juxtaposition exposes a mutually illuminating relationship between art and politics: Arendt's political theory has many aesthetic and existential dimensions; in fact, at moments of extreme lucidity she speaks in parables and poems, using examples from Franz Kafka, Rainer Maria Rilke, and Osip Mandel'shtam. Shalamov's literary work uses the same practices of estrangement, laying bare some common places in the political and historical narrative.

My approach comes partially in response to the situation in the early twenty-first century, which demands a rethinking of the political and specifically of the Soviet political legacy that persists in the practices of everyday life and in the new political and everyday rhetoric in Russia. Of course, this discussion has to move beyond the paradigm of the Cold War, but also beyond the scholarly and political context of the 1990s, which was characterized by the new access to the multiple archives and an important revisionary critique of the totalizing approach to Soviet history and of the implied "liberal subjectivity" of western and Russian historians of the previous decades. In the contemporary Russian situation, the excess of liberal subjectivity is hardly a threat, nor does it determine current historical paradigms. Rather the situation is characterized by the closing of archives and the rewriting of history books, by the censorship and self-censorship that is imposed on most political debate. A contemporary approach to Soviet and post-Soviet everyday practices requires an inter-disciplinary rethinking at the crossroads of political theory, anthropology, history, and literature.

In her last project, *The Life of the Mind,* Hannah Arendt proposed a distinction between "professional thinking," which emphasizes logical coherence of the scientific disciplines, and "passionate thinking," which explores the limits of knowledge and engages in a double movement between different modes of knowledge and between theory and experience.[8] Passionate thinking is an oxymoron that questions the emphasis on pathos, empathy, or acceptance of suffering, on the one hand, and yet does not equate thinking with scientific rationality, on the other. I believe that the understanding of the camp experience requires this kind of passionate thinking that is at once interdisciplinary and rigorous. A close reading of Shalamov's stories does not merely reveal, in a good old formalist fashion, "how a literary work is made"; it also shows how ideology is made and what forms of communication corrode or elude it. My reading will pay attention to the different ways of working through the Soviet clichés and "deaestheticizing evil," to the tactics of intonation and the uses of blemish, human error, mimicry, and minor gift exchanges that mark unofficial solidarities and elective affinities.[9]

Ethics of Intonation and Human Error

In one of Shalamov's few letters to Iurii Lotman, he writes about his desire to work on poetic intonation, a "completely underdeveloped topic in our literary studies."[10] At first there seems to be a degree of incommensurability between Shalamov's Kolyma world and his concern for "purity of tone." Intonation acquired great importance in the time of the terror. The writer, scholar, and student of formalism, Lidiia Ginzburg, recorded in her diary that people's degree of collaboration with and affirmation of Stalinism could not be found in the explicit pronouncements: "In the years of Stalin's terror the 'untruth' resided, not in the general ideological worldview, but often in the intonation, in the public display of one's agreement with the regime."[11] The practice of speaking in ideological clichés (in public and in private, including in personal diaries) persisted through the Soviet regime and beyond as a necessary incantatory practice; as with medieval icon painting, its interpretation depended on minor iconographic/intonational variations.[12] These minor variations revealed the degree of collaboration with the regime, or, in Arendtian terms, of complicity with banal evil.

Right after Iosif Stalin's death, at the dawn of the Khrushchev era, Soviet "thick magazines" were engaged in a passionate debate—not about the experience of the gulag or justice for the victims—but about "sincerity" of tone. The very term *thaw*, introduced by the writer Il'ia Erenburg, was connected to this discussion. In cultural politics Nikita Khrushchev's thaw was ushered in by a gentle revolution that did not turn the structure of society or Soviet discourse upside down but did affect its syntax and intonation. The unofficial (but never anti-official) thaw culture of poets and bards depended on the new intonation, which functioned like a password to an alternative network of Soviet friendships. The revolution in intonation—a rebellion in a minor key—was the first step in the Soviet unwritten contract with the state. Tone, like gesture, represented an invisible notation, unreadable to multiple "well-wishers" and informants, that could nevertheless serve as invisible glue to seal the imperfect informal networks of the Soviet time.

In his *Kolyma Tales* Shalamov seeks an uncompromising purity of tone that is linked to what Arendt called "the dignity of the defeated"— something that remains between the lines but shapes them like the prisoners' tracks in the Kolyma snow.[13] Shalamov's intonation is not the "sincere tone" and light touch of the thaw but a particular authorial tool that threatens the practices of Soviet mimicry. Repetitions in Shalamov do not perform ideology but open up the dimension of difference and the space for independent judging and imagination.

Intonation complicates the readability of the stories but also gives insight into the complexity of the gulag system of communication that is reflected in many documents. Purity of tone does not mean monologism or authorial omniscience but an aesthetic and ethical dissent against what Shalamov calls the "banalization" (*oposhlenie*) of the camp experience. To make the reader understand what it is like to return from "the hell of Kolyma," Shalamov fights against what he perceives to be the clichés of the Russian humanist tradition that teach acceptance of suffering and authoritarian morality: "Russian humanist writers of the second half of the nineteenth century carry a great sin in their soul [*nesut na dushe velikii grekh*], for the human blood shed in their name [*pod ikh znamenem*] in the twentieth century. All terrorists were Tolstoyan and vegetarian, all fanatics were the students of Russian humanists."[14]

Harsh as this verdict might appear, it is important to understand that Shalamov's reading focuses less on Lev Tolstoi's literary works than on his cultural mythology text, shaped largely by his prophetic late writing, the Soviet canon of socialist realism, and Aleksandr Solzhenitsyn's appropriation of Tolstoi.[15] In Shalamov's view, any kind of cliché and the discourse on the historic necessity of violence betray the "corpses of Kolyma." This issue comes up directly in the striking dialogue between Shalamov and Solzhenitsyn recorded in Shalamov's notebooks—a dialogue worthy of Fedor Dostoevsky's pen. In their conversations the two writers touch upon religion and spirituality, camp labor, faith, integrity,

Russia and the west, Thomas Jefferson, Voltaire, and the American book market, but it is the issue of the "banalization" of the camp experience that becomes crucial in Shalamov's final break with Solzhenitsyn. In the same entry in his notebooks Shalamov records that Solzhenitsyn knew that he (Shalamov) considered him to be a "polisher of reality." At the end, the writer of the *Kolyma Tales* cannot forgive the epic author of the *Gulag Archipelago* and other works of historical prose for "the impurity of tone that is not so much an aesthetic as an ethical issue."[16]

Shalamov's own prose focuses on the cracks in the process of polishing reality. Intonation for Shalamov is a trace of oral speech in the poetic form of the story that affects the stories' narrative voice and syntax, linking his unique artistic form to the collective experience. Shalamov wanted to avoid what he considered a conventional psychologism, dismissively dubbed "the surface peel [*shelukha*] of halftones in the representation of psychology."[17] This kind of psychologism domesticates and erases the modern specificity of the camp experience. Intonation in Shalamov's texts creates a special balance between the insider's voice and the estranging viewpoint. The narrator speaks as Pluto, the permanent resident of the underworld, not as Orpheus, an overly excited one-time visitor. Shalamov's stories are always in the present; the reader is put in the position of a fellow convict, a newcomer but not entirely an outsider. Creating this kind of visceral prose, that is not a description of experience but an experience in its own right, was for Shalamov an exhausting physical process akin to exorcism. He "screamed out every word of the story, screamed, threatened, cried, drying up tears only when the story was over."[18] Usually the stories begin and end in medias res, as if familiarizing the inhuman world of Kolyma with its radically changed scales of existence. However, "as if" here is crucial and is at the core of Shalamov's double estrangement. His stories are modern parables written in a documentary style reminiscent of the "literature of fact" of the 1920s and the poetics of OPOYAZ through which Shalamov learned his literary skills.[19]

But what is "literary" about it? Aesthetic and ethical moments coincide in Shalamov. Like the OPOYAZ members in the 1920s, he attacks conventional literary forms in order to explore the foundation of estrangement and the radical practice of judgment and imagination. His approach to his storytelling consists of aesthetic and ethical sculpting (*ustranenii vsego lishnego*) and involves the quest for "purity of tones" (*chistota tonov*); at the same time, he preserves traces of the singularity of experience and witnessing, including the author's misprints, repetitions, and individual blemishes, everything deemed irrelevant in the Hegelian-Marxist-Leninist understanding of the laws of history. To the great irritation of his helpful editors, Shalamov insisted on leaving misprints and repetitions in his texts.[20] For him they form another nonlinear "hypertextual" network that links the stories among themselves. Shalamov shared this peculiar poetics of misprint with other modernist writers who also addressed issues of totalitarianism—in particular, Vladimir Nabokov and Milan Kundera. Nabokov uses mistakes, misrecognition, and, directly, misprints, as in *Pale Fire* ("Life everlasting based on a misprint?") to create an ironic epiphany, a revelation with difference that incorporates human error and the crooked timber of humanity into the text. For Kundera, the Czech communist practice of removing the traces of *personae non gratae* from all photographs was never complete, leaving blemishes that open up spaces for another history, like the hat of the deposed leader kindly offered to another party member. I call it the "poetics of blemish," a crucial weapon of the weak and of the watched.[21] In Shalamov, the author's misprints similarly compose a theme with variations, a variation on the singularities and human errors that could represent a deviation from the collective teleology. Their preservation is the author's right, which he sometimes equates with a human right par excellence. In my view, these misprints and missteps should not be interpreted as unconscious "Freudian slips" that empower us readers to catch the author unawares. Rather, they can make us complicit in the alternative tactic of camp communication, if we are willing to be tactful readers.

Misprints, according to Shalamov, do not betray the author but compose his signature. In his *Kolyma Tales*, the "human errors" become triggers of secret narratives that tell stories of trickery and minimal liberation from the clichés of the banality of evil that permeate language and the everyday practices of Stalin's times.

Hannah Arendt: The Banality of Evil and the Art of Judgment

Arendt's reflection on the banality of evil will help to elucidate Shalamov's obsession with clichés and his insights into survival in the gulag, parallel but not equivalent to Levi's reflection on survival in Auschwitz. After the fall of the Soviet Union, Arendt's concept of totalitarianism was called into question and was discarded a number of times as a relic of the Cold War. More often than not, Arendt's concept of totalitarianism was understood literally as total state control and was turned into a strawman of total domination over all dimensions of life. The broader existential, philosophical, and aesthetic aspects of Arendt's conception of freedom and of totalitarian experience, of responsibility and judgment, received much less critical attention. For my own conceptual framework, three aspects of Arendtian thought are of primary importance.

The first is the radical strangeness of totalitarian domination that cannot be fully explained through a conventional social, psychological, or institutional rationalization. In line with Shalamov's notion of radically changed scales of experience, Arendt uses an aesthetic concept of estrangement in order to think about the power of the "ideology of terror" and its reliance on conspiracy theory.[22]

The second concerns the conception of "legality," conventional man-made laws versus the law of history and nature. Arendt argues that totalitarian ideology "pretends to have found a way to establish the rule of justice on earth—something which the legality of positive law admittedly could never attain."[23] This goal legitimizes any amount of (revolutionary) violence, since the end justifies the means. Arendt questions the basis of the Hegelian-Marxist framework for understanding the laws of history and the relationship between the state and the public sphere. Unlike Carl Schmitt, Michel Foucault, Giorgio Agamben, and other thinkers engaged in examining forms of domination and the critique of the Enlightenment project, Arendt underscores the totalitarian difference and does not blur the distinction between the Enlightenment project and the Stalinist project. Nor does she erase the difference between the conventional or democratic understanding of law and the prophetic conception of the true law of history. Stalinism, from the Arendtian perspective, can never be described merely as a culturally specific project of Soviet modernization, since such a description would make it historically inevitable and therefore excusable. Moreover, continuing in the tradition of the Enlightenment, she questions the inevitability of the connection between violence and law and develops a conception of law and politics based on the public memory of the common world that totalitarian ideology tries to destroy.

The third aspect involves her investigation of the "banality of evil" that sustains the totalitarian glue and the role of imagination that can undermine it. Imagination for Arendt is a form of *understanding* that could lead to individual acts of judging and paradigm shifts even in conditions of extremity. Here Arendt revises Kantian conceptions of "common sense" and imagination in order to develop her original theory of judgment. She focuses on a variety of aesthetic practices (from theatrical performance on the public stage to the art of thinking and the life of the mind) that work in counterpoint to the state's aesthetic totalwork. Such an understanding of practice presents an alternative model for thinking about everyday mythologies without domesticating and naturalizing them and allows for a variety of reactions, not limited to an enthusiastic embrace or heroic dissent. The task of the interpreter of everyday practices in conditions of extremity is to understand the minimal "zone" of deviation or noncompliance, the minor paradigm shifts that work in counterpoint to the official documentation of events.

In spite of Arendt's elaborate analysis of the total control of the state, she looks unflinchingly into the issue of individuals' capacity to judge for themselves and finds an unusual connection between judgment, imagination, and thinking. In her controversial account of the trial of Adolph Eichmann, the architect of the Final Solution responsible for the ideological basis of mass extermination, Arendt proposes to judge Eichmann as an individual, not as a devil, nor as a mere cog in the Nazi bureaucratic machine. In other words, she does not subsume Eichmann's case into her own theory of state terror. Eichmann appears as the ultimate organization man who speaks in clichés from the beginning to the very end. While in an ordinary context, Eichmann's behavior might be considered mere institutional conformism and traditional patriotism, in the context of the Nazi extermination machine this kind of clichéistic conscience leads to "thought and world defying banality of evil."[24] What does this mean? It does not suggest that evil is banal or that banality or everydayness is evil. Rather, Arendt draws our attention to the fact that an individual who authorized the worst crimes against humanity was an ordinary civil servant, neither a glamorous Shakespearean villain, nor the metaphysical embodiment of a Satan on earth. Arendt emphatically asserts that evil should not be mythologized; it should not be turned into a version of the negative sublime. In fact, the Israeli psychiatrist described Eichmann as absolutely normal. It is ironic that while in prison Eichmann was offered Nabokov's *Lolita* to read, a book which he rejected as "unwholesome" (this is perhaps the best defense that Humbert Humbert could have hoped for). Remarkably, in the afterword to *Lolita,*

Nabokov claims that true obscenity lies in the "copulation of clichés" and lack of curiosity and imagination, not in erotic subject matter.[25]

Arendt claims that the automatization of Eichmann's mind, his clichéistic consciousness and "failure of imagination" (understood broadly as moral imagination) led to the "colossal error in judgment" for which he bears individual responsibility.[26] Arendt does not subscribe to the concept of collective guilt that might blame everybody and hence nobody; for her, guilt is individual and particular.

While Eichmann's case can be explained sociologically, politically, and historically, it cannot be excused. To analyze the novelty of his existential position, Arendt uses aesthetic categories: the failure of imagination and banality. Arendt's conception of banality is reminiscent of Nabokov's critique of *poshlost'* and kitsch and the writings on kitsch and cultural commodification by Hermann Broch, Adorno, and Clement Greenberg.[27] In her last, unfinished project, *The Life of the Mind,* Arendt connects the question of ethics and responsibility directly to the issue of thoughtlessness on an unprecedented scale, reflecting in particular on "thoughtless" collaboration with the regime.[28]

An individual's capacity to engage in judging depends on the ability to mediate between a system of beliefs and lived experience, between consciousness and conscience. Judging requires a double movement—defamiliarizing experience through the practice of thought and defamiliarizing habits of thought in response to the changing experience. The space of reflective judgment is like a Möbius strip that moves seamlessly from the inside to the outside, from the known to the unknown.

The possibility of judgment is not determined by strict adherence to a moral code but by moral imagination. Even the most antisentimental witness of the camps, Primo Levi, a scientist and an agnostic, wrote about the role of curiosity and culture in Auschwitz.[29] First, like Shalamov, he disavowed any romantic or redemptive quality in aesthetic experience, but then he proceeded to explore a link between a capacity to survive and a cultivation of memory, curiosity, and imagination.

Of course, "failure of imagination" is hardly the sole explanation for the banality of evil. For Arendt the key lies in the destruction of the public realm and the public world and the resulting corruption of communication and intimacy with terror that conditions citizens' dependence on the regime and the proliferation of vicious circles of victimization. This is the irreducible political dimension of the totalitarian regime that cannot be domesticated. Yet the moral imagination might provide a form of necessary "perspectivism," an opening of other horizons.[30] Imagination is heteronymous and moves from one country to another without visa restrictions. It entertains the hypothetical; moves through leaps, lapses, and ellipses; engages in double vision. Imagination can be defined as what is inhuman in humans in the sense that it involves a capacity for self-distancing, for moving beyond individual psychology into the experience of the common world. Most important, imagination depends on cultural commonplaces but is not bound by the borders of a single system of coordinates and points beyond it.

Arendt did not have a chance to write about Shalamov, for his work appeared in translation only in the last years of her life. But his stories always engage the issues of the boundary—of the physical and mental "zone," and of the cultural common places that contribute to the banality of evil and the banality of good. Each story offers us an exercise in double vision, a creative document that stands in counterpoint to official historical documentation.

Rationing Clichés, Documenting Terror

The story "Dry Rations" opens almost like a fairy tale, with four convicts embarking on a mythical journey to explore a limbo region of the gulag zone and build a road through the snow. The story begins with them crossing beneath the camp gates with their familiar inscription: "Labor is a matter of honor, glory, courage, and heroism." Overwhelmed with joy at their momentous luck, they do not dare break the silence, as if afraid to discover that their short escape was somebody's error, a joke, or a misprint in some bureaucratic circular.

The official clichés of camp life frame the story like the barbed wire of the zone. In fact, since the Russian title is "Sukhim paikom," the translation should be "By dry rations." This elliptical adverbial construction indicates a mode of existence. The syntax of the title pushes us directly into the "rations" of camp language. "Dry rations" function as an "advance of short-lived liberation" that determines the time and space of the prisoner's journey outside the zone.[31] The rationing of food, labor, freedom, pain, punishment, and cruelty is central to camp life. Rationing was a form of rationalizing terror. The story proceeds by disrupting various clichés as well as official and unofficial rationalizations of camp existence.

The four unlikely fellow travelers represent a cross section of camp society. Yet they are not representative men in any shape or form, but singular individuals with uniquely (but not exceptionally) unlucky fates. Ivan Ivanovich, slightly older than his companions and described as "the most decent" prisoner, used to be "an excellent worker," almost a hero of camp labor. The reasons for his arrest are of the everyday order (*by-tovye*) and are not explained in detail. The youngest of the prisoners, Fedia Shapov, is a teenager from Altai with a not very strong "half-grown body." His crime was slaughtering a sheep on his own farm in order to feed his mother and himself.[32] Accused of sabotaging collectivization, he was sentenced to ten years in the camps. The third prisoner is a Moscow student named Savel'ev. Once a loyal member of the Young Communist League, he was accused of conspiring to create a counterrevolutionary cell that consisted of two members—himself and his fiancée. His romantic letter to his bride was used as evidence of anti-Soviet propaganda and agitation, for which he was given ten years of hard labor in Kolyma. The fourth convict is our narrator, a political prisoner from Moscow and a veteran observer of camp tactics, the prisoner without a biography.

Just as the convicts leave the gate of the zone with the uplifting slogan, they begin to ration their own efforts and debate the value and meaning of work in the camp. The narrator wonders whether "honest" work can still exist in the gulag context, and Savel'ev advances his own theory of surplus labor. First he speaks about the surplus of language that covers up the conditions of slave labor: "The only ones who call for honest work are the bastards who beat and maim us, eat our food and force us living skeletons to work to our very death. It is profitable to them but they believe in honest work even less than we do."[33]

The concept of "loafing" (*filonit'*) is crucial in Shalamov's camp world. His storytellers are not heroes of labor but "artists of the spade" and masters of dissimulation. A slang word for this "light labor" and the "artistry of the spade" is "Kant," a creative and survivalist approach to camp labor that manifests itself in seemingly harmless daily practices. The irony that the philosopher's name coincides with a reprieve from camp duties and with artistry instead of effort is not lost on Shalamov.[34] Love for "Kant" exemplifies the prisoner's parodistically anti-Marxist theory of surplus value; it is the surplus value of "loafing," of (relative) idleness and evasion that constitutes the prisoner's personal "capital" of disobedience.

Savel'ev teaches little Fedia the ways of camp survival through the tactics of language and labor. He tells him a story about one dissenting loafer who refused to work.

"They made a report. Said that he was 'dressed appropriately for the season.'"

"What does that mean: 'dressed appropriately for the season?' asks Fedia.

Savel'ev explains that this phrase was used when a prisoner couldn't fulfill the labor norm or died, but instead of listing all the items of clothing he was missing, boots and mittens and so on, the bureaucrats simply affirmed in their report that the prisoner was "dressed for the season," as a supposedly logical justification of inhuman labor.

"Well, they can't list every piece of summer or winter clothing you have on. If it's winter, they can't write that you were sent to work without a coat or mittens. How often did you stay in the camp because there were no mittens?"

"Never," said Fedia timidly. "The boss made us stamp down the snow on the road. Or else they would have had to write that we stayed behind because we didn't have anything to wear."

"There you have it."[35]

Behind a seemingly innocuous bureaucratic cliché, "dressed appropriately for the season" was a shortcut to cover up the naked truth that hardly anyone was ever dressed appropriately.

The prisoners bond together through an unofficial code of minimal camp decency that is never entirely deciphered. Neither prisoner transgresses certain ethical taboos of directly collaborating with the authorities and informing on the other prisoners or becoming a foreman (*brigadir*) and commanding the other prisoners. Somehow, in spite of the fact that they live at a time when everything is permitted and everything is possible, all four exercise inner restraint. They are most happy in the brief moments of loafing and storytelling—"storymaking-daydreaming" (*vran'e-mechtanie*), half-lies, half-dreams. Fedia particularly enjoys tales of the urban miracles, such as the Moscow metro. They let their imagination "go visiting" to escape the frost of Kolyma.

Yet there is a time bomb at the very heart of the story. The gasp of excessive freedom (relatively speaking, of course) for a convict in the zone is like a surfeit of bread for one who is starving: it can kill. As they are finishing their dry rations, the foreman from the camp arrives and immediately sees through their loafing and rationing tactics and orders them back to the camp. They have only one night left to daydream outside the camp. Ivan Ivanovich is the only one who continues working till twilight with the same tragic diligence.

The next morning Savel'ev finds Ivan Ivanovich hanged from a tree "without even a rope." The best worker among the four companions, the "decent man" Ivan Ivanovich chooses his own way out. The foreman panics and tries to distract the convicts from the sight of the corpse. Savel'ev, for whom, unlike the veterans of the gulag, the spectacle of death has not yet turned into daily routine, picks up an axe and brings it down on his own four fingers—only to be promptly arrested for self-mutilation, or rather, for the mutilation of a worker—since the body of an able gulag prisoner was considered state property.[36] Fedia and the narrator take Ivan Ivanovich's clean clothes and return to the zone, to the same berths in the same barracks.

Late at night the protagonist wakes up and finds Fedia in a stupor, composing a letter to his mother. The narrator reads it, eavesdropping "across Fedia's shoulder": "Mama,—Fedia was writing—mama, I live well. Mama, I am dressed appropriately for the season."[37]

This ending, with the central cliché of camp dissimulation—"dressed appropriately for the season," stuns us into silence. Like the convicts at the beginning of the story, we the readers are afraid to break into speech and rush to interpretation. Something in the narrator's intonation forces us to pause and rethink our assumptions.

Is Fedia knowingly telling half-truths to assuage his mother's fears? Or is he so shocked that he can only rehearse the official clichés in his most personal letter? Is this exploration of the limbo zone an initiation into the banality of evil or a lesson in dissent? Is Fedia's letter then an act of explicit conformity or of covert disobedience?[38]

This is an instance of Shalamov's signature intonation. What makes all the difference is that the word *mama* is repeated three times.[39] The "document" is interrupted. The intonation bursts open the letter's official clichés. In one line we have two types of repetition: repetition as mimicry of the camp clichés and repetition as lament. The invisible author eavesdropping over Fedia's shoulder makes minor notations that turn the bureaucratese of the letter into a lament: mama, mama, mama, like Anton Chekhov's broken string in the background. There is a desperation in the address here that expresses the sheer phatic function of language; this is not even a desire to communicate but simply a desire to test already fragile communication. Such nuance makes the story a great work of fiction and "hurts" moral imagination.

The catharsis of the story involves neither the death of Ivan nor Savel'ev's self-mutilation. It is the stunning ambivalence of Fedia's epistolary document that breaks the frame of the story and unhinges our frame of reference. Shalamov is not interested in ecstatic Dostoevskian scenes of suffering or Eisensteinian eccentric pathos. His stories deny the reader the instant gratification of empathy and communal purification, which might explain why some readers interpreted Shalamov as a cruel, or unemotional writer despite his frequent protestations to the contrary. More than instantaneous catharsis, he is engaged in the torturous peripeteias of camp luck.

The tragic predicament plays an important role for Shalamov, but his understanding of tragedy is modernist. It has a lot in common with the notion of tragic catharsis that was developed by the psychologist Lev Vygotskii, who was also close to the critics from OPOYAZ and was interested in the psychology of art. According to Vygotskii, "a work of art always contains an intimate conflict between its content and its form, and the artist achieves his effect by means of the form, which is capable of destroying the content."[40] In this understanding of the psychology of art, catharsis resides in the clash of ambivalence. Form "murders" the content, or rather transports it elsewhere into the domain of imagination, immortalizing the experience and disrupting the chain of victimization.

How does Shalamov give us a lesson in camp literacy and in understanding the documents of the gulag? Let us for a moment imagine the hypothetical historian of the future in some distant provincial archive looking at this letter to Fedia's mother. After going through many official documents, this historian rejoices at finding a personal one. The expression "dressed according to the season" might jar the historian a little, but then verifying the words in the dictionary, the researcher concludes that the peasant prisoner might have been *gramotnyi*, that is, well-educated in the new Soviet school built in his village in the Altai mountains. Fedia's "Soviet subjectivity" as expressed in his own words tells our imaginary historian that some (not all) "lived well" in the camp, especially those who knew how to work hard. Were Fedia's letter to reach its addressee, it would most likely be similarly misread.

Shalamov's story concerns the clash of two texts: Fedia's "document" of camp life and the story of how such a document came to be made. The aesthetic ambiguity turns into the ethics of judgment and understanding. In fact, the whole story is about the deviousness of language that has lost its meaning.

The story works through constant disruptions and subversions: of the prisoners' fears and expectations, of the reader's conventional framework, of the clichés of conventional novelistic redemption, and of Soviet reeducation.[41] The minimal "freedom" of the author and the reader is that they now share the other way of reading "across the shoulder" (*cherez plecho*) of the stupefied camp novice who learned about the temptation of nonconformity the hard way. Judging, in this literary form, is the ability to discriminate in reading, to acquire tact, to preserve multiple perspectives and multiple human fates, and to respect the choices. Judging is not about being judgmental but about giving imaginary space to the defeated and to their impossible human choices, leaving space and acknowledging the dreams of exit in a no-exit situation and according to the tactics of the zone. The secret of gulag communication is in the intonation, in the small successes of the condemned, in their varied stories' singular irreducibility to any masterplot. The story is also about the tactics of minimal singularity. Each prisoner reacts to the gasp of freedom by choosing a different tactic: suicide, self-mutilation, the resilient survival of gulag veteran and writer-witness, and Fedia's ambivalent lesson of pushing the boundaries of the zone. Each reaction is an unpredictable form of judging for oneself, a personal choice that does not agree with the official objectification and subjugation of the "human material." Thus "Dry Rations" concerns not a *liberal* subjectivity that some historians love to hate but a *liminal* subjectivity that bends the barbed wire ever so slightly and yet significantly. Shalamov works through the Russian and Soviet clichés as one works through trauma, grieving over every word, every turn of phrase.

Mimicry, Misprint, and Technologies of the Gulag

If the first part of Shalamov's *Kolyma Tales* concerns the early stages of the prisoner's gulag sentence and the difficult initiation into camp life and survival, the second part of the book deals with the difficulties of liberation and self-liberation after years in the zone. In "Lida," the hero of the story is a veteran survivor of the Kolyma camps who is approaching the end of his sentence but cannot see the end of the conspiratorial frames of the gulag system of well-wishers and informants, the "human chain" of enthusiastic perpetrators of the banality of evil. He is afraid that due to his political status, the end of his sentence will bring him not liberation but rather another imprisonment, another round in the vicious circles of gulag labor. Like Shalamov himself, who was rearrested many times, Krist is "branded" by the letter "T." The abbreviation "KRTD" appears in his file, a term applied to the most dangerous political prisoners. "T" stands for Trotskyism and, therefore, for the "death tribunal," giving his boss and anyone else who might discover this information in his secret file "poetic license" for endless persecution or even a license to kill him. Krist envisions the many eager little Eichmanns forming the human chain of informants that was the foundation of the "low tech" gulag system that relied, not on technology the same way the Nazis did, but on "relentless manpower."[42]

The perpetual question of "what is to be done" occupies Krist. His name notwithstanding, he is hardly a suffering hero or a charismatic redeemer. Krist, a survivor of "bookish Russia," does not believe in a single personal savior but thinks that in the world "there are many truths" and one must discover—co-create—one's own.[43] In the world of the camp where all scales have shifted to a radical degree, he has to rediscover what liberation means. For him survival is more than just a personal matter, it is a personal vendetta against the regime.

After months of torturous meditation, Krist comes up with a poetic license of his own. During one particularly intense night of thinking he experiences an "illumination" that comes to him "just like the best lines of a poem." The name of the solution is "Lida." Krist recalls an incident that happened several years before when he worked as a doctor's assistant (fel'dsher) in the camp hospital. One night the doctor on duty "from the political prisoners" had asked him for a small favor. It concerned a young secretary from the nonpolitical convicts whose husband had died in the camps and whose boss, the lieutenant, was threatening her after she refused to "live with him" (that is, have sex with him). The young woman hoped to hide in the hospital until the lieutenant was moved to another station. Krist asked to see her: "A not very tall, blond young woman appeared in front of Krist and bravely looked him in the eyes. Many people passed by Krist, many thousands of eyes were understood and figured out. It was very rare that Krist made mistakes. 'OK,' said Krist, 'put her in the hospital.'"[44]

It is important that neither the doctor nor Krist knew the woman beforehand. They understand each other with half-words and gestures, following some kind of unwritten code of honor among the noncollaborators. This was not a major act of disobedience, but a minor dissent, mimicry of the bureaucratic hierarchies that could cost them much or nothing, for the sake of a stranger. Lida managed to escape her pursuer. Krist and Lida never spoke about the incident again, although they occasionally exchanged knowing gazes. Now Lida is once again working as a secretary, typing passport forms and prisoners' files. Krist decides to ask her for a different kind of professional favor.

After his night of poetic revelation, Krist approaches Lida and tells her casually that she will soon type his documents of liberation.

"Congratulations," said Lida, and brushed off the invisible dust from Krist's fel'dsher's robe.

"You will type old convictions, there is such a line there, right?"

"Yes, there is."

"In the word 'KRTD,' drop the letter 'T.'"

"Understood," said Lida.

"If the boss notices when he signs it, just smile, say you made a mistake. Spoiled the form."

"I know what to say myself."[45]

Two weeks later, Krist is called to the office to receive his new passport. The letter "T" has disappeared from the nefarious abbreviation "KRTD." Was it a misprint, a human error? Krist's friends try to decipher his luck, but none suspects that Krist co-created his liberation with his own hands.[46]

Once again, catharsis occurs in the ellipsis, in what remains unsaid. Like a Greek tragedy, the story involves the confrontation of different understandings of law, with the improbable law of Krist's poetic justice gaining a temporary victory.

Minimal communication is the reaction against the banalization of speech in the camp and the impurity of tone : "The camp did not like sentimentality, did not like long and unnecessary preambles and various 'approaches.'"[47] As "veterans of Kolyma," Krist and Lida understood each other with half-words.

Lida's final action is not merely the return of a favor. It does not function within the economy of *blat* (the informal Soviet network of barter that existed among the privileged and the not-so-privileged in the circumstances of scarcity). Instead it belongs to the improbable circulation of minor gifts and acts of kindness among strangers that survived against all odds in the space of the zone.

Only the description of the night of Krist's feat of imagination compensates for the absence of explicit moral or ethical discussion. The impersonality of the gulag machine and the chain of informants who voluntarily perpetuate the banality of evil are not counteracted by a Tolstoyan or Solzhenitsyn-style morality tale that might turn into the banality of good but by minimal human solidarity and the exercise of extreme imagination. The epiphany of solution is described in aesthetic terms as a radical act of poetic composition, not as a religious conversion.[48] The inhuman creative effort that Krist expends to come up with a solution has to counterbalance the inhumanity of the system.

In each of Krist's moments of judging, ethics and aesthetics become closely intertwined even when it is a matter of life and death. Krist's first brief encounter with Lida is an "ethical encounter," as Emmanuel Lévinas understood it: it involves a face-to-face meeting that calls for an "anarchic responsibility" toward another particular human being.[49] But the story is not only about empathy; it is also about judging and co-creating a philosophy of composition in the gulag. This is not about the individual's romantic battle against the totalitarian system but about matching the "living chain" of denouncers with the chain of decent human beings who exchange gratuitous gifts. What breaks the vicious circle is an ingenious mimicry of the "low-tech" gulag system. In totalitarian circumstances, collaboration, survival, and belonging are all different forms of behavioral mimicry, and the nuanced distinctions are of crucial importance. In this case, however, mimicry is neither obedience nor the imitation of power; neither tautology nor parody. The best understanding of this kind of mimicry comes from the writer and lepidopterist Vladimir Nabokov. Mimicry in the Nabokovian definition is a "cryptic disguise" and a "non-utilitarian delight" that defies the Darwinian evolution of the fittest and the Hegelian laws of history: "The mysteries of mimicry had a special attraction for me. Its phenomena showed an artistic perfection usually associated with man-wrought things. . . . When a butterfly has to look like a leaf, not only are all the details of a leaf beautifully rendered but markings mimicking grub-bored holes are generously thrown in. 'Natural selection' . . . could not explain the miraculous coincidence of imitative aspect . . . nor could one appeal to the theory of 'the struggle for life' when a protective device was carried to a point of mimetic subtlety, exuberance, and luxury far in excess of a predator's power of appreciation. I discovered in nature the non-utilitarian delights that I sought in art."[50] Mimicry that "exceeds the predator's power of appreciation" persists as a form of trickery and as a homeopathic antidote to the gulag bureaucracy. Mimicry, in the words of Homi Bhabha, is at once "resemblance and menace": in Shalamov's story, it lays bare a clichéd conscience, a survivalist collaboration with the regime and its different forms of daily camouflage, revealing practices of creative "cheating" and judgment.[51] Such mimicry works as an example of Arendtian imagination that enlarges mentality and estranges the ethos of making everything permitted and possible, of domesticating terror through new and old master narratives.

In Shalamov's texts, the "human error and the authorial signature of the prisoner's illicit creativity coincide. Blemish and poetic license work like the prisoner's ephemeral individual traces in the virginal snow of Kolyma. The most striking expressive gesture of this minimal story is Lida's brushing off the invisible dust from Krist's medical uniform at the moment when he asks her to make a typo. This gesture is irreducible to any single moral symbol: it is at once a sign of gratitude, of wistful mutual understanding, of care, of the shamanism and mischief (*shamanism i shalost'*) that Shalamov believed to have been ciphered in his old Russian family name. In fact, the story performs a shamanic act of transforming the deficient official passport into an artistic document: "Poetic intonation is a literary passport, that personal 'brand' [*kleimo*], that provides the poet's place in history. We do not have a patent bureau and intellectual property rights for poetic intonation."[52] A writer's intonation functions like a fingerprint of his unofficial identity. Here Shalamov echoes Nabokov, another author obsessed with visas and watermarks. "Art is the writer's only passport," wrote Nabokov, the author of many tales of passportless spies.[53]

Poetic reflection for Shalamov is not a domain of autonomous literature but a practice of judging, of devising other horizons and reimagining a different system of coordinates for human existence. "In the visceral depth of any physical phenomenon we can find a poem and then switch this perception into real life."[54] Moreover, Shalamov's authorial ambiguity goes beyond the Aesopian language practiced by the intelligentsia of the thaw and afterwards; his unassimilable stories break open the nature of Soviet fabulization. His is the radical elaboration of Viktor Shklovsky's conception of art as a technique, in this case a technique of surprising survival through intense artistic and existential estrangement. Shalamov is one of Russia's great modern writers, but the modern track he follows is different from official Soviet modernization or the route that goes from the grave of the avant-garde to the socialist realist necropolis. His is not the modernism of self-expression, invention of personal language, and stoic inner freedom. Rather it is a public modernism that engages the political in a non-party-line manner, in the style of Primo Levi, W. H Auden, Albert Camus, and others.

Shalamov shares Arendt's view that clichés that produce the banality of evil as well as the banality of good not only package the experience but collaborate in the perpetuation of totalitarian horror. While opposing the clichés of both the authoritarian humanism of the nineteenth century and the no less authoritarian anti-humanism of the twentieth century's teleologies of universal happiness, Shalamov proposes a new form of imaginative documentary prose that does not describe but co-creates the experience. Shalamov and Arendt share one particular literary interest: the American writer William Faulkner. His statement, "The past is not dead, it is not even past," especially beloved by Arendt, reflects Shalamov's relationship to memory, and Faulkner is one of Shalamov's favorite writers who practice fractured and explosive prose. For Shalamov, as for Faulkner, past and present have equal urgency; the past explodes the present while the present actualizes the past. Memories for Shalamov are as real as bodily aches and pains. "Memory gnaws at you like a frostbitten hand at the first cold wind." Memory is a phantom limb, numb and undead.[55] This kind of memory, which is part of the "dignity of the defeated," works against Hegelian teleology of the law of history and the justification of historical violence.[56]

Arendt insists that in the aftermath of the totalitarian experience we lost the yardstick with which to measure the common world, and we lost touch with our own living tradition. The answer, however, is not the invention of a national tradition, or the resacralization of the disenchanted modern world and a prescriptive enforcement of moral rules. We cannot merely replace the yardstick or restore the broken vertebrae of common communication, covering up the scars. Rather we have to use our imagination to confront what might seem unimaginable. We have to "think without a banister" in order to understand the world that can no longer be measured with familiar yardsticks. Imagination might not be a panacea for the destruction of the public realm, but it can help keep the memory of another form of public solidarity alive. The larger-than-life collective inhumanity of twentieth-century mass movements requires a counterpoint: a creative and singular "inhumanity" of human imagination that can move outside the box of the temporal and spatial limitations of the present moment.[57] Judgment and imagination negotiate the space "between" and "beyond" collective and individual, precedented and unprecedented. Judging keeps imagination in check, imagination enlarges the possibilities of judgment, and so it goes back and forth. "Between" is never completely bounded by familiar yardsticks, but neither is "beyond" synonymous with boundlessness. Imagination opens unforeseen perspectives; but the moment they are transgressed or transcended they lose their horizon of wonder.

Rereading Shalamov in 2008 acquires a different urgency. It is no longer solely about the historical materials and the accuracy of the descriptions, but about the ways of understanding the Soviet legacy and the post-Soviet experience. In the present moment there is no widespread "gulag denial"; in fact, the brief opening of the archives and the activity of many Russian and international historians and researchers from Memorial made a lot of information publicly available. Yet in the new political climate, the increasing amount of information is in inverse proportion to the public's interest in understanding the past. There is an uncanny persistence of the authoritarian Eros in post-Soviet culture and the gulag legacy, which in this case means the legacy of unconfronted memories, of critical history turning into a protected domain of national heritage. The Soviet past is a realm of state-sponsored nostalgia, carefully orchestrated by contemporary "political technologists" who activate age-old training in self-censorship. When history becomes heritage, there is little space for critical questioning. Shalamov's work reveals how the gulag effect is created and how easy it is to domesticate terror and erase minor courageous acts as mere misprints in the official plot of history. In "The Gap between Past and Future," Arendt writes that the experience of freedom does not fit the historical, sociological, or philosophical narrative that protects its own internal logic at the expense of such disruptive experiences. Excluded from the conventional historiography, such experiences of freedom remain our other, forgotten heritage.[58]

Notes

1 Theodor Adorno, "Commitment," in Ernst Bloch et al., *Aesthetics and Politics* (London, 1980), 188–89.

2   Varlam Shalamov, "O novoi proze," *Sobranie sochinenii v shesti tomakh* (Moscow, 2004–2005), 5:157. All translations from Shalamov's essays are mine.

3   Shalamov's biography offers a tragic and ironic coda to the fate of the Russian and Soviet intelligentsia. Shalamov wrote that his name is related to two words—*shalost'* (whim, frivolity, play) and *shaman;* whether etymologically correct or not, this was his own poetic reinvention of his origins. The son of an Orthodox priest from Vologda in the Russian north, Shalamov rebelled against his father and, disappointed from an early age in all forms of institutional religion, chose literature instead. In February 1929 he was arrested at the underground printing press that printed the full text of Vladimir Lenin's testament criticizing Iosif Stalin. Shalamov received a five-year term for "KRTD," the abbreviation for "counter-revolutionary Trotskyist activity" covered under article 58. Later Shalamov would say that the "T" in this abbreviation stood for Lev Trotskii and tribunal as well as death sentence. (This letter "T" is a key cipher [for Trotskyist] in his story "Lida.") He is rearrested repeatedly in 1937, 1938, and then again in 1943. One of the reasons for Shalamov's later arrest was his having affirmed that the émigré writer Ivan Bunin had indeed received the Nobel Prize for Literature. Once again, as in the case of Lenin's testament, Shalamov was accused of "anti-Soviet propaganda" for stating the factual or documentary truth. See E[vgenii] A. Shklovsky, *Varlam Shalamov* (Moscow, 1991).

4   Dariusz Tolczyk explores the history of the dual image of the gulag in, *See No Evil: Literary Cover-ups and Discoveries of the Soviet Camp Experience* (New Haven, 1999). For the most recent documentary account of the history of the gulag, see Iu. N. Afanasiev, et al., eds., *Istoriia Stalinskogo Gulaga: Massovye repressii v SSSR* (Moscow, 2004); Anne Applebaum, *Gulag: A History* (New York, 2003); Michael Jakobson, *Origins of the GULAG: The Soviet Prison-Camp System, 1917–1934* (Lexington, 1993); Steven A. Barnes, "In a Manner Befitting Soviet Citizens': An Uprising in the Post-Stalin Gulag," *Slavic Review* 64, no. 4 (Winter 2005): 823–50. For a discussion of diaries from the time of the Great Terror, see Veronique Garros, Natalia Korenevskaya, and Thomas Lahusen, eds., *Intimacy and Terror: Soviet Diaries of the 1930s,* trans. Carol A. Flath (New York, 1995) and Sheila Fitzpatrick and Yuri Slezkine, eds., *In the Shadow of Revolution: Life Stories of Russian Women from 1917 to the Second World War* (Princeton, 2000); as well as writing on diaries: Jochen Hellbeck, *Revolution on My Mind: Writing a Diary under Stalin* (Cambridge, Mass., 2006). For the debate on "Soviet subjectivity" and approaches to Stalinist culture, see the journal *Ab Imperio* 3 (2002); and for a critique of applied Foucauldianism in the Russian context, see Laura Engelstein, "Combined Underdevelopment: Discipline and Law in Imperial and Soviet Russia," in Jan Goldstein, ed., *Foucault and the Writing of History* (Cambridge, Mass., 1994). For an insightful discussion of the "poetics of documentary prose," see Leona Toker, "Towards a Poetics of Documentary Prose—from the

Perspective of Gulag Testimonies," *Poetics Today* 18, no. 2 (Summer 1997): 201–7; and Leona Toker, "Documentary Prose and the Role of the Reader: Some Stories of Varlam Shalamov," in Leona Toker, ed., *Commitment in Reflection: Essays in Literature and Moral Philosophy* (New York, 1994), 169–93. I benefited greatly from the discussion at the conference "History and Legacy of Gulag" organized by Steven A. Barnes at the Davis Center at Harvard University, November 2006.

5   The lines come from the popular "Pesnia o rodine" (Song of our motherland), music by Isaak Dunaevskii, lyrics by Vassilii Lebedev-Kumach.

6   Varlam Shalamov, "O proze," *Sobranie sochinenii*, 6:148.

7   Ibid., 6:153.

8   Hannah Arendt, "The Abyss of Freedom and the Novus Ordo Seclorum," *The Life of the Mind*, vol. 2, *Willing* (New York, 1978), 198–99. These concepts are developed throughout Arendt's work; see *The Life of the Mind*, vol. 1, *Thinking*, 5–7. I develop a broader framework for these ideas in my forthcoming book, *The Other Freedom*.

9   Shalamov wrote that the "celebration of Stalinism is the aestheticization of evil [*estetizatsiia zla*]" in *Vospominaniia, zapisnye knizhki, perepiska, sledstvennye dela* (Moscow, 2004), 309.

10   Ibid., 933 (letter to Iu. M. Lotman). Shalamov's short texts on intonation include "Poeticheskaia intonatsia," 21–30, and "Vo vlasti chuzhoi intonatsii," in Shalamov, *Sobranie sochinenii*, 5:31–38. The study of intonation belongs to the interdisciplinary field of social linguistics, rhetoric, and social anthropology. The founder of Soviet musicology, Boris Asaf'ev (1884–1949), developed an interdisciplinary conception of intonation as a form of social communication and aesthetic innovation.

11   Lidiia Ginzburg, *Chelovek za pis'mennym stolom* (Leningrad, 1989), 310. Translation mine. This is further discussed in Svetlana Boym, *Common Places: Mythologies of Everyday Life in Russia* (Cambridge, Mass., 1994), 93.

12   By the late Brezhnev era, irony and doublespeak that relied on clichés were superseded by the *stiob* discourse that used ersatz irony and a different intonation. On the rhetoric of *stiob* and the legacy of the Soviet heritage in contemporary Russian culture, see Svetlana Boym, *The Future of Nostalgia* (New York, 2001), 154–56.

13   This concept is fundamental for Arendt and occurs in one of the epigraphs to her unfinished project "On Judging." It is discussed in Ronald Beiner, "Hannah Arendt on Judgment: Interpretive Essay," in Hannah Arendt, *Lectures on Kant's Political Philosophy* (Chicago, 1982), 131, and in Elisabeth Young-Bruehl, *Hannah Arendt: For Love of the World* (New Haven, 1982), 533.

14   Shalamov, "O novoi proze," 5:160.

15   Shalamov, *Vospominaniia*, 53–56.

16 In his notebooks Shalamov recounts several conversations with Solzhenitsyn, using only the initial "S" rather than identifying him using his full name. Consider, for example, the following account of "S" teaching a less successful Shalamov the way to publish his work abroad—an account that comes from Shalamov's notebooks:For America—said my new acquaintance quickly and instructively—the hero must be religious. They even have a law about this, so that no American publisher will take a story in translation where the hero is an atheist or simply a skeptic or a man of doubts.

— And what about Jefferson, the author of the Declaration of Independence?
— Well, but this was a long time ago . . . Now I looked through your stories and haven't found a single story where the hero was a man of faith. So, the voice was whispering, don't send it to America. The small fingers of my new friend quickly leaf through the typed pages.
— I am even surprised, how can you not believe in God?
— I don't have a need for such a hypothesis, just like Voltaire.
— But after Voltaire came World War II.
— That's precisely why . . .

Kolyma was Stalin's extermination camp. I experienced all its particularities. I could never imagine that in the twentieth century there could be a writer who would use his memoirs for personal reasons. Shalamov, *Vospominania*, 372–73.

In the next entries Shalamov observes: "The cheaper was the [literary] 'device', the more success it had. This is the tragedy of my life" (373). Contrary to Solzhenitsyn's observation, Shalamov does portray religious prisoners in the gulag, in particular the Old Believers, with great respect, but with a different intonation. When it comes to the complex and deeply personal issue of religious belief, Shalamov's response to Solzhenitsyn is recorded in his notebooks (373, 377). A friendlier dialogue between the two writers can be found in Shalamov's letters to Solzhenitsyn, 641–74.

17 Shalamov, "O proze," 6:152.

18 Shklovsky, *Varlam Shalamov*, 54.

19 In fact, Shalamov's discussion of documentary prose is not dissimilar from the 1920s discussions of the "end of the novel" and the new "prose of the document" (*proza dokumenta*), which is not accidental given Shalamov's studies and friendship with members of the formalist circle. Shalamov avoids ostentatious literary devices of narrative framing or explicit decorative tropes.

20 Shalamov, "O proze," 6:152; Shklovsky, *Varlam Shalamov*, 155–56.

21 Milan Kundera, *The Book of Laughter and Forgetting*, trans. Michael Heim (New York, 1986), 65–68. For a discussion of "poetics of blemish," see Boym, *Common Places*, 242.

22 In Arendt's view, totalitarian ideology tends to be quite successful due to the "common-sense disinclination to believe the monstrous" and because a great part of the population of the totalitarian country "indulges also in wishful thinking and shirks reality in the face of real insanity." Hannah Arendt, *The Origins of Totalitarianism* (New York, 1985), 437.

23 Ibid., 462.

24 Hannah Arendt, *Eichmann in Jerusalem: Report on the Banality of Evil* (New York, 1963), 252. See also Arendt, *Life of the Mind.*

25 Arendt, *Eichmann in Jerusalem*, 49; Vladimir Nabokov, "On a Book Entitled 'Lolita,'" *Lolita* (New York, 1977), 284.

26 Arendt, *Eichmann in Jerusalem*, 252.

27 Vladimir Nabokov, "On Philistines and Philistinism," *Lectures on Russian Literature* (New York, 1981). For a detailed discussion of cliché, *poshlost'*, and kitsch, see Boym, *Common Places*, 11–20. For a discussion of the banality of evil and radical evil, see Richard Bernstein, *Radical Evil: A Philosophical Interrogation* (Cambridge, Eng., 2002).

28 There is a form of thoughtlessness, as exhibited by Eichmann, which is not mere shallowness or stupidity but an ethical problem and a key to understanding war crimes from the point of view of the perpetrators. "Might the problem of good and evil, our faculty for telling right from wrong, be connected to our faculty of thought?" Arendt asks. Arendt, *Life of the Mind*, 1:5. On this issue, see Dana R. Villa, *Politics, Philosophy, Terror: Essays on the Thought of Hannah Arendt* (Princeton, 1999). On the connection between Arendt's political theory and aesthetic theory of estrangement, see Svetlana Boym, "Poetics and Politics of Estrangement: Victor Shklovsky and Hannah Arendt," *Poetics Today* 26, no. 4 (Winter 2005): 581–611.

29 Primo Levi, *The Drowned and the Saved* (New York, 1988), 138–39.

30 Hannah Arendt, "Understanding and Politics," *Partisan Review* 20 (1953): 392. For a more detailed discussion of imagination, see Hannah Arendt, *Lectures on Kant's Political Philosophy* (Chicago, 1992), 79–85; Beiner, "Hannah Arendt on Judgment: Interpretative Essay," 89–156; Howard Caygill, *The Art of Judgment* (London, 1989), 366–80. Arendt's reading of Kant with a focus on aesthetic judgment is rather eccentric to the tradition, yet crucial for her discussion of public freedom.

31 Varlam Shalamov, "Sukhim paikom," *Sobranie sochinenii*, 1:74.

32 Ibid., 1:77–78.

33 Ibid., 1:73.

34 "Kant is a widely popular camp term. It refers to something like a temporary rest, not a full rest . . . but the kind of work that does not make one labor to the limit of his possibilities, but instead easier, temporary work [*pri kotoroi chelovek ne vybivaetsia iz sil*]." Shalamov, "Kant," *Sobranie sochinenii*, 1:73.

35 Shalamov, "Sukhim paikom," 1:83.

36 Andrei Siniavskii wrote about the prisoners of the first Soviet gulag, the Solovki camp, who put their mutilated body parts into a log of wood produced for foreign export. These were their messages to western buyers about the nature of the labor and the product. Savel'ev's fingers sent a message that nobody might have received, yet it was his only means of horrific self-expression. Andrei Siniavskii, "Srez materiala," in *Shalamovskii sbornik* (Vologda, 1994), 1:224–28.

37 Shalamov, "Sukhim paikom," 1:87.

38 To complicate matters further, Fedia is telling the literal truth. Since he took Ivan Ivanovich's clothes, he now finds himself truly "dressed appropriately for the season." And, like the nameless convict in Savel'ev's story, he too has "loafed" appropriately for the circumstances.

39 I am grateful to Leona Toker for drawing my attention to this issue.

40 Lev Vygotsky, "Art as Catharsis," *The Psychology of Art* (Cambridge, Mass., 1971), 215. For another interesting discussion of the "aesthetic phenomenon of Shalamov," see E. B. Volkova, "Esteticheskii fenomen Varlama Shalamova," *Mezhdunarodnye Shalamovskie chteniia* (1997), 7–22; and E. B Volkova, "Paradoksy katarsisa Varlama Shalamova," *Voprosy filosofii*, 1996, no. 11: 43–57.

41 The title "Sukhim paikom" has a syntactic similarity with another Russian proverb that uses a similar adverbial expression that might be invoked here: "Man does not live by bread alone" (*Ne khlebom edinym zhiv chelovek*).

42 Varlam Shalamov, "Lida," *Sobranie sochinenii,* 1:320–21.

43 Ibid., 1:320.

44 Ibid., 1:325.

45 Ibid., 1:326–27.

46 The reasons Krist's fellow-*Zeks* propose for his good fortune are interesting in themselves. One sees there an accident of fate; the other believes it is a sign of the thaw, of the change in the political climate; the doctor sees the "will of god." Ibid., 1:327.

47 Ibid., 1:326. At the moment of liberation, Krist is afraid to speak, just like the convicts at the beginning of "Dry Rations" who were incredulous over their transient luck. The most important things are not to be profaned through impurity of tone.

48 "Revelation [*ozarenie*] arrived suddenly as usual. Suddenly but after an enormous effort—not only intellectual, not only of the heart, but of his whole being. It arrived the way poems or the best lines of a story came to him. One thinks of them day and night without a response and then revelation comes: the joy of the exact word, the joy of solution. Not the joy of hope—for Krist had already encountered too many disappointments, errors, and backstabbings. The revelation came: Lida." Ibid., 1:324. Both

metaphors and the materiality of writing play an important role in Shalamov's story. If the physical document at the center of the story, the passport with a typo, the document of the liberated Zek, were ever to be found in some imaginary archive, it would require a "thick description" and multiple layers of reading.

49 Emmanuel Lévinas, "Ethics as First Philosophy," in Séan Hand, ed., *The Levinas Reader* (Oxford, Eng., 1999), 84.

50 Brian Boyd and Robert Michael Pyle, eds., *Nabokov's Butterflies: Unpublished and Uncollected Writings* (Boston, 2000), 85–86. For more on the conception of "mimicry," see Boym, *Future of Nostalgia*, 265–66. The discussion of cryptic disguise occurs throughout *Speak Memory* and in Nabokov's own review of his text. See Vladimir Nabokov, *Speak Memory* (New York, 1989), 124–25; and Vladimir Nabokov, "Conclusive Evidence," *New Yorker*, 28 December 1998/4 January 1999, 126. For the discussion of Nabokov's aesthetics and ethics, see Boym, *Future of Nostalgia*, 259–83 and 337–40.

51 Homi K. Bhabha, "Of Mimicry and Man: The Ambivalence of Colonial Discourse," *The Location of Culture* (London, 1994), 85–92. Bhabha offers important insights into the hybridity and subversion of mimicry but his discussion is focused on the postcolonial and colonial contexts and has to be recontextualized when taken into the Stalinist context.

52 Varlam Shalamov, "Vo vlasti chuzhoi intonatsii," *Sobranie sochinenii*, 5:31.

53 Vladimir Nabokov, *Strong Opinions* (New York, 1973), 63. See also Boym, *Future of Nostalgia*, 266–74.

54 Varlam Shalamov, "Stikhi—vseobshchii iazyk," *Sobranie sochinenii*, 5:52–53.

55 William Faulkner quoted in Hannah Arendt, *Between Past and Future* (New York, 1969), 10; Shalamov, "O proze," 6:148.

56 Shalamov writes, paraphrasing Karl Marx: "History that first appeared as tragedy, reappears a second time as farce. But there is also the third embodiment of the plot: as absurd horror." Shalamov, *Vospominaniia*, 309. Marx's original aphorism from "Eighteenth Brumaire" paraphrases G. W. F. Hegel, who claimed that history repeats itself. Besides the striking insight that this observation offers, it is curious that Shalamov uses formalist literary vocabulary and speaks of historic "plots."

57 Thinking without a banister does not mean thinking without foundations, but rather, thinking without familiar props. For a discussion of banister, see an exchange between Hannah Arendt and Hans Jonas in Melvyn Hill, ed., *Hannah Arendt: The Recovery of the Public World* (New York, 1979), 311–15; and Hannah Arendt, "Basic Moral Propositions," from Lectures 1966 at the University of Chicago, Hannah Arendt's Papers, The Manuscript Division, Library of Congress, Washington, D.C., container 46, p. 024608.

58 Arendt, "The Gap between Past and Future," *Between Past and Future*, 3–4.

16 FREEDOM AS CO-CREATION

FIGURE 16.1 Svetlana Boym, "Chess Leviathan 2," *Another Freedom*, 2009.

Adventure and the Borders of Freedom

At the beginning of the twenty-first century we had difficulty imagining a new beginning. The future appeared frightening rather than liberating, while the past remained a domain of nostalgic utopias. For the first eight years or so our century seemed to have had a false start.

So how to begin again? Let us try to imagine freedom by thinking "what if" and not only "what is." Let us explore missed historical opportunities and highlight alternative spaces of freedom. This book is an attempt to rescue another history of freedom and propose a new vocabulary that goes beyond today's political debates. It explores the experience of freedom as cocreation in the world and as an adventure in political action and individual judgment, in public and private imagination and passionate thinking. The questions that concern me point to the paradoxes of freedom: What, if anything, must we be certain of in order to tolerate uncertainty? How much common ground or shared trust is needed to allow for the uncommon experiences of freedom? Can they be transported across national borders? If so, can we distinguish between firm boundaries and porous border zones and travel lightly between them?

Instead of vetting typologies and definitions we will engage in rigorous storytelling and follow cross-cultural dialogues between political philosophers, artists, dissidents, and lovers who address the very ground of the possibility of freedom and deliberate its boundaries. Many of these encounters took place in the wake of major historical cataclysms, wars, and revolutions, when the dreams of the new beginning and initial moments of liberation were followed by attempts to establish a regime of freedom. In all of them, experiments in thinking and imagination were also connected to life experiments, sometimes producing more contradictions than continuities. These experiments allow us to explore the relationship between freedoms in the plural (political freedoms, human rights) and Freedom in the singular (religious, artistic, or existential freedom) and look at the moments in which political and artistic understandings of freedom become intertwined. My freedom stories won't take the shape of military epics or romances of independence or martyrdom.[1] Neither will they function merely as cautionary morality tales. At best, they can shed some light on the dilemmas of freedom that are sometimes more difficult to confront than the discreet charms of power.

The experience of freedom has not been valued equally throughout history and across cultures. Even today freedom is out of sync with other highly desirable states of being, such as happiness, belonging, glory, or intimacy. While those states suggest unity and fusion, freedom has an element of estrangement that does not by definition exclude engagement with others in the public world but makes it more unpredictable.

Not only has freedom been a contested value, there has been no agreement as to what freedom would look like. Defining freedom is like capturing a snake: the snake sheds its skin, and we are left with the relic of her trickery as a souvenir of our aspiration. There was no god or goddess of freedom in any ancient mythology, only a belated Roman statue of Libertas, which caused many cultural scandals throughout the centuries. Her "liberty cap" covered the shaved head of a former slave, who acquired rights in the democratic city-states of antiquity, thus making an attribute of Liberty into a simultaneous memento of slavery. As late as 1855 Senator Jefferson Davis of Mississippi, soon to become the president of the Confederacy, objected to the idea of erecting a statue of Freedom wearing a liberty cap on top of the United States Capitol, arguing that this ancient badge of emancipated slaves would offend Southern sensibilities.[2]

The most famous American Statue of Liberty does not wear the memento of slavery either; instead, the traditional liberty cap is transformed into the crown of enlightenment, a beacon for the new modern world. The statue was a gift from a disenchanted Frenchman, who believed that Liberty no longer resided in Europe but only in the United States. To create the goddess of enlightenment, he was inspired, so it is said, by the body of his wife and the face of his mother. But his creation—accepted with great reluctance in the new world—soon shed its skin, metamorphosing into a goddess of immigrants, a tourist attraction, and a security threat. In other countries, like Russia, statues of Liberty were highly unpopular and lacked native iconography. Much preferred was Mother Patria, with classical breasts clad in prudent drapery not dissimilar to those of Lady Liberty.[3] Curiously, the Chinese Goddess of Liberty erected by dissenting students during the Tiananmen Square demonstrations in 1989 referenced both the American and the Russian monuments; it also bore an uncanny resemblance to a Soviet Peasant and Worker statue from the 1930s mass-reproduced all over the world. Quickly brought down by the government forces, this destroyed Goddess of Socialism with a Human Face had unpredictable multicultural features. Of course, all iconographies have their own pitfalls; in the case of freedom, they only point at the unrepresentable.

Having lived half my life on the westernmost point of Russia and the other half on the eastern edge of the United States, I am forever haunted by the specter of two worrying queens—America's Lady Liberty and Russia's Mother Patria. This kind of personal and historical double exposure prompts me to recognize the fragile space of shared dreams that sometimes must be rescued from both extremism and mediocrity. While examining cultural differences in various dialogues on freedom, I will not focus solely on the clash of cultures or external pluralism but will explore internal pluralities within cultures and trace elective affinities across national borders. The examination of freedom requires a creative logic of its own.

One should not forget that freedom has also been associated with invisible elements like the free air of the city and that this "free air" is hard to export or commodify. Freedom's inherent strangeness or noniconicity finds its best reflection in experimental art. The avant-garde artist Kazimir Malevich preferred a zero degree of representation, an image of the black square, an "embryo of multiple potentialities," while his rival Vladimir Tatlin designed the enigmatic monument To the Liberation of Humanity, known also as Monument to the Third Internationale, a tower of two mirroring spirals that resembled both a ruin of the Tower of Babel and a utopian construction site of the future. These artists believed that the new architecture of freedom would not require conventional technical drawings but could be built through experimental artistic technology. For many reasons ranging from the technical to the political, the monument to the liberation of humanity was never to be built. It remains a phantom limb of nonconformist art all over the world, an example of the improbable architecture of "what if."

The German American immigrant and political thinker Hannah Arendt described the experience of freedom as something fundamentally strange, a new beginning and a "miracle of infinite improbability" that occurs regularly in the public realm.[4] Since freedom is one of the most abused words in present-day politics, I will explore it as something "infinitely improbable" and, nevertheless, possible.

The new beginning marked by the experience Arendt describes is neither a return to nature and myth nor a leap into the "end of history." For better or worse, freedom is an ongoing human miracle. Arendt finds a new space for the experience of freedom—not inside the human psyche or in the domain of the will but in human action on the public stage. She traces the first positive appreciation of freedom back to ancient Greece, to the conception of public or political freedom. For her, "care for the common world" becomes a measure and limit of such freedom. The experience of freedom is akin to the theatrical performance that uses conventions, public memory, and a common stage but also allows for the possibility of the unprecedented and particular. Such experiences constitute our "forgotten heritage," which is frequently written out of the conventional historiography and therefore is something that every generation must discover anew.

The improbable element in the discussion of the experience of freedom is the word "infinite." Freedom is only possible under the conditions of human finitude and with concern for boundaries. In fact, since Aristotle, thinking of freedom begins with the disclaimer that freedom does not mean doing what one wishes, abolishing all boundaries and distinctions. Before thinking of "freedom from" and "freedom for" or negative and positive freedom we have to map the ground of possibility of the experience of freedom. Dreaming of borderlessness, we become aware of our fences and passages, bans and banisters, border zones and bridges where double agents are occasionally exchanged. But how do we understand a boundary: as a barrier or a contact zone, as a limit point or a horizon from which the world can be reimagined? Which boundaries are more important? Boundaries between cultures or between the individual and the state? Between private and public or within the self? Can there be a Russian freedom, an American freedom, a hyphenated freedom? Is one man's tyranny another man's national community of freedom? Touching upon contemporary debates around liberalism and its critics, around negative and positive conceptions of freedom, freedom of imagination and freedom of action, as well as of national and universalist understanding of rights of individuals and nation-states, this book will explore the border zones between political, religious, and cultural spheres, between economics and moral sentiments, between human rights and human passions.

The experience of freedom is akin to adventure: it explores new borders but never erases or transcends them. Through adventure we can test the limits but also navigate—more or less successfully—between convention and invention, responsibility and play. German sociologist Georg Simmel proposes an experimental spatial and temporal structure of adventure that in my view exemplifies the paradoxes of freedom. Adventure is an event, which both interrupts the flow of our everyday life and crystallizes its inner core.[5] Examples of adventure can vary: from the experience of foreign travel to the exploration of one's native modern metropolis, from a political action to an erotic experience or any life-transforming encounter. The concept will be further expanded to refer to the adventures of thinking, judging, of love and dissent. In adventure we "forcibly pull the world into ourselves," but at the same time allow a "complete self-abandonment to the powers and accidents of the world, which can delight us, but in the same breath can also destroy us."[6] Thus the relationships between inside and outside, foreign and native, center and periphery, core and everyday practice are constantly reframed. Adventure is like "a stranger's body" which foregrounds the most intimate.[7] Through the experience of adventure we enter into a dialogue with the world and with the stranger within us.

Adventure literally refers to something that is about to happen, ad venire, but rather than opening up into some catastrophic or messianic future, it instead leads into invisible temporal dimensions of the present. The temporal structure of adventure echoes the spatial one: it can be described as a time out of time, yet it also changes our everyday conception of what it means to be timely. Adventure might work against the linear conception of time, the time of modern progress or human aging; it challenges the implacable irreversibility of time without recourse to nostalgia. In the experience of adventure we can deflect the vectors of past and future and explore potentialities of the present, reenchanting modern experiences.[8] The adventurer pushes "life beyond the threshold of its temporal boundaries," but this "beyond" is never beyond this-worldliness. Neither transcendence nor transgression, adventure is a kind of profane illumination, to use Walter Benjamin's term. It pushes human possibilities but doesn't break them. It involves an encounter with the incalculable that forces us to change life's calculus and explore the dimensions of "what if."

Adventure opens up porous spaces of border zones, thresholds, bridges, and doors. It is not about experiences of the sublime but of the liminal that expand our potentialities. Adventure is described by Simmel as "a third something," neither an external incident nor an internal system. Similarly, the experience of freedom can be understood as "a third something," which calls for an adventure in thinking. I use "neither, nor" here to approach the sliding structure of adventure, but one can also describe it as "and, and" or "yet, and still" or "against all odds."

Albert Camus, a writer of working-class origins, French Resistance fighter, and one of the practitioners of existentialism, echoed Simmel's conception of adventure in his discussion of modern and ancient adventurers and rebels forging the idea of radical moderation. In The Rebel, Camus explores modern rebellion ranging from regicide and terror to resistance and artistic creativity. According to Camus, the ultimate adventure aims beyond the passionate romantic thirst for liberation toward the creative experience of freedom that might come with radical moderation. Moderation, in his unorthodox definition, is "a perpetual conflict, continually created and mastered by the intelligence," while "intelligence is our faculty not to develop what we think to the very end, so that we can still believe in reality."[9] "Intelligence" in this sense means something closer to "wisdom," a torturous but honest road between imagination and lived experience, between contemplation and action, that pushes the limits but does not destroy the space of the common trust or what Arendt called "the care for the world."

Many political thinkers have thought that defining freedom is as "hopeless" as trying to square a circle by simply inscribing one inside the other, yet forging into those asymptotic spaces of the adventurous and incalculable is a fundamental enterprise for the human condition.[10] It seems better to locate the experience of freedom in such asymptotic spaces than to square the circle once and for all. Recognition of such hopelessness is a sine qua non for my thinking about freedom. It is always a form of thinking out of or from within an impasse—an aporia, that is— turning obstacle into adventure in the broad sense of the word.

The adventure of freedom in this understanding is about reframing but not breaking and removing all frames. The word "frame" itself has had an adventurous past. "Frame" originates in "from," which suggests that it is made of the same timber as the object that it surrounds or that the two become codependent. Originally, "from" also had a meaning of "forward," "ahead," and "advance." I don't know how and why it evolved into the unfortunate direction of nostalgic introspection. Freedom frames can be unstable and unforeseen.

[…]

The Public World and the Architecture of Freedom

Hannah Arendt offers a cautionary tale of the appearance and disappearance of the public world: To live together in the world means essentially that a world of things is between those who have it in common, as the table is located between those who sit around it, the world like every in-between relates and separates men at the same time. What makes mass society so difficult to bear is not the number of people involved, or at least not primarily, but the fact that the world between them has lost is power to gather them together, to relate and to separate them. The weirdness of this situation resembles a spiritualistic séance where a number of people gathered around a table might suddenly, through some magic trick, see the table vanish from their midst, so that two persons sitting opposite each other were no longer separated but also would be entirely unrelated to each other by anything tangible.[11]

The "world" here appears uncanny, like a flickering ghost in a gothic tale. Yet it is also the measure and framework of human interaction, an everyday ground of common ethics and trust, obvious as the old dining table and not always visible due to its obviousness. In present-day terms, the "world" is rarely used without qualifiers: third world, second world, first world, old world, new world. To describe "the world" we have to come up with something like a retronym—a word introduced because an existing term has become inadequate, like "snail mail" in the era of e-mail. Has public worldliness become an endangered subject in contemporary thought? "Worldliness" refers neither to biological life nor to economic globalization; it is the realm of human artifice where the plurality of humanity manifests itself in its distinctiveness and multidimensionality, not merely in its agonistic otherness. Usually associated with the public sphere, which "gathers us together but prevents us from falling over each other,"[12] worldliness can be regarded more broadly as a realm of action and storytelling that speaks of fragility and finitude but also grants an extensive duration to the world beyond individual life-span or even the life-span of several generations. What is at stake here might not be the "immortality of the soul" or the mark of eternal life, but the survival of the manmade world. At its best, architecture and art can offer a "premonition of immortality," a "non-mortal home to mortal beings." Contrary to the poetic dictum that philosophy is about homecoming, there could be a different way of inhabiting the world and making a second home, not the home into which we were born but a home that we freely choose for ourselves, a home that contains a palimpsest of world culture.

Worldliness is often discussed together with architecture, material and metaphorical. Architecture inhabits philosophy just as much as philosophy inhabits architecture. Plato's Republic contains a mutual codependence between architectural and philosophical thinking. But Plato's protocinematic cave, where humans caught in the "world of appearances" watch the shadows of their existence on the screen, offers us a subterranean and unworldly metaphor for human existence. And this is not the only architectural possibility. Architecture is, after all, a form of poesis—a creative making of world culture that does not merely reify hierarchies but commemorates human labor and artifice and exceeds its immediate utilitarian function.[13] It is not by chance that myths of language and architecture overlap: the Greek labyrinth, the Biblical Tower of Babel, the Native American "world house" whose mistress is the playful serpent dancing with sympathetic humans. Most of these projects were unfinished works in progress, not unlike the avant-garde Monument to the Third International or the Monument to the Liberation of Humanity.

The architecture of freedom is a kind of transitional architecture traversed by storytelling that opens up spaces of desire and possibility.

The architecture of freedom frequently presents a combination of ruins and construction sites that reveals the fragility of manmade worlds. Architecture is not architectonics; it does not give to the world a system or a superstructure but rather a texture of concepts and common yardsticks.[14] To understand the forms of local cosmopolitanism and grassroots politics that provide insight into larger political structures in any country, it is most useful to examine the disputes around urban sites, monuments, and architecture, which can take the form of deliberation, oppositional demonstration, or orchestrated violent protest. Recent examples might include debates over the ground zero site in New York City, the discussions about public spaces and "the commons" threatened by corporate privatization in other American cities, mafia wars over real estate in the center of Moscow, or fights around squatters and "free states" like Christiania in Copenhagen or new "model" favelas and reorganized shantytowns in Latin America. Or, to think closer to home, during the financial crisis of 2008–2009 formerly middle-class Americans squatted in their own "foreclosed" suburban homes, expropriating like imposters the simulacra of their American dream. Debates around architecture provide a form of civic education based on care for the built environment, public memory, and forms of social justice.

"Worldliness" is not synonymous with "globalization." The word "globalization," first registered in 1959 at the beginning of space exploration, operates with an aerial picture of the Earth from outer space, or in contemporary terms, with a Google map view of the global flows of capital and populations. Worldliness suggests a different form of engagement with the world based not on virtual distance but on the interconnectedness and messiness of the human condition. Rethinking the concept of worldliness pushes us beyond the opposition between nature and culture, culture and civilization, or global and local; it is about thinking this-worldliness over other-worldliness. Fortunately, paradise has already been lost, so we have to start loving our less-than-paradisiacal world and accept the freedom of exile. The experience of freedom requires a renaming and remapping of this world and a challenge both to the metaphysics and to the notion of globalization.

The discovery of this-worldliness in the history of political thought is directly connected to a new appreciation of public freedom. It stemmed from a double perspective of slaves turned citizens in the Athenian city-state and was later developed by religious heretics, dissenters, and immigrants. Sociologist Orlando Patterson connected the positive conception of freedom to the particular circumstances in the Greek city-states. He observed that in most ancient and modern civilizations the native word synonymous with freedom does not necessarily carry a positive meaning. In ancient Egyptian the word for freedom signified "orphanhood."[15] Similarly in contemporary Chinese and Japanese, the native word for freedom was originally negative, suggesting privation or nonbelonging. This, of course, doesn't mean that there are other contemporary terms that reflect a more hybrid thinking. What was specific to the ancient Greek city-states was the fact that slavery was not necessarily a permanent condition; nor were captives murdered or sacrificed, as was the practice in many other ancient civilizations. Instead, in Athens slaves could be emancipated into citizens. Hence the negative term (a-douleia, simple noncoercion) developed into eleutheria (freedom). Of course, the first step after enfranchisement is a liberation from want and the satisfaction of basic human needs: shelter, food, minimal protection from violence, and liberation from immediate coercion. Freedom is the next step, but the relationship between freedom and liberation is never quite linear. My hypothesis (explored in chap. 1) is that the space of freedom was colonized from the space of the sacred and centered on the redefinition of sacrifice both in politics and in theater. The Athenian polis was supported by democratic practices and theatrical performances of tragedy and comedy. Tragedy educated democracy not only by providing the cathartic experience of a violent spectacle but also by showing the dangers of mythical violence through the twists of theatrical plots. At the center of Athenian tragedy is the issue of "corrupted sacrifice," which from its beginning as a sacred ritual becomes a deliberated act, opening into a space of negotiation and reflection in worldly theater.[16] Questioning violence and transforming the practice of human sacrifice into a space of deliberation would also be important in the later struggles for freedom of religion and freedom of consciousness that are fundamental for the early modern understanding of the idea.

The primal scene of the Greek eleutheria is public, not private; its setting is the public square (agora), not the inner citadel of the human psyche. Eleutheria was a combination of play and duty, an obligation and a potential for creative civic action. Ancient cultures did not have our contemporary understanding of the notion of individual freedom. Considerably later, the Greek Stoic philosopher Epictetus (c. 55–c. 135 CE), himself a freed slave who experienced many misfortunes in his life including physical handicap and exile, developed the doctrine of inner freedom as the individual's only refuge, an "inner polis" and an "acropolis of the soul." Uncannily, inner freedom mirrored the public architecture of the lost polis of the Greek city-state in the age of the Roman Empire.

If we look for the origins of the word "freedom" in several Indo-European languages, using etymologies broadly and poetically, we find some surprising results. The Greek word eleutheria and the Roman libertas have a common linguistic base in *leudhe/leudhi, signifying "public" or common space.[17] The Latin word for play, ludere, linked to illusion and collision, also goes back to this common base, as do libidia, love, and possibly Greek elpis, hope. The English word "freedom" is also connected to joy and friendship. Even the most explicitly antiarchitectural contemporary rhetoric of the "removal of barriers," off-shoring, and superhuman flow of capital also point back to a certain shared design and topography. "Trade" comes from treadth, a path, and "market" refers to a building where negotiations took place. Law, too, especially in the Greek conception of nomos—the boundary—was connected to a certain topography of cultural memory and was frequently used in the plural.[18]

Many historians have noted that the ancient Greek polis offered a limited space of self-realization that was available only to male citizens, but the polis gave shape to an aspiration, an ideal of freedom that spread beyond its walls. An understanding of spiritual freedom delineated by Epictetus reveals cross-cultural connections between East and West, between Indian, Persian, Hellenic, and Hebrew cultures. What is originally Greek is the concept of political freedom. Yet from the Middle Ages to the Enlightenment, debates on freedom, both spiritual and political, and on the preservation of the Greek philosophical heritage, became a cross-cultural affair. Among the first early medieval interpreters of Aristotle were Persian Muslim scientist, physician, philosopher, poet, and statesman Abu Ibn Sina (Avicenna [980–1037]) and the Spanish Egyptian Jewish philosopher, physician, and rabbi Moshe ben Maimon (Mussa bin Maimun or Moses Maimomdes [1135–1204]; the enumeration of adjectives and occupations is in itself amazing). In modern times, one might recall the passionate philosophical dialogue between Moses Mendelssohn and Immanuel Kant on the nature of progress and freedom of conscience beyond the Christian conception of universalism, and in the twentieth century the deliberation of civil disobedience and dissent from Gandhi to the American civil rights movement and East European, East Asian, Latin American dissidents.

There is no exclusive cultural patrimony of freedom; the concepts circulate and interact. The history of freedom is what Anthony Kwame Appiah calls "the case for contamination." Worldliness is not the same as cosmopolis, but the two notions overlap.[19] There are many vernacular cosmopolitans coming from different localities (with memories of inequality, but not entirely defined by a colonial or postcommunist or any other particular history) but sharing the preoccupation with worldly architecture.[20] Freedom is never about purity—ethnic or otherwise—but about contacts, contaminations, and border crossings. And so is what I would call "fascinating unfreedom," which takes different shapes but shares an eros of power and paranoic antimodern or post-postmodern ideology.

Agnostic Space: Freedom versus Liberation

To investigate the relationship between self and other and to explore the otherness inherent in the experience of freedom itself, I propose a distinction between agonistic and agnostic understandings of the public realm. This distinction once again highlights the connection between valorization of political freedom in ancient Greece and the emergence of tragic theater. The relationship between agonistic and agnostic is not in itself antagonistic but suggests a shift in the frame of reference and epistemological orientation. In ancient Greece, agon referred to action in an athletic contest, in politics, and in theatrical performances with its masked "protagonists." But the poetics of drama was based not only on agon but also on mimesis (imitation/performance), which, among other things, dramatized the encounter with luck, fate, uncertainty, and the everyday mysteries of the human condition (chap. 1). An agnostic understanding of the public realm puts more emphasis on the tragic and the comic aspects of human life that are not reducible to competitions, struggles, and contests that open into the space of the improbable and new. One can either dedicate the whole book to the distinction between agonistic and agnostic conceptions of the space of freedom or leave it to one extensive footnote and future deliberation.[21]

Agnostics (in my unconventional understanding of the term) do not think of political action as merely strategic or instrumental, but also as a form of public performance and encounter with the unpredictable beyond the political theology of the moment. If there is an agon among agnostics, it manifests itself as passionate opposition to antiworldliness or as charismatic advocacy for ultimate emancipation from worldly concerns (from Saint Paul to Saint Lenin). Possibly the only way to discover or rescue alternative frameworks of freedom for the twenty-first century is through thinking freedom neither as the means for an end nor as an end that justifies the means but simultaneously as means and ends, or as something that defies the mean-and-ends rationale altogether.

Poet and thinker Friedrich Schiller proposed a similar understanding of freedom in his work On the Aesthetic Education of Man, written two hundred years ago in the wake of the French Revolution. In response to revolutionary terror and postrevolutionary political disillusionments, Schiller argues that the political, aesthetic, and life realms are best mediated through the practice of play, which should be a foundation of a citizen's education. Only through serious play can one experience freedom both as a means and as an end of human existence because freedom is not merely an abstract goal but also an educational experience in shared humanity. Recognition of worldly play allows us to negotiate between chaos and cosmos, radical uncertainty and hopeful action, and also to acknowledge the multiple roles of others instead of typecasting them as friends or foes.[22] Aesthetic education is accomplished not merely through making art and teaching moral values but also through a variety of creative practices in the world. The word "aesthetics," like the word "politics," has been much maligned and too frequently used as an insult. I understand aesthetics in the original sense of the word, neither as an analysis of autonomous works of art nor as a connoisseurship of the beautiful but as a form of knowledge that proceeds through a particular interplay of sense, imagination, and reason and "the distribution of the sensible," to quote Jacques Rancière.[23] I will distinguish between aesthetic practice of the "total work," which strives to aestheticize politics and affirm total authorial control and aesthetics of estrangement, which is open to experiences of freedom, wonder, and renewal in art and politics (chap. 5).

It is not by chance that the moment of valorization of public freedom in the political realm coincided with the birth of theater in Western culture (chap. 1). As a parallel with the distinction between the agonistic and the agnostic, I will examine the culture of liberation and the culture of freedom, what in Greek tragedy began with the distinction between mania (madness, inspiration) and technê (skills, arts). Liberation (which might be a necessary first step in many struggles for independence) strives for dissolution of boundaries. Liberation can be of short duration but involve broad expansion and destruction. Freedom, on the other hand, requires a longer expanse of time but less expansion in physical space; it builds a creative architecture of political institutions and social practices that opens up virtual spaces of consciousness. Liberation is often engaged in a master-slave power struggle while freedom has many heterotopic logics. Liberation is antiarchitectural and at the end can become antipolitical as well, while the experience of freedom requires an unusual architecture of public memory but also spaces where desire can reside. The experiences of liberation and freedom also carry very distinctive moods, if we understand moods not as the transient ups and downs that color our daily life but instead as more fundamental experiences of modern temporality and of our interaction with the surrounding world (chap. 4). The mood of liberation might begin with anger, a thirst for justice and enthusiasm. The constant drive of liberation, however, might result in a form of paranoia and resentment and a need for an agonistic enemy in ever changing masks. The mood of freedom is what follows the enthusiasm of liberation. It starts with anxiety, which is then counteracted by a certain self-estrangement and curiosity, an openness to play but also care for the world. It may occasionally crash in despair but never stops at hopelessness.

Scenography of Freedom: Political Optics and Phantasmagoria

The architecture of freedom has a particular scenography. Neither brightly lit nor completely enlightened, it is a scenography of luminosity, of the interplay of light and shadow. Walter Benjamin, with his inimitable oblique lucidity, wrote about the importance of short shadows. They are "no more than the sharp black edges at the feet of things, preparing to retreat silently, unnoticed, into their burrow, their secret being."[24] Short shadows speak of thresholds, warn us against being overly short-sighted or long-winged. When we get too close to things, disrespecting their short shadows, we risk obliterating them, but if we make the shadows too long we start to enjoy them for their own sake.

Short shadows urge us to check the balance of nearness and distance, to trust neither those who speak of the essences of things nor those who preach conspiratorial simulation. Søren Kierkegaard spoke of "shadowgraphy" as a form of Platonic writing in this world. My shadowgraphy of freedom includes spaces of luminosity commemorating the fragile world of appearances. Writing about Walter Benjamin's life and art and that of other "men and women in the dark times," Arendt observed that in the circumstances of extremity, the illuminations come not from philosophical concepts but from the "uncertain, flickering and often weak light" that men and women kindle and shed over the lifespan given to them. This luminous space is the space of "humanitas," where "men and women come out of their origins and reflect each other's sparks"; by doing so they embrace social theatricality, not introspective sincerity.[25] The darkness of the human heart is not to be fully revealed in public; freedom is not about inquisitorial denunciation or smug claims of authenticity.

The demand of transparency defines political scenography in the contemporary media. But how transparent or realistic is such a demand? In the totalitarian regimes of the twentieth century, the private lives of individuals were supposed to be fully transparent for the authorities (at least in theory) while political life (bright colors of the parades and movies notwithstanding) was, in fact, completely obfuscated. In democratic societies, one would think that we can demand transparency from our political leaders and financial institutions, in which case transparency stands for accountability. At the same time, individuals' private lives must be protected from the demands of transparency, which in this case become synonymous with surveillance. In other words, what distinguishes democratic societies from authoritarian regimes, at least in theory, is the protection of nontransparency and privacy as personal rights, the public demand for political transparency and accountability, and the complex architecture that distinguishes one from the other. Today this story is complicated by both new technologies and media. The popular media's insistence on the public's right to know about politicians' private lives encourages mass voyeurism instead of democratic reflection, reselling the desire for transparency at a high price. At the same time, ordinary citizens' privacy is being invaded from every digital orifice, often under less-than-transparent guise. Thus, the moralism of complete transparency and authenticity can obscure the distinctions between public and private and distract attention from economic and public issues while indulging in the private indiscretions of politicians that appear to be more "media-friendly."

Even in modern architecture the uses of transparency are ambivalent: they hark back to the modern dreams of a technological progress that would transform architecture into a form of social engineering and the edifice of the new utopian collectivity. But we know that the architecture of transparency was used for both utopian communes and corporate structures, for both utilitarian and decorative reasons, for openness and for surveillance. In the end it appears that an understanding of transparency requires a complicated cultural optics. Transparent surfaces have become reflective and refracting mirrors and screens of our history and our technology, exposing the cracks and the patina of the medium itself.

The space of luminosity does not offer complete transparency or absolute clarity but might provide occasional lucidity. It helps to avoid the most stark delusions and to nurture a flickering hope in the preservation of the common world. Reflective chiaroscuro can be more reliable than blinding illumination in providing broad perspectivism and worldly insight.

Political philosophy—from Plato's cave to Thomas Hobbes's anamorphs, from Denis Diderot's theater of paradox to Marx's phantasmagoria of revolution—engaged with optical and theatrical metaphors that were integral to its arguments about freedom. To take one striking example, one could juxtapose Hobbes's Leviathan (1651) and Diderot's "Paradox of an Actor" (1770), since both share the Renaissance conception of the world as a theater in which all people are actors. Hobbes writes at the time of the English revolution of 1649 while Diderot foreshadows the events of the French Revolution and the Terror; both connect political and artistic judgment to theatrical spectatorship and to the recognition of artifice it entails.

Hobbes's Leviathan, the treatise on the "matter, form and power of commonwealth," opens with a famous reflection on the "art of man"—man's ability to imitate nature and create artificial monsters of Biblical proportions: "For by art is created that great Leviathan called a Commonwealth or State which is but an artificial man, though of greater stature and strength than the natural, for whose protection and defense it was intended, and in which the sovereignty is artificial soul."[26]

Such a baroque image represents a curious double figure of the body of the sovereign, made of his people. It/he is at once an artificial animal and the people who created him and obey him. Moreover, in the emblem the men greeting the sovereign happen to be wearing hats, less a sign of prostration before the divine monarch than a behavior of spectators, suggesting a peculiar form of political theatricality. The figure of the Leviathan or the state is not a political symbol but an ambiguous emblem, technically, a "catoptic anamorph" that actively engages the spectators and plays on their double vision. Hobbes was very interested in the theories of illusion making and perspective through "interactive optics" that revealed how a spectator can alter the event.[27] Catoptic optics—a precursor to the modernist revolution in vision—went beyond the study of three-dimensional perspective that can be politically manipulated by forcing the viewer to project empathetically and identify with a packaged illusion. By contrast, catoptic double play celebrated a theatrical artifice and creative perspectivism that combined invention and judgment.[28]

In other words, Hobbes represents not merely a theocracy based on fear, but also a theatocracy with an active spectator who consents to delegate some of his powers to the sovereign as part of a political pact, not as a divine entitlement. The emblem desanctifies the sovereign and at the same time endows it with contractual obligations. This is an example of an early modern theatrical body politics.[29]

Hobbes offers a special optics for looking at Diderot's "Paradox of an Actor" as a form of political art. It also connects the Renaissance and baroque to a certain strain of Enlightenment thought through the conception of play and the perception of the world as a theater. Diderot was working on "The Paradox of an Actor" while literally crossing the borders of Europe—on his way to see Catherine the Great, the "enlightened despot" of the Russian Empire. The text survived in the library of the Hermitage and was not made public for fifty years after it was completed, decidedly failing to enlighten the Russian court.

Unlike Hobbes, Diderot does not offer a treatise but a dialogue between the "men of paradox" using the Socratic method. The paradox is that a "natural actor," "a man or a woman of sensibility" who suffers on stage, gives a performance that is inferior to an "imitative actor" who recreates the scene from past observations. The best actor doesn't weep on stage but makes us weep, for the illusion is ultimately ours, not his. Diderot explains: "I want him [a great actor] to have a lot of judgment, for me there needs to be a cool, calm spectator inside this man, so I demand sagacity and no feeling, the power to imitate anything," says the "man of paradox."[30] This kind of actor who identifies with the "phantom," the spirit of theater itself, rather than of a particular character, is not unlike the Hobbesian anamorph, a figure of double vision, a performer and spectator at once, except that his doubleness is not only spatial or visual but also temporal. The great actor combines memory and imagination, observed moments of sublimity in the past with performance in the present.

Judging contemporary theater, Diderot advocates for tragedy and not for a "moving story" or tearful comedy. The best theater redefines the boundaries of the stage through movement and action; it transports us back and forth, beyond and inside, but it never obliterates the stage. Sense and sensibility are developed through e-motions that involve movements and peripeteias. From the perspective of the twentieth century, Diderot is arguably closer to the physical and intellectual theater of Vsevolod Meyerhold and Bertolt Brecht (minus the didacticism) than to Antonin Artaud. The answer to hypocrisy and injustice is not in emotion and sensibility but in the paradoxical politics of engagement and estrangement embodied in the actor's identification with the "phantom" and a certain existential irony.

In this respect Diderot's vision of the theater and more broadly of freedom is the opposite of Jean-Jacques Rousseau's, and their dialogue is at the core of debates for centuries to come. Rousseau and many generations of cross-cultural Rousseauists from all over the world share an antitheatrical prejudice and view the theater as the evil of insincerity and unfreedom. Is it possible that, being an insightful if somewhat resentful observer, Rousseau might have suspected that he was only a "natural actor" and not a natural man and thus wanted to ban theater so that nobody might judge his poor performance?

For Diderot, the advocacy of extreme sincerity on the social or political stage is in itself insincere and hypocritical if not downright manipulative and dangerous. Sincerity and empathy alone do not account for the exercise of free judgment that arises from mediation between experience and reflection, emotion and cognition.

Yet in the true spirit of paradox, Diderot doesn't offer an agonistic battle between the natural and the imitative actor. The experience of freedom comes when the actor surprises himself. Sometimes the imitative actor stops acting and forgets himself and is "overcome with sensibility," open to natural wonder and amazement. And the "natural man" begins to praise nature for being picturesque and for looking like a beautiful landscape, as if imitating art. So in the moment of freedom each actor exceeds himself, discovers the other within, and confronts his or her paradoxical inner plurality.[31]

But the real paradox involves transferring theater into life—not only through identification with feeling but also through estrangement and free play.[32] The paradoxicalist becomes a model personality for Diderot's version of playful Enlightenment unconstrained by scientific reason;

he is an adventurist in a Simmelian sense, a wanderer, a peripatetic conversationalist who enjoys the shadow play and luminosity of existence. The paradox of an actor becomes the paradox of a good citizen, not necessarily a revolutionary, but always a player on the world stage who embraces the phantom of world theater.

In the nineteenth and twentieth centuries the discussion of modern freedom is accompanied by the theater of phantasmagoria, which offers another kind of scenography, with specters of communism haunting Europe (and beyond) challenged by the ghosts of history. Marx, Baudelaire, and Dostoevsky pondered the phantasmagorias of modern urban life and their use in poetry, revolution, and terrorist movements of the nineteenth century (chap. 3). Arendt too described the memory of public freedom and public happiness in the twentieth century as a "fata morgana" and the return of worldliness as an uncanny postphantasmagoric realization.

The word "phantasmagoria" was invented for the theater of optical illusions, which were produced chiefly by means of the magic lantern or similar devices. One of the pioneers of phantasmagoria, Etienne-Gaspar Robertson, opened his spectacle in the Capuchine cloister in Paris in 1799 to a French audience haunted by the Revolution and Terror. Revolutionaries Jean-Paul Marat, Georges Danton, and Maximilien Robespierre as well as King Louis appeared as specters and skeletons in the phantasmagoric shows. In the words of Tom Gunning, "Phantasmagoria literally took place on the threshold between science and superstition, between Enlightenment and Terror."[33] It was also a combination of mystification and demystification, of new technology and historical violence, of haunting images and scientific explanations. While watching phantasmagoric presentations, the viewers could focus on the uncanny and mysterious haunting of the past, and their scientific elucidation, or on the ambivalence and play of such juxtapositions. Throughout the nineteenth century phantasmagorias haunted artists and political thinkers, offering many different optics and plots for dealing with the new experiences of modernization—from gothic romance to modernist allegory. Karl Marx uses phantasmagoria to describe the farce of the revolutions of the "Eighteen Brumaire" and the policies of Louis-Bonaparte (chap. 3). Marx's phantasmagoria evokes a gothic novel or a mystery play of the "world-historical conjuring of the ghosts of the dead."[34] The figure for phantasmagoria in Marx is the urban crowd, which for him is a great dissimulator. The crowd is a space where classes mix and where spontaneous and unpredictable associations beyond class struggle can emerge. Phantasmagoria in Marx is used negatively as a model of distorted perception, the "smoke and mirrors" behind which one can find the real and the undistorted. Theatrical metaphors are used similarly in a sarcastic fashion. The opposition is between the theatricalization of history and phantasmagoric optics and the higher vision of historic reality into which Marx had special insight. Marx, like Dostoevsky, disliked the everyday theater of modern life and was ready to sacrifice it for the future liberation of mankind. If many political thinkers and writers from Diderot on often used the metaphor of theater in speaking of revolution, Marx spoke of "the birth pangs" of the revolution as if revolution was a labor of nature or historic necessity. But phantasmagoria plays unforeseen tricks with Marx's dialectics and continues to haunt it. In the "Eighteenth Brumaire" as well as in "The Manifesto of the Communist Party," the ghost of the past is opposed not by living beings or existing social entities but by the "specter of communism" and the "spirit" of the revolution. The uncanniness of this resides in the fact that sometimes it is difficult to distinguish good ghosts from bad ghosts, the ghosts that should be with us and the ghosts that are against us.

Similarly in Feodor Dostoevsky's novel The Possessed (chap. 3), the phantasmagoria of Russian life created by terrorist conspirators must be eliminated, and yet it is shown as seductive and powerful. Dostoevsky, too, is fascinated by the gothic novel and the melodrama. While exorcizing some of the demons of terror and revealing the banality of actual terrorists, the novelist occasionally demonizes the experience of modern public life, demanding freer freedom and truer truth instead of the masquerade of modern appearances. Dostoevsky understands the power of charismatic seduction, which can never reveal its modus operandi and explain the inner working of its phantasmagoric fascination.

For the poet Charles Baudelaire, who coined the term "modernity" in his essay "The Painter of Modern Life," phanstasmagoria is no longer a bad word. It is constitutive of the experience of modern urban life, which cannot be merely unveiled and abolished. The poor, the injured, the war veterans, and the prostitutes are all present in the Baudelairian urban crowd, which is no longer cast as some gothic tale. The experience of urban phantasmagoria demands new plots, prose poems, and experimental essays that are open to chance encounters with unpredictable outcomes. Baudelaire's antiheroic modern wanderer is himself a phantasmagoria addict. Phantasmagoria contributes to the atmosphere of human liberty and cannot be completely destroyed for the sake of future liberation.

The debates on theatricality and phantasmagoria are echoed a century later in Theodor Adorno's correspondence with Walter Benjamin, in which he accuses Benjamin of becoming a phantasmagoric writer. Phantasmagoria for Adorno is once again the enemy of the revolutionary spirit: "A profound and thorough liquidation of phantasmagoria can succeed only if it is conceived as an objective category of the philosophy of history."[35] For Benjamin, phantasmagoria is an integral part of the dialectical image through which the past manifests itself in the present. Adorno's protestation notwithstanding, he refuses to disavow his phantasmagoric modern wanderer, the flâneur, who acts out the paradox of the actor on the city streets. Phantasmagoric ambivalence is a way of cohabiting or even co-creating with the ghosts of the past and the technologies of the present without the predictable agonistic plots of horror and romance. Phantasmagoric ambivalence is not a subjective fancy but a part of the phenomenology of modern experience that cannot be exorcised entirely—neither in the name of the objective laws of history nor in the name of the truer religion of the people (as in Dostoevsky). If approached critically and creatively, phantasmagoria ceases to be an obstacle for the everyday arts of freedom and instead becomes its manifestation; it opens up nonlinear potentialities of action and imagination by allowing us to recognize rather than exorcize our inner strangers.

Passionate Thinking, Judging, and Imagination

What, then, is the shape of free thinking, and how can we develop an eccentric methodology of "freedom studies"?

Many writers explored in this book were rigorous thinkers who participated in several systems of thought but chose not to belong to a single one. They were experimental essayists in the Socratic tradition of dialogue and peripatetic deliberation that questioned closed systems of thought, the exclusivity of analytical logic, and the scientific method. "Essay" meant at once a trial and an experiment. More than a genre, it was a mode of thinking and acting, an attitude towards truth. The essay is a reflection not merely of a style of thinking but also of thought's substance; the quest for freedom here is not a theme, not a form of writerly experience. In other words, Schiller's notion of play is a way of exploring freedom by way of freedom, for freedom must not be a betrayal of the imagination.

At a certain point in their lives, almost every "freedom thinker" went through a crisis of judging, a mind change or paradigm shift. A change of mind or change of heart was not considered by them to be a sign of weakness but a necessary right of passage for a free thinker. In the cases of Dostoevsky and Kierkegaard, this crisis of conscience resulted in a religious conversion or a "leap of faith," while for Tocqueville it provoked a turn away from institutional religion and toward a contradictory embrace of the "new political science" and critical and spiritual reflection for the sake of "educating democracy." Similarly, camp survivors and writers such as Primo Levi and Varlam Shalamov appealed to creative estrangement, curiosity, and imagination as a route of minimal self-liberation rather than to political or religious beliefs. So the paradigm shift involved in the exploration of freedom doesn't follow a predictable arc from atheism into religion or the other way around and can take the shape of either a conversion or an open conversation.

Arendt proposed a distinction between "nonprofessional," or passionate, thinking that searches for meaning based on reason's "concern with the unknowable," and "professional thinking," which searches for truth and is based on the intellect's concern with cognition. The origin of nonprofessional or "passionate" thinking is wonder and astonishment vis-à-vis the cosmos and the world. Professional thinking, on the other hand, has its existential root in unhappiness and "arises out of disintegration of reality and the resulting disunity of man and world, from which springs the need for another world, more harmonious and more meaningful."[36] Passionate thinking does not withdraw from "the world of appearances" into an interior invisible citadel or ivory tower. It bridges both vita activa and vita contemplativa, sometimes crisscrossing back and forth between the two.

A note of caution: the phrase "passionate thinking" could be misconstrued. It is not about sloppy and unrigorous thinking through suffering, passion, or identification. Rather, "passionate" here means yielding to the "nearness" of life, to everyday experience, relying upon one's curiosity and listening to worldliness. Passionate thinking is not thinking through mastery; it is fundamentally about understanding, not control. Understanding means yielding to the uncomfortable and incalculable.

Passionate thinking contains both adventure and humility, and a combination of thinking and thanking (life, being, existence), of reflection and "gratitude for being": "We will remember in Lethe's cold waters/That earth for us has been worth a thousand heavens," wrote Osip Mandelshtam in 1918.[37] Passionate thinking has to be versatile and mobile, since it mediates between philosophical knowledge and everyday experience, between politics and poetics.

The Russian poet Joseph Brodsky, once a prisoner and an underground poet in the Soviet Union, later an immigrant to the United States and a Nobel laureate, writes about his own difficulty in evolving from a "freed man to a free man": "Perhaps our [immigrant writers'] greater value and greater function are to be unwitting embodiments of the disheartening idea that a freed man is not a free man, that liberation is just the means of attaining freedom and is not synonymous with it. However, if we want to play a bigger role, the role of a free man, then we should be capable of accepting—or at least imitating—the manner in which a free man fails. A free man, when he fails, blames nobody."[38] The exiled writer stops being a victim perpetually in search of scapegoats. He can no longer resort to the culture of blame, or even of identity politics, as an ethnographic excuse.[39]

The "freed man" becomes free when he tries to break the chain of violence and coercion, of victim becoming a victimizer or slave becoming a master, when there is something other than revenge that drives him. A free man or woman is someone who has an uncanny double within them and cohabits with these foreigners within like Socrates with his talkative daemon. They have to be able to laugh at themselves but never stop at this moment of laughter. Conscience can be described somewhat dramatically as a neighbor or stranger who makes one feel at home or chez soi: "Conscience is the anticipation of that fellow who awaits you if and when you come home."[40] It is unclear whether the fellow daemon is your host or your guest as long as the home visit is not too unsettling. Such a conception of conscience resembles Diderot's vision of the imitative actor and adventurer at once. Inner plurality might force us to question the conception of the self as a fortress of sovereignty and autonomy, but such plurality is not a threat to individual integrity, quite the contrary: only a person who can change his or her mind can be a free thinker. Inner plurality is not the same as external pluralism; while not mutually exclusive, they are inherently contradictory. This relationship between inner plurality (of individuals and cultures) and external pluralism (encounter with the other, monolingual or polyglot) will be explored throughout this book.

Judging is the most urgent form of passionate thinking, which mediates between universal and particular, theory and practice; it is neither a systematic rationalism nor groundless decisionism but a border zone deliberation between precedent and unprecedented. The process of judging is not an applied art; one uses some existing laws and conventions and discovers others in the process. It requires a double movement—defamiliarizing experience through the practice of thought and defamiliarizing habits of thought in response to changing experience. The space of reflective judgment is like a Möbius strip that moves seamlessly inside out from the known to the unknown, from the familiar to the unpredictable, from the reliable to the improbable. Judgment orients itself from within and without using imagination.

The mysterious category of imagination has been crucial for the philosophical conception of freedom since the early modern era. With the help of imagination we can conceive of what our senses do not perceive, as if connecting the invisible within us to the invisible in the world, discovering the inner cosmos that enables us to confront the cosmos beyond our reach.[41] Imagination bridges the gulf between visible and invisible, or—to go beyond the metaphors of sight—also between the overheard and silenced, the well-thought-through and the unthinkable. It devises all kinds of "transports" through metaphors (which derives from the Greek metaphorein, to transport), similes, anamorphoses, allegories and symbols. Imagination entertains the hypothetical, moves through leaps, lapses, and ellipses and engages in double vision. Only through imagination does one have the freedom to picture otherwise, of thinking "what if" and not only "what is." Imagination navigates the space between emotional and rational, defying any single law but often developing laws of its own. Romantic and modernist artists believed that the capacity to imagine is the human way of imitating the act of creation itself, not merely the created world. Imagination is not entirely free of cultural common places but is not bound by the borders of a single system of coordinates; it is heteronymous and moves from one country to another without visa restrictions. Imagination bridges not only spatial but also temporal discontinuities, connecting "no longer" and "not yet" as well as "could have been" and "might become." It is not by chance that Kant considered imagination to be a "schemata" for cognition, the faculty that underlies different forms of human understanding and relations to the world. Imagination is a capacity to move beyond individual psychology into the common world and includes a capacity for self-distancing. In this sense I have defined imagination as what is in-human in humans, "in-" here being a polysemous prefix that refers to the inherently human capacity of self-distancing, the recognition of inner plurality in oneself and in the other.

But still, what is the relationship between the laws of imagination and the laws of the world? Thinking imaginatively and not proposing an analogy, Arendt suggests that the measure for those disparate, individual, imaginative judgments, the "tertium comparationis," is the care for shared worldliness, the "sensus communis" that is the foundation of cosmopolitan architecture. With this in mind, we might distinguish different tendencies in the act of imagination which are once again not antagonistic. A certain degree of self-distancing or estrangement is imperative in the act of imagining but here we can evoke different kinds of estrangement (which will be explored in chap. 5), estrangement from the world and estrangement for the world. (This is not the opposition between estrangement and belonging, or alienation and its overcoming, but between different horizons and trajectories of self-distancing.) One form of imagination might be associated with the intense experience of inner freedom and introspection and the other with a continuous double movement between the sheer energy of imagination and concern with the common world. We can provisionally call them "introspective" and "worldly" imagination. The potential danger of the introspective imagination based on estrangement from the world is that its laws might acquire a life of their own and occasionally take a form of rational delusion and develop a paranoic causality, which severs the connections between the private and public world. This might produce a dungeon imagination that walls itself against the world like Dostoevsky's Underground Man. The danger of the second kind of imagination, based on estrangement for the world, is that it would become too cautious and moderate and abandon the adventure of individual creativity.

Worldly imagination is theatrical, it works with phantoms of the world, restaging them with many overlapping shadows. It engages phantasmagorias but also, like Diderot's paradoxical actor, changes masks and angles of vision. Such imagination works through peripeteias rather than simply jump-cutting from one ecstasy to another. In this sense of the experience of freedom we are not looking at ineffable, sublime, or mystical illumination, which can produce terror and silence but for the aesthetic or creative practice that is agnostic and adventurous but not ineffable. In other words the most important characteristic of the worldly imagination is its perspectivism, an ability to change the systems of coordinates and reframe ideas, images, and grids for life.

Imagination might not be the panacea for building up the public realm, which also relies on collective solidarities, political rights, and flexible institutions. However, flights of imagination are not as unsafe as they are often made out to be; in fact, they are necessary in order to imagine the world anew, to make life worth living.

Arendt never ceased to repeat that, after the Second World War and the unimaginable scale of inhuman destruction in the twentieth century, we lost the yardsticks with which to measure our common world. The answer, however, is not in restorative nostalgia, the reinvention of national tradition, or the resacralization of the disenchanted modern world. We cannot simply restore the broken vertebrae of common communication, covering up the scars and gaps. So what is to be done? Arendt uses an architectural metaphor: she proposes to "think without a banister." What is the relationship between those two kinds of measure and support— excessively fragile yardsticks and excessively solid banisters? Could the banisters of social convention be the remainders of the lost yardsticks of tradition?

In the extreme circumstances of twentieth-century history, the banister of social common places and familiar clichés can turn into a scandala, an obstacle that leads to a moral scandal and foundation for the "banality of evil." One has to think through these radical breaks in the twentieth-century tradition that alter the way we measure things; otherwise one person's banisters can turn into another's barbed wire.

And yet, thinking without a banister does not mean thinking without foundations, but rather thinking without familiar props. In literal terms, banisters refer to the railing on a staircase. While occasionally skipping along a flight of stairs in a dancing gait, we have to preserve our bearings on the staircase (our home is shared, after all) and balance somehow between flying and falling. The experience of freedom occurs in this liminal space, and it is up to us to prevent the worst disasters from becoming a regular occurrence.

In light of twentieth-century history, the lost yardsticks of a living tradition cannot be replaced by comforting readymade banisters of a neoclassical style. We have to "think without a banister" in order to understand a world that can no longer be measured with familiar yardsticks. The larger-than-life collective inhumanity of twentieth-century mass movements requires a counterpoint: a creative and singular "in-humanity" of human imagination that can push the temporal and spatial limitations of the present moment.[42] Judgment and imagination negotiate the space of "between" and "beyond," collective and individual, precedent and unprecedented. Judging keeps imagination in check, imagination enlarges the possibilities of judgment, and so the process goes, back and forth. "Between" is never completely bounded by familiar yardsticks, but neither is "beyond" synonymous with boundlessness. The "beyond" opens unforeseen horizons; but the moment these horizons are transgressed or transcended, we lose the perspective of wonder. Freedom might be dangerous, but it is always interesting—in the literal sense of the word, inter-esse—suspended in between.

Notes

1   In the view of the political philosopher Michael Sandel there is a particular urgency for this today, when the "fundamentalists rush in where liberals fear to tread." Michael Sandel, *Public Philosophy: Essays on Morality in Politics* (Cambridge, MA: Harvard University Press, 2005), chapter 2 ("Beyond Individualism") and chapter 28 ("Political Liberalism"). This is exactly the space where the quest for the meaning of human life can occur and where tales of freedom have to be told.

2   Michael Kammen, *Spheres of Liberty: Changing Perceptions of Liberty in American Culture* (Madison: University of Wisconsin Press, 1986). Her other attributes are equally contradictory—the scepter, a symbol of self-control, and the cat, a symbol of a lack of restraint. In the eighteenth century, Liberty takes on the eclectic features of classical goddesses, Minerva, Eos, or Artemis, the Virgin Mary (in the French emblem, Marianne), or Mary Magdalene, as well as African and Native American queens. Throughout the book I follow Kammen's view and use the words "freedom" and "liberty" interchangeably in the contemporary context.

3   The first Soviet statue of Liberty built in the early Stalin era was quickly replaced by a more heroic monument to the medieval prince Iuri Dolgoruki, the legendary founder of Moscow. More on the avant-garde statues of liberty in chapter 5.

4   Hannah Arendt, "What Is Freedom?" in *Between Past and Future* (London: Penguin, 1979), 170.

5   Georg Simmel, "The Adventurer," On Individuality and *Social Forms*, ed. Donald Levine (Chicago: University of Chicago Press, 1971), 187-198. Simmel himself fit neither into the German academic establishment of his time nor into contemporary disciplinary systems of thought. Adventure was not only his topic but also an intellectual and existential modus operandi.

6 Simmel, "Adventurer," 193.

7 "It is a foreign body in our existence which is yet somehow connected with the center; the outside, if only by a long and unfamiliar detour, is formally an aspect of the inside." Ibid., 188.

8 Simmel's theory of adventure was at once a critique of the capitalist commodification of daily life but also an alternative to the Marxist conception of the public realm and civil society, and to Weber's and Lukacs's understanding of modernity as disenchantment and transcendental homelessness. In response to the Weberian disenchantment of the modern world enforced by the bureaucratic world of states and corporations, adventure promises reenchantment in a minor existential key.

9 Albert Camus, *The Rebel: An Essay on Man in Revolt* (New York: Vintage International, 1960), 295, emphasis in the original.

10 Arendt, "What Is Freedom?" 143-173.

11 Arendt, The Human Condition (Chicago: University of Chicago Press, 1957), 53. I discuss the differences between the Heideggerian and Arendtian conceptions of the "world" in chapter 4.

12 Ibid.

13 Arendt made the distinction in one of her public conversations: "People who believe that the world is mortal and they themselves are immortal are very dangerous characters because we want the stability and good order of this world." *Hannah Arendt and the Recovery of the Public World*, ed. Melvyn Hill (New York: St. Martin's Press, 1979), 311. See also Kenneth Frampton, "The Status of Man and the Status of His Objects: A Reading of The *Human Condition*," in *Labor, Work, and Architecture: Collected Essays on Architecture and Design* (London: Phaidon, 2002).

14 Aristotle compared philosophical reflection and judging with building. In his view, not all things can be determined by law, which does not mean that they don't use their own measures: "Where a thing is indefinite, the rule by which it is measured is also indefinite as the leaden rule used in Lesbian construction work. Just as this rule is not rigid but shifts with the contour of the stone, so a decree is adapted to a given situation." Aristotle, *Nichomachean Ethics* (Englewood Cliffs: Prentice Hall, 1962), 142. The molding on buildings on the island of Lesbos had a famous "undulating curve" accommodating beautiful irregularities of the stone. Lesbian construction work mastered the art of matching irregularities, and Aristotle reminds us that this was "a kind of equity" and justice, not a deviation from it.

15 Orlando Patterson, *Freedom in the Making of Western Culture, vol. 1* (New York: Basic Books, 1991), 37.

16 On the original conception of "corrupted sacrifice," see Froma I. Zeitlin, "The Motif of the Corrupted Sacrifice in Aeschylus' Oresteia," in *Transactions and Proceedings of the American Philological Association* 96 (1965): 463-508.

17 For the creative interpretation of *leudhe* / liberty, see Jean-Luc Nancy, *The Experience of Freedom* (Stanford: Stanford University Press, 1993). It is common among historians to distinguish between the Roman and later European tradition of liberty, which was a republican ideal, and the Anglo-American notion of freedom, which was perceived as noncoercion and noninterference resulting in a later liberal conception of individual freedom as a space outside politics.

18 Greek *nomos*–law–historically concerned drawing boundaries and respecting agreements, building a manmade space. Law can be seen as a response to violence or as a form of repression and prohibition, but it is also a part of collective existential topography. Similarly, economic and libertarian understandings of freedom also come from specific cultural and historical contexts. Adam Smith, the philosopher of the free market, believed in the connections between the wealth of nations, the invisible hand of the marketplace, and "moral sentiments," as did Friedrich Hayek, whose theory of the free market came into being in reaction to the bureaucratic autocracy of the Austro-Hungarian Empire. The public architecture of common memory is crucial in understanding conceptions and practices of freedom. More specific debates on the nature of the public realm and civil society, on private individuals and citizens, on state and the public sphere, are connected to cultural common places.

19 Cosmopolitanism is frequently reproached from a class position as elitist and as indifferent to one's specific surroundings. This accusation goes back to the Marxist critique of the internationalist aspirations of the bourgeoisie. In other words, as the accusation goes, the cosmopolitan citizen is a citizen of no country. Yet cosmopolitan citizenship is not the same as global corporation: it is not about "off-shoring" affection but rather about grounding it in the common world, in a particular place and language, not in a carefully guarded national territory.

20 For a cultural critic, the "world" might appear as an outmoded universalizing concept that does not take into account cultural pluralism. In fact, thinking worldliness does not exclude thinking about plurality within a common aspiration. On contemporary understanding of cosmopolitanism see Anthony Kwame Appiah, *Cosmopolitanism: Ethics in a World of Strangers* (New York: W. W. Norton, 2006); and Homi K. Bhabha, *A Measure of Dwelling: Reflections on Vernacular Cosmopolitanism* (Cambridge, MA: Harvard University Press, 2008).

21 In recent political theory there has been an attempt to offer a more complex understanding of agonism, redefining it as agonistic pluralism in opposition to a simple antagonism that presents the public realm as a battleground of powers, of friends and foes, of those who are with us and those who are against us. The agonistic understanding of the public realm was developed in the twentieth century by the German political thinker (and after Hitler's rise to power, the president of the Union of National Socialist Jurists) Carl Schmitt and by his recent followers, who propose a more subtle discussion of radical democracy and of differences between agonistic and antagonistic public realm and who apply Schmittian conservative political theology to the political philosophy on the left. See Carl Schmitt, *The Concept of the Political*, trans. George D. Schwab (1927, 1932; Chicago: University of Chicago Press, 1996; expanded ed. with an introduction by Tracy B. Strong, 2006). Among the most interesting recent work in this area that elaborates a more nuanced distinction between agonistic and antagonistic public realm (or treats "pluralistic agonism"), see Ernesto Laclau and Chantal Mouffe, in *The Challenge of Carl Schmitt*, ed. Chantal Mouffe (London: Verso, 1999). See also Chantal Mouffe, *Deliberative Democracy or Agonistic Pluralism*, Political Science Series, 72 (Vienna: Institute for the Advanced Studies, 2000). Bonnie Honig develops the agonistic conception, placing it in dialogue with feminism and multiculturalism in Bonnie Honig, *Democracy and the Foreigner* (Princeton: Princeton University Press, 2001). Proponents of agonistic thinking insist on the perpetuity of conflicts in society and deep divisions that cannot be happily resolved through mere consensus building, rational argument, and institutional practices. Taking conflict seriously, I will contest and deliberate throughout conceptions of the public realm and the space of freedom. Yet such cross-cultural examination also prompts me to reconsider some of the foundations of contemporary agonistic thought. While acutely aware of the need for pluralism, many agonistic thinkers are still deeply indebted to the uncomfortable marriage of the two Carls–Carl Schmitt and Karl Marx-whose respective conceptions of "political theology" and the "leap into the kingdom of freedom" often veered into antiworldliness, *politique du pire*, regarding modern public realm as a masquerade or phantasmagoria, a deceptive spectacle of inauthenticity (chap. 3). I would propose a different geneology of politics and political action oriented towards freedom and not only liberation.Hannah Arendt is an interesting example of an unconventional thinker who is inspired by the Nietzschean conception of agonism and creativity but not at all by Schmittian "political theology." Rather, in her work she advances the understanding of political action as artistic performance and combines some elements of Greek, Roman, and Enlightenment thought together with modern philosophy and aesthetics. See Dana R. Villa, *Arendt and Heidegger: The Fate of the Political* (Princeton: Princeton University Press, 1996); and Seyla Benhabib, *The Reluctant Modernism of Hannah Arendt* (Landham, MD: Row-man & Littlefield, 2003). I focus on the intertwining of the political and the aesthetic in Arendt's thought in chapters 4-6. I try to follow an alternative, non-Schmittian geneology of understanding the public realm, worldliness, and violence (chaps. 1, 3, and 6).

22 Johan H. Huizinga, *Homo Ludens: A Study of the Play-Element in Culture* (Boston: Beacon Press, 1955), 3; and Friedrich Schiller, *On the*

Aesthetic Education of Man, trans. Reginald Snell (New York: Frederick Ungar, 1965).

23 Yet the political and the aesthetic are never harmoniously reconciled. While the "science" of aesthetics was based on *"sensus communis,"* a shared human ability to self-distance and go beyond individual psyche into the realm of imagination, aesthetic and democratic understandings of the common sense and common good, of the end of life and freedom, have always been accompanied by conflict (chaps. 2, 6).

24 Walter Benjamin, "Short Shadows," in *Selected Writings, Volume 2 (1927-1934),* trans. Rodney Livingston, ed. Michael W. Jennings, Howard Eiland, and Gary Smith (Cambridge, MA: Harvard University Press, 1999).

25 Hannah Arendt, *Men in Dark Times* (New York: Harcourt Brace Hovanovich, 1968), preface, ix-x, and "Karl Jaspers: Laudatio," 80.

26 Thomas Hobbes, *Leviathan* (London: Harmondsworth, 1980), 3. [Boym's text originally contained an image of Hobbe's frontispiece at this point. -C. Vatulescu]

27 One of the most famous examples of anamorphism is Hans Holbein's painting of the ambassadors where a skull becomes visible from a certain perspective creating a counterpoint, a memento mori to the celebration of earthly riches.

28 Howard Caygill, *The Art of Judgment* (London: Basic Blackwell, 1989), 20-21. Hobbes was close to the Mersenne circle, which was preoccupied with physical and metaphysical implications of optics, perspective, and illusion making. Catoptics focused on what appeared to be distortions of perspective but were in fact exploring creative possibilities of double vision. This was an early example of phenomenological exploration of "interactive optics."

29 Optics for Hobbes is more important than imagination, which he first defines as "decayed sense" because it engages fancy and reason. In his later work Hobbes celebrates poetry and writes an autobiographical poem to tell the story of his life.

30 Denis Diderot, "Paradox of an Actor," *Selected Writings on Art and Literature,* trans. and with an intro. and notes by Geoffrey Bremner (London: Penguin Books, 1994). This is similar to Jonathan Lear's conception of irony. See Jonathan Lear, *Therapeutic Action: An Earnest Plea for Irony* (Other Press, 2003).

31 Ibid.

32 It is a kind of reverse mimesis: life is like a theater, a gentle epiphany of a "natural actor" who is on the verge of recognizing his own artifice. Diderot offers us a paradoxical and chiasmic encounter: while the man of estrangement and the self-possessed actor becomes overcome with sensibility, or when a "natural man" begins to praise nature for being picturesque and looking like a beautiful landscape. The ironic limits of

the dialogue are those moments of "excess" when opposites meet but only through the twisted parabolic peripeteia, creating complex optics and not breaking the glass in a violent fashion. Diderot's dialogues are not merely pedagogical; they offer amusing slices of prerevolutionary life. At one moment Diderot's paradoxicalists-critics decide to go to the theater and become spectators (instead of talkers) but there are no seats left in the theater, so they remain in the theater of life. They talk to each other, talk with themselves, daydream, keep silence, indulge in moments of empathy and feeling and then disavow emotions with humor. Echoing Locke and Hobbes, Diderot makes a direct analogy between the society and the theater: "It is the same with a play as with a well-ordered society, where everyone sacrifices some of his original rights for the good of the whole. Who will best appreciate the extent of this sacrifice? Will it be the enthusiast, the fanatic? Indeed not. In society, it will be the just man, in the theater, the actor who has a cool head." Diderot, "Paradox of an Actor," 114. See Eyal Peretz, "Identification with the Phantom"; book in progress.

33 Tom Gunning, "Illusions Past and Future: The Phantasmagoria and Its Specters," http://www.MediaArtHistory.org, a text for the First International Conference on the Histories of Art, Science and Technology, 2004.

34 Karl Marx, "The Eighteenth Brumaire of Louis Bonaparte" (1852), in Karl Marx and Frederick Engels, *Collected Works,* vol. 11 (New York: International Publishers, 1978), 99-197.

35 Theodor Adorno to Walter Benjamin, letter dated November 10,1938, in Walter Benjamin, *Selected Writings* (Cambridge, MA: Harvard University Press, 1997), 4: 100-101.

36 Hannah Arendt, *The Life of the* Mind, vol. 1, Thinking (New York and London: Harcourt Brace Jovanovich, 1977), 153. "Professional thinkers, whether philosophers or scientists, have not been pleased with freedom and its ineluctable randomness." See the chapter "The Abyss of Freedom and the *novus ordo seclorum,*" in *The Life of the Mind,* vol. 2, *Willing,* ed. Mary McCarthy (New York: Harcourt Brace Jovanovich, 1978), and "Willing," 2: 198-199. These concepts are developed throughout Arendt's work; see "Thinking," 1: 5-7.

37 Quoted by Arendt, *Life of the Mind,* 1: 185.

38 Joseph Brodsky, "On the Condition We Call Exile," in On Grief *and Reason: Essays* (New York: Farrar, Straus and Giroux, 1995), 34.

39 Unbeknownst to him, in his tale of transformation of a "freed man" into a "free man," Brodsky recounts the metamorphosis of Greek eleutheria.

40 Hannah Arendt, *Lectures on Kant's Political Philosophy,* ed. Ronald Beiner (Chicago: University of Chicago Press, 1982), 79-85. For a discussion of Arendt's theory of judgment, see Ronald Beiner, "Hannah Arendt on Judgment: Interpretative Essay," in *Lectures on Kant's Political Philosophy* (Chicago: University of Chicago Press, 1982), 89-156. For a reference to the "inhuman," see Hannah Arendt, "On Humanity in Dark Times:

Thoughts about Lessing," in *Men in Dark Times* (New York: Harcourt Brace Jovanovich, 1968), 24. Arendt's reading of Kant does not focus on moral imagination and categorical imperative but rather on his *Critique of Judgment* and on the connection between practical and theoretical reason in Kant. Her theory of freedom and judging is linked to Kant's work on the reflective and aesthetic judgment as developed in this volume.

41   Arendt discusses those issues in *The Life of the Mind*, vol. 1, *Thinking*, 98-109. In philosophy the theory of imagination plays an important role in the philosophy of Hume, Kant, Schiller and Shelling and then in the Romantic poetics of Coleridge, Wordsworth and Shelley. See Mary Warnock, Imagination (Berkeley and Los Angeles: University of California Press, 1976). I don't follow strictly the distinction between imagination and fancy or between primary and secondary imagination.

42   For a discussion of the banister, see an exchange between Hannah Arendt and Hans Jonas in Melvyn Hill, ed., *Hannah Arendt and the Recovery of the Public World* (New York: St. Martin's Press, 1979), 311-315; and Arendt, "Basic Moral Propositions," in *Lectures 1966*, University of Chicago, Hannah Arendt's Papers, the Manuscript Division, Library of Congress, Washington, DC, container 46, p. 024608. Kant gave at once the most lucid and the most labyrinthine definition of reflective judgment, one that is crucial for Arendt's revisionary theory: "Judgment orients itself according to something both within and without it, something which is neither nature nor freedom, in which the theoretical and practical are bound together in a way that is common but unfamiliar."

PART FIVE

THE OFF-MODERN
(2010–17)

The term Off-Modern occurs already in *The Future of Nostalgia* (pps. xvi–xvii, 30–31) but it matures into an independent project and a stand-alone interpretative method during and after Boym's work on *Another Freedom*. In 2008 the short *Architecture of the Off-Modern* was published with Princeton University Press and in 2016 *The Off-Modern* was posthumously published with Bloomsbury. In addition to selections from these two books, this last section of *The Reader* includes an article on an off-modern friendship, selections from a lecture about off-modern Jews and a transcript of a lecture-performance tour presenting the imagined, or off-modern history of a building that no longer exists. These last three are vivid examples of the way Boym was using "off-modern" as an operative interpretative tool, applicable to all cultural, artistic, and historic phenomena.

Set against "post," "neo," and "trans," "off" is defined as "a detour into the unexplored potentials of the modern project. It recovers unforeseen pasts and ventures into the side alleys of modern history to the margins of error of major philosophical, economic and technological narratives of modernization and progress." Boym examines these potentialities and errors, avenues forsaken but not foreclosed, as recovery sites that can begin to redeem the contemporary failures of modernity and enlightenment. Boym embraces both projects (modernity and enlightenment) with vigor, but her embrace is not of their evident successes but of their erroneous detours.

Such, for example, is the guided tour of the "residence" of Professor William Gilson Farlow, a cryptogamic botanist whose house on Quincy

Street in Cambridge Boym imagines to have survived the 1960 demolition which ushered Corbusier's Carpenter Center to that same lot. Boym thanks Harvard's "forward looking deans" who had declined Corbusier's bid so as to preserve a home on campus for cryptogamic experiments in Farlowe's spirit. Such experiments extract and reproduce, in laboratory conditions, the thoughts and ideas of a select number of Harvard's faculty, thus saving the university money and expenses. With deep humor Boym provides a powerful critique of Corbusier's cold, inappropriate mid-century modernist building. But in the very same sweep she tells an alternative story that renders the scientific option no better. Instead, in telling a history of "what if," Boym teaches us to embrace the beauty and potentiality of what is. Her last project consists of play with alternative histories—adventurous detours into obscure paths that, with the right gaze, disclose joyful meaning in the world.

Tamar Abramov

17 THE OFF-MODERN

History Out of Sync

In the twenty-first century, modernity is our antiquity. We live with its ruins, which we incorporate into our present. Unlike the thinkers of the last fin-de-siècle, we neither mourn nor celebrate the end of history or the end of art. We have to chart a new road between unending development and nostalgia, find an alternative logic for the contradictions of contemporary culture. Instead of fast-changing prepositions—"post," "anti," "neo," "trans," and "sub"—that suggest an implacable movement forward, against, or beyond, I propose to go off: "off" as in "off the path," or way off, off-Broadway, off-brand, off the wall, and occasionally off-color. "Off-modern" is a detour into the unexplored potentials of the modern project. It recovers unforeseen pasts and ventures into the side alleys of modern history, at the margins of error of major philosophical, economic, and technological narratives of modernization and progress. It opens into the modernity of "what if," and not only postindustrial modernization as it was.

The preposition "off" is a product of a linguistic error, popular etymology and fuzzy logic. It developed from the preposition "of," signifying belonging as in "being a part of," with the addition of an extra "f," an emphatic marker of distancing. The "off" in "off-modern" designates both the belonging to the critical project of modernity and its edgy excess. "Off" suggests a dimension of time and human action that is unusual or potentially off-putting. Through a humorous onomatopoeic exaggeration it describes something too spontaneous (off-the-cuff, off-handed, off the record) or too edgy (off the wall), verging on the obscene (off-color) or not in sync with the pace (offbeat). Sometimes "off" is about the embarrassment of life caught unawares. It is provisional, extemporaneous, and humane. Most importantly, "off" isn't a marker of margins but a delimitation of a broad space for a new choreography of future possibilities. Off-modern isn't antimodern; sometimes it is closer to the critical and experimental spirit of modernity than it is to contemporary neotraditionalism or postmodern simulations.

The off-modern isn't a lost "ism" from the ruined archive of the avant-garde, but a contemporary worldview and a form of historic sensibility that allows us to recapture eccentric aspects of earlier modernities, to "brush history against the grain," to use Walter Benjamin's expression. The off-modern project is still off-brand; it is a performance-in-progress, at once con-temporary and off-beat vis-à-vis the present moment.

After the Russian revolutions of 1917, theorist and writer Victor Shklovsky proposed to explore the lateral move in cultural history that can rescue a broader range of politics and arts. Modern artistic practice in this case isn't conceived as an autonomous activity (contrary to a common misunderstanding); it is a practice of estrangement and engagement; estrangement *for* the world and not *from* the world. The full implications of this radical world wonder haven't yet been fully explored, because this estrangement for the world doesn't follow systematic logic, and it doesn't fit into a familiar narrative of critical theory that was in part shaped by a mistranslation of Russian and East European formalists and structuralists. Shklovsky's favorite figure for such aesthetic and political practice was the knight in the game of chess. The knight moves forward sideways and traces "the tortured road of the brave," not the master-slave dialectics of "dutiful pawns and kings."[1] Oblique, diagonal, and zigzag moves reveal the play of human freedom vis-à-vis political teleologies and ideologies that follow the march of revolutionary progress, development, or the invisible hand of the market.

Like his contemporaries, Victor Shklovsky was fascinated by modernist science, from Einstein's theory of relativity, to the quantum and wave theories of light and Nikolai Lobachevsky's conception of a non-Euclidian geometry that doesn't accept the central axiom that parallel lines cannot meet. In the words of Vladimir Nabokov: "if the parallel lines do not meet, it is not because meet they cannot, but because they have other things to do."[2] In my off-modern interpretation, Shklovsky's zigzag is a path between two parallel lines, at once jagged and regular. It isn't a simple one-dimensional figure but an opening of an alternative intellectual tradition that brings together physics and poetics – from the ancient swerve of the Epicurean philosophers to the squiggle of the eccentric Enlightenment, from baroque anamorphoses to the Möbius strip, and from there to Deleuze's folds and veins in marble. The knight's move allows for a coexistence of different models of the universe side by side, not as a mere digital database or a salad bar of philosophical dressings but as a complex counterpointed composition that invites rigorous perspectivism and creative action.

The off-modern doesn't suggest a continuous history from antiquity to modernity to postmodernity. Instead it confronts the breaks in tradition, the loss of common yardsticks and disorientations that occur in almost every generation. The off-modern acknowledges the syncope and the off-beat movements of history that were written out from the dominant versions edited by the victors, who cared little about the dignity of the defeated. Off-modern reflection doesn't merely try to color the blank spots of history green or red, thus curing longing with belonging. Rather, it veers off the beaten track of dominant constructions of history, proceeding laterally, not literally, to discover missed opportunities and roads not taken.

An off-modern line of thinking takes us away from post-modernism and its discontents towards a broader reconsideration of modernities in the plural and over a long duration of time, from the early modern of the seventeenth century to the present. It is part of the twenty-first century cultural reflection on the "unfinished" project of modernity, "uneven" modernizations and "divergent" modernisms.[3] The off-modern is neither a new spatial turn to the margins or semi-peripheries of the West, nor a return to hip retro media. It tries to rethink the porous nature of historical time, making modernities out-of-sync less eccentric and more symptomatic for a twenty-first century experience.

Most importantly, the off-modern approach breaks away from the opposition between an artist and a master-theorist who maps and typologizes the modern and all its prefixes and suffixes. This is a contemporary exercise in aesthetic knowledge that crisscrosses (but never abolishes) the boundaries between artistic and critical practice; it follows the zigzag movements of an alternative cultural development explored by artists and writers themselves, often overlooked by theorists because it exceeds a specific plot of the history of the modern. The off-modern approach zooms in on the transitional periods of modern and contemporary history, moves off-center and foregrounds the heretics and misfits within well-known artistic and cultural movements. It unearths an alternative genealogy of the critical apparatus of modernity, harking back to Shklovsky's and Hannah Arendt's "estrangement for the world" that I understand as an aesthetic, existential, and political practice of passionate thinking and freedom, which strives neither for utopia nor for artistic autonomy, but for the transformation of this world.

The off-modern approach defies the "distant reading" and remote-controlled historiographic mappings of the modern and contemporary period; instead it engages in the embarrassment of theory and in a double movement between perspectivist estrangement and almost tactile nearness to artistic making. In short, the off-modern artist and theorist share an unconventional bond of *diasporic intimacy* familiar to contemporary immigrants.

Unlike the "altermodern," the term proposed by the writer and curator Nicolas Bourriaud in 2009, the off-modern doesn't define itself merely as a new modernity "reconfigured to an age of globalization, " "a new universalism" based on translations, subtitles and generalized naming.[4] The off-moderns aren't "early adapters" to the existing gadgets of posthistorical globalization or internet technology; they search for experimental platforms that would connect the world's public squares with the digital humanities of the future, for which no gadgets have yet been invented. Instead of the subtitled and translated languages of a new universalism, off-moderns focus on accents and affects, on material singularities and alternative solidarities between cultures that often circumscribe the center, creating a broad margin for peripheral scenographies. Examples can be found in the longstanding connections between Latin American, East European and South Asian modernities that didn't always go via Paris, London, or Berlin where metadiscourse to end all metadiscourses is perpetually enunciated, as if anew.

We will follow here some key aspects of the off-modern project, not "power points" but rather tangents with many possible bifurcations:

1 An alternative genealogy and understanding of the modern project, including art, theory and history.

2 Eccentric geographies, alternative solidarities and reemergence of cross-cultural public space.

3 Politics and arts of dissent are based on pluralities within cultures and identities, that is, do not belong in external pluralism or multiculturalism. This brings forth elective affinities between unlikely international bedfellows, and not their anxieties of influence and memories of domination.

4 Prospective nostalgia and critical urbanism that engages architectural and social concerns. A new scenography of

"modernization through preservation" where ruins cohabit with construction sites.

5   Alternative *new media* shaped by estranging artistic techniques and not only by new gadgets. Organization of humanistic platforms for knowledge and experience. Neither hyper- nor cyber- but another prefix that hasn't been invented yet.

6   Engagement with "human error" and human creativity, with artful and not just artificial intelligence. Reconsideration of affects, and productive embarrassment of theory and technology.

7   Not the end of criticism but passionate thinking, however belated and outmoded.

Cultural Exaptation

The off-modern perspective invites us to rethink the opposition between development and preservation, and proposes a non-linear conception of cultural evolution through trial and error.[5] The off-modern artist finds an interesting comrade-in-arms in contemporary science, in particular in Stephen J. Gould's subversive theory of exaptation that unsettles evolutionary biologists and proponents of intelligent design, technovisionaries and postmodernists. Exaptation can be seen as a rescue of the eccentric and unforeseen in natural history, a theory that could only have been developed by an imaginative scientist who sometimes thinks like an artist.[6]

Exaptation is described in biology as an example of "lateral adaptation," which consists in cooptation of a feature from some other origin. It happens when a particular trait evolves because it served one particular function, but subsequently may have come to serve another. A good example from biology would be bird feathers and wings that initially were used for temperature regulation, but later were adapted for flight. Exaptations are useful structures by virtue of their having been coopted – that is the *ex-apt* part of the term: they are apt for what they are for other reasons than their original use; they weren't built by natural selection for their current role. "Just because something arises as a side consequence does not condemn it to a secondary status," writes Stephen J. Gould. Exaptation isn't the opposite of adaptation; neither is it merely an accident, a result of human error or lack of scientific data that would in the end support the concept of evolutionary adaptation. (In fact, the word "evolution" itself is a product of linguistic exaptation and errors of transmission. Originally it meant the unfolding of a manuscript, an opening up of potentialities; the term wasn't originally favored by Darwin, who only used it a few times at the end of his work, and was adopted by his followers.) Exaptation questions the very process of assigning meaning and function in hindsight, the process of assigning the prefix "post" and thus containing a complex phenomenon within the grid of familiar interpretation.

Exaptation has mostly been studied in biological and technological evolutions. Bizarre as it may sound, our homey microwave ovens started their adventurous life as radar magnetrons. Edison's phonograph, which evolved into a cinematic apparatus, was born as a recording device for dictation; the Internet was introduced as a military communication exchange network. Of course, technological evolution moves much faster than biological evolution does, leaving us many discarded projects and possibilities. A bird's flight and the unpredictable beauty of a butterfly still amaze us, while Edison's phonograph and Technicolor film are now part of the exhibit at the museum of "Jurassic technologies" of the twentieth century. (Hopefully the art of cinema isn't going to end up on the same museum shelf with the toaster ovens).

The (as yet unwritten) history of invention and creativity abounds in unfulfilled projects of the *future antérieur*. The artistic equivalent of birds' wings could be found in the silk wings of Vladimir Tatlin's flying vehicle Letatlin, one of the most famous "failed" projects. Letatlin (in Russian, a play on the verb "letat" – to fly – and Le-Tatlin, the artist's pseudo-French signature), a cross between the mythical firebird and the prototype of Sputnik with silk wings, was a technical failure: it didn't fly, not in a literal sense at least, but it enabled many flights of dissident imagination. Its dysfunctional wings became phantom limbs of experimental architecture, art and technology in the second half of the twentieth century.

Perhaps the best things in life that money can't buy—like happiness, love, aesthetic appreciation and other such useless expenditures—are examples of exaptation. The off-modern foregrounds exaptation and deliberately places the provisional and prospective at the radius for new exploration. Sometimes exaptation can offer an artistic perspective on evolutionary biology that unsettles scientific determinism, yet also doesn't skew empirical evidence. Off-modern thinkers and artists recover many experimental paradigms in modernist science that might have been abandoned by the scientists themselves. Vladimir Nabokov found non-utilitarian delights in his study of butterflies, but also made a scientific conjecture about the patterns of butterfly migrations around the world that seemed, from an evolutionary or functionalist perspective, counterintuitive and improbable but was proven correct through a series of experiments fifty years later.

The strategy of off-modern exaptation is particularly apt at bringing together the *techne* of art and science and can thus produce an alternative form of new media. As Shklovsky explained in "The Knight's Move" in the fourth dimension of art, alternative geometrical and physical parameters are made probable and art is where provisionality itself takes form. The off-modern has the quality of a conjecture that doesn't distort the facts but explores their echoes, residues, implications and shadows that put the world off-kilter through creative erring.

Human Error

To err is human, says the Roman proverb, both excusing and celebrating human imperfection. Today "human error" has become a technical term designating the trace of an irrepressible humanity that even the most advanced machine or bureaucratic apparatus cannot control. Among a few remaining human traits that technology cannot duplicate are a sense of humor that forever resists "disambiguation," a sudden gasp of affect, a smile, a whim, a swerve. Human "ambiguation" will soon become a retronym like "snail mail."

Creative minds know how slight can be the line between flying and falling, between failure and co-creation. If only we always knew how to transform human error into a cognitive operation and a new form of passionate thinking! The practice of erring traces the jagged edges of evolution, making visible the act of change and its nonlinear outlines. It exposes the *pentimenti*, provisional compositional exercises, the palimpsests of forgotten knowledge and practice. Erring allows us to touch—ever so tactfully—the exposed nerves of cultural and human potentiality, the maps of possible, if often improbable, developments.

Playing with human error and improbable chance has been the realm of inventors and tricksters who cheated at the border-crossings of knowledge and culture. Of course, not all accidents of fate and aftereffects of human blindness are recuperable. One can distinguish between "dumb luck" – the luck of a gambler who risks his riches at the first opportunity, changing nothing in his worldview or the world around him – and a kind of "smart luck" that can be innovative and transformative. In the latter case, the receptivity to chancy error can lead to a kind of imperfect perfect moment, *kairos*, "an opening in the weaving of cloth, the weaving of time, the weaving of fate."[7] It requires a particular form of attentiveness or fine-tuning to the porosity in the cosmic cloth that can offer adventurous opportunities as well as awareness of the paradoxes and aporias of human existence.

Many scientific and artistic discoveries came about through this particular attuning to failures and errors. French chemist and microbiologist Louis Pasteur made a major contribution to the invention of vaccines while following what appeared at first as a botched experiment with chicken cholera. What Pasteur had to do is to grasp the scope of chance discovery. "Chance favors a prepared mind," concluded the scientist. The "prepared mind" in this case is an open mind that can reframe a failure into an invention. Similarly, astronomer James Christy, who spent years studying the orbit of Pluto, once stumbled upon an archive of images in the Naval Observatory that were ready to be discarded. The photographs had the following labels: "Pluto Image. Elongated. Plate no good. Reject." It took an attentive mind to realize that what appeared as a photographic error (the uncommon elongation) was no accident. Pluto had a moon[8].

Many artists were similarly "moonstruck" in their quest for chance encounters, not all of them successful. Ultimately, "smart luck" isn't mere luck; it might not be even about chaos and cosmos but also an insight into the sporadic nature of reality made up of chaotic dissolutions and possibilities, fluctuating together with us. In his study of tricksters and the relationship between art, mischief and myth, anthropologist Lewis Hyde writes: "a chance event is a little bit of the world as it is—a world always larger and more complicated than our cosmologies—and that smart luck is a kind of responsive intelligence invoked by whatever happens."[9] So, human errors aren't mere serendipities, examples of statistical randomness or a parapsychology of everyday life. Erring can trace unexpected connections between different forms of knowledge, art and technology, beyond the prescribed interactivities of specific technological media; erring can also make flexible cognitive maps based on aesthetic knowledge and ahead of software calculations. This practice is not to be confused with multitasking, which new neurological research shows can actually dull the brain, substituting surfing for thinking and more or less expensive gadgets for a paucity of ideas. Making lateral connections requires concentration, creative distraction, gadgetless daydreaming, and a longer duration of time than multitasking allows. Multitasking with clouds is, of course, an exception to the rule.

It isn't always possible to make exaptation into a deliberate practice, but at the very least one shouldn't miss a chance to engage in minor dissent, defying the framed world of the technological and bureaucratic apparatus. If we adapt too well —to the market, to the e-world, to the art world, to political regimes, to the particular institutions we inhabit— we might evolve to the point that the adventure of human freedom would become obsolete. The off-modern doesn't rush to imagine the apocalyptic posthuman future that captures the imagination of frustrated television producers. Artistic exaptation is a painstaking practice of human freedom.

Recently Mexican artist Gabriel Orozco made an off-modern chess game where the only figures on the board were knights. In this uncanny scenario the knight's move turns into the only rule of the game. As a static sculptural work poised in a perfect balance of provisionality and order, this can be considered the off-modern utopia *par excellence*. But in the unlikely case that these knight's moves in search of exaptations become institutional practices, the off-modern swerve would cease to exist.

Edgy Geography

The off-modern perspective affects our understanding of our historical and geographic relationships, as well as our political and even emotional ones, by revealing elective affinities and alternative solidarities through time and space. Off-modern art has both a temporal and a spatial dimension: some projects from different corners of the globe can appear belated or peripheral to the familiar centers of modern/postmodern culture. The off-modern has been embraced by international artists and architects from India to Argentina, from Hungary to Venezuela, from Turkey to Lithuania, from Canada to Albania. To give a few examples: the RAQs Collective from New Delhi, with their projects of porous time; Argentinian Guillermo Kuitca with his portable homes, mapped mattresses, and his reinvention of the avant-garde; the Hungarian documentary filmmaker Peter Forgacs and his documentary histories of "what if," made with the help of home movies; Albanian artist Anri Sala and his "out-of-sync" videos; New York artist Rebecca Quaytman and her "lateral moves" towards the forgotten tradition of the East European avant-garde; South African artist William Kentridge and his re-animation of an atonal Soviet opera; and experimental public performances using mimes and commedia dell'arte to enforce urban citizenship and the performance of law in Bogotá, Colombia, organized by the former mayor of the city, the mathematician, philosopher and unconventional theater director Antanas Mockus.

The seemingly peripheral situation of these artists, architects, and politicians reveals the eccentricity of the center; asynchronicity questions the progress of cultural trends and artistic movements that are supposed to succeed one another like well-behaved citizens in the express checkout line. The off-modern doesn't focus on the external pluralism and values of states, with their political PR and imperial ambitions, but on internal pluralities within cultures, tracing elective affinities, solidarities of dissent, and diasporic intimacies across national borders.

We might be living on the edge of an era when the accepted cultural myths of late capitalism and of technological or digital progress no longer work for us. We are right on the cusp of a paradigm shift, and to anticipate it we have to expand our field of vision. The logic of edginess is opposed to that of the seamless appropriation of popular culture, or the synchronicity of computer memory. This is a logic that exposes wounds, cuts, scars, ruins, the afterimage of touch. The edginess resists incorporation and doesn't allow for a romance of convenience. Clarification: the off-moderns are edgy, not marginal. They don't wallow in the self-pity or resentment that comes with marginalization, even when some of this is justified.

So the off-modern edge isn't a fault line, but a space. Thoreau once wrote that one has to have "broad margins" to one's life. The off-modern edges aren't sites of marginality but those broad margins where one could try to live deliberately, against all odds, in the age of shrinking space and resources and forever accelerating rhythms.

To be edgy, then, could also mean avoiding the logic of the cutting edge, even if the temptation is great. If you are just off the cutting edge of the butcher's knife, you'll end up being devoured before you are examined. The logic of the cutting edge makes one part of the bloody action movie so common in contemporary popular culture, where tears and affects are only computer generated. Edginess takes more time. Only at the risk of being outmoded could one stay con-temporary.

Black Mirrors

What if we use digital devices to multitask with clouds transforming their pixelated interfaces into reflective surfaces and black mirrors? The black mirror—an ancient gadget used by artists, magicians, and scientists from Mexico to India—offers an insight into another history of "technê" that connected art, science and magic, producing an enchanted technology of wonder. When a digital surface becomes a "black mirror," it reflects upon clashing forms of modern and premodern experience that coexist in contemporary culture. New "black mirrors" engage with pictorial and photographic genres of the past to document a confrontation of modern industrial ruins and virtual utopias.

The black mirror was an object of cross-cultural fascination, trade, conquest, and sometimes misappropriation. The Aztecs used black mirrors made of obsidian or volcanic glass in divination and healing practices. If a child was suffering from "soul loss," for example, the healer would look at the reflection of the child's image in a mirror and examine his shadows. After the discovery of the "new world," Europeans appropriated the obsidian mirror for anatomic theaters and occult practices, dissecting bodies and bringing ghosts back to life. Since the Renaissance, European painters and architects— including Leonardo da Vinci and Claude Lorraine—have used their own black mirrors to focus on composition and perspective in the landscape and to take a respite from color. Sometimes the artists have stared into the black mirror to take a break—to catch a breath, so to say—in order to purify the gaze from the excess of worldly information. The black mirror allowed them to suspend and renew vision.

In the nineteenth century black mirrors were rescued from oblivion and found their place in the new popular culture of the picturesque. English travelers carried miniature black-mirror-like opera glasses, framing and fetishizing fragments of landscape. Absorbed by the possibility of capturing the beauties of the world in the palm of their hand, voyeurs of the picturesque left the world behind. American doctor and spiritualist Pascal Beverly Randolph went beyond the picturesque. Believing in the mystical vitality of the black mirror, he supposedly used opium and his own and his wife's (and mistress's) "sexual fluids" – to use chaste Victorian language – to polish its surface.

At the turn of the twentieth century modern artists from Manet to Matisse resorted to the black mirror, not to reflect an image but to reflect upon sensation itself, on the ups and downs of euphoria and melancholia, or the syncopations of modern creativity. So, although the black mirror dims colors, it also sharpens perspective, not framing realistic illusions but estranging perception itself. The black mirror offers a different kind of mimesis and an uncanny and anti-narcissistic form of self-reflection, in which we spy on our own phantoms in the dim internal *film noir*.

I took a train journey through the American industrial landscape, multitasking with clouds on my digital screens. I used the digital surface as a "black mirror" to reflect nature and contemporary anxieties on the ground and in the air. The surface of my broken PowerBook looked like a Milky Way spotted with forgotten stars.

This project is *techno-erotic*—more erratic than erotic, engaged in errand and detour in order to question the new techno-evangelism. Surrounded by garrulous screens, we barely get a quiet moment for contemplation. The dim realm of personal chiaroscuro has given way to the pixelated brightness of a homepage, bombarded by hits and unembarrassed by total exposure. This new form of overexposed visuality hasn't been properly documented. When captured on camera, it appears ambivalent, confusing and barely readable.

I want to catch the digital gadgets unawares, confront them with each other with the alchemy of cross-purpose uses, to counterpoint different forms of modern and premodern experience, technological, existential and artistic.

Once upon a time, trains ran on time. These days they rarely do, but now we have a great opportunity to text about it. My train runs through ruins and construction sites of industrial modernity, factories, cemeteries of deceased cars and dismembered bicycles, service buildings that serve no purpose anymore with the palimpsest of graffiti on their walls. This landscape is the crisis of the picturesque.

With the Blackberry off, I get a respite from colorful virtual life. Distracted from "friending" or doing work, I stay in a state of contemplative slumber. I know that nostalgia isn't an answer to the speeded-up present, that time is irreversible and shadows will never conspire in the same way again. No longer a seductive digital fruit, my Blackberry reveals its second life as a melancholic black mirror that puts into sharp focus the *decaying non-virtual* world that is passing us by.

On *Off*

Off: a detour.

Off --the tip of your tongue tenses without touching anything. You're just about to bite your lower lip and suppress idle talk. But then reluctantly you let the sound go through. "Off" comes out almost as a sigh of relief.

Off is a product of a linguistic swerve, a mysterious evolution from the preposition of belonging to the signpost of mischievous eccentricity. It reminds us of the ancient theories of swerving, of atomic indeterminacy and enigmas of freedom.

"Off" is colloquial and particular, not abstract and equalizing the way "post" was. It is virtually untranslatable. Let each language find its own version of being "off" and being modern at the same time.

To a non-native English speaker "off" sounds like child's talk, somewhere between game and language: if you didn't know what "off" meant you could almost guess it. Sometimes "there is more mouth than meaning there" (so Nabokov characterized the kiss of one of his refugee-lovers). In Nano Moretti's film *Caro Diario*, the American beauty played by Jennifer Beals tries to find a synonym for this elusive preposition, and fails charmingly. When American immigrants talk among themselves in their native language (the pidgin mother tongue that through years of exile becomes a hyphenated American) "off" is often one word they use in English: "Sabes, el tipo es un poco 'off'"; "nu ona nemnogo 'off'." I hear in this the traces of foreign accents – of ouch, ouff, bo, oi, ay. In short, off is odd.

Being off is not to be *out* or *anti*. You're never completely off the hook. Being off is a form of virtuosity. You have to exercise a special attentiveness, the vigilance of sense, the virtuality of imagination and engagement in worldly practice, which is not to be confused with the virtual interfacing in which the main physical relationship is between you and the tender buttons of your PowerBook.

A history of words composed with "off" suggests a parallel modern history[10]. "Off-color" referred first to gems, and more specifically, to the industrial exploitation of the distant corners of the world and a democratization of jewelry – at a high price. Off-color gems were the cheaper ones. By analogy, if the high modernist museum was a gem of a white cube, the off-modern museum has to be off-white. It is a different space, more off-beat, with dimensions of spontaneity and excesses that do not fit the narrative of display. "Off" introduces a moment of chance;

it is both distancing and de-familiarizing, but also casts a short shadow next to the outlines of things. The off-modern space is where off-putting things are at home.

Off plays optical tricks with nearness and distance, belonging and straying off. Off doesn't enter into a clear binary opposition with anything, except in expressions like "lights on" and "lights off," meaning "out." But in our case, being off is very different from being out; it doesn't open into a dark space but into the multifarious world of luminous shadows and glimpses of the sun – neither blinding total illumination nor charismatic darkness, but a chiaroscuro, a shadow play. Off is not transcendental or transgressive, but mysterious and improbable.

The off-modern isn't ashamed of old-fashioned practices of thinking. Off-modern thinking combines logos and pathos, memory and imagination, expanding the regimes of the sensible wherever *techne*, muse, and gut guide us. Off-modern affects include different forms of reflective longing, balancing acts of tact and touch and of embarrassment – an outmoded form of self-consciousness, a paradoxical awareness of loss of control that deals with mishaps and challenges boundaries of body and space, of self and world.

At the same time, *off* is closer to the trans-sensical dimension of language as well as the realm of poetic puns and wordplay. We are warned that wordplay is bad for Internet searches; it requires constant disambiguation. Wordplay disorients the cookies installed in your hardware that collect information about you and send it to advertisers for niche marketing. So, off-moderns, beware, everything off the market price will be advertised to you. But you have the option to pursue the arts of human ambivalence, take a break off-grid and drift between the lines.

Notes

1 Victor Shklovsky, *The Knight's Move* (Dalkey Archive Press, 2007) and Victor Shklovsky, "Art as Technique," *Four Formalist Essays*, ed. and trans. Lee T. Lemon and Marion J. Reis (Lincoln: University of Nebraska Press: 1965), 3-24. In Russian, "Iskusstvo kak priem," O teorii prozy (Moscow: Sovetskii pisatel': 1983). For a detailed discussion see Svetlana Boym, "Poetics and Politics of Estrangement: Victor Shklovsky and Hannah Arendt," *Poetics Today* 2005, 26(4): 581-611.

2 See Vladimir Nabokov, *Lectures on Russian Literature* (New York: HBJ, 1981), p. 58.

3 I distinguish between modernization and modernity, but not in order to vilify the former and rehabilitate the latter. To discuss the concept of "world modernities," it is important to distinguish between *modernization*, which usually refers to industrialization and technological progress as state policy and social practice, and *modernity*—the word coined by Charles Baudelaire in the 1850s—which is a critical reflection on the new forms of perception and experience, often resulting in a critique of modernization and its accompanying unequivocal embrace of a single narrative of progress, without turning antimodern or postmodern or postcritical. This modernity is contradictory and ambivalent; it can combine fascination with the present with longing for another time, a critical mixture of nostalgia and utopia. Most importantly, reflecting on modernity makes us critical subjects rather than mere objects of modernization, and encompasses the dimension of freedom as well as a recognition of its boundaries.

The literature on modernity and modernisms is vast. The "unfinished project of modernity" is often associated with the work of Jürgen Habermas and Mikhail Bakhtin, and is linked to the discussion of the discursive public sphere in the work of the former and the unfinalizability of the cultural dialogue in the latter. See Jürgen Habermas, "Modernity— An Incomplete Project," trans. Seyla Benhabib in *The Antiaesthetic:Essays on Postmodern Culture*, ed. Hal Foster (Port Townsend, Wash.: Bay Press, 1983). "Uneven modernization" is part of the late Marxist discussion of the modern project in connection to social transformations of the present. For the best discussion of "alternative modernities" as well as for sympathetic critique of the Marxist model, see *Alternative Modernities*, edited by Dilip Parameshwar Gaonkar (a Public Culture Book) (Durham, NC: Duke University Press,1999). For other discussions of divergent and decentered modernities, see Julio Ramos, *Divergent Modernities: Culture and Politics in Nineteenth-Century Latin America*, trans. John D.Blanco (Durham and London: Duke University Press, 2001) and Chana Kronfeld, *On the Margins of Modernism: Decentering Literary Dynamics* (Berkeley: University of California Press, 1996). In the post-Soviet context, see Harsha Ram's "Futurist Geographies: Uneven Modernities and the Struggle for Aesthetic Autonomy: Paris, Italy, Russia, 1909-1914."

For a bold poetic rethinking of modern poetry and art, see the work of Marjorie Perloff, for example, *21st-Century Modernism: The "New" Poetics* (Oxford: Wiley-Blackwell, 2002) and Charles Altieri, *Painterly Abstraction in Modernist American Poetry: The Contemporaneity of Modernism* (Cambridge UK, 2009) For the crucial discussion of new avant-garde and a critique of the post-modern project see Hal Foster, *The Return of the Real: The Avant-Garde at the End of the Century* (MIT Press, 1990), and *Art Since 1900: Modernism, Anti-Modernism, Postmodernism* (with Rosalind Krauss, Yve-Alain Bois, and Benjamin Buchloh, Thames & Hudson, 2005), and his most recent work on art and architecture, *The Art-Architecture Complex* (Verso, 2011).

In my rethinking I am particularly indebted to the work of Andreas Huyssen and Reinhardt Koselleck that focuses on different understanding of historic temporality itself and on new modernities and the culture of amnesia. See Reinhart Koselleck *The Practice of Conceptual History: Timing History, Spacing Concepts* (Stanford University Press 2002) and Andreas Huysen, *Twilight Memories: Marking Time in the Culture of Amnesia* (New York and London: Routledge, 1995), and *Present Past: Urban Palimpsests and the Politics of Memory* (Stanford: 2003). I drew personal inspiration from Vilem Flusser's unconventional critique of technology that combines critique and creative freedom: Vilem Flusser, *Towards a Philosophy of Photography* (London: Reaktion Books, 2000).

My approach overlaps but never entirely coincides with all of the above, due primarily to my focus on the alternative genealogy of the critical apparatus of modernity, harking back to Shklovsky's and Hannah Arendt's "estrangement for the world" that I understand as an aesthetic, existential, and political practice. Moreover I develop a different off-modern vocabulary that embarrasses some of modern and contemporary theory, offering a creative reconsideration of the cultural evolution that is often "borrowed" from the artists and not overdetermined by the "bird's-eye view" of contemporary theorists.

4   To some extent, the theory of the altermodern still follows post-Marxist and post-postmodern logic, while the off-modern offsets this way of posthistorical thinking with the swerve and the knight's move that opens into alternative genealogies and conjectural histories. Bourriaud opposed the "modernism of the twentieth century which spoke the abstract language of the colonial west. " The off-moderns don't subscribe to such a definition of modernism in the singular.

5   Shklovsky observed that artists often borrow and reuse the features from their uncles and aunts and not only the giant grandparents. Innovation often follows the oblique moves of mimicry and ruse, and reuse of the features that were considered culturally irrelevant, residual, inartistic, or outmoded, placing them into an alternative configurations and thus altering the very horizons of interpretation.

6   Exaptation places eccentric imagination closer to innovation than the brutal struggle for the survival of the fittest, which extends from Darwin's theory of evolution to contemporary market capitalism.

7   Lewis Hyde, *Trickster Makes the World: Mischief, Myth and Art* (New York: North Point Press, 1998), 133.

8   Discussed in *Trickster Makes the World*, pp. 99-100.

9   Ibid., 140.

10 *Off*: By c.1200 as an emphatic form of O.E. *of* (see *of*), employed in the adverbial use of that word. The prepositional meaning "away from" and the adj. sense of "farther" were not firmly fixed in this variant until they left the original *of* with the transf. and weakened senses of the word. The meaning

"not working" is from 1861; verb sense of "to kill" first attested 1930. *Off the cuff* (1938) is from the notion of speaking from notes written in haste on one's shirt cuffs. *Off the rack* (adj.) is from 1963; *off the record* is from 1933; *off the wall* "crazy" is 1968, probably from the notion of a lunatic "bouncing off the walls" or else in ref. to carom shots in squash, handball, etc.

Off-base: "unawares," 1936, Amer. Eng., fig. extension from baseball in sense of "not in the right position" (1907), from the notion of a base runner being picked off while taking a lead; *off-beat*: "unusual," 1938, from *off* + beat (n.). From earlier sense in ref. to music rhythm (1927). *Off-Broadway*: 1953, "experimental theater productions in New York City." Even more experimental *off-off-Broadway* is attested from 1967. *Off-color*:1860, from *off* + color; originally used of gems; figurative extension to "of questionable taste, risqué" is Amer. Eng., 1860s.

Off-hand :1694, "at once, straightway," from *off* + hand. Probably originally in ref. to shooting without a rest or support. Hence, of speech or action, "unpremeditated" (1719). *off-key* : 1929, from *off* + musical sense of key (1). Fig. sense is from 1943. *off-limits*: OED says first attested to in 1952, in a U.S. military (Korean War) sense, but almost certainly from WWII (cf. Bill Mauldin cartoons), if not WWI. *off-line*: 1926, of railroads; 1950, of computers. *off-load* : "unload," 1850, from *off* + load (v.). Originally S.African, on model of Du. afladen.

Off-white: "white with a tinge of gray or yellow," 1927, from *off* + white. Off-peak: 1920, originally in ref. to electrical systems. *off-putting* 1578, "procrastinating," from *off* + put. The meaning "creating an unfavorable impression" is first recorded 1894. *Off-season* 1848, "a period when business is down," from *off* + season.

18 SCENOGRAPHY OF FRIENDSHIP

We live in a world of friending, not friendships. Friend has become a euphemism for something more or less than friendship; a "friend" is a conspicuous casual acquaintance who overcrowds our homepage, or an inconspicuous lover who likes to escape home.

The word friendship shares etymologies with freedom in English, *Freude* (joy) in German, and with *philia* (affectionate love) in Romance languages and Greek. In Russian, the word for "friend," *drug*, is related to "the other," but not a foreign other, for which there is another word, *inoi*. The aspect of otherness is important because there are many things friendship is not. Friendship, in my understanding, is neither a conventional intimacy, nor a brotherhood or sisterhood, nor a networking opportunity. Rather, it is an elective affinity without finality, a relationship without plot or place in our society, an experience for its own sake. It is not always democratic or egalitarian, but rather selective and not entirely inclusive.

Hannah Arendt wrote that friendship of a serious kind is what makes life worth living. Yet, she also emphasized that friendship should not be confused with romantic love for a "single one," which for her can become "a totalitarianism for two" because it makes the whole world around the lovers vanish. Nor is friendship the confessional intimacy advocated by Rousseau, an echo chamber of one's overflowing narcissism: "We are wont to see friendship solely as a phenomenon of intimacy, in which the friends open their hearts to each other unmolested by the world and its demands."[1] Friendship for her is, in fact, precisely about being molested by the world and responding in kind—by expanding, so to speak, the dimensions of existence and by co-creating on the worldly stage. This stage has a particular scenography. Neither brightly lit nor completely enlightened, it has a scenography of chiaroscuro, of the interplay of light and shadow.

Writing about men and women in "dark times," Arendt observed that in circumstances of extremity, the illuminations do not come from philosophical concepts but from the "uncertain, flickering and often weak light" that men and women kindle and shed over the lifespan given to them. This luminous space where "men and women come out of their origins and reflect each other's sparks" is the space of humaneness and friendship that sheds light on the world of appearances we inhabit. In other words, friendship is not about having everything illuminated or obscured, but about conspiring and playing with shadows. Its goal is not enlightenment but luminosity, not a quest for the blinding truth but only for occasional lucidity and honesty.

Philosophies of friendship go back to ancient Greece and Rome, where friendship was part and parcel of both vita activa and vita contemplativa, of politics and of philosophy (itself etymologically related to philia). These philosophies have alternated between the political and the apolitical, between the worldly and the utopian, but all of them, including contemporary analyses by Jacques Derrida, Jean-Luc Nancy, and Giorgio Agamben, speak mostly of male friendship. Friendship between women is somehow deemed to lack philosophical gravitas, even though ancient Greece had the occasional heroine—from Diotima, the teacher of Socrates, to the anonymous "Thracian maiden" who, as Arendt noted, laughed when philosophers barricaded themselves in inner fortresses or romantic huts on the tops of mountains.

Hannah Arendt's own unlikely relationship with Mary McCarthy provides a way to examine these issues in their specifics. The two women, who theorized and practiced friendship in a passionately non-euphemistic manner, had the type of relationship that can be described only through a series of expressions whose oxymoronic character allows us both to get to its passionate core and avoid the touchy-feely confessional mode for which the two had little patience—luminous opacity, diasporic intimacy, asymmetrical reciprocity, impolite tactfulness, homoerotic heterogeneity. Unlike recent philosophical reflections of friendship, what is offered here is not a theory but a theoretical fable that requires rigorous storytelling. Such storytelling works like a *fermenta cognitionis* (literally, "yeast of knowledge"), producing and rescuing insights and intimations that, in Arendt's description, are not "intended to communicate conclusions, but to stimulate others to independent thought, and this for no other purpose than to bring about a discourse between thinkers."[2]

"Oh": On Tact, Taste, and the Anchovy Paste

The story of their friendship begins with a misunderstanding. Hannah Arendt (1906–1975), political thinker and refugee from Nazi Germany, and Mary McCarthy (1912–1989), writer and political journalist, met in New York in 1944 and then again in 1945. Their second meeting turned into a war of words. Talking at a party about hostile French attitudes toward the Germans, McCarthy commented that she felt sorry for Hitler, who was so absurd as to desire the love of his victims. Arendt was enraged: "How can you say such a thing in front of me—a victim of Hitler, a person who has been in a concentration camp!" It was three years before the two women would talk again. Coming home from a meeting in which the two found themselves in the minority in a discussion of politics, Arendt approached McCarthy on the subway platform and said, "Let us end this nonsense. We think so much alike." At that point, McCarthy apologized for her comment about Hitler, and Arendt confessed that she had not in fact been in a concentration camp, but only an internment camp for enemy aliens in France. Theirs was no small talk. After this fortuitous encounter on the subway platform and mutual admission of mishaps and errors, the two very different women became friends for life. Theirs was not an agonistic competitiveness characteristic of the New York intellectuals of the time, but an agnostic erotics of difference.

In her text "Saying Good-Bye to Hannah," an unlikely funeral oration written right after Arendt's death in 1975, McCarthy tells a curious story of a rejected gift of friendship:

She had a respect for privacy, separateness, one's own and hers. I often stayed with her—and Heinrich and her—on Riverside Drive and before that on Morningside Drive, so that I came to know Hannah's habits well, what she liked for breakfast, for instance. A boiled egg, some mornings, a little ham or cold cuts, toast spread with anchovy paste, coffee, of course, half a grapefruit or fresh orange juice, but perhaps that last was only when I, the American, was there. The summer after Heinrich's death she came to stay with us in Maine, where we gave her a separate apartment, over the garage, and I put some thought into buying supplies for her kitchen—she liked to breakfast alone. ... I was rather pleased to have been able to find anchovy paste in the village store. On the afternoon of her arrival, as I showed her where everything was in the larder, she frowned over the little tube of anchovy paste, as though it were an inexplicable foreign object. "What is that?" I told her. "Oh." She put it down and looked thoughtful and as though displeased, somehow. No more was said. But I knew I had done something wrong in my efforts to please. She did not wish to be known, in that curiously finite and, as it were, reductive way. And I had done it to show her I knew her—a sign of love, though not always—thereby proving that in the last analysis I did not know her at all.[3]

Why is this story of an unrequited gift in the middle of the laudatio for a dear friend? The anchovy paste, that "foreign object," covers up and reveals intimate boundaries of friendship and tender paradoxes about taste and tact, love and knowledge.

In the spirit of Cabinet Magazine I did research on anchovies (and ate anchovy while writing this essay) to get a taste of this mysterious friendship. I learned that the anchovy is a small silvery fish from the Mediterranean and the Baltic Sea, though it is also known in India. Perhaps the anchovy paste functioned for Arendt like a Proustian madeleine, triggering the recovery of lost time and the memories she had of her lost European home. Yet there is something about the enforced attempt at an intimate recreation of home away from home that becomes intrusive. Nostalgia on steroids was not Arendt's style. She believed that one cannot imagine a perfect homecoming without self-delusion, and preferred the hospitality of plural homes to a return to a "single one."

Wikipedia informed me that anchovies were ancient Roman aphrodisiacs, but I let this intimation pass without comment, so as not to engage in over-reading; for this is not a cultural history of anchovy paste, but a cross-cultural story of friendship. The paste was not "shared" or consumed because true friendship is not always about instant gratification. To love a friend is to recognize the difference and estrangement of the other. It is important not to overly psychologize this kind of friendly love, not to exhaust it with the search for hidden meanings, repressions, or denials. Such total exposure would kill the play of light and shadow that constitutes that special realm of existence.

McCarthy thinks that Arendt didn't wish to be known as a private person in this kind of "finite way." But maybe this is another misrecognition? Perhaps the Arendtian "Oh" is not a rejection of the "sign of love," but only a repudiation of the conventional language of friendship and gift giving. In telling her story, McCarthy remembers a gesture of Arendt's own hospitality—offering McCarthy orange juice for breakfast (which Arendt herself never drank at that time) hoping, perhaps, that in this way a German Jewish refugee might make an American repatriate feel at home with her. This orange juice might have been Arendt's version of the "anchovy paste," an ordinary American drink that could help her soften her foreign accent. While the two women enjoyed giving each other presents for more than twenty-five years, and even writing about them, these friendly gift exchanges might not have been about reciprocity or giving the other the object of her desire. For such an object must remain unknowable, and friendly love, which is based on asymmetrical reciprocity, demands the recognition of the foreignness at the core of intimacy. This deeper intimation involves a perpetual de-reification of gifts.

Through the story of the anchovy paste, McCarthy is given knowledge about the boundaries of the other, and such recognition moves her to a deeper stage of friendship and a greater understanding of love's foreign language. The anchovy paste becomes a madeleine of memory for McCarthy herself; it allows her to suddenly hear the voice of a dead friend, even if the only thing she is saying is an undecipherable "Oh." As much as we learn about the anchovies, in the end, this is only a Kierkegaardian fish—a pretext for understanding, where what matters is the process and not the object itself. The recipes for friendship are always imprecise.

Tactfulness: Touching without Tampering

This story of friendship is about differences in taste, and about a particular balancing act between tact and touch. The word tact derives from touch, but, at first glance, the concept seems to have reversed its meaning and come to signify delicate distance and respect, a displacement of contact away from the domain of physicality and into the domain of sociability and the aesthetic arrangement of everyday life. But this is only at first glance. The more we look into the notion of touch itself, the more ambivalent it becomes. It was Aristotle who observed the elusiveness and mystery of touch in his De Anima. Unlike the other senses, we don't know what the "organ of touch" is and whether it is superficial or deep, visible or hidden. Can touch really be only skin deep, or is there a mysterious psyche somewhere that guides our tactile experiences? Touch appears to be at once the most syncretic of all senses and the least representable.

The organ and representation of tact are equally elusive. According to Derrida, tact is the "sense of knowing how to touch without touching, without touching too much where touching is already too much."[4] Tact, in other words, is connected to the art of measuring that which cannot be measured. In my view, tactfulness is less about abstinence than about conscious reticence, less about an interdict than about a deliberate choice not to violate certain boundaries and to touch without tampering. Tact points to the untouchable but also begs us not to forget the effect of touch, not to rush into the virtual or the transcendental.

When we read the letters between Arendt and McCarthy, we see how they not so much violate as play with boundaries—of truth and lies, of girls' talk and philosophical reflection, of erotic tenderness and epistolary distance. In one letter, Arendt makes an ironic comment on Rousseau, Sartre, and the "bad faith" embedded in the ostentatious proclamations of sincerity and authenticity that go together with a careful remaking of one's "sincere" confession: "It reminds me of what I heard recent scholarship unearthed about Rousseau—he did not have five children in the orphanage for the simple reason that he was impotent, which I think is most likely. Sartre's case [concerning his participation in the French resistance] is precisely the same. You tell a seemingly outrageous "truth" with a great show of sincerity in order to hide better what actually happened."[5] It is a parody of revelation: Rousseau's revealed secret hides from the paparazzi of the confessionate another, less glamorous, secret. Moreover, such revelation lays bare the scenography of "bad faith." Rousseau, who despised the theater of public life—advocating instead intimate identification and the total community of the "general will" which does not tolerate much dissent or difference—stages his own selective confession in the hope of gaining the public's empathy and identification. Arendt and McCarthy, who don't believe in the "dictatorship" of sincerity, don't play this game: their secrets are there to be shared between friends, as landmarks of their common world, intimate yet also connected to their broader public existence.

Diasporic Intimacy: Playing with Daimons

This kind of friendship resembles what I have called elsewhere a "diasporic intimacy," especially since we are speaking of friendship between an immigrant and an expatriate. Intimate means "innermost," "pertaining to a deep nature," "very personal," "sexual." Yet, "to intimate" also means "to communicate with a hint or other indirect sign; to imply subtly."[6] In contemporary American pop psychology, one is encouraged "not to be afraid of intimacy," which presumes that intimate communication can and should be made in plain language, that you can say "what you mean" without irony and double-speak. Diasporic intimacy, on the other hand, can be approached only through indirection and intimation, through stories and secrets. Spoken of in a foreign language that reveals the inadequacies of translation, diasporic intimacy is not opposed to uprootedness and defamiliarization but is constituted by it. In contrast to the utopian image of intimacy as transparency, authenticity, and ultimate belonging, diasporic intimacy is dystopic by definition; it is rooted in the suspicion of a single home, in shared longing without belonging. It thrives on the hope that human understanding and survival are possible, but this hope is not utopian.

Diasporic intimacy is not possessive but tender. Tenderness is not about complete disclosure, saying what one really means, and getting closer and closer. It excludes absolute possession and fusion. Not goal-oriented, it defies symbols of fulfillment. In the words of Roland Barthes, "tenderness ... is nothing but an infinite, insatiable metonymy" and a "miraculous crystallization of presence."[7] In tenderness, need and desire are joined. Tenderness is always polygamous, non-exclusive. "Where you are tender, you speak your plural."[8]

Most importantly, this form of diasporic intimacy and friendly love does not exclude *amor mundi* but constantly reconstitutes it. For Arendt, a conversation between true friends, "(in contrast to the intimate talk in which individuals speak about themselves), permeated though it may be by pleasure taken in the friend's presence, is concerned with the common world, which remains 'inhuman' in a very literal sense unless it is constantly talked about by human beings."[9] Arendtian friends don't only talk about themselves, but also take as an object of discourse the world, which they humanize and reinvent through language. Writing about Lessing, Arendt speaks of the friendship between a Jew and a German that for Lessing becomes a particular form of "worldliness," which she describes as a "vigilant partiality" that tests the boundaries between personal affect and worldly concern. In her texts, Arendt describes the common world in the twentieth century as something uncanny and on the verge of disappearance, comparing it to a table, which both unites and separates the people gathered around it but can also vanish, as in a spiritualist session. This conception of worldliness is not synonymous with globalization or universalism. It consists in the recognition not only of the external pluralisms of national, cultural, and religious identities, but of the inner pluralities within oneself and one's culture.

Who is talking when two friends like McCarthy and Arendt talk about the world? Reading the letters, we are impressed by the multiplicity of voices—tender attentiveness, impatient desire for the other's presence, mischief and playfulness, sharp intellectual observations, philosophical discussions. In other words, the voices of intimate friends, writers, political observers, philosophers, and adventurers. Only this worldly interspace of friendship allows for such exuberance of freedom that it does not conform to any divisions of labor, disciplines, or social roles.

With friends, one can take part in multiple dialogues and share solitudes. Arendt wrote that solitude is different from loneliness because in solitude we are in dialogue with ourselves and with the world, while loneliness makes us isolated and tongue-tied. When experiencing solitude, we are playing on our internal stage with what the Greeks called "daimons" (not to be confused with demons; daimons are not to be exorcized since they are the voices of our invisible selves.) When you speak with a true friend, she sees the daimons speaking over our shoulders, or perhaps our daimons confront each other in friendly recognition. With a single good friend, we are in good and diverse company. In such a deep friendship, we multiply, create, and discover our actual and potential selves, not fall back stubbornly into the claustrophobia of our supposedly "true self." Friendships are extensions of ourselves into the realm of liminal adventure.

In an essay on friendship, Giorgio Agamben comments on a mysterious passage in which Aristotle writes that friendship is not merely the pleasure of finding an alter ego but a revelation of the very "sensation of existence." In Agamben's reading, to find a friend is not to find another self; rather, "friendship is desubjectification at the very heart of the most intimate sensation of the self."[10] Agamben recalls a Renaissance painting by Giovanni Serodine in which the apostles Peter and Paul, on their way

FIGURE 18.1 Giovanni Serodine, "Parting of Saints Peter and Paul Led to Martyrdom," 1625-1626.

to martyrdom, are shown "so close to each other (their foreheads are almost stuck together) that there is no way they can see one another."[11] For Agamben, this closeness marks the space of friendship, a conception that is radically different from Arendt's—and would be incapable of illuminating the friendship between Arendt and McCarthy. The two women were no saints and their relationship is very far from a lovingly ascetic Christian proximity. Instead, their friendship is about affectionate, worldly theatricality with shadows and distances not commemorated in any painting. For such friendship, a different metaphor is more apt— not "desubjectification" and saintly proximity, but worldly play and open expansion of the self. Friendship is not utopian or teleological; it is worldly as well as lively. It belongs to the arts of existence of the broadest, non-disciplinary sort.

"Ach:" The Furrows of Friendship

McCarthy remembers Arendt as if she were a great actress on the existential stage:

> What was theatrical in Hannah was a kind of spontaneous power of being seized by an idea, an emotion, a presentiment, whose vehicle

her body then became, like the actor's. And this power of being seized and worked upon, often with a start, widened eyes, "Ach!" (before a picture, a work of architecture, some deed of infamy), set her apart from the rest of us like a high electrical charge. And there was the vibrant, springy, dark, short hair, never fully gray, that sometimes from sheer force of energy appeared to stand bolt upright on her head.[12]

In this wonderfully electric and theatrical portrait of Arendt, McCarthy doesn't stage any psychological drama but the life of the mind itself[13]. "Ach" is another interjection, this time expressing the wonder and astonishment of a true thinker. So much of this story of friendship is told through such interjections—in which one can almost hear the guttural sounds of the friend's dear foreign accent.

In the last paragraph of McCarthy's essay, the masks multiply only to reveal the friend's fragile body:

Her eyes were closed in her coffin, and her hair was waved back from her forehead, whereas she pulled it forward, sometimes tugging at a lock as she spoke, partly to hide a scar she had got in an automobile accident—but even before that she had never really bared her brow. In her coffin, with the lids veiling the fathomless eyes, that noble forehead topped by a sort of pompadour, she was not Hannah any more but a composed death mask of an eighteenth-century philosopher. I was not moved to touch that grand stranger in the funeral parlor, and only in the soft yet roughened furrows of her neck, in which the public head rested, could I find a place to tell her good-bye.[14]

This is an ending that refuses closure. The description is both more intimate and more estranging than customary—it violates the boundary of convention, but not of the impolite tactfulness of love. The immortal mask of a generic philosopher and the mortal and particular beloved body of a woman cohabit here. This is a body that is not one; it is at once public and private, untimely and contemporary, foreign and intensely familiar, with soft yet roughened furrows that belong to no traditional obituary. Only a woman writer and a time-tried friend could commemorate such furrows with vigilant partiality, before tears come.

Notes

1   Hannah Arendt, "On Humanity in Dark Times: Thoughts on Lessing," in *Men in Dark Times* (New York: Harcourt Brace & Company, 1968), p. 24.

2   Arendt, "On Humanity in Dark Times," op.cit., p. 10. The conception of worldliness and freedom in Hannah Arendt is further discussed in *Another Freedom: The Alternative History of an Idea* (Chicago: University of Chicago Press, 2010).

3   Mary McCarthy, "Saying Good-bye to Hannah," *The New York Review of Books*, 22 January 1976.

4   Jacques Derrida, *On Touching—Jean-Luc Nancy*, trans. Christine Irizarry (Stanford: Stanford University Press, 2005), p. 67.

5   Carol Brightman, ed., *Between Friends: The Correspondence of Hannah Arendt and Mary McCarthy 1949–1975* (New York: Harcourt Brace & Company, 1995), p. 172.

6   *American Heritage Dictionary* (Boston: Houghton Mifflin, 1985) p. 672.

7   Roland Barthes, *A Lover's Discourse: Fragments*, trans. Richard Howard (New York: Hill and Wang, 1978), pp. 224–225. For a discussion of diasporic intimacy, see my *Future of Nostalgia* (New York: Basic Books, 2001).

8   Barthes, *A Lover's Discourse: Fragments*, op. cit., p. 225.

9   Arendt, "On Humanity in Dark Times," op. cit., p. 24.

10 Giorgio Agamben, "The Friend," in *What is an Apparatus?*, trans. David Kishik and Stefan Pedatella (Stanford: Stanford University Press: 2009), p. 35. Agamben refers to some of the same texts on friendship as Arendt (though without reference to her work), but their conception of worldliness and the space of friendship is very different. See *Another Freedom*, op. cit.

11 Ibid., p. 30.

12 McCarthy, "Saying Good-bye to Hannah," op. cit.

13 In the tradition of Diderot's "Paradox of an Actor," Arendt is present there with her many mysterious phantoms that only a friend can recognize.

14 McCarthy, "Saying Good-bye to Hannah," op. cit.

19 VERNACULAR COSMOPOLITANISM: VICTOR SHKLOVSKY AND OSIP MANDELSHTAM

I would like to explore an alternative tradition of Jewish thought that Hannah Arendt called "passionate thinking," one that mediates between philosophy and experience, between judging and acting. In my investigation of the twentieth century's disasters and delusions I became fascinated with the thinkers and writers who in the most difficult circumstances of the mid-twentieth century Europe did not get history tragically wrong by aligning themselves with Stalinism or Nazism. These were lucid dissenters and fellow travellers who exercised an often-improbable art of judging that didn't follow prescriptive routes and defied the logic of extremity. During the difficult time of the post-revolutionary transition in the late 1920s one of these figures, critic and writer Victor Shklovsky, called for a "third way" of thinking that follows the zigzag movement of the knight in the game of chess and a double estrangement of theory and historical experience. His friend, poet Osip Mandelshtam, echoed this notion, speaking of the "honest zigzags" of the creative journey that makes one's work timely but not necessarily contemporary, in the sense of keeping some distance from the immediate political demands of the day

Does this strategy have anything to do with Jewish self-identification? Echoing earlier twentieth century writers, Italian historian Carlo Ginzburg wrote that all his life he was fascinated by distance and estrangement. For him these constituted the most pronounced feature of the Jewish perspective.[1] The figures of distancing and estrangement are abundant in the works of German/Eastern-European/Russian-Jewish writers.

Georg Simmel's stranger and adventurer, Walter Benjamin's flâneur and collector, Shklovsky's "strange man from a strange country," Hannah Arendt's pariah and "the girl from abroad" are a few of the best-known examples. In her essays of 1944 Hannah Arendt reflected on the pariah's and stranger's capacity for independent thinking and self-distancing, and at the same time she raised the question whether such contemplative freedom and the special intimacy of the pariah community might come at the expense of engagement with the world, *amor mundi*, and a concern for political rights.

I would argue that there is a different history of critical estrangement in the twentieth century that is not an estrangement *from* the world but also estrangement *for* the world; not a form of "negative identity" but of responsible artistic and political engagement with complex politics and history.

This alternative "off-modern tradition" helps us rethink the implications of the "linguistic turn" in theory in the political and historical context and reconsider means and ends of critical thinking in the humanities beyond "the end of history" that seems to mark in the twenty-first century. The off-modern writers tended to be not systematic but essayistic. They proceeded through parables, paradoxes, and "honest zigzags" rather than through Hegelian spirals, partaking in but not belonging to various theoretical movements, nor did they follow more familiar paradigms of Jewish idealism, Marxism, Zionism or a quest for messianic redemption. We often lack frameworks and vocabulary to account for the "third-way" thinking but it comes closest to thinking in freedom. Hannah Arendt believed that freedom is "our forgotten heritage" because it defies history that has been written by the victors.[2] Similarly passionate thinking is often a dissident thinking or free thinking that has escaped the history of theory in its post-modern version. It is not by chance that Shklovsky's invention of estrangement in response to the modern habituation involves the attitude towards surrounding objects, love, fear and war: "Habituation devours things, clothes, furniture, one's wife and the fear of war."[3] Artistic estrangement can make one's wife more lovable and the fear of war more real. The specific unexplored zigzag of modern thought that I will discuss here is this conjunction between the aesthetic practice of estrangement, and confrontation with the fear and cruelty of modern warfare and later totalitarian politics.

Inspired by Shklovsky's conception of the knight's move, I developed the idea of the off-modern. Most of us have heard that post-modernism died quietly in its sleep some time in the zero decade of the 21 century. In my quest for redefinition of the modern project I want to get away from the endless "ends" of art and history and of the prepositions "post," "neo," "avant" and "trans" of the charismatic postcriticism that tries desperately to be "in."[4] There is another option: not to be out, but off. As in off-stage, off-key, off-beat and occasionally, off-color. Off-modern involves exploration of the side alleys and lateral potentialities of the project of critical modernity. It brings into focus lateral and alternative modernities and alternative solidarities beyond the Western European and American systems of coordinates. *Off* in the off-modern comes from the prefix *of*, with an additional onomatopoeic "f"; it signifies both belonging to and estrangement of the project of critical modernity.

In my attempt to unearth the archaeology of "third-way" thinking and develop a new vocabulary, I will elaborate a series of oxymorons such as engaged estrangement, vernacular cosmopolitanism, uncanny worldliness, modernist humanism, brave fear—a series that affords what Freud called a "realistic assessment" of the historic dangers. My focus will be the work of Victor Shklovsky and Osip Mandelshtam in the prism of the twenty-first conception of the "off-modern." While the "linguistic turn" in literary and cultural theory followed Roman Jakobson's version of formalism that focused on binary oppositions and system building, Shklovsky's paradoxical theory of estrangement offers us another "turn" towards poetic and parabolic storytelling that brings together theory and history.

Modernist Humanism as a Double Estrangement

Victor Shklovsky's idea of vernacular cosmopolitanism emerges through the confrontation of his theory of estrangement and his experience in the military campaigns in Central Asia, Caucasus, Persia and Turkey during World War I as described in his autobiographical text *The Sentimental Journey.* (1921-23) Best known for his paradoxical literary science, Shklovsky was also an experimental writer who described himself humorously as "a half-Jew and a role player."[5] This is not an artistic alibi for staying outside politics. On the contrary, the experience of the campaign, the encounter with many local and displaced people of Jewish and non-Jewish extraction, and the first-hand knowledge of military and revolutionary violence transforms Shklovsky's theory of estrangement into an existential practice, a form of modernist humanism and an unconventional civic dissent.

It is little known that the founder of the Formalist theory had an adventurous albeit brief political career and wrote some of his early theoretical texts on the fronts of World War I, in the revolutionary underground and in exile. His love for poetry and poetics was hardly academic. Severely wounded twice, with seventeen pieces of shrapnel in his body, Shklovsky recited the avant-garde poetry of Velimir Khlebnikov while being operated on in the military hospital, hoping perhaps that this could help him estrange or at least be distracted from the pain.

Shklovsky embraced the revolutionary spirit, but as one of his critics would later comment, he "confused the revolutions." Or perhaps, he got it right? While a supporter of the February Revolution of 1917, he did not initially embrace the events of October 1917 and the storming of the Winter Palace. Shklovsky joined the Socialist Revolutionary party, which won the majority at the Constitutional Assembly, the revolutionary parliament that convened right after the storming of the Winter Palace. It is a well-known but frequently forgotten fact that the Constitutional Assembly was brutally dispersed by the Bolsheviks, thus putting an end to the variety of left and social democratic politics in Russia. After voting against the dispersal of the Constitutional Assembly Shklovsky joined the anti-Bolshevik underground (together with the writer Maxim Gorky, the future classic Soviet Socialist realist writer).[6] This was his own version of "socialism with a human face," if one were to apply an anachronistic definition. Threatened with arrest and possible execution, Shklovsky crossed the Soviet border on the frozen Gulf of Finland and eventually found himself in Berlin. There he revived his original theory of artistic estrangement and transformed it into the conception of the "third way" and the "knight's move."

In Shklovsky's early essay "Art as Technique," "estrangement" suggests both distancing (dislocating, *dépaysement*) and making strange.[7] Estrangement brings forth a new beginning and a transformation of vision, echoing Hannah Arendt's definition of freedom as a miracle of infinite improbability. In Shklovsky's view, shifting perspectives and making things strange can become an antidote to the routinization and automatization of modern life that leads to mass apathy and disenchantment: "Habituation devours things, clothes, furniture, one's wife and the fear of war."[8] Artistic estrangement can make one's wife more lovable and the fear of war more real. Estrangement is what makes art artistic; but, by the same token, it makes life lively, or worth living.

With hindsight we see that estrangement was not strictly speaking a mere technique or a set of stylistic techniques that define a structure of an autonomous artistic corpus. Rather, this is an artistic, and later political and existential, practice, a form of phenomenological experiment in living and thinking. It is not a foundation of a theoretical movement but a productive embarrassment of theory that can inspire free thinkers and artists. Thus the device of estrangement can both define and defy the autonomy of art. The technique of estrangement differs from scientific distance and objectification; estrangement does not seek to provide the "Archimedean point" from which to observe humanity. Estrangement lays bare the boundaries between art and life but never pretends to abolish or blur them. It does not allow for a seamless translation of life into art, nor for the wholesale aestheticization of politics. Art is only meaningful when it is not entirely in the service of real life or realpolitik, and when its strangeness and distinctiveness are preserved.

Shklovsky's understanding of estrangement is different from both Hegelian and Marxist notions of alienation.[9] Artistic estrangement is not to be cured by incorporation, synthesis, or belonging. In contrast to the Marxist notion of freedom that consists in overcoming alienation, Shklovskian estrangement is in itself a form of limited freedom endangered by all kinds of modern teleologies and utopian visions of the future.

In the post-revolutionary situation in the Soviet Union, when the world itself has been estranged by the state, Shklovsky proposes to practice double estrangement—mediating between conceptual and experimental practice. He proposes the figure of the knight in the game of chess to symbolize his non-Hegelian vision of cultural evolution.

Shklovsky's zigzag of freedom includes eccentric parallelism, paradoxes and subversive parables that come from the Bible and world literature. The "knight's move," however, is not a figure of what Daniel Boyarin and Jonathan Boyarin called "diasporic evasion."[10] Far from being a compromise, the third-route thinking and the knight's move evades limited master-slave dialectics of the "dutiful pawns and single-minded kings" offering instead a "tortured road of the brave" to those who dare to think independently.

Here is how Shklovsky paraphrases Marx' and Lenin's formula familiar to all Soviet citizens that "social being determines individual consciousness": "Material being conditions consciousness but conscience remains unsettled."[11] This key formulation was made in Shklovsky's "Third Factory" (1926) where the ideas of the improbable third-way thinking are explicitly put forth. The gap between conditioned consciousness and unsettled conscience exemplifies the work of double estrangement of theory and the historical circumstances of its production. This unsettled conscience will lead to the transformation of the arts of estrangement into the arts of judging and even dissent, opening up a space of moral reflection that defies the imperative of revolutionary violence.

Vernacular Cosmopolitanism and Critique of Revolutionary Violence

This gap is explored further in Shklovsky's unsentimental *Sentimental Journey* written by the "half-Jew and a role player" who becomes interested in vernacular cosmopolitanism. *A Sentimental Journey* is an amazing multi-generic text that recounts Shklovsky's many encounters with local people and records their tales of misfortune. Curiously the pioneer of estrangement Shklovsky doesn't frame his travels through Persia and Turkey as a journey to the exotic orient or to the land of the strange other. Rather unconventionally for a soldier of the Russian army he declares: "My orientation was local. There was one feature in 'the East' that reconciled me to them, there was no antisemitism here."[12] Shklovsky contrasts that to what he calls a "transsensical (*zaumnyi*) antisemitism" of the Russian Army, using a literary term to lay bare its irrationality. The literary term *zaumnyi* is used to estrange the common cultural forms of behavior and to defamiliarize what has become a form of habitual cruelty.

Shklovsky, like Babel, warned the locals about the pogroms against local Jews as well as other local people planned by the army and once even tried to stage a fake pogrom in order to avoid the real one. (No wonder his fellow soldiers considered him a brave man and a strange man.) The writer attributes this strangeness to his conflicting revolutionary and humanistic imperatives as well as to his half-Jewishness.[13] The son of a Jewish father and a half-German, half-Russian mother, Shklovsky plays with multiple identifications that allow him to engage with many dislocated and uprooted people that he encounters on his way. Possibly it is the experience of the Russian Army that made him identify himself with the Jews, since there he was not promoted to become an officer because he was considered "a son of a Jew and therefore a Jew."

In any case, when it comes to Jewish identification, we see a comedy of errors on all fronts. Shklovsky relates that when the British conquered Jerusalem, a delegation of the Assyrians came to visit Shklovsky carrying as a gift some sugar and *kishmish*: "Your people and my people would live together again. It is true we destroyed the Temple of Solomon a long time ago but we also restored it. They spoke that way because they considered themselves Assyrians and me, a Jew. In fact, they were mistaken: I am not quite a Jew and they are not the descendants of the Assyrians. They are Aramaic Jews."[14] The irony of the mutual mis-recognition resides in the fact that both sides see the other as "more" Jewish. And yet this encounter leads to deepened human connections. Recognition of estrangement does not preclude empathy, and this uncommon encounter shapes Shklovsky's perspective and expands his frame of references. Unlike his fellow soldiers, he is involved in constant conversation with the locals, sometimes enjoying their friendship or hospitality.

Shklovsky is fascinated by Jewish heteroglossia and by cultural plurality in general. He collects as much material as he can about the languages, habits and political situation of local minorities. Jews and non-Jews, Kurds, Armenians, Georgian Jews who speak a "tatar dialect" but also the more exotic Assyrians and Aissors-Nestorians will figure in many of Shklovsky's autobiographical parables of his relationship with the Soviet power, parables in which he identifies with those eccentric heretics.

Speaking as a half-Jew and a role player both in *A Sentimental Journey* and in his second autobiographical text, *Zoo, or Letters Not About Love*, Shklovsky offers us a series of political parables to understand the crucial problems of his time. The most pertinent example is Shklovsky's twentieth century parable of the revolutionary Shibboleth that is his response at once to structuralist linguistics and to the dilemmas of revolutionary violence. Shklovsky retells the famous Biblical tale (originally, of course, about intertribal Israelite warfare) as one in which the aggressors are Philistines:

The Jews set patrols at the crossing. On that occasion it was difficult to distinguish a Philistine from a Jew, both were in all likelihood, naked. The patrol would ask those coming through: Say the word "shibboleth."

But the Philistines couldn't say "sh"; and they were killed.

In Ukraine I ran into a Jewish boy. He couldn't look at corn without shaking. They told me the story. When they were murdering in Ukraine and needed to know if they were murdering a Jew they would ask them "say *kukuruza*." And the Jew would say: *kukuruzha*-- And they killed him.[15]

This was not merely a binary phonemic difference between two sounds, as Saussurian structuralist linguistics would suggest, but also a matter of life and death. The teller of the parable speaks from the gap between consciousness and conscience. Shklovsky's parables prefigure Jacques Derrida's discussion of shibboleth in his essay about Paul Celan. Shibboleth (a Hebrew word that also exists in Judeo-Aramaic, Pheonician and Syriac) functions as a password that demarcates a border-crossing. Shibboleth can become a "secret configuration of the places of memory."[16] Derrida doesn't dwell on the interesting case of intertextuality Celan's poem speaks about, "the estrangement of homeland--*die Fremde der Heimat*" nor about Celan's "Petropolis of the unforgotten which was Tuscany for your heart." The addressee of Celan's poem is, in fact, none other than Osip Mandelshtam, whom he was translating at the time, making the poem itself into a configuration of Jewish cosmopolitan memory, and returning us as well to the Biblical question of inter-"Israelite" mistrust and miscommunication.

Sentimental Journey abounds in descriptions of violence, presented in the most stark and unsentimental fashion. Violence is by no means excused or glorified as a part of the "necessary revolutionary sacrifice" for the sake of the future liberation of humanity. Nor are the numerous descriptions of dismembered bodies presented as examples of modernist aesthetic disfiguration or the "dehumanization of art." [17] In describing pillage, slaughter, pogroms and the daily cruelty that he witnessed at the front, Shklovsky redirects his estrangement. It no longer "dehumanizes" in Ortega-y-Gasset's sense but rather makes real the "fear of war"[18] that has become so habitual for soldiers and for the ideologues of violence. Thus, the technique of estrangement lays bare the senseless dehumanization of war. It is as if only through estrangement could the revolutionary writer Shklovsky rediscover that after all he is a humanist. Reporting the practices of wartime Communism--the execution of poet

Nikolai Gumilev, and the death of poet Alexander Blok--Shklovsky appeals to the Soviet citizens:

Citizens!
Citizens, stop killing! Men are no longer afraid of death! There are already customs and techniques for telling a wife about the death of her husband.
It changes nothing. It just makes everything harder.[19]

Similar address to the invisible "citizens" and a report on violence is found in Shklovsky's telegram to the military authorities about the pogrom of the Kurds:

That night I sent the TASK a panicky telegram:
"I have inspected Kurdistan units. In the name of the Revolution and Humanity, I demand the withdrawal of troops."
This telegram didn't go over too well—apparently it seemed naïve and funny to demand the withdrawal of troops in the name of humanity. But I was right.[20]

Haunted by the brutal materiality of war, Shklovsky sticks to the "literature of facts" and resists the transformation of violence into metaphor or a mere means to a beautiful end: "I wrote [A Sentimental Journey] remembering the corpses that I saw myself."[21] Shklovsky's "sentimental journey" is hardly sentimental in any conventional way, but it is extremely sensitive; it does not try to domesticate the fear of war; it individualizes the dead and the wounded, humanizing them through art.

Shklovsky speaks about dehumanization explicitly in his insightful and generally sympathetic portrait of Maxim Gorky: "Gorky's bolshevism is ironic and free of any faith in human beings...The anarchism of life, its subconscious, the fact that the tree knows better how to grow-- these are the things he couldn't understand."[22] Shklovsky never accepts the instrumentalization of human beings and had a keen concern for the "crooked timbre of humanity" (to paraphrase Kant). Shklovsky's modernist humanism is paradoxical and is based not on the nineteenth-century conceptions reflected in many psychological novels, but rather on anarchic spontaneity which preserves the "mystery of individuality," to use Simmel's term. This runs parallel to the interest in what Shklovsky calls "local laws" and conventions of art that for him are a part of the memory of world culture. Shklovsky's war memoirs estrange the revolutionary teleology and political theology of Lenin and Carl Schmitt alike offering an alternative way of reflecting on the modern experience without the sacrifice of human unpredictability, which brings Shklovsky close to the thought of Hannah Arendt and Georg Simmel.

Shklovsky wrote that the Soviet writer of the 1920s has two choices: to write for the desk drawer or to write on state demand. "There is no third alternative. Yet that is precisely the one that must be chosen ... Writers are not streetcars on the same circuit."[23] One of the central parallelisms that Shklovsky explores in *The Third Factory* is the unfreedom of the writer caught in the play of literary convention and the unfreedom of the writer working under the dictate of the state, specifically an authoritarian power. The two deaths of the author – one a playful self-constraint and the other the acceptance of the state *telos* – are not the same. Inner freedom and the space of the writer's creative exploration are shrinking in the context of public unfreedom. Shklovsky speaks about the secret passages in the walls of Parisian houses that are left for cats, an image that seems to refer to the shrunken literary public sphere in the 1920s. This is a forever shrinking space of freedom. The practice of aesthetic estrangement had become politically suspect already by the late 1920s; by 1930, it had turned into an intellectual crime. Later Shklovsky was accused of "cosmopolitanism" and of "practicing the cosmopolitan discipline of comparative literature," the accusation that followed him even after he (half-heartedly) denounced formalism in 1930.

In the case of Shklovsky we can observe a transformation of estrangement from the world into estrangement for the world, a distinction that comes from the work of Hannah Arendt. Estrangement from the world has its origins in the Stoic concept of inner freedom, in the Christian conception of freedom and salvation, as well as in romantic subjectivity and introspection. It suggests a distancing from political and worldly affairs. On the other hand, estrangement for the world is a way of seeing the world anew, a possibility of a new beginning that is fundamental for aesthetic experience, critical judgment, and political action. It is also an acknowledgement of the integral human plurality that we must recognize within us and within others. Like Shklovsky, Arendt uses an example of aesthetic practice to speak about public freedom; public or worldly freedom is a kind of art, but its model is not plastic but performing arts. Freedom for Arendt is akin to a performance on a public stage, that needs common language but also a degree of incalculabitiy, luck, chance, hope, surprise, wonder. Importantly, Arendt's conception of the art of freedom is just as different from the notion of a total work of politics as is the Shklovskian art of estrangement. It entails a non-Wagnerian conception of aesthetic practice that focuses on the process and not on the product. It depends on individual ability to estrange from oneself and see the stranger in the other. In other words, freedom is a recognition of inner plurality within individuals that allows for action and co-creation and not only for external pluralism.

Osip Mandelshtam: Co-creation with Fear and The Ends of Theory

"We will remember in Lethe's cold waters/ That earth for us has been worth a thousand heavens"—these words by Osip Mandel'shtam are used by Hannah Arendt in her discussion of worldliness and gratitude towards being. Contrary to the poetic dictum that philosophy is about homecoming, there could be a different way of inhabiting the world and making a second home, not the home into which we were born but a home that we freely choose for ourselves.

Joseph Brodsky described Osip Mandelshtam as a "homeless poet" and yet he was at home in the republic of "world culture." Like Shklovsky, Mandelshtam had unconventional politics, more committed to civic courage and artistic freedom than to a particular political party and state ideology which made him "nobody's contemporary" who was "out of pace" with his "brutal century." And yet it was Osip Mandelshtam who became one of the very few writers in the Soviet Union to write a satirical epigram on Stalin, for which he was severely persecuted and sent to the Gulag. Mandelshtam insisted that the poet has to always renew his beginnings and move in "honest zigzags," flirting with foreign speech and confronting the fear and the noise of time.[24]

Like Shklovsky, Mandel'shtam worked in many genres, including essays on the theory of literature and culture, as well as on linguistics and science. He was in dialogue with the members of the OPOYaZ circle, Jakobson, Shklovsky, Tynianov, with Henri Bergson and his conceptions of memory and virtual reality of imagination, as well as with experimental linguists, followers of Marr and his eccentric ideas of hybridity and grafting in the Indo-European and non Indo-European languages, as well as with experimental biologists and physicists.

Mandelshtam's semi-autobiographical novella *The Egyptian Stamp* (1928) takes place in the turbulent time between the February and October Revolution. It offers us a striking combination of Mandelshtam's theory of the "end of the novel" and of the radical novelistic practice that is not always loyal to the theory. Its main protagonist, a Chaplinesque figure named Parnok, is said to be "connected to the dance of modernity" only by a tenuous "safety pin." He embodies Mandelshtam's notion of "lyrical hermaphroditism," a poetic dialogue between masculine and feminine.[25] Parnok is a character with little personal biography; instead he is a walking bibliography, an amalgam of other failed heroes and heroines and avid readers, from Gogols' Akakii Akakievich to Madame Bovary and Don Quixote. His national origins are equally uncertain; he is one of the immigrants of the desolate city and yet he tries to become the city's saviour, a Don Quixote who opposes the violence of the lynch mob.

The narrator's own autobiographical ruminations run parallel to Parnok's but sometimes those parallels meet as in non-Euclidean geometry: "It is *terrifying* to think that our life is a tale without a plot or hero, made up of emptiness and glass, out the feverish babble of constant digressions, out of the Petersburg influenza delirium."[26]

Is this a description of a book of life or a modernist anti-novel? I notice that the Russian word for "terrifying" has actually nothing to do with terror, but rather with fear (*strashno*, from *strax*). This is neither terror nor sublime awe,and this kind of fear shouldn't be lost in translation since it is a key to Mandelshtam's evolving theory of prose and of the experience of Jewishness.

Mandelshtam declares that he will fearlessly speak about fear, both personal and historical. *The Egyptian Stamp* performs the end of biographical and historical genres by weaving together outtakes that contain his drafts, doodles and lateral memories.

I do not fear incoherencies and gaps
I shear a paper with long scissors.
I paste a ribbon as a fringe
A manuscript is always a storm, worn by rags, torn by beaks.
It's the first draft of a sonata.
Scribbling (*marat'*) is better than writing.
I do not fear seams or the yellowness of the glue.

I am a tailor, I am an idler.
I draw Marat in his stocking.
I draw martins.[27]

In this metaliterary digression about fear, fearlessness and a new literary form, the fear survives between the lines and doodles of the text, gradually acquiring form. Here the old-fashioned techniques of cutting and hemming used by the Petersburgian Jewish tailor and trickster Mervis merge with the new revolutionary technologies of cinematic montage to compose a modern fan of memory. The broad margins of Mandelshtam's text are filled with puns, allusions and daydreams. There is no opposition here between the text and marginalia; their relationship is not dialectical, but diagonal. Here the manuscript itself resembles a storm (*buria*) but this is a creative storm orchestrated by the poet himself in which the radical hero of the French revolution and martins cohabit on the same page. Such a creative storm works like a homeopathic pill against the storm of history, which the writer is not always able to divert, but at least the bold creativity offers a placebo from existential fears.

The stormy creative form proceeds through syncretic associations, what the aesthetic psychologist Vygotsky called "superordinary structures" characteristic of a child's imagination. "Superordinary structures" in this understanding are the modes of thinking and creating that follow neither everyday nor scientific logic; they do not recognize barriers and hierarchies between different conceptual orders and move freely from one cognitive or sensory code into another.[28] Yet this is not quite the same as the surrealist chance encounter. Here the emphasis is not on the revelation of unconsciousness but on the connections between individual dreams and cultural forms. The texts are both dialogical and a little glossolalic, because dialogues here do not happen on the level of characters or individuals but at the atomic level of the word itself, which is already a hybrid, a graft, a memory of other roots, accents, intonations, the soft timbre of the ghost writers of the past.

At the end *The Egyptian Stamp* explicitly confronts the relationship between fear, Jewishness and passionate thinking. In Mandelshtam's first autobiographical prose *Noise of Time* (1923) he describes his family as "tongue tied"; they spoke many languages with the same embarrassing accent. Tongue-tiedness is not always an impediment for creativity; it can be the onset of the new tongue, the beginning of an unforeseen liberation at least in literature. Moses, the great Biblical hero, had a speech impediment and was reluctant to take on the burden of history, to confront the tyrant and lead in the difficult road for liberation. In the *Egyptian Stamp* the tongue-tiedness becomes a part of the modernist texture that incorporates different forms of speech with syncopes and breaks.

One such revealing break comes at the end of the novella when the narrator moves from the third person to the first and recounts his own recurring childhood dream of escaping to the town Malinov (from "malina"—raspberry, an uncanny Raspberryville), possibly away from persecution or pogrom. The little Jewish boy finds himself fleeing in the wrong carriage with a Jewish family that's not his own and he is desperately trying to tie his shoes, over and over again. If only he could tie them in a perfect bow, everything would turn out ok. But he can't; his family ties are broken and he is tied up by fear.

Fear takes me by the hand and leads me. A white cotton glove. A woman's glove without fingers. I love fear, I respect it. I almost said: "With fear I have no fear." Mathematicians should have built a tent for fear, for it is the coordinates of time and space, they participate in it like the rolled up felt in the nomad tent of the Kirkiz. Fear unharnesses (unties) the horses when one had to drive and send us dreams with unnecessarily low ceilings.[29]

What happens here is both an estrangement and a poetic domestication of fear. Fear "unties" the horses and drives the narration. But this is no longer that terrifying emotion that would paralyze the boy, not even letting him tie his shoes. Fear is a part of the new system of coordinates; it is given space and time of its own and is respected, almost loved. Fear acquires its own nomadic architecture which provisionally houses it, without containing it fully. Such fear management produces a strange feeling of joy on the part of the narrator; there is almost a mutual attachment between him and the fear. The fear is personified into a strange Muse of Jewish luck. She leads the narrator by the hand on the dangerous modern journey. The narrator is guided by fear in order not to be driven by it. Fear estranges the novelistic form that dehumanizes the individual and enables the final metamorphosis and the work of poetic judgment.

Mandelshtam's contemporary Sigmund Freud contributed to the understanding of fear and its role in the modern psyche. Freud distinguished between "real fear" (i.e fear based on the realistic assessment of danger) and "neurotic fear", dividing the latter into two categories, fright and anxiety. The fear has an "object" and actually mobilizes self-defence—a combination of reasonable fear and resistance which can alert to existing dangers and enable the coping mechanisms. Fright is a sudden experience of danger without anticipation that can produce a traumatic response, while anxiety is a free floating dread without a specific object. Modernist theories made much more of anxiety without object than of the experience of "real fear" that alerts to existing dangers.

In Mandelshtam's experimental autobiographical prose we observe a transformation of free floating anxiety into the confrontation with "real fear." The nomadic architecture that the adult narrator creates to house his childhood fears allows him to lay bare some traumatic memories of escape from a pogrom that many Jewish children of his time might have shared. Such poetics of fear doesn't evolve into paranoia or suicide; quite the contrary. In Mandelshtam's tale coming to terms with fear saves the hero and possibly the narrator-writer from the fate of his literary predecessors, dreamers and obsessive readers of another time, Anna Karenina and Madam Bovary.

Let us examine this transformation step by step. Right after the discussion of the nightmarish road of fear, the last chapter of the novella moves to a more general discussion of the railroad and its role in modern literature and theory:

At the beck and call of my consciousness are two or three little words: "and there," "already," "suddenly,"; they rush about from car to car on the dimly lighted Sevastopol train, halting the platforms where two thundering frying pans hurl themselves at one another and crawl apart.

The railroad has changed the whole course, the whole rhythm of our prose. It has delivered it over to the senseless muttering of the French moujik out of Anna Karenina. Railroad prose like the woman's purse of that ominous moujik is full of the coupler's tools, delicious particles grappling iron prepositions and belongs rather among thing submitted in legal evidence; it is divorced from any concern with beauty and that which is beautifully rounded.[30]

We notice here obvious references to the ending of Tolstoy's novel *Anna Karenina*, only the perspective is radically different. We are not watching the road from the point of view of the suicidal heroine or desperate hero; psychological reflection gives way to reflection on the language and syntax of the prose itself. This is the moment where the novelistic dialogue doesn't happen on the level of the character but on the level of language itself. However, that's not merely the modernist gesture of dehumanization that Ortega y Gasset spoke about when he suggested that the center of gravity of the modern text is no longer the subject but the language itself. Neither is this the dramatization of the end of the novel as Mandelshtam saw it, representing the centrifugal force of modernity. Instead, I would argue that this is a radical case of "aesthetic therapy" where confrontation with fear and its double estrangement saves the hero and (possibly) the narrator from suicidal thoughts. This is the off-modern open-ending, not predetermined by an authorial moral universe and not guided by "the legal evidence" the way *Anna Karenina* was. The creation of the modernist literary architecture that encompasses fear allows the hero and the narrator to escape the suicidal outcome of the nineteenth-century "railroad prose." This is a striking example of the modernist humanism that Mandelshtam elaborates in his theoretical essays.

At the end, Mandelshtam claims that "with fear I have no fear" and follows the same serpentine road of the brave that was chosen by Shklovsky. *The road of self-reflective fear wouldn't lead to any kind of redemption, reconciliation, feel-good palliative or a happy ending.* On this road Mandelshtam's perception of Jewishness undergoes radical transformation. He writes from the particular historical moment between revolution and historic terror, and the deroutinization of fear is a first step towards lucidity and independent thinking. It might be scary and even terrifying to think that our life is a novella without a plot and a hero, made of Petersburg influenza delirium. But by the end of the text we realize that this influenza delirium is contagious and healing at once, it provides fear and inspiration, poison and cure, like a Derridean *pharmakon*. The confrontation with fear is a part of the "honest zigzag" of his passionate thinking that Mandelshtam follows through the last decade of his life. This thinking involves a personal transformation, an explicit rethinking of Jewish belonging in "The Fourth Prose" and the later poems and a further civic engagement with his "beast of a century."[31]

Nostalgia for World Culture and the Storm of History

Mandelshtam offers us his most complete version of his ars poetica and the practice of modernist humanism in his essay "Conversation about

Dante." His Dante is an experimental artist: Dante, the Dadaist who rhymes through different times and spaces. He is a temporal and spatial misfit, an exile and a citizen of the republic of letters who struggles with fear and anxiety that opens into a new historical understanding:

The inner anxiety and painful, troubled gaucheries which accompany each step of the diffident man, as if his upbringing were somehow insufficient, the man untutored in the ways of applying his inner experience or of objectifying it in etiquette, the tormented and downtrodden man — such are the qualities which both provide the poem with all its charm, with all its drama, and serve as its background source, its psychological foundation.[32]

This modern Dante is ill at ease in his time and a foreigner in his own land, almost like a wandering Jew. His untimely anxiety and tragic embarrassment are the human drives behind the *Divine Comedy*.[33] In Mandelshtam's story the central figure of the European culture comes out a little off; his embarrassing errors in etiquette in life and art made him a cultural survivor. What kind of form can the drama of tragic awkwardness and exile take? According to Mandelshtam, *Divina Commedia* is neither a total work nor even a unified formal corpus but a poetic laboratory for the future. At its core it is not "form creation"(formoobrazovanie) but "impulse creation" (poryvoobrazovanie), not the making of a new language but a dynamic grafting and hybridization, more estranging and vital than a neologism. This is a virtuoso performance with vectors directed towards the past and the future, like the mirroring spirals of the Tatlin Tower. Rather than looking at technology in a contemporary sense, Mandelshtam examines a variety of material practices that inspire Dante's metaphors such as seafaring, navigating, shipbuilding as well as minerology and meteorology. According to Mandelshtam, this material *ars poetica* both uses and estranges the techniques of other arts and probes the improbable. Such radical use of techniques of imagination allows a poet to prefigure quantum and the wave theories of light that will be discovered by the physicists some six hundred years later.

Mandelshtam focuses on mineralogy and meteorology to find the patterns of impulse creation that offer unpredictable shapes conventional logic doesn't accommodate--zigzags, serpentine lines, bifurcating lines in the stone, folds. Mandelshtam's off-modern exhibit number one is not a technological artifact but a simple stone caressed by the waves of the Black Sea and the poet's fluid imagination.

I permit myself here a small autobiographical confession. Black Sea pebbles tossed up on shore by the rising tide helped me immensely when the conception of this conversation was taking shape. I openly consulted with chalcedony, cornelians, gypsum crystals, spar, quartz and so on....Mineral rock is an impressionistic diary of weather accumulated by millions of natural disasters; however, it is not only of the past, it is of the future: It is an Aladdin's lamp penetrating the geological twilight of future ages...

Having combined the uncombinable, Dante altered the structure of time or, perhaps, to the contrary, he was forced to a glossolalia of facts, to a synchronism of events, names and traditions severed by centuries, precisely because he had heard the overtones of time.[34]

The Koktebel stone, a forgotten found object from Mandelshtam's happier past, brings back the memories of creative wandering. The small Crimean town of Koktebel preserved a hybrid heritage of Khazars, Tatars, Greeks, Italians, Jews, Russians, Ukrainians, Armenians and many others and at the turn of the century became a *patria chica* of cosmopolitan artists and poets including Annensky, Voloshin, Tsvetaeva, Akhmatova and others. This imaginary Koktebel souvenir now solidifies the fluid logic of the third way and a hybrid of meteorology and mineralogy. The trope of crystallization of the past for the sake of the future brings together Benjamin and Mandelshtam. Benjamin's "pearl diver" and Mandelshtam's sea stone-gatherer are half-brothers, only Mandel'shtam is not pursuing "dialectics at a standstill" or crystallization of the past for the sake of the future. Rather, his focus is on the impulses and graftings of the creative process. The amateur mineralogy to which Mandelshtam devotes many pages in the Conversation about Dante provides alternative shapes of evolution, bifurcating veins in the non precious stones, curvatures, zigzags, palimpsests, spirals without synthesis. These shapes point beyond the familiar paradigm of modern natural and political science and anticipate some of the thinking in Gilles Deleuze's "The Fold." World culture is imagined as a work in progress, constructed through impulses and unforeseen synchronicities and not through Hegelian dialectics or a museumification of the canon.

This palimpsest of free-willing zigzags also offers a temporary poetic remedy to the cruel irreversibility of time that lies at the heart of the human fear of mortality. At the same time it works in counterpoint to the linear progress and the forward march of history that in the 1930s was clearly not leading to a happy ending. The poet is filled with foreboding of an impending catastrophe but he doesn't wish to succumb to its inevitability. If we look for a single drive in Mandelshtam's corpus, we can find it not in the main body of the text but in outtake No 13, which was published only in the 1990s complete edition of Mandelshtam's essay together with its earlier versions. This fragment reads like a prophetic premonition of the poet's personal and historical anxieties:

> The foundation of the composition of all cantos of *Inferno* is the movement of the storm. It ripens as a meteorological phenomenon and all questions and answers revolve around it: beware, to be or not to be, will there be a storm.
>
> To be more precise it is about the movement of the storm, which passes us by, and definitely moves aside. *(mimo, obiazatel'no storonoj.)*[35]

Storona shares the root with estrangement *o-stranenie*. The storm passes "astray, "moves aside," laterally (storonoj). Perhaps, Mandelshtam didn't include this outtake because it could be read too "literally." At once too ominous and too optimistic, it reads like a political allegory particularly apt in the Stalinist Russia of the 1930s and an exercise in wishful thinking, of the dreams of conjectural history as changeable as the weather conditions. The impending storm hides in the *Divine Comedy*, like an anamorphose in baroque painting that is only visible from a certain lateral perspective. The storm, like a historic disaster, is not "written in [the] stone" of necessity; it can still go astray and spare the land. The logic here is quite different than Benjamin's more familiar description of the Angel of History. It is more lateral, impulsive and conjectural. In other words, the theoretical knight's move becomes a figure of historic hope that didn't come true.

The off-modern thinking of history is not made of the "aha" moments of inevitable disasters intuited by the great thinkers, but of such lateral moves. The experimental theorist and practitioner of new arts, Dante the dadaist, has many features of Mandelshtam and his various alter egos. In outtake 13 we find the poet's last "knight's move" and a hope for a non-teleological history of the fragile world culture.

In conclusion, we can only begin to outline the off-modern turn in contemporary theory through the eccentric writings of several "Jewish" thinkers and writers. These writers didn't embrace the binary system of thinking and defied political theology and teleology. Their outlook is non- or almost anti-messianic. They look for "the third way," lateral moves, everyday genres in literature and life. They invite us to rethink the relationship between aesthetics and politics through the experience of freedom, dissent and estrangement beyond the much misunderstood parallelism of Walter Benjamin in his opposition between aestheticizing politics (in Fascist Italy and Nazi Germany) and politicizing aesthetics (in the Soviet Union).[36] Aesthetics is not understood here as an analysis of autonomous works of art but as a form of knowledge that proceeds through a particular interplay of sense, imagination and reason. In the center is not the model of aesthetic autonomy (or specificity of the media) but rather the practice of estrangement and radical perspectivism that informs imagination and judgment in the public world.

In other words, Shklovsky and Mandelshtam explore what Arendt calls public "worldliness", this-worldly human culture and everyday life that is not regarded as an evil world of inauthentic appearances to be transcended and a longing for "world culture" (without much hope for the dream's fulfillment). Aesthetically they practice double estrangement of contemporary theories and practices but believe in a literary public realm, an imaginary community of the republic of letters that can never be entirely politicized.

Worldliness is not the same as cosmopolis, but the two notions overlap. The history of discourse about the world involves conversation across national borders and offers what Anthony Kwame Appiah calls "the case for contamination."[37] There are many vernacular cosmopolitans coming from different localities that require us to recognize inner pluralities within oneself and one's culture, not only of external pluralisms of national, cultural or religious identities.

Worldly modernist humanism here is often expressed "via negativa" and in a minor key; it works through rethinking scale (through anti-monumentalism) and offsetting any attempt at a total work through experimental compositions, unfinalizable parables and humor. Modernist humanism operates through the estrangement of cruelty, non-instrumentalization of the human being, foregrounding of embarrassment and human erring that resists any kind of revolutionary teleology that justifies violence. The relationship between aesthetics and politics has to be reexamined through the experience of freedom, dissent and estrangement. We have to return to the earlier original use of the word "aesthetics" not as an analysis of autonomous works of art but as a form of knowledge that proceeds through a particular interplay of sense, imagination and reason. The focus here is not on the model of aesthetic autonomy (or specificity of the media) but rather on the practice of estrangement and radical perspectivism that informs imagination and judgment. Looking back at twentieth-century history, Arendt proposed to estrange the immanency of disaster. To do so one has to "look for the unforeseeable and unpredictable," for "the more heavily the scales are weighted in favor of the disaster, the more miraculous will the deed done in freedom appear; for it is disaster, not salvation, that always happens automatically and therefore always must appear to be irresistible."[38]

Notes

1   Carlo Ginzburg, *Wooden Eyes: Nine Reflections on Distance* (London: Verson, 2002)

2   Hannah Arendt, "What is Freedom?" in *Between the Past and the Future* (New York, Viking: 1966).

3   Viktor Shklovsky, "Art as Technique" (1917) in Four Formalist Essays, edited and translated by Lee T. Lemon and Marion J. Reis, (Lincoln: University of Nebraska Press, 1965, 12.

4   Svetlana Boym, *Another Freedom: The Alternative History of An Idea* (Chicago, Chicago University Press, 2010).

5   Shklovsky was the son of a Jewish father and a German /Latvian/ Russian mother. He received no formal Jewish education yet he appears remarkably knowledgeable about the Bible. Throughout his life Shklovsky speaks explicitly about different Jewish languages, uses Biblical parables, discusses Jewish publishers and writers. Later in life he wrote about Russia's first Jews at the court of Peter the Great and contributed an account of Nazi atrocities against the Jews in Kislovodsk for Ehrenburg's *Black Book*.

6   More on Shklovsky, see Richard Sheldon, "Victor Shklovsky and the Device of Ostensible Surrender," in Viktor Shklovsky, *Third Factory*, edited and translated by Richard Sheldon (Ann Arbor, MI: Ardis) 1977 [1926]) , vii; and A.P. Chudakov, "Dva pervykh desiatiletiia," in Viktor Shklovsky, *Gamburgskii schet. Stat'i – vospominaniia – esse (1914-1933)*, edited by Aleksandr Galushkin and Aleksandr Chudakov (Moscow: Sovetskii pisatel', 1990), 17.

7   *Stran* is the root of the Russian word for country, *strana*, and the word for strange, *strannyi*, its Latin and Slavic roots superimposing upon one another, creating a wealth of poetic associations and false etymologies.

8   Viktor Shklovsky, "Art as Technique" (1917) in Four Formalist Essays, edited and translated by Lee T. Lemon and Marion J. Reis, (Lincoln: University of Nebraska Press, 1965, 12.

9   In his essays on the phenomenology of art, Hegel also speaks about freedom and alienation as well as art's particular role in mediating between different realms of existence. In a discussion of Dutch paintings, he calls art a "mockery" of reality, a form of irony. These ideas are close to the Formalists, yet Shklovsky by no means embraces the larger frame of the Hegelian system. In his later work, Shklovsky engages directly with Hegelian theories of literature. Speaking of Don Quixote, for example, Shklovsky, (in *O teorii prozy* (Moscow: Sovetskii pisatel')1983 [1925]: 370) observes that Hegel was not interested in "Don Quixote but in Don Quixotism," not paying attention to the particular strangeness of art. "In the words of Hegel there is no movement. Hegel had an impression that he sees from the hindsight of eternity everything, including the imperial police." The Brechtian V-effect can be read as a creative reinterpretation of Hegel.

10   Daniel Boyarin and Jonathan Boyarin, *Powers of Diaspora* (Minneapolis: University of Minnesota Press, 2002).

11   This translation has been slightly modified; the original is: "*Bytie opredeliaet soznanie, no sovest' ostaetsia neustroennoi.*" Viktor Shklovsky, *Third Factory*, edited and translated by Richard Sheldon (Ann Arbor, MI: Ardis, 1977 [1926]) The slogan "material being conditions consciousness" has been attributed in the Soviet sources to Feuerbach, Hegel, Marx and Lenin. Importantly, in Shklovsky's context, this slogan opened the 1924 declaration of a radical Constructivist group that declared that the writer had to serve the demands of the social and industrial revolution (LTsK [Literature section of Constructivists], "Tekhnicheskii Kodeks," quoted in T.M. Goriaeva, Politicheskaia Tsenzura v SSSR (Moscow: Rosspen, 2002), 123.

12   Viktor Shklovsky, "Sentimental'noe puteshestvie," in *Eshche nichego ne konchilos'* (Moscow: Propaganda, 2002 [1923]), 125. For English, see Viktor Shklovsky, *A Sentimental Journey: Memoirs, 1917-1922,* transl. by Richard Sheldon (Ithaca and London: Cornell University Press, 1984), "On 'Transsensical' (zaumnyj) Antisemitism," 81

13   Viktor Shklovsky, *A Sentimental Journey*, 195.

14   A Sentimental Journey, 112. Exactly what Shklovsky intends by "Aramaic Jews" here is unclear.

15   Victor Shklovsky, *Zoo, Or Letters Not About Love* (New York: Dalkie Archive), 45-46.

16   Jacques Derrida, *Shibboleth: pour Paul Celan* (Paris: Galilee, 1987).

17   It no longer "dehumanizes" but rather makes real the "fear of war. The term "dehumanization of art" was coined by the Spanish philosopher José Ortega y Gasset, who argued that in contrast to Renaissance art and the nineteenth-century novel, man is no longer at the center of modern art;

the new art does not "imitate reality," but operates through inversion, by bringing to life a reality of its own and realizing poetic metaphors. Ortega y Gasset wrote: "the weapon of poetry turns against the natural things and wounds or murders them" (See José Ortega y Gasset, *The Dehumanization of Art*, transl. by Helen Weyl (Princeton, NJ: Princeton University Press, 1968 [1925]) 35.

18   Viktor Shklovsky, 1965 [1917] "Art as Technique" in *Four Formalist Essays*, edited and translated by Lee T. Lemon and Marion J. Reis, 3-24 (Lincoln: University of Nebraska Press, 1965 [1917]), 12.

19   Viktor Shklovsky, *A Sentimental Journey*, 238

20   Viktor Shklovsky, *A Sentimental Journey*, 101.

21   Viktor Shklovsky, *A Sentimental Journey*, 60.

22   Viktor Shklovsky, "Sentimental'noe puteshestvie,"195-196.

23   Viktor Shklovsky, *Third Factory*, edited and translated by Richard Sheldon (Ann Arbor, MI: Ardis, 1977 [1926]), 47-49.

24   See Osip Mandel'shtam, "Fourth Prose," in *Mandel'shtam: The Complete Critical Prose and Letters*, edit. Jane Gary Harris, trans. Jane Gary Harris and Constance Link (Ann Arbor: Ardis, 1979) 312-325.

25   Svetlana Boym, "Dialogue as Lyrical Hermaphroditism, " *Slavic Review*, 1991.

26   Osip Mandelshtam, "The Egyptian Stamp" in *The Noise of Time*, translated and edited by Clarence Brown (New York: Penguin, 1993), 161. Translation is modified by Svetlana Boym.

27   Osip Mandelshtam, "The Egyptian Stamp," 149.

28   Charles Isenberg, *Substantial Proofs of Being: The Prose of Osip Mandelshtam*, (Slavica Publishes, 1987), 168

29   Osip Mandelshtam, "The Egyptian Stamp," 162

30   Osip Mandelshtam, "The Egyptian Stamp," 162

31   The poem is translated into English as "My Age," and begins in translation, "My Age, My Beast." http://www.poetryconnection.net/poets/Osip_ Mandel'shtam/8104, accessed 11/8/2015.

32   Osip Mandel'shtam, "Conversation about Dante," in *Mandel'shtam: The Complete Critical Prose and Letters,* edit. Jane Gary Harris, trans. Jane Gary Harris and Constance Link (Ann Arbor: Ardis, 1979) 406.

33   Mandelshtam first writes about the impulse-creation in his essay on the great Jewish actor Mikhoels whose Jewish mask also resembles the theater of Greek antiquity and who performs through the "vibration in his thinking fingers, animated like [poetic chlenorazdel'naia] speech." (448, vol. 2)

34   Osip Mandel'shtam, "Conversation about Dante," 439. Most importantly, Mandelshtam is not interested in creating a museum of the past but in

perpetuating a certain social architecture that for him constitutes a form of contemporary humanism, where the contemporary is always a little out of step with the present moment to rhyme with the past and the future. In his visionary essay of 1922 "Humanism and the Present" (*Gumanizm i sovremennost'*) Mandelshtam does not think of humanism in the terms of the nineteenth-century psychology and biography-centered literary culture, but in broad Renaissance terms. His humanism is a form of social architecture which does not use human beings as a material for the authoritarian pyramids but exist for humans and in the human scale. Here Mandelshtam extends his temporal range from Assyria and Babylonia to the contemporary moment, challenging the use of the word "revolution" and putting it in the service of humanism and never subscribing to the doctrine of the necessary violence of the revolution: "There are epochs which maintain that man is insignificant, that man is to be used like bricks or mortar, that man should be used for building things, not vice-versa-that things be built for man…. Nevertheless, there is also another form of social architecture whose scale and measure is man. It does not use man to build, it builds for man. Its grandeur is constructed not on the insignificance of individuality but on the highest form of expediency, in accord with its needs." Osip Mandelshtam, "Humanism and the Present," in *Mandel'shtam: The Complete Critical Prose and Letters,* edit. Jane Gary Harris, trans. Jane Gary Harris and Constance Link (Ann Arbor: Ardis, 1979) 181

35   Osip Mandelshtam, Sobranie Sochinenij, Vol.4, 103

36   Benjamin's reflection is obviously more complex than alluded here and changed from one essay to another. This issue is discussed in detail in Svetlana Boym's *Another Freedom*, Chapter 5.

37   Kwame Anthony Appiah, *Cosmopolitanism: Ethics in the World of Strangers* (New York: WW.Norton: 2006).

38   Arendt, "What Is Freedom?" in *Between Past and Future*, 170.

20 CRYPTOARCHITECTURE: CORBUSIER AT 50, A TOUR WITH SVETLANA BOYM

On the evening of April 4th 2013, Svetlana gave a unique, one-off performance, "Cryptoarchitecture: A Tour with Svetlana Boym," in the basement of the Carpenter Center of Visual Arts at Harvard University.

That year marked the 50th Anniversary of the Carpenter Center, Le Corbusier's only building in North America. On that occasion, Katarina Burin and I co-curated Brute, an exhibition engaging the building through new commissions by artists, a speculative exhibition model deploying objects and artworks from Harvard University collections, as well as a series of events, screenings and performances. The exhibition format was regarded as a non-hierarchical process of inquiry and collaboration, and, to that end, we invited Svetlana to give a presentation as part of the final event of our program. She decided her talk would take its cues from the various species of fact and fiction unleashed by the show, spaces of dubious authenticity, gender, questionable histories, associative networks of object, archive and image errata… in short, a space where Svetlana felt right at home.

Imagine, if you will, Svetlana's delivery on that April evening: a Russian accent full of warmth, humor, and a deadpan affectation pierced by the occasional giggle. Novelist, image-maker, writer, scholar, teacher, confidante—Svetlana lobbied ardently for spaces of "play" in her work, pushing the confines of genre, expectation and discipline. That evening she proposed an alternate history of the Carpenter Center, one where a local female architect, rather than "the rationalist Frenchman of Swiss extraction," was hired to renovate the Farlow House, the original 1910 wood carpenter's gothic on the grounds of what became the Carpenter Center. Her talk is a playful satire of the Academy, radicalizing the "quiet historic setting," one *idea triggering the next, building in associative breadth into a rebus-like structure. From intellectual property debates (the "faculty genome project") to sporous fungi, phantom limbs, Leif Erikson, Le Corbusier's ghost in the Charles River, Russian-American relations, budget conscious deanery (one of whom was in the audience, sporting a look of strained, beatific confusion) and, of course, cryptogamic love.*

I was disturbed to realize later that the talk was not documented on video, but now feel that Svetlana would appreciate the images our imaginations conjure and bring to bear upon her incantations in reading the record of this one-time event—her baroque twists of fact and fiction flowering (or "mushrooming") out into the deep red hush of Le Corbusier's Carpenter Center basement, a sporous mold, alive and growing within the institutional cracks.

Amie Siegal

Dear Friends and colleagues

Welcome to the Farlow-Sears Center for Digital Fine Arts at 24 Quincy Street, the home of the Faculty Genome project and the cryptogamic library of the late Dr. Farlow.

Professor Farlow, a noted cryptogamic botanist, was a lover of arts and music and bequeathed his collection to our Center. Here is the photograph of the original Farlow House in colonial style, decorated by Lois Lilly Howe, the first woman member of the Boston Architectural Association.

Today we are celebrating the 50th anniversary of the renovation of the Farlow House, done with the help of Ms. Lois Howe's longtime partner, Ms. Eleanor Manning. Skylight design by Ms. Molnar. And the work was curated by Katarina Burin. We will mention, too, the generous support of Ms. Clara Endicott Sears, a noted philanthropist and cryptogamist, sometimes mistaken for a Shaker.

The addition to the Farlow House was completed in 1963. A gracious red brick building with updated infra-structure makes for a harmonious ensemble with other notable buildings on Quincy street such as Harvard's Faculty Club and the Fogg Museum.

In 1993, the Architectural Digest magazine commented: "The Farlow Sears Center anticipates the new urbanism of the late 1980s and prefigures a moderate postmodern architecture without the excesses of a Gerry or a Koolhaas." Architectural historian Ilana Goldberg[1] wrote in House and Garden Magazine: "The Farlow Sears Building bypassed the controversial *architettura bruta* and the so called international style, building an organic bridge from the European Bauhaus to the American Garden-House."

Here we see the Farlow Sears Center reflected in the work of Olga Carr.[2] The project is presented on the seventh floor of the exhibition *Brute* next to the cryptogamic orangerie. These images come from *Multitasking with Clouds: Puddle Architecture*, where we recognize a classical Harvardian window.

Let us not forget that fifty years ago the remarkable Farlow House was threatened with demolition. Several projects for the center for visual arts were developed for the site including ones by Louis Kahn and Le Corbusier. While the latter was certainly not without interest[3] it showed a complete disregard for the history of the site and the remarkable contributions of the aforementioned local women architects. We are very grateful to our forward looking deans for preserving Harvard's historical heritage. The new addition to the Farlow Sears Building is perfectly suited to house our undergraduate MegaLab and the new Faculty Genome Project.

A few words about the Faculty Genome Project:

From Education X to Education Y: the Faculty Genome Project (FGP)

1 **SGS**s (Sensitive Genomic Swipes) are developed to collect the embryos of new ideas directly from the faculty member's brain under local anesthesia.

2 Organically conceived **FEI**s (Faculty Embryo Ideas) are grown in the meta-dish under the supervision of the Council of Deans, appointed by the President.

3 **ECC** (Embryo Creative Commons) is cultivated through cryptogamic fertilization of faculty ideas.

Net Gain: 44% Budget Cuts on faculty and student travel, art supplies, research grants and library acquisitions.

Community Development: Faculty and Students enjoy advanced digital technology in a quiet historical setting.

We think of this project as the most recent continuation of the cryptogamic experiments of Dr. Farlow.

Let us now revisit the history of the site. Here is a photograph from the Farlow archive. The first renovation to Dr. Farlow's House was done in the early 1910s by the most distinguished Boston woman architect at the time, Lois Lilley Howe. She was born on September 25, 1864 in Cambridge, Massachusetts, the eldest of four children. From a young age, Howe showed an interest in architecture. The workers building Sanders Theatre on Harvard Yard in 1876 dubbed her "the little superintendent" for her constant comments on their project. As a teenager she proposed a redesign of the staircase in her parents' house. In 1888, Howe entered MIT's School of Architecture and after graduation opened her own firm at 73 Tremont Street in Boston. In her first job she shared the office with two men, but at the end of the first year these two men left her "high and dry. One of the best things that happened to me", observed

Lois Howe in her address to MIT alumnae. Later she worked exclusively with women: Mary Almy and Eleanor Manning became her partners in 1913. In 1901, Howe became the second woman elected to the A.I.A. (American Institute of Architects). She was the first woman elected to the Boston Society of Architects. Howe's later work used the English Garden City model to develop a New England version of Garden City architecture. Contemporary Boston architect Graham Gund purchased one of Howe's houses and said that it had a "certain gutsy Thomas Jefferson quality about it, grandness of texture and a sense of simple and free-flowing spaces." So, once again we are thankful that the work of such a remarkable architect is housing our Center.

Here you see Lois Howe in her family circle with the family dog William James and Lois' beloved cat Gertrude.[4]

Lois Lilley Howe passed away in Cambridge on September 13, 1964 just twelve days short of her hundredth birthday. Before her death she saw her last dream come true—the completion of the Farlow Sears Center, done with the generous support of old friend and eccentric cryptogamist, Clara Endicott Sears.

Howe was friendly with Dr. and Mrs. Farlow and shared many of their interests in garden architecture and cryptogamic botany. Professor Farlow was a Renaissance Man, versed in both art and science. Born near Boston, Massachusetts on December 17, 1844, he was equally gifted in both science and music, but decided to embrace the new audacious discipline of cryptogamic botany. In 1879 Farlow was appointed Professor of Cryptogamic Botany at Harvard and did remarkable research on fungi and algae. His two major works *Host Index to Fungi in the United States* (1888) and the *Bibliographical Index of North American Algue* (1905) remain indispensable reading for all of us, taking nostalgic walks on the Charles River and gathering mushrooms in the Cambridge woods.

Following Farlow's marriage to Lilian Horsford in 1900 their home became a haven for visiting botanists. Later, in the 1940s, it turned a lady's lounge and salon—anticipating The Radcliffe Center for Advanced Studies. Lois Howe was friendly primarily with the beautiful and rebellious Mrs. Lilian Farlow, who was an active amateur historian. Together they explored the secret gardens of Cambridge and their mysterious archeology.

In my research I managed to get hold of the minutes of *The Forty Fourth Meeting of the Cambridge Historical Association*: "MRS. WILLIAM GILSON FARLOW spoke on the traces of houses built here by the Northmen in the year 1000, discovered and identified by her father, Eben Norton Horsford". Eben Norton Horsford (1818–1893) was an American scientist who is best known for his reformulation of baking powder, his interest in Viking settlements in America and the monuments he built to Leif Erikson. Horsford travelled extensively in Scandinavia, became interested in Viking visits to North America (such as Leif Erikson's) and was determined to prove that North America had been discovered not by a Mediterranean Catholic (like Cristobal Colon (possibly a converso)), or Americo Vespurri, but by an Aryan.

I need not remind you that according to this theory, Vikings simultaneously founded Ancient Russ - the Novgorodian kingdom, or Rurik, Igor and Olga - and travelled to what would later become America. We can conjecture then that had they succeeded, they would have found the largest empire of Ame-Rossia that would have expanded from Novgorod to Cambridge.

Back now to the meeting of the Cambridge Historical Association: Mrs. Farlow continued her father's work and can be seen as the founder of crypto-architecture, even if she herself did not use the term. Some remains of old Northmen's buildings were found during the inauguration of 29 Garden Street in Cambridge in the trash of the landscape institute.

So What is Cryptogamy?

Cryptogam refers to a plant or plantlike organism that reproduces by means of spores and not through the production of flowers or seed. Cryptogamae are the opposite of the Phanerogamae (Greek φανερός, *phaneros* = "visible") or Spermatophyta (Greek σπέρμα, *sperma* = "seed" and φυτόν, *phyton* = "plant"), or: seed plants. This classification has been deprecated in Linnaean taxonomy.

In local popular culture, from the American Civil War to the Cold War, cryptogamic plants are viewed as alien and dangerous. But in other parts of the world they were known for their mysterious healing powers as well. The legendary Slavic Raskovnik was considered to be a poison and cure at once. In Serbian, Bulgarian and Slovak mythologies Raskovnik is believed to unlock the mysteries of love. The problem is that this medicinal plant disguises itself and can only be identified by a rare Ruthenian hedgehog known as *eshiechek* that became endangered after the last Balkan war.

Cryptogamic science reaches its peak at the turn of the 19th century—the time of historicism, *art nouveau* and aestheticism. It is a poetic intercourse between art and science.

Mordecai Cooke in his celebrated *Romance of Lower Plants* speaks of cryptogamic love that is not concerned with procreation but with creation; it is a love for love's sake, art for art's sake. For Louis Menand, a Harvard Professor, cryptogamic science is a beautiful and useless aristocratic science that harks back to the biblical paradise.

But I am getting ahead of myself. *The Book Without a Name*, a rare copy of which is found in the Widener Library, reminds us to slow down and be attuned to the ancient art of curiosity. From Socrates to Newton, this art of attunement is the highest achievement of cryptogamy. (Cryptogamic history doesn't reproduce itself according to the laws of conventional evolution, but mushrooms into unknown potentialities.)

In the twentieth century cryptogamy became the foundation of the imaginative practice that influenced many local writers, such as Vladimir Nabokov, who took frequent walks between various houses built by Lois Howe on Craigie and Quincy Streets.

He recalled this in *Speak, Memory*: "I discovered in nature the non-utilitarian delights that I sought in art. Both were a form of magic, both were a game of intricate enchantment and deception."[5] Vladimir Nabokov walked by the Viking plaque near the Charles River and dreamed of Amerossia – the continent that would join northern Russia with New England.

Charles River walks have become an important ritual for the cryptogamists and fellow travelers. On one breezy February day in 1969 Borges walked by Dr. Farlow's house, then passed Dunster house and found himself on the river, where a mysterious stranger spoke with an Argentine accent. This was none other than Borges' younger self. Borges the younger dreamed of the brotherhood of all men, while Borges the elder doubted the existence of a single individual. The event has been recorded thirty years later by Borges the younger.

In the early 1960s Vera Nabokov recalls her husband Vladimir relating an amusing episode of running into a pensive man in glasses mumbling to himself in French. The writer recognized the words *merde* and *artist* but couldn't make sense of the whole sentence. The two men greeted each other, barely cracking a smile, the way Europeans who despise small talk do.

The man was none other than Corbusier – and he had much to be upset about. In 1947 his UN project did not materialize. Corbusier, jet-setting around the world, made a stop in Boston. He proposed a building for the Center for Visual Art with assistance from his old friend Louis Sert. The hope was that the Carpenters would support the new center for so called "environmental studies". Luckily, our venerable deans intervened on time! Quoting the Bauhaus dictum they said: "We believe that everybody at Harvard is talented, everybody is an artist, and there is no need to destroy our architectural heritage to prove it. There is no place for that kind of contemporary art next to Harvard yard."

However, Corbusier persisted. He proposed the design for the prospective Carpenter Center. He commented that accomplishing anything in the United States was just as difficult as working in the Soviet Union. He wanted to build a Cambridge sibling to his Moscow Tsentrosoiuz building, offering a virtual ramp to connect the two Cold War rivals. One marked facet of Le Corbusier's design is the use of concrete *pilotis* to elevate the building above the ground. In his final design, he aligned some of the *pilotis* with the existing trees, which, I would argue, is an explicit reference not only to European Bauhaus but also to the American garden house in the spirit of Lois Howe. Corbusier rejected Harvard's brick architecture; he believed that only the light-colored concrete is capable of reflecting the morning sun and capturing the elongated shadows of the afternoon. Clearly the rationalist Frenchman of Swiss extraction knew very little about cryptogamic light.

And yet, to be objective, we can say that Corbusier's project is not without merit. The model for the Carpenter Center has been venerated in architectural circles for the past fifty years. It became a masterpiece of paper architecture joining the legendary Tatlin Tower, the most famous un-built monument in history, one that became a phantom limb of non-conformist art all over the world.

As is the case with Tatlin's Tower, we are not sure if the Carpenter Center was a viable engineering endeavor and whether it could have been built at all. Our team made a counterfactual reconstruction with this computer generated image of the building. The department could have been called The Department of Visual Media and Sensory Geography, and would have housed a collection of analog celluloids from obscure countries that no longer exist, where classes in snail film-making and streetwalking on ruined maps would have been offered.

Prof. Ross McElwee, otherwise known for his photographic memory, shot an unusual counterfactual documentary where he cast an unemployed Yugoslav actor, Slobo Raskovnikov, to play Vlada Petric, the director of the fictional Harvard Film Archives.

That Film Archive, in the basement of the so called Carpenter Center, was an outmoded European transplant, a utopian place where lonely immigrants from Cambridge could wander into the darkness of a movie theater and feel at home. There were rumors that in the 1980s and 90s the Film Archive went through an experimental phase under the leadership of the Yugoslav avantgardist Vlada Petric. Here the Yugoslav director Dushan Makaveev dreamed of making a film that documents one day in the life of the Kremlin's crows and walls, and the Hungarian Miklos Janczo threatened to make the longest take in the history of cinema without ever leaving the basement. For our exhibition today the team of the Farlow-Sears researched and simulated an antique paper version of the Film Archive Program. I have a few copies here.

Amie and Katarina lovingly reconstructed Corbusier's ramp that nobody dared to cross to the other side of the looking glass and from there on to Prospect Street. Marina Rechny, professor of Sensory Ethnography, conducted a rigorous cryptogramic research on the memory of the Charles River. I will share with you her uncanny discoveries.

Experiment in Multitasking with Clouds

I take regular walks on the Charles River as a kind of urban ritual. On a cool March day in 2011 I began to photograph shadows on the rippled surface of the river frolicking and touching each other. When I came home I discovered a face made of skywater, litter and light. I continued my pilgrimages to the river over March and April and only once or twice in a thousand images there would be an intimation of face, a promise of a chance encounter. A face recognition device on the camera never helped. Only the human eye could make out the human likeness. The probability of the figuration was almost equal to the "human error" in the technological process, a teasing contingency

caught by the camera. I realized that I wasn't capturing ghosts but a material flow of reflections which inspired religion, science and art. The images evoked beginnings of creation or pentimenti for an unknown painting and architecture.

Dr. Pnina Grietzer, a scholar of Biblical Studies, suggested that the images evoke the second day of creation and the separation of waters, but it is unclear who is in the likeness of whom, who is a creature and who a creator.

Over the next three months Marina was able to encounter 10 clear likenesses that could not be reproduced through similar scientific experiments. The Cryptic disguise she practiced was a unique co-creation. We invited people to stop the film, but few found ready-made revelations.

This experiment raises many questions: Is this a dream of paradise or a nightmare of the diluvium? Is this an expression of crypto love or of crypto architecture? Can we recognize these faces? Is this a daydreaming Viking or a distracted Lilian Hornsfeld, bored at the meetings of The Cambridge Historical Society? Is this a vacationing UFO or somebody much more familiar to us?

Well, there is no doubt in my mind that this image can only be the ghost of Le Corbusier. His ghost guided me through my own unrealized project. I followed the route of Vikings backwards from the Charles to the Moskva River, in search of the Moscow sibling of the unrealized Carpenter Center, the sibling that would give us the best sense of what the building would have looked like.

Le Corbusier's one and only building in the former Soviet Union was meant to be a laboratory of revolutionary architecture. Instead it became an archive of unrealized possibilities. Built for the Trade Union Center, it housed the Russian State's Statistical Bureau.

I went back to Moscow for the first time in ten years, navigating the local puddles to the Corbusier building. Instead of the constructivist concrete it was clad in red volcanic stone from the Caucasus. The Moscow building shared the *piloti* with the unrealized Cambridge project—the phantom limbs of the International Style. I couldn't find the entrance to the building. Its open and lifted first floor, the model for the public sphere of the future garden city, was fenced. In fact, there were several fences there, both solid and porous. Behind these fences the building was dreaming.

Victor Shklovsky, a contemporary of Corbusier and a noted cryptogamist wrote a fable about revolutionary art and the wind: "A peasant asks Nickolas the Wondermaker to give him total control over the weather so he could perfect the revolutionary art of agriculture. The Wondermaker grants his wish, but in the next season the peasant grows the worst crop ever. 'Did you try to regulate the wind?', asked the Wondermaker. 'The wind that moves the clouds, pollinates the grains and plays the games of chance?!'"

"Dear Future Comrades," appeals Shklovsky "leave the wind alone. Let it blow. It's impossible to regulate the unknown."

On a breezy Sunday in the fall of 2012 with my camera in hand I made an oblique route around the fenced Corbusier building. "The building is closed," said the security guard. "No photography." Once again, I failed to enter the Corbusier building. All I managed to capture was a gust of wind.

Well, I am happy to come full circle from dreams to reality and back to our Farlow-Sears Center of Digital Fine Arts and the home to the Faculty Genome Project. It's fine to scratch phantom limbs, and today we can all scratch the model of the carpenter center with a mixture of pleasure and pain, remembering that some dreams should remain dreams and reality cannot plagiarize them.

Disclaimer

An all persons fictitious disclaimer is a disclaimer in which a work of media states that all persons portrayed in it are fictitious. This is done to reduce the possibility of legal action for libel from any person who believes that he or she has been libeled via their portrayal in the work (whether portrayed under their real name or a different name).

Such a disclaimer often reads similarly to the following:

Most characters appearing in this work are not fictitious. Any resemblance to real persons, living or dead, is deliberate. The wording of this disclaimer differs from jurisdiction to jurisdiction, and from country to country, as does its legal effectiveness.

Origins

The disclaimer originated with the 1932 MGM movie, *Rasputin and the Empress*, which insinuated that the character Princess Natasha had been raped by Rasputin. Princess Natasha's character was supposedly intended to represent Princess Irina of Russia, and the real Princess Irina sued MGM for libel. After seeing the film twice, the jury agreed that the princess had been defamed. Princess Irina and her husband Felix Youssoupoff were reportedly awarded $127,373 in damages by the English Court of Appeals in 1934 and $1 million in an out-of-court settlement with MGM. As a preventive measure against further lawsuits, the film was taken out of distribution for decades. Prompted by the outcome of this case many studios began to incorporate an "all persons fictitious" disclaimer in their films in order to try to protect themselves from similar court action.

Ironic Use

Because the disclaimer is intended for serious purposes, it is often the subject of comedic satire. The Three Stooges' parody of Nazi Germany, "You Nazty Spy", stated that "Any resemblance between the characters in this picture and any persons, living or dead, is a miracle." The sequel "I'll Never Heil Again" states that: "[t]he characters in this picture are fictitious. Anyone resembling them is better off dead". In the film *An American Werewolf in London*, and in Michael Jackson's *Thriller* the disclaimer refers to "persons living, dead or undead". An episode of the TV series *Red Dwarf* included a news report saying an ancient scroll had been found containing such a disclaimer for the Bible. The novel *Breakfast of Champions* by Kurt Vonnegut features a truncated version of the disclaimer referring to the novel's existentialist themes: "All persons, living and dead, are purely coincidental, and should not be construed".. The memoir *A Heartbreaking Work of Staggering Genius*, by Dave Eggers, because of its autobiographical nature, features the following play on the usual disclaimer: "Any resemblance to persons living or dead should be plainly apparent to them and those who know them, especially if the author has been kind enough to have provided their real names and, in some cases, their phone numbers. All events described herein actually happened, though on occasion the author has taken certain, very small, liberties with chronology, because that is his right as an American." Richard Linklater's 1990 feature film *Slacker* ends with "This story was based on fact. Any similarity with fictitious events or characters was purely coincidental." All episodes of *South Park* open with a tongue-in-cheek disclaimer that begins by stating, "All characters and events in this show – even those based on real people – are entirely fictional. All celebrity voices are impersonated – poorly." In the beginning of the 2009 American comedy-drama film *(500) Days of Summer*, a disclaimer is given: "Any resemblance to people living or dead is purely coincidental ... Especially you, Jenny Beckman ... Bitch." (The film is about a failed romantic relationship.)

Disclaimers can occasionally be used to make political or similar points. One such chilling disclaimer is shown at the end of the industrial/political thriller *The Constant Gardener*, signed by the author of the original book, John Le Carre: "Nobody in this story, and no outfit or corporation, thank God, is based upon an actual person or outfit in the real world. But I can tell you this; as my journey through the pharmaceutical jungle progressed, I came to realize that, by comparison with reality, my story was as tame as a holiday postcard.". The 1969 film *Z*, which satirizes the military dictatorship ruling Greece at that time, has this notice: "Any resemblance to actual events, to persons living or dead, is not the result of chance. It is DELIBERATE." The novel *The Lost Honour of Katharina Blum* by the German nobel laureate Heinrich Böll was originally preceded by the following disclaimer: "The characters and action in this story are purely fictitious. If the depiction of certain journalistic practices should have resulted in similarities with the practices of the Bild newspaper, these similarities are neither intended nor coincidental but inevitable." For legal reasons this disclaimer was later removed in the English edition.

Notes

1   [Ilana Goldberg is one of the names by which Svetlana often referred to herself. -T. Abramov]

2   [Olga Carr, too, was one of Svetlana's alter egos. - T. Abramov]

3   [This is Le Corbusier's design for the Carpenter Center, the house of the Harvard Film Archive and Harvard's VHS department which stands there today, in the place of the Farlowe House. - T. Abramov]

4   [This image is one of Svetlana's beloved cat, Koshka. -T. Abramov]

5   Vladimir Nabokov, *Speak Memory* (Vintage, NY), 1986, 125.

PART SIX

AFTERIMAGES: SVETLANA BOYM'S IRREPRESSIBLE CO-CREATIONS

To most people Svetlana Boym was known as a writer: a prolific writer of books marked by originality, insight, and irreverence for intellectual pieties, no matter how fashionable.[1] The media artist side of her presented in this section was chronologically last of her artistic personas. A whole string of these bifurcated the bios at the end of Boym's monographs. In the first, *Death in Quotation Marks* (1991), she introduced herself as a playwright and assistant professor of comparative literature at Harvard University. In the second, *Common Places: Mythologies of Everyday Life in Russia* (1994), she was also a writer and filmmaker. In her third, most well-known monograph, *The Future of Nostalgia* (2001), she was again a writer, and this time, full professor at Harvard, but also, as the back cover blurb reminds us, "a native of St. Petersburg who lived in Cambridge, Massachusetts." "Native" was a word she would have pronounced with an accentuated accent and that she wore as a mask, as another persona. Her creativity was hard to contain and performative—the whole world was her stage—thus all her authorial and artistic personas. It is just at the end of *Another Freedom* (2010), her last monograph, that she introduced herself to readers as a media artist.

Her biographies were not accidental inconsistencies but sustained exercises in self-fashioning, and lately, she told me during our last conversation, self-editing. "There are writers with biographies and writers without biographies," she often quoted Boris Tomashevskii's quip as an intriguing prelude to her influential critique of "the death of the author."[2] So it is fitting to consider Boym's art in relation to her writing and to her biographies, her crafted fashioning, and editing of herself. Far from any sort *Gesamtkunstwerk*—a concept she detested, these were co-creations, whose contingent coexistence inspired thoughts on difference and a heightened sensitivity to the beauty of cracks, hinges, borderlines, and transit zones.

Co-creation was a concept she developed and lived for many years, and theorized at length, equating it with freedom, in her last book.[3] Among her co-creators were the people around her as well as thinkers, artists, and philosophers with whom she engaged passionately. For her digital art, co-creators were also "the unmemorable landscapes" registered in her cosmopolitan travels. Some of her most successful art projects, such as *Hydrant Immigrants* (see plates 2–5), took place at the hinge between writing, photography, autobiography, and scholarship. She paired images of New York City hydrants with fragments of interviews she conducted over the years with immigrants (herself included), a project that stemmed from her essay "On Diasporic Intimacy."[4] Readers have in the meantime become more familiar with the crafted montage of voices used to going unheard. The genre has just won Nobel Prize recognition in Svetlana Alexievich's haunting work. Yet in Boym's *Hydrant Immigrants* the playfulness, humor, and attention to that double movement of echo and dissonance (between, art and life, figural and literal, word and image) makes each photo text diptych fully her own. Her signature grows even more unmistakable in the repetitions with significant differences that organize most of her pieces in series, her preferred mode of working and exhibiting.

Besides turning fellow immigrants and hydrants into co-creators, Boym also turned to broken technologies, such as printers out of black ink, for inspiration. She welcomed chance and imperfection to stunning visual and intellectual results, in her art as well as in daily life. Like most of us, she made typos in the process of writing. The only handout from her class that I still have, for a seminar on the death of the author, preserves a trace of her impetuousness in a misprint. Boym rarely wasted precious time fixing typos. Instead she composed a manifesto on human error and wrote an exquisite theory of the "misprint" that addresses what she saw as a gap in our ethical reckoning with the Gulag.[5] Her last artistic project, *Phantom Limbs* (see Plates 13–15), was a celebration of literal erring. During her ritual walk to the Charles River over the space of two years, she took thousands of photographs of water surfaces, among which she discovered ten "faces of litter and light." *Phantom Limbs* also tracked the conceptual and practical consequences of "human error" and the beauty and humanity that can be rediscovered in it. One way she told of her life-changing encounter with theory was the shiver of terror she felt while reading Michel Foucault's description of the face of man drawn in the sand being washed out to sea in the last paragraph of *The Order of Things*. I heard this story in her theory seminar, long after she had stopped worrying and learned to love that bomb. Yet I wonder if some of the intimations of faces—wry, incomplete, and cracked—that she rescued in her last project were not recovering some of the face washed out in that formative early terror.

Boym even turned into a co-creator the process that some of us are still going through years after her passing—mourning. So we can learn to mourn for Svetlana, from Svetlana. This may seem improbable not only because she was the embodiment of vivacity, but also because she entered academic discourse through a critique of what she perceived as "the peculiar necrophilia that dominates literary theory." This is the first line of the book jacket of her first book, where she continued: "Whether it be under the banner of 'anatomy of criticism' or 'death of the author,' students of literature seem fated to form a Dead Poets' Society."[6] I came to study with her a decade after she published that book, and my first impression of comparative literature at Harvard was that I was going to get at least a certificate, if not the whole PhD, in mourning. Comparative literature was still shaken by the revelations of Paul de Man's collaborationist past, revelations made in the wake of his death and of his public mourning by some of the most highly regarded names of the day. There was a sense that mourning was not just hard but also hard to get right.[7] It was a mined territory, and one could easily blunder. Against this background, enter Boym's spontaneous work of mourning for Jacques Derrida created on the day of his death, a work she dedicated to Barbara Johnson.

Touching Writing (see Plate 1) shows Boym at work co-creating, even while mourning. It is a creative act all the way down to the concrete sense of producing a new object. Next to the image, she wrote:

> In the absence of a mourning ritual, I found myself taking photographs of the fallen page, touching the words in the light, casting shadows,

animating the lines. According to legend, the sixteenth-century Venetian painter Titian discovered the secret of depicting the warmth of the human body when he held his fingers up to the light and marveled at the reddish aura around them. He tried to capture this aura in his paintings, smudging the lines of the body with a touch of red. In my photographs I am projecting this light touch into the writing, conjuring up ghosts.[8]

There is much to be said about this work that projects Boym's fingers, described in the larger piece as warm, foreign, and ghostly, playing with a text that so famously denied its outside, its *dehors*. Suffice it to say that this play with light is no light play, but a distillation of a lifetime of rigorous engagement with Derrida that began in *Death in Quotation Marks*. For me, what matters is that her mourning is an act of co-creation, an act whereby she conjures his ghost at the risk of her own warm fingers turning ghostly. Boym artfully handles the essential part of mourning we so often avoid, the fear of seeing our own mortality in another's. When she created the piece, she described it to me as a hand extended toward her mentor, Barbara Johnson, who at the time was retreating from the public life of the university as the illness that was to claim her life a few years later advanced. Boym placed herself in the middle, between a mentor just disappeared and one about to step into the shadows. Animating the words of the departed while extended to the living, her hand, turned medium, glows transparent in the process of making.

On Svetlana Boym's website (www.svetlanaboym.com) you can find her art and learn that it has been shown in galleries in New York as well as at an installation at the Berlin Schlesischer Busch Watchtower. She had solo shows in Ljubljana, Glasgow, Copenhagen, Kaunas, and Cambridge. She gave lectures/performances: the Sigmund Freud Museum in Vienna, the Artists Space and MoMA in New York City, the Kunsthalle Wien (Vienna), the Carpenter Center for the Visual Arts (Harvard University), the City of Women Festival (Ljubljana), the Maison des sciences de l'homme (Paris), and the Institute of Contemporary Art (Moscow).

Yet there exists a more personal, miniature retrospective of her art, one that she sent to a few friends, pasted in between the lines of a story she was working on in her last months (Figure 27.1, pp. 408–501, present volume). "Remembering Forgetting: Tale of the Refugee Camp" tells of her return to the outskirts of Vienna to find the refugee camp she inhabited after leaving the Soviet Union in 1981. The story contains a succinct artist statement: "Since the late 1990s I've been documenting my travels through the world, collecting errors, overexposures, chance encounters. I have been taking pictures of the places that I would otherwise not remember."[9] The story spins this statement into a narrative, illustrates it, and performs it into an *ars photographica*. Indeed, the story contains not just images of the refugee camp but also some of Boym's seemingly unrelated iconic images. Out of her series *Family Album* (see Plate 6) (which showcases not just particular photographs but the experience of looking at an album and the contingent moment of coming across a picture distorted by the overlay of a half-raised sheet protector, see Plate 6) she chose the 1990s shine of an album page of plastic slide pockets. In one photo, most of the pockets are shining empty. Only two slides are left—one barely visible, the other just a white cardboard frame, with the film missing. A few pages later, there is the peacock she discovered with delight—accompanied by a flood of references to Charles Baudelaire's "The Swan" and to Vladimir Nabokov's "Mademoiselle O"—among new construction in my NYC neighborhood, a photo that made its way into her *Leaving New York (Cities in Transit)* series (see Plates 8–9). In the same series, a dandelion explodes the façade of a communal apartment in *Leaving Sarajevo* (see Plate 7).

"Remembering Forgetting" gives a key to this collection of seemingly disparate images, as to much of Boym's media art, in the record of a short exchange that followed a presentation she gave at the Vienna Kunsthalle. A seemingly grumpy—if insightful—man in the audience asked her: "'Why do you photograph the same landscape in different places?' 'I don't know,' I said. 'These are just transits, warzones, afterimages of something we see and forget.'"[10] Later on, upon visiting the camp near Vienna, she admits that the return did not prompt any rush of *mémoire involontaire*, no immigrant madeleine—"*bulochka* soaked in the camp tea."[11] So the story gets titled "Remembering Forgetting" after this signature line: "Only I don't remember any of that and I'd rather not fill the gaps with a plausible fiction."[12] What the visit does bring her, however, is an experience of "almost ecstatic photographing." Returned to Boston, upon reflection and creative manipulation of the photographs, she has a revelation:

Upon my arrival back in Boston, I found myself staring at the images of the camp, rescuing and highlighting the cracks in the wall.
Everything I photographed all over the world was there: the stains on

the concrete walls, sickly poppy flowers and dandelions, half-readable signs, the pinecones in a disowned shopping cart and a dove, the color of urban ruins. . . . Wandering through the invisible ruins of the camp I discovered the landscape of my own photographs that travelled with me from one continent to another.[13]

This paragraph comes as close to a key to her art as we may ever get: The memory that has been lost, repressed, not just by her but by all the other fellow immigrants she interviews, comes back to haunt them, superimposing itself over everything. It frames the world in its likeness. The narrator quotes an art historian friend and fellow immigrant who recalls the camp yard as a Kazimir Malevich black square.

That the story reached this blanket Freudian interpretation of all her fellow immigrants' psyches and afterimages surprised me. Boym distrusted any one interpretational paradigm, and when her students got too Freudian for her taste in their readings, she would sometimes jokingly quote Joseph Brodsky's admonishment to his imaginary reader, at the end of his brush with an Oedipal scene: "Exit Sigmund Freud."[14] In "Remembering Forgetting," she comments: "We never saw the Vienna that we dreamed about, the city of Mozart and Sigmund Freud. We remained extraterritorial. Like the Freudian unconscious our transit camp had no outside; it was a place out of place and a time out of time."[15] Yet this world without outsides was not her geography—she found cracks, and from there exits, even if just through the friction she created by comparing a literal and a figurative no-exit space, like in the sentence above. Just as she had found an improbable exit as an eighteen-year-old out of Brezhnev's Soviet Union, she found the exit to the refugee camp and later returned to Vienna repeatedly.

Few artists have as much insight into their art, or articulate that insight as eloquently, as Boym did. The texts of her manifestoes, interviews, mixed media art, scholarship, and short stories provide some of the most exquisite keys to her art. Often an integral part of the art, the writing never falls into the trap of explication, as her art never falls into the trap of illustration. There is too much humor, irony, dialogism, and assumed contingency for that. Whether literal or figurative, the keys, while always beautifully wrought, sometimes remind us more of locks that no longer exist than open any locks at hand. Sometimes they open little side gates into her wanderer's world, revealing other gates nested like Matryoshkas. And sometimes they intimate the contours of locks to exit doors we did not even imagine possible. Yet as anyone who had the honor to have

Boym as a house guest knows, she could always be trusted to repeatedly lose and find keys—yours and her own—literally and figuratively. There was no guarantee of a happy ending to the sequence of finding and losing: some keys did end up lost for good. Yet there was a guarantee that losses would be followed by searches, conversations, flaneries, and contingent discoveries. This last section records some of their afterimages.

Cristina Vatulescu

Notes

1. This is a shortened version of "Afterimages: Svetlana Boym's Irrepressible Cocreations" originally published in *diacritics*, 43:3 (2015), pp. 98–109. Reproduced by kind permission of *diacritics*.

2. Boym, *Death in Quotation Marks*, p. 24

3. Boym, "Freedom as Cocreation," introduction to *Another Freedom: The Alternative History of an Idea*, pp. 1–36.

4. Boym, *The Future of Nostalgia*, pp. 251–58.

5. Boym, *Another Freedom*, pp. 255–84.

6. Boym, *Death in Quotation Marks*, book jacket.

7. In my first year of graduate school, we read de Man's own prescriptions on mourning, with his dichotomy between "true mourning" and bad mourning "the pathos of terror" in several classes (de Man, "Anthropomorphism and Trope in the Lyric," p. 262). Bad mourning was excoriated. Proposed good examples were held to close scrutiny: Derrida's *Adieu to Levinas*, Lyotard's *Mémorial immémorial*, the numerous tributes at de Man's memorial, and their varied rewritings by their famed authors once de Man's past came to light, collected in *Yale French Studies* 69: "The Lesson of Paul de Man."

8. Boym, "Touching Writing," October 8, 2004, *Svetlana Boym: Nostalgic Technology*, http://www.svetlanaboym.com/touching.htm.

9. Boym, "Remembering Forgetting: Tale of the Refugee Camp" (unpublished manuscript, 2015), p. 5.

10. Boym, "Remembering Forgetting: Tale of the Refugee Camp," p. 7.

11. Ibid., p. 20.

12. Ibid., p. 4.

13. Ibid., pp. 20–21.

14. Joseph Brodsky, *Less than One*, p. 27.

15. Boym, "Remembering Forgetting: Tale of the Refugee Camp," p. 4.

Works Cited

Bartos, Adam, and Svetlana Boym. *Kosmos: A Portrait of the Russian Space Age.* New York: Princeton Architectural Press, 2001.

Boym, Svetlana. *Another Freedom: The Alternative History of an Idea.* Chicago: Chicago University Press, 2010.

Boym, Svetlana. *Common Places: Mythologies of Everyday Life in Russia.* Cambridge: Harvard University Press, 1994.

Boym, Svetlana. *Death in Quotation Marks: Cultural Myths of the Modern Poet.* Cambridge: Harvard University Press, 1991.

Boym, Svetlana. *The Future of Nostalgia.* New York: Basic Books, 2001.

Boym, Svetlana. *Ninochka: A Novel.* Albany: State University of New York Press, 2003.

Brodsky, Joseph. *Less than One.* New York: Farrar Straus Giroux, 1985.

Brooks, Peter, Shoshana Felman, and J. Hillis Miller, eds. "The Lesson of Paul de Man." Special issue, *Yale French Studies*, 69 (1985).

de Man, Paul. "Anthropomorphism and Trope in the Lyric." In *The Rhetoric of Romanticism*, 239–62. New York: Columbia University Press, 1984.

Derrida, Jacques. *Adieu to Emmanuel Levinas.* Translated by Pascale-Anne Brault and Michael Naas. Stanford: Stanford University Press, 1999.

Lyotard, Jean-François. "Mémorial immémorial." In *L'exposition imaginaire: The Art of Exhibiting in the Eighties*, edited by Evelyn Beer and Riet de Leeuw, 247–71. The Hague: Rijksdienst Beeldende Kunst, 1989.

Tomashevskii, Boris. "Literatura i biografiia." *Kniga i revoliutsiia*, 4 (1923): 6–9.

21 TOUCHING WRITING (HOMAGE TO JACQUES DERRIDA, OCTOBER 8, 2004)

For Barbara Johnson

On the day of Jacques Derrida's death I found on my bookshelf a fallen page from Of Grammatology with pencil marks and scribbled Russian words in the margins. The text spoke about "the end of the book and the beginning of writing" and about metaphorical transports. I remembered that one of the first courses I ever took in English was Barbara Johnson's Deconstruction in the Fall of 1983. Ironically the first theoretical text I studied in English happened to be Gayatri Spivak's translation of Of Grammatology. For a recent immigrant from Russia, this was a strange "beginning of writing" in a foreign language. My English and my entire way of thinking would never be the same.

In the absence of a mourning ritual, I found myself taking photographs of the fallen page, touching the words in the light, casting shadows, animating the lines. According to legend, the sixteenth-century Venetian painter Titian discovered the secret of depicting the warmth of the human body when he held his fingers up to the light and marveled at the reddish aura around them. He tried to capture this aura in his paintings, smudging the lines of the body with a touch of red. In my photographs I am projecting this light touch into the writing, conjuring up ghosts.

Note: Related images appeared on the cover of PMLA journal in March 2005 (a special forum on Derrida)

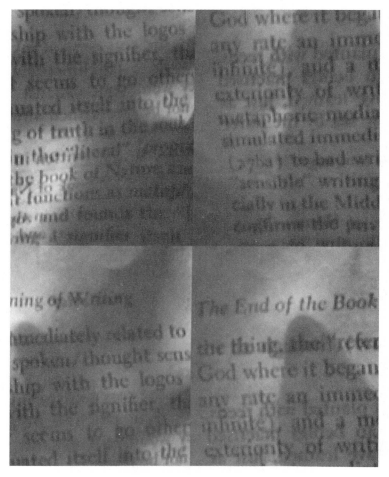

FIGURE 21.1 Svetlana Boym, "Homage to Derrida," *Touching Writing*, 2004. Digital Photograph

22 IMMIGRANT HYDRANTS

Description: 15-20   22″ × 17″ photographic prints

Dialogues, complaints, appeals, outbursts, and snippets of recollection of New York immigrants of different backgrounds (including the author's own) are recorded and recreated from the hydrant's point of view.

Note: See "On Diasporic Intimacy" in Boym, *The Future of Nostalgia*

FIGURE 22.1 Svetlana Boym, "Chemiak," *Hydrant Immigrants*, 2007-2015. Photographic prints, 17 × 22in.

Of course they are real. It's art! I don't know what it means and it's none of my business. My job to tell people what they can and cannot touch. I am with the security apparatus. And you?

FIGURE 22.2 Svetlana Boym, *Hydrant Immigrants*, 2007-2015.
Photographic prints, 17 × 22in.

My country was colorful
and awful, here it's bland
and livable. I went for
the shades of grey..

23 FRAMING THE FAMILY ALBUM

When I immigrated from USSR, we were not allowed to carry family albums. Photographs with more than three people in the picture were considered 'suspicious grouping.' Each picture we took with us thus became unique and unrepeatable. I began to rephotograph those pictures caught between two cultures--one of sparcity of objects and the other of excess, one of archival obsession and the other of obsolescence.

I still don't have a proper family album but I constantly reframe photographs and play with foreign words that don't translate into my mother tongue.

"Frame" comes from "from" which meant "forward," "ahead" and advance; I don't know how and why it evolved into the unfortunate direction of nostalgic introspection. Framing can be unstable and unforeseen.

FIGURE 23.1 Svetlana Boym, *Touching Photographs*, Date Unknown. Photographic print 22 × 11in.

FIGURE 23.2 Svetlana Boym, "Mama on the Bridge," *Touching Photographs*, Date Unknown. Digital Photograph.

FIGURE 23.3 Svetlana Boym, "Mama, Fira, Fania," *Touching Photographs*, Date Unknown. Digital Photograph.

24 NOSTALGIC TECHNOLOGY: NOTES FOR AN OFF-MODERN MANIFESTO

A Margin of Error

"It's not my fault. Communication error has occurred," my computer pleads with me in a voice of lady Victoria. First it excuses itself, then urges me to pay attention, to check my connections, to follow the instructions carefully. I don't. I pull the paper out of the printer prematurely, shattering the image, leaving its out takes, stripes of transience, inkblots and traces of my hands on the professional glossy surface. Once the disoriented computer spat out a warning across the image "Do Not Copy," an involuntary water mark that emerged from the depth of its disturbed memory. The communication error makes each print unrepeatable and unpredictable. I collect the computer errors. An error has an aura.

To err is human, says a Roman proverb. In the advanced technological lingo the space of humanity itself is relegated to the margin of error. Technology, we are told, is wholly trustworthy, were it not for the human factor. We seem to have gone full circle: to be human means to err. Yet, this margin of error is our margin of freedom. It's a choice beyond the multiple choices programmed for us, an interaction excluded from computerized interactivity. The error is a chance encounter between us and the machines in which we surprise each other. The art of computer erring is neither high tech nor low tech. Rather it's broken-tech. It cheats both on technological progress and on technological obsolescence. And any amateur artist can afford it. Art's new technology is a broken technology.

Or shall we call it dysfunctional, erratic, nostalgic? Nostalgia is a longing for home that no longer exists or most likely, has never existed.

That non-existent home is akin to an ideal communal apartment where art and technology co-habited like friendly neighbours or cousins. Techne, after all, once referred to arts, crafts and techniques. Both art and technology were imagined as the forms of human prosthesis, the missing limbs, imaginary or physical extensions of the human space.

Many technological inventions, including film and space rocket were first envisioned in the science fiction; imagined by artists and writers, not scientist. The term "virtual reality" was in fact coined by Henri Bergson, not Bill Gates. Originally it referred to the virtual realities of human imagination and conscience that couldn't be mimicked by technology. In the early twentieth century the border between art and technology was particularly fertile. Avant-garde artists and critics used the word "technique" to mean an estranging device of art that lays bare the medium and makes us see the world anew. Later the advertisement culture appropriated avant-garde as one of the styles, as an exciting marketable look that domesticates, rather than estrange the utopia of progress. New Hollywood cinema uses most advanced technology to create the special effects. If artistic technique revealed the mechanisms of conscience, the technological special effect domesticates the illusions and manipulations.

Has Art itself become a mere outtake, a long footnote to the human history? In the United States it is technology, not culture, that is regarded to be a space for innovations. Art, it seems, has overstayed its welcome. But the amateur artists, immigrants from the disintegrated homeland, survive against all odds. Often they cross the border illegally and like the diasporic repo-men try to repossess what used to belong to them, re-conquer the space of art.

The amateur artists aspire neither for newness nor for a trendy belatedness. The prefixes "avant" and "post" appear equally outdated or irrelevant in the current media age. The same goes for the illusions of "trans." But this doesn't mean that one should try desperately to be in. There is another option; not to be out, but off. As in off-stage, off-key, off-beat and occasionally, off-color. One doesn't have to be "absolutely modern," as Rimbaud once dreamed, but off-modern. A lateral move of the knight in game of chess. A detour into some unexplored potentialities of the modern project.

Broken-tech art doesn't thrive in destruction. At times, I go so far as to hit my computer, give it a mild spanking, push it to the limit. I want to handle it manually, like a craftsman handles his tools but without craftsman's faith in the materials. Yet I never wish to annihilate the computer and return to the anxieties of leaking pens and inkblots on the grid-paper of my childhood. Broken-tech art is not Luddite but ludic. It challenges the destruction with play.

Short Shadows, Endless Surfaces

In the early twentieth century French photographer Jacques-Henri Lartigue wanted to make photography do what it couldn't do: to capture movement. The blurs on the image are photographic errors, nostalgia for what photography could never be, longing for cinema. Yet photography shouldn't become as garrulous as a film. It offers an elliptic narrative without a happy ending. Its fleeting narrative potentialities would never find their scriptwriters and producers. There would always be a cloud or two, a crack on the surface of the picture, a short shadow that evades the plot.

With his inimitable oblique lucidity Walter Benjamin wrote about the importance of short shadows. They are "no more than the sharp black edges at the feet of things, preparing to retreat silently, unnoticed , into their burrow, their secret being." Short shadows speak of thresholds, warn us against being too short-sighted or too long-winged. When we get too close to things, disrespecting their short shadows, we risk to obliterate them, but if we make shadow too long we start to enjoy them for their own sake. Short shadows urge us to check the balance of nearness and distance, to trust neither those who speak of essences of things nor those who preach conspiratorial simulation.

Broken-tech art is an art of short shadows. It turns our attention to the surfaces, rims and thresholds. From my ten years of travels I have accumulated hundreds of photographs of windows, doors, facades, back yards, fences, arches and sunsets in different cities all stored in plastic bags under my desk. I re-photograph the old snapshots with my digital camera and the sun of the other time and the other place cast new shadows upon their once glossy surfaces with stains of the lemon tea and fingerprints of indifferent friends. I try not to use the preprogrammed special effects of Photoshop; not because I believe in authenticity of craftsmanship, but because I equally distrust the conspiratorial belief in the universal simulation. I wish to learn from my own mistakes, let myself err. I carry the pictures into new physical environments, inhabit them again, occasionally deviating from the rules of light exposure and focus.

At the same time I look for the ready-mades in the outside world, "natural" collages and ambiguous double exposures. My most misleading images are often "straight photographs." Nobody takes them for what they are, for we are burdened with an afterimage of suspicion.

Until recently we preserved a naive faith in photographic witnessing. We trusted the pictures to capture what Roland Barthes called "the being there" of things. For better or for worse, we no longer do. Now images appear to us as always already altered, a few pixels missing here and there, erased by some conspiratorial invisible hand. Moreover, we no longer analyse these mystifying images but resign to their pampering hypnosis. Broken- tech art reveals the degrees of our self-pixelization, lays bare hypnotic effects of our cynical reason.

Errands, Transits

We are surrounded by the anonymous buildings of our common modernity, a part of the other International Style not commemorated in masterpieces but inhabited in the outskirts of Warsaw, Petersburg, Berlin, Sarajevo, Bratislava, Zagreb, Sofia. These buildings, often indistinguishable from one another, even in my own photographs, compose an outmoded mass ornament of global culture. That is only at the first glance, of course. If we look closer we see that no window, balcony or white wall is alike. People in these anonymous dwelling places develop the most nuanced language of minor variations; they expose singular and unrepeatable out takes of their ordinary lives: a lace curtain half-raised, a dusty lampshade in retro colours of the 1960s, a potted flower that knew better days, a piece of a risqué underwear hung on a string here and there. The inhabitants of these buildings dream of elsewhere, homesick and sick of home. The satellite dishes spread out over the ruined balconies like desert flowers.

A Critic, an Amateur

If in the 1980s artists dreamed of becoming their own curators and borrowed from the theorists, now the theorists dream of becoming artists. Disappointed with their own disciplinary specialization, they immigrate into each other's territory. The lateral move again. Neither backwards nor forwards, but sideways. Amateur's out takes are no longer

FIUGRE 24.1 Svetlana Boym, *Not Working*, c.2005. Photographic print, 10 × 7½ in.

excluded but placed side-by-side with the non-out takes. I don't know what to call them anymore, for there is little agreement these days on what these non-out takes are.

But the amateur's errands continue. An amateur, as Barthes understood it, is the one who constantly unlearns and loves, not possessively, but tenderly, inconstantly, desperately. Grateful for every transient epiphany, an amateur is not greedy.

25 CITIES IN TRANSIT

This project is about global errands and technological errors. In collecting errors, I defy the understanding of photography as an art of mechanical or digital reproduction. The making of each print becomes a mini-performance of intervention and imperfection. The photographs are pulled out prematurely from the printer, leaving the lines of passages. "Communication error!" screams the disgruntled computer voice. This "human error" makes each print unrepeatable and uniquely imperfect. The process is not Luddite but ludic, not destructive but experimental. An error has an aura.

This series of "ruined prints" shows various ruins and construction sites of global modern architecture. Most of them come from cities that have survived wars, revolutions, terrorist acts, and economic crises— from Sarajevo to New York. I present portraits of cities in transit, taking pictures near the ports and train stations, questioning disaster tourism and juxtaposing the panoramic and the intimate. The more intimate images include scaffoldings with the dream homes of the future, the construction site in Manhattan, the home of an immigrant peacock, and the real estate pictures of sold and foreclosed homes from 2008.

All images, except three, are "straight" photographs. In the case of Sarajevo and Petersburg, I looked back at old snapshots of the damaged buildings re-photographing them and retaining the original blemishes and the glare.

Part of the book project "Nostalgic Technologies."
See also: The Off-Modern Manifesto

FIGURE 25.1 Svetlana Boym, "Leaving LA," *Cities in Transit*. Photographic print, 17 × 22in.

26 PHANTOM LIMBS

Installation: 11 photographs mounted on glass and a video of the river flow. Visitors to the installation are encouraged to stop the flow for a second and see if they get a ready-made revelation.

Memories of the Charles River 2011-2013

I take walks on the Charles river as a part of a daily ritual. I photograph whatever catches my eye, or just I walk camera-free, making mental notes on pictures not taken. On breezy March day I see only shadows on the river surface, separating and touching each other, escaping my viewfinder.

I persist and follow a few dry tree branches in the skywater. My memory card is filled with crooked abstractions in black, white and blue, phantom limbs without roots.* At home, while saving the images to my computer, I see something I haven't noticed before. A face made of litter and light, is staring back at me.

I am drawn to eyes on the photograph. I ran back to the same spot on the river to capture the face again, this time with the right exposure. No luck. Occasionally there is an intimation of a figure, watered down features, near-misses of a chance encounter. Face recognition device on the camera doesn't help me either. This must have been something purely accidental, a *human error* of sorts.

One thing I know for sure is that they are not ghosts. On the contrary, the photographic unconsciousness of my camera recorded a material flow of reflections which inspired religion, science and art.

After a thousand photographic takes, captured over a period of two months, I manage to find ten faces. Who are they? Pentimenti for an unknown creation? Drowned characters in search of an author or some winking imaginary friends? Did I conjure them into existence or did they find me? Can you see them now?

Six years ago I broke my limbs right around the place on the Charles river where the faces first appeared to me. Limb refers to a human bone and a tree branch thus connecting us to the world. My leg healed but sometimes I still feel a mysterious itch in my phantom limb.

Bereshit (*Arameic: in the beginning.*)

In the beginning was a tease
Rhymed clouds
Rippled visions
Teared limbs
A creature and a creator
Share
a tear
of skywater
a cloudy likeness
That blurrs the picture
But bonds them in the afterimage
(The poem ends here.)
But I want to begin again
In a middle of my road take a detour,
blow the soapbubble of time
Touch a clowning shadow on the river
Nature's emoticon
Your face

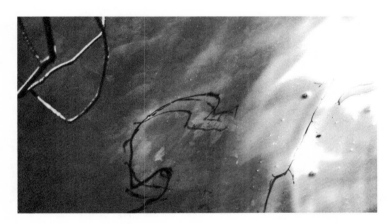

FIGURE 26.1 Svetlana Boym, "Bereshit Face," *Phantom Limbs*, 2013.

27 REMEMBERING FORGETTING: TALE OF A REFUGEE CAMP

The little that remains of the memory of my refugee camp *circa* 1981 is in extreme close up: a breach in the concrete wall with barbed wire, a foot in a darned sock dangling from the upper bunk bed, an unzippable suitcase filled with obsolete things, a roll of the foreign toilet paper, pink like the Fairy in the *Wizard of Oz*. And no establishing shot.

To tell you the truth, none of these things bothered me for 27 years. I happily forgot my forgetting. My immigration from Leningrad to Boston had a few detours, gaps and loose ends. But the point was not to travel down memory lane but to move on, to begin again. Why remember the unmemorable?

In the Soviet Union of the 1980s *leaving* was a code word . If you whispered it with mysterious gravitas, there would be no need to ask further questions. To leave meant to flee once and for good. You knew well your point of departure but not necessarily your destination. To leave was an intransitive verb that marked a break in space and time. You might as well be going to the Moon or to the Underworld. Farewell parties in the 1970s-1980s resembled funerals in their finality.

I decided to emigrate at the age of twenty and had to leave the country without my parents. I met my future husband, Moscow architect Constantin Boym, in Koktebel, Crimea, in 1979. After a ten -minute conversation in the line for beer and sundried roach he asked me if I cared to join him in emigrating to America. So goes the family legend, but the truth is a bit more complex. Constantin was a well-known "paper architect" and had applied to leave the Soviet Union permanently a year earlier; he was looking for a companion, for it was rumored in Moscow that there was a shortage of nice Jewish girls in America. After an impulsive non-deliberation, which combined my ardent desire to leave the country and a somewhat less ardent desire to teach a lesson to my non-responsive Leningrad boyfriend, I applied for a marriage license three weeks after Constantin and I met. A year and a half later, in January 1981, after a grueling process of exclusion and harassment, our much more grown-up selves received permision to depart permanently. This was not a romantic story, but an emigrant one. We were stripped of citizenship and were told that we would never be able to return even to see our families. The "personal search" to which we were subjected at Soviet Customs lasted many hours and included intimate parts of our bodies and of our personal belongings. The custom officers enjoyed the procedure. They fingered every scratch on the few family pictures, counted the number of permitted individuals in the group photos, penetrated every seam in our clothes, patted the inside lining of our oversized suitcases with rusty zippers in search of "the second bottom. " Since then I travel light, but more often than not, the zipper on my carry-on bag doesn't come together till the last minute.

My father remembers the moment of my departure with a cinematic clarity. It took place at a Moscow airport, at the gate reserved specially for those who were "leaving for permanent residency." I said the my last good-bye and moved behind the glass through which my parents could still see me go through the next Customs gate. A family standing in line behind me consisted of a young couple with a baby and a baby carriage and a grandfather carrying a large manuscript that was invaluable to him. "Either the manuscript or the baby carriage," said the Customs officer. Whatever that manuscript was, this was one thing the older man could not part with. "To hell with you," the young mother shouted and pushed away the baby carriage. At that moment I disappeared behind the glass. The baby carriage rolled slowly into the empty corridor and down the steps. An uncanny afterimage, courtesy of Sergei Eisenstein.

It was another seven years before my parents saw me again. In my family we generally leave longing behind along with personal belongings, and we treat nostalgic tales with a grain of salt.

My "journey to freedom" was short in time and cosmic in proportion. This was one of the first times in my life that I traveled by plane to the other side of the border. At the Vienna airport I caught a glimpse of the spring sky framed by the ramp and a frivolous sign that said "Duty Free" but which I couldn't decipher. We were greeted by the representative of a refugee-assistance organization and quickly herded onto unmarked buses with darkened windows and transported to the outskirts of Vienna, or someplace else. We had no idea where we were and didn't ask indiscrete questions.

The first impression of the camp was disappointing. The place resembled a provincial military hospital, a monastery. Is this what West looks like? Neither terrifying nor exhilarating, just banal. Among the transient residents of the camp were Soviet Jews from Central Asia to Leningrad, Poles, Crimean Tartars and a Russian Protestant escaping religious persecution. The camp was operated by several Jewish philanthropic agencies and guarded by Austrian soldiers with friendly German Shepherds. The latter were supposed to protect us from attacks from the outside. From what I remember, we worried little about that and just wanted to catch some rest and dream about the future. We took walks in the camp yard but never went outside the walls. Men shred past erotic dreams to fall asleep and women kept their dreams to themselves. We ate plenty of comfort food and Austrian sweet breads and filled out many forms that itemized our hyphenated identities. Movies were shown all the time, and they mixed with our scarce memories.

I would like to give you a more detailed description of the camp, to provide you with snippets of conversation between the emigres on the upper bunkbeds and emigres on the lower bunkbeds, their tired jokes and discussions of the meaning of existence, to convey the anxious whispers of the social workers and armed guards, provide lifelike images of narrow beds with broken springs, the archives of classified documents next to the trash storage, ruined warehouses in the walled monastic yard where brown pigeons peck at the cones of the local evergreens. I'd like to share with you the taste of the sweet bread soaked in weak tea, the homey camp pasta with Viennese sausage and a flickering image of the sun-kissed athletic men and women building a city on the sand with song and dance. Only I don't remember any of that and I'd rather not fill the gaps with plausible fiction.

We never saw the Vienna that we dreamed about, the city of Mozart and Sigmund Freud. We remained extraterritorial. Like the Freudian unconscious our transit camp had no outside; it was a place out of place and a time out of time. I don't know how long we stayed there. It felt like we were in a time capsule, a place where there was no present, only the repressed past and the unknown future. I actually had a good camera with me, probably a Zenith with a high precision lense and a long zoom. It never occurred to me to use it. The camera was meant to be sold at the flea market in Rome together with Ukranian linens, nesting dolls and caviar, to make some money for rainy days "in the West." I had studied photography as a teenager, experimenting with reflections on rippling water and urban panoramas. It never even occurred to me to photograph anything in the camp. There was nothing there "to write home about". New immigrants like to make cheerful pictures next to other people's houses and bright cars. The camp didn't seem worthy of a photograph.

* * * * * *

Fifteen years after leaving the camp I became a photographer. I returned to photography as suddenly as I had dropped it before. My digital camera has a few special effects that imitate the old Leica, but I don't use them. Since the late 1990s I've been documenting my travels through the world, collecting errors, overexposures, chance encounters. I have been taking pictures of the places that I would otherwise not remember.

Once during my presentation at the Vienna Kunsthalle commemorating the twentieth anniversary of the fall of the Berlin Wall, a man in the audience asked me:

"Why do you photograph the same landscape in different places?"
"I don't know, I said. These are just transits, warzones, afterimages of something we see and forget."
"So is this your first time in Vienna?" He continued, changing the subject.
"No. The first time was in 1981. In a refugee camp," I said surprising myself.
"Really? What was it like?"
"I don't remember much."
"Where was it?"
"Nobody knew."

It was then, during my second visit to Vienna that I decided to find the address of my former camp. Just to take a picture of it, to fill the gap. This would be a photographic project, not a nostalgic trip down memory lane.

Curiously, my former husband Constantin - we went our separate ways in 1986 - shared the excitement of my quest. Ironically, it was the break of my second, American, marriage that sent me back to retrace emigration.

My initial research into the location of our camp proved futile; the more I prodded, the more mysteries I encountered; they hid one inside the other like the nesting dolls that we carried in our overburdened suitcase. It was clear that the break in my personal memory went together with a lacuna in collective history. The extraterritorial refuge for extralegal immigrants was not to be found on Viennese maps or in archival records. Our story was deeply embedded in the inconvenient histories of the Cold War as as well as in improbable adventures and acts of courage of many individuals who brushed that history against the grain.

The city of Vienna that we didn't get to visit in the 1980s was a magnificent sleepy capital of the fallen Hapsburg empire, which had disintegrated after the first World War, and after the Second World War turned into a small "non-aligned" country at the crossroads of East and West. Vienna carried its war scars quietly, observing the code of silence when it came to confronting its recent history. Black-and-white documentary footage showing the Viennese happily greeting Hitler, a native son, in 1938, were not very popular during the 1980s, when Austrians preferred to see themselves as victims of Nazism and avoided going through the "management of Nazi memory" as did the Germans. Equally not addressed were the years of the occupation of the city by the Red Army, which liberated Vienna from the Nazis in 1945 and remained in the city until 1948, almost turning Austria into one of the Eastern Bloc countries. It was no coincidence that postwar Vienna became a stage-set for many Cold War movies, from the shadowy black-and-white *Third Man* to the colorful James Bond in *Living Daylights*. Sometimes when film directors couldn't get a permit to film in the Soviet Union, they would film the backdrop for Petersburg-Petrograd-Leningrad in the baroque squares of Vienna. In the 1970s-1990s Vienna became an inconspicuous transit point for the many refugees from Eastern Europe.

I began to understand what our Vienna transit might have looked like from the outside with the help of the article "Mysteries of the Vienna Airport" written by the journalist Joe Nocera for the Harper's

Monthly (May, 1982) Trying to make sense of the dramatic transport of refugees from the Soviet Union, Nocera came to a paradoxical conclusion. Each country involved in our transit was creating its own diplomatic half-fiction. This included the Soviet Union, the USA, Israel and Austria. These half-truths didn't impede the process of emigration but actually enabled it. In other words, if there had been a hypothetical classified information leak, or if a particularly enterprising investigative journalist had revealed all the arrangements made between the Soviet Union, Austria, the USA and Israel, our transit might not have taken place.

First and a foremost a humanitarian shelter, the camp was also a site of awkward political arrangements. The Austrian chancellor at the time, Social democrat Bruno Kreisky, agreed to take on a humanitarian role in the passage of the Soviet Jews but did so obliquely. The first transit camp organized by the government of Bruno Kreisky with the assistance of the several Jewish philanthropic agencies, including JA, Joint and HIAS was at Schoenau Castle close to Vienna. The camp at Schoenau Castle was closed after the terrorist groups Black September and the Eagles of Palestine attacked a train carrying Jewish emigres from Ukraine via Bratislava to Vienna (September 1973.) To make a long and controversial story short, the terrorists took hostages, and in order to secure their release the chancellor of Vienna agreed to close the camp at Schoenau Castle. But Kreisky kept his commitment to house the refugees, only he moved them to undisclosed and heavily guarded locations, first to the military barracks in Woellersdorf and then to somewhere in the territory of the Red Cross in the district of Simmering.

Since I didn't have the exact address of the camp I began to wander through Simmering with the help of Google Earth. After all, the family of the founder of Google, Sergei Brin, went the same immigrant route as I did. Simmering harks back into history; it was a medieval village with a famous brewery and a church. Later, Simmering became an industrial district of Vienna known for its material recycling industries and the Gasometer featured in the exemplary Cold War film, *The Living Daylight,* a James Bond movie. I came across several local-newspaper articles reporting on protests against placing a transit camp for Jewish refugees in Simmering: "We will not cease to protest against this camp which is a danger for all of us, particularly for our children, " stated Angelika Kneth, 34, mother of four children, who objected to the presence of armed guards and barbed wire near a kindergarten. The Interior Minister of Kreisky's Social Democrat government, Otto Roesch, tried to reassure local residents: "We have to fulfill a humanitarian task. Everybody must understand that it is our duty to help other people." As ironies of history go, it was later disclosed that Mr. Roesch had once been a Nazi storm trooper, but later, as a minister in the Social Democratic government of Bruno Kreisky, he played a humanitarian role in the transit of Soviet Jews.

My main lead in my search for material traces of the camp was the Austrian documentary filmmaker with a Russian last name, Alexander Schukoff, who made a film about the district of Simmering in 1977-78, a few years after the opening of the camp. I hoped that after filming for a year in the neighborhood he might have its address. "This is what you would have seen if you had been allowed to leave the camp. I give you a bigger window now, " said Mr. Schukoff, graciously offering me his film as a gift. The film was a poetic meditation on the metropolitan city's working class district that the Viennese rarely visit. Located between the cemetery and the airport, it was home to the Viennese fiakers who do nostalgic sight-seeing tours of Vienna and at night return to unspectacular Simmering, which looks like Eastern Europe. Local residents, young and old, complain of boredom, of the fact that nothing has ever happened in Simmering.

Schukoff's film makes no mention of the refugee camp that existed for ten years on the street around the corner. The director confessed that he had no information about it. What about the neighborhood protests in 1974? He was doing *cinema verité, not investigative journalism*. While being faithful to the ebb and flow of local daily life, he might have missed the biggest Cold War story that was unfolding in Simmering, and in Vienna at the time. Or perhaps he got the story right: the camp remained extraterritorial. It existed "off" the Viennese map, disconnected from the rest of the city. *Cinema verité* captured the site's eerie invisibility.

I decided to look for more history in the archives of the HIAS (Hebrew International Aid) , one of the organizations that supported our transit and resettlement in the United States. The associate director greeted me with open arms but warned me that he didn't have the address of the camp in Simmering. He ordered the Vienna files from the 1980s. They contained everything declassified, excluding personal files. Among the documents that caught my attention were: a check from an Italian man who wanted "to support the Jewish people after World War II," a passionate letter from a case worker who advocated allowing the refugees to choose their ultimate destination, another letter documenting the mysterious disappearance of the HIAS Hungarian translator who turned out to be a double agent and escaped with a large sum of money and a telefax from the Austrian Interior Ministry that demanded that the refugees in the camp be informed about their rights to ask for political asylum. Since I already knew that at the time most Western European countries tried their best not to offer the political asylum to Soviet Jews, I copied the telefax and buried it in my folder as another example of half-truth practiced by the Austrian government. As for the Hungarian double-agent, apparently he remained at large. And the passionate case worker was in the right. Apart from those few intriguing documents, most of the HIAS files were tantalizingly unrevealing. They contained the minutes of the organization's administrative meetings, requests for new furniture for the HIAS offices, and instructions on how to handle the "noshrim" or *dropouts* whose numbers were growing. I was puzzled by the terminology.

"Who were those "dropouts?" I asked the associate director of HIAS. "You." He answered, smiling.

Dropouts in the files always came in the plural, while we, the refugees, wanted to think of ourselves only in the singular. Over the span of seven years I graduated from a *dropout* into a *refugee*, from a *non-resident alien* into a citizen. Dropouts were those of us who "dropped out" of going to Israel, the destination on their exit visas, chosing the limbo of the refugee camps and hoping to get across the Atlantic. The HIAS files revealed that the *dropouts* didn't always follow orders, tried to outsmart their superiors and deviated from instructions. Still they were well- protected, taken care of and nourished in the camp with no address somewhere off the Viennese map, between the airport and the train station.

I looked up a few of my fellow *dropouts*, whom I didn't know at the time but who subsequently became my friends. None of them was particularly interested in finding the location of the camp. The idea of the "camp reunion" left them cold. They approached the conversation with a dose of healthy skepticism.

Why revisit the camp now? We were very tough then because we knew how to forget; if we start remembering now we could risk our immigrant resilience. Obsession with the past might shortshrift our future. "Is there is a change in your life now that makes you look back at that first big break?" one friend asked.

"I just want to take a picture of it," I said, not too convinced myself.

My former camp mates had their own blind spots next to vivid memories. Most interviews happened surreptitiously, in transit or in between other important tasks; they were not fully recorded. I asked my witnesses to draw pictures of the camp as they remembered it on a napkin. Now this strange collection of paper ephemera, stained with garlic oil and cappuccino, offers a collective memory map of what the camp might have looked like.

Masha Gessen, political journalist, age 14 at the time of immigration, recalls her disappointment at the sight of Austrian guards with German shepherds: "I thought I was emigrating to the "West" and then I found myself in the camp. I thought that my parents had deceived me; the West was the camp." By contrast, Masha's younger brother, writer and editor Kostya Gessen, age 6 at the time, enjoyed his stay "It wasn't a camp," he said. "More like a hotel, yes, a nice hotel with a yard. I had a good time there." The singer Regina Spektor, who wasthe same age as Kostya, didn't think it was a nice hotel: "there was no floor there, just bunk beds everywhere, " she recalled.

My witnesses couldn't agree on the geometrical shape of the camp yard. Historian of Russian art Anna Wexler-Katznelson., age 6 at the time of emigration, claims that the camp yard resembled a black square just like the famous painting by Kazimir Malevich. Artist Vitaly Komar who passed through the camp as a grown up, said that the yard had the shape of a mandala. At present Vitaly is working on the artistic project of transforming and sometimes reconciling symbols of different religions. The shape of the yard echoed the speaker's artistic psychic geography. "Of course, I was keeping records in the camp, said Vitaly. My notebooks with little squares were with me. Only my records had nothing to do with the place I was in. I was putting down my thoughts on art."

Curator and artist Anton Vidocle, age 15 at the time of emigration, commented that the camp looked like a high school, sort of like PS1 in New York. He had no recollection at all of his departure from Moscow, but a "photographic memory" of the camp movie theater and the new suit with red stripes that he wore there. He knew all along that the dogs and the armed guards were on our side and were protecting us from the outside. He wasn't scared of them. He remembers most fondly an erotic conversation he eavesdropped on in the collective ward. "It must have been the retelling of the famous *Story of O*, the erotic classic. I was completely taken by it." My former husband Constantin noticed the unusual shape of the pre-war window in the camp ward. Not being able to fall asleep, he peered through it chasing glimpses of the outside world. He saw a stranger walking on a dark street. "That's the West, I thought," said Constantin . "All I wanted is to be that man strolling somewhere outside the camp. " "Look, maybe it doesn't matter what actually happened in the camp," he added at the end. "What matters is the camp of memory. Or art."

Indeed, why seek a physical confirmation for our unbelievable stories? The immigrant is a bit of a trickster, who moves laterally, like a knight in the game of chess, in order to survive. Maybe it would have been more accurate to recreate the camp of our escape dreams that transported us beyond the thick concrete walls. Such a camp wouldn't require a precise address.

It dawned on me that my campmates and I might have been afraid of a question that I never dared to ask. Why did you leave? Or worse: Did you ever imagine what your life would have been without emigration?

I always believed that I couldn't. My emigration began long before the actual departure and has lasted long after the arrival. I might have started expatriating myself when I still lived in Leningrad as a teenager and heard for the first time my grandmother's story about her time in the Gulag.

My grandmother, Sara (Sonya) Goldberg, a secondary school teacher in Leningrad, was rounded up in 1948 during Stalin's so-called anti-cosmopolitan campaign, aimed largely at Soviet Jews, including atheists and those who had changed their names and claimed other ethnicities in their documents. Grandma Sonya considered herself "lucky" after she had been released; thanks to Stalin's death, she spent only six years in the Gulag, instead of ten. Fifteen years later she was "rehabilitated" for the "absence of the content of the crime."

My grandmother's story had many blank spots because for twenty or so years nobody in the family talked to her about her life in the camps. Without conversations, memories turn into stones or fairy tales. I inherited her blind spots and her fears and have carried them with me through life. She didn't know either where her camp was located within the vast zone of the Gulag. She never talked about how she resisted arrest and tried to cut her veins. Instead she remembered tricking the informants in the camp who wrote reports to the authorities, and mostly she loved to recall her friendship with the actress Tatyana Okunevskaya and how at difficult moments they had talked to each other with the help of Chekhov: "One day we will see diamonds in the sky. You will see that day will come."

What I gathered from the fragmented tale of the camps that she told me when I was 11 was that there was another unwritten history and another secret territory outside the official maps, a camp zone where millions of Soviet citizens were detained without having committed any crime.

In the 1970s my grandmother became a kitchen dissident. While cooking her soup, made with the skinniest and cheapest chickens that she got in the market for one ruble and five kopeks, she listened to Voice of America. For years she cried over the death of Kennedy and the Soviet tanks in Prague in 1968. Sometimes she imagined what they were saying on the radio, since the sound was jammed. She would just stand there whispering something to a faraway addressee, a prayer or a poem, as she looked through the unwashed window into our dark Leningrad yard.

My emigration can be considered political since I took part in several demonstrations protesting human rights violations, yet at the age of 20 my understanding of the political was rather vague. It was a blend of the existential dreams of liberation that we saw in foreign movies and a rebellion against local coercion and claustrophobia of the Brezhnev era, known as the Era of Stagnation, that threatened to destroy all of our teenage ideals of justice.

I could blame the great Italian director Michelangelo Antonioni for seducing me with his long cinematic takes that promised an unforeseen freedom of movement. My father organized a film club in the Palace of Culture in the Petrograd district of Leningrad, and this club became his cozy little homeland. In his words, it was a state within a state that also provided good babysitting for the children of the club goers, rebellious Leningrad pre-teens like myself. Almost no American films were shown in such film clubs but there were plenty of Polish and Czech existential tales as well as films by Italian communist film makers, filled with existential mysteries and wonder. I loved *Passenger (Profession: Reporter)* more than the others. It was the story of a journalist (played by Jack Nicholson) who chose to radically change his life and adopt the identity of a dead man. At the end he encounters a beautiful and mysterious woman (played by Maria Schneider) and finds his match in the existential adventure of life and death. I didn't watch the film for the complex plot of mistaken identity but for the long takes and eccentric vistas into a foreign life. I was particularly taken by the free spirited and edgy Maria Schneider, who criss-crosses borders somewhere in the Pyrenean mountains, just to study architecture or to meet strangers. I never saw women and borders like that. The film was explained to us as a "Marxist critique of bourgeois alienation" but it felt more like a cultural luxury, a quest for freedom and creative living. There was a breeze in the heroine's hair and the long duration of a non-obligatory time that shaped my dreamscape. I had to emigrate, go through several transit camps and work hard for years before I could enjoy that kind of artistic wanderlust.

My first border crossing didn't resemble anything I had seen in the movies. Yet movies remain among my most vivid memories of the camp. The camp's film collection included Holocaust movies and various comedies on Jewish subjects. We were extremely ignorant since any study of Jewish culture was effectively prohibited in the Soviet Union, condemned as either "cosmopolitan" or Zionist propaganda; the two contradictory terms were used interchangeably. We knew that we didn't want to try on the exotic East European Jewish attire from another time, which appeared foreign or even kitschy to us. When the representative of the Jewish Agency asked me in the camp if I planned to go to Israel, I answered that I didn't want to go to the country of *Fiddler on the Roof*. This was an embarrassing mixture of ignorance and chutzpa. I didn't realize then that I had just left one of the film's homelands, Russia, and was about to arrive for permanent residency in the United States, where the poor fiddler found his cinematic home. All pain apart, some of our camp experiences had an element of absurdity to them and resembled a chance encounter between the *Fiddler on the Roof* and the *Third Man*.

In 2012 I decided to cross the border back, to go to Vienna for the third time and properly scout the location. Before my departure I nervously looked through copies of the "Vienna files" that I had obtained with a kind permission of HIAS. I reread the article from the New York Times, perused the case of the cunning Hungarian spy, unfolded the telex the Austrian Minister of Interiors who seemed to suddenly care about the plight of the refugees they had sent to who knew where. Just as I was ready to put it back into my drawer , I spotted faint typewritten letters right in the fold at the bottom of the page: *Transit Camp, 66 Dreherstrasse, Vienna 11.* I couldn't believe my eyes. I had possessed the address of our transit camp for a year. It was hidden in plain view, in the fold of the xerox in my desk drawer .

A chance encounter in Vienna brought the last key witness in my investigation. During the first week of my stay I met a local journalist married to a Russian artist. I told him about my investigation.

"Yes, the camp on 66 Dreherstrasse," he said, looking into my eyes. "It was an ugly place."

This was no small talk. The man did his civil service there in 1985, when it again became an office of the Red Cross.

We both remembered cracks in the concrete wall with the barbed wire, anonymous hospital rooms, a "prison yard" with sickly trees.

"Have you ever asked what was there before? I prodded.

"No. In Vienna, we don't do that,"

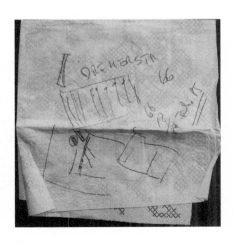

He took a napkin and drew a picture of the narrow bunk bed with broken springs that left scars on his body. There was something else there that haunted him even more than those springs: blank forms and signs written in Cyrillic, instructions that he couldn't understand. Unreadable, they became the stuff of his dreams. By 1985-86 the former transit camp ceased to exist as emigration from the Soviet Union had fizzled. That stained napkin with the drawing of springs protruding from the bunk beds might have been the last afterimage of our unphotographed transit.

66 Dreherstrasse, it said on the napkin. On a sunny wintry day in January 2012 I returned to the camp. From the window of an old car I got an oblique glimpse of a village church and lacy curtains on dark windows, evocative as they were unrevealing. The journey felt like a road movie with long takes and no denouement.

"Sorry, there is not much here," said my Viennese friend who drove me to Simmering. He left me alone to wander along the deserted Dreherstrasse. The main building that housed the camp hadn't survived but the territory did, complete with fences, warehouse shags, packaging from recycling machines, archives of trash. I found a shopping cart filled with evergreen pine cones, a moving altar to an immigrant genius loci.

In 2006 a part of the former camp territory had been developed into an ecological-e housing. The new buildings bore the names of exotic fruits in Italian: *Melanzana, Pera, Melone*, turning the history of the site into a delicious pastoral. The new buildings were surrounded by an ecologically correct fence behind which was abandoned territory with high grass, weeds and withered dandelions growing next to the thick concrete wall *circa* 1970s. There was still occasional barbed wire left and and rusting remains of the old infrastructure for the security cameras. Between the ecological fence and the concrete walls of the former camp, Simmering teenagers were playing a ball game, oblivious to the past and the future, the way teens are.

The adults were not so different. Nobody working or living on the site had any knowledge of what was there before. "A military hospital? A monastery? Something like that." I was stopped and questioned by the local residents once I took out my camera. I quickly excused myself, claiming to be an architectural photographer interested in the former Carmelite monastery. The owner of a new lighting design firm politely invited me in and guided me through his recently redesigned interiors made to "evoke some history." The office had a nice retro feel of the mid-century Modern style with a few historicist echoes. It still preserved those unusually shaped windows recalled by Constantin . Once again I was struck by the intimate proximity of the refugee camp and the ordinary residences of Simmering; yet even in memory they occupied non-contiguous and incommensurable spaces of experience. I was tempted to tell the retro-loving designer about the camp in his former office but I was afraid that he might ruin my memory card.

Did I recognize anything when I revisited the camp territory? To be honest, no new reminiscence came to me, no taste of sweet bread soaked in camp tea could breach my forgetting. Yet photographing the former camp territory was strangely ecstatic. It felt like quenching an old thirst. It wasn't for the sake of recovered memory or history, just for its own sake.

Upon my arrival back in Boston, I found myself staring at the images of the camp, rescuing and highlighting the cracks in the wall.

Everything I photographed all over the world was there: the stains on the concrete walls, sickly poppy flowers and dandelions, half-readable signs, the pinecones in a disowned shopping cart and a dove, the color of urban ruins, finishing her comfort food, in haste. Wandering through the invisible ruins of the camp I discovered the landscape of my own photographs that traveled with me from one continent to another.

I didn't know until then that I had been a subject of my photographs and not only the photographer. I stumbled upon an uncharted emotional geography mapped over the inconvenient history. Somehow the walls of the camp stood both for liberation and for confinement, for memory and for forgetting; they became a canvas for our improbable hopes.

After many turns and returns I recognized my point of departure. It was not my house in Leningrad but this forgotten refugee camp that I carried with me as I traveled light. Unmemorable and unmonumental, the camp became a ruin in reverse, a palimpsest of my future transits, a hidden backdrop to my second home.

T.S Elliot described such departure in his *Fourth Quartet*:

We shall not cease from exploration
And the end of all our exploring
Will be to arrive where we started
And know the place for the first time.

SOURCES

All images © Estate of Svetlana Boym

I. The Theater of The Self (1984-1991)

1 Osip Mandels'tam and the Drama of Writing

"Dialogue as 'Lyrical Hermaphroditism': Mandel'shtam's Challenge to Bakhtin," *Slavic Review*, vol. 50, no 1 (Spring, 1991): 118-26. Used with permission of the American Association for the Advancement of Slavic Studies.

2 "Petersburg Influenza: Notes on *The Egyptian Stamp* by Osip Mandel'shtam," Seminar Paper for Comparative Literature 206, taught by Professor Donald Fanger, 1984, pp. 13-15.

© Estate of Svetlana Boym

3 The Death of the Revolutionary Poet: Vladimir Maiakovskii and Suicide as Literary Fact

From *Death in Quotation Marks: Cultural Myths of the Modern Poet* (Cambridge, MA: Harvard University Press, 1991): 26-28, 29-34, 120-21, 123-25, 137-48, 149-51, 152-58, 159-160, 162, 163-66. Copyright © 1991 by the President and Fellows of Harvard College.

4 Marina Tsvetaeva and the Cultural Mask of the Poetess

From "Loving in Bad Taste: Eroticism and Literary Excess in Marina Tsvetaeva's 'The Tale of Sonechka.'" In *Sexuality and The Body in Russian Culture*, ed. by Jane T. Costlow, Stephanie Sandler, Judith Vowles (Stanford, CA: Stanford University Press, 1993): 160-61, 163-76. Copyright © 1993 by the Board of Trustees of the Leland Stanford Jr. University. All rights reserved. Used by permission of the publisher, Stanford University Press, sup.org.

5 Public Personas and Private Selves of Cultural Critics
From "The Obscenity of Theory: Roland Barthes' 'Soirees de Paris' and Walter Benjamin's 'Moscow Diary,'" The Yale Journal of Criticism, vol. 4, no 2 (1991): 105-07, 111-12, 114-16, 117, 119-120, 123-125. Used with permission of John Hopkins University Press.

II. Living in Common Places and Rethinking What Matters (1992-1995)

6 "The Poetics of Banality: Tat'iana Tolstaia, Lana Gogoberidze, and Larisa Zvezdochetova." *Fruits of Her Plume: Essays on Contemporary Russian Woman's Culture* (1993): 59-85. Used with permission of M. E. Sharpe Press of the Taylor Francis Group.

7 *Common Places: Mythologies of Everyday Life in Russia* (Harvard University Press, 1994) Copyright © 1994 by the President and Fellows of Harvard College.
"Theoretical Common Places," pp. 1-5.
"Archaeology of the Common Place: From Topos to Kitsch," pp. 11-20.
"Living in Common Places," pp. 121-130, 139-148, 150-59, 163-67.

8 "Paradoxes of Unified Culture: From Stalin's Fairy-Tale to Molotov's Lacquer-Box." *South Atlantic Quarterly* 94.3 (1995): 821-836.
© Estate of Svetlana Boym

III. That Historical Emotion (1996-2001)

9 "On Diasporic Intimacy: Ilya Kabakov's Installations and Immigrant Homes." *Critical Inquiry*, Vol. 24, No. 2, Intimacy (Winter, 1998), pp. 498-524. Used with permission of University of Chicago Press.

10 *The Future of Nostalgia* (Basic Books, New York: 2001) Reprinted by permission of Basic Books, an imprint of Perseus Books, LLC, a subsidiary of Hachette Book Group, Inc.
"From Cured Soldiers to Incurable Romantics," pp. 3-18.
"Restorative Nostalgia: Conspiracies And Return To Origins," pp. 41-48.

"Reflective Nostalgia: Virtual Reality and Collective Memory," pp. 49-55.
"Vladimir Nabokov's False Passport," pp. 262-266, 277-282.
"Nostalgia and Global Culture," pp. 345-55.

11 "Conspiracy Theories and Literary Ethics: Umberto Eco, Danilo Kis and *The Protocols of Zion*." *Comparative Literature*, Vol. 51 no. 2, 1999: 114-121. © Estate of Svetlana Boym

12 "Kosmos: Remembrances of the Future." pp. 83-84, 89-93 © Estate of Svetlana Boym

This essay first appeared in *Kosmos*, (Princeton: Princeton Architectural Press, 2001).

IV. Freedom, Subjectivity, and the Gulag (2002-2010)

13 "My Grandmother's First Love," *Harvard Review,* No. 22 (Spring, 2002): 20-29. http://www.jstor.org/stable/27568600 © Estate of Svetlana Boym

14 "How was 'Soviet subjectivity' constructed?" English original © Estate of Svetlana Boym. Published in Russian translation as: "Kak sdelana 'sovetskaia sub'ektivnost' '? *Ab Imperio, no.* 3 (2002), 285-296.

15 "Banality of Evil," Mimicry, and the Soviet Subject: Varlam Shalamov and Hannah Arendt." *Slavic Review* 67, no. 2 (Summer 2008): 342-63. Published with permission of the American Association for the Advancement of Slavic Studies.

16 "Introduction: Freedom as Cocreation." In *Another Freedom: The Alternative History of an Idea*, 1-7,10-30. Chicago: Chicago University Press, 2010. Used with permission of the publisher.

V. The Off-Modern (2010-2017)

17 *The Off Modern*. International Texts in Critical media Aesthetics Vol. 20. Founding Editor: Francisco J. Ricardo. New York: Bloomsbury, 2017.

"History out of Sync," pp.3-7
"Cultural Exaptation," pp.9-11
"Human Error," pp.13-15
"Edgy Geography," pp. 25-26
"Black Mirrors," pp. 171-173
"On *Off*," pp. 133-134

18 "Scenography of Friendship." *Cabinet*, 36 Winter 2009/10.

This essay originally appeared in Cabinet magazine, at http://cabinetmagazine.org/issues/36/boym.php and is reprinted with permission.

19 "Vernacular Cosmopolitanism: Victor Shklovsky and Osip Mandelshtam." This essay was published under the title "The Off-Modern Turn: Modernist Humanism and Vernacular Cosmopolitanism in Shklovsky and Mandelshtam," in Shai Ginsburg, ed., *Jews and the Ends of Theory*, Fordham University Press, 2018.

20 Cryptoarchitecture: Corbusier at 50, A Tour with Svetlana Boym. © Estate of Svetlana Boym

VI. Afterimages: Svetlana Boym's Irrepressible Co-creations

21 "Touching Writing (Homage to Jacques Derrida, October 8, 2004)" © Estate of Svetlana Boym http://www.svetlanaboym.com/touching.htm

22 "Immigrant Hydrants" © Estate of Svetlana Boym http://www.svetlanaboym.com/diaspora.htm

23 "Family Album" © Estate of Svetlana Boym http://www.svetlanaboym.com/unforeseen.htm

24 "Nostalgic Technology: Notes for an Off-modern Manifesto" © Estate of Svetlana Boym http://www.svetlanaboym.com/manifesto.htm

25 "Cities in Transit" © Estate of Svetlana Boym http://www.svetlanaboym.com/cities.htm

26 "Phantom Limbs" © Estate of Svetlana Boym http://www.svetlanaboym.com/limb.htm

27 "Tale of a Refugee Camp." This story originally appeared in Tablet magazine, at http://www.tabletmag.com/jewish-arts-and-culture/ books/176945/camp-tale, and is reprinted with permission. The version that we print here is slightly different from the *Tablet* version, both in its title and through text additions, all of which reflect Svetlana Boym's choices. We are grateful to Masha Gessen for agreeing to the publication of this version.

BIBLIOGRAPHY

Svetlana, Boym (Winter 2015). "Like New: An Immigrant's Tale," *Five Points*, Vol. 16, No. 2. http://fivepoints.gsu.edu/issue/five-points-vol-16-no-2/
Svetlana, Boym (2012). *Soviet Everyday Culture: An Oxymoron?* Edited by Dmitri Shalin, 1–30. http://digitalscholarship.unlv.edu/russian_culture/8
Svetlana, Boym (2011) "Cosmos: Remembrances of the future." In *Star City: The Future Under Communism*. Józefów: MAMAL Foundation, 186–213.
Svetlana, Boym (2011). "Off-Modern Homecoming in Art and Theory." In *Rites of Return. Diaspora Poetics and the Politics of Memory*, 151–65.
Svetlana, Boym (2011). "Ruins of the Avant Garde: From Tatlin's Tower to Paper Architecture." In *Ruins of Modernity*, edited by Julia Hell and Andreas Schönle, Durham: Duke University Press.
Svetlana, Boym (2011). *Ruins. [An Anthology of Essays]*. Edited by Brian Dillon, London, England; Cambridge, MA: Whitechapel Art Gallery; MIT Press.
Svetlana, Boym (2010). "The Off-modern Mirror." *E-flux Journal*, Vol. 19, No. 1–9. http://www.e-flux.com/journal/the-off-modern-mirror/
Svetlana, Boym (2010). *Tobias Putrih & MOS: without out* [curator Jane Farver; essays by Svetlana Boym and Timothy Hyde ; and an interview by Svetlana Boym with Michael Merdith and Tobias Putrih] http://collections.si.edu/search/results.htm?q=record_ID:siris_sil_939311
Svetlana, Boym (2010). *Another Freedom: The Alternative History of an Idea*. Chicago: University of Chicago Press.
Svetlana, Boym (Winter 2009–10). "Scenography of Friendship: Hannah Arendt, Mary McCarthy and Anchovy Paste." *Cabinet*, special issue "Friendship," no. 36.
Svetlana, Boym (Summer 2008). "Banality of Evil, Mimicry, and the Soviet Subject: Varlam Shalamov and Hannah Arendt." *Slavic Review*, Vol. 67, No. 2, pp. 342–63. http://www.jstor.org/stable/27652847
Svetlana, Boym (2008). *"Ruinophilia: The Love of Ruins,"* Entry in the *Atlas of Transformation*. Adopted from Svetlana Boym, *Architecture of The Off-Modern*. New York: Architectural Press, http://monumenttotransformation.org/atlas-of-transformation/html/r/ruinophilia/ruinophilia-appreciation-of-ruins-svetlana-boym.html
Svetlana, Boym (2008). *Architecture of The Off-Modern*. Princeton: Architectural Press.
Svetlana, Boym (2008). "Tatlin, or, Ruinophilia." *Cabinet Magazine*, Vol. 28 (2007).

Svetlana, Boym (2007). "Inserts: Photos." *Ulbandus Review*, Vol. 10, No 146–8 http://www.jstor.org/stable/25748169.

Svetlana, Boym (2007). "Nostalgia and its Discontents," [Adapted from *The Future of Nostalgia*] ISAC, University of Virginia, http://www.iasc-culture. org/eNews/2007_10/9.2CBoym.pdf

Svetlana, Boym (2006). *Territories of Terror: Mythologies and Memories of the Gulag in Contemporary Russian-American Art*. Boston: Boston University Art Galleries.

Svetlana, Boym (2005). "Politics And Poetic Of Estrangement: Victor Shklovsky and Hannah Arendt." *Poetics Today*, http://poeticstoday.dukejournals.org/ content/26/4/581.short

Svetlana, Boym (Wednesday, 23 February 2005) "Anri Sala," ARTMARGINS. http://www.artmargins.com/index.php?option=com_content&view= article&id=177%3Amodernities-out-of-sync-the-tactful-art-of-anri-sala&Itemid=68

Svetlana, Boym (2003). *Ninotchka: A Novel*. Albany: SUNY Press.

Svetlana, Boym (2002). *Obshchie mesta: mifologiia povsednevnoi zhizni*. Novoe literaturnoe obozrenie.

Svetlana, Boym (2002). "Kak sdelana sovetskaia sub"ektivnost'?." *Ab Imperio*, Vol. 3, 285–96.

Svetlana, Boym (Spring 2002). "My Grandmother's First Love." *Harvard Review*, No. 22, 20–29. http://www.jstor.org/stable/27568600

Svetlana, Boym (Summer 2002). "Dubravka Ugrešić." *BOMB*, No. 80, 74–80. http://www.jstor.org/stable/40426709

Svetlana, Boym (2001). *Kosmos: Remembrances of the Future* - photographs by Adam Bartos, text by Svetlana Boym. New York City: (Princeton Architectural Press)

Svetlana, Boym (2001). "Nostalgia," Entry from the *Atlas of Transformation*, Adoptation and elaboration from Svetlana Boym, *The Future of Nostalgia*. New York: Basic Books, http://monumenttotransformation.org/atlas-of-transformation/html/n/nostalgia/nostalgia-svetlana-boym.html

Svetlana, Boym (2001). "Nostalgia, Moscow style: Authoritarian Postmodernism and Its Discontents." *Harvard Design Magazine* Issue 13. http://www. harvarddesignmagazine.org/issues/13/nostalgia-moscow-style

Svetlana, Boym (2001). *The Future of Nostalgia*. New York City: Basic Books.

Svetlana, Boym (2000). "Leningrad into St. Petersburg: The Dream of Europe on the Margins." In *Europe and the Other and Europe as the Other*. Brussels: Peter Lang, 311–25.

Svetlana, Boym (1999). "Conspiracy Theories and Literary Ethics: Umberto Eco, Danilo Kiš and The Protocols of Zion." *Comparative Literature*, Vol. 51, No. 2, 97–122 http://www.jstor.org/stable/1771244

Svetlana, Boym (1999). "Nostalgic Memorials and Postmodern Survival in Russia." In *POSTMODERN STUDIES*, 143–70.

Svetlana, Boym (1999), "Ilya Kabakov: The Soviet Toilet and the Palace of Utopias." *ARTMargins Online*.

Svetlana, Boym (January 19, 1999), "Istoria w Sadowo-Parkowom Stile." (История в Садово-Парковом Стиле) Журнал "Итоги"(Магазин "Итоги"), 45–49.

Svetlana, Boym (1999). "From the Toilet to the Museum: Memory and Metamorphosis of Soviet Trash." In *Consuming Russia: Popular Culture, Sex, and Society Since Gorbachev*, edited by .Adele Barker. Durham: Duke University Press, 383–96.

Svetlana, Boym (1998). "Estrangement as a Lifestyle: Shklovsky and Brodsky." In *Exile and Creativity: Signposts, Travelers, Outsiders, Backward Glances*, edited by Susan Suleiman. Durham: Duke University Press, 241.

Svetlana, Boym (1998). "On Diasporic Intimacy: Ilya Kabakov's Installations and Immigrant Homes." *Critical Inquiry*, Vol. 24, No. 2, 498–524. http://www.jstor.org/stable/1344176

Svetlana, Boym (1996). "Everyday Culture." *Russian Culture at the Crossroads: Paradoxes in Postcommunist Consciousness*, edited by Dmitri N. Shalin. Boulder: Westview Press.

Svetlana, Boym (1996). "Estrangement as a Lifestyle: Shklovsky and Brodsky." *Poetics Today*, Vol. 17, No. 4, 511–30, http://www.jstor.org/stable/1773211

Svetlana, Boym (1996), "Unsettling Homecoming." In *Fieldwork. Sites in Literary and Cultural Studies*, 262–67.

Svetlana, Boym (1995). "From the Russian Soul to Post-Communist Nostalgia." *Representations*, Vol. 49, 133–66. http://www.jstor.org/stable/2928753

Svetlana, Boym (1995). "Post-Soviet Cinematic Nostalgia: From 'Elite Cinema' to Soap Opera." *Discourse*, Vol. 17, No. 3, 75–84, http://www.jstor.org/stable/41389386.

Svetlana, Boym (1995). "Paradoxes Of Unified Culture, From Stalin Fairy-Tale To Molotov Lacquer-Box." *South Atlantic Quarterly*, Vol. 94, No. 3, 821–36.

Svetlana, Boym. (1995). "Paradoxes of Unified Culture." In *Socialist Realism Without Shores*. Durham: Duke University Press, 120–34.

Svetlana, Boym (1994). *Common Places: Mythologies of Everyday Life in Russia*. Cambridge, MA: Harvard University Press.

Svetlana, Boym (1994). "From Russia with a Song: From 'Back in the USSR' to 'Bye-Bye Amerika.'" *New Formations*, Vol. 22, 33–58.

Svetlana, Boym (1994). "The Archeology of Banality: The Soviet Home." *Public Culture*, Vol. 6, No. 2, 263–92, http://publicculture.dukejournals.org/content/6/2/263.citation

Svetlana, Boym (February/March 1994). "Strange Hybrid." *Boston Review*, 22–24.

Svetlana, Boym (1994). "Zametki na zadannuu temu." (Заметки на заданную тему) *Magazin Seans* #9: 68–70.

Svetlana, Boym (1993). "Loving in Bad Taste: Eroticism and Literary Excess in Marina Tsvetaeva's The Tale of Sonechka.". In *Sexuality and the Body in Russian Culture*, 156–76.

Svetlana, Boym (1993). "Perestroika of Kitsch: Sergei Solov'ev's Black Rose, Red Rose." In *Inside Soviet Film Satire: Laughter with a Lash*, edited by Andrew

Horton. Cambridge: Cambridge University Press, 125–37. http://ebooks.
cambridge.org/chapter.jsf?bid=CBO9780511527135&cid=CBO9780511527
135A024

Svetlana, Boym (1993). "Power Shortage: The Soviet Coup and Hurricane Bob."
In *Media Spectacles*, edited by Marjorie Garber, John Matlock and Rebecca L.
Walkowitz. New York: Routledge.

Svetlana, Boym (1993). "Stalinism and Soviet cinema." In *Stalinism and Soviet
Cinema*, edited by Richard Taylor and Derek W. Spring. Hove: Psychology
Press.

Svetlana, Boym (1993). "Tat'iana Tolstaia, Lana Gogoberidze, and Larisa
Zvezdochetova." In *Fruits of Her Plume: Essays on Contemporary Russian
Woman's Culture*, 59.

Svetlana, Boym (1993). "Salat pod russkim sousom." (Салат под Русским
Соусом) Short Story (Сборник "Чего хочет женщина"). Moscow, 144–58

Svetlana, Boym (1992). "Stalin's Cinematic Charisma: Between History and
Nostalgia." *Slavic Review*, Vol. 51, No. 3, 536–43, http://www.jstor.org/
stable/2500060

Svetlana, Boym (1991). "The Obscenity of Theory: Roland Barthes' 'Soirées de
Paris' and Walter Benjamin's 'Moscow Diary.'" *The Yale Journal of Criticism*,
Vol. 4, No. 2, 105.

Svetlana, Boym (1991). "Dialogue as 'Lyrical Hermaphroditism': Mandel'shtam's
Challenge to Bakhtin." *Slavic Review*, Vol. 50, No. 1, 118–26, http://www.
jstor.org/stable/2500603

Svetlana, Boym (1991). *Death in Quotation Marks: Cultural Myths of the Modern
Poet*. Cambridge, MA: Harvard University Press.

Svetlana, Boym (1990). "Paradoxes of Perestroika." *Agni*, Vol. 31/32, 16–24,
http://www.jstor.org/stable/23009360

Svetlana, Boym (Winter 1989). "Return to Reality: Aragon, Maykovsky
and Politics of Poetry." *Social Discourse Research Papers in Comparative
Literature*, Vol. 2, No. 4.

Svetlana, Boym (1988). "Literariness of the Poet's Life: The Case of Four
Rimbauds." In *Proceedings of 12th Congress of International Comparative
Literature Association*. Munich.

Svetlana, Boym (Fall 1986). "Inscriptions on the Poet's Monument." *Harvard
Review*, Vol. 1, No. 1, 65–81.

INDEX

Note: Page numbers in *italics* refer to figures.

and modernist
humanism   419–22, 432
everyday/everday life   5, 116, 137
aesthetics of   164–72,
182 n.56–7, 199
and art   7, 105, 128–32
byt   72–3, 112, 116, 125, 137–8
and camp sensibility   126,
146, 148
Certeau on   105
and cultural critics   96–7, 105–6
and cultural
"untranslatables"   138–9,
176 n.3
and ideology   111–13, 185
and literariness   108 n.11
materiality of existence   103–4
psychopathology of   161–4
of Stalinist elite   190
women's invention of   126–8
evil   282. *See also* banality of evil
exaptation   393–7
exile/exiles/*emigrés*   200, 214 n.1,
248, 274 n.66
and "bad taste"   202
by choice   255–7
diasporic intimacy   202–3,
204–6, 210
and homecoming   248–51
and mimicry   251–2
Soviet home in exile   207
experimental art
and freedom   357

faction   284 n.2
fairy tales   189
Family Album (Boym)   461
Farlow House   387–8, 441, 442, 444
Farlow, Lilian   445, 446–7
Farlow Sears Center   442–3, 445
Farlow, William Gilson   387–8, 442,
445–6
fashioning   44–5
of cultural critics   96–7, 105–6
notion of   97
Faulkner, William   346

fear
co-creation with   428–32
confrontation with   6
Freud on   430–1
female eroticism   91–2, 130
female relationships   80, 86–91
feminine poetry/writing   21–3, 119
femininity
cultural myths of   56–7, 80–5,
108 n.9, 117–20, 128–32
Flaubert, Gustave   116, 120, 178
n.23, 320
"Fop's Blouse" ("Kofta fata")
(Mayakovsky)   51–2
Foucault, Michel   315,
316–17, 459
Fourier, Charles   153
freedom   5
Anglo-American notion
of   382 n.17
architecture of   357, 360–5
boundaries of   357–60
as co-creation   4, 5, 9, 353–4
conception of   355–7
economic and libertarian
understandings of   382 n.18
etymology of   364
native words synonymous
with   363–4
scenography of   367–74
shrinking space of   426
vis-à-vis judgment and
imagination   374–80
vs. liberation   365–7
free indirect discourse   320
Freidin, Gregory   28
Freud, Sigmund   42, 245, 246,
247, 430–1
Friedländer, Saul   189
friendship   406–7
between women   407–15
fright   431. *See also* fear
The Future of Nostalgia (Boym)   3, 5,
8, 199, 457
Futurism   52–3
as feminine   57

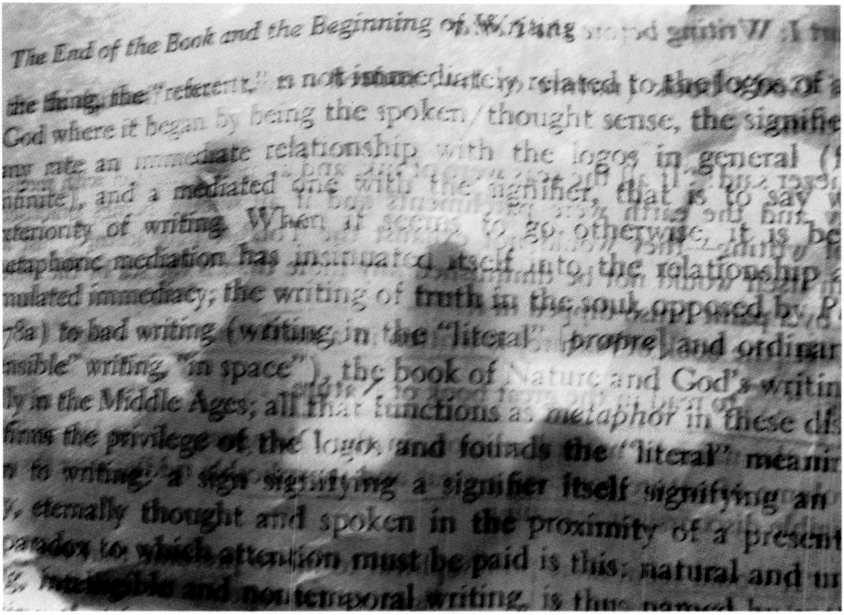

PLATE 1 Svetlana Boym, "Homage to Derrida," *Touching Writing*, 2004. Digital Photograph.

PLATE 2 Svetlana Boym, *Hydrant Immigrants*, 2007-2015. Photographic prints, 17 × 22in.

When we came to America, we wanted to live
in the center of the city. And then we
learned that there was downtown, uptown,
hell's kitchen, but no center. We rented
an attic in the theater district but our
ceiling cracked and we leak.

We met again, ten or so years later. One
of us became a commercial artist, the
other a technical writer. We wanted to be
just an artist and a writer, but what are
you gonna do? This is America.

PLATE 3 Svetlana Boym, *Hydrant Immigrants*, 2007-2015. Photographic prints,
22in.

PLATE 4 Svetlana Boym, *Hydrant Immigrants*, 2007-2015. Photographic prints, 17 × 22in.

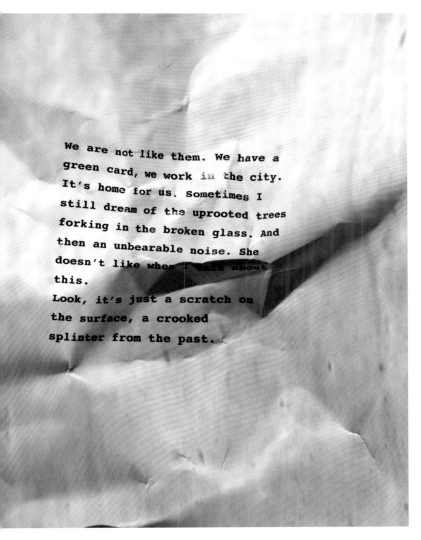

We are not like them. We have a green card, we work in the city. It's home for us. Sometimes I still dream of the uprooted trees forking in the broken glass. And then an unbearable noise. She doesn't like when I talk about this.

Look, it's just a scratch on the surface, a crooked splinter from the past.

ATE 5 Svetlana Boym, *Hydrant Immigrants*, 2007-2015. Photographic prints, × 22in.

PLATE 6 Svetlana Boym, "Slides (Two Empty)," *Touching Photographs*, Date Unknown. Digital Photograph.

PLATE 7 Svetlana Boym, "Leaving Sarajevo," *Cities in Transit*, 2009. Photographic print, 17 × 22in.

PLATE 8 Svetlana Boym, "New York Peacock," *Cities in Transit*, 2009. Photographic print, 17 × 22in.

PLATE 9 Svetlana Boym, "Leaving New York (Trash)," *Cities in Transit*, 2009.
Photographic print, 17 × 22in.

PLATE 10 Svetlana Boym, "Leaving Venice," *Cities in Transit*, 2009. Digital photograph.

PLATE 11 Svetlana Boym, "Leaving Leningrad," *Images without Black*, Date
unknown. Photographic print, 22 × 17in.

PLATE 12 Svetlana Boym, "Santa Barbara #3," *Images without Black*, 2003.
Photographic print, 22 × 17in.

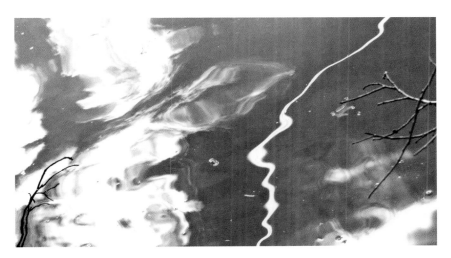

PLATE 13 Svetlana Boym, "Bereshit," *Phantom Limbs*, 2011-2013. Photographic print, 26 × 17 in.

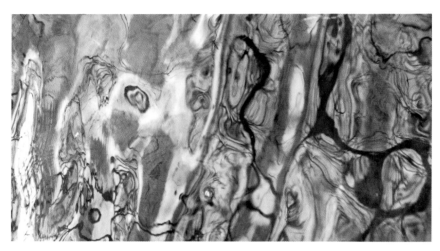

PLATE 14 Svetlana Boym, "Bereshit Couple," *Phantom Limbs*, 2011-2013. Photographic print, 26 × 17 in.

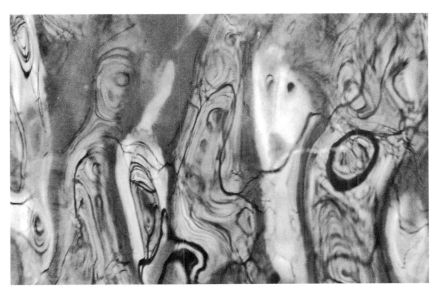

PLATE 15 Svetlana Boym, "Bereshit Visions," *Phantom Limbs*, 2011-2013. Photographic print, 26 × 17 in.

PLATE 16 Svetlana Boym, *Not Working*, c.2005. Digital Photograph.